EPIDEMICS AND GENOCIDE IN EASTERN EUROPE

EPIDEMICS AND GENOCIDE IN EASTERN EUROPE

1890–1945

Paul Julian Weindling

OXFORD
UNIVERSITY PRESS

OXFORD
UNIVERSITY PRESS

Great Clarendon Street, Oxford OX2 6DP

Oxford University Press is a department of the University of Oxford.
It furthers the University's objective of excellence in research, scholarship,
and education by publishing worldwide in

Oxford New York

Athens Auckland Bangkok Bogotá Buenos Aires Calcutta
Cape Town Chennai Dar es Salaam Delhi Florence Hong Kong Istanbul
Karachi Kuala Lumpur Madrid Melbourne Mexico City Mumbai
Nairobi Paris São Paulo Singapore Taipei Tokyo Toronto Warsaw

and associated companies in Berlin Ibadan

Oxford is a registered trade mark of Oxford University Press
in the UK and certain other countries

Published in the United States
by Oxford University Press Inc., New York

British Library Cataloguing in Publication Data

Data available

Library of Congress Cataloging in Publication Data

Weindling, Paul.
Epidemics and genocide in eastern Europe, 1890–1945 / Paul Weindling.
Includes bibliographical references and index.
1. Epidemics—Europe, Eastern—History—19th century. 2. Epidemics—Europe, Eastern—
History—20th century. 3. Bacteriology—Germany—History—19th century.
4. Bacteriology—Germany—History—20th century. 5. Genocide—Europe, Eastern—
History—20th century. I. Title
RA652.W43 1999
614.4′943′09041—dc21 99-34520
ISBN 0-19-820691-7

1 3 5 7 9 10 8 6 4 2

Typeset by Best-set Typesetter Ltd., Hong Kong
Printed in Great Britain
on acid-free paper by
Biddles Ltd.
Guildford and King's Lynn

For my mother, Erica Weindling.

In memory of Julian Weindling (born 13 Jan 1875 in Klasno, Wieliczka; resident of Zakopane), his wife Amalia, and their daughter, Nusie; their fate unknown

CONTENTS

List of Illustrations   viii

List of Maps   x

List of Tables   x

Acknowledgements   xi

Note on Names of Places and Persons   xiv

Foreword   xv

I. MICROBES AND MIGRANTS

1. Disease as Metamorphosis   3
2. Eradicating Parasites   19
3. Cleansing Bodies, Defending Borders   49
4. The First World War and Combating Lice   73

II. CONTAINMENT

5. Defending German Health: Technical Solutions   111
6. The Sanitary Iron Curtain: The Relief of Polish and Russian Typhus   139
7. German–Soviet Medical Collaboration   183
8. The Demise of Internationalism   209

III. ERADICATION

9. From Geo-medicine to Genocide   225
10. Delousing and the Holocaust   271
11. 'Victory with Vaccines': Human Guinea-pigs and Louse-feeders   322
12. From Medical Research to Biological Warfare   373
13. Clinical Trials on Trial   393

APPENDICES

I. Typhus Statistics in Germany, Poland, Russia, and the Ukraine   428
II. Typhus Vaccines and Sera, 1876–1944   435

Select Bibliography   437
Index   451

LIST OF ILLUSTRATIONS

1. 'JEWS–LICE–TYPHUS'. German propaganda poster in the
   Generalgouvernement, 1940   2
   Biblioteka Jagiellonska, Cracow.

2. Prussian Hygiene Institute, Posen, opened 20 April 1913   50
   Nachlass 156 (E. Wernicke), k. 5: Mp. 'Fotos v. Hygiene-Inst.', Nr 1. Staatsbibliothek zu
   Berlin—Preussischer Kulturbesitz—Handschriftenabteilung.

3. Typhoid inoculation at the front, c. 1915   74

4. 'Louse-table of Professor Hase'. Text in Yiddish. Hase was the Prussian army
   military entomologist, and expert on lice   101
   Frey, 'Bilder aus dem Gesundheitswesen in Polen (Kongress-Polen)', 20

5. Environmental damage due to military operations near Smorgon (east of
   Vilna) and in the Baranowitschi Forest. Photographs by German Foresters   107
   Bundesarchiv R 168/172

6. Medical-hygienic course for Polish District Medical Officers in Posen,
   Easter 1920. In centre: Prof. Dr Erich Wernicke, Director of the former
   Prussian Institute of Hygiene   116
   Nachlass 156 (E. Wernicke) K. 5. Mp. 'Fotos v. E. Wernicke' Nr 25. Staatsbibliothek zu
   Berlin—Preussischer Kulturbesitz—Handschriftenabteilung.

7. The German sanitary train, photographed by Peter Mühlens   161
   Staatsarchiv, Hamburg 352 Bernhard Nocht Institut 23 Bd

8. A Railway wagon with corpses of persons attempting to flee, photographed
   by Peter Mühlens   173
   Staatsarchiv, Hamburg 352 Bernhard Nocht Institut 23 Bd

9. Bodies of famine victims, photographed by Peter Mühlens   174
   Staatsarchiv, Hamburg 352 Bernhard Nocht Institut 23 Bd

10. German mothers honour Behring, Marburg 1940   238
    Bildbericht für die Teilnehmer der Behring-Erinnerungsfeier 4.–6. Dezember 1940
    Marburg-Lahn, Behring-Archiv.

11. The Behring Memorial   239
    Bildbericht für die Teilnehmer der Behring-Erinnerungsfeier 4.–6. Dezember 1940
    Marburg-Lahn, Behring-Archiv.

12. The Guard of Honour at the tomb of Behring   240
    Bildbericht für die Teilnehmer der Behring-Erinnerungsfeier 4.–6. Dezember 1940
    Marburg-Lahn, Behring-Archiv.

13. German propaganda poster: 'Typhus the Scourge of the East'   278
    Das Vorfeld, 3 (1943).

14. German propaganda poster: 'The Path of Horror', depicting how a Jewish
beggar-woman reputedly infected forty-two persons with typhus 278
Das Vorfeld, 3 (1943).

15. German propaganda poster. Inscribed in Ukrainian: 'Beware of Typhus. Do Not
Come Near to Jews' 285
Yad Vashem Archives, Jerusalem, No. 4613/119. Copyright: Sifriat Hapoalim.

16. Military delousing certificate, 1943 286

17. Behring Institute, Lemberg 340
Behring-Archiv, Marburg.

18. Celebrating the Behring Institute: Richard Haas explaining the work of the
Behring Institute to Reichsminister Hans Frank 340
Behring-Archiv, Marburg.

19. Louse-feeders at the Behring Institute, Lemberg 341
Behring-Archiv, Marburg.

20. Epidemic warning-signs at Terezín 404
Yad Vashem Archives, Jerusalem.

21. 'Human laundry', Belsen 405
Prof. Keith Mant.

22. 'Janet Vaughan with one of her patients' 405
Prof. Keith Mant.

LIST OF MAPS

1. Border control stations *c.* 1910   57
   Staatsarchiv, Bremen
2. Epidemic situation in Eastern Europe in 1922   113
   League of Nations Health Organization
3. Typhus in Russia, 1921–4   151
   E. Rodenwaldt, *Welt-Seuchen Atlas* (Hamburg, 1952)

LIST OF TABLES

7.1. The German–Soviet Institute for Racial Research   192
11.1. Buchenwald Prisoner Vaccine Researchers: 'Kommandoliste
       Block 50'   370

ACKNOWLEDGEMENTS

Numerous archivists, librarians, colleagues, and friends assisted me on my historical odyssey into lice and typhus. It is a pleasure to thank them for their generous
assistance and advice.

Isaac Arbus, E. H. Strach, and H. Kafka discussed their experiences of typhus.
Rabbi Ephraim Oshry described delousing at Kovno. Claudette Bloch-Kennedy
described the Raisko botanical laboratory of Auschwitz and her visits to the neighbouring SS-Hygiene Institute. Keith Mant described his investigations of
Ravensbrück. Alice Ricciardi-von Platen, medical observer at the Nuremberg
Medical Trial, shared her recollections of the typhus researchers in the dock. I am
grateful to Gertraud Rudat and Hartmut Mrugowsky for providing access to their
father's description of typhus prevention in the Second World War.

I owe an especial debt to Susan Solomon (University of Toronto) who has organized a workshop for the past six years on Weimar German–Soviet medical collaboration at the Institute for the History of Medicine of the Free University, Berlin,
with generous support from the Institute's Director, Rolf Winau and from Peter
Schneck of the Humboldt University. She generously provided copies of documents from Moscow. Over the years I have enjoyed the erudite company of Michael
Hubenstorf (now Toronto), who is engaged on a fundamental reappraisal of
German bacteriology, and of other participants in the group, particularly Jochen
Richter. Wolfgang Eckart of the University of Heidelberg hosted a research workshop on German medicine in the east, and we have periodically exchanged ideas
and information about German tropical medicine.

Michael Burleigh (University of Wales, Cardiff) gave insightful opinions on an
early version of the text, prompting me to rethink the book into one more firmly
focused on the German medical obsession with the east. Steven Aschheim (Hebrew
University of Jerusalem) prompted me to clarify some crucial issues in a near final
draft. David Rechter (Oxford Centre for Postgraduate Hebrew Studies) and Lynn
Hirsch commented on the First World War chapter, allowed me to consult copies of
materials relating to the General Government of German-occupied Poland, and
provided copious references to historical studies on medical and biological representations of Jewish identity.

Alfons Labisch (Düsseldorf) gave access to his Institute's collections on military
medicine, including the film *Kampf den Fleckfieber*, and guidance on other collections like the Gerstein and Oskar Vogt papers. Karl-Heinz Leven, himself the
author of a pioneering account of typhus and German military medicine, provided
access to the Aschoff papers. Several long-standing colleagues have supported
research visits: Reinhard Spree and Flurin Condrau to Munich, and Dietrich Milles
to Bremen.

It is a pleasure to record my intellectual debts to current and former doctoral students, particularly to John Clark (now University of Kent) with whom I began to explore the history of entomology; to Viviane Quirke, who has overlapping interests in the history of the Pasteur Institute in the Second World War and to Robert Atenstaedt, who has written the definitive account of trench fever.

Rainer Liedtke advised on aspects of migration history in Hamburg and Barbara Leidinger made available copies of her publications on Bremen hospital history. The Librarians of the Hamburg Bernhard Nocht-Institute provided access to archives and literature. Stefan Wolf made available his important study of the Institute's history. Howard Markel kindly sent the text of his book on quarantine in New York, drawing on perceptions of US immigration controls in the Yiddish press.

Dr Schultze assisted by Ilona Kalb of the archives of the Humboldt University, Berlin provided frequent access to the papers of Zeiss. Marion Kazemi and the Director of the Max Planck-Gesellschaft Library and Archives made available to me the papers of Hase and Haber. I am most grateful for the assistance of the archivists of Bayer-Leverkusen, the Behringwerke, and DEGUSSA. I owe especial thanks for considerable advice from Joseph Staerck of the Behring-Archiv, Marburg, who arranged for generous access to the Behring-Archiv and guided me to several sites associated with Behring. B. Wolff of Wehrmedizinische Bibliothek, Sanitätsamt der Bundeswehr, Bonn sent copies of the Arbeitstagung-Ost of German military medical officers. Bettina Winter of the archives of the Landeswohlfahrtsverband, Hessen provided information on euthanasia installations. Gabrielle Moser (Greifswald) drew my attention to sources on typhus in the Soviet zone.

I enjoyed lively discussions with Marta-Aleksandra Balińska (Paris) about the Polish history of medicine and about her great-grandfather Ludwik Rajchman. Maria Kordas (Wrocław) and Wanda Kemp-Welsch (Oxford) assisted with Polish texts. Latterly, Maria Kordas conducted interviews of great significance with louse-feeders. Ute Caumanns of the German Historical Institute, Warsaw kindly located one of the typhus posters.

My visit to Israel was facilitated by Raphael Falk (Jerusalem) with the support of the Van Leer Foundation. Bazi and Jochi Doron translated Hebrew and Yiddish survivors' accounts. I am immensely grateful to the archivists and librarians at Yad Vashem for advice and guidance in my use of their extraordinarily rich collections on the Holocaust.

In Paris I benefited from assistance provided by Ilana Löwy and Anne-Marie Moulin of INSERM U-186, to whose group I first presented my initial paper on the topic of typhus and the Holocaust. It has been a great pleasure to visit the archives of the Institut Pasteur under the direction of Denise Ogilvie, whose guidance and erudition I gratefully acknowledge. Claire Ambroselli, Lion Murard, and Patrick Zylberman advised on medicine in Vichy France.

I am grateful to Mattias Tyden (Stockholm) for information on Gerstein's Swedish contacts, and to Tore Tennøe (Oslo) who shares an interest in Gerhard Rose.

In the United Kingdom I wish to record my thanks to Alexandra McAdam Clark (MRC archivist) and to PRO archivists who provided access to MRC papers during their transfer. Silvia Frenk (Cambridge) kindly made available information on the MRC holdings. The Wiener Library, London has been an essential scholarly resource.

For advice on materials in the United States I wish to thank the Rockefeller Archive Centre and especially Tom Rosenbaum and Darwin Stapleton; Virginia Harden and John Parascandola provided helpful initial guidance concerning federal archives. Charles Roland (Montreal) assisted with Polish sources. The rare books and manuscripts section of the Countway Library, Boston under the genial Richard Wolfe proved to be an outstanding resource with its magnificent collections, expert advice, and scholarly dedication.

I have also drawn on the resources of various specialist libraries, including the Senckenbergische Bibliothek, Frankfurt, the New York Academy of Medicine, the Archiv des Österreichischen Widerstandes, and the excellent library at the Austrian State Archives. I wish to convey my appreciation to all the archivists who patiently responded to the requests of a researcher with a keen academic appetite for files on his topic.

This work was mercifully not carried out as a formal project nor has it benefited from a specific grant, and I therefore enjoyed exceptional freedom in developing its conceptualization and scope. I have three basic debts: to the Wellcome Trust for financing my employment, to the Wellcome Unit for the History of Medicine at the University of Oxford, and finally to Oxford Brookes University for taking me on board. Completion of this book on an appropriately dismal theme coincided with the closure of the Unit which had nurtured a distinguished generation of historians engaged on fundamental and innovative projects in the social history of medicine. My migration to Oxford Brookes has meant that the School of Humanities has provided resources during the production of the book, as well as a vibrant intellectual environment. I am grateful for valuable editorial in-put at Oxford University Press, and I especially wish to thank Sarah Ridegard, Paul Smith, and Helen Rappaport.

The brilliant opening academic conference of the US Holocaust Museum in 1993 impressed me with the importance of drawing on survivors' testimonies. The Museum has taken due account of medicine as part of Holocaust history. The 1995 conference at the YIVO Institute on Jewish Medical Resistance developed my understanding of ghetto medical services, not least because of the survivors' memories.

My family—Julia, my daughters Silvia and Miranda, and baby Felix patiently endured my obsession with lice. My mother many years ago had impressed me with her experiences of the discomfort of bedbugs in prison in Bucharest on an unsuccessful attempt to escape post-Anschluss Austria. She has been mercifully fortunate, but others were not: hence the dedications.

NOTE ON NAMES OF PLACES AND PERSONS

Where there is a commonly recognized name in English, e.g. Cracow or Vilna, this has been used throughout. Otherwise, place-names are generally given in the language of the prevailing political authority: for example, Lemberg under Austrian rule, from 1919 Lwów, then under Soviet occupation during 1939–41 Lvov, and again Lemberg under German occupation. At times usage varies in accordance with the sources: thus the Austrians used the name Oswiecim prior to Polish independence, while under German rule Auschwitz is appropriate. I have exceptionally retained German forms of Polish or Russian place-names when the equivalent is unclear or when these were part of plans for post-conquest economic development.

The names of persons are given according to their national identity, e.g. Ludwik Hirszfeld rather than Ludwig Hirschfeld. Self-styled forms have been used, e.g. Serge Balachowsky. I have kept the idiosyncratic listing of names and national identity used by Balachowsky in his listing of Buchenwald vaccine researchers. Where the original forms of names are unclear, these are given as in the sources used.

FOREWORD

Delousing became routine during the First World War, based on the recent discovery that lice spread typhus. By the time of the Second World War migrants and deportees had become conditioned to expect the ordeal of delousing at border crossings, ports, railway junctions, and on entry to camps. The Nazis stigmatized ethnic undesirables as human vermin and as poisoning the Aryan race. As racial therapy became intertwined with the control of epidemics from the east, the preventive strategies of sanitary experts merit scrutiny. The cruel fiction that the crematoria of Auschwitz were for delousing raises the question as to how the medical eradication of parasites was linked to genocide.

In confronting typhus we see twin processes of sanitary policing, and its racialization with typhus characterized as a *Judenfieber*. Preventing epidemics involved a battery of sanitary technologies to cleanse, disinfect, fumigate, and cremate. The campaigns against lice dragooned civilians into compliance with draconian sanitary regimes, and ethnic minorities became vulnerable to extortion, destruction of personal property, and racial violence. The campaigns were predicated on a metaphorical divide between the advanced sanitary conditions of Western Europe, and a pathogenic and primitive east. The Second World War saw megalomaniac racial engineering of the genocidal *Generalplan Ost*, involving plans for 'clearance' and transplanting of reinvigorated ethnic German stocks in the occupied eastern territories. This had as its corollary what amounted to an anti-epidemic *Seuchenplan Ost*, first to segregate and then to eradicate the human carriers of epidemic infections. Medical experts and subordinate troops of disinfectors targeted ethnic foes as the sources of infections, menacing the health of German 'colonists' in the east, the German heartlands, and the predatory forces of the army and SS.

A brief historiographical review, and some explanation of the gestation of this work will—I hope—be helpful. My intial concerns were with the sanitary and symbolic significance of borders, transport, and sanitary policing. Two groups merited special attention: the migrants crossing Germany from eastern Europe on their way to the United States, and the ethnic German 'colonists' in Russia. The Treaty of Versailles was traumatic for the German sanitary experts, while the Allies recognized that the central European successor states required national hygiene installations. The new hygiene institutes and delousing stations could provide a virtual iron curtain (or what the Germans called 'an epidemic protection wall') to prevent typhus as a devastating new 'Black Death' from the east. Graphic reports by League of Nations Epidemic Commissioners, depicting the Russian famine and typhus epidemic of 1921 as a 'Holocaust' poised to engulf the new Europe, prompted my first reflections on the genocidal significance of the disease. The Commissioners' reports alluded to tensions between measures sponsored by the Allies and those of a German epidemic relief expedition in Russia. I set out to examine how the

German medical experts appeared on the international stage of epidemic control, and to compare German responses to epidemics from the east to those of British, French, and United States sanitary experts. Medical élites established new sanitary infrastructures and powers, amounting to a distinctive form of medical imperialism. Yet the exterminatory medical Sonderweg still required explanation.

At first my approach to delousing was in its use as a means of sanitary conditioning of people forced to submit to baths, the shaving of hair, and to fumigation of clothing and possessions. Yet delousing was far more than a regime of social control. Resistance and evasion, and long-standing customs need to be taken into account. Issues arise concerning differing ideologies, interests, and affiliations among the sanitary experts and the perpetrators of genocide. The relations between medical views of infectious micro-organisms and anti-Semitism prompt review of German bacteriology. Nazi enthusiasts exaggerated the anti-Semitism of the pioneers of bacteriology. There were distinguished bacteriologists who were Jewish (including Ferdinand Cohn, the Breslau botanist who coined the term 'bacterium', Paul Ehrlich, and August von Wassermann). The interaction of medicine and ideas of racial purification involved not only the transfer of techniques but the deployment of a medical voccabulary to strengthen the racial metaphor. Moreover, the racial aims were complex: among the rationales motivating the medical advocates of expanding German *Lebensraum* was the sustaining of ethnic German communities in the east. The material on typhus prompts consideration of a great diversity of medical strategies, perceptions of the disease, and popular evasion of public health measures.

The whole idea of a self-evident disease with a single agent of transmission—the louse—did not accord with the medical discourse on bacteria, viruses, and geographical factors. Why did the mentalities of those in command of epidemic control strategies vary? How did scientific and racial impulses interact in medical programmes to combat epidemics from the east? What popular responses were there to the coercive regimes of delousing? It became necessary to take account of multiple strategies of the prepetrators, evasion, resistance, and an ability to turn the German fear of typhus to advantage. Virtually every survivor's account of the Holocaust confronts not only death but also the malignant shadow of disease. The rich sources demand a complex account, but I hope one that a patient reader will appreciate as more authentic than just the operationalizing of an exterminatory medical strategy.

The survivors who pioneered Holocaust history provided powerful testimony of how medical science was poised between assistance and destruction. In 1946 Marc Dvorjetski described how typhus and a range of other diseases were fought by Jewish sanitary services in the Vilna ghetto, which replicated advanced models of social and preventive medicine. Dvorjetski evocatively raised the issue of the different types of Jewish medical resistance. One may legitimately ask, resistance to what? Answers were provided by Désiré Hafner in a medical dissertation in 1946, where he argued that the Nazis used typhus as a powerful means of extermination in the camps, and by Isaiah Trunk's trenchant study, published in 1953, of typhus in the

Warsaw ghetto. Trunk argued that: 'In their campaign of annihilation against the Jewish population of Poland, the Nazis employed not only the well-known technique of "deportations" to the death camps, but also used bacteria . . . By deliberate design the German authorities created conditions in the ghettos which made the outbreak of epidemics inevitable.'[1] Ludwik Hirszfeld, an eminent serologist, drew the same conclusion about the murderous intent of German sanitary measures from his experiences on the Health Council of the Warsaw ghetto. In 1946 the chemist Primo Levi and the bacteriologist Lucie Adelsberger contributed analyses of how malnutrition, water shortage, and inadequate sanitation resulted in louse infestation, rampant scabies, and lethal diarrhoea. Adelsberger noted that it was not possible to survive more than six months on the normal diet, and memorized records on decreases in blood protein and ascorbic acid with progressive starvation. She noted how the dangers of the camp sharpened the will to survive and resist disease, particularly among those who although starving had not wholly succumbed to malnutrition. Survivors accused the Germans of having deliberately fanned the flames of infectious disease among overcrowded, starved, and physically exhausted ghetto internees and concentration camp prisoners.[2] Hermann Langbein, the prisoner-secretary to the Auschwitz physician Eduard Wirths, and Eugen Kogon, the prisoner-secretary of Buchenwald bacteriologist Erwin Ding, highlighted how in the permanent subterranean struggle against the SS, it was disease and death which provided opportunities for subterfuge and sabotage.[3] While eradicating the filth and disease of eastern peoples was a leitmotif of the German mission in the east, epidemics were caught up in a struggle between experts seeking to impose control measures, and popular strategies of evasion and resistance. The topic gained in cultural significance, as Alex Bein, a historian of Zionist ideas, examined how biological notions of the parasite came to pervade Nazi racism.[4]

Between the 1960s and 80s historians of Nazi Germany were preoccupied by political mobilization, the build up of the war economy, and with the genocidal role of bureaucrats and the Nazi élite. Medical questions, racial sensibilities, the mentalities of experts and their underlings, and sheer individual idiosyncrasy were eclipsed as structure, function, and ideology came to dominate Holocaust history. Disease and disability regained attention by 1990 for several reasons. Nazi

[1] M. Dvorjetski, *Le Ghetto de Vilna (rapport sanitaire)* (Geneva, 1946); D. Hafner, *Aspects pathologiques du camp de concentration d'Auschwitz-Birkenau* (Tours, 1946), cited by C. Romney, 'Les Témoignages des médecins déportés à Auschwitz', *La Pensée et les hommes*, 39 (1992), 95–112; I. Trunk, 'Epidemics and Mortality in the Warsaw Ghetto, 1939–1942', *Yivo Annual of Social Science*, 8 (1953), 82.

[2] H. Hirszfeldowna (ed.), *The Story of One Life* (Fort Knox, Ky., n.d.), 216–73; L. Hirszfeld, *Historia jednego życia* (Warsaw, 1946); L. De-Benedetti and P. Levi, 'Rapporto sulla organizzazione igienico-sanitaria del campo di concentramento per Ebrei di Monowitz (Auswitz—Alta Slesia)', *Minerva Medica*, 2 (1946), 535–44; L. Adelsberger, 'Medical Observations in Auschwitz Concentration Camp', *Lancet* (2 Mar. 1946), 317–19.

[3] E. Kogon, *Der SS-Staat. Das System der deutschen Konzentrationslager*, 23rd edn. (Munich, 1993); H. Langbein, *Menschen in Auschwitz* (Vienna, 1972); id., *Against All Hope. Resistance in the Nazi Concentration Camps* (London, 1994).

[4] A. Bein, 'The Jewish Parasite. Notes on the Semantics of the Jewish Problem with Special Reference to Germany', *Leo Baeck Institute Yearbook*, 9 (1964), 3–40.

euthanasia at last received serious historical attention as crucial in the genesis of genocide; the concern with the radicalization of the Holocaust on the eastern peripheries raised questions as to the role of racial experts in the east. The critique of modernity meant that the Holocaust became a product of calculated, rational planning rather than racist irrationalism. Finally, Marxist concerns with the socioeconomic structures of fascism were displaced by a new stress on Nazi Germany as a racial state and on the grandiose fascist masterplans to rejuvenate society. The disintegration of opaque sociological categories meant that greater significance was ascribed to individual experiences of 'ordinary men' as perpetrators, and to those of the victims.

The 1980s saw the rise of studies of Nazi medicine, often in protest against lingering authoritarian values and the remnants of racial ideas in the medical establishments in the two Germanies. The initial focus was on the eugenic component of public health and population policies in the emerging German welfare state. Medical and social assistance were increasingly coercive involving detention, invasion of the body with forced sterilization, and ultimately destructive of human life. My analysis of these developments, *Health, Race and German Politics between National Unification and Nazism*, was written very much from the position of a *Primat der Innenpolitik* of the responses by professional élites to the social misery of a rapidly industrializing nation. Bacteriology and tropical medicine (as opposed to social medicine), and the German borders (as opposed to urban public health) provide scope for a complementary study which deal far more directly with genocide.

It was possible to weave a new fabric of racialized medicine from some anomalous loose ends. Mark Adams, the historian of Soviet genetics, in 1985 caught sight of some material on the Moscow Institute for Racial Pathology buried in a footnote in my paper on the Kaiser Wilhelm Institute for Anthropology, Human Heredity and Eugenics; he prompted me to work up the materials on the German racial laboratory in Moscow.[5] But this research only became viable with the collapse of the Berlin Wall, when a range of historical sources became accessible, such as the papers of Heinz Zeiss and of the German embassy in Moscow, documenting German–Soviet medical co-operation.[6] Earlier attempts at comparing 'socialist' Weimar eugenics and Soviet eugenics, notably by Loren Graham, have had to be reconceptualized by investigating 'geo-medicine' and 'racial pathology' as nationalist constructs.[7]

The wave of historical research on eugenics, psychiatric abuses, and population policies neglected bacteriology as an apparently value-neutral sphere, and of

[5] P. J. Weindling, 'Weimar Eugenics in Social Context; the Founding of the Kaiser Wilhelm Institute for Anthropology, Human Heredity and Eugenics', *Annals of Science*, 42 (1985), 303–18; id., 'German–Soviet Co-operation in Science: The Case of the Laboratory for Racial Research, 1931–1938', *Nuncius. Annali di Storia Scienze*, 1 (1986), 103–9.

[6] Id., 'German–Soviet Medical Co-operation and the Institute for Racial Research, 1927–ca.1935', *German History*, 10 (1992), 177–206.

[7] L. R. Graham, 'Science and Values: The Eugenics Movement in Germany and Russia during the 1920s', *American Historical Review*, 22 (1977), 113–64.

diminishing importance given that infectious diseases were on the decline. But a whole new perspective came to be opened up, requiring a reconsideration of what had hitherto been marginalized. Tackling how experts in infectious diseases sought to defend the German heartlands and to colonize areas for German settlement prompted me to confront the issues of infectious disease and genocide. It became possible to add a medical dimension to the work of Michael Burleigh and Wolfgang Wipperman on the German 'racial state', as they mapped the contours of *Ostforschung* and the German sense of a historic mission in the east. The history of German Jewry has gained in subtlety and sophistication, well exemplified by Aschheim's depiction of the German-Jewish ambivalence over the *Ostjuden*. These developments meant that it was possible to build on a substantial literature on German nationalist opinions on the Polish question and the post-First World War territorial settlement.[8] The idea of a Jewish parasite acquired new meanings in the positivistic and professionalized realm of microbiology and disinfection.

Christopher Browning pointed out the force of medical arguments to confine Jews to ghettos.[9] The transition from ghettoization to extermination raises complex issues concerning the rationales and procedures of delousing and epidemic control. The rallying cry of stamping out epidemics clearly meant eradicating the racially inferior carriers of lice. Lüdger Wess, who investigated links between the clique of Generalgouvernement sanitary bureaucrats, identified by Browning, and the Hamburg Tropical Institute, concluded that ghettoization was only the most conspicuous tip of a vast iceberg represented by typhus in the Holocaust.[10] Longer-term responses to typhus as an epidemic hazard from the turn of the century had to be taken into account, along with the ideas and actions of 'ordinary doctors', disinfectors, and purveyors of hygienic technologies when confronting epidemics from the east. To recover how disease was manipulated, it became necessary to examine the structures of medical expertise and public health organization, and the distinctive roots of biological forms of racism in bacteriology and eugenics.

Holocaust historians have moved away from seeing the perpetrators' sole motive as the irrationalism of an exterminatory *völkisch* racism, regarding this as insufficient to explain the imposition of Nazi genocide. Emphasis on the rational elements of modernity—especially the 'solution' of a range of socio-economic problems—has provided interpretative space for the role of eugenics and bacteriology, neatly conflated as 'racial hygiene'. As Steven Aschheim has perceptively remarked, there is no clear link between popular anti-Semitism and the Holocaust.[11] Historians of Auschwitz, notably Deborah Dwork and Robert van Pelt,

---

[8] S. E. Aschheim, *Brothers and Strangers. The Eastern European Jew in German and German Jewish Consciousness, 1800–1923* (Madison, Wis., 1982); M. Burleigh, *Germany Turns Eastwards. A Study of Ostforschung in the Third Reich* (Cambridge, 1988).

[9] C. R. Browning 'Genocide and Public Health: German Doctors and Polish Jews, 1939–1941', in id., *The Path to Genocide. Essays on Launching the Final Solution* (Cambridge, 1992), 145–68.

[10] L. Wess, 'Menschenversuche und Seuchenpolitik—Zwei unbekannte Kapitel aus der Geschichte der deutschen Tropenmedizin', 9/2 (1993), 10–50.

[11] S. E. Aschheim, *Culture and Catastrophe. German and Jewish Confrontations with National Socialism and Other Crises* (New York, 1996), 118.

have pinpointed the changing functions of this inferno within the context of German *Ostraumpolitik* and the strategies for securing living space for a constricted and degenerating population.[12] Their account combines ideological (including medical) issues with chillingly vivid detail on the killing installations. Necessarily meticulous research has been conducted on the camp as an inferno produced by a genocidally twisted variant of town planning, and Jean-Claude Pressac has disentangled the genocidal gas chambers from delousing installations.[13] The broader context of typhus becomes relevant as Zyklon was stockpiled in the camp for use by a well-drilled brigade of disinfectors before the genocidal gas chambers were devised. Sanitary experts had to protect the highly vulnerable racial élite from outbreaks of infection. 'Normal' sanitary science had a lethal potential in shaping exterminatory practices.

Interest in the genocidal activities of German technical experts in the east represented a shift from ideological fanatics to expert groups and specialist occupations. Again, survivors' historical work has pointed the way forward. Kogon noted how Hitler had drawn a distinction between the sporadic nature of the traditional pogrom and his visions of relentless power once anti-Semitism was conceived as a science. One direction was that taken by historians of the German army in the east, demonstrating that genocide was not limited to the exterminatory special detachments. While this ultimately went in the direction of 'ordinary men' (or as Daniel Goldhagen specified 'ordinary Germans'), racial strategists gained in importance. This was confirmed by renewed emphasis on the *Generalplan Ost*, and Götz Aly argued that economic *Raumplanung* provided the impetus for deportations and genocide.[14] To overcome somewhat exaggerated claims made for the Holocaust as a product of economic rationalism, the debate shifted back to racial strategies in the east, throwing open the question of the complex ideological inputs to race.

As far as this account is concerned, the evidence pulls in three directions: the narrative moves backwards from the experiences of typhus victims in the Holocaust, and then forwards via medical concepts of the parasite; and there is a shift from tropical medicine in Africa and the Middle East to Eastern Europe. Medical *Ostpolitik* was shaped by German concerns to develop sanitary defences against diseases from the east, by outrage at the loss of these defences and a new vulnerability to epidemics with the Versailles settlement, and efforts to compensate by developing medical outposts in Russia and to sustain ethnic German communities. The selection of issues—epidemic control measures and medical research in the east, disinfection procedures, medical entomology and notions of the parasite, poison gas technology, and cremation—arise from their unique conjunction in the Auschwitz crematoria and as part of epidemic 'control' measures in the east. But

[12] R. J. van Pelt and D. Dwork, *Auschwitz 1270 to the Present* (New Haven, Conn., 1996).

[13] J.-C. Pressac, *Auschwitz: Technique and Operation of the Gas Chambers* (New York, 1989); id., *Les Crématoires d'Auschwitz. La machinerie de meutre de masse* (Paris, 1993).

[14] G. Aly, *Endlösung. Völkerverschiebung und der Mord an den europäischen Juden* (Frankfurt/M., 1995); D. J. Goldhagen, *Hitler's Willing Executioners. Ordinary Germans and the Holocaust* (London, 1996).

viewed contextually from the 1890s they only sporadically interact until the emergence of the genocidal *Seuchenplan* at the time of the German invasion of the Soviet Union in 1941. Even then, the genocidal measures were marked by controversy among SS and military bacteriologists, technical incompetence, and widespread resistance and evasion from groups targeted for disinfection.

Judging the record of German bacteriologists in the immediate post-Second World War era, the Allies were torn between attempts to evaluate German expertise, and the ethical condemnation of human experiments. The Nuremberg Medical Trial avoided prosecuting German doctors for genocide, and typhus figured prominently as part of the medical research programmes of the SS. The Germans turned their academic feuding and careerism into spurious resistance. The onset of the Cold War marked the death knell for a vigorous policy to prosecute medical war crimes, and the burial of the genocidal significance of anti-typhus measures. It is time to exhume the body of a decayed mentality of combating epidemic threats from the east as a sanitary therapy for German racial ills.

I
MICROBES AND MIGRANTS

1. 'JEWS–LICE–TYPHUS'. German propaganda poster in the Generalgouvernement, 1940

1

Disease as Metamorphosis

i. Fevered Visions

He was seized by the wish not to have a face. Not because he was afraid that someone would denounce him; no, he suddenly felt that he had a repugnant sinister face. The face from the poster 'JEWS–LICE–TYPHUS'.

The Nazi image of the parasite shot a pang of terror through Marek Edelman, when he saw the typhus poster in a Warsaw tram. Having survived the Warsaw Ghetto uprising he was revolted by how German propaganda whipped up anti-Semitism by depicting the Jewish body as malign and pathogenic. The posters and a grotesque anti-Semitic exhibition of spring 1943 marked the culmination of an anti-Semitic press campaign accompanying the destruction of the Ghetto. Bacteriologists gave scientific precision to the concept of the parasite by associating Jews with lice as carriers of the typhus germ. The Germans, who themselves were terrified by the prospect of epidemics, exploited the fear of disease to advance their strategy of establishing racial hegemony in the East.[1]

Despite the Nazi tactic of denigrating Jews as lice, the morbid image of the insect could be brushed aside in a spirit of defiance: 'I wished I were an insect'—the whim of Sala Pawlowicz marked how the freedom of insect existence could be preferable to the brutalizing ordeals of slave labour in a German armaments factory. Observing a single, scurrying insect made her envious. By way of contrast, the campaigners against insect predators used images of collectivities—of insect swarms spreading epidemics—or of a stylized, single monstrous bug. The Germans intended the macabre Auschwitz poster 'One louse—your death' to ensure compliance with mass delousing procedures.[2] Yet was there a hidden subtext, as the skull's grim features warned of impending death from 'disinfection'?

While the representation of typhus was shaped by the politics of genocide, the experience of delirium challenged the racialized view of disease. The sick experienced a delusion, which could strengthen the will to overcome the annihilating circumstances. It was when in the grips of the disease that the afflicted could transcend the confines of the racially condemned body. Contracting typhus while on a

---

[1] H. Krall, *Shielding the Flame. An Intimate Conversation with Dr. Marek Edelman, the Last Surviving Leader of the Warsaw Ghetto Uprising* (New York, 1986), 15; Edelman, opening address to YIVO/New School 1996 conference on Jewish Medical Resistance during the Holocaust; L. Wess, 'Menschenversuche und Seuchenpolitik—Zwei unbekannte Kapitel aus der Geschichte der deutschen Tropenmedizin', 9/2 (1993), 41 for the poster campaign. J. M. Glass, '*Life Unworthy of Life*' (New York, 1987), xix.

[2] The poster was plastered all over the camp in 1943 according to L. Adelsberger, *Auschwitz. A Doctor's Story* (Boston, 1995), 50; L. J. Micheels, *Doctor #117641. A Holocaust Memoir* (New Haven, Conn., 1989), 140–1.

death march in the last gasps of the war, Sala feverishly imagined her liberation. Her vision of a strange, wonderful land where her murdered family were reunited at her splendid wedding enabled her to escape psychologically all the deprivations, the coercive discipline, and medical stigma. Succumbing to the disease induced a sense of freedom from the burdens of the body as an object of racial persecution.

The term 'typhus' derived from the ancient Greek for smoke, vapour, or stupor, because of the delirious state characterizing the disease. While its external sign was a distinct rose-like rash, physicians observed a muttering delirium, a comatose stupor, and tremors which culminated in a feverish crisis. The military film *Kampf dem Fleckfieber* showed patients as passive and vegetative.[3] In this lethal form Renzi Rosa Berkowitz became unconscious when sick with typhus in a camp at Zibulowka in Transnistria, and her baby froze to death.[4] Everyday norms were rejected: a medical prisoner in Theresienstadt, Dr A. Weiss, noted that during incubation of the fever there were signs of nervous strain, depression, and revulsion against eating.[5] Although the coma stage could resemble death, when the delirium was at its height patients had crazed dreams, wild visions, or acute phobias—their bodies might twist in emaciated coils, and they might sob, scream, and stammer incoherently. When fever struck the skeletal Bogdan Wojdowski in the Warsaw Ghetto he felt engulfed by the green gas of the sky.[6]

Yet bouts of typhus meant the body could feel pleasantly released and dismembered with limbs floating freely, transcending the grim brutality of the camps and the racialized human physiology. The memory of the sensations remained powerfully vivid. An Auschwitz prisoner, Wiesław Kielar, commented on his experience of typhus: 'I was delirious but my delirious dreams were not altogether unpleasant.'[7] Claudette Bloch remembered that fever brought on a vision of being seated in an armchair at home in the presence of her mother—she lay exhausted in a truck after three days' continuous marching from Auschwitz to Ravensbrück.[8] Struck down by fever, Esther Brunstein 'recalled the images of all that was dear to me, bidding farewell to my loved ones and my young life'.[9] Fragmentary accounts of individual experiences suggest that it would be a trap to accept unreflectingly the Nazi medical categories. At the point when disease was most acute, the delirium constituted a spiritual resistance—a triumph of the individual will against medical genocide.

For the afflicated, the disease could be a refuge: a concentration camp internee— Dr Hanus Kafka, deported from Theresienstadt via Auschwitz to Kaufering near Dachau where he contracted typhus in January 1945—dreamed feverishly of being

---

[3] The film was produced during 1941–2: *Kampf dem Fleckfieber*, Leonaris-Film Dr Georg Munck AV Medien Gmbh.

[4] Yad Vashem Archives (YVA) 03/2461 testimony of Renzi Rosa Berkowitz née Engler.

[5] A. Weiss, *Le Typhus exanthématique pendant la deuxième guerre mondiale en particulier dans les camps de concentration* (Paris, 1954), 45, 53, 58–9.

[6] Adelsberger, *Auschwitz*, 52–3. B. Wojdowski, *Bread for the Departed* (Evanston, Ill., 1997), 271–3.

[7] W. Kielar, *Anus Mundi: Five Years in Auschwitz* (London, 1981), 102.

[8] Interview with Claudette Bloch Kennedy, 28 Feb. 1997. Dr Kennedy recollects the disease as malaria; her friends considered it typhus.

[9] E. Brunstein in: 'Belsen in History and Memory', *Journal of Holocaust Education*, 5 (1996), 214.

tossed about in a ship heading to a land of freedom.[10] Dr Isak Arbus, an imprisoned Polish army medical officer, while ill with typhus in 1940 hallucinated that the Germans were retreating.[11] A sick physician wandered between visions of international medical conferences and the typhus barracks in Birkenau. Lucie Adelsberger, who had researched at the Robert Koch Institute on immunology and allergies until her dismissal in 1933, recorded how, as a patient at Birkenau, she experienced doubling of the self: 'I remember observing every single detail in the Gypsy block during my bout with fever while at the same time sojourning in the Engadin behind Sils-Maria in the Malojan heights with the sun playing over Segantini's grave and myself gazing out onto the bluish-pink fields of the Bergell Valley.'[12] There is a sharp rift between the disease as experienced, and the public health discourse of prevention and eradication. The surreal distortions experienced by the emaciated sick contrasted with the rigid categories of scientific hygiene—with glorification of the wholesome and well-formed body, and of rigidly defined diseases with a single pathogen, and uniform symptoms, and the afflicted reduced to being encephalated animals with skeletal, deranged features.

While the experience of typhus took quite distinctive forms during the Holocaust, intense psychological impulses were evident at other times. Typhus patients often had to be restrained. During the Russian civil war cases were recorded of a patient shooting wildly around an improvised military hospital, or crossing the snows of the Siberian Steppes clad only in a shirt under the impression of running away from lice. An unloved wife accused her medical husband of an all-consuming passion for anatomy, and the starving phantasized of banquets, or dived into a black ocean of morbid despair, floundering in apocalyptic struggles between life and death. An English nurse in Serbia during the First World War hallucinated with images of the idyllic countryside back home. The body felt fractured in a world of disassociations—a sick nurse touched her three faces; patients complained that another person was in the bed, asked for their chin to be removed for shaving, or for their legs to be hung up as if clothing in a wardrobe. After recovery from the disease, character changes would persist, as well as lethargy, disorientation, transient delusions, memory loss and absent-mindedness punctuated by further delusions, and even bouts of paralysis, and finally of personality change.[13]

[10] S. Pawlowicz, *I Will Survive* (London, 1966), 100–1, 108, 200–1. Personal communication from E. H. Strach, 22 Sept. 1995 concerning the memoirs of Dr Hanus Kafka.

[11] I. Arbus, 'Memoirs of Heroic Deeds of Jewish Medical Personnel in the Camps', paper to YIVO/New School 1996 conference on Jewish Medical Resistance during the Holocaust, and personal communication.

[12] Adelsberger, *Auschwitz*, 52–3. Segantini was an Italian landscape painter, and the editors of her memoirs suggest that Adelsberger recalled his triptych 'Life, Nature, Death'. On hallucinations see also T. Radil-Weiss, 'Men in Extreme Conditions: Some Medical and Psychological Aspects of the Auschwitz Concentration Camp', *Psychiatry*, 46 (1983), 259–69.

[13] For patient experiences see Alexandra Rachmanowa, *Studenten, Liebe, Tscheka und Tod* (Salzburg, 1931); 327–9, 335, 341 for a patient's account of an isolation ward in Russia in 1919; 378–9 for delirium of political persecution; 333–5 for fellow patients' delirious states and suicide; K. Schneider-Janessen, *Arzt im Krieg. Wie deutsche und russische Ärzte den zweiten Weltkrieg erlebten* (Frankfurt/M., 1993), 179, 181; F. Farnborough, *Nurse at the Russian Front* (London, 1974), 182, 240–1, 324; M. Krippner, *The Quality of*

The challenge of disease heightened the will to resist. Moshe Koerner who suffered two months' sickness with typhus when deported with the Czernowitz ghetto to Mogilev in the Ukraine observed that moral strength and an individual will to survive kept the sick alive in the midst of disease, dirt, and squalor.[14] Various types of medical resistance were elucidated by the physician Marc Dvorjetski, who had rejected the office of head of the sanitary police in the Vilna ghetto because he did not wish to be identified with the ghetto police force.[15] While Dvorjetski's focus was mainly the activities of physicians and nurses, he also included the concept of popular spiritual resistance. A colleague who concealed typhus cases in the Vilna ghetto hospital, Abraham Wajnryb, regarded resistance as a spectrum in the struggle to survive against persecution, including individual survival and an organized 'operation typhus' to control and conceal the disease.[16]

The determination to transcend not only the sickness but also the exterminatory conditions of the camps revealed by survivors' testimonies contrasted with the objective medical view of rampant infections. Persons considered as infected or as carriers of infected lice were subjected to brutal sanitary procedures of delousing, disinfection, and quarantine. The responses to typhus in the Holocaust derived from a broader hygienic paradigm. Quarantine of individuals or of whole communities, and fumigation against foul airs had become routine by the seventeenth century. Yet what was novel was that from the 1890s hygienic propaganda demonized insects as pathogenic vermin, as *Ungeziefer*. Medical scientists assigned specific diseases to insect species, and concocted a battery of preventive measures using chemicals and gases which were far more powerful than those deployed for the cordon sanitaire during the Enlightenment. In the past lice had been regarded as medically benign, or commended for sucking out foul humours from the body.[17] But such coexistence gave way to a sanitary war on insect parasites. As hygienic campaigns alerted the public to the risks of insect pests and parasites, their monstrous images instilled the fear of a pathological descent into the pitiful condition of the verminous *Ungeziefer*.

The Hamburg-based medical entomologist, Erich Martini, reflected that lice and fleas, linked to dust, filth and damp, replaced the demon harbingers of past plagues.[18] Insects were feared as sexual predators. When in 1911 Franz Kafka's Galician actor friend, Yitshak Löwy, confided that he had gonorrhoea, Kafka focused

Mercy. Women at War in Serbia 1915–18 (Newton Abbott, 1990), 49–50, 62–3; M. D. Mackenzie, 'Louseborne Typhus Fever', in A. Hurst, *Medical Diseases of War* (London, 1944), 235–60; Weiss, *Typhus exanthématique*, 45, 53, 58–9. Micheels, *Doctor #117641*, 164.

[14] YVA 03/914 testimony of Moshe Koerner.

[15] M. Dvorjetski, *Le Ghetto de Vilna (rapport sanitaire)* (Geneva, 1946), 15; id. (also Dworzecki), *Histoire de la resistance anti-Nazie juive (1933–1945)* (Tel Aviv, 1965). id., 'Le Résistance médicale juive et la médecine nazie à l'époque de la catastrophe', *Revue d'histoire de la médecine hébraïque*, 15 (1952).

[16] A. Wajnryb, 'Medizin im Ghetto Wilna', *Dachauer Hefte*, 4 (1993), 99–101.

[17] R. Hoeppli, *Parasites and Parasitic Infections in Early Medicine and Science* (Singapore, 1959), 164–5; on living lice as remedies, ibid. 201–2; H. Zinsser, *Rats, Lice and History* (Boston, 1935), 186–7.

[18] E. Martini, 'Praktisch-entomologische Erinnerungen aus dem Weltkriege', *Zeitschrift für hygienische Zoologie*, 32 (1938), 51–8, 65–78, 77.

his repulsion on a fear of lice: 'When my hair touched his as I moved my head towards his, I became afraid of the possibility of lice.'[19] That Kafka's father derided visiting Jewish actors as *Ungeziefer* showed how commonplace it was to condemn traditional customs as diseased and depraved.

By 1914 medical propaganda warned how swarms of lice, flies, and other dreaded bugs carrying as yet undetermined diseases threatened civic order, military efficiency, and the emotive issue of infant deaths.[20] The publication of Kafka's fable *Metamorphosis* in 1915, dissecting the experience of an awakening as an indeterminate species of bug, occurred at a crucial turning-point in the history of medical offensives against infectious diseases.[21] Kafka drew on the widespread concern with insect predators: bedbugs were medically suspect, and deprived their hosts of sleep. The most vicious threat to European civilization was vested in the *Kleiderlaus*, known to the English as the body louse.

By the time of the First World War, bacteriologists demonized lice as carriers of the newly discovered micro-organism causing typhus. Biologists extended their expertise to the human hosts of insects, and classified supposedly surplus people, notably migrants, pedlars, Jews, and gypsies, as human parasites menacing national hygiene. Soon, an epidemic of posters in central European cities warned of the dangers of *Ungeziefer*. Cohorts of bacteriologists explored the hidden empire of micro-organisms, while claiming that they were defending European civilization against the microbial hordes; disinfection squadrons policed borders, sealed infected areas and penetrated into contaminated housing in order to burn, poison, or otherwise disinfect infested possessions.

The hygiene experts who masterminded mass delousing bombarded soldiers and civilians with scientifically tested disinfectants and sanitary measures. These amounted to a modernistic campaign against traditional customs: beards and long hair were condemned as habitats of insect parasites. The dictates of hygiene demanded clearance of any insect refuge—including the voluminous domestic ornamentation derided by modernists. Seen in a wider social context, hygiene was a rationalizing force, affecting every aspect of living conditions from a post-coital douche to prevent sexually transmitted diseases to the fumigation of food stores in immense warehouses. The Western nations' pride in being in the vanguard of medical progress was accompanied by derision for Eastern peoples clinging to archaic habits, dress, and beliefs. Modernist notions of clearance spurred the

[19] H-G. Koch, M. Müller, and M. Pasley (eds.), *Franz Kafka. Tagebücher* (Frankfurt/M., 1990), 93; S. Gilman, *Franz Kafka. The Jewish Patient* (New York, 1995), 161.
[20] Kafka's fictitious insect had an indeterminate form, which makes it impossible to pin down with any zoological precision; commentators have suggested some type of bed bug, beetle, cockroach, and a louse as candidates. *Ungeziefer*—a term that Kafka's father had employed to denounce visiting Jewish actors. Cf Diary for 21 Oct. 1913: 'Ehrenfels's seminar ... I keep thinking of the black beetle', M. Brod (ed.), *The Diaries of Franz Kafka* (Harmondsworth, 1972), 234. S. Corngold, *The Commentators' Despair: The Interpretation of Kafka's Metamorphosis* (Port Washington, NY, 1972) for various identifications (see p. 228 for Wilhelm Stekel's view of the insect as a louse, representative of sadistic fantasies).
[21] The story was first drafted from Nov. to Dec. 1912—a crucial time in the identification of the body louse as vector of typhus.

relentless process of stripping away all the habitats of the swelling ranks of parasites.

ii. The Disappearance of a Disease

Exhuming a corpus of medical debates and interventions by Western Powers in Eastern Europe between the 1890s and the aftermath of the Second World War involves dissecting mentalities rather than hard statistics of the spread of epidemics. For underlying the numbers of telegrams by alarmed medical officers in remote eastern provinces reporting suspected typhus cases among itinerant workers, gypsies, *Ostjuden*, or prisoners of war was the medical stigma surrounding ethnic undesirables. Similarly, it is less a question of analysing the statistical fluctuations of epidemics, or of assessing whether delousing, quarantine, or vaccines were most effective in saving lives and preventing infections. For the fear of what in 1900 was a virtually dormant disease was so magnified as to legitimate draconian control measures.

Bacteriologists sought to classify and control a 'Third Reich' of insect and microbial organisms through mass prevention and eradication programmes. Public health experts conceded that quarantine, destruction of personal possessions, and sanitary controls infringed civic liberties and disrupted economic life; but that the priorities of scientific advance and disease control overrode individual casualties. Typhus was feared as a new Black Death, poised to eradicate European civilization. Bacteriologists enforced delousing routines to contain migrants from the east in their place of origin, in sealed trains, on disinfested ships or in transit camps on borders, at railway junctions, and in ports. National and international concerns conspired to impose ever more rigorous sanitary measures. At the domestic level, the anxieties were generated by domestic social tensions in Germany and the right-wing demands for acquiring *Lebensraum* in the east. International sanitary controls on migrants seeking to escape persecution and poverty also shaped delousing. The nativist lobby among the 'WASPs' in the United States urged the exclusion of 'lousy' eastern Jews, and a chain of disinfection stations imposed stringent measures on German borders and in ports. Immigration of 'surplus peoples' from Europe became restricted in the early twentieth century, as migration and border controls intensified the suspicion that transmigrants were disease carriers. Public health officials saw the movement of poor and persecuted populations from the Eastern margins of Europe as a threat to the improved levels of public health within Germany and in the wider world.

Sanitary authorities and bacteriologists increased their powers by magnifying epidemic threats. How was the malignant monster of an epidemic visualized? Why were certain groups seen as potential epidemic risks and subjected to the hygienic rites of showers, shaving, and the burning of their possessions? What strategies of control and repression lay behind the draconian routines of delousing? And how was the tragic amalgam of stigma and medical science that constructed typhus overcome by resistance, evasion, and collective solidarity? The metamorphosis of humans into parasites had a multiplicity of outcomes involving diverse contexts, technologies, transpositions, deceptions, and tragedies.

The sociologist Theodor Adorno interpreted Kafka's *Metamorphosis* as prefiguring dehumanization and the biological regression of the concentration camps.[22] The grotesque deception of a delousing installation was supported by signs 'to the baths' and 'to disinfection', by false shower heads, dummy pieces of soap, the issuing of towels, 'changing rooms' with numbered hooks, and verbal exhortations that after delousing would come hot soup and other comforts. The Nazi transformation of cleansing into killing exploited expectations of delousing as a routine and widespread medical procedure for migrants. The modern rituals of hygiene facilitated the destruction of persons stigmatized as parasites on an unprecedented scale. 'I wished I were an insect'—a whim but also a token of inner resistance, marking a refusal to accept hygienic regimentation and genocide.

The formulating of typhus as a specific disease with a defined biological basis reveals much about the ideas, convictions, and allegiances of medical élites. The 'microbe hunter' magnified diseases so that these took on gargantuan proportions of a monstrous menace, thereby glorifying the researcher as a medieval knight slaying the dragon of pestilence. The medical literature endowed typhus with dimensions that made the disease as real an enemy as a hostile nation-state, a colonial territory, a devious villain, or—to invoke another biological set of myths—a parasitic and alien, marauding race.[23] Bacteriologists encountered the hazards of louse-infested persons, worked with the pathogenic germs in laboratories, and faced the toxic effects of chemical disinfectants like formaldehyde; they might contract diseases carried by rats who lived among corpses and dead animals stored for pathological examination, or inhale the lethal germs.[24] There was a scramble for authority over the hitherto hidden realm of bacteria. The 'great man' view of medical history required great diseases to tame and eradicate—so the heroic discoveries of Robert Koch and his disciples were proclaimed as national triumphs, despite uncertainties about the cure and control of many diseases.

Medical advances resulted in the redefinition of the disease first in terms of its pathological effects on the body, and then in terms of biology. Until the 1830s typhus was a general term for a set of feverish symptoms, high fever, red spots or a rash, and delirium. Between the 1830s and 50s clinicians and pathologists used evidence from autopsies to distinguish between 'typhoid' as a water-borne disease arising from poor sanitation, and 'typhus' or *Fleckfieber* as a disease of poverty and overcrowding. When epidemiologists accepted the distinction, German statistics on 'typhus' actually referred to typhoid, whereas the category *Fleckfieber* (literally

---

[22] Corngold, *Commentators' Despair*, 46–7.

[23] For the historical background see I. Löwy, 'Immunology and Literature in the Early Twentieth Century: *Arrowsmith* and *The Doctor's Dilemma*', *Medical History*, 32 (1988), 314–32.

[24] Geheimes Staatsarchiv Preussischer Kulturbesitz, Berlin (hereafter GSTA) Rep 76 VIII B Nr 3017 Hygiene Institut Posen. Die Bauten, 19 Dec. 1903 for rat infestation.

'spotted fever') denoted typhus. Karl Joseph Ewald in 1880 and Koch's assistant Georg Gaffky in 1884 isolated the bacterium causing typhoid. Whereas typhoid declined due to improved water quality and food hygiene, reduction in typhus rates required eradication of a hidden and unknown cause.[25]

Although typhus had an array of symptoms, not least a distinctive rash, it proved to be elusive, when it came to the application of the strict causal criteria of Koch's bacteriology. Unlike the Koch school's triumphs in locating the bacteria of anthrax, cholera, diphtheria, or tuberculosis, no typhus germ could be proven: for it was impossible to carry out Koch's procedures concerning the cultivation of bacteria and their injection into a laboratory animal to replicate typhus. Establishing a bacteriological cause for a disease was only a first stage; it had to be determined whether the spread of the bacteria could be checked by disinfection, isolation, and sanitary improvements. Therapies were very difficult to attain, as Koch found to his cost in launching his controversial tuberculin 'cure' for tuberculosis in 1891. When Emil Behring, assisted by Shibasaburo Kitasato, Erich Wernicke, and Paul Ehrlich, pioneered a serum to 'cure' diphtheria in the 1890s, this was hailed as constituting a model to prevent and control all infectious diseases. But the euphoria surrounding this innovation rapidly dissolved into debates about the virulence of the bacillus, and the effect of climatic and other physical and social factors. Typhus exposed medical impotence as the germ remained frustratingly invisible and the disease appeared to be unresponsive to sera, chemical therapies, or vaccines.

Bacteriologists commanded an arsenal of disinfectants and hygienic weapons—showers, chemical poisons, and incineration facilities—to tame and eradicate typhus. Yet the fear of contracting typhus and of its rapid spread resulted in medical delusions concerning methods of control. The irony was that the disease spontaneously disappeared from the European heartlands by the early twentieth century without medical intervention other than as part of a general sanitary 'clean up'.[26] Isolated cases and localized epidemics flared up, but it was questionable whether the disease could spread like wildfire throughout the German Reich with its developing sanitary infrastructure as long as rudimentary personal hygiene and sanitation were sustained.

Even if no conclusive proof could be established concerning the role of lice in spreading typhus, lice infestation was deemed to be an entrenched problem. Poverty had long been linked with lousiness and the role of lice in spreading dis-

---

[25] Notably William Gerhard in Philadelphia, P. C. A. Louis in Paris, and Alexander Stewart observing the diseases in Glasgow and Paris during the 1830s, with confirmation from William Jenner 1849–53; A. P. Stewart, *Some Considerations on the Nature and Pathology of Typhus and Typhoid Fever Applied to the Solution of the Question of the Identity or Non-identity of the Two Diseases*, in *Selected Monographs* (London: New Sydenham Society, 1886), 159–226; U. Lindemann, 'Die Geschichte der Krankheitsbezeichnung "Typhus" und der Wandel der Typhuslehre im 19. Jahrhundert in Deutschland', diss. med. dent. FU Berlin, 1986; J. Vögele, 'Typhus und Typhusbekämpfung in Deutschland aus sozialhistorischer Sicht', *Medizinhistorisches Journal*, 3 (1998), 57–79.

[26] P. J. Weindling, 'Medicine and the Holocaust: The Case of Typhus', in I. Löwy (ed.), *Medicine and Change: Historical and Sociological Studies of Medical Innovation* (Montrouge and London, 1993), 447–64.

eases was sporadically suspected before the twentieth century. Poor law work-houses had 'louse ovens' where the inmates' rags were disinfected. The grandmaster of classification, Carol Linnaeus, identified lice in 1758 as 'pediculus', demeaning them with the Latin for 'foot slaves'. Lousiness was dignified in medical Latin as 'pediculosis'; infestation was taken as a general sign of ill health while being associ-ated with boils, carbuncles, and other skin infections. Worse still was 'Phtiriasis' when the lice penetrated the swellings. Lousiness was accompanied by so much dis-comfort that heavy infestation was regarded as an epidemic condition, irrespective of whether the lice carried infections.[27]

Nineteenth-century sanitary regulations for migrants involved a general cleans-ing rather than specific measures against epidemic diseases apart from an insis-tence on smallpox vaccination. A Prussian decree of 1835 required compulsory disinfection of the sick and of all persons in attendance, and of their excreta, cloth-ing, lodgings, and possessions by means of washing, fresh air, burning, boiling, and spraying of disinfectants like chlorine. When thoroughly carried out, these mea-sures destroyed clothing and personal possessions and harmed the respiratory organs. Typhus required a full-scale disinfection as a disease attributed to mias-matic foul air in enclosed spaces like hospitals and workhouses.

Lice were visibly pathogenic. A poor law physician at Insterburg in East Prussia described in 1866 notable cases of louse infestation: impetigo disfigured the skin with viscid and foul-smelling sores, matted scabs and crusts formed at the nape of the neck, a condition known as *plica Polonica* and associated with poor Jews; lice congregated beneath the skin causing swellings and abscesses, and a rough, black discolouring of the skin resulted from haemorrhaging due to louse bites.[28] 'Louse rash' was linked to swellings known as furuncula, and eczema-like skin inflamma-tions. Lice could breed so rapidly that they coated the body in a virtual black fur— whether death arose from the infection or sheer loss of blood was a moot point.[29] Although accusations had long been made that lice were a cause of plague, leprosy, and beri-beri, conclusive experimental evidence was lacking.[30]

The pre-bacteriological emphasis was on the social environment where infec-tion occurred: typhus was synonymous with 'gaol fever', 'ship fever'—prison ships were referred to as floating tombs, 'camp fever', 'hospital fever' or even 'factory fever'. Such terms reflected concern with crowds and filth in public institutions. The disease was attributed to impure air, but the causes were exacerbated by over-crowding and starvation. Liberal-minded physicians attributed epidemics to igno-rance, and social and environmental conditions rather than to a single ferment, germ, or parasite. The radical Berlin pathologist, Rudolf Virchow, diagnosed the Silesian 'famine fever' in 1848–9 as a symptom of oppression by the autocratic Prussian state. His nationalist remedy for what he described as louse-infested,

[27] E. Friedberger, *Zur Entwicklung der Hygiene im Weltkrieg* (Jena, 1919), 159–63.

[28] Cited by Hoeppli, *Parasites and Parasitic Diseases*, 354–6.

[29] E. H. Strach, personal communication 22 Sept. 1995.

[30] G. H. Nuttall, 'The Part Played by *Pediculus Humanus* in the Causation of Disease', *Parasitology*, 10 (1918), 68–71.

overcrowded, and dirty Poles was a good dose of German education and liberal political reform to inculcate a sobre regime of hard work and cleanliness: he aimed to cure the social malaise underlying the spread of the fever.[31] Virchow defined typhus as a group of diseases attacking the nervous system, emphasizing the psychological aspects of the illness. His analysis of local living and climatic conditions was typical of the pre-bacteriological era of medical surveys of the intertwined climatic, socio-economic, and biological factors.

Although outbreaks of typhus among laundresses meant that vermin-infested clothes were suspect, the prevailing medical concern with environmental conditions meant that no causal link between typhus and lice was made. Virchow observed that the poor huddled around stoves to keep warm in winter, and he noted how they were crawling with lice, which he saw as symptoms of general uncleanliness. The less frequent changing of clothes and seasonal reluctance to wash during the colder months accounted for the winter peak in typhus. A classic work on the epidemiology of fevers by Charles Murchison established that fevers spread rapidly in a locality or house, and that personal belongings and clothing could be 'saturated with the typhus poison'.[32] That migrant labourers were known to be susceptible to only mild attacks of typhus was attributed to acquired resistance to the disease in areas where it was endemic, while the non-immune would have a blazing fever and risked death. The dying down of epidemic infections created a fear that the scourges of dearth and disease would return with increased intensity. Pasteur's nascent science of immunology showed that the absence of disease increased vulnerability to infection: if immunity had not been acquired earlier in life, the effect of typhus would be severe.

As typhus, cholera, and malaria were endemic in parts of Eastern Europe, preventive strategies were intensified in the 1890s. The severity of sanitary controls on state frontiers accompanied the emergence of more rigid disease categories and the search for specific causes. Hygienic reformers prescribed local sanitary improvements—the reduction of overcrowding, the provision of washing and public laundering facilities, education and the inculcation of the rudimentary facts of hygiene—whatever was necessary to prevent unwashed and ragged populations huddling together for warmth and comfort. The medical historian, Georg Sticker, observed that police eradication measures against rats and fleas were in vain: far more important was inculcating a sense of cleanliness among the people.[33]

The shift from the reforming liberalism of Virchow's cellular pathology to bacteriologically based concepts of infection meant that typhus was transformed from a

---

[31] R. Virchow, 'Mittheilungen über die in Oberschlesien herrschende Typhusepidemie', *Archiv für pathologische Anatomie und Physiologie und für klinische Medicin* (1849), ii. 143–322, tr. in L. J. Rather (ed.), *Rudolf Virchow. Collected Reports on Public Health and Epidemiology* (Canton, Mass. 1985), i. 205–319.

[32] C. Murchison, *A Treatise on the Continued Fevers of Great Britain*, 3rd edn. (London, 1884), p. xx; Nuttall, 'The Part Played by *Pediculus Humanus* in the Causation of Disease', 47 citing observations made by James Lind in 1833 on laundresses.

[33] G. Sticker, *Die Bedeutung der Geschichte der Epidemien für die heutige Epidemiologie. Ein Beitrag zur Beurteilung des Reichsseuchengesetzes* (Giessen, 1910), 37.

morally and politically construed disease as arising from poor education and social deprivation to being perceived as caused by a specific but still mysterious micro-organism.[34] Some public health experts continued to stress the importance of environmental factors, others considered that general cleansing measures were out of step with advances in the bacteriological understanding of specific diseases. Yet typhus initially eluded the pioneers of bacteriology: Koch believed that the infectious typhus substance was spread by dust, and that ventilation with open windows and doors was the best defence against the disease—an etiology revived during the Second World War; he also thought that relapsing fever might be spread by bugs and fleas (wrongly, as lice were the culprits), and (rightly) as best combated with insect powder.[35] Hans Zinsser, the American bacteriologist and eloquent biographer of the disease, commented, 'Before the true causes of the disease were uncovered, almost every known microorganism had, at some time or another, been implicated.'[36]

Because there was no known cause of typhus, the routine bacteriological tests could not detect the presence of any causal micro-organism. In 1877 Koch had puzzled over a case of typhus as he was unable to detect any 'microcci'.[37] In 1904 the Reich Health Office established guidelines for the prevention of typhus; but the hazards of body lice as the vector in transmitting the infection were overlooked. In 1907 the authorities still suspected that typhus was transmitted by an air-borne germ. Patients had to have their ears, nose, and eyes disinfected with powerful chemicals; their possessions were doused in chlorine, or steamed, boiled, or burned, and rooms were gassed with formaldehyde.[38] The more that bacteriological testing became routine, the less visible typhus became: it could not be detected by conventional procedures and general hygienic improvements diminished its incidence.

Virchow sanguinely observed how 'the threatening spectre of hunger typhus epidemics' erupted only intermittently.[39] Epidemics occurred in 1876–7 in Upper Silesia, in 1878 in Berlin, and finally in 1881 in West Prussia (a province with a substantial Polish population). The Prussian authorities accused vagabonds of importing the disease, and denounced the overcrowding and poor living conditions of railway navvies and of road-building gangs.[40] The sporadic cases of typhus were attributed to migrant apprentices, seasonal labourers from the east, tramps,

[34] A. Hirsch, *Handbook of Geographical and Historical Pathology* (London, 1883), i. 545, 574.

[35] R. Koch, 'Die Bekämpfung der Infektionskrankheiten, insbesondere der Kriegsseuchen. (Rede, gehalten zur Feier des Stiftungstages der Militärärztlichen Bildungsanstalten am 2. August 1888)', *Gesammelte Werke von Robert Koch*, ii, pt. 1, pp. 281–2; id., 'Seuchenbekämpfung im Kriege', ibid., 291–2.

[36] H. Zinsser, *As I Remember Him. The Biography of R.S.* (Boston, 1940), 217.

[37] Möllers, *Koch*, 108–9; Heymann, *Koch*, 225–6.

[38] 'Bekanntmachung betreffend Desinfektionsanweisungen für gemeingefährlichen Krankheiten', *Reichsgesetzblatt*, 17 (1907), 95 ff., includes 'Desinfektionsanweisung der Fleckfieber (Flecktyphus)' (124–32); E. Roesle, *Über Wohnungsdesinfektion mit Formaldehyde, speziell mit Lingnerischen Apparate* (n.p., n.d.).

[39] Rather, *Virchow*, i. 319, 418.

[40] M. Pistor, *Geschichte der preussischen Medizinalverwaltung*, 117. For a similar accusation by the Reich Health Office see A. Roche (ed.), *The Imperial Health Manual* (Dublin and London, 1896), 228–9.

and pedlars.[41] Attention turned to the borders—so as to keep out all carriers of epidemic disease.

From 1894 typhus disappeared from the Prussian army.[42] In Germany typhus rates slumped to just one case in 1901, and between 1901 and 1914 there were seven deaths, mostly of migrant workers crossing from Russia.[43] The incidence of typhus was remarkably low in Germany if compared to 390 deaths in England and Wales between 1899 and 1913, 147 deaths in Scotland between 1905 and 1914, and 1,043 deaths in Ireland, renowned for endemic typhus, between 1899 and 1913.[44] The stigma attached to the Irish as typhus carriers was similar to German resentment of Eastern European migrants. Epidemiologists identified Belfast and Dublin, along with Liverpool and Glasgow, as the last strongholds of typhus.[45] Yet without an identified bacteriological cause there was nothing to screen for: prior to the First World War British port health regulations dealt with cholera, yellow fever, and plague, but ignored typhus.[46] British medical officials brushed off US demands for tougher procedures as presumptuous interference, whereas the German port health authorities complied as fitting in with their desires for tighter controls. By 1900 typhus displaced cholera as the most feared epidemic disease which could engulf Europe.

Environmental explanations were challenged just before the outbreak of the First World War by the discovery of a specific pathogenic organism being deposited by the body louse. Infection occurred not from louse bites but when the human host scratched the micro-organisms into the flesh where the louse had drawn blood. Bacteriologists distinguished typhus from other louse-borne diseases like relapsing fever. The role of the louse as a carrier of the typhus germ was revealed amidst the frenzy of rising war fever between 1910 and 1914. Observations on lice were made during Spanish epidemics, and by Richard Otto, a German bacteriologist, based on Crimean and Balkan evidence. The hunt for the causal organism was pursued by means of epidemiological and experimental observations on colonial subjects. Although bed bugs, lice, and fleas were suspect as carriers of typhus, in 1903 the Spanish researcher Cortezo postulated the louse as the carrier, and in 1907–11 researchers in India, Algeria, and Egypt linked louse infestation to outbreaks of relapsing fever among natives who (reputedly) hardly ever washed or changed their clothes.[47] In 1909 Charles Nicolle, the Director of the Pasteur

---

[41] H. Hetsch, 'Flecktyphus in Deutschland im 19. Jahrhundert', *Zeitschrift für Hygiene*, 124 (1942–3), 241–9.

[42] H. H. Ries, 'Über die geschichtliche, insbesondere die kriegsgeschichtliche Bedeuting des Fleckfiebers', med. diss., Hamburg, 1944, 45.

[43] Bundesarchiv Koblenz (hereafter BAK) R 86/1039 Bd 1.

[44] Nuttall, 'The Part Played by *Pediculus Humanus*', 45; Hirsch, *Handbook*, i. 555.

[45] B. Luckin, 'Evaluating the Sanitary Revolution: Typhus and Typhoid in London, 1851–1900', in R. Woods and J. Woodward (eds.), *Urban Disease and Mortality* (London and New York, 1984), 102–19.

[46] e.g. *Regulations as to Cholera, Yellow Fever and Plague (Ships Arriving from Foreign Ports)* (London: Local Government Board, 1907). For a novel concern with typhus: R. J. Reece, 'Port Sanitary Administration', *British Medical Journal* (1922), 1–10 (as offprint).

[47] Nuttall, 'Part', 58–9.

Institute of Tunis, noticed the absence of typhus at the native hospital where newly admitted patients were bathed and dressed in clean hospital clothing. He demonstrated that lice feeding on experimentally infected chimpanzees could infect healthy chimpanzees.[48] In 1913 researchers at the Pasteur Institute, Algiers proved that when louse-infested persons scratched themselves, the bursting of lice near an abrasion would induce relapsing fever, and they conjectured that scratching in infected louse faeces caused typhus. Three natives were 'voluntarily' infected with crushed lice, and the diagnosis of typhus was confirmed by infecting monkeys and finding suspected typhus germs in the bodies of the implicated lice.[49]

By the outbreak of war in 1914 the lethal role of the louse was beginning to be accepted, but the evidence was inconclusive as to whether head lice (similar to the body or clothes lice apart from their habitat), fleas, and bed bugs were culprits in spreading typhus, and it was still not known whether typhus could also be transmitted by person-to-person contact.[50] Austrian military regulations in 1911 and civil legislation of 1913 commanded eradication (*Vertilgung*) of *Ungeziefer*, as lice, bugs, and fleas were the likely culprits of typhus and relapsing fever. Lice were accused of sucking the blood of the sick and then injecting the contagious particle by biting the healthy. Dousing clothes in petrol, and immersing infested persons in warm baths after rubbing them down with medicated soap were prescribed.[51]

The question whether the louse was the sole vector of typhus prompted more human experiments—when infected typhus blood was injected or crushed nits were used to innoculate persons by scarification.[52] The possibility of direct infection by droplets of saliva expelled by coughing in the air was debated. Experiments on prisoners were inconclusive. The disciples of Pasteur, Alexandre Yersin and J. Vassal in Indo-China, tried to prove the transmission of typhus by the direct injection of typhus blood in humans. The causal microorganism was by no means obvious. In Algeria in 1914 distinctive 'microbes' (the Germans preferred to speak of bacteria) were identified in the lice living on the sick, but Nicolle, Georges Blanc, and Ernest Conseil in Tunis found this pathogen in typhus-free districts.[53]

[48] C. Nicolle, C. Comte, and E. Conseil, 'Experimental Transmission of Exanthematic Typhus through Body Lice', in N. Hahon, *Selected Papers on the Pathogenic Rickettsiae* (Cambridge, Mass., 1968), 37–40; M. Huet, *Le Pommier et l'olivier. Charles Nicolle, une biographie (1866–1936)* (n.p., 1995), 86–95; L. Gross, 'How Charles Nicolle of the Pasteur Institute Discovered that Epidemic Typhus is Transmitted by Lice: Reminiscences from My Years at the Pasteur Institute in Paris', *Proceedings of the National Academy of Sciences of the USA*, 93 (1996), 10539–40.

[49] Experiments of E. Sergent, H. Foley, and C. Vialette, *Archives de l'Institut Pasteur de l'Afrique du Nord*, 1/3 (1921), reported as 'Experimental Transmission of Typhus to Man', *Lancet* (4 Mar. 1922), 445; J. R. Busvine, *Insects, Hygiene and History* (London, 1976), 239–42; Nuttall, 'Part', 61.

[50] His, *Front*, 37.

[51] *Vorschrift über die Verhütung und Bekämpfung der Infektionskrankheiten im k. u. k. Heere* (Vienna, 1911), 63–5, 128–9; W. Prausnitz, *Desinfektion* (Vienna, 1914), 4 concerning Gesetz betreffend die Verhütung und Bekämpfung übertragbarer Krankheiten, 20–1.

[52] Nuttall, 'Part', 48–50. The first such experiment was a fatal self-experiment by Moczutovski in 1900. 'Experimental Transmission of Typhus to Man', *Lancet* (4 Mar. 1922), 445; *Archives des Instituts Pasteur de l'Afrique du Nord*, 1/3 (1921).

[53] R. P. Strong, G. C. Shattuck, A. W. Sellards, *et al.*, *Typhus Fever with Particular Reference to the Serbian Epidemic* (Cambridge, Mass., 1920), 44–57.

The eventual discovery of the causal organism of typhus was an opportunity to commemorate researchers who died 'on active service'. The double-barrelled name of the pathogen (*Rickettsià prowazeki*) causing typhus derived from two heroes of research into the louse-based transmission of the typhus 'virus', Howard Taylor Ricketts and Stanislaus von Prowazek. Ricketts found that the body louse had an important role as a vector of typhus in studies of the Mexican epidemic of 1910, when he succumbed to typhus. In 1916 his name was bestowed on the class of invasive micro-organisms smaller than the smallest known bacteria and which came to be known as 'rickettsiae'.[54] The characteristics of rickettsiae remained controversial, so that the idea persisted that typhus was a group of diseases rather than a single disease with a unique pathogen. Variants of typhus were discovered, notably rat-borne typhus in America and scrub typhus in Asia. Bacteriologists modified their notions of a uniform disease with a single cause by paying attention to varying forms of the disease and types of causes, for example, inhaling dust containing louse faeces.

iii. International Controls

The factual observations of medical researchers should not obscure how typhus has to be approached at a symbolic level as a set of metaphors; these expressed in the objective terms of medical science the threats of alien, non-European behaviour, culture, and social conditions. The fear of an epidemic spreading like wildfire legitimated international administrative responses, designed to exclude, contain, and segregate the ethnically 'primitive'. The perception of typhus as a potential menace to socio-economically advanced European nation-states was far greater than its actual incidence measured in terms of reported cases. Despite the *Angst* surrounding a cataclysmic typhus epidemic, and localized outbreaks of the disease, the expected epidemic apocalypse never occurred, and arguably never could have occurred given that typhus could be checked by regular washing and laundering of clothes. By the twentieth century diseases like malaria and typhus were relegated to endemic pockets on the margins of Europe, where cholera was tamed, and plague was more an object of historical study than an actual threat. Bacteriologists hoped that an effective system of medical controls on borders and an improved sanitary infrastructure would guard the European continent from alien 'Asiatic' infections.

Innovative branches of medicine like pathology and parasitology imposed systems of order and control on micro-organisms and their insect carriers. The modern body politic was kitted out with elaborate border controls and passports,

---

[54] *Contributions to Medical Science by Howard Taylor Ricketts (1870–1910)* (Chicago, 1911); V. A. Harden, 'Rocky Mountain Spotted Fever Research and the Development of the Insect Vector Theory, 1900–1930', *Bulletin of the History of Medicine*, 59 (1985), 449–66; id., *Rocky Mountain Spotted Fever. History of a Twentieth-century Disease* (Baltimore, Md., 1990), 109; H. da Rocha Lima, 'Zur Aetiologie des Fleckfiebers', *Berliner klinische Wochenschrift*, 53 (1916), 567–72, tr. in N. Hahon (ed.), *Selected Papers on the Pathogenic Rickettsiae* (Cambridge, Mass., 1968), 74–8.

and trimmed with the formalities of medical inspection, delousing, quarantine, and compulsory vaccination. The controls were all the harsher as typhus carriers were identified either by the presence of lice (which may or may not have been infected) or by the indirect and much disputed Weil–Felix serological test. Sanitary authorities policed national frontiers, and international conventions regulated disinfection and quarantine measures, while medical relief organizations sought to eradicate typhus at source. Escape from racial persecution and social misery became ever harder, as typhus spurred German public health officials to seal the nation's eastern borders against refugees from the east.

The internationalism of medicine boosted the status of medical officials with conferences, sanitary agreements, and exchange visits to colleagues' laboratories and sanitary facilities. Maritime health agencies employed bacteriologists to police the spread of bacteria and of their human and animal hosts. Port and city health officers and the new institutes for tropical medicine competed to magnify their facilities and powers. Disinfecting goods and the quarantining of persons and livestock were to prevent plague, cholera, and typhus invading the European heartlands, by excluding undesirable germs, parasites, and their human hosts. Bacteriologists rallied to the defence of national borders, claiming that they were sustaining European civilization against the microbial hordes; disinfection squadrons sealed off infected areas and penetrated into contaminated housing in order to burn or disinfect infested possessions. The harder out-migration became, the more social tensions built up: those who might otherwise have migrated were stigmatized as parasites, providing a scientized form for the persecution of social outcasts—of Jews, gypsies, and of the multiplicity of ethnic minorities throughout Europe whose sporadic distribution stained the map of nation-states. The First World War drastically reduced migration from the east, and the Versailles Treaty favoured ethnically homogeneous nation-states. Sanitary techniques once designed to promote European settlement in overseas colonies were harnessed to sustain national integrity against epidemics from the east.

Typhus control and eradication measures constituted a medical discourse on the barbaric threats to European civilization from the Asiatic margins.[55] The fear of an epidemic conflagration meant that various waves of epidemics like plague, 'Asiatic' cholera, and typhus were conflated as leading to global devastation. Dostoyevsky concluded *Crime and Punishment* (written during 1865–6) with the imprisoned Raskolnikov dreaming that Europe had succumbed to an unknown and terrible plague from the depths of Asia, as a new kind of microscopic germ infected villages, whole towns, and peoples, leading to insanity and an epidemic of violent killing; only a few chosen people would survive to start a new race. Horrific new plagues combined known characteristics of various diseases but in a composite and more lethal form. National ideologues attributed immense power to the invisible bacterial foes. The boundaries blurred between sober observation and racial

[55] That Hippocrates in the fifth century BC characterized 'the Asiatics' as cowardly and mentally feeble was noted by German advocates in support of a renaissance of environmental epidemiology. Hippocrates, 'Airs, Waters, Places', 16.

demonology, suggesting that social ills could be attributed to a macabre world of grotesque diseases and human parasites.[56]

Delousing and disinfection procedures were scientized rites of purification for supposedly parasitical populations. In 1868 Virchow reflected on medieval fears of Jews having poisoned wells, when seeking to raise support for the victims of a typhus epidemic in East Prussia:

Epidemics and the persecution of the Jews belong together from a certain internal necessity—a sad example of how the human intellect, even in a quite justified direction of research, is diverted into a totally wrong approach through prejudice, the innocent ultimately having to pay for the guilty.[57]

Medical science advanced on lines which rendered Virchow's observations prophetic. All proportions came to be in disarray as the microscopic underworld of pathogenic germs became magnified into the grotesque *homo parasiticus*.[58] The historical journey from the cleansing of migrants to their eradication was underway.

---

[56] A. Bein, 'The Jewish Parasite. Notes on the Semantics of the Jewish Problem with Special Reference to Germany', *Leo Baeck Institute Yearbook*, 9 (1964), 3–40.

[57] R. Virchow, 'On Hunger Typhus and Related Forms of Disease. (Lecture read on the 9th of February 1868 for the Benefit of Typhus Cases in East Prussia)', in L. J. Rather (ed.), *Rudolf Virchow. Collected Essays on Public Health and Epidemiology* (Canton, Mass., 1985), i. 443.

[58] Bein, 'The Jewish Parasite', 18, 21, 35.

2

Eradicating Parasites

i. Racial Therapies

In July 1941 Hitler proclaimed himself the discoverer of the Jew as the 'ferment of social decay'. He compared himself to Robert Koch, the Nobel-prize-winning bacteriologist. Just as Koch had proved specific bacteria caused infectious diseases, so Hitler claimed to have detected how the 'Jewish race' as a 'bacillus', 'virus', 'toxin', or consumptive 'parasite' poisoned and infected the German body politic.[1] Convinced that infectiousness was an attribute of Jewish racial inferiority, the lethal threat of the Jewish pathogens justified resort to a strong antidote: Hitler prescribed elimination of 'Jewish bacteria' to revive the vitality of the Aryan race.[2]

When Hitler assumed the mantle of Koch, he believed that his armies were poised to capture the city of Kiev—a delusion confounded by fierce resistance until late September 1941.[3] While conquest of the east held out enticing prospects of natural resources and *Lebensraum* for German settlers, the invading German forces confronted climatic extremes and epidemic hazards. Bacteriology became entangled with the genocidal campaign to clear vast areas of Eastern Europe for settlement by racially valuable German stock. The Nazi war machine mobilized tropical medicine and bacteriology to provide a shield of immunity against lethal diseases in the east.

Hitler's medical rhetoric drew on an evolving body of German medical triumphs. Nazi medical propagandists projected an image of the German physician as a guardian of racial health and as an intrepid warrior against disease. Nazi medical historians attributed German scientific breakthroughs in the battle against bacteria to innate cultural superiority. They demonstrated that scientific advance arose less from experimental skills and more from a special 'racial' affinity for nature. As Germanic cultural heroes, bacteriologists were celebrated as heirs to 'storm and stress' romantic philosophers, seventeenth-century nature mystics, and

---

[1] P. Burrin, *Hitler and the Jews. The Genesis of the Holocaust* (London, 1994), 136. For further examples of the Jew as a 'ferment of decomposition' see R. A. Koenigsberg, *Hitler's Ideology. A Study in Psychoanalytic Sociology*, 3rd edn. (New York, 1992), 9–11, and on the national body as diseased, 16–19, and consumed by parasites, 19–20; H. Picker, *Hitlers Tischgespräche im Führerhauptquartier* (Stuttgart, 1976), 79, 1 Dec. 1941.

[2] R. A. Pois, *National Socialism and the Religion of Nature* (London, 1986), 59, 122–5, 131; S. E. Aschheim, *The Nietzsche Legacy in Germany 1890–1990* (Berkeley, Calif., 1992), 70–3.

[3] Kiev did not fall until the week after 19 September 1941, when German troops entered the city. The Germans massacred mainly Jewish children, women, and the elderly at the ravine of Babi Yar. A. J. Mayer, *Why Did the Heavens Not Darken? The Final Solution in History* (New York, 1988), 242–3, 248–9, 265–8. For the strategic significance of Kiev to Hitler See B. A. Leach, *German Strategy against Russia 1939–1941* (Oxford, 1973), 209–13.

Reformation iconoclasts like Paracelsus who claimed transcendent mastery over the natural forces of decay and disease. The physician was transmuted from a healer of the sick individual into a national Führer figure armed with new scientific powers over nature and human life. This vein of complex and evocative images was tapped to justify the extermination of 'parasites' and experimentation on racial inferiors.

A militant cohort of Nazi physicians and scientists rallied to Hitler's call for a struggle against diseased parasites. But the fusion of medical thinking on disease with Nazi ideology was frequently strained: medical officials could not agree on the origins and dissemination of epidemics, disinfection technologies, the merits of various vaccines, poison gases and of DDT, the value of cremation, and the viability of germ warfare, let alone over the racial predisposition to disease. Even among the well-drilled ranks of the SS, there were clashes over the constituting factors of race and disease. Key Nazi concepts like the *Volksschädling* developed in the context of differing methods for dealing with human parasites.

Hitler's sense of continuing the legacy of Koch's bacteriological breakthroughs was consistent with camouflaging genocide by means of the terminology and technologies of disinfection. The centenary of Koch's birth in 1943 was celebrated by depicting Koch as a Führer figure and his school as a monolithic scientific orthodoxy. The notion of a triumphal bacteriological *Blitzkrieg*, launched in 1892 by the 'unassailable' Koch school was a myth propounded by Nazi propagandists keen to heroize the German medical genius. There were dissident undercurrents in the portrayal of Koch. Influential epidemiologists pointed out the medical limitations of bacteriology in not taking account of biological variations and environmental circumstances. The focus on Koch obscured how diverse approaches in German hygiene had persisted.

ii. The Rise of Bacteriology

The Nazi image of Koch as a loyal servant of Prussia and the Reich, a fervent patriot, and a dutiful military medical officer has generated a dichotomy between bacteriological hygiene as militarist and state-oriented, or a more liberal, municipally based prioritizing of environmental factors and social conditions.[4] Koch's bacteriology has been portayed as being in conflict with the environmentalism of Max Pettenkofer, the holder of the first German chair in hygiene since 1865, and by 1882 as sceptical of Koch's 'fungus hunting'.[5] Set against the typology of a state-sponsored and militarist bacteriology was liberal and municipal support for bacteriological innovations: doctors and the public enthused over what amounted to social bacteriology. The Berlin municipal authorities backed the new therapies of

[4] A. Labisch. *Homo Hygienicus. Gesundheit und Medizin in der Neuzeit* (Frankfurt/M., 1992), 132–41.
[5] Heymann, *Robert Koch*, ii. 89. The other Bavarian universities of Erlangen and Würzburg also established teaching positions in hygiene in 1865. See H.-H. Eulner, *Die Entwicklung der medizinischen Spezialfächer an den Universitäten des deutschen Sprachgebietes* (Stuttgart, 1970), 154–5.

Koch's tuberculin and Behring's serum therapy in the 1890s. The boundary of state and municipality was in any case blurred in the Hanseatic city states of Bremen and Hamburg, as well as in Berlin with the police presidium's medical powers. The Prussian official responsible for universities, Friedrich Althoff, masterminded schemes linking state, municipal, and philanthropic resources: such mixed funding provided Paul Ehrlich with the Frankfurt serum testing and experimental therapy institute.[6] The ranks of Koch disciples contained a multiplicity of viewpoints, and Althoff supported the careers of Koch, Behring, and Ehrlich despite their manifold disagreements.

Far from any 'last stand' by the environmentalist Max von Pettenkofer at the time of the Hamburg cholera epidemic of 1892–3, an entrenched faction among the hygiene experts continued to support von Pettenkofer's localism and resisted Koch's laws for a uniform bacterial cause of each infectious disease.[7] In Berlin Koch was succeeded as professor of hygiene by Max Rubner, who was renowned for studies of the physiology of nutrition. In Munich, von Pettenkofer's successor from 1892, Eduard Buchner, investigated the effects of environmental factors in eradicating bacteria, demonstrating the importance of air, sun, and light in preventing tuberculosis. How an infection was ignited aroused an environmentalist counter-attack on the new bacteriology. Holistic critics pointed out how germs could lie latent, and that a disease could assume a variety of forms, contingent on local conditions. Adolf Gottstein, a lapsed bacteriologist, municipal medical officer in the Berlin district of Charlottenburg (and from 1919 ministerial director of the Prussian Medical Department) argued that improved housing and diet would enhance the body's powers of resistance to disease.[8] Bacteriology did not displace environmental reform.

Koch's mission was to discover causal links between a bacteriological species and a disease, so that a disease could be prevented by tracing how its causal bacteria spread. Bacteriologists refined their theories of causality, as their screening procedures taught them that exposure to a microbe did not necessarily result in an outbreak of disease. In 1903 Wilhelm von Drigalski, a military medical officer and former assistant to Koch, elaborated the concept of carriers as apparently healthy persons who harboured pathogenic bacteria, which he compared to domestic pet animals. The implications were that the healthy as well as the sick had to be screened. In 1903 a small army of bacteriologists was drafted into the area of Trier, Alsace-Lorraine, and the Saar to eliminate typhoid. They had special powers to track down the carriers of pathogenic bacteria. Such endeavours resulted in

---

[6] For the complexities of state supervision of the Berlin Magistrat see W. Ribbe, *Geschichte Berlins* (Munich, 1987), ii. 745; W. U. Eckart, 'Friedrich Althoff und die Medizin', in B. vom Brocke (ed.), *Wissenschaftsgeschichte und Wissenschaftspolitik im Industriezeitalter* (Hildesheim, 1991), 375–404.

[7] cf. R. J. Evans, *Death in Hamburg. Society and Politics in the Cholera Years 1830–1910* (Oxford, 1987), 490–507 for the argument that Koch's state-oriented bacteriology triumphed over Pettenkofer's localist environmentalism.

[8] A. Gottstein, *Das Heilwesen der Gegenwart, Gesundheitslehre und Gesundheitspolitik* (Berlin, 1924), M. Stürzbecher, 'Aus der Geschichte des Charlottenburger Gesundheitswesens', *Bär von Berlin* (1980), 43–113.

elaborate medical controls, and reached fever pitch during the First World War. Under the Weimar Republic, Neufeld the Director of the Prussian Institute for Infectious Diseases conceded that bacteriologists had over-extrapolated their model of infection and control.[9]

Although Nazi propagandists projected the image of Koch as a Germanic racial warrior, it is worthwhile examining how the historical record of bacteriologists' triumphs over the 'Third Reich' of micro-organisms in Imperial Germany was manipulated under Nazism.[10] Was an ideology of disease extermination revolving round the concept of *Ausrottung* (i.e. extermination) central to bacteriology, and did this link bacteriology to genocide? Did the legacy of Koch's bacteriology boost racial hygiene and how did this relate to 'geo-medicine'—the revamped term for Pettenkofer's environmentalism with explicit links to expansionist geo-politics? Did the Nazification of bacteriology misrepresent the founders of bacteriology as anti-Semitic, and did bacteriologists assist Hitler's racial crusade against the Jewish 'virus'? The responses of bacteriologists to 'Asiatic' epidemics indicate whether there was an inherent exterminatory potential in bacteriology and in related fields like parasitology.

Most founders of German bacteriology were fervent nationalists and imperialists, but only exceptionally were they anti-Semites. In 1876 Koch, then an unknown physician in the predominately Polish Eastern Marches, sought advice from the Breslau botanist Ferdinand Cohn, who remarkably for a university professor at the time was Jewish. Koch sent Cohn his preparations of anthrax bacilli, and continued to seek his guidance. Cohn had since 1868 pioneered study of bacteria by applying his skills in plant physiology, discovering that bacteria were plant species, and he developed techniques to culture and classify bacteria. Cohn facilitated Koch's transformation from an obscure provincial medical officer into a dynamic researcher at the Reich Health Office.[11] That Koch had few Jewish assistants arose not from any personal antipathy to Jews but because assistants' posts were filled by seconded military medical officers at a time when the Prussian army opposed promotion of Jews to the regular officer corps.[12] Koch was on cordial terms with the waywardly brilliant Ehrlich and the director of his serological department, August von Wassermann (both Jewish); his assistant and intended successor Carl Fraenkel (who in 1908 Germanized his name to Fraenken) had a Jewish background. Among the early bacteriologists, religion was no barrier to academic cooperation among converts to an exciting new branch of medicine, but this was to change. The Nazi

[9] J. A. Mendelsohn, 'Cultures of Bacteriology: Formation and Transformation of a Science in France and Germany, 1870–1914', Ph.D. thesis, Princeton, 1996, 560–775.

[10] W. Boelsche, *Das Liebesleben in der Natur* (Jena, 1905), is p. iii, 'Vom 'dritten Reich' und seine Liebe'.

[11] B. Heymann, *Robert Koch, i, Teil 1843–1882* (Leipzig, 1932), 220–3; P. Cohn, *Ferdinand Cohn. Blätter der Erinnerung* (Breslau, 1901), 181–91; J. Seide, 'Le Grand Botaniste et Bactériologiste Ferdinand Cohn', *Revue d'histoire de la médecine hébraïque*, 5 (1950), 23–52.

[12] K. Demeter, *The German Officer-Corps in Society and State 1650–1945* (London, 1965), 224–30. But note that Jews could be commissioned as Prussian reserve-officers, and the situation varied in each state.

biography of Koch by Hellmuth Unger, an influential poet-physician and advocate of euthanasia, suppressed mention of Cohn's name.[13]

The Nazi medical ideologists lavished even greater attention on Koch's renegade assistant, Emil Behring, whose somewhat manic personality was portrayed in terms of heroic struggle. Behring was an ardent nationalist, but he was not conspicuously anti-Semitic. Although the partnership between Behring and Ehrlich in developing serum therapy rapidly dissolved into bitter scientific and commercial disputes, Behring later sought to collaborate with Ehrlich on a remedy for tuberculosis. Behring's ideas of disinfecting blood and his development of blood serum therapies for diphtheria and tetanus led to theories of differential immunity in which heredity was a factor. But medical ideas of cleansing blood were not necessarily linked to racial purity.[14] Nazi historians posthumously recruited Behring, admiring his *Kampfgeist* as he clashed with the noted liberal Virchow. They delineated Behring's Germanic psychology, and discovered that not only had Behring corresponded with the racist philosopher, Eduard von Hartmann, but also that in unpublished writings on German national psychology, Behring gave vent to anti-Semitism: 'The Jew speaks German, but does not think as a German'.[15] Behring's wife, Else, had a partially Jewish family background, and his outlook was that of a conservative nationalist rather than of an anti-Semitic activist. In 1941 the author of a popular biography overcame Behring's deficiencies in the matter of anti-Semitism by having Behring's sister deliver anti-Semitic utterances, when it came to Behring's rivalry with Hans Aronson (vilified as a Jewish protégé of the liberal Virchow) over serum therapy. In 1942 the comment on the un-German Jew was highlighted in a series of sketches of 'physicians in the struggle for Germany'; the overall ideological thrust of dragooning Behring into the campaign against racial undesirables in the east was conveyed by the final portrait in this Germanic medical gallery which was of a Bromberg physician, Siegfried Staemmler, who was killed by Poles early in September 1939.[16]

While the key figure of Koch remained immune from the virus of anti-Semitism, other bacteriologists felt unease about the east. Carl Flügge, who argued that Silesia's vulnerability to epidemics necessitated a hygiene institute, confided to the Prussian Ministerial Director, Althoff, his revulsion from the 'alien species' among the population of Breslau. A colleague, Friedrich von Müller, classed Flügge as an antisemite among the ranks of the Breslau medical faculty. Flügge was a staunch friend of Koch, while seeking a compromise between Koch's bacteriology and Pettenkofer's environmentalism. When appointed to the chair of hygiene in Berlin in

[13] H. Unger, *Robert Koch. Roman eines grossen Lebens* (Berlin, n.d.), 100–22. L. Glésinger, 'Robert Koch et les Juifs', *Revue d'histoire de la médecine hébraïque*, 59 (1963), 15–24.

[14] For such a leap via notions of blood see S. Gilman, *Franz Kafka. The Jewish Patient* (New York, 1995), 110.

[15] H. Zeiss and R. Bieling, *Behring. Gestalt und Werk* (Berlin, 1941), 118–21, 141–8, 481–96.

[16] O. Gerhardt, *Stationen einer Idee. Behrings schicksalsvoller Weg* (Berlin, 1941), 11, 54, 56; H. O. Kleine, *Ärzte kämpfen für Deutschland* (Stuttgart, 1942), 252–61, 295–7.

1909, Flügge intensified support for racial and social hygiene. Yet he stopped short of ideas of racial purity, and he worked with several Jewish assistants. Among these was Bruno Heymann, who pioneered poison gas for delousing and researched a pioneering biography of Koch, which the Nazis exploited.[17]

Of the early bacteriologists, Ferdinand Hueppe, a lapsed Koch disciple, was the most noted exponent of Aryan ideology in writings on the racial hygiene of the ancient Greeks. He condemned Jewish ritual slaughter of animals, ostensibly because he regarded meat that had been bled as of lower quality. Hueppe's trenchant critique of Koch's bacteriology and advocacy of predisposition and racial factors in disease led him to formulate a theory of 'constitutional hygiene'. He advocated state measures to promote diet and exercise, and gained the admiration of the racial ideologue Houston Stewart Chamberlain, who had scientific pretensions as a botanist.[18] Yet Hueppe worked with Jewish assistants in Prague, and was careful to mount his attacks on Jewish traditions in scientific terms so as to appear to be correcting outmoded customs. While Hueppe can be ranked as a nationally minded critic of bacteriology, he remained closely linked to the scientifically oriented racial hygienists rather than to the racist and anti-Semitic ultra-right.

German Jewish doctors and scientists contributed much to their nation's world leadership in medical science. Religious background was generally irrelevant in developing bacteriology. The first generation of bacteriologists were 'ordinary Germans' in that they were zealous patriots and devoted to the national culture of the educated bourgeoisie; a virulent, deeply rooted, and widespread anti-Semitism was not evident amongst their ranks. Cohn and Koch spoke a common language of scientific patriotism. Cohn combined experimental hygiene with anti-Catholicism, and advocacy of Darwinism and evolutionary sociology. In 1874 in a speech to the Breslau meeting of German Scientists and Doctors, Cohn prophesied that a general staff of doctors would defend the peoples' health and national life against the invisible enemies in the air, soil, and water. By 1890 Koch was the acclaimed chief of this general staff.[19]

Despite Cohn's prophecy, a unified phalanx of Koch disciples did not materialize. The Koch school polarized into nationalist and liberal factions: one, more militarist in ethos, shifted from bacteriology to racial hygiene and geo-medicine, and another politically more liberal group was more orthodox in sustaining Koch's principles of causal bacteria. Before 1914 Rhoda Erdmann and Lydia Rabinowitsch-Kempner, both incidentally Jewish, worked at the Institute for Infectious Diseases,

[17] GSTA Rep 92 Nachlass Althoff B Nr 41 Bd 2 Flügge to Althoff 24 Nov. 1886, 29 June 1894; F. von Müller, *Lebenserinnerungen* (Munich, 1953), 92–3; H. Horn and W. Thom, *Carl Flügge (1847–1923). Integrator der Hygiene* (Wiesbaden, 1992), 26 consider that Flügge was not anti-Semitic given that he had several Jewish assistants; G. Henneberg, K. Janitschke, M. Stürzbecher, *et al.* (eds.), *Robert Koch, ii. Teil 1882–1908. Nach Fragmenten von Bruno Heymann* (Berlin, 1997), 10–16, 30–1.

[18] F. Hueppe, *Zur Rassen- und Sozialhygiene der Griechen im Altertum und in der Gegenwart* (Wiesbaden, 1897); Gilman, *Jewish Patient*, 135, 197–8; Weindling, *Health, Race and German Politics*, 110, 130, 170–3, 228.

[19] F. Cohn, 'Der Zellenstaat', *Deutsche Rundschau*, 27 (1881), 62–80; K. Litthauer, *Ueber Einrichtung von Desinfectionsanstalten* (Leipzig and Berlin, 1889), 3.

the bastion of Koch's ideas. In 1917 a political moderate, Fred Neufeld, took over as director of the Institute, and the 1920s saw a number of left-wing radicals among the ranks of bacteriologists. The expanding discipline of bacteriology provided Jewish researchers with career opportunities in state and municipal laboratories. Michael Hubenstorf has documented how the polarization in bacteriology culminated in one-third of the staff of the 'Prussian Institute for Infectious Diseases, Robert Koch' having to emigrate after 1933.[20]

Political values intruded into bacteriology in terms of explicit party political allegiances—for example, in Behring's conservative municipal politics, and in Koch's role as an agent of the Reich Health Office at the time of the Hamburg cholera epidemic; the conservative minister Gustav von Gossler pressured Koch into publicizing tuberculin therapy. Yet in contrast to Virchow as a liberal politician, bacteriologists were not so much political activists as supporters of a depoliticizing strategy to remove the causes of diseases as a means of reducing social conflict. Professors of hygiene mobilized the public to support educational campaigns against such scourges as syphilis or tuberculosis, and to accept disinfection and isolation.[21] Reservoirs of germs came under attack—whether harboured by prostitutes and vagrants, or in contaminated food and infested housing. Hygienic campaigns were predicated on the faith that once disease-producing hazards were eliminated, then orderly social life could flourish.

Military, state, municipal, and (as at Gelsenkirchen in the heart of the Ruhr) industrialists' recognition of the utility of Koch's work meant that his bacteriological procedures won official acclaim in Imperial Germany. The Prussian military authorities deployed bacteriologists, drilled in Koch's rigorous methods, and the armies of Baden, Bavaria, and Austria-Hungary, and the Reich navy followed suit. Koch was satirized for regimenting colonies of bacteria into categories of immutable species. He battled for the victory of his school by warning the military medical establishment that typhus as a disease of war could exterminate whole armies composed of the youthful male 'buds of the nation'. Koch's doctrine of specific bacterial causes meant that he rejected that diseases like typhus and tuberculosis were caused by generalized social misery.[22] Whereas reformers demanded costly intervention to counteract social deprivation and the spread of diseases, bacteriology required the targeted eradication of infective bacilli, or some means of curbing their reproduction. Bacteriology held out prospects of a technical solution to

[20] M. Hubenstorf, 'Aber es kommt mir doch so vor, als ob Sie dabei nichts verloren hätten', 355–460, 394–5.

[21] P. J. Weindling, 'Hygienepolitik als sozialintegrative Strategie im späten Deutschen Kaiserreich', in A. Labisch and R. Spree (eds.), *Medizinische Deutungsmacht im sozialen Wandel des 19. und frühen 20. Jahrhunderts* (Bonn, 1989), 37–56.

[22] R. Koch, 'Die Bekämpfung der Infektionskrankheiten, insbesondere der Kriegsseuchen. (Rede, gehalten zur Feier des Stiftungstages der Militärärztlichen Bildungsanstalten am 2. August 1888.)', *Gesammelte Werke von Robert Koch*, ii, pt. 1, pp. 277–8, 280–1. A. Hirsch attacked the narrowness of this approach in the following year: Hirsch, *Über die historische Entwicklung der Öffentlichen Gesundheitspflege. Rede gehalten zur Feier des Stiftungstages der militärischen Bildungsanstalten am 2. August 1889* (Bad Reichenhall, 1967).

economically burdensome diseases. Moreover, imperialists welcomed bacteriology as a means of control of infectious diseases in otherwise inhospitable colonial
contexts. Hygiene had a dual character as a scientific discipline, and as a creed of
national salvation to transcend political conflicts and to strengthen Germany as a
world power.

Bacteriologists were scientific empire builders. Koch and his former assistant
Bernhard Nocht in Hamburg built up institutions with expanding responsibilities
over environmental conditions and housing, trade, and transport. Koch devised a
battery of medical and social countermeasures against potential epidemics. He
supported public education to improve general hygiene, notification of infectious
diseases, disinfection measures, water filtration, effective sewer systems, and quarantine. Despite the rigour of his causal criteria, he did not advocate a single experimental strategy to cure diseases, to the exclusion of general hygienic measures. The
bacteriologist was as much a scientific missionary preaching commandments of
hygienic behaviour, as a medical police officer with powers to confine, isolate, and
detain in tracking down pathogenic germs.[23]

Although bacteriologists claimed that animal and human experiments were in
the long-term interest of the nation, they differed in their experimental ethics.
Koch first tried his new tuberculin cure on himself, and others tested sera on their
children. The enthusiasm for experimental medicine gave rise to ethical abuses and
public protest. Medical experiments were carried out on the socially vulnerable as
prisoners, the mentally ill, prostitutes, children, and native peoples under colonial
rule. During the 1890s anti-vivisectionists denounced doctors for implanting
worms in children and injecting gonococci for the study of the resulting inflamma-
tions.[24] Anti-vivisectionists protested that the poor were treated as 'experimental
rabbits' in public hospitals. The debate concerning human experiments raged on,
as laboratory-based medicine was condemned as soulless and mechanistic. After
the Nazi takeover experimentalists welcomed the removal of democratic checks to
their activities.

Koch supervised experiments with Atoxyl, an arsenical compound, in German
East Africa and Uganda from April 1906 until November 1907 in order to treat
sleeping sickness. In 1903 how a species of tsetse fly spread the disease was discovered, and the German colony appeared to be increasingly vulnerable to the spread
of the disease from Uganda. Because Koch considered that repeated and large doses
of Atoxyl were necessary, he established the first German 'concentration camp' for
sleeping sickness therapy in the north-west of the colony. He was convinced that
the British should also be persuaded to establish 'concentration camps' as part of a
'rational epidemic prevention'. The British in neighbouring Uganda came to use

---

[23] C. E. Rosenberg, *Explaining Epidemics and Other Studies in the History of Medicine* (Cambridge, 1992), 299.

[24] B. Elkeles, 'Medizinische Menschenversuche gegen Ende des 19. Jahrhunderts und der Fall Neisser', *Medizinhistorisches Journal*, 20 (1985), 135–48; ibid., *Der moralische Diskurs über das medizinische Men-schenexperiment im 19. Jahrhundert*, (Stuttgart, 1996) P. J. Weindling, *Health, Race and German Politics between National Unification and Nazism, 1870–1945* (Cambridge, 1989), 168–9.

the term 'segregation camp'. Concentrating the sick and treating them was to protect German settlers, who were vulnerable to infection transmitted by tsetse flies. But the Germans stopped short of outright coercion. They found that if they used force, then natives would conceal the sick, and escape all medical controls. Moreover, Koch respected native wishes that no postmortems be carried out, not least because this would have rendered the German doctors suspect of cannibalism. Because the disease attacked the nervous and motor systems, some patients were chained—Koch stressed that the patients were brought by their relatives, who had chained or yoked them like slaves because the fever had resulted in the sick burning down huts. He pointed out that patients submitted freely to the treatment as the untreated would die, even though the injections were painful and massive doses (but occasionally moderate doses) resulted in total and permanent blindness. It was necessary to calculate by trial and error the threshold of danger, and several other drugs were tested including chemical dyes supplied by Ehrlich, inducing pain but no beneficial effects.[25]

The cohort of Koch's former assistants included anti-Nazis like Drigalski, who was dismissed from his post as medical officer of Berlin in 1933. Other assistants, although not Nazi Party members, held key positions after 1939. Robert Kudicke was seconded from the East African Guards in 1905 and had experimented in the sleeping sickness camps in 1906–7, running his 'concentration camp' with the support of a local sultan. Kudicke was to be drafted from the Institute for Experimental Therapy in Frankfurt to supervise the Warsaw Hygiene Institute in 1940. The question arises whether Kudicke transferred racist views about African native peoples to the Jews of Warsaw; were the German sleeping sickness concentration camps similar to the 'death camps' in the Belgian Congo, or can one believe the German reports that a successful therapy was pioneered?[26] Claus Schilling from 1904 directed a department for tropical medicine at Koch's Institute and was to be executed in 1946 for malaria experiments at the Dachau concentration camp. Another of Koch's last assistants in German East Africa, Bernhard Möllers wrote a Koch biography during the war, and portrayed a unified and patriotic Koch school. This was possibly at the instigation of the Reich Health Office, and using the materials collected by the persecuted Heymann.[27]

That a strand of bacteriology spawned links to eugenics arose from Koch's denial that bacteria could become less virulent: notions of inherited predisposition to

[25] Möllers, *Koch*, 299–301, 314, 335, 391 (for biography), 698; M. Lyons, *The Colonial Disease. A Social History of Sleeping Sickness in Northern Zaire, 1900–1940* (Cambridge, 1992), 109–10, 120, 152; M. Marquardt, *Paul Ehrlich* (London, 1949), 141–6; R. Koch, M. Beck, and F. Kleine, 'Bericht über die Tätigkeit die zur Erforschung der Schlafkrankheit im Jahre 1906/07 nach Ostafrika entsandten Kommission', *Arbeiten aus dem Kaiserlichen Gesundheitsamte*, 31 (1911), 10, 80–1, 111–16, 119–20; Koch, 'Anthropologische Beobachtungen gelegentlich einer Expedition an der Viktoria-Nyanza', *Zeitschrift für Ethnologie*, 40 (1908), 449–70; id. *Gesammelte Werke*, ii, pt. 2, p. 936 (memorandum of 18 Nov. 1907 on sleeping sickness in East Africa); W. U. Eckart, *Medizin und Kolonialimperialismus. Deutschland 1884–1945* (Paderborn, 1997), 161–74, 340–9.
[26] Lyons, *Colonial Disease*, 120.
[27] B. Möllers, *Robert Koch: Persönlichkeit und Lebenswerk 1843–1910* (Hanover, 1951); Henneberg, *Koch*, 21–31.

diseases, and of a diseased constitution, were invoked to explain why some people succumbed to a disease and others did not. Koch and Pasteur were hailed as the Newtons of pathology. The prestige of bacteriology prompted the pioneer of German racial hygiene, Alfred Ploetz, to attempt to identify and eradicate the germs of deviant behaviour.[28] Leading hygienists and pathologists rallied to the German Society for Racial Hygiene, when it was founded in 1905, exploring links between disease, inherited predisposition, and the environment. Members of the Berlin chapter of the Racial Hygiene Society in 1913 included Alfred Blaschko—a liberal-minded dermatologist and leprosy expert, Flügge—by then Director of the Berlin Institute of Hygiene, Karl Kisskalt—shortly to become professor of hygiene at Königsberg and a disciple of the Pettenkofer school, Arthur Korff-Petersen—assistant at the Institute of Hygiene and Secretary of the Berlin chapter, and Philalethes Kuhn—a bacteriologist in the colonial troops in the Cameroons. The Munich chapter was based at the Hygiene Institute under the ultra-conservative professor Max von Gruber, and among its ranks were Ignaz Kaup—a Lamarckian eugenicist, and the bacteriologist Wilhelm Rimpau. The Bremen medical officer Hermann Tjaden and the distinguished Freiburg pathologist Ludwig Aschoff were also members of the German Racial Hygiene Society.[29] The key role of the Berlin and Munich Hygiene Institutes in the racial hygiene movement indicates how notions of inherited disposition and immunity boosted the racial element within bacteriology. Bacteriologists did not just concentrate on infective micro-organisms, as many cultivated interests in racial anthropology. The Austrian bacteriologist, Stanislaus von Prowazek was deeply interested in ethnography, having travelled to the German colony of Samoa in 1911.[30] Colleagues at the Hamburg Institute of Maritime and Tropical Diseases shared his interest in race and disease.

At least for Koch and his close disciples, ethnicity was an irrelevant factor in the spread of disease. Koch remarked on the presence of 'negroes', for example, on board ships where cholera erupted, but he did not regard race as increasing susceptibility to disease. As with many German medical men, notably the liberal-minded Virchow, he conducted extensive anthropological observations, and when in Africa Koch avidly photographed native peoples. Koch returned in triumph from East Africa to give anthropological and medical lectures to the Colonial and Anthropological Societies.[31] Yet he did not link ethnicity and disease, not least because he wished to shift attention to the means by which bacteria were transmitted as in human faeces, dust, contaminated water and soil, and away from the generalities of social misery or of imprecise racial ideas.

While Koch can be exonerated from implanting racial values in bacteriology, his human experiments and authoritarian prescriptions raise the question to what

---

[28] For the impact of Koch and Pasteur on the genesis of racial hygiene see my *Health, Race and German Politics*, 71, 167.

[29] Deutsche Gesellschaft für Rassen-Hygiene, 'Mitgliederliste vom 31. Dezember 1913'. List kindly supplied by Widukind Lenz via Florian Tennstedt, and analysed in *Health, Race and German Politics*, 148–9.

[30] Berhard Nocht-Institut (herafter BNI), 6a 352—8a Schriftwechsel Prowazek/Nocht/Rocha Lima Nr 6c Reise Prowazek, Südsee 1911. 6d Prowazek Manuskripte.

[31] Möllers, *Koch*, 703.

extent bacteriology and the associated science of parasitology contained an exterminatory rationale? In 1877 Koch considered wholesale eradication (*gänzlich auszurotten*) of the disease of anthrax by preventing the reproduction of the bacilli and the spread of the spores. But he regarded destruction of all substances containing anthrax bacilli as impracticable. He suggested ways of hindering the bacilli from developing spores—a bacteriological strategy which was akin to eugenic sterilization. The total extermination of a species of bacteria—and beyond this of the host species of carriers—was not envisaged, as Koch hoped to free the human race from an 'angel of death'. The vision of emancipating the human race from invasions by primitive parasites occurred repeatedly in Koch's work; but such rallying cries for bacteriologically based programmes of disease control cannot be read as a call for exterminating a pathogenic species—whether of animal or plant microorganisms let alone an ethnic group.[32]

The terminology of eradication made only few appearances in Koch's work, which was primarily concerned with control and disinfection. In 1901 Koch discussed the suppression and eradication of both typhus and typhoid: although invoking the rallying cry of *Ausrottung*, Koch considered that the diseases of war could be effectively contained rather than eradicated. He focused on how the germs might reproduce, and so any medical campaign had to be conducted on a search-and-destroy basis against the carriers of the infective parasite. It was on this basis that he masterminded the campaign to eliminate typhoid in the Trier region. By 1902 Koch took a more radical stance. He considered that a battery of diseases—malaria, typhoid, cholera, dysentery, and diphtheria—could be not just controlled and suppressed but totally eradicated if the animal or human carriers could be identified. He argued in 1904 that destroying rats was the most effective way of combating plague, and joined other experts in tropical medicine in supporting poison gas experiments.[33] In 1909 he mistakenly condemned crocodiles as a reservoir of sleeping sickness trypanosome, and recommended their destruction as a source of polluted blood by means of arsenic poisoning or finding their nests and destroying the eggs. He considered various measures for destroying the tsetse fly as vector.[34] Koch demonstrates how the rhetoric of extermination—of *Vernichtung*, *Vertilgung*, or *Ausrottung*—invaded the vocabulary of hygiene. Koch's initial hesitations concerning eradication were diminishing, but he still saw disease control measures as specific to areas where diseases were prevalent rather than projecting any 'final solution' to the problem of infectious diseases in the sense of total eradication of a species of pathogenic organism.

Koch was pessimistic about the possibility of eradicating a disease by

---

[32] Koch, 'Die Aetiologie der Milzbrand-Krankheit, gegründet auf die Entwicklungsgeschichte des Bacillus Anthracis', *Beiträge zur Biologie der Pflanzen*, 2 (1877), 277–310. For extermination see *Medical Classics*, 218 (1938), 777, 815.

[33] GSTA Rep 76 VIII B Nr 2895, report by Koch, Feb. 1904.

[34] Ibid., Nr 2900, Unterdrückung des Typhus und dessen Ausrottung, 14 Aug. 1901 [title of a report by Koch]; Koch, 'Seuchenbekämpfung im Kriege', *Gesammelte Werke von Robert Koch*, ii, pt. 1, pp. 290–5; id., Beck, and Kleine, 'Bericht', 7, 46–7, 126–9; Lyons, *Colonial Disease*, 51.

vaccination in individual cases let alone for purposes of wholesale disease extinction. His vision of disease control was authoritarian—he required compulsory notification, testing, quarantine, and disinfection of households: it became chillingly racist in German East Africa, but it was not genocidal. The concept of the parasite, the origins of the techniques of disinfection—including what became a lethal trinity of showers, poison gases, and crematoria, the eastern bacteriological strategy of disease prevention, and the cleansing of migrants crossing Germany from Russia require further scrutiny to evaluate the tortuous path from Koch's bacteriology to the bloodbath in the wake of the capture of Kiev.

iii. Dissecting the Parasite

Bacteria were not the only threat identified by medical researchers: advancing up the evolutionary scale, minute protozoa causing malaria, worms, insects, and rodents became ranked as medical foes. The Nazi appropriation of the biological parasite raises the question whether this was merely political abuse of scientific terminology or whether more complex processes were involved. In the most sustained examination of this problem, Alex Bein explored the historical semantics of the Jewish parasite and the process of the biological labelling of explanations of character and behaviour. Bein regarded the natural sciences as objectively neutral: the racialization of language corrupted 'biological realities', and the originally biological concept of the *Schädling* lost its objectivity amidst the rhetoric of racial myths.[35]

Such an interpretation overlooks the extensive cross-fertilization between scientific and socio-political concepts. Nineteenth-century biology pulsated with nationalist ideas: the botanist Cohn spoke of cell states, colonies, and the division of labour in ways reflecting the imperial order and biological principles. More than just a linguistic transposition occurred as nationally minded scientists gained new powers to tackle parasites and pathogens. Definition of the parasite was contingent on medical expertise required by states to police borders and hygienically regulate populations.

Bacteriologists forged the image of the parasite in terms suited to their expansionist medical research agendas, state security, and imperialist *Weltpolitik*. The preyed-upon host and the sustenance-drawing parasite provided a malignant image attributing sickness to exploitation by a predator. The label of parasite transformed the free organism or the benign messmate into a cunning predator, living off its victim. Sanitary reformers denounced a motley range of unwanted inhabitants as cancerous growths or as parasites on the body politic—not merely drawing nourishment from the host, or polluting morals, but draining, infecting, and sapping the vigour of an otherwise healthy organism.[36] Bacteriologists conceptual-

[35] A. Bein, 'The Jewish Parasite. Notes on the Semantics of the Jewish Problem with Special Reference to Germany', *Leo Baeck Institute Yearbook*, 9 (1964), 30; id., *Die Judenfrage. Biographie eines Weltproblems* (Stuttgart, 1980); id., *The Jewish Question* (Rutherford, 1990).

[36] C. Herbert, 'Rat Worship and Taboo in Mayhew's London', *Representations*, 23 (1988), 1–24.

ized the nation as an organism with the bacteriologically schooled physician as its guardian.

Armed with precision lenses and powerful chemical stains, protagonists of biology probed ever deeper into minute forms of life.[37] Museum cabinets provided the student of parasitology with ranks of insect pests and parasites; specimen jars preserved infested organs in formaldehyde. Medical museums regimented such human foes as pathogenic insects and tapeworms, and other symbiotic mess-mates.[38] Disease was 'domesticated' as bacteriologists reduced the severity of disease outbreaks—and no longer attributed these to sin. The newly revealed realm of plant-like bacteria and animal-like protozoa provided a glimpse into an ancient and savage world of primeval forms of life, with disease as part of the Darwinian struggle.[39]

Biological techniques of differential staining isolated the invasive micro-organisms, and revealed the devious behaviour of animals drawing sustenance from their hosts. Zoologists charted an underworld of amazing ingenuity and variety of the minute suckers, hooks, and claws. Progressive-minded biologists condemned parasites for jeopardizing the independence and vigour of higher animals. Alternation of generations meant that certain stages of development, characterized as 'sexless nurses', posed burdens on their human hosts. During the 1860s Friedrich Küchenmeister, a physician in Saxony, dissected the intestines of an executed murderer to demonstrate that apparently distinct species of cystic worms and tapeworms were really different stages in the development of a single species of tapeworm. His catalogue of human parasites revealed complex life-cycles and the ways in which tapeworms spread and sapped the vigour of their host.[40]

Rudolf Leuckart, a zoologist, launched parasitology as an international science; he competed with the celebrated liberal pathologist, Virchow, in tracking down the route whereby the fleshworm, *Trichinella*, invaded human muscles. Their discovery of the pathway through tissue led to stringent meat inspection laws: from 1864 microscopical examination of pork (often consumed as raw mince for breakfast) began in many parts of Germany. Leuckart emerged as a leading Darwinian zoolo-gist, interpreting the characteristics of parasites in evolutionary terms; he chal-lenged notions of spontaneous generation by swallowing worm eggs and recovering adult parasites from his faeces. Leuckart warned how the abundant

[37] On the origins of biology as a science see M. Dittrich, 'Progressive Elemente in den Lebensdefini-tionen der romantischen Naturphilosophie', *Communicationes Historiae Artis Medicinae*, 73–4 (1974), 73–85; I. Jahn, R. Löther, and K. Senglaub, *Geschichte der Biologie* (Jena, 1982), 511–22; L. Nyhart, *Biology Takes Form. Animal Morphology and the German Universities, 1800–1900* (Chicago, 1995).

[38] S. Rideal, *Disinfection and Disinfectants* (London, 1895), 219–23. The disinfecting properties were originally noted in 1886, but German work dates from H. Aronson, 'Ueber die antiseptischen Eigen-schaften des Formaldehyds', *Berliner klinische Wochenschrift*, 29 (1892), 749–51.

[39] I. Jahn, 'Zoologische Gärten in Stadtkultur und Wissenschaft im 19. Jahrhundert', *Berichte zur Wis-senschaftsgeschichte*, 15 (1992), 213–25; Beneden, *Parasites*, 129.

[40] F. Küchenmeister (tr. E. Lankester), *On Animal and Vegetable Parasites of the Human Body. A Manual of their Natural History, Diagnosis and Treatment*, 2 vols. (London, 1857); id., *Parasiten des Menschen*, 2nd edn. (Leipzig, 1878); D. I. Grove, *A History of Human Helminthology* (Wallingford, 1990), 11–13, 46–8, 802–3.

forms of human parasites threatened free existence in a liberal society. In 1870 Leuckart moved to Leipzig, establishing the world's first parasitological laboratory, where a small army of students were drilled in the new discipline: an estimated 10,000 students heard him lecture and 800 more advanced students conducted practicals.[41]

Parasitologists embarked on a mission to liberate the German people of tapeworms, fleshworms, eye diseases like trachoma, and skin infestations from itchmites. The botanist Ernst Hallier of Jena rallied to the *Vernichtungskrieg* by discovering colonies of microscopic fungi and spores spreading over human eyes, mouth, and genitalia, and experimenting on how to prevent infections.[42] Animal infestations like liver fluke from sheep caused hefty losses to livestock farmers and threatened human health by causing fevers and general malaise. Botanists catalogued a range of pests damaging crops and forests. Hallier launched his specialist *Zeitschrift für Parasitenkunde* in 1869. Zoologists showed their medical utility by discovering disease-causing parasites and animal vectors of disease.

The key to parasitology was life-cycle research: skilful demonstration of alternation of generations and intermediate forms, and of the tortuous routes by which worms migrated laid to rest religious notions of miraculous spontaneous generation. Parasitologists debunked beliefs in worms generated by corpses and intestines by undertaking studies of complex life-cycles: the alternation of generations involved changes in bodily form facilitating their passage to a new host organism.[43] Zoologists detected how the predatory stowaways cunningly changed both their 'dress' and 'railway trains' in an itinerant life-cycle.[44] Tapeworms were revealed as widespread throughout fish and animal species, their eggs being disseminated by excreta of their host. Zoologists exposed cooks and butchers as prone to tapeworms, and discovered species of worms in human eyeballs, hearts, brains, and muscles. Wandering worms were said to have lodged in a man's brain lobe and near optic nerve centres—a nationalist diagnosis was that 'Two spirits seemed to haunt and speak to him, the one a German, the other a Pole. Filthy images were called up before his imagination.'[45]

[41] From 1855 professor of zoology and comparative anatomy in Giessen, and from 1870 in Leipzig. R. Leuckart, *Die menschlichen Parasiten und die von Ihnen herrührenden Krankheiten. Ein Hand- und Lehrbuch für Naturforscher und Aerzte*, 2 vols. (Leipzig and Heidelberg, 1863, 1876), 2 edn. (1879); Leuckart (tr. W. E. Hoyle), *The Parasites of Man and the Diseases which Proceed from Them. A Text-book for Students and Practitioners* (Edinburgh, 1886); J. Farley, 'Parasites and the Germ Theory of Disease', *Milbank Quarterly*, 67, suppl. 1 (1989), 50–68; J. Ettling, *The Germ of Laziness. Rockefeller Philanthropy and Public Health in the New South* (Cambridge, Mass., 1981), 15–17; Grove, *Helminthology*, 50–1, 580–90, 805. R. Virchow, *Lehre von den Trichinen* (Berlin, 1865); Nyhart, *Biology Takes Form*, 169, 173, 175; K. Wunderlich, *Rudolf Leuckart. Weg und Werk* (Jena, 1978), 41, 73–9.

[42] E. Hallier, *Die Pflanzlichen Parasiten des menschlichen Körpers für Ärzte, Botaniker und Studirende zugleich Anleitung in das Studium der niederen Organismen* (Leipzig, 1866); id., *Gährungserscheinungen. Untersuchungen über Gährung, Fäulniss und Verwesung mit Berücksichtigung der Miasmen und Contagien sowie der Desinfection* (Leipzig, 1867).

[43] J. Farley, 'Parasites and the Germ Theory of Disease', *Milbank Quarterly*, 67, suppl. 1 (1989), 50–68.

[44] P. J. van Beneden, *Animal Parasites and Messmates* (London, 1876), 196 for the railway metaphor.

[45] R. Hoeppli, *Parasites and Parasitic Infections in Early Medicine and Science* (Singapore, 1959), 83 on eye-worms.

Such liberal-minded zoology arose as a response to public panic in 1863, when fleshworms were found in pork.[46] When the causes of a disease were not known, an imaginary parasite (often a worm) was a convenient explanation: tooth worms, corpse worms, ear worms, heart worms, worms in urine were widespread in folk belief; early modern medical scientists speculated that diseases were induced by sub-microscopic invisible worms. The philosopher Arthur Schopenhauer believed that lice were spontaneously generated from filth, putrefying substances and decomposing perspiration. Concerned that the nation's health was being sapped by malignant parasites, doctors attributed a 'Russian disease' involving fatal swellings to lethal worms carried by the wind across the steppes.[47]

The fight against the unwelcome animal colonists of the human body infused public health measures in the slums, in the Prussian lands bordering on Russia, and in the frenetic grab for colonies. German medical researchers competed with British, French, and American medical rivals to rid choice parts of the globe of insect predators. Tropical researchers demonstrated how mosquitoes deposited filarial worms which congested the lymph glands causing the gross swellings of elephantiasis; how blood-sucking flies spread sleeping sickness; and how certain mosquitoes transmitted malaria and yellow fever. Eye and gut infections, body sores, and a range of fevers were attributed to a battery of insect enemies like black flies, sandflies, and mosquitoes.[48] Zoologists scored notable triumphs in detecting how parasites gave rise to deficiency diseases. The comparative anatomist Theodor Bilharz, newly moved to Egypt, discovered in 1851 threadlike parasitic worms lodged in human veins of the gut, liver, and bladder—initiating work on the chronic disease popularly known as 'snail fever' or, because of a redundant taxonomic grouping, 'schistosomiasis'.[49] The parasitologist Leuckart showed how the hookworm could be the culprit of an apparently anaemic lethargy, present in the warm bowels of the mines of Europe.[50] The sheer variety of predators—worms, insects, and micro-organisms—fed the classificatory appetites of parasitologists.

Heroic discoveries were accompanied by imperialist rhetoric: swarms of parasites 'migrated', 'wandered', and 'colonized'. The invading animal and plant 'colonists' had to be isolated, contained, and eradicated in order to prevent the spread of diseases and to make room for human colonists. The rising prestige of tropical medicine was reflected in demands for segregation of populations and clearance of the insect vectors. German specialists in tropical medicine saw their work as protecting settlers overseas, as well as ensuring that epidemics should not

---

[46] Beneden, *Parasites*, 218, 246.

[47] H. Hoeppli, 'Imaginary Parasites and Their Role in Medicine', in Hoeppli, *Parasites and Parasitic Infections* 59–89, also 116, 130–3, 347; A. Hase, 'Pseudoparasitismus und Pseudoparasitismus', *Zeitschrift für hygienische Zoologie und Schädlingsbekämpfung*, 32 (1938/9), 353–9.

[48] J. R. Busvine, *Disease Transmission by Insects. Its Discovery and Ninety Years of Effort to Prevent It* (Berlin, 1993); F. Delaporte, *The History of Yellow Fever. An Essay on the Birth of Tropical Medicine* (Cambridge, Mass., 1991).

[49] J. Farley, *Bilharzia. A History of Imperial Tropical Medicine* (Cambridge, 1991), 48–50.

[50] J. Ettling, *The Germ of Laziness. Rockefeller Philanthropy and Public Health in the New South* (Cambridge, Mass., 1981); Farley, *Bilharzia*, 72–5.

reach the European heartlands. Medical scientists considered Germany vulnerable to parasitic and infectious diseases through its ports and ethnically mixed Eastern regions.

The perception of insects underwent a metamorphosis. Nineteenth-century naturalists extolled the virtues of industrious and orderly insect societies as a stage in progressive evolution. The collective discipline of ant and bee societies aroused admiration as models of industry, and religious awe at their beauty and grace. Some speculated that fleas might come to be of medical utility (supplementing leeches which had a role in control of inflammation): but hopes of improvement were terminated, when insects were reclassified as biological predators. From the 1880s the benign wonder at insect life gave way to belligerence. The fly was no longer welcomed as a domestic playmate for young children, but was demonized as the cause of infant deaths.[51]

Insects were meticulously dissected, and magnified by ever-more powerful microscopes; the development of minute organs was charted; Koch pioneered techniques of micro-photography, and his fellow virtuoso Ehrlich deployed aniline dyes (as the arsenical derivative Atoxyl) to stain tissues and cleanse them from infections. Investigators revealed that the causes of disease: inheritance, instinct, sexuality—and by extrapolation of an array of psychological and social problems—lay in the microscopic world of chromosomes and bacteria. Arising from newly discovered laws of reproduction and biological inheritance worked out on the parasitic worm *Ascaris*, and on insects (initially crane flies, and then fruit flies[52]), eugenicists feared the onset of degeneration due to the unnatural effects of modern civilization. Horror of marauding, parasitic cockroaches, lice, and bedbugs reached a fever pitch from the 1890s. The life-cycle and parasitic habits of worms and insects demonstrated how the intestines and other organs provided a nurturing habitat: as the housing movement sought to rid the modern city of decaying slums, and sanitary reformers sought to flush away the pathogenic bodily excreta, so the body was to be purged of its festering mass of parasites. Scientists detected pathogens on insects or in insect excrement, and showed how flies dispersed the eggs of parasitic worms: they reviled insects as purveyors of filth and disease.[53] As Austrian medical regulations of 1897 indicated, eradication of insects became a medical requirement.[54]

The characteristics of the animal parasite were transposed into the human realm: biological reformers targeted a social problem group of vagrants, alcoholics, mental defectives, and the chronically ill as reservoirs of germs and biological parasites—not only did they spread diseases but their superfecundity and degenerate

---

[51] N. Rogers, 'Germs with Legs: Flies, Disease and the New Public Health', *Bulletin of the History of Medicine*, 63 (1989), 602–3; Beneden, *Parasites*, 129.

[52] The German neo-Darwinist, August Weismann focused on crane-flies, and geneticists on fruit flies.

[53] J. C. Riley, 'Insects and the European Mortality Decline', *American Historical Review*, 91 (1986), 844–5; G. S. Graham-Smith, *Flies in Relation to Disease. Non-Bloodsucking Flies* (Cambridge, 1913).

[54] F. Schürer von Waldheim and J. Kafka (eds.), *Aerzte-Codex. Eine Sammlung von den Arzt betreffenden österreichischen Gesetzen, Verordnungen, Erlässen, Entscheidungen, etc.* (Vienna, 1897), 227–8.

offspring posed threats to future generations. The Belgian zoologist Pierre van Beneden linked the animal parasite to paupers in a defining study, translated into German as *Die Schmarotzer* in 1876.[55] This term, hitherto used to deride freeloading spongers, became incorporated into biology and medical propaganda. The public was alerted to how marauding insect swarms consumed valuable crops and spread infectious diseases, penetrating the defences of the body by sucking blood or infecting food.[56] Hygiene experts targeted insects as visible pathogens.[57] Public health posters magnified vicious-looking predators, warning against the danger of fleas, flies, mosquitoes, and other pests.[58] A sanitary war was declared: insects had to be eradicated and their haunts cleared. Suspicion surrounded cracked and crumbling buildings where bugs might creep in the crevices just as witches were once believed to lurk on the margins of small communities.

A new breed of scientific experts sought to place medicine on a rational biological basis. The notion of 'applied biology' linked the biological sciences to public health, pest control, agriculture, and forestry. Hygiene was a composite science which drew on such specializations as parasitology (a term first used in 1882), disinfection (placed on a more scientific basis by Koch in 1881), and—to cleanse the germs of crime and insanity—eugenics (Galton's term dating from 1883) or race hygiene (a favoured German term coined in 1895). Protagonists of applied biology claimed that scientific eradication of parasites and pests would provide immense savings for the national economy, and would promote sobriety, hygiene, and the fitness of future generations. Medical entomology as a new science of insect eradication appealed to imperial and economic interests.[59]

The medically qualified entomologist Karl Escherich admired the United States for its advances in applied biology. Forests, instead of being romantically extolled as a primeval paradise, became reservoirs of insect pests, which were poised to devastate crops, orchards, and trees. Biologists rallied to the call for applying the laws of hygiene to forests and wastes to prevent epidemics arising from the uncontrolled breeding of pests. Alarmed by the plague of nun moths in 1913, Escherich called for biology and medicine to be applied in a discipline of 'forest hygiene', so that Germany could catch up with its international competitors in deploying modern methods of insect eradication.[60] Even though the Reich Health Office in 1913 cautioned that the fly as a danger to national health was

---

[55] Beneden, *Parasites*; id., *Die Schmarotzer* (Leipzig, 1876).

[56] Farley, 'Parasites'; A. Lipschütz, *Die Schmarotzer des Menschen* (= Arbeiter-Gesundheitsbibliothek, no. 25) (Berlin, 1910).

[57] N. Rogers, 'Germs with Legs: Flies, Disease and the New Public Health', *Bulletin of the History of Medicine*, 63 (1989), 599–617.

[58] cf. British Museum (Natural History) posters 'The Fly Danger', 'The Mosquito Danger'.

[59] W. B. Herms, *Medical and Veterinary Entomology* (New York, 1915), pp. vii, 1–5. This text dates from *c.* 1909.

[60] K. Escherich, *Leben und Forschen. Kampf um eine Wissenschaft*, 2nd edn. (Stuttgart, 1949), 78–9, 115–25; BAK R 86/3444 pamphlet of the Deutsche Gesellschaft für angewandte Entomologie; S. Jansen, 'Männer, Insekten und Krieg: Zur Geschichte der angewandten Entomologie in Deutschland, 1900–1925', *Geschlechterverhältnisse in Medizin, Naturwissenschaft und Technik* (Bassum, 1996), 170–81.

exaggerated, biologically minded patriots rallied to the crusade for medical entomology.[61]

The Prussian Law on Infectious Diseases prescribed that rats, mice, and other parasites were to be exterminated as a plague control measure. Medical officers conducted surveys of vermin, especially of rodents, and spoke of a *Vernicht-ungskrieg*.[62] Such counter-measures also targeted more minute species of vermin: once the dangers of lice as carriers of relapsing fever and typhus were discovered, inspectors ascertained the prevalence of fleas, bugs, and lice in beds and bedding of lodging houses and tenements. Hoteliers feared travellers infesting their beds with unwanted insect guests. Medical entomologists considered the weight, texture, and habits in the wearing of clothing in order to gain insight into the seasonality of louse infestation and typhus. They examined the distribution of lice on clothing, discovering that infestations were common around the waist, wrists, thighs, and buttocks. School medical officers from the turn of the century warned against clothes lice migrating to new habitats in cloakrooms. Person-to-person contact, and hair brushes and towels came under scrutiny.[63] The prevalence of rat fleas was linked to temperature changes. Hygienists sought to regulate social space, as too close proximity—the sharing of bedding and clothing—was (especially if linked to sexual dangers) immoral, unhygienic, and posed threats to communal health. Predatory insects became indicators of filth, disease, and primitive culture, as bacteriologists and medical zoologists prescribed the reform of social behaviour and a reordering of social relations in line with the dictates of their discoveries.

iv. Cleansing Bodies

A German entomologist organizing the conversion of saunas into delousing installations in the Baltics complained in 1943 of the popular superstition that an absence of lice was damaging to health. Doctors confronted an entrenched popular tolerance of lice, because of the belief that lice suck out foul humours from the body— this was a relic of ideas of disease as an imbalance of humours against which bacteriologists waged protracted academic war.[64] Scientists condemned customs such as nit-picking or the combing out of lice from hair as woefully primitive. Hygienic reformers censured Turkish baths because of associations with male prostitution and opium. Ritual cleansing as a religious rite was defective from modern hygienic perspectives. Bacteriologists viewed Germany's eastern border as a divide

---

[61] BAK R 86/3444 Schädliche Insekten response of Reich Health Office 22 Oct. 1913 to literature on the house-fly.

[62] G. Sticker, *Die Bedeutung der Geschichte der Epidemien für die heutige Epidemiologie. Ein Beitrag zur Beurteilung des Reichsseuchengesetzes* (Giessen, 1910), 37.

[63] Nuttall, 'Biology of *Pediculus humanus*', 87–8, 91–2, 96–9. The London County Council sponsored inspectors from 1909 who scrutinized the sheets of hundreds of beds for lice.

[64] F. Steiniger, 'Dorfbäder als behelfsmässige Entlausungsanlagen', *Zeitschrift für hygienische Zoologie*, 35 (1943), 57–62, 58; id., 'Soll man bestehende Badeanstalten in Entlausungsanlagen umbauen?', *Zeitschrift für hygienische Zoologie*, 35 (1943), 93–6, 94.

between civilized hygiene and disease-prone 'Asiatic' barbarism.[65] Once scientists defined cleanliness as biologically essential for civilized life, then the human carriers of insects were stigmatized as vermin. Religious notions of disease as punishment for evil were transmuted into biological possession by insect parasites.

Concepts of disease and of disease-spreading agents were reformulated in line with medical discoveries of bacteria and disease-carrying animals. The traditional notion of a fever was of a visionary trance-like state, purifying the soul from polluting inner demons. The science of hygiene imposed cleansing rituals of purification.[66] Disease as demonic possession by a monstrous force meant a shift away from correcting malfunctions in the body, or an imbalance of humours, to the construction of systems of attack and defence against invasive parasites. Biologically minded doctors cautioned how animals were reservoirs of pathogenic insects and worms. Mid-nineteenth-century anthropologists argued for diverse human races on the basis of the species of parasites that they harboured, and indeed Charles Darwin cited evidence for distinct species of lice, infesting different 'races of man'.[67] The presence of lice and other vermin became an index for cultural backwardness. Public health reformers portrayed how the character of cities was polluted by the underworld of rats as an archetypally cunning and thieving criminal population, spreading plague, and exhibiting vice and psychopathic behaviour. Pasteur captivated his fellow countrymen by his medical triumphs over rabid dogs and other depraved animal pests as national perils.[68]

Salvation was at hand from the purveyors of experimental hygiene, who demanded external cleansing with washing and disinfecting bodies, clothes, and overcrowded tenements. Scientists martialled new weapons for inner disinfection as vaccines, sera, and drugs.[69] Public health enthusiasts intensified their efforts to cleanse not only the open spaces in the urban environment, but also to locate the hidden carriers of disease lurking in the deepest recesses—in cracks and crevices of buildings, in clothing and underwear, in hair and folds of skin, and embedded in the organs, tissues, and fluids of the body. The body was to be as carefully tended as a municipal park with the removal of unwanted bacterial flora from hair, teeth, mouths, throats, and other habitats. Just as diseased paupers preyed upon society, so it was said that insect parasites utilized the human body as a crèche or lying-in asylum. Pasteur's triumph over rabies raised the hope that vaccines could weaken the force of invasive microbes; but for the moment defending the body from the pathogenic micro-organisms by improved personal and domestic hygiene had to suffice.

---

[65] For classic discussions of the dichotomy between magic and religion, and more broadly of dirt and disease see M. Douglas, *Purity and Danger. An Analysis of the Concepts of Pollution and Taboo* (London, 1966); N. Elias, *The Civilising Process* (New York, 1978).

[66] Riley, 'Insects', 849.

[67] C. Darwin, *The Descent of Man and Selection in Relation to Sex*, 2nd edn. (London, 1879), 169–70.

[68] For the identification of the proletariat with rats see C. Herbert, 'Rat Worship and Taboo in Mayhew's London', *Representations*, 23 (1988), 1–24; K. Kete, '*La Rage* and the Bourgeoisie: The Cultural Context of Rabies in the French Nineteenth Century', *Representations*, 22 (1988), 89–107.

[69] G. Vigarello, *Concepts of Cleanliness*, 208 on Jules Verne.

Sanitary reformers sought to prevent disease by means of chemical technologies and sanitary engineering.[70] The nineteenth-century effort to make the metropolis habitable involved provision of pure running water, sewers, housing free from damp and dirt, and public amenities like parks, wash houses, public baths, and showers.[71] From the 1890s electricity provided a cleaner source of power, and the demise of horse-drawn transport reduced the prevalence of flies. Washing and steam ironing of clothes eradicated all sorts of parasites, and fleas disappeared with the advent of carpet sweepers and vacuum cleaners. Advances in chemical technologies and understanding of the bacteria-killing powers of disinfectants meant that the risk of contagion from crowded institutions could be minimized. Free circulation of fresh air explained why typhus was not directly transmissable from person to person, as diluting the poison of the fever.[72] Human swarms in the burgeoning cities needed to be sanitized by reducing the risks of person-to-person infection.

Sanitary evangelists preached the virtues of the power of soap and water, denouncing dirty skin and clothing as attracting lice. Soap consumption rose, public baths and wash-houses spread, and a torrent of disinfectants and antiseptics poured onto the German market from the 1860s.[73] From the 1880s steam, hot air, chemicals (like carbolic acid), and gases were deployed to destroy germs and vermin in a war against contagious disease. In 1881 Koch demanded systematic studies of chemicals to find out which could best destroy different strains of bacteria. Among substances tested were sodium cyanide (which was to achieve importance in delousing), although Koch preferred formaldehyde (produced in a patent solution by the Schering chemical works as 'Formalin') as more effective in killing bacteria.[74]

Manufacture boomed of antiseptic oils, powders, sprays, and gases, and of disinfection, filtration, and sterilization machinery. German producers of medical hardware attained a commanding international position. A major supplier of equipment for medical laboratories, the firm of Lautenschläger, had offices in Berlin and Odessa.[75] The bacteria-killing virtues of soap, disinfectants, mouthwashes, and toothpaste were publicized in health exhibitions. Koch's new Berlin

---

[70] G. Göckenjan, *Kurieren und Staat machen. Gesundheit und Medizin in der bürgerlichen Welt* (Frankfurt/M., 1985), 110–30; R. Otto, R. Spree, and J. Vögele, 'Seuchen und Seuchenbekämpfung in deutschen Städten während des 19. und frühen 20. Jahrhunderts. Stand und Desiderata der Forschung', *Medizinhistorisches Journal*, 25 (1990), 286–304.

[71] E. H. Gibson III, 'Baths and Washhouses in the English Public Health Agitation, 1839–48', *Journal of the History of Medicine*, 9 (1954), 391–406; B. Ladd, *Urban Planning and Civic Order in Germany, 1860–1914* (Cambridge, Mass., 1990), 60–7; B. Ladd, 'Public Baths and Civic Improvement in Nineteenth-century Germany', *Journal of Urban History*, 14 (1987–8), 372–93.

[72] A. Newsholme, *Fifty Years in Public Health. A Personal Narrative With Comments* (London, 1935), 38–9.

[73] For a bibliography of early disinfection see E. J. Waring, *Biblioteca Therapeutica* (London, 1878), i. 149–52.

[74] Koch, 'Ueber Desinfection', *Mitteilungen aus dem kaiserlichen Gesundheitsamte*, 1 (1881), 234–82.

[75] The addresses were given as Oranienburger Strasse 54, Berlin and Preobrajenskaya Strasse 13, Odessa.

Institute of Hygiene included a public museum. Professors of hygiene devised disinfection apparatus using steam, hot air, poison gases in canisters, and sprays.[76] A new vocabulary of destruction with terms like 'disinfestation' and 'deratization' accompanied painstaking studies of the efficacy of lethal machines and gases.

The dermatologist Oskar Lassar pressured municipalities to provide steam and chemical disinfection chambers and baths. Lassar contributed to the first public disinfection installation opening in Berlin in 1886. Disinfection ensured that the sanitary infrastructure did not actually spread diseases: hospital wards, waiting-rooms, and clinics all posed risks, and the ambulance system, extended at the time of the Hamburg cholera epidemic of 1892, was backed up by the disinfection of carriages, blankets, and the clothing of the personnel.[77] By the 1890s refuges for vagrants disinfected clothing every night. Hygiene experts demanded disinfection stations in all towns and mobile disinfection machinery in the countryside: they prophesied that if disinfection of household effects would take place every time a labourer moved, then typhus (whatever its cause) would be eliminated.[78]

Baths diminished the number of invisible, but invasive pathogens.[79] Such hygienic innovations had to be cost-effective, efficient, and (as disinfection became loathed as damaging possessions and causing unpleasant odours) neither obnoxious nor destructive. Liberal sanitary reformers took up the cause of the shower. Historical precedents confirmed the hygienic advantages of regular washing: enthusiasts attributed the ancient Teutons' vigour to cold baths, and praised medieval cities for having large numbers of bathhouses, some equipped with contraptions resembling the modern shower. The nineteenth-century sanitary reformers turned washing into a regimented and invigorating activity, and zealots indulged in 'air baths' with nude drill, undeterred by snow and other climatic extremes. Psychiatrists used cold douches as a routine therapy (and at times to subdue patients) in mental hospitals.

The shower joined the battery of new sanitary technologies. From the 1820s water closets with automatic flushing and steam laundries were introduced into large state hospitals.[80] The public shower cubicles of the later nineteenth century derived from hydropathic 'rain baths' which had been in vogue at spas and as medical therapies. Since 1849 the spa doctor Vincenz Priessnitz in Austrian Silesia recommended the open air 'Douche écossaise'—abbreviated by Germans as

---

[76] U. Koppitz and W. Woelk, 'Die Desinfektionsmaschinerie', *Paedagogica Historica*, 33 (1997), 833–60.

[77] The first disinfection facility in Berlin was in the Reichenbergerstrasse; the second on the Prenzlauer Allee, opened in 1888. *Das Medicinische Berlin. Ein Führer für Studirende und Aerzte* (Berlin, 1892), 55; *Bericht über die Gemeinde-Verwaltung der Stadt Berlin in den Jahren 1889 bis 1895* (Berlin, 1900), pt. 3, pp. 152–6.

[78] Nuttall, 'Part', 85; Litthauer, *Ueber Einrichtung von Desinfectionsanstalten* (Leipzig and Berlin, 1889), 9.

[79] Vigarello, *Concepts*, 202–25.

[80] E. Ackerknecht, *A Short History of Psychiatry*, 2nd edn. (New York, 1968), 45, 63–4; A.-H. Murken, *Vom Armenhospital zum Grossklinikum* (Cologne, 1988), 56–7, 67, 96. For cold baths as punishment see Len Smith, 'Provision for Pauper Lunatics in the West Midlands, 1815–1850', unpub. paper for Exeter conference, 1996, 18.

Dusche—to harden the body against illness, as hot water had degenerative and immoral associations.[81]

Military showers heralded an era of hygiene for the masses. The Prussian army instituted one bath tub for each squadron in 1843, and from 1852 a campaign began to introduce showers for all soldiers; but only in 1879 did the shower triumph over Europe's most powerful army. Showers required a carefully designed circuit through a dressing-room, entrances and exits so that the men could efficiently undress and shower in cohorts, and a timed sequence of showering, soaping, rinsing, and drying; the water had to be at the correct temperature for the time of year, and the showers were ventilated whilst avoiding exposure to the cold. Precisely timed shift systems enabled a company of a hundred men to shower in thirty minutes using ten showers.[82] The Reich navy followed suit in the 1890s when on-board distillation apparatus and steam power facilitated the use of showers.

Lassar became convinced that parasitic skin diseases could be prevented by regular showers, and realized that the military shower could provide the people with an economic, weekly wash. At the Berlin Public Health Exhibition of 1883 Lassar presented 'the bath of the future': his model 'people's bathhouse' was a hydropathic panopticon of ten corrugated shower cubicles under central surveillance, an arrangement publicized as having hygienic, physiological, and economic advantages. These showers were a popular attraction, and inspired a campaign to make cleanliness accessible to all social classes. Since 1873 the Berlin Society for Public Baths had ministered to the homeless. After writing in 1886 to each of Germany's 1,030 medical officers, Lassar discovered that there was on average one public bathing institution for 30,000 persons, and in Hamburg there was one for 64,000 inhabitants. From 1888 public showers were provided, and in 1899 Lassar, a liberal who understood the power of association, launched a National Society for the Construction of Public Baths. Over 1,300 dignitaries from 120 German towns joined at its foundation; patrons from the nation's academic, military, and financial élites included Althoff, Virchow, the bacteriologists Koch, Gaffky, and Friedrich Loeffler, military and naval leaders, and commercial magnates. The physiologist Rubner pointed out that cleanliness was not only a sign of education and morality, but also essential to health as invasive parasites preferred dirty skin. The Society advertised showers as costing a tenth of a visit to a bathhouse or swimming-pool, and proclaimed that every German should shower once a week.[83]

To achieve this target showers were to be established at post offices, railway sta-

---

[81] A. Martin, *Deutsches Badewesen in vergangenen Tagen* (Jena, 1906); H. Prignitz, *Wasserkur und Badelust*, figs. 77–84; E. G. Eder, *Bade- und Schwimmkultur in Wien* (Vienna, 1995), 151–5. The Scottish physician William Cullen prescribed cold water showers. The fashion for hydrotherapeutic showers was exemplified by Darwin's enthusiasm for hydropathic showers to calm his anxieties over his evolutionary heresies during the 1850s.

[82] Hoffmann and Hollmann, 'Die Brausebäder in der Armee und bei der Marine', *Gesundheits-Ingenieur*, 22 (1899), 280–4.

[83] C. Kolski, 'Oscar Lassar als Gründer der "Deutschen Gesellschaft für Volksbäder" ', in N. Goldenbogen, *et al.*, *Hygiene und Judentum* (Dresden, 1995), 78–89; Rubner in *Veröffentlichungen der Deutschen Gesellschaft für Volksbäder*, 1 (1899), 50.

tions, factories, and schools so that bathing should no longer be a luxury but available to all.[84] The application of water, suitably filtered and reinforced by steam or pressure systems, and of powerful disinfectants, would provide environments free from the evils of dirt and disease. Cold showers would harden the body against infections and regenerate national health.[85]

Sanitary measures against parasites, bugs, and vermin became routine. In 1909 Hitler became disgusted at the *Ungeziefer* and insanitary conditions in a cheap lodging house. He encountered a cleansing regime in a Viennese shelter for the homeless, when he became an object of bacteriological hygiene. Here the poor were separated by sexes, lined up for a shower, clothes were disinfected, and then soup was served. From 1909 to 1913 Hitler lived in an ultra-modern hostel for male workers, complete with a disinfection chamber for delousing new arrivals.[86]

As the mania for showers spread, doctors condemned alternative rites of cleansing. On the Eastern margins of Europe, the fear arose that hordes of human parasites—filthy, diseased, and primitive peoples—could shatter the fragile health of European cities.[87] German Jews derided *Ostjuden* or *Asiaten* for their religious traditionalism and cultural backwardness. Public health reformers, associating Jewish traditionalism with dirt, odours, and disease, condemned the Jewish ritual bath, or Mikveh, as spreading disease.[88] Such baths were primarily taken to cleanse body and soul after menstrual periods or pregnancy. Medical rationalists condemned immersion in ritual baths as superstitious, and the location of Mikveh in cellars, due to the requirement of spring water or natural running water, gave rise to accusations of putrid darkness, dampness, and filth.[89] Physicians (some Jewish, plunging into a rationalist frenzy of emancipatory zeal to lift restrictive burdens of ritual traditions) accused the baths of spreading sexually transmitted diseases and chronic infections. Spiritual cleansing and the hygienic shower were pitted against each other in a clash of religious and secular values. Yet despite cramped and insanitary conditions, medical officers often observed that Jews had lower rates of disease, and less infant and child deaths when compared to other ethnic groups living in similar poverty.

[84] Vigarello, *Concepts*, 220–5; Ladd, *Urban Planning*, 63–7; *Veröffentlichungen der Deutschen Gesellschaft für Volksbäder*, 1 (1899); O. Lassar, 'Über den Stand der Volksbäder', *Gesundheits-Ingenieur*, 25 (1902), 94–6; BAP 15.01 10963 Das Badewesen 1887–1906; Prignitz, *Wasserkur*, 196–8. Showers were installed in primary schools in Hannover from 1890, see Tamm, *Hannover und Linden*, 205.

[85] Rubner in *Veröffentlichungen der Deutschen Gesellschaft für Volksbäder*, 1 (1899), 52–4.

[86] J. S. Jones, *Hitler in Vienna 1907–13. Clues to the Future* (London, 1983), 133–4; B. Hamann, *Hitlers Wien. Lehrjahre eines Diktators* (Munich, 1996), 213–19, 222–8, 231–4.

[87] O. Lubarsch, *Ein bewegtes Gelehrtenleben* (Berlin, 1931), 141. The eastern stereotype has complex historical roots; see, for example, L. Wolff, *Inventing Eastern Europe. The Map of Civilization and the Culture of the Enlightenment* (Stanford, Calif., 1994).

[88] S. E. Aschheim, *Brothers and Strangers. The Eastern European Jew in German and German Jewish Consciousness, 1800–1923* (Madison, Wis., 1982), 3, 11, 28. Wojdowsky, *Bread*, 142: 'To the *mikva*? *Tate*, the only thing you get at the *mikva* is typhus.'

[89] Alfred Martin, *Deutsches Badewesen in vergangenen Tagen* (Jena, 1906), 138–43 on Jewish baths; T. Schlich, 'Medicalisation and Secularisation: The Jewish Ritual Bath as a Problem of Hygiene (Germany 1820s–1840s)', *Social History of Medicine*, 8 (1995), 423–42; J. M. Efron, 'Der reine und der schmutzige Jude', S. L. Gilman, R. Jütte, G. Kohlbauer-Fritz (eds.), *'Der Schejne Jid'. Das Bild des 'jüdischen Körpers' in Mythos und Ritual* (Vienna, 1998), 75–85.

Despite lack of sanitation and running water in airless and congested living and working conditions, immigrant households could keep themselves clear of vermin to an extent that surprised medical observers; in addition to rabbinically sanctioned mikvehs, plunge baths and 'sweat' or Russian baths were popular.[90]

Franz Kafka's diary entry for 27 October 1911 noted that Jewish ritual baths in Russia were for washing spiritual dirt from the soul rather than the external body, which could remain filthy and stinking. Kafka vacillated between conflicting canons of hygienic belief: while admiring the spiritual values of the Eastern Jews, he followed a modern biological creed of health, subjecting his body to a daily ritual of exercise and a complex dietary regimen.[91] Kafka's outlook was symptomatic of how disease-ridden populations were condemned for their ignorance and superstition, as they clung to highly ritualized religions. Doctors condemned rites from the communion cup to circumcision as unhygienic. Modern techniques of cleansing and purification conflicted with traditional lifestyles of the migrant labourers known as *Schnitter* who crossed into Germany at harvest-time, peripatetic pedlars, gypsies, and vagrants. Many Eastern Europeans sought refuge from persecution and chronic poverty by finding a niche in the swarming metropols of Berlin or Vienna, or crowding the packed holds of steamers to the New World. Cleansing and containing the flow of migrants added to the problems of parasites and diseased bodies. Bacteriologists declared war on pathogenic micro-organisms, on their insect and animal carriers, and finally on human reservoirs of infectious diseases.

v. The Disinfecting Fires

Doctors came to control the border procedures between death and disposal of bodies. Public health officials were concerned that corpses could harbour infections. Radical and secularizing medical reformers aroused public enthusiasm for cremation. Rudolf Virchow in 1845 and a fellow liberal hygienist, Carl Reclam, praised cremation as an ideal disinfecting process. Medical arguments were in the forefront of their campaign; a key text was by the Prussian military physician Johann Peter Trusen.[92] Jakob Moleschott, a materialist biologist, argued in 1852 that cremation provided a means for phosphoric acid in the bones to replenish the soil. Cemeteries were condemned as fouling drinking water and polluting the air and soil.

Cholera left corpses posing a risk of infection. Hallier, the botanist, studied the

---

[90] Dwork, 'Health Conditions', 28–30; W. A. Mansheimer, 'The Sanitary Condition of Mikvehs and Turkish Baths', *Collected Studies from the Bureau of Laboratories (Foot of East 16th Street) City of New York*, 9 (1916–19), 407–13; M. Grunwald, *Die Hygiene der Juden. Im Anschluss an die Internationale Hygiene Austellung, Dresden 1911* (Dresden, 1911).

[91] My thanks to Ritchie Robertson for comments on Kafka's lifestyle and attitudes to the Ostjuden.

[92] J. P. Trusen, *Die Leichenverbrennung als die geeignetste Art der Todtenbestattung* (Breslau, 1855); J. Heldwein, *Die Geschichte der Feuerbestattung und Deutsche Krematorien* (Frankfurt/M., 1931), 42–6; H.-J. Zeidler, 'Die Hygiene des Bestattungswesens', *Veröffentlichungen aus dem Gebiete des Volksgesundheitsdienstes*, 61/5 (1938).

process of decomposition of corpses, and in the light of the discoveries by Pasteur, stressed the dangers of traditional burial vaults as reservoirs of plague and other infections.[93] Such findings fuelled the cremation movement. The Saxon medical officer and expert on animal and plant parasites of the human body, Küchenmeister, celebrated the first cremation by a Siemens oven in October 1874 in Dresden; he campaigned for cremation on hygienic grounds, while seeking a supportive blessing from the churches.[94] Küchenmeister and Reclam collaborated with the engineer, Friedrich Siemens, in developing efficient and hygienic cremation procedures with the installation of a new type of enclosed oven in Gotha in 1878. The engineering firm Topf of Erfurt, established in 1873 as a producer of boilers and furnaces, took advantage of the new market opportunity and opened a division for cremation ovens.[95] Topf was to be one of the main suppliers of cremation furnaces to Auschwitz.

Images of fire and disease were fused: medical scientists deployed evocative imagery of flames and fire-fighting, projecting themselves as the nation's saviours from epidemic conflagrations. Koch explained the origins of epidemics with the notion of embers scattered on a thatched roof requiring fast and effective counter-measures.[96] Disinfectors were compared to a fire brigade. Behring compared 'catching' infectious diseases (*ansteckende Krankheiten*—*anstecken* also meant to light a fire) to images of raging forest fires which medical science could now quell. The populist imagery of blood and fire evoked belief in a purging, cataclysmic conflagration.[97] Cremation gained medical credibility as ideas of fire and cleansing became linked.

Germany was the leading nation in the international cremation movement. Cremation societies were established in 1874 in Dresden, Berlin, Vienna, and Zurich, as well as London. By 1875 only one body had been experimentally cremated in Dresden, when the Prussian House of Representatives was petitioned to legalize cremation for sanitary reasons, because of the pollution of ground water: the state advised by the Prussian Medical Department defended the sanitary regulations pertaining to cemeteries as fully adequate. There was no law to prevent the construction of incinerators, only regulations against the burning of bodies. By persistent lobbying, cremationists, who were as dedicated a pressure group as temperance reformers, anti-vivisectionists, vegetarians, or the public bath

---

[93] E. Hallier, *Gährungserscheinungen. Untersuchungen über Gährung, Fäulniss und Verwesung mit Berücksichtigung der Miasmen und Contagien sowie der Desinfecktion* (Leipzig, 1867), 102–3.

[94] F. Küchenmeister, *On Animal and Vegetable Parasites of the Human Body. A Manual of their Natural History, Diagnosis and Treatment* (London, 1857); Küchenmeister, 'Die Räthlichkeit der Verbrennung von Thier- und Menschenleichen', *Handbuch von der Verbreiting der Cholera und die Schutzmassnahmen gegen sie* (Erlangen, 1872), 456–527; Küchenmeister, 'Die erste Leichenverbrennung (die der Leiche der Lady D.) im Siemensschen Regenerativ-Ofen. Geschehen am 9. Oktober 1874 abends 7 Uhr zu Dresden', *Deutsche Klinik*, 44 (1874); Küchenmeister, *Die Todtenbestattungen, der Bibel und die Feuerbestattung* (Stuttgart, 1893).

[95] J.-C. Pressac, *Les Crématoires d'Auschwitz. La machinerie de meutre du masse* (Paris, 1993), 93–4, 136.

[96] Koch, 'Bekämpfung', 286.

[97] E. von Behring, 'Einleitende Bemerkungen über die ätiologischen Therapie von ansteckenden Krankheiten', *Gesammelte Abhandlungen zur ätiologischen Therapie von ansteckenden Krankheiten* (Leipzig, 1893), pp. vii–viii.

enthusiasts, gradually eroded official restrictions. While Prussian officials continued to oppose cremation, the transport to less prohibitive *Länder* of corpses and of
urns containing ashes was permitted from 1900.[98]

Cremation appealed to freethinkers and reforming elements among German
Jews. While orthodox traditionalists condemned cremation as an affront to the
spiritual integrity of the body and soul, liberal and modern-minded Jews favoured
cremation as materialistic and secular in ethos, indicating a denial of belief in res-
urrection. There were lively debates around 1900 over whether urns could be
buried in Jewish cemeteries, and proportionally fewer Catholics than Jews opted
for cremation.[99]

Hygiene conferences and exhibitions were opportunities for international meetings of cremationists at Turin in 1880, and at the health exhibitions at Berlin in 1883
and Dresden in 1911. The Dresden and Berlin cremation societies campaigned on
economic and medical grounds, avoiding divisive religious questions.[100] In 1892 the
Berlin authorities asked the Prussian state for permission to build a crematorium
to burn bodies in the event of a cholera epidemic. Koch and Virchow ordered
excrement from cholera victims to be burned, and the physician and parliamentary
representative, Paul Langerhans, pressed the case. Among the medical arguments
for cremation was that germs thrived in dead bodies, particularly victims of infectious diseases: the cholera vibrio could live for three weeks and typhoid bacteria for
eight weeks, while anthrax spores had considerable longevity. The hygienic advantages of cremation included the eradication of pests like worms and insects.[101] That
Robert Koch was cremated in 1910 before being laid to rest in a mausoleum in his
former institute was fitting for a hero of hygiene.[102] The legalizing of cremation in
various German states extended the doctor's authority by virtue of having to testify
that no postmortem was necessary.

Corpses required stringent disinfection, to be sealed in coffins and securely
buried at a depth at which the body could not pollute groundwater.[103] A municipal

[98] M. Pistor, *Geschichte der preussischen Medizinalverwaltung* (Berlin, 1909), 271–3. GSTA Rep 76 VIII
B Nr 3389 Die Leichenverbrennung, 1875–92, Bl. 15 for petition by Prof. Karl Binder.

[99] F. Wiesemann, 'Jewish Burials in Germany—Between Tradition, the Enlightenment and the
Authorities', *Leo Baeck Institute Yearbook*, 37 (1992), 29–30; F. Rosner, 'Embalming and Cremation in
Judaism', *Koroth*, 8 (1985), 218–35. T. Schlich, 'Der lebende und tote Körper', in Gilman, *et al.* (eds), *Der
Schejne Jid'*, 145–57.

[100] *Friedrich Küchenmeister. Sein Leben und Lebensarbeit* (Bottrop, 1936).

[101] Thalmann, *Urne*, 17–38 for an overview of medical arguments; J. Heldwein, *Die Geschichte der
Feuerbestattung und Deutsche Krematorien* (Frankfurt/M., 1931), 42–5; 'Feuerbestattung und Hygiene',
Die Flamme, 31 (1914), 508–10. For a critical view see R. Abel (ed.), *Handbuch der Hygiene* (Jena, 1913), i.
379–84; GSTA Rep 76 VIII B Nr 3390, 1892–1905, *Haus der Abgeordneten* (30 Jan. 1993), 645–6, 1195–9; also
(1892–3), Drucksachen Nr 61. *Die Flamme*, 78 (1892), 1125–6, 1231.

[102] H. Unger, *Robert Koch. Roman eines grossen Lebens* (Berlin, 1936), 274–5.

[103] W. von Drigalski, *Im Wirkungsfelde Robert Kochs* (Hamburg, 1948), 291–3; BHSTA MInn 62407
Vollzug des Gesetzes betr. die Bekämpfung gemeingefährlicher Krankheiten. On carrier cases see A.
Newsholme, *Fifty Years in Public Health. A Personal Narrative With Comments* (London, 1935), 214–16. In
the United States the case of 'Typhoid Mary'—a domestic servant who was a lethal disease carrier—
became a *cause célèbre*. See A. M. Kraut, *Silent Travellers. Germs, Genes and the 'Immigrant Menace'* (New
York, 1994), 97–104; J. Walzer Leavitt, *Typhoid Mary: Captive to the Public's Health* (Boston, 1996).

medical officer remarked that the only time many bodies were first washed was as a corpse laid out after death.[104] Crusaders for hygiene supported the cremation as a means of hygienic disposal of the dead, using new technology of gas or electric ovens. In 1902 a massive petition was presented to the Reichstag, denouncing cemeteries as a danger to public health. The petition, headed by the public health reformer, Theodor Weyl, and signed by over 3,000 doctors, resulted in grudging official acceptance of cremation. In 1911 Prussia passed a law regulating cremation, although still placing bureaucratic obstacles in its way: cremation had to be the express wish of the deceased and an elaborate autopsy was required. As with the state's resistance to removing the controls on abortion and birth-control, officials felt that a Christian ethos needed to be sustained whether around marriage or death: a furore erupted over the regulation that virginity was to be noted when an autopsy was carried out.[105] The lack of a national law placing cremation on an equal footing to burial fired the indignation of cremationists. Certain states (like Bremen and Mecklenburg-Schwerin) had no law, and others had elaborate regulations designed to hinder cremation. Notwithstanding bureaucratic obstacles, by 1912 there were thirty-four German crematoria (mostly municipally owned), which incinerated 8,858 bodies.[106]

The speech on cremation in the ancient world by the folklorist Jakob Grimm to the Prussian Academy of Sciences in 1849 marked a turning-point in justifying cremation from historical precedents.[107] Nationalists regarded cremation as a reincarnation of Teutonic burial rites.[108] Controversy smouldered over the terminology of cremation—words like *Krematorium* and 'columbaria' were deemed inadequately German. Ersatz-terms included *Feuerhalle* or *Feuerbestattungshalle*.[109] The image of the purging and purifying flame fitted in with the Germanic and Nordic veneration of fire and light as life forces. Medical notions of 'the flame as the best means of disinfection' were fused with Nordic racism and the idealization of nature. Cremation became contested territory between nationalists and freethinking progressives. Sanitary reform was as much a matter of *Weltanschaung* as technical expertise.

vi. The New Pesticide

The lethal trinity of showers, crematoria, and poison gas chambers had their origins in sanitary reform. Applied biologists developed poison gas as a hygienic

---

[104] I. Tamm, *Hannover und Linden*, 206.

[105] GSTA Rep 76 VIII B Nr 3391, 1906–22, *Gesetz betreffend die Feuerbestattung vom 14. September 1911* (Berlin, 1911).

[106] Abel, 'Feuerbestattung', 382. BAP 15.01 Nr 11732 Die Leichenbestattung 1915–21; *Die Flamme*, 36/4 (Apr. 1919).

[107] Jacob Grimm, 'Ueber das Verbrennen der Leichen', in Grimm, *Kleinere Schriften*, ii. 211–313.

[108] Karl Blind, *Fire-Burial among our Germanic Forefathers: A Record of the Poetry of History of Teutonic Cremation* (London, 1875). My thanks to Ruth Richardson for this reference.

[109] *Die Flamme*, 31 (1914), 11; 'Zur Verdeutschung das Wort Krematorium', ibid. 32 (1915), 877–8.

technology of pest eradication. Hydrocyanic acid was a German invention: Carl Wilhelm Scheele discovered 'acidum berolinense' during the 1780s. It became known as 'prussic acid' because it was a derivative of the prussian blue dye—hence the colloquial name of *Blausäure*. In 1813 a Berlin apothecary had suggested that rags soaked in this acid should be fixed to Prussian bayonets, so as to create a deadly gas cloud.[110] Modern use of the gas originated in the United States: in 1886 D. W. Coquillett of the US Department of Agriculture in Los Angeles pioneered hydrocyanic acid to destroy insect pests ravaging Californian citrus orchards; he experimented with generators, airtight tents, and dosages so that foliage would not be injured.[111] Since 1898 the gas was used to fumigate mills, ships, and domestic dwellings, and in South Africa from 1904 for railway carriages. Prompted by overseas initiatives, German agriculturalists and the Biologische Reichsanstalt—an imperial research and advisory establishment for applied biology—sponsored a series of trials, although damage to plants suggested that the gas was too strong for general pest control.[112]

The medically qualified entomologist, Escherich, overcame the hesitation of German officials. Inspired by a visit to pest control installations in the United States in 1910, he became a tireless campaigner to develop applied entomology, combining North American concepts of economic utility with a nationalist rhetoric of the defence of the sick German forest.[113] Escherich criticized the caution of the Reich Biological Institute, while admiring the ability of the Americans to apply scientific technologies. In 1913 an Imperial Bureau of Entomology was founded in London, instilling *Angst* in the Germans that they were being left behind in the development of 'applied biology'. Escherich warned that resources for applied entomology available to the Reich Biological Institute remained sparse. In 1914 he founded the German Society for Applied Entomology to develop pest eradication. This society involved nationally minded biologists, seeking opportunities to harness their

[110] U. Müller-Kiel, *Die chemische Waffe im Weltkrieg—und jetzt,* 2nd edn. (Berlin, 1932), 68; J. R. Partington, *A History of Chemistry* (London, 1962), 233–4; G. Peters, *Blausäure zur Schädlingsbekämpfung* (Stuttgart, 1933), 8–13, 16–17.

[111] E. O. Essig, *A History of Entomology* (New York, 1931), 468–94.

[112] BAK R 168/172 Versuche mit Blausäure 1906–1918, correspondence with Graf Arnim Schlagenthin 29 May 1906, 12 May 1907; J. Moritz, 'Versuche betr die Wirkung von gasförmiger Blausäure auf Schildläuse insbesondere auf die San José Schildlaus', *Arbeiten aus der Biologischen Abteilung für Land und Forstwirthschaft der Kaiserlichen Gesundheitsamt,* 3/2 (1902); R. Scherpe, 'Einfache Verrichtung zur Vertilgung tierischer Schädlinge an Feld- und Gartengewächsen mittels gasformiger Stoffe (insbesondere Blausäure)', *Arbeiten aus dem kaiserlichen Biologischen Anstalt für Land- und Forstwirtschaft,* 5/6 (1907), 351–3; W. G. Johnson, *Fumigation Methods* (New York, 1910); L. O. Howard and C. H. Popenoe, 'Hydro-cyanic Acid against Household Insects', *US Department of Agriculture Farms Bulletin,* 699 (1916); W. Heckenast, *Desinfektionsmittel und Desinfektionsapparate* (Vienna and Leipzig, 1917), 107; L. Schwarz, 'Die Entwicklung des Blausäureverfahrens in der Schädlingsbekämpfung', *Zeitschrift für Desinfektionsund Gesundheitswesens,* 22 (1930), 304–8; Testa, *Blausäuredurchgasungen von Seeschiffen* (Hamburg, 1925).

[113] 'Einfache Vernichtung zur Vertilgung tierischer Schädlinge an Feld- und Gartengewächse mittelst gasformige Stoffe (insbesondere Blausäure)', *Kaiserliche Biologische Anstalt für Land und Forstwirtschaft. Arbeiten der Anstalt,* 5 (1907), 351–3; K. Escherich, *Die angewandte Entomologie in den Vereinigten Staaten* (Berlin, 1913). Cf. L. O. Howard, *Fighting the Insects. The Study of an Entomologist* (New York, 1933); id., *A History of Applied Entomology* (Washington, DC, 1930), 265–6.

science to German agriculture, forestry, and colonial expansion.[114] Escherich saw the war as a struggle to defend German territory and culture, so that a victorious greater Germany could be the international 'Führer' of science and culture.[115]

'Forest hygiene', with its holistic concept of the sick forest, was a counterpart of 'racial hygiene'. The agricultural geneticist Erwin Baur linked agricultural improvement to nutritional and eugenic issues.[116] The scientific approach to pest control—*Entwesung*, literally de-existifying—had its counterpart in negative eugenic demands for human sterilization and the movement for compulsory euthanasia of the mentally and physically disabled, whose lives were deemed as no longer in the national interest.[117]

Scientists agreed that hydrocyanic acid (HCN) did not harm plants, but that it was highly poisonous to animals, rapidly immobilizing their capacity to absorb nutrients from the blood and paralyzing the central nervous system. Unconsciousness and convulsions followed, then the respiratory centre and the circulation failed, resulting in death. However, lower doses than fatal concentrations allowed the body's defence mechanisms to work. But there were great drawbacks to HCN. The parasitologist Hallier in the 1860s dismissed cyanide compounds as favourable to the spread of bacteria, as the gas was not harmful to plants. HCN neither killed bacteria nor cleansed. Because the gas was ineffective as a disinfectant, clothing had to be additionally disinfected.[118]

The chemical manufacturer, Deutsche Gold- und Silber-Scheidungsanstalt, vormals Roessler (Degussa), took the key role in the introduction of HCN into Germany. Degussa originated from a family firm specializing in metal refining, founded during 1873 in Frankfurt am Main by the progressive liberal Heinrich Roessler. This was a high-profile company in the centre of Frankfurt, which developed considerable expertise in cyanogen products.[119] An important source of cyanogen was the Kolin factory in Bohemia with which Degussa had a contract since 1903.[120] Degussa's American subsidiary, the Roessler and Hasslacher Chemical Company in New York, provided a channel for information about North American

---

[114] K. Escherich, *Die angewandte Entomologie in den Vereinigten Staaten* (Berlin, 1913), 131–7; *Neue Deutsche Biographie*, 4 (1957), 649; E. Teichmann, 'Cyanwasserstoff als Mittel zur Entlausung', *Zeitschrift für Hygiene*, 83 (1917), 449–66; K. Escherich, 'Über die Ziele und Aufgaben der "Deutschen Gesellschaft für angewandte Entomologie" ', *Zeitschrift für angewandte Entomologie*, 1 (1914), 14–19.

[115] Escherich, 'Der Krieg', *Zeitschrift für angewandte Entomologie*, 1 (1914), 32.

[116] J. Harwood, *Styles of Scientific Thought. The German Genetics Community 1900–1933* (Chicago, 1993), 214–16.

[117] For Entwesung see W. Heerdt, 'Zyklon Verfahren', *Der Praktische Desinfektor*, 13/2 (1921), 9–11.

[118] E. Hallier, *Gährungserscheinungen. Untersuchungen über Gährung, Fäulniss und Verwesung mit Berücksichtigung der Miasmen und Contagien sowie der Desinfection* (Leipzig, 1867), 96; E. von Skramlik, 'Ueber die Desinfektionswirkung von Cyanwasserstoff', *Zeitschrift für Bakteriologie, Parasitenkunde und Infektionskrankheiten*, Abt. 1, vol. 83 (1919), 386–91. The point was publicized by the War Ministry in guidelines of 9 July 1919, BAP 15.01/9367.

[119] Degussa, *It All Began in Frankfurt. Landmarks in the History of Degussa AG* (Frankfurt/M., 1989); id., *Im Zeichen von Sonne und Mond. Von der Frankfurter Münzscheiderei zum Weltunternehmen Degussa AG* (Frankfurt/M., 1993), 143–9; J. Brillot, 'L'argent sans mémoire: Degussa-Degesch', *Le Monde Juif*, 151 (1994), 7–81; K.-H. Roth, 'Ein Spezialunternehmen für Verbrennungskreisläufe: Konzernkisse DEGUSSA', *1999* 3/2 (1988), 8–44.

[120] Degussa Direktion DL 5/24 Bl. 149.

uses of HCN. In April 1914 Roessler became interested in cyanide fumigation in the Sicilian orange groves.[121] Degussa was at the centre of an international network in the manufacture and deployment of HCN, when the war on agricultural pests was extended to the carriers of human diseases.

Expertise in hygiene and liberal notions of social reform facilitated the development of sanitary technologies of the shower, cremation, and hydrocyanic acid to sweep away insect pests. Although powerful weapons in the armoury of hygiene, in Imperial Germany their use remained sporadic. The campaigns of sanitary reformers and bacteriologists demanded a generalized cleansing rather than targeting a specific ethnic group. By way of contrast, measures were more draconian on Germany's colonial and eastern peripheries. Yet, as the cases of Koch and Kudicke suggest, the pioneers of bacteriology generally disdained rabidly racist rhetoric. It was indeed Hitler who could claim originality in discovering the Jew as a bacillus of social decay.

[121] Ibid., 5/11, Bl. 14 Roessler, note of 9 Apr. 1914.

3

Cleansing Bodies, Defending Borders

i. Bastions of Bacteriology

Bacteriologists rallied to the defence of Germany's frontiers and monitored the spread of epidemics; they aimed to prevent the passage of animal and human carriers of bacteria. State, university, and municipal institutes for hygiene and disinfection were to guard the health of the nation. The regulations for Prussian medical officers issued in 1901 laid down prevention and control of infectious diseases as their main task. In 1902 every Prussian province was commanded to send a medical officer for training in bacteriology at Koch's Institute for Infectious Diseases. A hundred Prussian district medical officers were then equipped with microscopes. When it emerged that these medical officers lacked the time for routine diagnostic work, in 1907 Prussia established ten provincial bacteriological stations to undertake diagnostic tests and disinfection to cover vulnerable points on the eastern and western borders, in ports and in cities.[1] The universalization of bacteriological institutes arose from a multiplicity of factors: military, industrial, and regional interest groups supported the building up of a network of diagnostic and epidemic monitoring stations. Their diverse forms indicate that the hygiene institutes arose opportunistically and sporadically.

Army and naval medical officers were seconded to posts in hygiene institutes, launching the most talented into academic careers. Thus at the Army Experimental Station at Posen, the young military medical physician Emil Behring experimented on disinfectants to neutralize the toxic effects of bacteria. Leading military doctors held honorary positions at the Berlin medical faculty and Koch retained a military rank. His first assistants at the Imperial Health Office—Friedrich Loeffler and Gaffky—were seconded from the Prussian army whose chief medical officer Alwin von Coler appreciated the potential of bacteriology for the newly organized Prussian sanitary corps. His assistants at the Berlin University Institute of Hygiene—the military medical officers Kirchner (the future ministerial director of the Prussian Medical Department), Behring and Wernicke (pioneers of serum therapy), and the naval medical officer Nocht—took the lead in building the nation's bacteriological defences.[2] When the Prussian Institute for Infectious Diseases was founded for Koch in 1891, it had military subventions, trained military medical officers, and

---

[1] *25 Jahre Preussische Medizinalverwaltung seit Erlass des Kreisarztgesetzes 1901–1926* (Berlin, 1927), 95, 115; Prinzing, *Epidemics*, 112–13.

[2] Labisch, *Homo Hygienicus*, 137–40; id. and F. Tennstedt, *Der Weg zum 'Gesetz über die Vereinheitlichung des Gesundheitswesens' vom 3. Juli 1934* (Düsseldorf, 1985), i. 18–20, 52–5; Möllers, *Koch*, 400–2.

2. Prussian Hygiene Institute, Posen, opened 20 April 1913

fulfilled strategic tasks. Many professors in medical faculties held rank as reserve officers, so that medical scientists and their institutes and staffs could be readily mobilized in the event of war.[3]

The bacteriologists' footsoldiers—the newly conscripted brigades of disinfectors—gained in status. Pest control was traditionally carried out by *Kammerjäger* (literally, chamber hunters), an epithet drawn from the romance surrounding the *Leibjäger* or huntsmen in royal service.[4] Medical disinfectors competed with the *Kammerjäger*, as cities martialled squads of disinfectors, armed with powerful and

---

[3] B. Latour, *The Pasteurization of France* (Cambridge, Mass. and London, 1987); P. J. Weindling, 'Scientific Elites in *fin de siècle* Paris and Berlin: The Pasteur Institute and Robert Koch's Institute for Infectious Diseases Compared', in A. Cunningham and P. Williams (eds.), *Laboratory Medicine in the Nineteenth Century* (Cambridge, 1992), 170–88.

[4] BHSTA MWi 760 Kammerjägergewerbe.

destructive chemicals. Koch undertook systematic tests in order to find out which disinfectants were suitable for different bacteria and circumstances, whether for clothes, beds or washing, or for ships and railway carriages.[5] The Hamburg Sanitary Exhibition of 1883 displayed new municipal steam disinfection installations. Disinfection was improved by the experiments of Koch and his associates. Special courses were laid on to train disinfectors: by 1890 Berlin and neighbouring Charlottenburg employed sixty disinfectors. The Prussian district medical officers law of 1901 required trained disinfectors, and to meet this need in 1901 the bacteriologist Flügge opened Prussia's first state disinfectors school, which was attached to the hygiene institute in Breslau in Silesia. By 1903 600 budding disinfectors were being trained in provincial disinfection schools in Prussia to use steam and formalin equipment.[6] Procedures were codified in a Reich decree of 1907, as medical scientists, aided by zoologists, botanists, chemists, and engineers, developed ever more powerful chemicals and incinerators.

Whereas demands for a national law against epidemics had been rejected in 1868 and 1876, by 1894 the Prussian and Reich authorities decided that advances in bacteriology necessitated a revised law for the registration of severe cases of infection. The Reich law for notification of infectious diseases required registration of every case of typhus, cholera, yellow fever, plague, smallpox, and leprosy as well as epidemics of dysentery, diphtheria, and trachoma. Foreigners suffering from these diseases were liable to deportation from Germany.[7] Scarlet fever, measles, tuberculosis, and whooping cough were far more prevalent than the more exotic acute epidemic infections, but they were ranked as socially less disruptive, and were left to individual states to devise counter-measures. In Prussia legislation was delayed until 1905: conservative opposition to the costs of disinfection and liberal hostility to excessive police powers made it necessary to drop tuberculosis and sexually transmitted diseases from the requirement of compulsory notification.[8] Medical officials recognized that the law infringed individual liberty as it was framed in the general interest, although compensation was granted to quarantine persons and for destroyed possessions.[9]

The fear arose that if Germany would wage a major war or acquire new territories for settlement, then like an atavistic throwback to a primitive past age, an epidemic spreading like wildfire from the east could attack the nation's political,

[5] R. Koch, 'Ueber Desinfection', *Mitteilungen aus dem kaiserlichen Gesundheitsamte*, 1 (1881), 234–82; id. and G. Gaffky, 'Versuche über Desinfection des Kiel- oder Bilgeraums von Schiffen', *Arbeiten aus dem kaiserlichen Gesundheitsamte*, 1 (1886), 199–201.

[6] GSTA Rep 76 VIII B Nr 35 wissenschaftlichen Deputation für das Medizinalwesen Bl. 351–70 Desinfections-Ordnung f.d. Krankheiten des Menschen 28 Oct. 1991; Pistor, *Geschichte der preussischen Medizinalverwaltung*, 108; *25 Jahre*, 136–41.

[7] Pistor, *Geschichte der preussischen Medizinalverwaltung*, 95–106; GSTA Rep 76 VIII B Nr 3403, containing the 1835 regulations; Maurer, *Ostjuden*, 357.

[8] GSTA Rep 76 VIII B Nr 3405 betr d. Pr Gesetz zur Bekämpfung ansteckender Krankheiten, newspaper criticisms, e.g. *Die Post* (19 Feb. 1903) and 9 Apr. 1903 on excessive powers of doctrinaire medical officials. Blaschko letter of 27 Feb. 1903 concerning STDs. The law was passed on 26 Aug. 1905.

[9] M. Kirchner, *Die gesetzlichen Grundlagen der Seuchenbekämpfung im Deutschen Reiche unter besonderer Berücksichtigung Preussens* (Jena, 1907), 188.

military, cultural, and economic superiority. Physicians carried out border controls on transmigrants from the east as potential carriers of 'Asiatic epidemics'. Port sanitary officers screened immigrants, cargoes, and shipping, supervised 'deratization' of ships, and quarantined migrants who unlike settled populations had no political rights. Bacteriologists were concerned about persons crossing the frontier from Russia importing infectious diseases. 'Asiatic' cholera, smallpox, and trachoma (an eye infection resulting in blindness) were the main hazards, but from the 1890s typhus and leprosy joined the ranks of infectious enemies, and polio first appeared in epidemic form in 1908.

The superiority of German scientific medicine was seen as a means of securing German hegemony among the hybrid nationalities of the Prussian eastern provinces. Koch moved to the Grand Duchy of Posen in 1869 under a Prussian scheme to promote German settlement; the predominance of the Polish population meant that he hired a Polish maid to interpret when treating patients who could not understand German. After patriotically serving in the Prussian army during 1870, state officials supported his career in public health when he returned to Posen as medical officer of Wollstein. He encountered typhus and anthrax, and observed how the peasants spread anthrax by avoiding registration and by digging up infected cattle carcases.[10]

Medical nationalism was heightened by a sense of mission to extend German culture in the east. Propagandists for German scientific achievements in cell biology suppressed the Polish–Jewish identities of 'German' medical researchers like the pathologist Robert Remak and the Warsaw-born botanist Eduard Strasburger. A largely mythical history of German achievements in medical science achieved widespread acceptance. A similarly nationalist ethos pervaded bacteriology. Military, state, university, municipal, and commercial interests supported bacteriologcal institutes in the eastern provinces. Cohn built up a network of bacteriologists in Silesia, which was especially vulnerable to cholera. While Cohn elucidated the structure, reproduction, and movement of bacteria, he encouraged the practical application of bacteriology in such spheres as preventing the fouling of water and (later, from 1893) in evaluating the effects of formaldehyde on bacteria. Developing the medical aspects of bacteriology fulfilled Cohn's sense of dedicated patriotism and of communal duty and pride in Breslau, where he became honorary citizen. Cohn's academic relations with Koch blossomed, as he secured for Koch the post of municipal medical officer in Breslau. When the move in 1879 turned out to be financially unsatisfactory for Koch, the Breslau medical faculty proposed him for a new chair of hygiene.[11]

---

[10] B. Möllers, *Robert Koch: Persönlichkeit und Lebenswerk, 1843–1910* (Hanover, 1950), 67–92; Staatsbibliothek Preussischer Kulturbesitz Berlin, Wernicke papers, box 2, R. Koch to Wernicke 13 Nov. 1907 on his early career in Posen.

[11] B. Kisch, 'Forgotten Leaders in Modern Medicine. Valentin, Gruby, Remak, Auerbach', *Transactions of the American Philosophical Society*, 44 (1954), 141–317; Möllers, *Koch*, 108–9, 113–19; Cohn, *Cohn*, 185–7; H. P. Schmiedebach, *Robert Remak (1815–1865)* (Stuttgart, 1995); H. Harris, *The Birth of the Cell* (New Haven, Conn., 1998), 136, 146–8.

In 1880 Koch took charge of the bacteriological laboratory of the Reich Health Office in Berlin; yet he remained preoccupied with preventing diseases from the east. After a stormy period as Berlin's first professor of hygiene from 1885, he assumed command of the Prussian Institute for Infectious Diseases in 1891—just prior to the Hamburg cholera epidemic which confirmed his abilities to defend Prussia against bacteriological incursions. Bacteriologists rallied to building up defence systems against epidemics from the east and put in place more rigorous medical screening of transmigrants. Flügge was well acquainted with conditions in Russia having relatives in St Petersburg; the bacteriologist Martin Hahn (who was to succede Flügge in Berlin) travelled in Russia to gauge the risk of cholera.[12] Moreover, advocates of Lebensraum endorsed bacteriology to improve medical protection for German settlers in the east or in the tropics.

Koch relished his role as an international medical fire-fighter against epidemic flare-ups. In 1896 he returned to the eastern margins—to the Baltic district of Memel to tackle the worsening problem of endemic leprosy, which it was feared could spread to the rest of Germany. He stressed that this was an infectious disease. Noting that pedlars, rural workers, and beggars were most susceptible, he prescribed compulsory isolation in a new 'leprosorium' (a modern type of leper colony), disinfection, public education by teachers and the clergy, and training in bacteriology for the district medical officer.[13] Concern over infections in the east provided a springboard for notable careers. The military medical officer and former assistant to Koch, Martin Kirchner, entered the Prussian medical administration, and travelled to Russia in 1897 to find out the extent of the worsening leprosy problem. His solution was a network of Prussian bacteriological monitoring stations. These efforts culminated at the International Leprosy Conference held in Berlin in 1897 when bacteriologists argued that the disease was not inherited.[14]

The development of hygiene institutes in the provinces of Silesia and Posen demonstrate the multiplicity of social interests supporting new bacteriological installations. Silesia with its overcrowded and insanitary living conditions aroused especial concern. In 1885 Ernst Noack, a medical officer at Oppeln in Upper Silesia, proposed establishing a state bacteriological station.[15] What was initially pressure from a concerned physician on the peripheries became a more generalized Prussian state and military strategy to strengthen the nation's bacteriological defences. While the University of Breslau only gained a hygiene institute in 1887, it rapidly became the centre of a network of disease control agencies. From 1889 the hygiene institute at the University of Königsberg provided cover in East Prussia. Medical officers in the eastern provinces of Gumbinnen in East Prussia and Marienwerder in West Prussia were reinforced by laboratories, quarantine institutes, and

[12] GSTA Rep 92 Althoff B Nr 41 Bd 2 Nachlass Althoff, Flügge to Althoff 30 July 1991, Bl. 38.

[13] Koch, 'Die Lepra-Erkrankungen im Kreise Memel', *Gesammelte Werke von Robert Koch*, ii, pt. 2, pp. 670–81.

[14] Kübler and M. Kirchner, 'Die Lepra in Russland. Eine Reisebericht', *Arbeiten aus dem Kaiserlichen Gesundheitsamte*, 13 (1897), 403–55.

[15] GSTA Rep 76 VIII B Nr 3080 Oppeln 1885–1906, Noack to Kultusministerium 30 Jan. 1885.

diagnostic stations.[16] New disinfectants were deployed in densely populated eastern districts: in 1898 the bacteriologist Flügge devised the 'Breslau apparatus' for formaldehyde, after having tested it in over 130 fumigations involving meticulous calculations and regimented procedures. He considered that hygiene institutes should advise and train physicians in the use of disinfectants in each administrative district.[17]

In 1901 a station for bacteriology and food hygiene was established during a typhoid epidemic at Beuthen in the densely populated industrial region of Upper Silesia, close to the Russian border and the Austrian border town of Auschwitz. The Beuthen Hygiene Station was partly supported by the Prussian state, and Flügge supervised disinfection and diagnosis to advanced standards; the municipality provided free rooms, gas, and water, and the Upper Silesian Mining Association contributed towards the running costs. Municipalities on border crossing points like Myslowitz were asked to contribute as the station was responsible for bacteriological diagnoses of human and animal diseases, medical examinations, training disinfectors, and providing steam disinfection ovens and formalin apparatus.[18] Courses updated physicians and taught disinfectors the basics of bacteriology.[19]

More than just disease control was at stake: such hygiene institutes were to inject a dose of German culture into the 'eastern marches' with a dissident Polish population on the Russian border. The province of Posen lacked a university: the Posen Hygiene Institute, established during 1899, spearheaded a phalanx of cultural institutions—the Kaiser Wilhelm Library, a Kaiser Friedrich Museum, and the Royal Academy were founded in Posen between 1901 and 1903. When the town of Bromberg in the province of Posen gained a bacteriological station, this was seen as reinforcing its German character. The crowning glory came when the Kaiser selected Posen for a new royal residence, so conferring additional dignity on the 'Royal Institute of Hygiene' where lectures on infectious diseases were linked to imperial celebrations.

The initiative for the hygiene institute came not from state officials but from the ultra-nationalist Association to Advance German Values in the 'Ostmark' or Eastern Marches (a new but deliberately archaic term for the provinces of Posen, West Prussia, and East Prussia, drawing inspiration from the crusading era of the

---

[16] *25 Jahre*, 100–22.

[17] C. Flügge, 'Die Wohnungsdesinfektion mit Formaldehyd', *Zeitschrift für Hygiene*, 29 (1898), 276–305; Horn and Thom, *Flügge*, 32–3; E. Wernicke, 'Die neueren Fortschritte auf dem Gebiete der Wohnungsdesinfektion', xii. Hauptversammlung des Preussischen Medizinalbeamten-Verein am 28. u. 29 September 1900, offprint in *Arbeiten aus dem kgl. Hygienischen Institut in Posen, Hy. bakt. Abt. 1900–1907*, Nachlass Wernicke.

[18] GSTA Rep 76 VIII B die Errichtung und die Verwaltung des Hygienischen Station in Beuthen 1901–5, Oberschlesischer Berg u. Hüttenmännischer Verein to Flügge 12 Feb. 1902. Flügge memorandum Oct. 1902. *Zeitschrift des oberschlesischen Berg- u. Hüttenvereins*, 40 (1901), 356–8. Flügge to Koch 28 Mar. 1901 cited in Horn and Thom, *Flügge*, 27.

[19] GSTA Rep 76 VIII B Nr 3065 Kultusministerium to Regierungs-Präsident Oppeln 13 Oct. 1910. Nr 3065 Flügge to Althoff 24 Oct. 1900.

Teutonic Knights). The municipality of Posen wished to cultivate an academic stratum in order to mediate between the state and its highly divided population of German Protestants, Polish Catholics, and Jews.[20] Polish doctors resented the build-up of medical institutes at Posen as part of intensified policies of Germanization which included the replacing of Polish and Jewish medical officers by German Protestants. Local groups of German and most Jewish physicians clamoured for an institute of pathology, which would boost medical education and research. They overcame Roman Catholic protests against autopsies in public hospitals as defiling the body.[21]

The Eastern Marches Association had a hefty membership among German doctors, whom it tried to attract to predominately Polish towns by financial subsidies.[22] The Prussian official Althoff conceived of a scheme in which the state funded the Posen hygiene institute because of the risks of epidemics from Russia, whereas the municipality of Posen supported a pathologist to promote research into infectious diseases and medical education.[23] The director, Erich Wernicke, had worked closely with Behring on diphtheria and tetanus serum as an assistant in Koch's Berlin Hygiene Institute from 1890 until 1893, and from 1895–6 at the Kaiser Wilhelm Academy of Military Medicine. His service as a military medical officer shaped his nationalist outlook, and he was appointed to Posen in April 1899.[24] In keeping with the social parameters of civic support, Wernicke developed a wide-ranging programme of what amounted to social bacteriology. He established Prussia's second State Disinfectors School in 1903, convinced that doctors were akin to generals who were duty-bound to train cohorts of disinfectors as the infantry of disease prevention. He bombarded local physicians, disinfectors, teachers, and the public with sermons and tracts on bacteriology, domestic and school hygiene, baths and showers, diet, and the dangers of alcohol as a racial poison.[25]

The Posen Hygiene Institute was to combine practical work with advanced research in its departments of pathology and chemistry. Wernicke was reinforced

[20] R. W. Tims, *Germanizing Prussian Poland. The H-K-T Society and the Struggle for the Eastern Marches in the German Empire 1894–1919* (New York, 1941), 11, 35. The Society was called the Deutscher Ostmarkenverein from May 1899. See A. Galos, F.-H. Gentzen, and W. Jakobczyk, *Die Kakatisten. Der Deutsche Ostmarkenverein (1894–1934)* (Berlin, 1966).

[21] O. Lubarsch, *Ein bewegtes Gelehrtenleben* (Berlin, 1931), 160–1.

[22] Tims, *Germanizing Prussian Poland*, 193–5, 200–1.

[23] GSTA Rep 76 VIII B Nr 3004 die Einrichtung und Verwaltung des (staatlichen) hygienischen Instituts in Posen 1898–1900, Bl. 14 Verein der Aerzte Regierungs-Bezirk Posen, 1898; Bl. 23 'Die Notwendigkeit eines hygienischen Instituts für Posen', *Das Volk*, 16 June 1898; Bl. 31–2 'Ueber die Anlage eines hygienischen Instituts Posen', *Die Ostmark*, 3 (June 1906), 61–3; Nr 3007 die Einrichtung und die Verwaltung des (staatl.) Hygienischen Instituts in Posen 1911–25; Wernicke, 'Das Posener Königl. Hygienische Institut', 1911, cited as offprint; Lubarsch, *Gelehrtenleben*, 125, 152, 158 for Polish opposition.

[24] E. Wernicke, 'Behrings Serumtherapie bei Tetanus', *Deutsche Militärärztliche Zeitschrift* (1893), cited as offprint.

[25] Id., 'Bemerkungen über die Ausbildung von Desinfektoren und über Desinfektorenschulen', *Klinisches Jahrbuch*, 2 (Jena, 1903), 305–14; id., *Die Bekämpfung der Infektionskrankheiten. Ein Rückblick und Ausblick* (Posen, 1905); Wernicke papers, Probetext for 'Die Wohnung in ihrem Einfluss auf Krankheit und Sterblichkeit', *Krankheit und soziale Lage* (Munich, 1912).

by the pathologist Otto Lubarsch, a Protestant but of Jewish ancestry, a founder of the Pan-German League in 1890, and long-standing member of the Eastern Marches Society. The appointment at Posen fired Lubarsch's sense of mission to strengthen German values in the province, yet also exposed how controversial bacteriology continued to be. Along with certain local medical officials, he disliked Wernicke's blinkered adherence to Koch's teachings which took no account of variation in disease forms and environmental conditions. Scientific civil war erupted within the Posen Institute as Lubarsch became a noted advocate of an anti-bacteriological constitutional medicine, based on the importance of a body's physiological and metabolic processes.[26]

Military contacts were cultivated when a regimental medical officer, who had grown up in the region, was seconded for training in bacteriology from 1905 until 1909—that this medical officer, Eugen Gildemeister, was to be director of the Robert Koch Institute during the Second World War indicates that the eastern bacteriological arena was crucial in the training of nationally minded research cadres.[27] The passing of the Prussian law to prevent infectious diseases in 1904/5 extended epidemic prevention to the surrounding province of Posen. The popularity of hygiene bore fruit in parliamentary pressure to expand the institute, a victory achieved in 1913.[28] The Posen scheme demonstrates how an alliance of ministerial bureaucrats, medical researchers, and German patriots tackled the combating of infectious diseases on a scientific basis. The Poles and *Ostjuden* could be redeemed by a sound hygienic lifestyle, thereby consolidating national interests.

ii. Cleansing Migrants

Civic and provincial networks of bacteriologists rallied to defend German urban health from the threat of eastern migrants. Since the early 1870s the port city state of Bremen (a major migration centre) introduced controls on the health of transmigrants—especially quarantine to prevent the spread of smallpox—and by the 1880s doctors cultivated an interest in bacteriology. The Bremen authorities intensified quarantine and isolation when the cholera epidemic erupted in Hamburg in 1892, demonstrating that bacteriologically based measures could be effective in

---

[26] Lubarsch, *Gelehrtenleben*, 126, 133, 156–7, 531–5. He is characterized as 'a Jew' by Chickering (p. 233—his autobiography explains that he was of Jewish descent, his parents having converted and suppressed any 'specifically Jewish' characteristics). See ibid., 2–4.

[27] In 1909 Gildemeister joined the Imperial Health Office, 1913–14 member of the Posen Institute, 19 Nov. 1916 on active service. See GSTA Rep 76 VIII B Nr 3007 *Bericht . . . Etatsjahres 1913*.

[28] GSTA Rep 76 VII B Nr 3005 die Einrichtung und Verwaltung des (staatlichen) Hygienischen Instituts in Posen 1901–4, 'Geschäftsbericht für das Rechnungsjahr 1902'; Nr 3006 ibid. 1904–19, Kommandierung eines Militärarztes 25 Feb. 1905, 9 June 1906, Wernicke on the Seuchengesetz; Nr 3011 Beamten, appointment of Wernicke on 5 Apr. 1899; Nr 3018 Die Bauten des (staatlichen) Hygienischen Instituts in Posen 1911–20, on rebuilding and municipal grants.

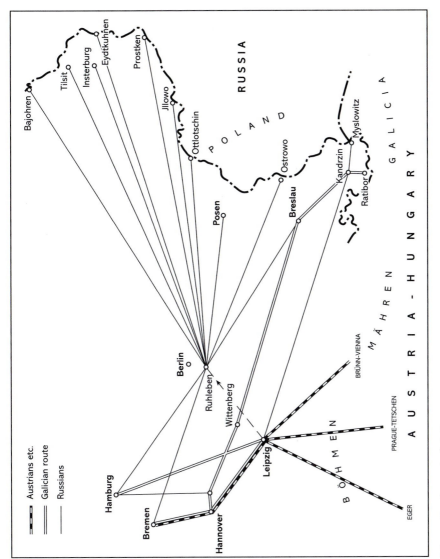

MAP 1. Border control stations c.1910

warding off an epidemic; a Bremen bacteriological institute opened in 1893.[29] The port cities of Danzig and Stralsund established bacteriological laboratories, and Hamburg in 1900 founded Germany's flagship institute for maritime and tropical diseases.[30] Prussia established a quarantine station near Memel to prevent the spread of plague, cholera, and yellow fever, and arranged for health checks on sea-sonal farm workers crossing from Russian Poland.[31] The Prussian municipalities of Berlin-Charlottenburg, Cologne, Erfurt, Gelsenkirchen, Halle, and Wiesbaden agreed with provincial state authorities to fund bacteriological stations. By 1910 Prussia had achieved a chain of bacteriological stations on its frontiers and each major city had its hygiene institute.

Germany's aspirations as a world power in commerce and international politics spurred on the build-up of its bacteriological defences. If nation-states could have been antiseptically sealed, then the masterminds of bacteriology would have been contented; but the movement of people and goods on an ever greater scale meant that new hygienic defence systems had to be devised. The Prussian measures were part of a wider network of bacteriological controls. International agreements enforced disinfection of persons, baggage, and cargoes, especially when coming from areas vulnerable to infections. Sanitary conventions aimed to prevent plague and cholera decimating the European heartlands by insisting on disinfecting goods and quarantining persons and livestock. Ever more elaborate border formalities of medical inspection, quarantine, and compulsory vaccination for smallpox on Germany's eastern frontier were imposed.

Sanitary controls were part of an international system to ensure that the move-ment of migrants and goods did not undermine state security. At the International Sanitary Conference held at Washington in 1881, the United States began a cam-paign to allow foreign countries (notably the USA) to check on health conditions in port cities of other countries. The conference projected three international agen-cies to take responsibility for sanitary notification: in Vienna (for Europe and Africa), in Havana (for the Americas), and one somewhere in Asia. The first inter-national sanitary convention to achieve widespread support was concluded in 1893 for control of ships passing through the Suez Canal and for pilgrimages to Mecca. Sanitary controls in the Danube estuary and the gulf of Genoa and on the Turkish borders were to prevent cholera, yellow fever, and plague (but not typhus). Interna-tional sanitary authorities in Alexandria (commanded until the war by the German

---

[29] *Erster Bericht über die Thätigkeit des Bakteriologischen Instituts zu Bremen von seiner Gründung im Jahre 1893 bis zum Ende 1897* (Bremen, 1898); B. Leidinger, 'Auswanderergeschäft und Gesundheitspoli-tik—Auswandererkontrollen in der Allgemeinen Krankensanstalt Bremen um 1900', *Stadt, Krankheit und Tod. Städtische Gesundheit während der Epidemiologischen Transition* (Berlin, 1998), cited as preprint. For the contrast between Bremen and Hamburg see Evans, *Death*, 299–305. Leidinger points out that Evans overlooks extensive medical controls on transmigrants prior to 1893.

[30] GSTA Nr 2998 das staatl. Medizinal-Untersuchungsamt in Stettin; Nr 3002 das bakteriologische Untersuchungsstelle bei der Regierung Stralsund; Nr 3003 die Errichtung von Untersuchungsanstalten zu Zwecken des Gesundheitswesens in der Provinz Posen, circular to Regierungspräsidenten concern-ing municipal precedents Bl. 1–5, 21 Oct. 1901.

[31] *25 Jahre*, 131–3.

hygienist Emil Gotschlich) and Tangiers were to warn of epidemics. Controls were imposed on travellers, luggage, and transportation at times of epidemics. In 1905 the International Office of Hygiene was established in Paris on the model of the International Bureau of Weights and Measures. It correlated information on sanitary regulations and the incidence of disease. Germany did not join what it condemned as a French dominated organization, permeated by the scientific misconceptions of Pasteur.[32]

Emigration to the United States provided a solution to European problems of impoverished, persecuted, and 'surplus' populations. Emigration offered escape from economic misery the Russian pogroms unleashed in 1881, and tsarist repression. Five million migrants (including an estimated one million Jews) from Eastern Europe passed through the ports of Hamburg, Bremen, and Bremerhaven between 1880 and 1914, boosting the profits of German shipping companies.[33] The increasingly stringent United States sanitary regulations exerted a powerful influence on German port health measures. The US port health officials demanded rigorous medical controls on migration routes from the German–Russian borders to the US medical inspection and quarantine stations. The Federal Government assumed responsibility for immigration in 1890, and public protests that the influx of Eastern Europeans might turn the youthful nation into 'the hospital of the nations of the earth' led to a law requiring immigrants to undergo medical inspections before departure and arrival. In 1892 the federal authorities opened the Ellis Island immigration station to enforce rigorous medical controls to defend America's health.[34]

The screening for parasites applied to both persons and goods: Germany only admitted American pork imports after 1890, when the US Congress passed an act requiring microscopical examination of all pork for export.[35] There was a macabre symmetry between the German terror of an invasion of parasites from infested American pork, and the fears of native-born Americans of pollution from inferior Eastern European racial stock. Ideas of defending nations as biological organisms from bacterial invasions coincided with medical attempts to reinforce quarantine and medical surveillance of migrants.

Public health experts in the United States urged draconian disease control

---

[32] N. Howard-Jones, *Les Bases scientifiques des conférences sanitaires internationales 1851–1938* (Geneva, 1975); R. Carvais, 'La Maladie, la loi, et les mœurs', in C. Salomon-Bayet (ed.), *Pasteur et la révolution pastorienne* (Paris, 1986), 279–330, 413–22; M. Hahn, 'Allgemeine Epidemiologie und Prophylaxe', in E. Friedberger and R. Pfeiffer (eds.), *Lehrbuch der Mikrobiologie (mit besonderer Berücksichtigung der Seuchenlehre)*, i (Jena, 1919), 227–69.

[33] The statistics are from J. Sielemann, *Eastern Jewish Emigration via the Port of Hamburg 1880–1914* (typescript, n.d.). For Bremen see P. Marschalck, *Inventar der Quellen zur Geschichte der Wanderungen, besonders der Auswanderung, in Bremer Archiven* (Bremen, 1986); A. Armgort, *Bremen-Bremerhaven-New York. Geschichte der europäischen Auswanderung über die Bremischen Hafen* (Bremen, 1991); and Leidinger, 'Auswanderergeschäft'. See also Markel, *Quarantine*, table 6.2; S. Joseph, *Jewish Immigration to the United States from 1881 to 1910* (New York, 1914); S. Kuznets, 'Immigration of Russian Jews to the United States: Background and Structure', *Perspectives In American History*, 9 (1975), 35–124.

[34] A. Kraut, *Silent Travellers. Germs, Genes and the 'Immigrant Menace'* (New York, 1994), 51.

[35] Grove, *Helminthology*, 590; J. R. Mohler and A. Eichhorn, *Meat Hygiene*, 388–97.

measures, as the new bacteriology opened up the enticing prospect of disease eradication. The medical officer of Providence, Rhode Island, Charles Chapin, praised
Koch's discovery of the tuberculosis bacillus: 'if we can prevent the spread of
contagion at all we can prevent it entirely'.[36] Chapin denounced general sanitary
cleansing of rooms and objects, and instead targeted medical resources on specific
disease vectors; he favoured vaccination, formalin and steam disinfection, and
insect eradication. His views were supported by fellow disciples of bacteriology,
Alvah H. Doty, health officer of the Port of New York, and Milton J. Rosenau, director of the Marine Hospital Service's Hygienic Laboratory.[37] Others objected that
bacteria varied just as diseases varied in virulence. While wholesale eradication of
any species of disease remained a chimerial dream, bacteriological stress on a single
causal pathogen precipitated intervention: bacteriologists envisaged a world order
in which they would have a key strategic position in preventing diseases.

The combined effect of typhus and cholera scares in New York during 1892
toughened up medical controls not only at the entry points to the US but also in
Europe. In spring 1892 New York officials were alarmed by typhus cases from a
shipload of refugees fleeing the Russian pogroms; the officials intensified pressure
for restricting immigration. The Hamburg cholera epidemic in the summer of 1892
resulted in seventy-six deaths of migrants due to contaminated drinking water
on ships sailing to the United States. The nightmare of cargoes of cholera carriers
aroused public pressure in New York to impose quarantine and medical screening
for steerage passengers to weed out 'the diseased, defective, delinquent and dependent'. Anti-Semitic prejudices against Russian Jewish refugees underlay agitation
for tougher epidemic controls to secure a temporary cessation of all immigration.
Sanitary inspectors targeted Russian Jews as typhus hazards, ignoring that other
Eastern Europeans, Italians, and Irish immigrants were also possible typhus carriers. The US quarantine laws had a hidden subtext of anti-Semitism given that the
violent Russian pogroms were at their height, and that 1891 and 1892 were peak
years for Jewish Russian migration. The percentage of Jewish migrants to the US in
1891 climbed to 12.3 per cent of immigrants, representing 69,140 persons—but by
1893 numbers had more than halved.[38]

The 'nativist' campaigners against immigration of ethnic undesirables to the US
pressured German shipping companies and state medical authorities to impose
ever more elaborate routines of quarantine and disinfection. The vice-president
of the National Board of Health called for 'detention stations . . . with the closest
possible medical inspection' and 'fitted up with all sorts of modern appliances to
combat the disease' as well as for 'inspectors, physicians, nurses, together with

---

[36] Chapin's pronouncement of 1888 was quoted by F. L. Soper, a post-Second World War advocate of
eradication programmes in Soper, 'Eradication Versus Control in Communicable Disease Prevention', in
J. A. Kerr (ed.), *Building the Health Bridge. Selections from the Works of Fred L. Soper, M.D.* (Bloomington,
Ind., 1970), 330–6.

[37] J. H. Cassedy, *Charles V. Chapin and the Public Health Movement* (Cambridge, Mass., 1962), 66–9,
103–5, 126–41. For an approach based on prevention see M. J. Rosenau, *Preventive Medicine and Hygiene*
(New York, 1913).

[38] These efforts have been evocatively analysed in Markel, *Quarantine*, 103, 317–20, 412–15.

means for boiling the immigrants' clothing.'[39] Even shipments of rags for paper-making had to be disinfected by boiling, steam, or sulphuric acid gas. Although the controls were at first intended to permit immigration of the great majority of transmigrants, the Federal authorities steadily tightened up the immigration laws and regulations, extending observation periods and medical checks.

US Marine Hospital Service officials renewed demands for an agreement for sanitary supervision of migrants to the United States before embarkation from European ports, but encountered stiff opposition from Britain, France, and Germany.[40] The US Quarantine Act of February 1893 stipulated that no ship could leave a foreign port without a bill of health signed by the US consul. Medical officers were attached to consulates in Bremen and Hamburg, and were trained in European bacteriological laboratories. In 1894 the bacteriologist Kinyoun left his laboratory on Capitol Hill to attend a course at the Pasteur Institute, spent three weeks with Koch, and inspected laboratory facilities in Hamburg.[41] US Marine Hospital Service and immigration officials exerted pressure on the Bremen and Hamburg medical authorities to toughen up procedures. In 1899 Doty set off to Bremen from Ellis Island with the mission of preventing trouble from 'a poor class of Russians'; for such persons might be passed as healthy by the medical officer of the shipping company, even if incubating diseases.[42] US officials wished to take over quayside inspections in the ports of embarkation, but this was rejected by the British and German medical authorities as an unwarranted interference in national sovereignty. The Italian authorities, having managed to conceal a cholera epidemic in Naples, were more compliant; but although US immigration officers in Italian ports vetted migrants on departure, this did not prevent passengers from being turned back at Ellis Island.[43] Thus the US authorities had to work indirectly to alleviate the pressure on US points of entry. A fine of $100 for every immigrant refused entry spurred shipping companies to sharpen up medical screening prior to embarkation.

Informal liaison between US and German port health experts led to the Germans adopting ever more elaborate medical procedures. The US inspection system was organized on a federal basis and was more scientific, centralized, and intensive than that of the Germans. The German measures were left to shipping companies; although sporadically monitored by the *Länder*, the inspections were less routinized, much depending on the whim of the medical officer at the frontier or quayside.

[39] STAB A.3 N.3 No. 89 betr die Einwanderungs, Quarantänegesetze des Vereinigten Staaten von Nordamerika im Allgemeinen. 1893–1932, 'Against Immigration. Doctors Give Important Testimony', *New York Tribune* (2 Dec. 1892).

[40] Williams, *Public Health Service*, 438–9.

[41] B. Furman, *A Profile of the United States Public Health Service 1798–1948* (Washington, DC, 1973), 211–19.

[42] STAB A.4 No. 164 Massnahmen zur Verhinderung der Einwanderung Typhus oder Blatternkranker in die USA, 1899, 'Inspection of Immigrants: Dr Doty to Go to Bremen with a Suggestion for Improvement', *Washington Evening Star* (5 Oct. 1899).

[43] STAB A.3 N.3 No. 89, The Immigration Commission, *Brief Statement of the Conclusion and Recommendations of the Immigration Commission with Views of the Minority* (Washington, DC, 1910), 17.

The Ellis Island reception facilities became more elaborate with a palatial new station in 1900, a hospital in 1902, and a 450-bed contagious diseases hospital in 1911. The expanded US Public Health Service and Marine Hospital Service maintained a staff of over forty physicians on Ellis Island by 1911. Line inspection controls on migrants—up to 10,000 persons per day—became ever more stringent to weed out the sick and the disabled. The steep steps to the Ellis Island Registry Hall tested physical condition.[44] From 1905 all eyelids were everted for trachoma and heads were checked for favus (a fungal infection of the scalp). From 1906 Federal law imposed a six-day quarantine period before embarkation, having a decisive effect on the arrangements in Bremen and Hamburg. From 1907 immigrants suffering from tuberculosis, epilepsy, or physical disabilities were banned as part of efforts to weed out 'idiots', diseased poor persons, polygamists, anarchists, prostitutes, epileptics, and the insane, and illiteracy was soon added to the list; by 1915 Wassermann blood tests to screen for syphilis were introduced. The draconian controls on passengers in steerage contrasted to token medical checks for higher classes of passengers—medical authorities linked poverty (rather than race) of the steerage passengers with potential disease and mental defects.[45]

The German medical controls attempted to screen large numbers of passengers at low cost. As rival shipping lines like Cunard, HAPAG (the acronym for Hamburg Amerikanische Paketfahrt-Aktiengesellschaft), and the Bremer Lloyd competed, they had to balance the expense of inspection and accommodation with the need to prevent outbreaks of infections on board ship. HAPAG was technologically innovative, pioneering new sanitary procedures (as well as oil as a cleaner, lighter, and more efficient fuel).[46] With a rapid rise in migrants, in the cholera year of 1892 HAPAG opened migration halls housing 1,400 people at a time in eight quayside sheds to house, feed, and medically screen the migrants, and to disinfect their baggage. Yet the quayside halls rapidly became overcrowded, and their lack of adequate sanitation and washing facilities meant that they could become a source of infections.

'Gentlemen. I forget that I am in Europe' was Koch's expression of revulsion at the primitive, insanitary conditions in Hamburg. Although Koch pointed to 'the Russian emigrants' as the source of the cholera 'invasion' in August 1892, he did not blame them for a lack of cleanliness. Indeed, it was because the transmigrants began cleaning their possessions that infected water polluted the harbour, adding to the inevitable sewage. Koch denounced the Hamburg authorities for not disinfecting the waste water before discharge from the migration halls into

---

[44] A. M. Kraut, 'Plagues and Prejudice: Nativism's Construction of Disease in Nineteenth- and Twentieth-Century New York City', *Hives of Sickness. Public Health and Epidemics in New York City* (New Brunswick, NY, 1995), 65–94.

[45] STAB A.3 N.3 No. 89, copy of 'An Act to Ammend an Act to Regulate the Immigration of Aliens into the US', approved 20 Feb. 1907, copy from Auswärtiges Amt, Deutsche Botschaft Washington, 7 Feb. 1907. See also 'An Act to Regulate the Immigration of Aliens in and the Residence of Aliens in the United States' for exclusion of the illiterate and extension of US powers of inspection.

[46] F. Venn, *Oil Diplomacy in the Twentieth Century* (Basingstoke, 1986), 3; F. E. Hyde, *Cunard and the Atlantic, 1840–1973* (London, 1975), 104–18.

the river Elbe from where Hamburg's drinking water was taken without being filtered.[47]

Although sporadic anti-Semitism flared up during the Hamburg cholera epidemic of 1892, such prejudices did not infect expert opinion. Koch identified Russian migrants as the source of the epidemic, but their race and religion were irrelevant. Other doctors stressed the effects of local insanitary conditions, or considered that cholera came from the Middle East via French coastal traffic. Richard Evans in his study of the Hamburg cholera epidemic of 1892 assumes that *Ostjuden* brought cholera to Hamburg; but this is more a matter of conjecture than epidemiologically proven. Jews were in an overall minority among Eastern European migrants during the 1890s; even though in 1892 numbers of Jewish migrants were high (and possibly exceeded those of other religions), because there were cholera outbreaks in Russia at the time there was no proof that Jewish rather than other migrants and travellers from Russia (or indeed from other cholera areas) were the carriers of cholera. Transmigrants did not 'cause' cholera in other port cities, notably Bremen. Russian Jews were scapegoated for the failure of the Hamburg authorities to provide filtration. But there is no conclusive proof for the view held at the time by anti-Semites that Russian Jews caused the Hamburg cholera epidemic.[48]

The cholera crisis prompted the German authorities to seal the eastern borders: protests from the shipping companies and the German Jewish Central Committee for Russian Jews resulted in the concession of the hygienically controlled route across Germany, channelling migrants to cross to ports of embarkation. Poles (including Jews) had been expelled from Germany in the 1880s, and German nationalists and anti-Semites demanded closure of the eastern border. German Jewish organizations were prepared to provide assistance, but agreed that eastern Jews should not settle in Germany.[49]

The medical inspection, cleansing, and quarantine for migrants from the east varied according to general epidemiological conditions, the sporadic pressures applied by US agencies, and local idiosyncracies. Prussian medical authorities guarded against migrants sparking off outbreaks of disease among those in transit or igniting a major epidemic in Germany itself. Border stations functioned as collecting centres for migrants, and were the portals for the hygienically controlled route to Ellis Island. Procedures began on Germany's Eastern frontiers, as a prelude to transfer in segregated carriages or sealed trains via the 'Central Control Station' at Ruhleben on the outskirts of Berlin or, for persons crossing from Austria, via a state control station at Leipzig. These collecting points at railway junctions ensured

---

[47] R. Koch, 'Ueber den augenblicklichen Stand der bakteriologischen Choleradiagnose', *Zeitschrift für Hygiene und Infektionskrankheiten*, 14 (1893), 319–38; id., 'Wasserfiltration und Cholera', ibid., 393–426; id., 'Die Cholera in Deutschland während des Winters 1892/93', *Gesammelte Werke von Robert Koch*, ii, pt. 1, p. 214.

[48] R. J. Evans, *Death in Hamburg. Society and Politics in the Cholera Years 1830–1910* (Oxford, 1987), 280–4, 299–300.

[49] Aschheim, *Brothers and Strangers*, 31–5, 60–2.

that the migrants did not defile the metropolis.[50] Sick migrants were weeded out at the border control stations, and from 1891 at Ruhleben, where shipping companies financed large-scale facilities for delousing and disinfecting baggage. The Hamburg Senate established disinfection facilities for incoming passengers and shipping, as well as smaller medical control stations on rivers and canals.[51] The North German Lloyd shipping company provided disinfection and quarantine facilities at the Bremen Allgemeine Krankenhaus and Bremerhaven for passengers without a disinfection certificate from Ruhleben.[52] While Koch demanded destruction of the 'infectious substance', he cautioned that the arbitrary medical checks were all too often senseless: light cases of cholera were often overlooked and medical certificates could be forged.[53]

As the flow of migrants magnified sanitary problems, the Hamburg authorities pressed for enlarging migration halls, as the original barracks in Hamburg, designed for 150 passengers, were at bursting point. In 1900 the pavilion system to prevent cross-infection (an innovation derived from isolation hospitals) was adopted. The new pavilions were constructed with dormitories, each for twenty-two passengers. Further rebuilding, jointly financed by the Hanseatic states and the shipping companies, took place between 1905 and 1906 to cope with the more stringent US immigration laws requiring prolonged quarantine and documentation of body size, facial colour, the colour of hair and eyes, and place of birth. But neither religion nor race was registered. Port health officers scrutinized facilities so that they should be in line with modern hygiene.[54]

From 1894 HAPAG and Lloyd combined to finance five control stations on the Russian–German border at Bajohren, Eydtkuhnen, Illowo, Ottlotschen, and Prostken, and 'registration stations' were sited at Leipzig, Myslowitz, and Oderberg-Ratibor. The companies modernized the control stations and opened new ones between 1904 and 1906 at Insterburg, Ostrowo, Posen, Tilsit, and Thorn.[55] The more modern control stations incorporated bathing, disinfecting, and medical facilities. The hygiene institutes of Breslau and Posen trained disinfectors and saw that medical facilities at the migration stations were up to standard.[56] The border stations regulated the through-flow of migrants like valves in a sewage system, so that travellers would not have to stay more than the required five days at the port emigration camps, where overcrowding was a health hazard.

[50] Dwork, 'Health Conditions'.

[51] STAH A 10 Bd 1 betr Cholera-Schiffs u Auswandererüberwachungs Dienst. The medical control stations were at Altona, Hamburg, Lauenburg, Wittenberg, Potsdam, and Berlin. *25 Jahre*, 135–6.

[52] Leidinger, 'Auswanderergeschäft'.

[53] Koch, *Gesammelte Werke*, ii, pt. 2, pp. 870, 875 (opinion of 28 Nov. 1894).

[54] STAB 4, 21–502 Auswanderungswesen, Bd 1 1904–13, report by Tjaden 13 Apr. 1905, and 27 Sept. 1906 on US laws; Sthamer, *Die Auswanderer in Hamburg* (Hamburg, 1904); Sielemann, *Emigration*; STAB 4, 21–503 Norddeutschen Lloyd to Gesundheitsrat Bremen 14 Jan. 1914 on modifications in isolation facilities. The US authorities recorded data on numbers of Jewish immigrants from 1898.

[55] Z. Szajkowski, 'Sufferings of Jewish Emigrants to America in Transit through Germany', *Jewish Social Studies*, 39 (1977), 105–16.

[56] GSTA Rep 76 VII B Nr 3005 die Einrichtung und Verwaltung des (staatlichen) Hygienischen Instituts in Posen 1901–4, 'Geschäftsbericht für das Rechnungsjahr 1903'.

The trains went directly to the halls on the quayside from where, after quarantine, passengers joined their ships. The routine work of German port medical staff involved examining eyes for trachoma and the scalp for pellegra. Especially when there were cholera epidemics in Russia, transmigrants had to undress and be rubbed down with a disinfectant for a compulsory shower. Then came screening for skin diseases and fevers while naked; clothes and possessions were returned after disinfection. In Bremen doctors noted the passengers' physical appearance, temperature, and whether a bath was necessary.[57] In Hamburg, wooden benches, zinc crockery, bedding, stoneware washing facilities, tiled shower cabinets with hot and cold water, and various types of toilets were designed to maintain hygiene at the lowest possible cost. On the men's side, showers could cope with 120 persons per hour; on the women's side, six showers and four bathtubs immersed sixty-eight persons per hour. Disinfection of clothing and luggage took longer than the cleansing of bodies, so a waiting-room and blankets had to be provided. Sanitary authorities dragooned eastern populations into expecting disinfection as part of the experience of migration. New techniques of disinfection with bactericidal antiseptics like carbolic acid, lysol, and paraffin emulsion were deployed—although partially effective against lice, the disinfectants could cause skin reactions and were not fully effective against the tenacious nits (the louse eggs). Any concern with lice was merely incidental until 1913, when the link with typhus began to be recognized.[58]

Despite the anxiety concerning epidemics, in 1905 the vast majority (5,272 out of *c*.112,000) of migrants turned back at the border control stations and at Ruhleben had eye diseases; a further 98 were refused passage because of the condition of their hair, and 146 were condemned as too decrepit, but only 40 persons were denied passage for harbouring infectious diseases like cholera, plague, and typhus.[59] Epidemic infections were rare when compared to eye infections and chronic disabilities, suggesting that the perception of epidemic threats was much magnified. In any case, infectious diseases prompted tough preventive measures, as when the Hamburg authorities suspended a shipping route across the Baltic from Libau because of the number of cholera cases arriving on this route.

The sanitary procedures were the targets of much medical criticism at the time. The Hamburg Institute for Maritime and Tropical Diseases, founded in 1901, agitated for more effective (but not necessarily severe) hygienic controls on migrants. The Tropical Institute ensured constant interaction between medicine for the colonies, port health, and domestic public health provisions. The German Colonial Society, the Reich, port and municipal authorities, and military and naval authorities drummed up support for tropical medicine. Koch, who in 1896 worked on cattle plague in Africa, was enthusiastic. Nocht remained in Hamburg after the cholera epidemic of 1892 in the new post of port medical officer to take a key role in developing Hamburg's medical relations with the wider world. Once the Colonial

---

[57] STAB A.4 No. 320, extract from Stationsbuch der Desinsfectionsanstalt des Norddeutschen Lloyds, 1906–8.
[58] Nuttall, 'Combating Lousiness', 523–4, 530, 544.
[59] STAB A.4 No. 300a, report by Tjaden and Nocht, 20 July 1906.

Society in 1898 decided that it would support a specialist department for tropical medicine, rivalry flared between medical leaders in Berlin and Hamburg. In 1901 Nocht succeeded in establishing a tropical institute in Hamburg: this was a national response to the opening of the Liverpool School of Tropical Medicine and the London School of Tropical Medicine in 1899, as well as a regional triumph over Koch's scheme for a Berlin Institute of Tropical Medicine. Situated since 1914 as a massive bastion between the harbour and the red light district of St Pauli, this disease-detection and research agency reinforced medical aspirations for an imperial role. The symbiosis of state, public, and commercial interests boosted the Hamburg Institute: the Reich Colonial Office subsidized its medical facilities, and the Colonial Society financed the Institute's journal for maritime and tropical diseases.[60]

The Hamburg Institute advised on national regulations to eradicate parasites on board ships. The rat was known to carry plague bacilli, and it became a target for bacteriologists. The Reich Health Office supported Nocht's experimental studies of different poison gases to kill rats, checking whether grain cargoes were damaged. The aim was to replace the vagaries of rat-catchers and other traditional pest control methods by uniform scientific procedures.[61] Nocht disputed the efficacy of the American-developed Clayton machinery for gassing with sulphuric acid. He preferred the far more toxic carbon monoxide gas for which he devised generator equipment. The Hamburg Institute developed regimes of disinfection and pest eradication by gassing, as a means of securing Germany's borders. The international sanitary convention of 1912 required the fumigation of ships at least once a year. The term 'deratization' made its debut in the vocabulary of international hygiene in 1912—the term 'delousing' was soon to follow.

Despite the efforts of authorities to regulate screening procedures for transmigrants, numerous abuses occurred. During the 1880s a racket was conducted on the Austro–German border, when at Oświęcim clothes were taken away for 'disinfection' and valuables were pinched. The Prussian system of controlled transmigration did provide some degree of personal security, whereas those hazarding 'wild' crossings of the Prussian–Galician border risked blackmail and theft.[62] The medical controls on transmigrants were draconian but erratic, because of large numbers, the economic interests of the shipping companies, and differing views of what was medically necessary. Having escaped tsarist repression and terrifying

---

[60] Evans, *Death* ignores the crucial role of Nocht as a link between Hamburg and the wider world. W. U. Eckart, 'Von der Idee eines "Reichsinstituts" zur unabhängigen Forschungsinstitution. Vorgeschichte und Gründung des Hamburger Instituts für Schiffs-und Tropenkrankheiten 1884–1901', in R. vom Bruch and R. A. Müller (eds.), *Formen ausserstaatlicher Wissenschaftsförderung im 19. und 20. Jahrhundert* (Stuttgart, 1990), 31–52; id., *Medizin und Kolonialimperialismus. Deutschland 1884–1945* (Paderborn, 1997), 79–90; L. Wess, 'Tropenmedizin und Kolonialpolitik: Das Hamburger Institut für Schiffs- und Tropenkrankheiten 1918–1945', 1999, 8/2 (1992), 38–61; S. Wulf, *Das Hamburger Tropeninstitut 1919 bis 1945* (Berlin, 1994). For schools of tropical medicine see Farley, *Bilharzia*, 20–30.

[61] STAH Hafenarzt I Nr 135 Verwendung von Kohlenoxydhaltigen Gasen (Generatorgas) für Rattenvertilgung 1899–1905; BAP 15.01 1165 Desinfektion der Schiffe 1903–10; *Reichsgesetzblatt* (1907) 511; Koch, *Gesammelte Werke*, ii, pt. 2, pp. 902–5 (Koch to the Kaiserliches Gesundheitsamt President 29 Sept. 1901).

[62] Dwork and van Pelt, *Auschwitz*, 57.

pogroms, migrants could expect prison-like regimentation by German medical personnel, border guards, and officials. Most control centres were guarded and encircled by walls. After disembarking from the packed trains, disinfection involved the separation of male and female passengers and consequent breaking up of families, the confiscation of all clothing and possessions, rubbing down with strange, slippery substances, and a shower (hopefully, of a tolerable temperature). The 'dirty' and 'clean' sides of the sanitary circuit were rigorously policed by coarsely behaved attendants. Although much attention was given to disinfection of sewage because of the cholera risk, the accommodation was rudimentary. While one migrant reflected on being transmuted into 'dumb animals, helpless and unresisting', passengers' terror led to protests and evasion.[63]

Each control station had its own idiosyncratic medical routine. Where baths were compulsory, there were inspections of the naked body, but at Myslowitz only eyes, hair, and forearms were examined. In Bajohren, Insterburg, and Tilsit, throats were inspected, and only at Posen was the temperature taken. Compulsory baths involved being rubbed down with various bactericidal soaps and disinfectants. Most stations had only the older steam disinfection equipment rather than the more modern hot air chambers. Some stations disinfected all clothing and personal effects, some exempted clean clothes, and at others the doctor selected items for disinfection. Different substances—like carbolic or creosote—were sprayed or painted on clothing. Despite the pressure from the authorities to improve hygienic conditions for steerage passengers, the problems of overcrowding, lack of sanitation and washing facilities, and infestation persisted. A Russian Jewish emigrant of 1908 recalled that 'the atmosphere was so thick and dense with smoke and bodily odours that your head itched and when you went to scratch your head . . . you got lice in your hands.'[64]

Whether such varied procedures were effective in weeding out the diseased and protecting the health of the German population was dubious. In 1905 the Bremen medical officer Tjaden recommended a general medical inspection rather than disinfection, and in the following year Tjaden and the Hamburg port medical officer Nocht inspected the control stations on the eastern border. They had no confidence in the haphazard medical screening on the frontiers as capable of detecting persons incubating diseases, and they condemned the hygienic routines as so severe as to encourage 'wild transmigrants' illegally to make their own way across Germany. The controls often went beyond what was medically necessary—Nocht and Tjaden considered that the germs were inside rather than on the body, and that even after bathing such vermin as headlice remained. They condemned chemical disinfection

---

[63] Mary Antin, *A Promised Land* (Boston, 1912), 174–7: description of two weeks' experience of quarantine in Hamburg in 1894, cited by Markel, *Quarantine*, ch. 1; U. Weisser (ed.), *100 Jahre 1889–1989 Universitätskrankenhaus Eppendorf* (Tübingen, 1989), 43.

[64] STAH II F6 Unterbringung der Auswanderer vor deren Einschiffung Bd I 1886–1906, Bd II 1906–8, Bd III 1908–38; Sthamer, *Die Auswanderer-Hallen in Hamburg* (Hamburg, n.d. [1900/4]); B. Nocht, *Die Auswandererobdach und die gesundheitspolizeiliche Überwachung der Auswanderer in Hamburg* (Hamburg, 1901); Sielemann, *Emigration*; Kraut, 'Germs, Genes'; quotation by Sophia Kreitzberg in B. C. Hamblin, *Ellis Island. The Official Souvenir Guide* (Santa Barbara, 1994), 12.

as useless and steam disinfection as only partially effective. Bacteriologists were sceptical of general cleansing measures, and wished to alleviate rather than intensify the disinfection procedures.[65]

At some stations the transmigrants were held in the control stations and at others they were allowed to lodge nearby. Arrangements differed for provision of food, and whether alcohol was allowed. In order to remove the sheer terror from the procedures, Nocht and Tjaden recommended that baths ought to be voluntary, and only soiled underclothes ought to be disinfected. They singled out the system at Ratibor as ideal, with medical inspection of eyes, hair, skin, arm movements, breathing, and temperature, while recognizing that increased medical personnel and equipment like thermometers would be necessary. They argued that if the sanitary controls were relaxed, more transmigrants would comply, thereby minimizing evasion and contacts with the German population. The Prussian authorities accepted that control station doctors should have discretionary powers over baths and disinfection, and that only in exceptional cases should doctors insist on total nudity.[66]

The transmigrant system was criticized as exploiting emigrants for commercial ends. Socialists argued that there was greater leniency at German control stations for migrants who had booked passages with German shipping companies than for those intending to embark from the Netherlands, Belgium, or Britain.[67] The Hamburg medical authorities criticized the quarantine halls as overcrowded and the screening procedures as too lax.[68] The densely packed immigrants in dirty, prison-like conditions increased the risks of infection, even while undergoing disinfection procedures or medical examinations. Bremen introduced medical inspection of all transmigrants in 1907, as a preliminary for selective disinfection. Tjaden warned that a mysterious 'infective substance' was invading the crowded migration halls.[69] Complaints against poor-quality food and the overfull halls led to violent protests. Facilities designed to cope with 5,000 persons at one time were flooded with thousands of extra persons—a situation that was profitable to the shipping company but which was constantly criticized by the port medical officer. For those unfamiliar with modern medical routines, medical inspections could be terrifying, arousing fears of robbery and murder.[70] In Hamburg sick children were carted off to the new but remote Eppendorf Hospital, which banned visits and provided no information to relatives. Migrants hated the medical controls, insanitary

---

[65] STAB A. 4, 21–502; A 4 No. 290 betr Besichtigung der Auswanderer-Kontrollstationen an der russischen österreichischen Grenze und in Ruhleben und Leipzig, report by Nocht and Tjaden 20 July 1906.

[66] STAB A. 4 No. 290 betr Besichtigung der Auswanderer-Kontrollstationen an der russisch-österreichischen Grenze und in Ruhleben und Leipzig, report by Nocht and Tjaden 20 July 1906. Prussian MdI report of 19 Apr. 1907; STAB 4, 21–502 Auswanderungswesen, Bd 1 1904–13, Tjaden report 'Auswandererungswesen in Bremen', 10 June 1907, pp. 6–7.

[67] M. Just, *Ost- und südosteuropäische Amerika-Wanderung 1881–1914* (Wiesbaden, 1988), 30–1, 77–85, 106–14.

[68] STAH F6 Bd II. Szajkowski, 'Sufferings'.

[69] STAB 4, 21–470 Fleckfieber (Flecktyphus) und Läusebekämpfung, Tjaden report 21 Nov. 1908.

[70] J. Wertheimer, *Unwelcome Strangers. East European Jews in Imperial Germany* (New York and Oxford, 1987), 50–1.

conditions, and forced removal to quarantine facilities as severing ties of kinship and violating the personal sanctity of the body.[71] Medical routines were to prevent epidemics in Germany, and to reassure the German public that the transmigrants posed no threat to the nation's health.

The hygienic routines provided a general cleansing, rather than delousing as specifically targeting typhus. In 1905 it was decreed that at times of typhus epidemics, migrants could only cross Germany in special carriages without upholstery, and all towelling had to be burned as part of disinfecting routines.[72] But this changed in 1913 when the news of Nicolle's discovery of the louse-borne aetiology of typhus coincided with the Balkan Wars, arousing fears that diseased Serbian migrants might travel through Germany and spread typhus. Sanitary controls were introduced in the event of a case of typhus occurring within twenty kilometres of a military barracks.[73] By May 1913 delousing was on the medical agenda for the Hamburg migration station.[74]

Initially designed to safeguard migrants and to ensure a smoothly running system of mass emigration, the medical controls became steadily more restrictive. Quarantine and disinfection procedures like the compulsory showers exceeded what made sense in terms of contemporary medical theories. Migrants could find their taste of the new hygiene bewildering and utterly terrifying. But as disease and vermin became welded together by medical science, migrants in time became not only conditioned to expect sanitary controls and disinfection, but also wary as to what these might involve in terms of the loss of possessions and personal indignities.

Mary Antin, who crossed from Plotzk in Russia to Boston in 1891, provided a classic description of sanitary procedures. Holocaust historians see these as prefiguring the utterly humiliating and brutal delousing of Auschwitz, and above all of the cruel genocidal deception of the gas chambers.[75] Antin's description conveys the fear of the travellers at their segregation, their commercial exploitation—they were charged two marks for being disinfected, and their feelings of humiliation at the medical and administrative procedures. She was subjected to a general cleansing rather than to delousing as a typhus control measure—for the connections between lice and typhus were unknown. A German physician on the border at Eydtkuhnen showed a glimmer of pity, when advising her on how to gain assistance. Otherwise, the sanitary controls at the border station of Eydtkuhnen were perfunctory.[76] The cleansing Mary Antin experienced on the outskirts of Berlin,

[71] Just, *Amerika-wanderung*, 114. Howard Markel has examined these perceptions in the Yiddish-American press; see H. Markel, *Quarantine: East European Jewish Immigrants and the New York City Epidemics of 1892* (Baltimore, Md., 1996).

[72] BHSTA M Inn 62407 Vollzug des Gesetzes betr die Bekämpfung gemeingefährlicher–Krankheiten, *Anweisung zur Bekämpfung ansteckender Krankheiten im Eisenbahn Verkehr* (Berlin, 1905).

[73] BHSTA MA 95773 Bekämpfung gemeingefährlicher Krankheiten, Reichskanzler to Bayer. Staatsministerium 30 Apr. 1913.

[74] STAH II F6 Unterbringung der Auswanderer vor deren Einschiffung Bd III 1908–38, letter from Hafenarzt 26 May 1913.

[75] D. Dwork and R. van Pelt, *Auschwitz*, 52–4.

[76] M. Antin, *From Plotzk to Boston* (Boston, 1899; repr. Saddle River, NJ, 1970), 22–46.

and the fumigation of her baggage were primarily to prevent cholera. There was no sense of combating a specifically 'Jewish disease': the rationales derived from cholera disinfection procedures and were formulated on the basis of Koch's discovery of the comma bacillus. The bacteriologist Flügge wrote in 1886 that it was necessary to eliminate the possibility of contact with soiled objects and linen, that infective material can cling to the hands, and that insects could spread the disease. Hence the requirement for 'rigid and properly applied cleanliness'.[77] The cholera prevention measures experienced by transmigrants had to undergo some considerable change before they became equivalent to the delousing procedures of the Nazi concentration camps.

iii. The Jewish Bacilli

Although the German and American press sensationalized how *Ostjuden* imported infections, such was the official disinterest that transmigrant regulations and statistics did not generally record religion or race. Bacteriologists during the 1890s were largely unconcerned about religion, except if rituals like communion spread germs.[78] What mattered was the contact with infectious pathogens, as race and notions of constitutional susceptibility were irrelevant to the Koch school of bacteriologists.

There were sporadic attempts to gain acceptance for anti-Semitic notions of the Jew as a parasite by deploying the rhetorical force of bacteriological discoveries. It is tempting to construct an identikit picture of a scientized anti-Semitism by presenting sporadic outbursts of prejudice as a coherent and pervasive movement. A much-cited instance in the litany of scientific racism is that in 1892 the Italian physiologist Paolo Mantegazza noted in the liberal Austrian newspaper *Neue Freie Presse* that anti-Semites characterized Jews as alien 'tubercular growths, ulcers' and as 'swollen and presumptuous parasites' in 'our European body'. Mantegazza, however, rejected these accusations as grotesque distortions. He viewed many characteristics attributed by anti-Semites to Jews such as immunity to cholera as unfounded, and he saw no reason to condemn Jews as inadequately patriotic.[79]

Yet public prejudice against Russian Jewish refugees fleeing from the Eastern European pogroms increased during the 1890s: racial biology reinforced stereo-

[77] C. Flügge, *Micro-organisms with Special Reference to the Etiology of the Infective Diseases* (London, 1890), 442–51.

[78] D. Dwork, 'Health Conditions of Immigrant Jews on the Lower East Side of New York: 1880–1914', *Medical History*, 25 (1981), 1–40; A. M. Kraut, 'Silent Travellers: Germs, Genes and American Efficiency', *Social Science History*, 12 (1988), 377–94; A. M. Kraut, *Silent Travellers. Germs, Genes and the 'Immigrant Menace'* (New York, 1994); V. A. Harden, *Inventing the NIH: Federal Biomedical Research Policy 1887–1937* (Baltimore, Md., 1986), 11–16; H. Markel, ' "Knocking Out the Cholera": Cholera, Class and Quarantines in New York City, 1892', *Bulletin of the History of Medicine*, 69 (1995), 454 for the mortality of migrants.

[79] P. Mantegazza, 'Der Antisemitismus', *Neue Freie Presse*, nos. 10448–9 (23–4 Sept. 1893); Bein, 'Jewish Parasite', 13; M. B. Hart, 'Moses the Microbiologist: Judaism and Social Hygiene in the Work of Alfred Nossig', *Jewish Social Studies*, NS 2 (1995), 72–97.

types of Eastern Europeans as living in filth and squalor and as clothed in dirty and verminous rags. Hereditary biology and bacteriology cross-fertilized with loathing of Jews as an alien culture and religion to generate a biological stereotype of the Jewish race as pathogenic. In 1895 the Reichstag debated whether 'those Jews who were not German citizens'—a euphemism for *Ostjuden*—could be allowed to cross frontiers. Anti-Semitic Reichstag delegates condemned Jews as 'parasites on the German oak', a 'deathly enemy', bringers of 'misfortune or *Unheil*', and as threats to 'the spiritual and moral health of the German Volk'; the onslaught culminated in Jews being denounced as 'cholera germs'.[80] Nationalists drew exterminatory senti-ments from one of their inspirational propagandists, Paul Lagarde: 'One does not negotiate with trichinae and bacilli; trichinae and bacilli are not chosen to be edu-cated, they are exterminated as quickly and as thoroughly as possible.'[81]

Anti-Semitic propagandists demanded the sealing of borders to undesirables from the east. Anti-Semitic extremists in Vienna denounced Jews as 'parasites', 'insects', and 'grasshoppers', which had to be poisoned by insect powder.[82] The con-cept of *Sozialparasitismus* among ant societies, developed by the entomologist Escherich, was taken up by anti-Semites to denounce Jews as parasitic vermin.[83] Anti-Semites added potency to their diatribes with scientific terms to strengthen their bitter rhetoric, and derided Jews as congenitally diseased. Despite such bor-rowings, anti-Semitic rhetoric did not as yet pollute mainstream medical science. Bacteriologists refuted the allegations of Jews as corrupters of blood, and Jewish traditions could be depicted as in keeping with modern hygienic laws.[84] Jewish physicians studied specifically Jewish medical problems and Jewish anthropolo-gists used biology and physical anthropology to define the characteristics of a Jewish race, and to promote Jewish health and racial regeneration.[85]

When world war erupted, typhus as a disease threat had a visible cause in the louse, and eastern migrants had a reputation as louse-infested. There were new bacteriological institutes to guard Germany's health, and the search for more pow-erful pesticides led to increasing awareness of the potentialities of hydrocyanic acid. Emigration from persecution and poverty in Eastern Europe prompted German doctors and state officials to prevent the importation of diseases by ever more rigorous (although not necessarily severe) medical screening and disinfec-tion. Overall, the medical controls were permissive, designed to allow migrants to pour out of Russia, to cross Germany, and embark from German ports as a

---

[80] Reichstag, 47 sitting (27 Feb. 1895), Antrag Frh. v. Hammerstein, Fr v. Manteuffel auf Vorlegung eines Gesetzentwurfs nach welchem Israeliten, die nicht Reichsangehörige sind, die Einwanderung über die Grenzen des Reichs untersagt wird; Hilberg, *Destruction*, 18–20.

[81] *Völkischer Beobachter* (22 Dec. 1941), quoted by Pois, *National Socialism*, 123–4; P. de Lagarde, *Juden und Indogermanen, eine Studie nach dem Leben* (Göttingen, 1887), 339.

[82] B. Hamann, lecture at St Antony's College, Oxford, 1997.

[83] A. Schickedananz, *Sozialparasitismus im Völkerleben* (Leipzig, 1927), 121–2; Bein, 'Jewish Parasite', 21.

[84] Hart, 'Moses the Microbiologist'; M. Grunwald (ed.), *Die Hygiene der Juden. Im Anschluss an die Internationale Hygiene-Ausstellung Dresden 1911* (Dresden, 1911).

[85] Hart, 'Social Science and National Identity: A History of Jewish Statistics, 1880–1930', Ph.D. thesis, UCLA, 1994, 101–2. My thanks to David Rechter for this reference. Gilman, *et al.*, *'Der Schejne Jid'*.

profitable trade for shipping companies, provided they did not spread diseases. In a changed international situation of war and post-war turbulence, medical controls led to immigration restrictions; international agencies intervened in Eastern Europe to impose rigorous disease-control measures on migrants to discourage emigration. Hitler's bacteriological rhetoric accelerating extermination marked the culmination of a process of sealing borders against ethnic undesirables from the East.

4

The First World War and Combating Lice

i. The Medical War

The introduction of a battery of new medical terms—*Entlausung*, 'delousing', or *dépouillage*—marked the international declaration of sanitary war on the louse. Armed with the discovery that the louse was the carrier of typhus, German military hygienists set out to ameliorate the squalid conditions in the trenches on the Western Front. They built up defences against incursions by rats, lice, and mosquitoes, and derided North African French troops as typhus carriers. Although the Russian advance of August 1914 was swiftly reversed by the Central powers, it brought the threat of 'Asiatic' epidemics into the European heartland. When the German and Habsburg troops invaded Russian territory, they were exposed to an alien epidemiological regime. Typhus was rife in the Balkan and Turkish theatres of war, and the Austro-Hungarian and Serbian armies were soon immobilized by a raging epidemic. The confrontation with alien species of disease carriers led to draconian delousing of civilians and racial stigmatization; in the Near East German hygiene experts came to the threshold of genocide.

Bacteriologists were confident they could prevent epidemics, and laid down hygienic routines governing the daily rituals of washing, sanitation, food hygiene, and care of clothing in the trenches. The wearing of the same clothes for protracted periods, and failure to wash were condemned as jeopardizing fitness. The military links to bacteriology enabled a medically well-trained regiment of professors and researchers to be mobilized. The war against the unseen enemy of invisible bacteria meant that the belt of hygiene institutes on the Prussian and Austro-Hungarian eastern flanks was deployed for military tasks. These eastern defences served the war effort by providing bacteriological diagnosis, epidemiological monitoring, and disinfection technologies.

The entry of typhus onto the international medical agenda can be seen in the preparations for a major war by the German and Austro-Hungarian bacteriologists during the Balkan Wars of 1912 and 1913. In 1912 forty-seven doctors were dispatched from Bohemia and ten from Moravia to assist the Bulgarian army, and they were reinforced by an Austrian bacteriological expedition.[1] Typhus erupted in Sarajevo in 1913, as returning Muslim soldiers supposedly spread the disease in Bosnia.

---

[1] Österreichisches Staatsarchiv (ÖSA)—Allgemeine Verwaltungsarchiv, Ministerium des Inneren, KuK MdI S Nr 29 Statthalterei Wien 2 Dec. 1912 concerning the bacteriological expedition; Statthalterei Prag, 30 Nov. 1912.

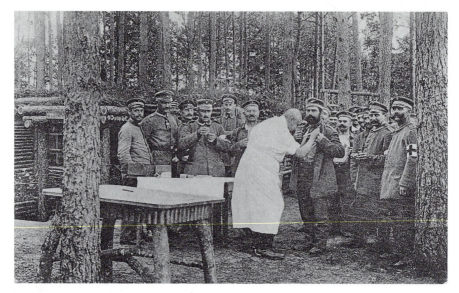

3. Typhoid inoculation at the front, *c.*1915

Medical authorities responded by isolating and disinfecting the sick.[2] The Austro-Hungarian authorities stationed bacteriologists in crucial areas: early in 1914 a bacteriologist was sent to Ragusa in Dalmatia, having just completed a course in microbiology at the Pasteur Institute. Anti-typhus measures were intensified in the Bukovina and around Lemberg in the east.[3] In August 1914 Austrian bacteriologists were called up from the hygiene and pathology institutes at Graz, Lemberg in Galicia, Czernowitz in the Bukovina, and Prague to staff mobile field laboratories.[4]

The maritime and colonial links of experts in tropical medicine provided expertise in combating epidemics in the east. Peter Mühlens, who as a naval medical officer had trained with Koch and Nocht, was recalled to the Hamburg Tropical Institute from the Health Office, Jerusalem. He alerted the Tropical Institute regarding the hazards of typhus in Constantinople and Bulgaria. A special typhus study commission, consisting of the Austrian Stanislaus von Prowazek, the Hamburg internist Carl Theodor Hegler, and Henrique da Rocha-Lima, who was departmental head at the Tropical Institute, studied typhus in Turkish prison camps from June

[2] ÖSA KuK MdI Nr 34B, Bericht der Landesregierung für Bosnien und die Hercegovina 1 July 1914.

[3] ÖSA KuK MdI S Nr 39 KK, Statthalterei Zara 5 Mar. 1914, concerning the appointment of Wenzel Neumann; ÖSA/AdR Staatsamt für soziale Verwaltung, Karton 1588, 1918 Infektionskrankheiten, Flecktyphus, Abwehrmassnahmen, Czernowitz 6 June 1914.

[4] ÖSA KuK MdI Nr 39 Institute Bakteriologie in genere 1911–1918, Einrückung der bacteriologischen Fachmänner zum Militärdienst, reports from Prague 18 Aug. 1914, Lemberg 12 Aug. 1914.

1914.[5] Other German bacteriologists returned with experience in Asia and Africa: Emil Gotschlich, who had moved from Flügge's hygiene institute in Breslau to a position as director of the Alexandria sanitary office, was expelled from Egypt; he communicated the experimental studies by Nicolle and Conseil on typhus transmission by the louse.[6] Colonial-style sanitary regimentation was to be applied in Eastern Europe.

The network of hygiene institutes was rapidly mobilized for strategic tasks. Gildemeister, who had only left active military service to work at the Posen Hygiene Institute in May 1913, was recalled as a military hygienist, and the Prussian War Ministry allowed him to retain command over the bacteriological laboratory in Posen.[7] The military medical authorities built up model hygiene facilities in occupied Poland and Serbia with the idea that these could locate and quell epidemics at their source. Experts in hygiene monitored the quality of drinking water, and devised new sanitary routines and contraptions, including toilets secure from flies and cesspits. They improvised ingenious machines for delousing uniforms and personal effects. The serum researcher Emil von Behring was awarded the Iron Cross for his vaccine to control tetanus arising from wound infections. Serbia and the Eastern front posed severe problems of a multiplicity of infections exacerbated by wounds, gangrene, and frostbite, as the central powers encountered typhoid, dysentery, typhus, cholera, and malaria. By 1915 *Ungeziefer* were a general topic of conversation among soldiers. Any military advance required doctors to oversee disinfection of billets, the establishing of isolation hospitals for the infectious, and the separation of civilians from the troops.[8]

Medical experts on all sides were well aware that epidemics resulting from wars could cause higher casualties than military action. How typhus devastated Napoleon's campaign of 1812 in Russia was frequently cited as a warning not to disregard epidemic hazards. Such cautionary historical precedents gained international currency when the standard treatise on military medical history by the German epidemiologist Friedrich Prinzing was published in English by Oxford University Press in 1916; it was edited by a Danish epidemiologist and sponsored by the Carnegie Endowment for Peace Studies.[9] International communication

---

[5] P. Mühlens, 'Vier Jahre Kriegshygiene in der Türkei und auf dem Balkan', *Vor Zwanzig Jahren. Zweite Folge. Von den Dardanellen zum Sues* (Leipzig, 1935), 141–59; R. P. Strong, G. C. Shattuck, A. W. Sellards, and H. Zinsser, *Typhus Fever with Particular Reference to the Serbian Epidemics* (Cambridge, Mass., 1920), 58; W. Sackmann, 'Fleckfieber und Fleckfieberforschung zur Zeit des Ersten Weltkrieges. Zum Gedenken an Henrique da Rocha Lima (1879–1956)', *Gesnerus*, 37 (1980), 113–32.

[6] BAK R 86/1040 Bd 7. R 86/2605 report by Gotschlich on typhus, 5 Jan. 1915; B. Nöske, *Emil Gotschlich (1870–1949). Sein Leben und wissenschaftliches Werk* (Giessen, 1996).

[7] GSTA Dahlem Rep 76 VIII B Nr 3007 *Bericht . . . Etatsjahres 1913, Bericht . . . Etatsjahres 1914.*

[8] W. Hoffmann (ed.), *Die deutschen Ärzte im Weltkriege* (Berlin, 1920), 105–7; P. Mühlens, 'Kriegshygienische Erfahrungen', *Deutsche Medizinische Wochenschrift*, 65 (1939), 1589–94; G. Frey, 'Das Gesundheitswesen im Deutschen Verwaltungsgebiet von Polen in den Jahren 1914–1918', *Arbeiten aus dem Reichsgesundheitsamt*, 51 (1919), 583–4; 'Das Ungeziefer!', *Frankfurter Zeitung*, 5 (Jan. 1915) in BAK R 86/3444 Schädliche Insekten.

[9] F. Prinzing (ed. H. Westergaard), *Epidemics Resulting from Wars* (Carnegie Endowment for International Peace) (Oxford, 1916). I am informed by the archivist of Oxford University Press that no papers have survived relating to this publication.

networks in the medical sciences were sustained. The neutrality of the Netherlands and Sweden assisted the flow of medical information in periodical literature to all sides. The embassies of neutral Spain and (until entering the war in 1917) the United States facilitated the interchanges of epidemiological information and medicines. The Germans asked the American embassy in St Petersburg to distribute a pamphlet by the bacteriologist Fred Neufeld on the origins and prevention of epidemics in the hope of eradicating typhus at source.[10] Disease prevention cut across frontiers and fronts: the Rockefeller Foundation allied with the American Red Cross and the organization-builder Herbert Hoover to mount medical relief programmes in France, German-occupied Belgium, Poland, Serbia, and Russia. The US ambassador in Berlin chaired a committee for the relief of Poland with support from the Rockefeller Foundation. American-Jewish funds came via Holland to assist impoverished Polish Jews, for whom emigration via Holland or Scandinavia became virtually impossible.[11]

The mobilization of port sanitary agencies established a crucial link between the pre-war medical screening of Eastern European migrants and the wartime anti-typhus measures. The Hamburg Institute for Maritime and Tropical Diseases housed a reserve military hospital, and took a lead in implementing delousing. The Hamburg medical entomologist and former military assistant at the Prussian Institute for Infectious Diseases, Erich Martini, improvised delousing with flat-irons and ovens on the eastern front in October 1914.[12] The Tropical Institute devised mass delousing routines between January and March 1915 when typhus epidemics raged in German prisoner of war camps. Medical observations were carried out in the camps, and the technical assistant at the Hamburg Tropical Institute, Hilda Sikora, experimentally demonstrated the cause of typhus in a heroic experiment on herself. The Bremen port medical officer, Tjaden, drew on his experience in the surveillance of transmigrants, by advising on sanitary arrangements for hospital trains from the east.[13]

The Serbian typhus epidemic placed the disease on the international medical agenda. Prowazek was sent from Hamburg to occupied Serbia, and Rocha Lima was dispatched to Constantinople, as part of the German military assistance for the Ottoman forces. The few isolated cases became a highly lethal epidemic; over 200,000 refugee civilians succumbed to typhus in six months. Troops suffering from typhus were held in overcrowded and filthy conditions. Mortality was as high

---

[10] AA R 66178 Sept. 1916, concerning F. Neufeld, *Seuchenentstehung und Seuchenbekämpfung* (Vienna, 1914). Note: archive files lack folio numbers except where given; items are identified by date and contents.

[11] J. W. Gerard, *My Four Years in Germany*, 211–12; H. H. Fisher, *America and the New Poland* (New York, 1928), 77–8; *Halbjahresbericht des Verwaltungschefs bei dem Generalgouvernement Warschau für die Zeit vom 1. Oktober 1917 bis 31. März 1918*, 79. I am grateful to Lynne Hirsch for making available to me copies of the Generalgouvernement medical reports.

[12] E. Martini, 'Praktisch-entomologische Erinnerungen aus dem Weltkriege', *Zeitschrift für hygienische Zoologie*, 32 (1938), 51–8, 65–78.

[13] STAB 4, 21–470 Fleckfieber (Flecktyphus) und Läusebekämpfung, Agreement of Generalarzt Hoffman and Tjaden 19 Jan. 1915.

as 70 per cent in affected areas with an estimated 150,000 deaths. Seventy thousand Austrian prisoners died in overcrowded camps with poor sanitation: foul, unwashed clothes swarmed with vermin, as the sick lay together on straw and mud.[14]

Hindenburg's victory at Tannenberg in East Prussia on 25 August 1914 had the medical side-effect of bringing large numbers of Russian prisoners of war into Germany, prompting concerns that they harboured diseases. The medical crisis was compounded by the Russian destruction of sanitary installations. The Russian attack of August 1914 prompted German medical officials to denounce the Russian occupation of East Prussia as spreading disease.[15] They accused the tsarist administration of corrupt neglect of public health services, resulting in the poor health status of Jews and a sanitary nightmare of foul water, overcrowding, and dirty conditions in Russian-Poland. Sporadic disinfection procedures by the heavy-handed Russian administration had provoked popular resistance. Only after the declaration of war in 1914 did the Russian authorities permit the formation of a hygiene committee in Warsaw.[16]

Typhus was unfamiliar to all but a few specialists. Martini realized that it was necessary to overcome the soldiers' sense of shame from louse infestation on the Eastern Front.[17] The Prussian Medical Department expected outbreaks of typhus, but was overconfident that routine sanitary measures could easily control the problem.[18] Only when typhus had reached epidemic proportions in prisoner of war camps was it properly diagnosed and managed. On 4 December 1914 the first case of typhus was identified in the Russian prisoner of war camp in Cottbus, which was ominously only 100 kilometres from Berlin. Nocht alerted the military authorities that the louse was in all probability the main carrier of typhus; he warned that Germans were threatened with infection from the French because the disease was endemic in North Africa, and on the Russian and Serbian fronts.[19] Medical publications on the dangers of lice began to appear during the first months of 1915. Scientists felt that the military should have operationalized delousing far more rapidly than was in fact the case.[20] While military authorities imposed draconian measures fearing another unknown means of contagion, medical scientists tried to stabilize the situation by providing unassailable proof that the louse was sole vector. By

---

[14] R. P. Strong, G. C. Shattuck, A. W. Sellards, and H. Zinsser, *Typhus Fever with Particular Reference to the Serbian Epidemics* (Cambridge, Mass., 1920); R. P. Strong, 'The Anti-typhus Campaign in Serbia Considered in Connexion with the Present Typhus Epidemic in Poland', *International Journal of Public Health*, 1 (1920), 7–33, 188–210.

[15] GSTA Rep 76 VIII B Nr 3770 Reichsgesundheitsrat Ausschuss für Seuchenbekämpfung 13 Jan. 1915; Rep 76 VIII B Nr 3483, RMdI to the Kaiser, 24 Mar. 1915; K. Schwabe, *Wissenschaft und Kriegsmoral* (Göttingen, 1969), 30–1.

[16] Frey, 'Gesundheitswesen', 584, 589, 628, 719; id., *Bilder aus dem Gesundheitswesen in Polen (Kongress-Polen) aus der Zeit der deutschen Verwaltung* (1919) (= Beiträge zur Polnischen Landeskunde, ser. B, vol. 7).

[17] E. Martini, 'Läuse und Flecktyphus', *Der praktische Desinfektor*, 31 (1939), 43–5, 54–7.

[18] GSTA Rep 76 VIII B Nr 3766 Kirchner, MdI 14 Nov. 1914.

[19] Bernhard Nocht Institut Hamburg (hereafter BNI), 6a Nocht to Raalzow, 6 Dec. 1914. For lectures by Mühlens and Nocht in Nov. 1914 see Martini, 'Erinnerungen', 55–6.

[20] Martini, 'Erinnerungen', 56–7.

spring 1915 the Posen professor of hygiene Wernicke instructed Field Marshal von Hindenburg on how the body louse spread typhus.[21]

ii. Heroes as Victims

In March 1915 the president of the Reich Health Office convened a conference in Berlin on the combating of typhus. The assembled military doctors and bacteriologists stood to honour their colleagues who had sacrificed their lives for the Fatherland in the campaign against typhus. Special mention was accorded to bacteriologists, who had once served alongside Behring and Koch: Georg Jochmann of the Prussian Institute for Infectious Diseases had used his sickness to illustrate that typhus did not spread by person to person contagion.[22] Prowazek's martyrdom occurred in his field laboratory among prisoners of war at Cottbus; he had dedicated himself to microbiology in the spirit of Koch whom he venerated as a saint. Two future leaders of Nazi geo-medical research were deeply affected by the loss of Prowazek—Ernst Rodenwaldt idolized Prowazek as a scientific hero, and Heinz Zeiss (an assistant at the Hamburg Institute of Tropical Medicine) wrote that as a soldier Prowazek had fallen in the daily work of 'scientific trench warfare, as a field grey pioneer of science'.[23] For his part Prowazek had observed the metamorphosis of Rocha Lima into a Prussian soldier; in 1916 Rocha Lima, who had contracted typhus but survived, called the parasite identified as the cause of typhus *Rickettsia prowazeki* to commemorate Prowazek and the American Ricketts.[24] Ten out of fifty German medical officers in occupied Poland were to die from typhus, and colleagues praised their sacrifice in defending Germany from typhus.[25] The rhetoric of typhus pulsated with notions of valour and heroic mortal combat, spurring bacteriologists to impose ever tougher medical measures.

The conference of March 1915 represented the culmination of three months' protracted struggle against typhus. In December 1914 Nocht ordered Prowazek to

---

[21] GSTA Rep 76 VIII B Nr 3770 Reichsgesundheitsrat Ausschuss für Seuchenbekämpfung 13 Jan. 1915. BNI 6b von Prowazek, Rocha Lima to Nocht 5 Jan. 1915. Wernicke Papers, box 1 'Fleckfieberforschung und Bekämpfung in Osten als Obergeneralarzt u. berat. Hygieniker bei der 8 u. 11 Armee im Felde' (dated 1 Oct. 1926), p. 7.

[22] BAK R 86 1040 Bd 4 Aufzeichnung 27 März 1915, pp. 3–4; R. R. Breger, 'Aerztliches Heldentum', *Berliner Tageblatt* (15 Aug. 1915). Other deceased medical researchers included Georg Cornet (1858–1915) for many years assistant to Koch, Lüthje (a clinician from Kiel), and Paul Heinrich Römer (1876–1915), a former assistant and co-worker with Behring. P. Musehold, *Streiflichter aus dem Wirken des Sanitätskorps in Weltkriege* (Oldenburg, 1927), 59.

[23] BNI 6b von Prowazek, Prowazek to Nocht 15 Jan. 1915, Zeiss to Nocht 23 Feb. 1915, Rodenwaldt to Nocht 19 Feb. 1915. E. Rodenwaldt, *Ein Tropenarzt erzählt sein Leben* (Stuttgart, 1957), 50–2, 55; H. Unger, 'Prowazek, der Erforscher des Fleckfiebers', *Die Gesundheitsführung. Ziel und Weg* (1942), 256–60.

[24] BNI 6b von Prowazek, Prowazeck to Nocht 15 Jan. 1915; H. da Rocha-Lima, 'Zur Aetiologie des Fleckfiebers', *Deutsche medizinische Wochenschrift*, 42 (1916), 1353; id., 'Zur Aetiologie des Fleckfiebers', *Berliner klinische Wochenschrift*, 53 (1916), 567–72 tr. in N. Hahon (ed.), *Selected Papers on the Pathogenic Rickettsiae* (Cambridge, Mass., 1968), 74–8; J. R. Busvine, *Insects, Hygiene and History* (London, 1976), 233–9; W. His, *Die Front der Ärzte* (Bielefeld and Leipzig, 1931), 102; Strong, *Typhus*, 47–9.

[25] Frey, 'Gesundheitswesen', 591, 595; Frey, *Bilder*, 129.

assess delousing methods so as to find alternatives to bathing and shaving as impractical in winter. Nocht sought advice from the entomologist, Martini, and experiments were carried out delousing Russian prisoners using benzyl chloride.[26] Prowazek and Rocha Lima observed Russian prisoners of war in Cottbus to prove that the body louse was the vector of the disease, and that irritating louse bites prompted the scratching in of the infectious germ. Instead of person-to-person infection, the body louse was found to be a devious and prolific enemy: at the Russian prisoner of war camp of Schneidemühl the medical professors Ludolf Brauer and Wilhelm His counted up to 6,000 lice on an individual.[27] In January 1915 concern that typhus in the Russian army might spread to Germany spurred the Prussian public health authorities to target the louse.[28]

Military medical experts suspected lice of inhabiting the contaminated clothes of vagabonds, and infesting the inhabitants of Russian Poland and Austrian Galicia. When not feasting on blood from their human hosts, lice found habitats in the folds of clothing and favoured the bandages of wounded soldiers.[29] It was known that naphtaline was an effective moth-proofing agent in clothes, and chemists were instructed to find an impregnating substance to deter lice. The economic opportunities were attractive to the chemical industry and there were hundreds of foul-smelling patent products seeking to capture the military market. New brands like 'Lausemors' and 'Nik-o-laus' were ready for Christmas 1914 as gifts for loved ones at the Front. The advertisements of products with bellicose names like 'Feldgrau', 'Antipax', 'Insektentod', and 'Läuse-Panzer' raised the prospect of wholesale destruction and eradication of lice, which was far more than they could actually achieve—when tested most lacked repellant effect. The officially approved substance 'Globol', devised by Nocht and the disinfection chemist Josef Halberkann, was worn in packets on the body, but had to be abandoned once it was found that it attracted lice.[30] Chemical amulets as charms against lice were popular in Poland and Russia, where mercury belts and gas capsules were favoured.[31] Medical scientists were alarmed by the useless waste of such products, and instead attacked lice with baths, sharp brushes, and razors.[32]

Because of the labour shortage, Russian prisoners worked in German agriculture, factories, and mines.[33] Any infection carried by the Russians posed a threat to German civilians. By March 1915 there were 500,000 Russian prisoners of war of whom 27,500 had contracted typhus. Epidemics raged in twenty-five out of forty-one prisoner of war camps. Six per cent of those with typhus had died, although

---

[26] BNI 6a Nocht to Martini 28 Jan. 1915; Karl Küstermann to Nocht 10 May 1915.

[27] His, *Front*, 40, 52–6.

[28] BNI 6a Minister of Interior, decree of 27 Jan. 1915 communicated to Hamburg Senat by Reichsamt des Innern 30 Jan. 1915. Rocha Lima to Nocht 5 Jan. 1915.

[29] His, *Front*, 38.

[30] BAK R 86/1040 Bd 3 for six pages of manufacturers' advertisements; Nuttall, 'Combating Lousiness', 489–90 for German rejection on patent remedies.

[31] Nuttall, 'Combating Lousiness', 519–59.

[32] BNI Hamburg 6b von Prowazek, Nocht to Raalzow 9 Dec. 1914.

[33] J. Oltmer, *Bäuerliche Ökonomie und Arbeitskräfte im Ersten Weltkrieg* (Sögel, 1995), 337–42.

mortality rates were much higher for the German medical and nursing personnel. From 19 December 1914 the camps were sealed off from German soldiers and civilians as far as possible. In 1914 there were only fourteen cases of civilian typhus, but in 1915 573 cases were reported using a system of telegrams, registration forms, and medical inspection. The German medical authorities prioritized defending civilians in the Fatherland from infection, leaving Russians to be tended by their own doctors.[34]

Conflict erupted over the treatment of prisoners of war: the Germans maintained that prisoners were well cared for, while the British and French, whose soldiers were at especial risk from typhus, protested that conditions were atrocious. A British report of April 1915 denounced the insufficient food and clothing, bedding on mouldy straw, and exposure to cold in ten of the sixteen typhus-ridden camps holding British prisoners.[35] The British complained that it was only when typhus spread to German civilians that improvements were eventually made.

In August 1915 the Germans rejected protests of the French concerning health conditions in prisoner of war camps. The German Foreign Office argued that it was not bad conditions within the camps that had caused the epidemic but as typhus came from Russia, the Russians were culpable.[36] The Germans viewed Russian soldiers as indolent because they delayed in registering that they were sick, and allowed mild cases of typhus to be left as undiagnosed. Moreover, the Foreign Office accused the Russians of general neglect of an estimated 200,000 German prisoners, causing their deaths in filthy, cramped, and unhygienic camps which lacked washing facilities and basic sanitation. In January 1916 the Germans informed the neutral Spanish embassy about their success in typhus prevention, urging the Russians to reciprocate with similar hygienic measures.[37]

There were special quarantine arrangements for Russian prisoners on the Ostgrenze with baths, disinfection, and observation for twenty-one days. The same treatments were to be provided for Germans as for Russian prisoners, and German camp doctors praised Russian doctors for their valuable assistance.[38] While such optimal assessments concealed the grim reality of worsening conditions with chronic shortages of food and fuel, they diverge sharply from the murderous treatment of Russian prisoners during the Second World War.

Delousing was organized on a massive scale. For only by processing large numbers of prisoners—in batches of 1,000 per day—could risks of reinfestation be

[34] BAK R 86/1040 Bd 7 13 Jan. 1915 Beratung des Reichsgesundheitsrats; R. Otto, 'Fleckfieber', in W. Hoffmann (ed.), *Handbuch der ärztlichen Erfahrungen im ersten Weltkriege* (Leipzig, 1922), 405 for registration statistics; GSTA Rep 76 VIII B Nr 9 Mar. 1917.

[35] *Annual Report. Local Government Board* (1914–15), p. xliv.

[36] AA R 66177 note of 25 Aug. 1915 sent via the Spanish embassy. Note of Jan. 1916.

[37] BAK R 86/1040 Bd 4 meeting of 27 Mar. 1915, 20; comments by Fred Neufeld; A. Hase, *Praktische Ratschläge für die Entlausung der Zivilbevölkerung in Russisch-Polen. Nach eigenen Erfahrungen* (Berlin, 1915).

[38] AA R 66178 betr ansteckende Krankheiten note verbale 28 Jan. 1916; G. H. Davis, 'The Life of Prisoners of War in Russia, 1914–1921', in S. R. Williamson and P. Pastor, *Essays on World War I. Origins and Prisoners of War* (New York, 1983), 167–9; R. Nachtigal, 'German Prisoners of War in Tsarist Russia. A Glance at Petrograd/St Petersburg', *German History*, 13 (1995), 198–204.

minimized. The one camp which had remained free from typhus was where from the start prisoners had the opportunity to bath while clothing was fumigated in adjacent ovens. The doctor in charge at the Cottbus camp pointed out that the infected could mix with those free from the disease provided both groups were deloused. The experience in handling Russian prisoners of war prompted the establishing of mass bathing facilities and disinfestation ovens or fumigation chambers as a routine measure to maintain louse free conditions.[39] Clothes were disinfected, the prisoners were shaved under the armpits and around the genitals, given hot baths, and rubbed with antiseptic soap and with a grey ointment to asphyxiate and loosen the lice, while liberal amounts of carbolic acid or creosol soap solutions were used.[40] A standard delousing drill was devised.

Delousing involved rigorous controls, while clothing and possessions were disinfested. The division between the 'unclean' and 'clean' sides of each installation was meant to be absolutely impenetrable apart from through the showers, but it was in practice difficult to sustain. A thorough process of disinfecting and louse and nit eradication had to take place; there were special procedures for different parts of the body, and for types of objects for which steam, dry heat, or louse powder might be most appropriate.[41] A 'transport' had to be held in quarantine, the temperature of all prisoners had to be taken and anyone with a fever was isolated; everyone had to be bathed every third day, the hair was to be shorn and burned, and the skin was to be rubbed down with an antiseptic like lysol or paraffin oil. If lice managed to survive this, each person had to be isolated and rigorously deloused by hand. Underwear and clothing had to be changed and disinfected. Soldiers, prisoners, and civilians were subjected to similar measures.[42]

The Prussian authorities called on the German Society for Peoples' Baths to supply delousing facilities for civilians.[43] Delousing became an integral part of military hygiene: bathing and showers were prescribed with steam for clothes, and lysol for footwear and leather articles. Above all it was vital to ensure stringent separation of persons who were hopefully louse free after cleansing. Flügge, the Berlin professor of hygiene, drew on extensive experience in epidemic control in Silesia, as he laid down stringent delousing procedures in January 1915, involving washing, the regular changing of clothes and underwear, the cutting of hair, and the disinfection of buildings. The routine demanded total nudity, and special attention to the hair, skin folds, and the 'Schamgegend' where the lice might lurk in pubic hair or

[39] BAK R 86/1040 Bd 4, Reichsgesundheitsamt, *Aufzeichnung über die am Sonnabend, den 27. März 1915 im Dienstgebäude des Kaiserlichen Gesundheitsamts abgehaltene Sitzung des Reichs-Gesundheitsrats über die Bekämpfung des Fleckfiebers* (Berlin, 1915).

[40] BNI Hamburg 6a Prowazek to Nocht 15 Jan. 1915, 21a Flecktyphus, Prowazek to Nocht 25 Jan. 1915.

[41] Uhlenhuth and Olbrich, 'Anleitung zu Improvisation und Betrieb von kleinen und mittleren Entlausungsanstalten', *Medizinische Klinik*, 28 (1915) cited as offprint in BAK R 86/1040 Bd 5.

[42] For experiences of Ukrainian refugees in an Austrian camp see J. Reder, *Das Fleckfieber nach dem heutigen Stande seiner Lehre und nach Beobachtungen in den Epidemien des k.k. Flüchtlingslagers Gmünd* (Leipzig and Vienna, 1918), 97–9.

[43] GSTA Rep 76 VIII B Nr 3767, Prussian MdI to Deutsche Gesellschaft für Volksbäder, 21 Dec. 1915; *Die Volksbäder und die Bekämpfung der Läuseplage* (Berlin, 1916). The Prussian Ministry of the Interior ordered 1,600 copies: see letter of the Society's General Secretary 16 May 1916.

between the bottom cheeks. If any person resisted the shaving of all their hair (and it was noted that women often protested), then a louse-killing substance like petroleum or eucalyptus oil was to be used on those parts of the body defended from more radical hygienic intervention. (It was later discovered that petroleum caused skin irritation and was ineffective in destroying nits.)[44] Clothing, bed linen, and mattress covers had to be placed in ovens or steam chambers. For disinfestation of rooms either steam or canisters of sulphuric acid or sulphur dioxide were used. Items of low value were burned: the ominous tone in which the rags and straw bedding of paupers were condemned conveyed how techniques of eradication were preferred to cleaning and welfare.[45]

Clothing became a sanitary battle zone. In 1911 Max Rubner, the Berlin professor of physiology, had calculated the higher temperatures of a sweaty overheated skin during summer months. Lice reputedly disliked hot skin and retreated to cooler outer-garments in the summer, while preferring warmer bodies in winter when clothes were changed with less frequency.[46] Doctors, nurses, disinfectors, and washerwomen were to wear washable overalls, rubber shoes, rubber gloves, and face masks, and to have all openings in the clothes greased with anisol or stuffed with cotton wool and tied as securely as possible to prevent penetration by lice. Total coverage in elaborate suits of smooth rubber or oilcloth with as few openings as possible were recommended so that the lice would find it difficult to creep around the protective clothing. A heated international debate erupted about the preventive qualities of silk underwear as being too slippery for lice, as silk found favour among certain hygienists, who warned that lice had a predelection for fibrous and rough textured fabrics. However, experimental studies led George Nuttall (the Cambridge medical entomologist, sometime colleague of Flügge in Breslau, and student of rat-fleas and plague) to conclude, 'lice will lay even on black sateen and smooth silk, especially when the choice is limited'.[47] A stark contrast emerges between the bare and shaved bodies accompanied by invasive examinations for those undergoing delousing, and the attempts to devise an outer covering of defensive clothing so as to make the bodies of medical staff and disinfectors impregnable to lice. Between these states of total nudity or total covering of the body required for mechanical disinfection procedures lay the simple alternative of regular changing and laundering of clothing—an option which did not require regimented louse extermination.

When nurses unbandaged the wounded from the front, the bandages might contain hundreds of lice.[48] Mobile sanitary installations and portable delousing apparatus were required. A scheme was drawn up in 1915 for a delousing train with

---

[44] A. Hase and W. Reichmuth, *Grundlagen der behelfsmässigen Entlausungsmassnahmen* (Berlin, 1940), 7.

[45] BAK 86/1040 Bd 4 Merkblatt 'Kleiderläuse' 21 July 1915; Nuttall, 'Combatting Lousiness', 551 for criticisms of sulphur dioxide.

[46] M. Rubner, 'Die Kleidung', *Handbuch der Hygiene*, 1 (1911), 600–6. Nuttall, 'Biology', 89.

[47] *Annual Report of the Local Government Board* (1911–12), lxxv–lxxviii; Nuttall, 'Biology of *Pediculus humanus*', 134.

[48] BAK R 86/1040 Bd 4 meeting of 27 Mar. 1915, 31–3. For the comments of a military nurse see M. von Rohrer, *Im Krieg gegen Wunden und Krankheit* (Brünn, n.d. [c.1943]), 189–92, and illustration of clothing for louse-ridden transports.

carriages for disinfection, showers and dressing and undressing compartments. In 1915 there was much opposition to chemical gases for delousing, although Nocht defended the use of chemicals, and Rodenwaldt recommended the sulphur dioxide method devised by Martin Hahn, both rising stars in the galaxy of hygiene professors. Chemical gases were denounced as explosive, harmful to the nervous system, inefficient, and difficult to organize in remote areas, whereas soap, dry heat, and steam from locomotives were preferred.[49]

Elaborate delousing measures were not always practicable, and troops on active service had to improvise. Rodenwaldt claimed success in delousing clothing by using pans in Belgian jam factories. But the buildings had been so damaged that it was impossible to make them airtight for disinfection using gas. Dairies with facilities for steam-treating milk, breweries, and factories were converted into washing, delousing, and laundering stations.[50] As soon as any building behind the front was louse free, frontline troops might move in, causing reinfestation. Moreover, any troop movement from the east was hazardous, as stringent delousing was not always observed.[51] The success of the German sanitary defence system was marked by the few outbreaks of typhus in the west.[52] As the German hold on eastern territories consolidated, ever more draconian delousing strategies were devised.

No soldier recovering from typhus, typhoid, or dysentery was allowed home leave, and complete disinfection of all kit was necessary. The prewar delousing stations established by shipping companies were reinforced for soldiers, as part of a strategy of hygienically sealing off the east. The eighteen delousing stations between Eydtkuhnen and Rosenheim for disinfecting uniforms and kit could cope with up to 45,000 men per day. Delousing certificates became essential travel documents. Parcels from the east had to be left unopened for fourteen days so that the lice would starve. Foreign workers were deloused, washed, medically inspected, and vaccinated against smallpox once they had passed through the border delousing controls. Public baths were converted into delousing stations, in order to make up for the lack of delousing facilities and equipment.[53]

The louse infestation crisis prompted a biologist, Albrecht Hase, to petition the medical department of the Prussian War Ministry that he should be authorized to undertake zoological studies of lice in order to work out practical control measures. Hase's offer was accepted, and although without medical qualifications, he was called up with the rank of a military medical officer.[54] At the University of Jena, Hase had close links with the Social Darwinist, eugenicist, and ultra-nationalist, Ludwig Plate, indicating how the biology of louse control became entangled with

---

[49] BAK R 86/1040 Bd 4, Meeting 27 Mar. 1915, 27–31.

[50] E. Friedberger, 'Beschreibung einer Korps-Feldwäscherei, Entlausungs- und Badeanstalt auf dem westlichen Kriegsschauplatze', *Zeitschrift für Hygiene*, 81 (1916), 1–14.

[51] BNI 6a Rodenwaldt to Nocht 10 Feb. 1915.

[52] O. von Schjerning, *Die Tätigkeit und die Erfolge der deutschen Feldärzte im Weltkriege* (Leipzig, 1920), 3–8.

[53] GSTA Rep 76 VIII B Nr 3771 Ministry of Interior decree 15 Apr. 1915; BAK R 86/1040 Bd 6 Besprechung 9 Apr. 1918; H. Roetzle, *Das Sanitätswesen im Weltkrieg 1914–18* (Stuttgart, 1924), 113–14.

[54] BAK R 168/293 Hase Personalakte; A. Hase, 'Feldzug gegen Insekten. Kriegserinnerungen', *20 Jahre Schädlingsbekämpfung*, 21–33.

racial hygiene.[55] Hase set up an experimental station in the prisoner of war camp of Hammerstein, West Prussia in March 1915 where he studied louse-infested Russians. He examined the differences between head lice and body lice, and, to the amusement of his fellow officers, observed the movement and speed of lice over different terrain, and tried to establish whether head lice carried typhus germs.[56] Between September and December 1915 he conducted 3,000 experiments using about 25,000 lice and nits, establishing that the latter could survive bombardment by many different types of chemical disinfectants. His aim was to devise delousing procedures on the scale of a factory.[57]

Hase developed the biological characterization of the louse as the carrier of typhus, and a menacing stereotype of louse-infested humans. He showed the rapidity with which lice could move, and their ingenuity in penetrating earthworks in order to creep into trenches or under walls. Lice were devious, hardy, and deceptive, able to sham death, so duping doctors into believing that their delousing procedures were effective. He found that certain soldiers remained free from louse infestation, and studied how Russians and Poles became accustomed to lice bites.[58] Other biologists gave attention to precise description of the sex organs of lice, their mating behaviour and variations in the numbers and fertility of eggs. Despite casualties and occasional infertility, a female could lay eight eggs per day over a fertility period of forty days, resulting in a potential 4,160 offspring.[59] As hostility to the louse increased, so did recognition of its prevalence. In heavily infested populations, there could be 500 lice per person, and occasionally infestation rates could be much higher. Campaigns were stepped up against other insect foes, like bedbugs, fleas, mosquitoes, flies, and itch-mites, even if as in the case of bedbugs no links to any disease could be identified. The predatory insect world posed a threat to military efficiency and national health. Entomology was placed on a war-footing as the German Society for Applied Entomology displayed blown-up diagrams and pictures of monstrous insect enemies, that looked like armour-plated tanks bristling with vicious weaponry.[60]

Residual doubts surrounded the exclusive role of the body louse as vector of

[55] Postcard, Hase to Plate, Sanierungsanstalt Sosnowice, 16 Aug. 1917, Author's collection.

[56] Hase, 'Feldzug', 24; id., *Beiträge zur Biologie des Kleiderlaus* (Flugschriften der Deutschen Gesellschaft für angewandte Entomologie 1) (Berlin, 1915). Against headlice as vectors of typhus see Otto, 'Fleckfieber', 425.

[57] Id., 'Experimentelle Untersuchungen zur Frage der Läusebekämpfung', *Zeitschrift für Hygiene und Infektionskrankheiten*, 81 (1916), 319–78.

[58] Id., 'Praktische Ratschläge für die Entlausung der Zivilbevölkerung in Russisch-Polen', sent 22 Oct. 1915. Hase's work was reported on in *Deutsche Tageszeitung* (4 Feb. 1916); His, *Front*, 39–40.

[59] H. Sikora, 'Beiträge zur Biologie von *Pediculi vestimenti*', *Centralblatt für Biologie*, 76 (1915), 523–37; J. Müller, 'Zur Naturgeschichte der Kleiderlaus', *Das Oesterreichische Sanitätswesen*, 27 (1915) issued as reprint. See also G. H. F. Nuttall, 'The Copulatory Apparatus and the Process of Copulation in *Pediculus Humanus*', *Parasitology*, 9 (1916–17), 293–324; A. Bacot, 'A Contribution to the Bionomics of *Pediculus Humanus (vestimenti)* and of *Capitulus Capitis*', *Parasitology*, 9 (1916–17), 228–58.

[60] Hase, *Beiträge zur Biologie des Kleiderlaus* (Flugschriften der Deutschen Gesellschaft für angewandte Entomologie 1) (Berlin, 1915). This work was described by Howard, *Applied Entomology*, 488 as 'the best study of this insect that has been made'. Hase, 'Ungeziefer', in W. Hoffmann (ed.), *Handbuch der ärztlichen Erfahrungen im ersten Weltkriege* (Leipzig, 1922), 306–27.

typhus germs, and the pathogenic role of *Rickettsia prowazeki*, challenging the official fixation on delousing. Certain military medical officers conducted a rearguard action against bacteriology in favour of Pettenkofer's theories of local environmental causes of infectious diseases.[61] Some medical officers implicated all louse species and other insects as vectors, various causal micro-organisms were still candidates. One reason for the difficulty in identifying the microbial foe was the causal organism's minute size. For what were variously termed the Chlamydozoa by Prowazek, Strongyloplasmata by Lipschütz or Rickettsia by Rocha Lima were recognized as 'viruses' with distinctive characteristics in the way that they could pass through bacterial filters or develop within cells; others merely considered 'virus' to mean an 'unknown pathogen'. Fritz Munk (a Berlin physiologist) and Rocha-Lima in 1917 conceded the difficulties of distinguishing rickettsiae from other microscopic bodies such as tissues, granulations, or coagula.[62] Although many German bacteriologists accepted the causal role of rickettsiae, others argued that there were various species, or that they merely accompanied the as yet unascertained cause of typhus.[63] By the end of the war it still had not been possible to culture the rickettsiae and so to prove experimentally (and satisfy Koch's postulates) that the louse-borne rickettsiae caused typhus. The medical evidence against louse-borne transmission of the typhus 'virus' makes the official fervour of the delousing campaigns all the more remarkable. Military authority backed the notion of hordes of invasive bacterial foes.

The 'natural powers of resistance', and the defence systems of the body were much debated: did ethnic differences or the deterioration of the physical conditions of prisoners of war enhance susceptibility to typhus?[64] Typhus was caught up in a protracted feud between Pasteurian and Koch schools of bacteriologists who disputed whether infection could be rendered less acute. The disease was much more severe for those who did not come from areas where typhus was endemic and where a mild form of the disease might have been contracted at an early age. Hase in 1915 examined those who had been bitten continuously but suffered no ill-effects, or who became immune to the effects of louse-bites, indicating that Russian tolerance of louse-infestation was due to a process of natural immunization commencing in childhood.[65] This meant that Germans were particularly at risk, and explained why deaths from typhus among physicians from 'civilized' non-immune areas were exceptionally high—hence the high death toll from typhus among district medical officers in German-occupied Russian-Poland.[66]

---

[61] F. Wolter, 'Über den Flecktyphus als Kriegsseuche', *Berliner klinische Wochenschrift*, 52 (1915), no. 31.

[62] R. P. Strong, 'The Significance of Rickettsia', *International Journal of Public Health*, 1 (1920), 346–51; Strong, *Serbian Epidemics*, 52–61; Otto, 'Fleckfieber', 424–6.

[63] G. H. F. Nuttall, 'The Part Played by *Pediculus humanus* in the Causation of Disease', *Parasitology*, 19 (1917), 57.

[64] BAK R 86/1040 Bd 4 meeting of 27 Mar. 1915, 16.

[65] A. Hase, 'Weitere Beobachtungen über die Läuseplage', *Centralblatt für Bakteriologie, Parasitenkunde und Infektionskrankheiten*, 1 Abt. Orig., 77 (1915), 153–63; reported in Nuttall, 'The Part', 73.

[66] *Halbjahresbericht des Verwaltungschefs bei dem Generalgouvernement Warschau für die Zeit vom 1. Oktober 1917 bis 31. März 1918*, 27. This report notes seven deaths, but Frey (above) concludes that until the end of the war there were ten deaths of German medical officers.

While louse control meant improving the external defences against typhus, efforts continued to probe the body's internal defence mechanisms. In 1915 the Austrian medical officers Edmund Weil and Arthur Felix, working in a field laboratory in Sokal on the Galician border, discovered a distinctive bacillus in the urine of typhus sufferers. Although their assertion that this 'Proteus-X10 bacillus' was the true cause of typhus was disproved, the clumping phenomenon (agglutination) that they demonstrated in conjunction with a related 'X-19 bacillus' became accepted as a useful diagnostic test. Felix carried out further tests in the German Red Cross Hospital in Constantinople, and worked in Russia and the Ukraine. As in its initial stages the symptoms of typhus differed little from influenza, the use of the Weil-Felix agglutination reaction provided a simple and effective test for typhus using blood serum.[67]

Whereas serum therapy and chemical drug therapies for typhus proved to be disappointments, greater success was claimed for experimental vaccines and injections with blood from recovered patients so as to promote immunity. Nicolle injected himself with a mixture of typhus bacilli and blood serum. He then injected children as hopefully more resistant, but to his alarm they developed typhus.[68] In March 1917 Richard Otto, a bacteriologist trained at the Prussian Institute for Infectious Diseases and under Ehrlich at Frankfurt am Main, was ordered to produce a typhus vaccine. This was initially drawn from the blood of those who had contracted typhus. Such convalescent sera had first been deployed by E. Legrain in 1895. The success of Otto's vaccine was uncertain, although he hoped that it reduced the risk of death from typhus. Zeiss claimed that it prevented infection of about two hundred persons in Asia Minor. Rocha Lima used a vaccine derived from the miniscule louse faeces: although it was not possible to produce this on a large scale, it was a prototype for a vaccine produced from louse guts.[69] Uncertainties surrounding vaccines contrasted to the fervour for delousing.

Military hygienists were confident in their heroic achievements. Even in remote and vulnerable theatres of war like Turkey and the Balkans, bacteriologists claimed that they brought typhus under control. The German scientific victory over typhus was celebrated at the congress for internal medicine held in Warsaw in May 1916.[70] Systematic delousing, and surveillance and isolation of civilians kept the German armies free of typhus—448 German soldiers died from typhus out of 32,875 deaths

---

[67] E. Weil and A. Felix, 'Zur serologischen Diagnose des Fleckfiebers', *Wiener klinische Wochenschrift*, 29 (1916), 33–5; A. Felix, 'Die Serodiagnostik des Fleckfiebers', *Wiener klinische Wochenschrift*, 29 (1917); id., 'Serologische Untersuchungen an Fleckfieberkranken aus der asiatischen Türkei', *Zeitschrift für Immunitätsforschung*, 26 (1917), 602–19; H. Zeiss, 'Zur Aetiologie des Fleckfiebers', *DMW* (1917), 1227; Otto, 'Fleckfieber', 435–41; ÖSA/AdR Staatsamt für soziale Verwaltung Karton 1588, 1918 Infektionskrankheiten, A. Ghon, 'Flecktyphus, Einführung der Serodiagnose nach Weil-Felix' to Oberster Sanitätsrat 12 Feb. 1918.

[68] Gross, 'Nicolle'.

[69] Hoffmann, *Weltkrieg*, 149–51; Otto, 'Fleckfieber', 454–9.

[70] W. His and W. O. Weintraud (eds.), *Verhandlungen der ausserordentlichen Tagung des deutschen Kongresses für innere Medizin in Warschau am 1. und 2. V. 1916* (Wiesbaden, 1916); K. Reicher, 'Ausserordentliche Tagung des Deutschen Kongresses für innere Medizin zu Warschau, 1. und 2. Mai 1916', *MMW* 63 (1916), 777–80, 814–16.

from infectious diseases.[71] But this medical victory was illusory. Typhus was perceived to be a major threat to military and civilian health, but—at least for the
German army—caused only a low incidence when compared to typhoid, dysentery, and malaria. Moreover, rampant influenza caused an estimated 176,000 deaths
in Germany and marked a defeat for hygiene—rendered all the more traumatic by
the German military collapse.[72] Civilians under occupation experienced steadily
worsening shortages of food and fuel, and rocketing rates of disease, as the German
medical authorities ignored the far more prevalent disease of tuberculosis. Typhus
epidemics raged in Warsaw's densely populated districts during the winter of
1916–17, and disease rates worsened throughout 1918 as typhus spread from the city
to the countryside.

iii. Allied Strategies

The strains of war exposed contrasts between the sanitary policies of the British,
relying primarily on personal hygiene, the more bacteriologically oriented
Americans, and the Central Powers, favouring draconian measures which culminated in deployment of poison gases. The shock of encountering typhus in Serbia
forced the disease onto the Allies' medical agenda. Serbia became a mecca for international medical relief teams from Britain, France, Russia, and the United States.
The American Red Cross Sanitary Mission (supported by the Rockefeller Foundation), the British Red Cross, and hospitals organized by Lady Muriel Paget—
amounting to over 300 British doctors and nurses, a hundred French doctors, and a
Russian medical mission divided the country into fourteen sanitary districts.

The Scottish Women's Hospitals were among the first on the scene in January
1915, seeking to establish 'clean beds and clean linen' for the sick and wounded, and
this philosophy of laundering and washing remained the crucial feature of the
British control measures. Once a typhus hospital was established, the nurses wore a
special white combination garment tucked into high riding boots, and tight-fitting
caps to protect themselves against the louse, which had just achieved international
celebrity as the carrier of typhus.[73] British isolation wards aimed to eliminate lice by
strict routines of washing and shaving patients and disinfecting their belongings. A
delousing train was improvised by a British military doctor in April 1915. A team of
Royal Army Medical Corps doctors established a line of quarantine stations,
restricted contacts between soldiers and civilians, and carried out strategic disinfection of railway carriages and public buildings.[74]

The US contingent combined a high level of scientific expertise with implement-

---

[71] Wernicke Papers, box 1 'Fleckfieberforschung und Bekämpfung in Osten als Obergeneralarzte u.
berat. Hygieniker bei der 8. u 11. Armee im Felde' (dated 1 Oct. 1926), p. 11; His, *Front*, 42–3.

[72] Möllers, 'Grippe', in Schjerning (ed.), *Handbuch*, 574–5.

[73] E. S. MacLaren, *A History of the Scottish Women's Hospital* (London, 1919), 90–7; L. Leneman, *In the
Service of Life. The Story of Elsie Inglis and the Scottish Women's Hospitals* (Edinburgh, 1994), 17–23.

[74] Krippner, *Quality*, 71, 74–5; Roksandic, *Sanitäre Wacht*, 27–8.

ing tough measures. The American Red Cross typhus relief team director, Richard Strong, considered that rigorous medical intervention would eradicate typhus from Serbia, and that 'the whole race of the Serbian people' would begin to remedy their insanitary habits so as to avoid inspections and isolation. Conditions were atrocious; he described how at the Military Hospital at Belgrade, 'Excreta, sputum and pus-soaked dressing were scattered everywhere within and without the building. Vermin, especially the body louse were omnipresent.'[75] His teams conducted house-to-house inspections, removed typhus cases to hospitals, disinfested clothing, houses, and persons, arranged mass showers and baths, sprayed liberal amounts of petroleum brought from the United States, and instructed the people in how to avoid typhus. The American Mission agreed an 'eradication' programme with medical, police, and military authorities, requiring general delousing of populations, control of railway travel, the use of trains with wooden rather than upholstered seats, the disinfestation of all public transportation, cafés, and restaurants, and an educational campaign.[76] The Serbian railways converted goods waggons into sanitary units with boilers, steam disinfestation of clothing, and showers. Batches of several hundred people had their hair clipped, their clothes deloused and their bodies scrubbed, prior to spraying with petroleum or carbolic. Turkish baths, makeshift barrels, and ovens were transformed into delousing installations.[77] While there was never popular enthusiasm for delousing, a measure of consent was secured: 'It was not that the great majority enjoyed taking a bath or being deloused, or having their clothing deloused. In fact, many had not had a bath for over a year; in some instances their faces betrayed surprise, in others fear, when the water from the shower bath touched their bodies.'[78]

Strong was professor of tropical medicine at Harvard University, and brought into Eastern Europe an experimental and racist mentality. In 1906 he tested a new cholera vaccine on Filipino prisoners, causing ten deaths out of the twenty-four inoculated. He continued coercive experimentation, boosted by racial prejudice and contempt for traditional medicines.[79] Strong was attracted to Serbia as an experimental field, where he hoped to confirm the bacteriological cause of typhus; although Nicolle could not be released from Tunis because of a typhus epidemic there, his team included the innovative bacteriologists, Zinsser and Harry Plotz, who were keen to test an experimental vaccine: but they failed to find the hoped-for *Bacillus typhi exanthematici* (typhus being non-bacterial) or indeed to confirm the presence of rickettsiae.[80] For a programme of human experiments, Strong consid-

---

[75] Countway Library Boston (hereafter CLB), Archives GA 82, Strong papers, box 35, Strong to Kober 9 Mar. 1915; Strong, 'Typhus Fever', p. 10; box 36b Strong to Mabel Boardman 5 May 1915, 3 June 1915; RAC Rockefeller Foundation 1/100/32/259 memo of 19 May 1941.

[76] Strong, 'Typhus Fever', 23; RAC Rockefeller Foundation 1/100/32/259 Study of Typhus Fever.

[77] Strong, *Serbian Epidemics*, 25–31, 88–9; Nuttall, 'Combating Lousiness', 463 on the origins of railway van disinfectors; H. Zinsser, *As I Remember Him. The Biography of R.S.* (Boston, 1940), 209–25.

[78] Strong, *Typhus*, 25–31, 88–9.

[79] K. A. Campbell, 'Knots in the Fabric: Richard Pearson Strong and the Bilibid Prison Vaccine Trial, 1905–1906', *Bulletin of the History of Medicine*, 68 (1994), 600–38.

[80] CLB, Strong papers box 36b, Strong to Mabel T. Boardman, Chairman American Red Cross, 3 June 1915; Nicolle to Strong 30 Mar. 1915, 2 Apr. 1915, 7 Apr. 1915 telegram that 'tout est arrangé'.

ered using Austrian prisoners of war for experimental infection with typhus, but hesitated—as they were not free agents such experimentation might be considered as constituting ill-treatment. Serbian or Montenegran volunteers were called for, and one volunteer from the Commission was available. Strong remained a key figure in US military medicine, and he gave international health a pronounced militarist and research-oriented character. His clinical trials of plague vaccine prisoners in Manilla were targeted by the German defence at the Nuremberg Medical Trial.[81]

The British parasitologist, Nuttall, arrived at sanitary solutions to the problems of louse control. Nuttall's career was thoroughly international in the United States and in German hygiene institutes, including work with Flügge on anthrax. In 1897 he turned to the study of the role of insects in spreading disease.[82] He assumed a commanding position as a military medical expert, as prior to the war the Local Government Board funded his collection of lice from vagrants and the destitute. Hase and Nuttall were passionate about parasitology as an applied branch of biology, but drew very different conclusions about disease prevention at the front.

Both Britain and Germany saw close integration of medical research with military strategy. In Britain the Medical Research Committee devoted its resources to war work; protozoologists, bacteriologists, and entomologists confirmed the aetiology of the typhus as louse-borne. Controversy persisted on the possibility of airborne infection, the species of lice involved, and the precise location, type, and characteristics of causal rickettsiae. With a majority consensus on both sides that the louse was the cause of the disease, it became necessary to find out more about the insect and how it carried an invasive pathogen in order to draw up preventive strategies. Arthur Bacot, from August 1915 honorary consulting medical entomologist to the Army Medical Department, and Nuttall shared a common scepticism of the continuous stream of such worthless specific insecticides as 'Oxford grease', preferring the simpler method of preventing infestation by regular washing and laundering.[83]

Typhus was effectively kept at bay from the Western front, although there erupted a milder louse-borne disease called by British troops 'trench fever' (which did not actually kill the infected louse), and relapsing fever, another louse-borne infection, which incapacitated rather than killed those afflicted. The Germans encountered a similar fever which they named after the localities of White Russia and Volhynia. In September 1915 the Royal Army Medical Corps experimentally

[81] CLB Strong papers, box 36a 'Preliminary Plan in Regard to Determining the Method of Transmission in Typhus Fever'. T. W. Jackson to Strong 3 Sept. 1915 concerning Plotz; Strong, *Serbian Epidemics*, 86–7. STAN Rep. 502A, KV Verteidigung, Handakte Fritz Nr 28, Einwand der 'Freiwilligkeit' der versuchspersonen bei Menschenversuchen in Ausland.

[82] P. J. Weindling, 'The First World War and the Campaigns against Lice: Comparing British and German Sanitary Measures', in W. Eckart and C. Gradmann, *Die Medizin und der Erste Weltkrieg* (Pfaffenweiler, 1996), 227–40; G. H. F. Nuttall, 'On the Role of Insects, Arachnids, and Myriapods as Carriers in the Spread of Bacterial AND Parasitic Diseases of Man and Animals: A Critical and Historical Study', *Johns Hopkins Hospital Reports*, 8 (1900), 1–37; Howard, *Applied Entomology*, 468.

[83] M. Greenwood, 'Arthur William Bacot 1866–1922', in id., *The Medical Dictator and Other Biographical Studies* (London, 1936), 174–213.

inoculated a healthy soldier with blood from a trench fever patient's vein, so establishing that the disease was carried in the blood, and experiments on volunteers led to the conclusion that the body louse was the agent of transmission.[84] There was severity in dealing with colonial subjects, when forcible disinfection was employed: the Egyptian Labour Corps were stripped, shaved of body hair, and marched to disinfecting trains.[85] Yet Nuttall, for all his knowledge of modern methods, rejected such regimentation to reach historically founded conclusions. His motto was a sixteenth-century English text: 'The best is for to wasshe the ofetimes, and to chaunge oftentymes clene lynen.' He commended washing and laundered clothes as the keys to louse control, backed up by hot-air and steam disinfestation, while doggedly resisting modern technical panaceas of chemicals and poison gases.[86]

Despite the German condemnation of Russian sanitary provision in Poland and in the Russian prisoner of war camps, there was rapid development of disinfection facilities in Russia, in order to counter the spread of epidemics from the Front to the interior. Experiments with eradicating insects on corpses in mortuaries and in night shelters (a favourite source for the collection of lice for parasitological research) led to the use of chemical, gas, and hot air delousing procedures. Mass baths for soldiers impressed German medical experts who held Russian medical science in high esteem. Delousing, involving the building of bath houses, laundries, and disinfection chambers at strategically important railway junctions, was extended to civilians as part of policies of 'desinsectisation' to destroy all disease-carrying insects.[87]

All sides developed mobile showers, and motorized and railway van disinfecting units which could delouse hundreds of soldiers. Indeed, the larger the numbers of men deloused at one time the better, as re-infestation risks diminished, and men were dragooned through hot air and bathing huts, despite the risk of coke fumes. Fumigation chambers were improvised, and billets and transport vehicles had to be cleaned and sprayed with insecticides. The Allies and the Central Powers deployed a similar range of measures against lice. But two elements were distinctive on the

[84] G. H. Hunt and A. C. Rankin, 'Intermittent Fever of Obscure Origin Occurring Among British Soldiers in France—the so-called Trench Fever', *Lancet* (1915), ii. 1133; Zinsser, *Rats, Lice,* 298; W. Byam, *Trench Fever—a Louse Borne Disease* (Oxford, 1919); R. P. Strong, *Trench Fever. Report of the Commission of the Medical Research Committee of the American Red Cross* (Oxford, 1918); McNee, Renshaw, and Brunt, 'Trench Fever', *British Medical Journal,* (1916), i. 225; Werner, *MMW* 63 (1916), 287, 402; Jungmann, *Das wolhynische Fieber* (Berlin, 1919); T. von Wasielewski, 'Fünftagefieber', Schjerning (ed.), *Handbuch,* 532–6; CLB, Strong papers, box 36 for Osler's role in publishing Strong's report. For an overview see R. L. Atenstaedt, 'The Medical Response to Trench Fever in the First World War', M.Phil. diss., Wellcome Unit for the History of Medicine, Cambridge University, 1994.

[85] M. Harrison, review of Eckart and Gradmann, *Die Medizin und der Erste Weltkrieg, Social History of Medicine,* 10 (1997), 489–91.

[86] 'Lice, their relation to disease, and biology and means of combating lousiness among soldiers', *Army Council Instructions,* 1918. Nuttall, 'Combating Lousiness', 417, 573 quoting F. J. Furnivall (ed.), *The Book of Quinte Essence (AD 1460–1470)* (London, 1866), 19.

[87] BNI 6a Nocht to Raalzow 9 Jan. 1914; Blau, 'Die planmässige Insektenbekämpfung bei den Russen', *Zeitschrift für Hygiene,* 83 (1917), 343–88; J. F. Hutchinson, *Politics and Public Health in Revolutionary Russia, 1890–1918* (Baltimore, Md., 1990), 125–6, 128–32, 136, 186–8; W. P. Davenport, 'Discovery of the Typhus Germ', *ARA Bulletin,* ser. 2, no. 26 (July 1922) concerning research by V. Barikan and N. Kritch.

German side—the German interest in the use of poison gases for delousing, and mounting racial prejudice against the Polish Jews. Typhus worsened as the military situation deteriorated, and medical animosity against the eastern Jews—derided as treacherous vermin—intensified.

iv. Gas Warfare

The more moderate Allied sanitary strategies prompt the question whether there was a medical *Sonderweg* characterizing German responses to typhus, or were German responses dictated by the rationales of internationally accepted scientific knowledge and hygienic practices? Two factors stand out as distinctive in the German response—the development of poison gas and the ideology of *Lebensraum*. The extermination of rats, lice, moths, bedbugs, and beetles became caught up in the spiralling web of chemical and gas warfare. The Germans first deployed chlorine gas in April 1915 at Ypres. A medical vocabulary camouflaged the chlorine programme under the code name of 'Disinfection'.[88] This rhetoric was symptomatic of the interaction between medical and military uses of hygienic technologies. The sanitary problems, decomposing corpses, and ubiquitous parasites accompanying trench warfare spurred the development of gas warfare to remedy the military stagnation in the west. Troops used gas on the eastern front in the advance on Warsaw and to capture Riga, inflicting heavy losses on the poorly equipped Russian armies.[89]

Chemical weapons undermined the traditional chivalry of man-to-man combat, just as chemical fumigants destroyed the fairytale ethos surrounding ratcatchers. Delousing meant waging an elaborate sanitary war on a tenacious foe of Lilliputian proportions.[90] Total war bequeathed a legacy of pest eradication methods that subjected enclosed environments created by modern technology—ships, railway carriages, factories, warehouses, and apartment blocks—to an all-pervasive gas that destroyed organic life while leaving material objects intact.

Immersion in a lethal gas was a baptism of destruction and cleansing—a macabre rite of purification in the name of the extinction of parasites and the conservation of resources. One of the leading companies, DEGESCH, had as its symbol a triple cross. This represented a stylized bug; but the symbol also had religious overtones, analogous to the double cross of Lorraine used as the icon of the public anti-tuberculosis campaigns. The triple cross marked a national crusade against pests.

The military use of hydrocyanic acid (HCN) as an offensive weapon in the field was problematic as the gas was lighter than air and so tended rapidly to dissipate. The low level of concentrations that could be attained in the field meant that here the gas was harmless. All sides feared deployment of bombs, grenades, and shells filled with HCN, eradicating troops in the trenches like the rats that infested

[88] J. A. Johnson, *The Kaiser's Chemists. Science and Modernization in Imperial Germany* (Chapel Hill, NC and London, 1990), 191.
[89] E. M. Spiers, *Chemical Warfare* (Basingstoke, 1986), 14–15, 30.   [90] Eksteins, *Rites*, 161–9.

frontline positions. Winston Churchill favoured shells filled with a syrup derived from HCN known as 'Jellite' and in 1916 the French filled grenades with this acid.[91] A French prisoner spoke of the gas while in a feverish delirium, and the Germans added silver oxide to their gas mask filters to neutralize the gas. The German chemical warfare specialists, who twice rejected proposals to deploy HCN as a weapon, took pride in their defensive triumph.[92]

The German armies preferred HCN for delousing equipment, because patent delousing preparations were so dubious.[93] Bruno Heymann, a long-term associate of Flügge at the Berlin Hygiene Institute (and biographer of Koch), developed disinfection techniques; he was the first to conduct trials in 1915 on HCN as an inexpensive means for the extermination of lice. He pointed out parallels between fumigating trenches and the Californian orange groves.[94] Other gases used for delousing were explosive and inflammable, and damaged paintwork of buildings and ships. This was the case with the foul-smelling sulphur dioxide. Steam could damage footwear, furs, and paper money and notebooks—all habitats favoured by lice. On the other hand, too weak gases or steam might not be all-pervasive, and allow lice to survive in crevices of a building. The Germans became adept at improvising fumigation and gas chambers by sealing off all rooms, and then devising methods by which steam or gas could be conducted. The German army pressed for a simple and effective means of delousing which could be deployed on the Eastern front.[95]

The chemical manufacturers Degussa built up relations with the Society for Applied Entomology. In March 1915 Escherich drew the attention of Degussa to the commercial opportunities in the development of gassing for sanitary purposes. Its chemist, Adolf Andres, co-operated with Richard Heymons of the zoological institute of the Agricultural College, Berlin in experimental gassings against agricultural pests in July 1916. Schemes were floated for an institute for applied entomology in Berlin or Frankfurt am Main which would combine industrial, state, and scientific resources. The venture had an eastern profile with plans for tests in Turkey and the Middle East.[96] Andres discussed HCN fumigations with officials at the Medical Department of the Prussian War Ministry in November 1916. The ministerial official Oberstabsarzt Professor Heinrich Hetsch suggested that preliminary tests be carried out at the Berlin Hygiene Institute, where Heymann was experimenting with the effect of the gas on nits, and—crucially— that the Degussa personnel consult with Fritz Haber, the chemist and gas warfare

[91] L. F. Haber, *The Poisonous Cloud. Chemical Warfare in the First World War* (Oxford, 1986), 22, 41–2, 62–3. The French mixed HCN with arsenic trichloride to prevent the gas from rising.

[92] Haber, *Poisonous Cloud*, 117–18 and 262 for production statistics; Müller-Kiel, *Die chemische Waffe*, 69–71.

[93] Heckanast, *Desinfectionsmittel*, 143–4; Haber, *Poisonous Cloud*, 205.

[94] B. Heymann, 'Die Bekämpfung der Kleiderläuse', *Zeitschrift für Hygiene*, 80 (1915), 299–322.

[95] BNI Hamburg 6a Zusammenstellung einiger Verfahren zur Vertilgung von Kleiderläusen, Berlin 4 Mar. 1915; Reichs-Gesundheitsrat, *Aufzeichnung*, 27–9.

[96] Direktion Degussa DL 5.1/15 Bl. 17, 58 experiments on Rittergut Damerow, Bl. 65 betr Gründung eines neuen Instituts für angewandte Entomologie in Berlin.

supremo.[97] Haber turned sporadic experimental forays into pest control into a carefully planned and highly resourced campaign.

Commercial chemists and biologists conducted experiments on pest eradication and delousing in hospitals, ambulances, and barracks using HCN. Hase, the entomologist commissioned by the Prussian War Ministry Medical Department, was in touch with Escherich and Degussa experts from November 1916, evaluating trial gassings of body lice and bedbugs in Frankfurt and at the state grain research institute in Berlin.[98] In December 1916 Degussa experts fumigated a hospital train using HCN. In April 1917 Escherich joined forces with Bavaria's largest firm of millers for the first large-scale gas disinfestation of a mill in order to exterminate the flour-moth (*Mehlmotte*)—Escherich proclaimed this as a grand triumph because even the moth eggs were destroyed.[99] Gas fumigation was a weapon to defend both food and fuel reserves. The socialist newspaper *Vorwärts* endorsed the new product.[100]

The war had excluded Degussa from access to the world market for cyanide products, so delousing promised to be a profitable new outlet.[101] Degussa supported German and Austro–Hungarian military medical experiments on different strengths of the gas, and on the time taken at various temperatures to kill insects.[102] In September 1916 the military entomologist Hase began experiments at Korelitschi on the Serwetsch Front in occupied Russian-Poland, using HCN to exterminate bedbugs. After Escherich's triumphant mill gassing, Hase resumed his bedbug gassings in May 1917, this time with greater success. He was helped by the pharmacologist Ferdinand Flury, who headed a department of toxicology for developing chemical weapons under Haber and devised a gas mask against HCN fumes. The Chemical Department of the Prussian War Ministry favoured experiments in occupied areas to circumvent the safety restrictions of the Prussian

[97] Direktion Degussa DL 5/19 Bl. 14 Andres, Rücksprache mit Kriegsministerium u. im Hygienischen Institut wegen Räucherung mit Blausäure, 1–5 Nov. 1916. Bl. 17a on the lack of effect of hydrocyanic acid on bacteria. M. Szöllösi-Janze, *Fritz Haber 1868–1934. Eine Biographie* (Munich, 1998).

[98] Peters, *Blausäure*, 42; E. Teichmann, 'Cyanwasserstoff als Mittel zur Entlausung', *Zeitschrift für Hygiene*, 83 (1917), 449–66; *Sonne und Mond*, 146; Hase, *20 Jahre*, 28–31; Direktion Degussa, November–Dezember 1916, DL 5/19 Bl. 93–4 A. Andres, Unterredung mit Prof. Dr A. Hase, 29 Dec. 1916.

[99] Escherich, *Leben und Forschen*, 295–6. Direktion Degussa DL 5/19 Bl. 36 A. Andres report on the grain moth gassing by Heymonns and Plötz 23 Nov. 1916, Bl. 52 betr Räucherung des Lazarettzuges (Verein der schlesischen Maltheserritter) mittels Blausäure am 30 Nov. 1916.

[100] BAK R 86/4050 'Entlausung mit Blausäure', *Vorwärts* (14 Oct. 1917).

[101] M. Szöllösi-Janze, 'Von der Mehlmotte zum Holocaust; Fritz Haber und die chemische Schädlingsbekämpfung während und nach dem ersten Weltkrieg', J. Kocka, H.-J. Puhle, and K. Tenfelde, *Von der Arbeiterbewegung zum modernen Sozialstaat* (Munich, 1994), 658–75, 662; J. A. Johnson, 'Vom Plan einer Chemischen Reichsanstalt zum ersten Kaiser-Wilhelm-Institut', in R. Vierhaus and B. vom Brocke (eds.), *Forschung im Spannungsfeld von Politik und Gesellschaft* (Stuttgart, 1990), 499; also *Wer Ist's* (1907 edn.).

[102] The experts included Teichmann, Hase, Heymann, Hetsch, Oskar Bail, and Josef Cancik in Prague, and Hoffmann and Lohmann of the Hamburg Zoological Museum. 'Die Verwendung von Blausäure Gas zu Ungeziefer-Vertilgung' (9 July 1917); 'Entlausung mit Blausäure', *Vorwärts* (4 Oct. 1917) on its recent use in the army; E. Teichmann 'Cyanwasserstoff als mittel zur Entlavsung', *Zeitschrift für Hygiene*, 83 (1917), 449–66; O. Bail and J. Cancik, 'Ungezieferbekämpfung mit Blausäuredämpfen', *Centralblatt für Bakteriologie, Parasitenkunde und Infektionskrankheiten*, 1 Abt. vol. 81 (1918), 109–24; A. Müller, '25 Jahre Blausäure-Durchgasung in Deutschland', *Der praktische Desinfektor*, 34 (1942), 23.

Ministry of Agriculture. The Prussian Ministry of the Interior supported HCN delousing installations at Vilna late in 1917 and in October 1918 at Riga.[103] At Vilna Hase favoured a 'ruthless and dictatorial strategy' for fumigating civilian homes, clothes, and possessions. Experiments in southern Poland showed how up to 10,000 men in military hospitals and barracks could be deloused in 24 hours.[104] German occupying troops rapidly made widespread use of HCN in Eastern Europe. The gas was hailed as an ideal method of dealing with gypsy dwellings and infested railway carriages.[105] German methods were quickly followed: the professor of hygiene at the German University of Prague drummed up support for the formation of fumigation squads on the German model, and organized gassings of railway carriages at Sarajevo and of the Austrian fleet on the Adriatic.[106]

HCN had many economic and practical advantages: it was cheap, did not damage woven fabrics, leather and metal of uniforms, and penetrated all folds and pockets, as well as bedding and crevices. There were no risks of explosions or fire. Haber calculated that the gas would save fuel reserves, which would otherwise be squandered on hot air or steam disinfestation, and that HCN pest eradication in food stores and warehouses protected precious foodstuffs at a time of widespread malnutrition.

But the gas was also deadly. Deploying HCN required laborious safety precautions, first sealing the space for fumigation, and afterwards airing thoroughly. The gas was produced by mixing sodium cyanide, sulphuric acid, and water in wooden tubs (Bottichen)—a dangerous and complex procedure—or it was supplied from the exterior of buildings in pipes. The public health authorities insisted that the gas be used only under medical supervision by specially trained experts. Despite its hazards the Hamburg medical authorities drew up plans to use HCN acid in June 1917.

HCN was rapidly put into service during 1917 with the backing of the medical department of the Prussian War Ministry. Haber had a staff of 1,500 with 150 scientists for military poison gas research at the Kaiser Wilhelm Institute for Physical Chemistry and other institutes. He was anxious to maintain his research empire after the war, and saw pest control with HCN as a means of increasing agricultural productivity, already boosted by his synthesis of ammonia fertilizer. At the Kaiser Wilhelm Institute for Biochemistry Otto Warburg analysed the effects of HCN on the cellular metabolism, and physiologists found effective detoxicants and devel-

---

[103] GSTA Rep 76 VIII B 3775 Prussian MdI meeting of medical officers 26 Oct. 1918, report of Lentz. Szöllösi-Janze, *Haber*, 384.

[104] BAK R 168/172 comment of Stabsarzt Wirth of the Medical Department, 12 Apr. 1917; A. Hase, 'Über die Bekämpfung der Bettwanzen (*Cimex lectularius* L.) mittels Cyanwasserstoff (Blausäure)', *Zeitschrift für angewandte Entomologie*, 4 (1917/18), 309; id., *Die Bettwanze, ihr Leben und ihre Bekämpfung* (Berlin, 1917); id., 'Feldzug gegen Insekten', *20 Jahre*, 21–31. On Flury see D. Stoltzenberg, *Fritz Haber* (Weinheim, 1994), 253, 264.

[105] BAK 168/172 report to Degussa on fumigating of railway carriages in Constantinople, 3 Mar. 1917; M. Hahn, 'Zur Technik der Vergasung mit Cyanwasserstoff. II. Zusatz', *Hygienische Rundschau*, 29 (1919), 818–21.

[106] M. Stoecker, 'Blausäure Räucherung in den alten Oesterreich', *20 Jahre*, 16–18.

oped safety equipment.[107] Although Haber failed to secure support for linking a proposed Kaiser Wilhelm Institute for Gas Research to an institute for pesticide research, a Technical Committee for Pest Control was launched in February 1917 with the backing of the Prussian Ministries for War, the Interior, Agriculture, Finance, and Education, and from Roessler of the Degussa company. Haber thereby integrated the efforts of scientists, public health experts, industry, and the army.[108]

The committee, known as 'TASCH' (Technische Ausschuss für Schädlings-Bekämpfung[109]), was a branch of the Chemical Department of the Prussian War Ministry. Various ministries, scientific institutes, and the German Society for Applied Entomology, represented by Escherich, manned the TASCH committee, while Haber presided.[110] As Haber's centralized TASCH organization challenged Escherich's Society for Applied Biology, Haber clashed with Escherich in July 1917 over whether gassings required supervision of a trained entomologist (demanded by Escherich and Heymons) or whether a troop of soldiers—preferably with experience of combat—was adequate (as maintained by Roessler, Haber, and the War Ministry). For security and safety reasons Haber insisted that TASCH should have a monopoly over gassings, while for a combination of professional, academic, and localist reasons, Escherich backed separate Bavarian delousing squadrons and promoted a rival scheme for a national research institute for biological pest control.[111]

The Degussa chemical concern was a powerful force for extending the uses of the gas as it continued to experiment on fumigation procedures, and to seek the endorsement of military authorities in Bavaria and Württemberg, and Austria and Switzerland. Although keen that the TASCH organization should consider no other product than HCN, Degussa was reluctant to accept restrictions on its pest control team, and a dispute flared with Haber in November 1917.[112] Degussa's power was strengthened by its monopoly of the key ingredient, sodium cyanide, which had the distinction of having been tested by Robert Koch for bactericidal properties.[113]

[107] W. Richter, *Kampfstoffwirkung und Heilung* (Leipzig, 1939), 155–61, 233 for a review of research findings in the 1920s and 30s; F. Flury and W. Heubner, 'Über Wirkung und Entgiftung eingeatmeter Blausäure', *Biochemische Zeitschrift*, 95 (1919), 249–56; BAK 168/172 the KWG's role noted by Haber 5 Oct. 1918.

[108] BAK R 168/172 Besprechung am 15 Feb. 1917 betr. Schädlingsbekämpfung. Szöllösi-Janze, 'Von der Mehlmotte zum Holocaust', 665–8; id., *Haber*, 383; *Sonne und Mond*, 146.

[109] i.e. Technical Committee for Combatting Parasites.

[110] Direktion Degussa DL 5/20, Bl. 4 protocol of meeting of Haber, Roessler, Gagezow, Du Bois, Just 1 June 1917.

[111] BAK R 168/172 TASCH meetings of 9 July 1917 and 17 Nov. 1917; Szöllösi-Janze, 'Von der Mehlmotte zum Holocaust', 668–9; id., *Haber*, 381–93; Direktion Degussa DL 5/20 Bl. 81 Bericht über die Besprechung Blausäureräucherungen b. Kriegswirtschaftsamt 2 July 1917.

[112] Direktion Degussa DL 5/21 Bl. 102 report on TASCH meeting 9 July 1917; Bl. 178 report on TASCH meeting of 17 Aug. 1917. Bl. 187 on contacts with the Württemberg War Ministry; Bl. 196 on Teichmann, DL 5/22; Bl. 35 Besprechung mit Geh. Haber, 17. Nov. 1917; Bl. 109 on contacts with the Bavarian Military Medical Academy, 22 and 25 Nov. 1917.

[113] R. Koch, 'Ueber Desinfection', *Mitteilungen aus dem kaiserlichen Gesundheitsamte*, 1 (1881), 234–82. Direktion Degussa Bl. 1 on bactericidal testing of hydrocyanic acid, 2 Jan. 1919.

In April 1918 TASCH demanded that the state restrict access to poisonous substances, so giving it an enhanced role. Haber gained the support of the Reich Economic Office for TASCH to undertake research. But Degussa sought new sources of the gas as well as seeking to manufacture delousing chambers and other fumigation equipment. Relations between Degussa and TASCH deteriorated; Degussa kept its position as supplier of sodium cyanide while it continued to innovate concerning the composition and uses of HCN against different pests. Degussa's position was strengthened as it ingeniously exploited sugar refining as a major new source of HCN acid. In April 1918 Degussa agreed a contract with the Dessau Sugar Refiners, to produce HCN from decomposing molasses by a process of heating and purification.[114]

The ingenious harnessing of biology for the war-effort generated the new concept of *Biotechnik*: in 1917 such applied research at the University of Jena covered sewers, fish farming, and—at Hase's promptings—pest control.[115] The rise of interest in genetics and eugenics, and demands for a national institute of racial research, reflected the mood for practical utilization of biology. Biologists felt that they had a crucial role in protecting the nation's wealth—including the treasury of human inheritance, and the safeguarding of food and raw materials, which were vital for the war and to maintain a fit and fertile population. Hygiene as a biologically based discipline covered a spectrum from eradicating insect pests by gas fumigation to patriotic schemes for raising the birth-rate.[116]

v. Sanitizing *Lebensraum*

Medical experts became involved in planning for an eventual German victory. Annexing a slice of occupied Russian Poland and erecting a Polish buffer state were tantalizing options. The mirage of a German Asiatic empire had enticed enthusiasts for war during the autumn of 1914: the Eastern Marches Association and the Pan-German League (both with a substantial medical cohort) envisaged supplementing overseas colonies with acquisition of chunks of Poland, as well as dominance over the Ukraine, Crimea, and the Caucasus.[117] German medical officers embarked on a campaign to raise standards of public health in occupied Russian Poland, and in the *Verwaltungsgebiet Oberost* including the area around Vilna, while supporting expeditions to secure German influence in the Ukraine and Transcaucasus. As bacteriologists observed that typhus was more prevalent in what

---

[114] Direktion Degussa 5/24 Bl. 48 on Dessau, 18 Apr. 1918; Bl. 6 on HCN machinery 20 Mar. 1918.

[115] H. Penzlin (ed.), *Geschichte der Zoologie in Jena nach Haeckel (1909–1974)* (Jena, 1994), 28–9; A. Hase, 'Die Zoologie und ihre Leistungen im Kriege 1914/1918', *Die Naturwissenschaften*, 7 (1919), 105–12.

[116] R. Bud, *The Uses of Life. A History of Biotechnology* (Cambridge, 1993), 32–6; A. Hase, 'Über technische Biologie: ihre Aufgaben und Ziele, ihre prinzipielle und wirtschaftliche Bedeutung', *Zeitschrift für technische Biologie*, 8 (1920), 23–45; Weindling, *Health, Race and German Politics*, 328–30, 337–8.

[117] A. Lange, *Das Wilhelminische Berlin* (Berlin, 1967), 642–7; Tims, *Germanizing Prussian Poland*, 272–5.

had been Russian- (as opposed to German-) Poland, their priority was to improve sanitary conditions in occupied territories.[118]

The German civil government or Generalgouvernement of German-occupied Russian-Poland, established on 5 January 1915, made epidemic control a strategic priority. Its chief medical officer, Gottfried Frey, had grown up experiencing the tensions between Germans and Poles in West Prussia, and had administrative experience in the border region of Upper Silesia.[119] Frey was supported by nearly fifty German district medical officers, by the medical entomologist Martini who was appointed typhus commissar, and by six state-examined disinfectors seconded from the army with the brief of training Polish disinfectors. Frey took an environmentalist view of controlling infectious diseases, and launched an ambitious programme of improving sanitary conditions, installing toilets and drains, purifying the water supply, and building mortuaries. He was proud to have supplied an arsenal of 165 mobile and 127 mobile steam disinfection machines and 320 formalin chambers from Germany to the Generalgouvernement. The Germans established over 300 quarantine stations and isolation hospitals: persons suspected of being infected were detained, and anyone who had been in contact with a typhus case was to be deloused and kept under observation for fourteen days. Hospital pharmacies distributed German medicines, bandages, and other medical equipment. Municipal baths were renovated, and collective baths were replaced by individual showers to assist delousing.[120] Between July 1916 and November 1918 over three and a half million civilians were deloused and over 480,000 dwellings were fumigated.[121] The fear of typhus prompted ever more stringent procedures, lethal gases, and disinfection methods—provoking evasion, hostility, and resistance.

Bacteriological tests for the Generalgouvernement were initially carried out by the existing battery of Prussian hygiene institutes and bacteriological stations at Beuthen, Breslau, and Posen. A hygiene institute, using earlier Polish facilities, was opened in Łódź in November 1915, where the Jewish quarter was singled out for its insanitary condition, and medical laboratories were established in Płock and Ostroleka; military hygiene institutes in Warsaw, Białystock, Thorn (Toruń), and Brest-Litovsk carried out bacteriological tests for the area to the east of the Vistula. The German authorities planned for Warsaw a massive hygiene institute, staffed

[118] E. Gildemeister, *Bericht über die Untersuchungstätigkeit des Hygienischen Instituts in Posen während des Krieges (1. Aug. 1914 bis 31. Dez. 1918)* (= *Veröffentlichungen a. d Gebiet der Medizinalverwaltung*, 14/7) (Berlin, 1921).

[119] M. Stürzbecher, 'Zur Biographie von Gottfried Frey', *Bundesgesundheitsblatt*, 5 (1962), 125–7. Frey was from Jan. to 24 Feb. 1915 assistant to the Prussian medical officer, Abel. *Vierteljahrsbericht der Zivilverwaltung für Russisch-Polen vom 5. Januar (dem Tage der Einrichtung der Verwaltung) bis zum 25. April 1915*.

[120] Frey, *Bilder*, 46–64; 2. *Vierteljahrsbericht der Kaiserlichen Deutschen Zivilverwaltung für Polen links der Weichsel für die Zeit vom. 26. April bis zum 20. Juli 1915*, 22 concerning the Łódź Jewish district. The Łódź Hygiene Institute was directed by the medical officer Dr Wolf, the bacteriologist was Dr Croner, and there were three food chemists.

[121] *Halbjahres Bericht des Verwaltungschefs bei dem Generalgouvernement Warschau für die Zeit vom 1. April bis 30 September 1918*.

largely with Polish bacteriologists.[122] With bacteriology linked to environmental notions of disease control, the cleansing of bodies, dwellings, and localities were priorities.

The German medical authorities condemned Russian Poland and Lithuania as brimming with typhus carriers, whereas the Baltic and the Ukraine were considered relatively healthy: this verdict reinforced anti-Polish and especially anti-semitic stereotypes.[123] The Germans' condemnation of the dirty and ragged condition of Jews overlooked that the Russian retreat was accompanied by plunder and burning, and how the war caused widespread economic misery: the acute effects of the war were interpreted as due to immutable racial character. The scientific stigmatizing of traditional customs and rites of purification erupted in racial hostility. The Austrian authorities herded refugees into overcrowded collecting camps where despite sanitary regimes of forced showers and quarantine, large numbers died from typhus.[124]

The more contact the German soldiers had with eastern populations, the greater became medical anxieties over the risks of contracting typhus. Prostitutes—and especially Jewish prostitutes—were denounced as a source of lice and other vermin, and subjected to regular medical controls. The troops in Russian Poland were held to be at particular risk from sexually transmitted diseases; while the prostitutes were denounced as *verseucht*, this overlooked that the incidence of syphilis and gonorrhoea was far higher in German cities from where most soldiers came than in the rural eastern areas.[125]

German military medical experts blamed high rates of typhus among civilian populations on popular ignorance and stubborn lack of compliance with military medical directives.[126] The decline of typhus was correlated with the formation of the sanitary brigades, as *Seuchentruppen* (sometimes called 'storm troops') consisting of one or two physicians and five nurses trained in disinfection methods, cleansed dwellings, clothes, and persons in the villages of Russian Poland, Romania (where the German armies suffered most from typhus in an epidemic early in 1917),

[122] Frey, 'Gesundheitswesen', 623–5; id., *Bilder*, 41–4, 46, 64–7. GSTA Dahlem Rep 76 VIII B Nr 3007, *Bericht . . . Etatsjahres 1914* (1915), 5–6, note of 11 Feb. 1918, Der Verwaltungchef Warschau, Abwickelungsbehörde Berlin, 23 Aug. 1919; E. Gildemeister, 'Bericht über die Untersuchungstätigkeit des Hygienischen Instituts in Posen während des Krieges (1. Aug. 1914 bis 31. Dez. 1918)', *Veröffentlichungen aus dem Gebiet der Preussischen Medizinalverwaltung*, 14/7 (1921); Bettke, 'Die Tätigkeit der Medizinaluntersuchungsämter und Medizinaluntersuchungsstellen im Geschäftsjahr 1917 nach den Jahresberichten der Anstalten zusammengestellt', *Veröffentlichungen aus dem Gebiet der Preussischen Medizinalverwaltung*, 14/8 (1921); Anlage 3, *Vierteljahrsbericht des Verwaltungchefs bei dem General-Gouvernement Warschau für die Zeit vom 21. Juli bis zum 1. Oktober 1915* for list of German district medical officers, including the bacteriologist Höfer in Plock.

[123] Otto, 'Fleckfieber', 406.

[124] W. Mentzel, 'Weltkriegsflüchtlinge in Cisleithanien 1914–1918', in Heiss and Rathkolb (eds.), *Asylland*, 17–44; A. Carlebach, 'A German Rabbi Goes East', *Leo Baeck Institute Yearbook*, 6 (1961), 60–121.

[125] Aschheim, *Brothers and Strangers*, 146–8. On prostitution in occupied Poland see M. Hirschfeld (ed.), *Sittengeschichte des Weltkrieges* (Leipzig, 1930), i. 346–50, 356–7, 369, 398–9; ii. 239–42 on louse infestation; P. J. Weindling with U. B. S. L. Slevogt, *Alfred Blaschko (1858–1922) and the Problem of Sexually Transmitted Diseases in Imperial and Weimar Germany* (Oxford, 1992), 76–93.

[126] Hoffmann, *Weltkriege*, 138.

and Lithuania.[127] The newly trained Polish disinfectors were accused of corruption and bribery, using their powers of search to locate illicit distilleries and hordes of blackmarket goods, and then blackmailing the owners.[128]

It is worth comparing the German sanitary measures to those of the Austro-Hungarian military government of Serbia. The civilian population in Serbia, typically denounced by a medical officer as 'filthy and lousy', was subjected to rigorous delousing and education about the dangers of *Ungeziefer*. The *Salubritätskommissionen* established typhus isolation wards and delousing installations. Military doctors saw their role as apostles of civilization, engaged in *Kulturarbeit* to achieve sanitary 'rebirth' by means of steam and baths. A highly sensitive problem was to locate typhus among Muslims, especially women, because of religious prohibitions to medical inspection by male doctors. The government arranged for immune Serbian women to undertake such inspections. The Austrian military medical officers took pride in respecting local piety, improving the overall health of the Serbian population, and thereby defending the health of the occupying troops and preventing the spread of epidemics to the fatherland.[129] The tone of the Austrian military doctors was more moral than racial in spreading their gospel of hygiene.

The more authoritarian policies of delousing and isolation were imposed in German-occupied Poland, the worse the typhus rates became. In the winter of 1917–18, the Oberkommando-Ost, governing the region beyond the river Bug, appointed 'Typhus Commissars' and 'Epidemic Commissars' with powers over large 'epidemic control areas' to suppress the disease. The system was extended to the Generalgouvernement in spring 1918, as Polish doctors became district medical officers, thereby freeing German doctors to concentrate on the strategically important task of epidemic control.[130] Based in Vilna, the bacteriologist Richard Otto had an extensive laboratory for serum research and hospital facilities, and Hase (recently recovered from relapsing fever) ran an entomological laboratory there during 1918. Otto supervised thirty disinfection squads: in Vilna these consisted of a German doctor, seven German soldiers, and thirty-six local inhabitants, ensuring that in one year 200,000 persons were deloused. Between January and August 1918 the squads disinfected 19,000 dwellings in 1,670 places, seeking out the sick concealed in stables and sties, and detaining 6,000 persons in quarantine.[131]

Whole communities were deloused. Men were shaved of all hair from their heads and bodies, while women's heads were generally only shaved; healthy adult women might be allowed to retain their hair, and rabbis and women teachers (as

[127] Otto, 'Fleckfieber', 407–9; Musehold, *Sanitätskorps*, 59. On Romanian experiences see H. Bruns, 'Fleckfiebererfahrungen', *Deutsche medizinische Wochenschrift*, 65 (1939), 1762–6.

[128] Frey, 'Gesundheitswesen', 612.

[129] Roksandic, *Sanitäre Wacht*, 29–31, 40–7, 131–5, 176–7; 'Sanitärer Wideraufbau Serbiens. Festschrift anlässlich einjährigen Bestehens des k und k Militär-General-Gouvernements in Serbien', *Der Militärarzt*, 51 (1917), nos. 2–3 (= 3 Feb. 1917), 4–5 (10 Mar. 1917), 6 (14 Apr. 1917).

[130] *Halbjahres Bericht des Verwaltungschefs bei dem Generalgouvernement Warschau für die Zeit vom 1. April bis 30 September 1918*.

[131] Otto, 'Fleckfieber'.

community leaders) might be accorded the privilege of being deloused without medical supervision.[132] The hygienic fanaticism was mitigated by sporadic efforts to respect Jewish customs, but orthodox Jews were forcibly shaved, and young women felt violated by compulsory haircutting as only married women tradition-ally had short hair while wearing wigs. In Warsaw a special delousing facility was opened where Jews could pay to be deloused without having to be shaved.[133] Given that medical opinion was divided over whether head lice carried typhus germs, then the shaving of hair was in any case of dubious efficacy.

German medical officers sought to convert priests, teachers, and rabbis to the doctrine of the louse-borne aetiology of typhus. Co-operation with Jews was in keeping with the German and Austrian armies' promise of civic rights to Jews, and German rabbis ventured east to liaise between the army and Polish rabbis. These German rabbis, Emanuel Carlebach and Pinchas Kohn, considered that outward reforms were necessary to preserve inner spirituality.[134] Polish rabbis were sum-moned to Warsaw in 1916, where they were much relieved to be addressed by a German military doctor on the importance of delousing; he tried to persuade them that the baths and haircuts were not against religion, and showed them greatly enlarged photographs of lice. Hase's anti-lice posters, issued with a Yiddish text, reputedly adorned the antechambers of synagogues, baths, schools, and cafés. The Bavarian Pinchas Kohn co-operated with Frey in producing the Yiddish pamphlet. They outlined the dangers of *Fleckentyphus*, and persuaded Jews, 'aso reinlich Volk', to abide by the hygienic commandments of the delousing regulations: they were urged to shave hair and beards, and burn the wigs of orthodox married women when infested, and not to offer hospitality to wandering beggars. Although thou-sands of copies were issued for discussion by rabbis and teachers, Frey considered that the primitive religious culture of the Jews meant that the pamphlet had no impact.[135] The German bacteriologists attempted to modernize the rabbi's role as a community leader by turning him into a medical educator.

Although German medical officers continued to seek support from rabbis for delousing, they condemned ritual baths, describing the water as brown, stinking, and rarely changed, and washing and sanitary facilities as covered with decades of filth. The medical officers encouraged Jewish communities to improve the water quality and the sanitary installations, and to add showers and delousing facilities. Modernization of the baths involved adding central heating and electric lighting, new benches, steam sterilization of basins, hot air delousing ovens, and electrically driven water pumps. The German sanitary authorities were proud that 188 delous-ing centres were opened in Polish towns, the cost being borne by municipalities in

---

[132] Ibid., 445–54; GSTAD Rep 76 VIII B Nr 3565 Die Vorkehrungen im Inlande gegen die Einschlep-pung gemeingefährlicher Krankheiten aus dem Auslande, visit by Lentz and Neufeld, report of 22 June 1918; Frey, 'Gesundheitswesen', 593–5, 648.

[133] GSTA Rep 76 VIII B Nr 3565, report of Neufeld 14 June 1918.

[134] A. Carlebach, 'A German Rabbi Goes East', *Leo Baeck Institute Year Book*, 6 (1961), 60–121.

[135] *Vierteljahrsbericht bei dem Generalgouvernement Warschau für die Zeit vom 1. April 1916 bis zum 30. Juni 1916*, 19; Frey, 'Zu den Juden in Polen', text in 'Gesundheitswesen', 632–5, 724–5 on the lack of impact; id., *Bilder*, 70–1; I. B. Singer, *Mayn Tatns Bays-Din-Shtub* (Tel Aviv, 1979), 300.

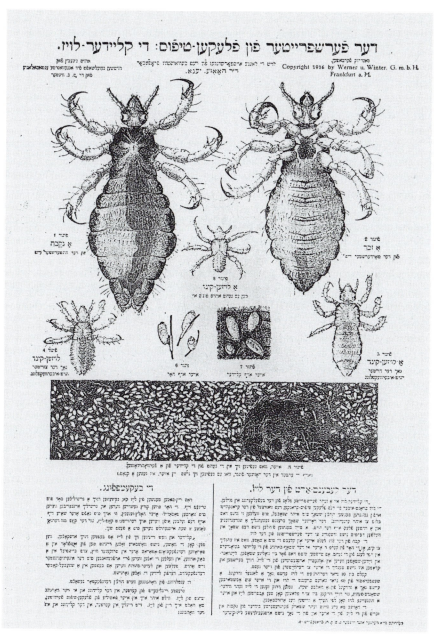

4. 'Louse-table of Professor Hase'. Text in Yiddish. Hase was the Prussian army military entomologist, and expert on lice

the hope of overcoming popular resistance. Jewish schools were criticized for their cramped and airless conditions, and the Germans claimed to have inculcated a new hygienic culture among Jewish schoolchildren, compelling them to bath weekly. The Jewish districts of Warsaw and Łódź were condemned by the Germans as the sources of typhus, from where it was spread by beggars and ragtraders. Łódź was surrounded by thirty-five 'louse forts', where persons were incarcerated before being marched off for delousing. As the epidemics spread, so the throughput at a large new delousing installation in Warsaw in 1917 was increased from a couple of hundred to 1,500 persons per day, despite the worsening fuel shortages which disrupted delousing by freezing pipes.[136]

Subjecting Jews to the medically administered rituals of bathing and haircutting involved domestic intrusions to enforce alien 'German hygiene', the closing of Jewish schools and synagogues, and of shops and markets; beggars were arrested, clothing was burnt, and rag collecting was outlawed.[137] Communities perceived delousing as a collective punishment. The hatred of delousing installations meant that some were burned down as acts of local resistance. The Generalgouvernement medical reports became increasingly anti-Semitic, by 1918 concluding that cleanliness could only be achieved if the Jews were replaced by another race.[138] German medical officers condemned the ritual washing and laying out of corpses, as well as traditional burial customs in which coffins were not sealed. Hygiene violated religious and personal sanctity. The Germans insisted that no Jewish-owned shop could open unless the owner's family was deloused, and accused the Jewish owners of sending their children a number of times rather than going themselves. The Germans compiled lists of Jews who were to be forcibly washed and deloused every week. Pedlars and other peripatetic occupations were condemned for spreading typhus. Wilhelm His, professor of internal medicine at the University of Berlin, attacked Jews as natural spies, smugglers, and swindlers, and ethnic Poles denounced Jews as responsible for epidemics.[139] Heroization of medical researchers was accompanied by demonization of eastern Jews as an alien species, carrying lethal germs.

The need to remedy manpower shortages at harvest time by importing workers into Germany posed further sanitary problems. Since the winter of 1915 the War Ministry and the Warsaw Generalgouvernement agreed that all workers from occupied Poland and Russia should be deloused; but delousing was not fully

---

[136] Frey, 'Gesundheitswesen', 647, 710–11; id., *Bilder*, 69–91; *Vierteljahrsbericht bei dem Generalgouvernement Warschau für die Zeit vom 1. Juli 1916 bis zum 30. September 1916*, 16; *Vierteljahrsbericht bei dem Generalgouvernement Warschau für die Zeit vom 1. Oktober 1916 bis 31. Dezember 1916*, 20; *Halbjahresbericht bei dem Generalgouvernement Warschau für die Zeit vom 1. Oktober 1916 bis 31. März 1917*, 29.

[137] *Vierteljahrsbericht bei dem Generalgouvernement Warschau für die Zeit vom 1. April 1916 bis zum 30. Juni 1916*, 19.

[138] *Halbjahresbericht des Verwaltungschefs bei dem Generalgouvernement Warschau für die Zeit vom 1. Oktober 1917 bis 31. März 1918*, 29.

[139] His, *Front*, 39, 91–4; Otto, 'Fleckfieber', 443–5; Frey, 'Gesundheitswesen', 615, 623–4, 631 on avoidance of disease notification; 637–9, 725–6 concerning burial rites; 650 on health education; 722 on delousing as punitive; 723 on Polish anti-Semitism; 726 on ritual baths; 729 on resistance to delousing; id., *Bilder*, 117–24.

effective, and typhus was often misdiagnosed as influenza by inexperienced German doctors. The Prussian medical authorities complained in 1917 that Russian agricultural workers arrived louse-infested, and that their barracks were filthy. Between September 1916 and March 1918 over 11,000 Polish-Jewish workers were transferred to Germany, resulting in outbreaks of typhus being attributed to them. A mild epidemic of typhus in Warsaw in 1916 was disregarded as primarily affecting the Jewish population; but a severe epidemic of typhus in Warsaw during 1917 had a radicalizing effect on the German authorities, arousing racist hostility to Jews.

The proclamation of the Kingdom of Poland on 5 November 1916—envisaged as a German client state—meant that a separate Polish medical department was established in September 1917. Cooperation with the Austrian military government in Lublin led to a public health department from February 1917, and to the appointment of fifty Polish medical officers by the summer of 1917. These developments culminated in the proclamation on 4 April 1918 of a Ministry of Public Health, Social Welfare, and Labour Protection under Witold Chodźko, a Polish psychiatrist. The German medical officers increasingly limited their medical activities to epidemic control, so devolving all other areas of public health to Polish doctors. The Germans thus claimed to have laid the foundations of a modern public health administration in Poland.[140] Yet the German reports concluded that Jewish physicians were unsuited to epidemic control, lacking the courage to run isolation hospitals. Moreover, the authorities denounced impoverished and starving Jewish vagrants for moving from the cities to rural areas, thereby spreading typhus.[141]

Jews and Poles were to be restricted to a self-governed region rather than allowed free movement throughout Germany. Prejudice against Polish Jews as typhus carriers infected the German and Austrian civilian authorities, who linked supposed Jewish indolence to disease. As eastern refugees poured into Vienna, the Austrian authorities feared a pogrom in 1915 because Jews were accused of spreading typhus. Many refugees were held in 'concentration camps', and their detention was justified by fears of typhus, although the camp internees and Jewish welfare organizations protested that they were treated worse than animals. The authorities dreaded that the concentration camps could generate epidemics, posing a danger not only to the inmates but also to the population at large.[142]

German nationalists invoked the long-standing demand for a *Grenzschluss* to exclude *Ostjuden* as necessary to contain typhus. Although there were virtually no cases of typhus among the Jewish *Gastarbeiter*—according to one set of statistics

[140] Frey, 'Gesundheitswesen', 584, 591, 731–3; id., 'Bilder', viii; *Halbjahresbericht des Verwaltungschefs bei dem Generalgouvernement Warschau für die Zeit vom 1. April 1917 bis zum 30. September 1917*, 28.

[141] *Halbjahresbericht des Verwaltungschefs bei dem Generalgouvernement Warschau für die Zeit vom 1. April 1917 bis zum 30. September 1917*, 32–3.

[142] ÖSA/AdR, Bundesministerium für soziale Verwaltung/Volksgesundheit (= BMfsV/Volksgesundheit), Karton 1588, 1918 Infektionskrankheiten, Flecktyphus in Konzentrationslagern, Magistrat Wien to k.k.n.ö. Statthalterei 13 Jan. 1917; also 11. Feb. 1915 Betreff: Konzentrationslager; D. Rechter, 'Galicia in Vienna: Jewish Refugees in the First World War', *Austrian History Yearbook*, 27 (1997), 113–30.

eight cases out of 6,000 until the end of 1916—the demand for sealing the frontier did not diminish.[143] In March 1918 there was a Reich conference on preventing typhus imported by Polish-Jewish unskilled workers. The Director of the Prussian Medical Department, Kirchner, denounced Jewish workers as dirty, unreliable, lazy, and opportunistic, and as possessed of 'a special number of morally degenerate characteristics' they were vilified as the worst possible type of worker. Kirchner, a protégé of the bacteriologist Koch, condemned the Eastern Jew as pathogenic. The medical official Frey, while denying anti-Semitism, reported that typhus was considered in Poland to be a *Judenfieber*, because of its very high incidence among the Jewish population (95 per cent of all cases in 1915–16) even though Jewish mortality rates were lower. Medical advice that Polish Jews constituted an epidemic risk meant that the Reich authorities decided to close the borders to these workers. By 1918 the medical staff of the Warsaw Generalgouvernement wearily complained that it was pointless to delouse Polish Jews, as they very quickly became reinfested.[144] For their part Jews regarded enforced baths for the frail, the elderly, and children as liable to spread disease: a Vilna resident's diary noted, 'To become sick—but to be clean.'[145]

Delousing was to secure the expansion of German power in the east. As Pan-Germanic annexationists fought moderate patriots believing that Germany was waging a war of self-defence, the ultra-nationalist wing of eugenicists supported schemes for German settlement in the east, displacing the eastern populations that they so despised. Jews and Poles were to be expelled to make way for an expected 1.5 million German settlers from Russia.[146] Plans for a wide-ranging population policy were linked to territorial expansion. The Nordic wing of racial hygienists—the geneticist Erwin Baur, and the public health professors Max von Gruber, Fritz Lenz, and Philaletes Kuhn—advocated settlement in the East for selected groups of high eugenic quality. While on active service Kuhn and Lenz were involved in delousing and typhus prevention, as they kindled hopes for a Germanic Utopia in the east.[147] Their demands kept in step with the ultra-right-wing Vater-

[143] E. Zechlin, *Die deutsche Politik und Juden im Ersten Weltkrieg* (Göttingen, 1969), 260–77. For German Jewish responses see Z. Szajkowski, 'Jewish Relief in Eastern Europe 1914–1917', *Leo Baeck Institute Yearbook*, 10 (1965), 24–56; Aschheim, *Brothers and Strangers*, 175–7; T. Maurer, 'Medizinalpolizei und Antisemitismus. Die deutsche Politik der Grenzsperre gegen die Juden im Ersten Weltkrieg', *Jahrbuch für die Geschichte Osteuropas*, 33 (1985), 205–30.

[144] Frey, 'Gesundheitswesen', 642–3; *Vierteljahrsbericht des Verwaltungschefs bei dem General-Gouvernement Warschau für die Zeit vom 1. Januar 1916 bis zum 31. März 1916*, 16 for the report that 90 per cent of all typhus cases were among the Jewish population. The figure rose to 95 per cent in the next quarterly report. GSTA Rep 76 VIII B Nr 3774 Drews of Prussian Ministry of the Interior (MdI) to Reichskanzler 18 Feb. 1918; Prussian MdI 20 Apr. 1918; BAK R 86/1040 Bd 6 Besprechung 9 Mar. 1918; GSTA Rep 76 VIII B Nr 3775 Prussian MdI meeting of medical officers 26 Oct. 1918. For comparison of the epidemics of 1916–21 to 1940–41 see Hagen, 'Das Gesundheitswesen der Stadt Warschau September 1939 bis März 1941', Archives of National Institute of Hygiene Warsaw. Hagen believed there was a 'Jewish epidemic' of 1916–18, and a 'Polish epidemic' of 1918–21.

[145] Aschheim, *Brothers and Strangers*, 181; Szaikowski, 'East European Jewish Workers', 900.

[146] I. Geiss, *Der Polnische Grenzstreifen 1914–1918. Ein Beitrag zur deutschen Kriegszielpolitik im Ersten Weltkrieg* (Lübeck, Hamburg, 1960), 5, 151–60, 177.

[147] F. Lenz, 'Über Naphthalinentlausung und ihre Methode', *MMW* 62 (1915), 1550–1.

landspartei of General Ludendorff and Admiral Tirpitz in 1917, agitating for extensive annexations.[148]

Military associates of Ludendorff supported the expansion of German medical
installations in Russia, and envisaged German influence over satellite states extending to Persia. The Treaty of Brest-Litovsk in March 1918 initiated a phase of Ostpolitik, combining the notion of Lebensraum with co-operation with eastern vassal
states. The political arrangements had a medical sub-plot—to contain Russia as an
'Asiatic' and barbarian state, by imposing quarantine measures, a *Pestcordon*, or a
medical 'Chinese Wall' on the new frontier. Russia's frontiers were rolled eastwards
as Germany occupied an area from the Baltic to the Black Sea with Austria–
Hungary also taking a belt of land stretching to the Sea of Azov.[149] Lands to the west,
notably independent Ukraine, were regarded as a vast German reservoir of much
needed grain and cattle.

In 1918 the German military mission in St Petersburg dispatched medical assistance to prisoners of war held in remote areas like Tashkent.[150] Medical experts were
drafted into Germany's shortlived eastern empire of the Crimea, Georgia, and the
Ukraine to contain epidemics, to consolidate German influence, and to secure
grain and oil. As the German military tentacles extended beyond the Crimea to
strategic outposts like Baku, a network of field hospitals and lazarettos was
provided for cases of dysentry, malaria, cholera, and finally influenza. Hahn, the
bacteriologist with long-standing Russian links to the Nobel oil company, was in
the Crimea and Ukraine in March 1918; and His, the Berlin professor of internal
medicine, was in Ukraine from July until September 1918.[151] The hospitals of ethnic
Germans in Russia were given renewed support. In 1918 a field hospital was
established in Tiflis by the German military expedition; after the withdrawal of
the troops the military doctor remained, so that the hospital provided the nucleus
for future German intervention.[152]

The alliance with the Ottoman Empire resulted in stringent epidemic measures
as well as efforts to establish a permanent German medical presence in Asia Minor.
German medical experts were concerned that Turkish troops had introduced
typhus into the Balkans, and so medical support for the Ottoman Empire was a
means of defending Germany's health.[153] As part of a programme of military and
technical assistance to the Ottoman Empire, German medical advisers imposed a
sanitary strategy of baths and delousing, initially deploying fumigation chambers

---

[148] BAK R 86/1039 Fleckfieber 1917–19; M. Gruber (ed.), *Zur Erhaltung und Mehrung der Volkskraft. Arbeiten einer vom ärztlichen Verein München eingesetzten Kommission* (Munich, 1918).

[149] W. D. Smith, *The Ideological Origins of Nazi Imperialism* (New York and Oxford, 1986), 192–4; K. Schwabe, *Wissenschaft und Kriegsmoral* (Göttingen, 1969), 167; J. W. Wheeler Bennett, *Brest-Litovsk, the Forgotten Peace. March 1918* (London, 1936).

[150] GSTA Rep 76 VIII B Nr 2996 Gumbinnen, Bl. 313 Lebenslauf Ernst Josef Gottlieb Reissland who was in Russia from 1915 until repatriation in 1920, eventually appointed at Gumbinnen to compensate for his interupted career.

[151] His, *Weltkriege*, 226–42; R. G. Suny, *The Baku Commune 1917–1918* (Princeton, NJ, 1972), 280–7.

[152] Eckart, 'Medizin und auswärtige Kulturpolitik'; H. W. Neulen, *Feldgrau in Jerusalem. Das Levant-korps des kaiserlichen Deutschlands* (Munich 1991).

[153] BNI 6b von Prowazek, Nocht to Raalzow 9 Dec. 1914.

used in the Balkan wars.[154] Nocht drafted a substantial medical contingent of 'his men' from the Hamburg Tropical Institute into the Turkish army, including Mühlens, Rodenwaldt (who had studied racial hygiene and anthropology, and had served in Togo and the Cameroons), Claus Schilling, Viktor Schilling, and Zeiss to test new drugs and disinfecting equipment. German bacteriological laboratories were opened in Constantinople, by Viktor Schilling in Aleppo, and by Rodenwaldt and 'Pasha Zeiss' in Adrianople and in the coastal city of Smyrna, where they concocted anti-cholera and anti-typhus sera. Mass delousing overcame what Rodenwaldt condemned as Muslim piety in not killing lice, and the revulsion against bathing in water which was not absolutely fresh meant the body was contaminated. Rodenwaldt maintained the network of German and military hospitals, ensuring that the Turks supplied the necessary iron beds, sanitary equipment, and even a delousing train. Inspired by German archaeological ventures at Troy, he gained the backing of scientists in Berlin, Frankfurt, and Hamburg, and the ministerial official Friedrich Schmidt-Ott in Berlin for a scheme for a German Hygiene Institute, situated on the coast south of Smyrna. They planned to combine with botanical, zoological, and archaeological research.[155] The German aim of an eastern outpost was to persist.

By 1917 Rodenwaldt, Zeiss, and their Turkish colleagues felt beleaguered because of widespread pauperization, and the spread of louse-infested beggars. The poor were rounded up, deloused on the German trains, but soon became reinfested.[156] Epidemics provided a pretext for genocide. Turkish physicians took a crucial role in planning and carrying out brutal expulsion of the Armenians from the area near the front lines in the Caucasus. They unleashed a genocidal regime of forced marches, starvation, and torture. Protecting the health of populations against epidemics became a pretext for murder of the deported Armenians. Typhus experiments on Armenians took place at a hospital in Erzincan in Central Turkey, where serum was injected from typhus patients; a German Red Cross mission doctor defended such practices. It was alleged that children were killed in Red Crescent Hospitals: what purported to be a steam bath at Trabzan was used to kill infants with some kind of fatal gas.[157] Mühlens, having insisted on elaborate anti-epidemic measures in Syria and Palestine, blamed the Armenians for upsetting his hygienic arrangements in Aleppo; the 50,000 Armenians who were held in miserable conditions in the city, were accused of bringing an epidemic of typhus, as well as typhoid,

[154] H. Becker, *Äskulap zwischen Reichsadler und Halbmond* (Herzogenrath, 1990), 37–9.

[155] BNI 10 Weltkrieg 1914–18 Teilnehmer, series of photographs of Tropical Institute members on active service including 'Pasha Zeiss' in Turkish military uniform and of Mühlens as adviser to the 4th Turkish Army. Photocopies with the author, although this file is currently missing. *Sanitätsbericht über das Deutsche Heer (Deutsches Feld- und Besatzungsheer) im Weltkriege 1914/18*, 2 (Berlin, 1938), 799–809; Otto, 'Fleckfieber', 410; Wernicke papers Box 3 Nocht to Wernicke 16 Mar. 1916; Rodenwaldt, *Tropenarzt*, 117–21, 157–65, 187; Becker, *Äskulap*, 39, 243, 389–91, 410.

[156] Rodenwaldt, *Tropenarzt*, 172–5.

[157] V. N. Dadrian, 'The Role of Turkish Physicians in the World War 1 Genocide of Ottoman Armenians', *Holocaust and Genocide Studies*, 1 (1986), 169–92; id., *The History of the Armenian Genocide* (Providence, 1995), 219–300 for 'the Issue of German Complicity'; personal communication from V. N. Dadrian, 3 June 1997.

5. Environmental damage due to military operations near Smorgon (east of Vilna) and in the Baranowitschi. Forest. Photographs by German Foresters

dysentery, and cholera. Mühlens urged their 'removal', fearing that the Armenians would infect the troops. Deprived of all sanitary facilities, Armenians not only died from epidemics and debility, they were herded into far worse concentration camps for eventual liquidation in the desert.[158] 'Pasha' Heinz Zeiss was medical adviser to the Fourth Turkish army from 1915, and in 1917 he too was stationed in Aleppo, where Turkish operations culminated in the Armenian concentration camps. The question arises whether the German medical witnesses of this slaughter became so hardened that they enforced genocidal measures in the Second World War.[159] Certainly, Germany was to offer a refuge: Dr Nazim and Benhaeddin Sakir, the leading genocidal physicians, took refuge in Berlin where Sakir was assassinated by an Armenian avenger in April 1922.[160]

The military experience in Eastern Europe, Southern Russia, and the Middle East whetted the medical appetites for new colonies. The Germans adopted not only regimented and widespread delousing, but also poison gas. Zeiss regarded medical science as a weapon to restore the nation's political might. His experience of military combat and the associated scientific triumphs infused him with a sense of dedication in a struggle for Germanic ideals.[161] The racial medical Utopia which inspired the ardour of militaristic bacteriologists abruptly evaporated with the shock of Germany's military 'betrayal' in November 1918. International isolation meant that national survival became linked to uneasy coexistence with Germany's new constellation of eastern neighbours. As the European map was redrawn, peace brought new epidemic hazards.

[158] Mühlens, 'Vier Jahre', 152; H. Becker, *Äskulap zwischen Reichsadler und Halbmond* (Herzogenrath, 1990), 185–93, 197–204.

[159] W. His, *Die Front der Ärzte* (Bielefeld and Leipzig, 1931), 134, 152–4 on Viktor Schilling in Aleppo, where he ran a bacteriological laboratory and undertook serological research; p. 169 concerning the Armenian massacre. For Zeiss's war service with Schilling see BAK R 86/744 Bl. 25–30 Heinrich Zeiss Lebenslauf in letter of Zeiss to Reichsminister des Innern 4 Apr. 1933. On Aleppo as pivotal in the massacre see G. Chaland and Y. Ternon, *The Armenians. From Genocide to Resistance* (London, 1983), 17, 63. For German military doctors and the Turkish army see H. Becker, *Äskulap zwischen Reichsadler und Halbmond* (Herzogenrath, 1990), and pp. 200–3 for German military criticisms of the Turks. On Schilling in Nazi Germany see P. Voswinckel, 'Von der ersten hämatologischen Fachgesellschaft zum Exodus der Hämatologie aus Berlin', *Exodus von Wissenschaften aus Berlin*, 552–67.

[160] Dadrian, 'Armenian Genocide', 173.

[161] H. Zeiss, 'Feuerbestattung und Nationalsozialismus', *Zentralblatt für Feuerbestattung*, 6 (1934), 1–5.

II
CONTAINMENT

5

Defending German Health: Technical Solutions

i. Sealing Borders

Confident in an imminent German victory in 1918, the Prussian medical department planned elaborate sanitary measures on the extended frontiers. The returning troops and civilians were to undergo a rigorous medical regime of small-pox vaccination, delousing, disinfection of clothing and possessions, and twenty-eight days' quarantine at a border station, followed by medical examination for tuberculosis and sexually transmitted diseases on arrival at their final destination. The strain posed by the German offensive in the west and the Allied breakthrough in Bulgaria in September 1918 meant that the German hold on the eastern conquests weakened, and medical controls disintegrated. By May 1918 medical officers agreed to reduce quarantine to twenty-three days, then to ten days with two bouts of delousing; and by the time the Baltic provinces were evacuated in 1919, the demoralized officials conceded that just one or two days were necessary.[1]

Demobilization, the realignment of borders, and population transfers generated immense sanitary upheavals. Torrents of war-wounded, the psychologically traumatized, the bereaved, the starving, and stateless, homeless, and displaced refugees streamed back into a beleaguered, politically convulsed, and disease-ridden Germany. Typhus deaths soared, reaching a peak in March 1919 in Prussia, when over a thousand cases and nearly a hundred deaths were recorded, although in the medical chaos typhus was often confused with influenza.[2] From further east came repatriated German nationals, 150,000 German prisoners of war, and 10,000 Russian captives deported from East Prussia. More refugees flooded in after Germany ceded the provinces of Posen, West Prussia, and Upper Silesia to the new Poland. From the east came 120,000 ethnic Germans from Russia, Baltic Germans displaced by Bolshevik incursions, Jewish refugees from the Russian civil and Russian–Polish wars, Russian escapees from Polish camps, German socialists disillusioned with the Russian revolution, and Russian contingents seeking a safe haven. Seasonal Polish workers, *Schnitter*, were still needed to help with the German harvest. Confronted by such a motley *Völkerwanderung*, the medical officers of the border districts demanded selective entry policies based on racial

[1] GSTA Rep 76 VIII B Nr 3564, 1913–18, Reichsgesundheitsrats, Ausschuss für Seuchenbekämpfung, 28 Feb. 1918, 28 Mar. 1918, PrMdI 30 Apr. 1918, 18 May 1918, Nr 3565, Reichskanzler decree 19 July 1918 implementing 10 days' quarantine. Nr 3566, 4 and 12 Nov. 1919 RMdI discussions on the Baltic evacuation.
[2] O. Peiper, 'Das Fleckfieber in Preussen 1918–1920', *Veröffentlichungen aus dem Gebiete der Medizinalverwaltung*, 19 (1921), 3–23.

criteria; they favoured the 'morally superior' Germanic refugees, while excluding *Ostjuden* on the pretext that they were diseased and criminal.[3]

The shrunken German borders were at first characterized as 'green' or open borders, and refugees escaping the Russian Revolution crossed freely. Medical officers demanded that the frontiers be defended against 'undesirable elements' importing typhus and cholera into Germany from the East.[4] The fear of disease, crime, and radical subversion militated for ever tougher border controls so that by 1919 passports, visas, and quarantine became the norm. Poland and Russia were characterized as *verseucht*, posing epidemic threats to the existence of an unfairly victimized Germany, and the anti-Semitic press targeted Jews as carriers of diseases. The medical officer of Liegnitz depicted the situation as a battle to defend German order, cleanliness, and prosperity against barbaric *Unkultur*.[5] The strategy was to secure the eastern border with a chain of medical inspection and delousing stations, and so defend the metropolitan centres of Breslau and Berlin against the floods of diseased refugees.[6]

German medical experts consoled themselves that, despite losing the war, they had won the battle against infectious disease. For until the ravages of influenza, the *Heimat* had remained largely free from epidemics.[7] Outbreaks of typhus, cholera, typhoid, dysentery, malaria—and war-specific variants like trench fever—had been contained. It could not be claimed (especially given the high casualty rates in battle) that epidemics killed more than military action. But the peace left Germans, who faced shortages of food, fuel, soap, and other essentials, exposed to infectious and chronic diseases. German medical officials condemned *Ostjuden* and Polish workers as 'bacillus carriers', and feared that 'the German race' was threatened with extinction by starvation and sickness arising from the Allied blockade and the economic and political burdens of the Versailles Treaty. Nationalists lamented territorial losses of vital *Lebensraum* in the East. Germany was isolated internationally, and medical officials feared their nation's vulnerability between a revanchist France and a rapidly militarizing Poland: the weakened physical constitution of the *Volk* would be unable to resist the epidemics from the East.[8] German national organizations resolved to strengthen the spirit of Germandom in the scattered 'colonies' in eastern Europe, while preferring their expatriate racial brethren to stay in place rather than add to the burden of the Reich's medical problems.

Public health and social welfare programmes were designed to remove the causes of poverty and persecution, which had spurred the mass emigration prior to

---

[3] GSTA Rep 76 VIII B Nr 3567 Medizinalbeamte der Grenzmark Posen/Westpreussen 24 Jan. 1921. For comments on Polish workers see Willführ, 'Fleckfieber', 62–3; B. Pinkus and I. Fleischhauer, *Die Deutsche in der Sowjetunion* (Baden-Baden, 1987), 156.

[4] GSTA Rep 76 VIII B Nr 3776 Ministerium für Volkswohlfahrt 21 July 1920.

[5] Willführ, 'Fleckfieber', 60; Maurer, *Ostjuden*, 108–11, 802–3.

[6] *25 Jahre*, 170. These were at Eydtkuhnen, Prostken, Gross-Kosslau bei Neidenburg, Gross-Boschpohl bei Lauenburg i. Pommern, Schneidemühl, and Stentsch.

[7] Hoffmann, *Weltkriege*, 98; His, *Front*, 245.

[8] BAP 15.01/9405 Gesundheitliche Wirken der Kriegs- und Nachkriegszeit Bl. 93, meeting in Reich Health Office on health and nutritional conditions, 3 July 1923.

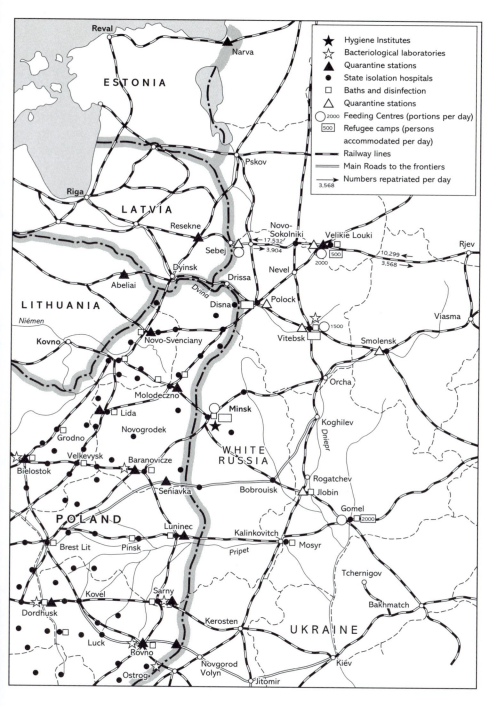

Legend

★	Hygiene Institutes
☆	Bacteriological laboratories
▲	Quarantine stations
●	State isolation hospitals
□	Baths and disinfection
△	Quarantine stations
◯ 2000	Feeding Centres (portions per day)
500	Refugee camps (persons accommodated per day)
▬▬	Railway lines
═══	Main Roads to the frontiers
→ 3,568	Numbers repatriated per day

Reval
Narva
ESTONIA
Pskov
Riga
LATVIA
Resekne
Novo-Sokolniki
Velikie Louki
Rjev
17,532
3,904
Sebej
500
2000
10,299
3,568
Dyinsk
Drissa
Nevel
Abeliai
Dvina
Disna
Polock
LITHUANIA
Viasma
Niémen
Kovno
Novo-Svenciany
Vitebsk
Smolensk
Molodeczno
Orcha
Lida
Minsk
Koghilev
Novogrodek
Dniepr
Grodno
WHITE RUSSIA
Velkevysk
Baranovicze
Rogatchev
Bielostok
Seniavka
Bobrouisk
Jlobin
Gomel
POLAND
Luninec
Kalinkovitch
2000
Brest Lit
Pinsk
Mosyr
Pripet
Tchernigov
Kovel
Sarny
Bakhmatch
Dordhusk
Kerosten
UKRAINE
Luck
Rovno
Kiév
Ostrog
Novgorod Volyn
Jitomir

0   50   100 km

MAP 2. Epidemic situation in Eastern Europe in 1922

the First World War. Draconian border controls were imposed by Austria and Germany to keep out diseased undesirables. The medical checks on the border of the rump state of Deutsch-Österreich became more rigorous to ensure that only ethnic German 'colonists' or refugees from the South Tyrol were admitted while *Ostjuden* were excluded. Anti-Semites demanded that Jewish refugees be expelled from Austria or be interned in 'concentration camps', and organized Austrian anti-Semitism increased.[9] During 1918 the sanitary surveillance or *Perlustrierung* demanded by the Austrians for returning soldiers and civilian refugees on the borders of the Bukowina and Galicia was intensified.[10] The aim was to defend the Austrian heartlands. The new 'German Austrian' Ministry for Public Health, or *Volksgesundheit*, which began its work in August 1918, was (like the medical department of the new Prussian welfare ministry under Gottstein) administered by eugenically minded public health experts. From October 1918 until May 1919 the Ministry was directed by the racial hygienist Ignaz Kaup who was keen to exclude racial undesirables in the fight against infectious diseases. Kaup intensified disinfection procedures to eliminate *Ungeziefer* at special 'cleansing stations'.[11] His successor, the socialist anatomist—and eugenicist—Julius Tandler, continued to enforce defences against the import of infections by the returning troops from Russia, Poland, the Balkans, and Italy, by providing a bathing train and special carriages for the sick and wounded.[12]

German military medical and state authorities channelled refugees from Russia into 'reception camps': these were a hybrid between the transmigrant collecting stations and the Austrian concentration camps for refugees.[13] The priority was '*seuchenhygienische Abwehr*' involving the medical surveillance of the Eastern border, and subjecting all refugees and seasonal workers to thorough medical inspection and delousing under police supervision. Former prisoner of war camps were converted as *Heimkehrerlager* or *Sammellager* for the reception of refugees from Poland and Russia. The atrocious conditions were meant to deter refugees from descending on Germany. In January 1919 a 'collecting camp' for returning soldiers was opened at Eydtkuhnen (one of the former HAPAG transit stations).[14] Hospitals in border districts provided quarantine, bathing, and delousing facilities;

---

[9] B. Hoffmann-Holter, 'Jüdische Kriegsflüchtlinge in Wien', Heiss and Kolb, *Asylland*, 45–59; M. Grandner, 'Staatsbürger und Ausländer. Zum Umgang Österreichs mit den jüdischen Flüchtlingen nach 1918', Heiss und Kolb, *Asylland*, 60–85; G. Heiss, 'Ausländer, Flüchtlinge, Bolschewisten: Aufenthalt und Asyl 1918–1933', Heiss und Kolb, *Asylland*, 86–108.

[10] ÖSA/AdR, BMfsV/ Volksgesundheit, Kt. 1905 Fasz. Nr 71/2, Desinfektion 1919, k.k. Ministerium des Inneren Regelung der Fürsorge für Zivilheimkehrer in Ostgalizien und in der Bukowina.

[11] ÖSA/AdR, BMfsV/ Volksgesundheit, Kt. 2880 Fasc. 19. The text of a poster ran: 'Schutz gegen Fleck-Typhus. Wer mit Ungeziefer behaftet ist, gehe vor Betreten einer Wohnung in die Reinigungs-Anstalt'. In Jan. 1919 the military *Reinigungs-Anstalt* was at Gudrunsstrasse 87, 10th district of Vienna, and a civilian *Reinigungs-Anstalt* was in the Steinbauergasse, 12th district.

[12] *50 Jahre Ministerium für Soziale Verwaltung 1918–1968* (Vienna, n.d.), 16–29; K. Sablik, *Julius Tandler. Mediziner und Sozialreformer* (Vienna, 1983), 140–51; J. Tandler, *Das Volksgesundheitsamt in der Zeit von Mitte Mai 1919 bis Mitte Mai 1920* (Vienna, 1920), 7–8.

[13] BAK R 86/2401 Heimkehrer, Flüchtlinge und Kriegsgefangenelager.

[14] GSTA Rep 76 VIII B Nr 3565, OP Königsberg 25 Jan. 1919.

at Meseritz disinfection was carried out, and at the twin town of Obrawalde there were delousing facilities. Quarantine camps processed soldiers at Prostken and refugees at Frankfurt am Oder and Hammerstein, where the security was draconian and the appalling conditions were made worse by outbreaks of typhoid and typhus.[15] Bacteriologists from the Reich Health Office and Robert Koch Institute monitored conditions in the camps in order to prevent the spread of disease to surrounding areas.[16] A typhoid epidemic in Frankfurt am Oder, blamed on incoming refugees, exacerbated the situation. Beleaguered Germans in Lower Silesia agitated for increased bacteriological facilities to prevent the *Ostseuchen* brought by the waves of refugees from the lost territories.[17]

German states intensified their anti-immigration policies. In October 1921 the Prussian Minister of the Interior declared the policy of restricting immigration from the East; he hoped that those 'undesirable elements' already in Prussia could be persuaded to re-migrate or return to the East. In any case stricter border controls and delousing were necessary before a labour permit could be issued. The *Ostjuden* were disinfected in Berlin under the auspices of a Jewish aid committee.[18] Medical authorities attributed outbreaks of typhus to the collapse of delousing on the frontiers. In January 1919 German soldiers, who had fought their way back from Lithuania, refused to be deloused, and when at the end of 1919 the remnants of the German Baltic troops returned, typhus rates again rose. Delousing the recalcitrant soldiers was made more difficult because troops stationed on the border were loath to impose regimented delousing; and at the border crossings of Prostken and Lyck guards were simply lacking. Revolutionary councils of soldiers had to be persuaded to apply sanitary regulations. Delousing procedures could cost a traveller not only a seat in a train, but also luggage and possessions. Showers were an ordeal when water pipes were defective, and fuel for heat and light was unavailable.[19]

German bacteriologists accused the Poles of destroying the German epidemiological defences, and of mounting a crude form of human biological warfare—by deporting ethnic Germans who were infected with typhus into Germany without any effort to delouse them. German medical officers stigmatized Poland as saturated by typhus, and were alarmed that the shift westwards of the Polish border brought the threat of typhus close to the heart of Germany.[20] Bacteriologists

[15] Ibid., 3567, Heeresabwickelungsamt Posen 26 Oct. 1920; RP Schneidemühl 12 Oct. 1920; Nr 3570, Bericht über die Tätigkeit des Roten Kreuzes im Quarantänelager Frankfurt am Oder, 8 Mar. 1922 on the unsuitability of the camp for long-stay inmates. BAK R 86/2401 Bd 1 RGA report by Frey, Gesundheitliche Verhältnisse in den Heimkehrlagern 2 Jan. 1923.
[16] GSTA Rep 76 VII B Nr 3567, tour of Hamel and Frey to Heilsberg, Königsberg, and Tilsit.
[17] GSTA Rep 76 VIII B Nr 3077, Medizinisches-Untersuchungsamt Breslau, laboratory director to Ministry 21 June 1922.
[18] GSTA Rep 84a Bekämpfung gemeingefährlicher Krankheiten Nr 1236 Bl. 156–7 statement of Minister of the Interior.
[19] GSTA Rep 76 VIII B Nr 3565, RP Allenstein (Dr Lembke) 29 Jan. 1919 and 31 Jan. 1919. PMdI 17 Feb. 1919; Peiper, 'Fleckfieber', 11.
[20] BAK R 86/1040 Bd 6 Report in the *Kreuzzeitung*, Berlin 6 Apr. 1919 concerning 'Flecktyphus als polnisches Kampfmittel'; Frey, 'Medizinalwesen', 654.

6. Medical-hygienic course for Polish District Medical Officers in Posen, Easter 1920. In centre: Prof. Dr Erich Wernicke, Director of the former Prussian Institute of Hygiene

mourned the loss of the flagship hygiene institute in Posen/Poznań, and of an ancillary bacteriological station in Bromberg/Bydgoszcz. Poznań was a centre of radical Polish councils, and the bacteriologist Wernicke narrowly escaped execution—once because of assistance from Polish sewer workers to whom he had often distributed cigars. When Piłsudski invited Wernicke to stay on, the handover was orderly: German staff worked from February 1919 to March 1920 under supervision of the Polish Ministry of Health, so that the official transfer of power on 1 October 1919 did not disrupt the bacteriological services. Wernicke ran two courses for contingents of Polish medical officers. In 1920 the Germans left what they regarded as adequate equipment for the routine functioning of the institutes, although the Poles argued that the totality of the equipment ought to have been handed over. Confusion arose over whether the hygiene institutes were formerly institutes of the Prussian state (and thus their equipment could be legitimately repatriated to Germany), or whether as municipal facilities all their contents were due to Poland. The Poles appealed to the allies that they were bereft of medical laboratory facilities. The nationalist resolve of the German staff hardened. Wernicke was transferred in 1921 to a new Prussian Hygiene Institute at Landsberg an der Warthe to police the frontier *Grenzmark* against epidemics.[21]

[21] GSTA Rep 76 VIII B Nr 3007, Einrichtung und Verwaltung des (staatl) Hygiene Institutes in Posen, Reichs- u. Staats Kommission für die Überleitungen 28 May 1925. Nr 3018, Die Bauten des Hygiene Institut Posen 1911–20, Überleitungskommissar für die Abwickelung der Medizinalverwaltung in Bereich der Provinz Posen, 2 Nov. 1920. Nr 3020, Staatliche Medizinaluntersuchungstelle in Bromberg 1912–25, Gottstein directive on equipment 21 Nov. 1920, 7 Dec. 1922. Wernicke Papers, photographs of course participants for Polish medical officers, 1919 and Easter 1920. Information from Edith Geyl-Wernicke, daughter of Erich Wernicke, Mar. 1997.

Once the Prussian military medical department gave up its wartime responsibility of protecting Germany from epidemics, officials argued over the costs of the internment camps. Prussia had exchanged its frontier with tsarist Russia for the complexities of the new border with Poland and the Polish corridor to the Baltic, leaving East Prussia as an exclave between Poland and Lithuania. As the Reich only paid for the effects of the war or the implementation of the peace treaty, the Prussian officials sniped back that they were in the frontline of epidemic prevention, safeguarding the health of the nation from a danger which threatened all Germany.[22] Military and civilian authorities and refugees fought over the costs of delousing each person passing through a camp.[23] While the state aimed to have a delousing station in every Prussian frontier district, many districts and municipalities resisted the financial burdens of having to pay for quarantine and disinfection facilities. The Königsberg camp was municipally owned but run by the German Red Cross, and the municipality of Lauenburg did not wish to be burdened by a camp harbouring the risks of infection.[24] The 'loss' of the Memel coastal strip meant relinquishing a quarantine station and a leper colony.[25] In order to secure the eastern medical defences, Prussia offered in April 1921 to take over several camps still owned by the army or by HAPAG and the Norddeutsche Lloyd shipping companies at Eydtkuhnen, Prostken, and Tilsit on the border of East Prussia.

The proliferating system of border camps was turned to anti-Semitic ends, as the Prussian Ministry of the Interior targetted *Ostjuden* as a group of undesirables. In 1919 registration was imposed, and the Minister of the Interior began to prepare 'concentration camps' for *Ostjuden*. In March 1920 several hundred eastern Jews were rounded up by the Berlin police, and denounced as a degenerative 'cancerous sore' on the national body. Camps at Stargard and Cottbus, once used for prisoners of war, as well as at Ingolstadt in Bavaria, were used for brutal internment of 'criminal *Ostjuden*'; most were refugees or transmigrants hoping to cross to America but lacking a visa. The camps were infested with bedbugs, and the atrocious food and defective sanitation caused high rates of sickness. Sporadic pogroms erupted in German cities, and in 1923 some Jews were expelled.[26] Parallel efforts were mounted to detain Jews on the Prussian borders as a response to the Polish persecution, military drafts, and the Russian–Polish war driving Jewish refugees into East Prussia. A limited right of asylum was recognized by government decrees in November 1919 and June 1920, on condition that Jewish organizations provided welfare. The Prussian Ministry of Interior conceded that Jews could remain in Prussia as 'an alien and unequal culture'. But by the winter of 1920 the Reich wanted a camp for

[22] GSTA Rep 76 VIII B Nr 3565, PMdI to Reichskanzler 19 Nov. 1918, 5 June 1919 PMdI Sitzung betr die Behandlung der Rückwanderer in Ostpreussen, 5 June 1919.

[23] Ibid., 3568, 7 Apr. 1921.

[24] Ibid., 3567, Landrat Lauenberg, 25 Nov. 1920 refusing to pay for a delousing station on the Polish border. Nr 3569, RMdI 23 Feb. 1922. Nr 3571, RP Köslin concerning delousing at Lauenburg, 17 Oct. 1922.

[25] *25 Jahre*, 157.

[26] Aschheim, *Brothers and Strangers*, 199, 240, 242–3; Maurer, *Ostjuden*, 416–35; L. Heid, *Maloche— nicht Mildtätigkeit. Ostjüdische Arbeiter in Deutschland 1914–1923* (Hildesheim, 1995), 200–3.

'undesirable elements' in order to solve the problem of foreign aliens. The Prussian authorities demanded that Jewish refugees be deported from Königsberg to internment camps at Eydtkuhnen, Heilsberg, and Preussisch-Holland, as a means of 'hygienic control', accusing Jews of importing cholera and typhus. Parliamentary pressure mounted against the 'floods' of *Ostjuden* who were subsumed into a nightmarish horde of psychopaths and Bolsheviks.[27] When Ostjuden from Schneidemühl and Stentsch congregated on the eastern border, the Berlin police added communism and crime to the burdens of racial pollution and infection. Given the lack of delousing facilities at Schneidemühl, Jews represented 'a grave threat to the population of Germany'. The police demanded that Jews be detained on the frontier at Eydtkuhnen, and dispatched in sealed trains to internment camps. A programme of expulsions was instigated with Stargard in Pomerania designated as a transit camp, as resentment festered against the refugees.[28]

The Poles took over the former German camps on their territory. Ruth Fry, a Quaker aid worker described a delousing camp near Warsaw in 1922: 'It was installed by the Germans and the arrangements for disinfection are very good, but the barracks where the people live are abominable. Large, dark sheds, where whole families have just a space of floor in two tiers, one above the other. Just the worst kind of refugee accommodation that I have seen in so many places.'[29] More powerful disinfection technologies were intended to tackle the atrocious conditions in the refugee and internment camps. Although the new disinfection technologies were first adopted as emergency measures, public health officials soon favoured their deployment on a routine basis.

ii. The Zyklon Solution

After the war hydrocyanic acid gas was deployed for pest control: Hase, the zoologist, reflected that the measures to combat lice among the eastern Jews could be transferred to bug and louse control among the urban slums. There were political motives, as nationalists combated a pincer movement of communism spilling over from the east, and filth, disease, and revolution which threatened to pollute the German heartlands. While the hygienic monitoring of the new frontiers was to

---

[27] GSTA Rep 76 VIII B Nr 3566, PMdI 1 Nov. 1919, Nr 3567, OP Ostpreussen 17 Dec. 1920 to MVW. Severing RMdI, 13 Jan. 1921 ordering internment of Ostjuden at Eydtkuhnen. Prussian Grenzpolizeidirektor MdI 'ob Ostjuden überhaupt anzunehmen sind . . . ?', 13 Jan. 1921. MdI 22 Jan. 1921 concerning Königsberg. Nr 3568, Henning of RMdI on proposals for camps and a Reichsstelle zur Regelung des Fluchtwesens, 7 Sept. 1920. Nr 3571, RMdI betr. Sonderausweise für menschliche Flüchtlinge 17 Nov. 1922. Dr Kaehler (Greifswald), *Haus der Abgeordneten*, Drucksache Nr 2932 (29 Nov. 1922), betr Einwanderung der Ostjuden nach Deutschland.

[28] GSTA Rep 76 VIII B Nr 3568, Polizei Präsident Berlin betr Ostjuden auf d. Schlesischen Bahnhof in Berlin. 17 Nov. 1921 Severing, RMdI. 21 Feb. 1921. RP Schneidemühl 30 Dec. 1920. Preussischer Landtag, Anfrage Nr 270, 20 Aug. 1921, reply by MVW 6 Sept. 1921. The internment of *Ostjuden* occurred at Stargard and Cottbus only after the socialists left the government in 1921; see Aschheim, *Brothers and Strangers*, 242; Maurer, *Ostjuden*, 417.

[29] A. R. Fry, *Three Visits to Russia* (London, 1942), 20.

keep epidemic infectious diseases at bay, efforts were made to cleanse the domestic environment in order to eradicate incipient communism, and to sustain health and national vitality. The post-war crises saw a radicalization of eugenic ideas, as eugenicists sought to cleanse the nation's gene-stock by incarcerating and indeed sterilizing the antisocial.[30] New disinfection technologies provided a bacteriological counterpart, as disease-carriers were regarded as socially disruptive, and the chronically degenerate as prone to infectious diseases. Scientists rallied to calls for mobilizing Germany's medical, scientific, and technological resources to remedy post-war social ills. The Angst surrounding an epidemic menace was transposed from an external 'Asiatic' menace to an internal pool of chronic degenerates.

By January 1919 sanitary controls on the frontiers collapsed: only the delousing stations at Illowo and Prostken were functioning. Delousing stations in towns and cities were the next line of defence. Hydrocyanic acid delousing stations in Berlin, Munich, and other cities coped with the floods of infested soldiers from the east.[31] In November 1919 the Prussian state conducted a survey of louse infestation, which was attributed as much to the nation's internal ills—such as shortages of soap, fuel, and underwear, youth delinquency, and the housing crisis—as to migrant workers and Polish Jews.[32] The field experience acquired by public health experts contributed to municipal use of prussic acid. For example, Wilhelm Hoffmann (who turned from military medicine to becoming chief medical officer for Berlin) was impressed by the gas.[33] Delousing stations consisted of shower facilities and a hydrocyanic gas chamber: such a 'sanitary bath' was pioneered for demobilized troops in Frankfurt am Main in 1918.[34] Although Nocht (who had invented a carbon monoxide method of pest control) warned that hydrocyanic acid was dangerous, procedures were agreed for the fumigation of ships.[35] The demobilization of troops who were familar with delousing meant that pesticides and fumigation became accepted in civilian society. When accidents occurred, the blame was placed on human error in ignoring warning notices or not observing instructions. To overcome the problem of inadequately trained personnel, state medical officials took on a regulatory and supervisory role.[36]

The municipality of Frankfurt am Main, taking a cue from the entomological crusaders Escherich and Hase, exhumed in March 1920 the wartime plan for a pest

[30] Weindling, *Health, Race and German Politics*, ch. 5: 'Revolution and Racial Reconstruction'.

[31] GSTA Rep 76 VIII B Nr 3776, *Tägliche Rundschau*, 20 Jan. 1919. Ministry of Interior discussion 3 May 1919.

[32] Peiper, 'Fleckfieber', 18–23.

[33] Hoffmann, *Weltkriege*, 146–9; O. Bail and J. Cancik, 'Ungezieferbekämpfung mit Blausäure-dämpfen', *Centralblatt für Bakteriologie, Parasitenkunde und Infektionskrankheiten*, 1 Abt, vol. 81 (1918), 109–24; Hetsch, *Ungeziefervertilgung mit Blausäuregas* (= *Deutsche Militärärztliche Zeitschrift* no. 1 (1918)).

[34] 'Berichte über Blausäure-Entwesungskammern', *Zeitschrift für Desinfektion*, 21 (1929), 105–12.

[35] STAH II J2 Bd V 1912–19, Bl. 212–18. Nocht's method was found not to kill fleas.

[36] STAB 4, 21–491 Deutsche Gesellschaft für Schädlingsbekämpfung, C. M. Hasselmann, 'Zur Frage der Ueberwachung von Blausäure und Zyklondurchgasungen durch den beamteten Arzt', *Zeitschrift für Medizinalbeamte* (1925), 921–46.

control institute to carry out tasks for the municipality, industry, and agriculture, and to serve as a national centre for research in applied zoology. Fritz Roessler, directing the Degussa chemical manufacturers, lobbied to place the venture under the former Strassburg zoologist Ernst Bresslau, whose work had once been supported by the industrialist F. A. Krupp, as likely to gain additional funds from industry. The image was presented of a devastated national economy plagued by insect pests. Biological experts magnified their own worth by arguing that virtually all the delousing products were an irrational waste of money, and that pest control workers were themselves parasites on the national economy. They agitated for a national research institute for pesticides on the grounds that it was rational and cost-effective.[37] While there was an exaggerated sense that the nation was threatened by typhus, there were very real dangers for those in the frontline of the campaign, as medical officers, nurses, and disinfectors were liable to contract typhus.[38]

The wartime TASCH organization only partially fulfilled Haber's aspirations for a national pesticides agency. Between April 1917 and March 1919 TASCH commissioned Degussa to fumigate a series of mills, while refining the methods of gas storage and release. A 'gas squad' (*Kompagnie für Schädlingsbekämpfung*) under a Reich Commissar for Pest Control fumigated barracks and mills throughout northern and central Germany and in the occupied eastern territories. These military brigades were transformed into specialized civilian teams for fumigating barracks during demobilization; by June 1919 the gas brigades were dissolved (with the exception of a naval contingent) as a step towards state-regulated commercialization. Profits were invested in research, as Haber simplified fumigation procedures and developed protective equipment and measuring devices.[39]

Haber regarded TASCH as more a managerial body than a scientific committee. He planned to commercialize TASCH by attracting capital of a million marks, while intending that all profits should be reinvested in research on pest control. From its inception Haber argued that TASCH should attain the status of a limited company.[40] Any organization which was saving the nation millions of marks had to be profitable. Haber located five firms willing to invest over one million marks to found a German Company for Pest Control (Deutsche Gesellschaft für Schädlings-bekämpfung, i.e. DEGESCH) with just under one-half of the capital coming from

[37] Stadtarchiv Frankfurt am Main, Akten des Magistrats, Hygienisches Institut V 320 Bl. 138–49 betr. Abtrennung der Abteilung für Schädlingsbekämpfung 18 Mar. 1920. Bl. 140–54 Ernst Bresslau, Schaffung und Errichtung einer Forschungstätte für angewandte Zoologie. Bl. 157–9 Roessler to Oberbürgermeister Voigt; H. E. Ziegler and E. Bresslau, *Zoologisches Wörterbuch* (Jena, 1912).

[38] Willführ, 'Fleckfieber', 58, 86–7.

[39] D. Stoltzenberg, *Fritz Haber* (Weinheim, 1994), 456–8; H. W. Frickhinger, 'Blausäureräucherung im Dienste der Mehlschädlingsbekämpfung', *Zeitschrift für angewandte Entomologie*, 4 (1917/18), 310–20; BAP 15.01/9367 Bericht über die Gründungsverhandlung einer Deutschen Gesellschaft für Schädlings-bekämpfung vom 5. Oktober 1918. Reichswirtschaftsministerium 2 Oct. 1919. GSTA Rep 76 VIII B Nr 3775, agreement 30 Jan. 1919 concerning TASCH and the Kriegsministerium.

[40] BAK R 168/172 Tasch meeting of 12 Apr. 1917.

Degussa. The Chancellor endorsed the scheme for a state-regulated national monopoly organized as a commercial company with the backing of the chemical industry.[41] In October 1918, with the military situation disintegrating, the state's economic resources collapsing, and a liberal Chancellor in place, Haber salvaged the gas fumigation organization by restructuring it as part of a new system of integrating industry with the state. By way of contrast, the industrialist Carl Duisberg favoured a sharper division between the state and commercial sphere. The Reich Economic and Health Offices supported the development of a commercial organization oriented to public health, but insisted that any monopoly should be restricted to hydrocyanic acid.[42]

Pest control was deemed necessary at a time of political instability to clean up in the wake of the insurrectionary brigades on the left and right. Hase was repulsed by the spectacle of revolution in Vilna, erupting in November 1918, when the cleansed troops came into contact with 'totally depraved and unhealthy human masses'. Demobilized in December 1918, on return to Berlin early in 1919 Hase joined Haber's institute. One of his first tasks was to advise in April 1919 on fumigating the Reichstag building with hydrocyanic acid gas, after occupation by revolutionaries and vagrants since November 1918; but the enormity of sealing the Reichstag meant that Hase opted for a forty-day isolation of the building in order to starve the lice. Hase flattered himself that the Weimar Republic was the result of his louse control methods determining the move of the constitutional assembly to Weimar from May to September 1919 (overlooking that police control of the railway communications, the size of theatre in Weimar, and the city's symbolic cultural value all prompted the move).[43] Self-magnified pest-control experts exaggerated their importance as defenders of the nation.

Newspaper adverts and flyposters on the sewer columns publicized delousing facilities. Health authorities pleaded with the workers and soldiers councils to permit sanitary controls. Although delousing the whole population of Berlin was contemplated, a more targeted approach was adopted: delousing stations were established in city night shelters for the homeless, hospitals, and barracks. Socialists demanded that health inspectors and public health centres should enforce mass delousing to counteract the lack of clothes, soap, and general deprivation. Nationalists despaired at the lack of parental supervision of youth delinquents, who swelled the army of the infested. The medical entomologist Martini and the Berlin internist His urged delousing the influx of Polish Jews, that a national typhus

---

[41] BAK 168/172 16 Feb. 1918, Haber memo to Reichswirtschaftsamt. Reichskanzler 30 Apr. 1918.

[42] BAP 15.01/9367 betr die Deutsche Gesellschaft für Schädlingsbekämpfung 1918–22, Staatssekretär des Reichswirtschaftsamtes 22 Apr. 1918 and 23 Apr. 1918. Reichsgesundheitsamt betr Regelung der Verwendung hochgiftiger Gasen 13 June 1918. Sitzungsbericht über die Besprechung im Reichswirtschaftsamt am 15. Januar 1919 betreffend den Entwurf einer Verordnung über die Schädlingsbekämpfung mit hochgiftigen Stoffen. Direktion Degussa DL 5.25 Bl. 82 negotiations with Heerdt of Tasch, 5 Feb. 1919. BAK 168/172 memo of Haber Feb. 1918.

[43] Stoltzenberg, *Haber*, 462–3; MPG Haber Sammlung 540 Hase to Heerdt 27 Apr. 1956; 541, Hase to MPG 11 Sept. 1956; 548, Hase 'Die Rolle der Läuse in der neueren Geschichte und in der Reichstaggebäude 1918/19'; BAK R 168/293 Hase Personalakte.

commissar be appointed as in Poland, and that demobilized doctors should form a special anti-typhus corps.[44]

Among those who had experience of delousing routines was Hitler: during the war he was impressed by the use of gas for the extermination of rats and lice, and, blinded in a British gas attack in October 1918, defeat came as an apocalyptic trauma.[45] Gas disinfestation became part of the programme to restore order after the revolutionary upheavals. In the military transit camp (or DULAG) of Lechfeld in Bavaria, there were repeated outbreaks of typhus with the arrival of troop trains from Ukraine: after a turbulent period when the soldiers ran riot, in June 1919 the camp medical officer ordered immediate delousing showers and disinfection after disembarkation from the trains, and plastered the camp with propaganda posters on the hazards of lice and typhus.[46] During May 1919 (when the Munich Soviet was crushed by the ultra-nationalist Freikorps) the Health Commission of the First Bavarian Army trained twenty-seven disinfectors, who set about gassing barracks, schools, and mills to clear up in the wake of the freecorps and revolutionaries. The Lechfeld camp was a focus for the delousing corps in June 1919.[47] The Bavarian reception camps for soldiers from the east combined delousing with political cleansing, giving Hitler the opportunity of showering returning troops with nationalist invective. Hitler was an 'informant' for the 'enlightenment squad' at Lechfeld in 1919, charged with inculcating sound nationalist opinions among demobilized troops who might have been 'infected' with Bolshevism while in the east. He attended a political course in August 1919; by September 1919 he was referring to Jews as 'racial bacilli', and he joined the Deutsche Arbeiter Partei, convinced that the health of Germany required eradication of Jews as a type of racial tuberculosis.[48] The concept of the parasite was transferred from applied biology to militant ultra-nationalist campaigns for cleansing the nation of numerous species of social parasites.[49]

Applied biology and emergent Nazism came into contact through forestry, as delousing helped to sustain right-wing nationalism under turbulent conditions. General von Kahr agreed that the Bavarian delousing and gas disinfestation troops should continue during 1920 with the technical support of the entomologist Karl

[44] GSTA Rep 76 VIII B Nr 3776, Prussian Ministry of the Interior meeting, 10 Mar. 1919. Nr 3768, decree of 22 Nov. 1919.

[45] A. Hitler, *Mein Kampf* (London, 1974), 183; Eksteins, *Rites*, 308; I. Kershaw, *Hitler* (Harmondsworth, 1998), 96–7, 102–5.

[46] Bayerisches Hauptstaatsarchiv Abt IV (Kriegsarchiv) (hereafter BHK), for Hitler see Kriegsministerium Referatsakten nos. 309, 314; MKr 10112 Fleckfieber 1914–19, telegram of 16 Mar. 1919. on typhus among returning soldiers; MKr 10113 MdI, Med-Abt 3 June 1919, report by Dr Furst; 23 June 1919 Fleckfieber in Lager Lechfeld.

[47] BHK MKr 10059 Gesundheitliche Massnahmen 1919–21, reports of 18 May 1919, 1 June 1919, 19 July 1919. MKr 10067 Report of Gesundheitskommission I Armee Korps 18 June 1919.

[48] Hitler, *Mein Kampf*, 195–202; E. Jäckel, *Hitler. Sämtliche Aufzeichnungen 1905–1924* (Stuttgart, 1980), 176 for Hitler's speech in Salzburg 7 Aug. 1920. Kershaw, *Hitler*, 121–5.

[49] A. Bein, 'The Jewish Parasite. Notes on the Semantics of the Jewish Problem with Special Reference to Germany', *Leo Baeck Institute Yearbook*, 9 (1964) 3–40.

Escherich in Munich.[50] Escherich's brother Georg had worked with Hase on fumigation while in charge of the Bialowies forest in eastern Poland, which was steeped in nationalist myths. The German occupation had combined rapacious logging, depleting forest animals including the legendary bison, with gassing experiments by Hase, intent on sanitizing the great forest. A team of botanists also assessed the damage that poison gas could do to vegetation around Vilna and Baranowitschi (see plate 5).[51] Georg Escherich returned to Bavaria to organize an armed militia to support a militant conservative centrism, known as the *Organisation Escherich* or *Orgesch*. His more academic brother Karl initially supported the Orgesch movement, but after it was banned by the Allies, he joined the Deutsche Arbeiterpartei in 1922–3 prior to the Putsch of November 1923. Although Escherich did not rejoin the Nazi Party when it was refounded in 1925, during the Third Reich he could claim that he had once been close to Hitler.[52]

In 1919 the official view was that the use of poison gas for disinfestation would bring the public benefits of the wartime development of poison gases, while allowing the chemical industry a market to deploy its new products. Pesticide development could secretly sustain military poison gas research.[53] DEGESCH was founded in April 1919 and became a commercial organization under Reich control. Haber resigned from TASCH, being succeeded by Walter Heerdt, an innovative chemist with American experience of gas fumigation. In 1919 Haber became Reich Commissar for Pest Control, a position that lasted until DEGESCH became an independent company in 1920. Heerdt then became Director of DEGESCH, maintaining good relations with Haber, as well as seeking US approval for innovative fumigation techniques.[54]

Direct state control was replaced by regulation. A government commissar was to attend all DEGESCH board meetings, and the residual TASCH (now under the control of the Reich Economic Ministry) initiated research financed from DEGESCH profits. Investment in DEGESCH was secured from Degussa and the

---

[50] BHK MKr 10067 Desinfektionswesen 1919–21, Vertrag of Regierung Oberbayern with Stadt München 24 Mar. 1920.

[51] S. Schama, *Landscape and Memory* (London, 1995), 48, 64–5; BAK 168/172 report of 21 May 1918 indicating that gas did not damage vegetation apart from pine trees.

[52] The BDC file for Escherich contains only a membership card of the Reichsschaft Hochschullehrer im Nationalsozialistischen Lehrer-Bund, dated 1 Dec. 1933. Munich University Archives, Akten des Akademischen Senats der Universität München betr. Karl Escherich, Personalakte E II N, protest by Escherich 27 Nov. 1946, 2 Jan. 1947 on DAP membership, 8 Mar. 1948 legal defense concerning DAP membership, Escherich 12 Mar. 1948.

[53] Rittmeister Dueb was Haber's key contact in the founding of TASCH. BAP 15.01/9367 betr die Deutsche Gesellschaft für Schädlingsbekämpfung 1918–22, Reichskanzler, Staatssekretär des Reichswirtschaftsamtes 23 Apr. 1918. Entwurf einer Verordnung über die Schädlingsbekämpfung mit hochgiftigen Stoffen von Januar 1919: Begründung. Bericht über die Gründungsverhandlung einer Deutschen Gesellschaft für Schädlingsbekämpfung vom 5. Oktober 1918.

[54] Stoltzenberg, *Haber*, 460–1; W. Rasch, '80 Jahre Mehlmotten—40 Jahre Mehlmottenbekämpfung. Ein geschichtlicher Rückblick', *Die Mühle*, 93/25 (1956), 349–50. NAW RG 90 Records of the Public Health Service, box 384, Heerdt to Surgeon General US Public Health, 31 Oct. 1923.

Holzverkohlungsindustrie AG Konstanz, both taking a quarter share; eighth shares were taken by the chemical firms BASF, Hoechst, and Bayer; further holdings were acquired by AGFA, the Casella dye works, and by three smaller chemical factories. In May 1920 DEGESCH moved its operations to Frankfurt am Main as a centre of the chemical industry.[55] The company became a purely commercial undertaking, rather than the national institution as envisaged by Haber. After financial difficulties during the inflation Degussa became the sole owner in 1922, formalizing the transition from the war economy to the Weimar Republic.[56]

Degussa was careful not to rely on any single source of HCN. Despite the break-up of the Habsburg Empire, Degussa retained close relations with the Kaliwerke Kolin, and by 1919 it held a fifth of the shares in this key supplier.[57] Degussa had its own production plant in Frankfurt, but as manufacture in the city centre was considered dangerous, production was scaled down, leaving DEGESCH to concentrate on marketing and gassing.[58] Supplies from the Dessau sugar refiners and Kolin ensured that the rapidly expanding demand for hydrocyanic acid could be met during the boom years of the 1920s and in the changed circumstances of the Third Reich.[59]

Gas warfare has been interpreted as a modernistic cultural impulse equivalent to cubism in modern art.[60] The spread of poison gas for pest control was plotted in terms of cubic metres gassed, as if the nation consisted of modernistic spatial structures requiring sealing and gassing. TASCH disinfested in all 3,102,000 cubic metres of national space; in the one and a half years between April 1919 and December 1920 DEGESCH carried out gassings over an area of 11,567,000 cubic metres, nearly nine million of which were military barracks. By 1920 it was calculated that 21 million cubic metres had been fumigated with hydrocyanic acid. The vast totals provided an accounting method as the gassing was charged by the cubic metre.[61] National space was chemically dissected and subjected to medical regulation.

Haber's prestige was boosted in 1919 by the award of the Nobel Prize for chemistry—one of three Nobel prizes for German scientists in 1918 and 1919 making plain the Swedish displeasure at the allied boycott of German science. While French newspapers denounced the award to such an *exterminateur*, the German press celebrated a national victory.[62] Haber had discovered how to manufacture ammonia by combining nitrogen and (significantly for HCN research) hydrogen,

---

[55] *Frankfurter Zeitung*, 424 (11 June 1920); Stoltzenberg, *Haber*, 459–60; Szöllösi-Janze, *Haber*, 391.

[56] *Sonne und Mond*, 146.

[57] Degussa Direktion 5/26 Bl. 170 on Degussa's shareholding of 2,013 out of 10,000 shares in Kaliwerke Kolin. 5/29 Bl. 35 for the Zykon B purification process from molasses.

[58] Degussa Direktion DL 5/28 Bl. 135 in 1924 the Dessau sugar refinary supplied 76 tons of hydrocyanic acid and 23 tons were produced in Frankfurt.

[59] H. Schlosser, 'Geschichte der DEGESCH', unpub. MS 1961.

[60] Eksteins, *Rites*, 161–9.

[61] K. B. Lehmann, 'Bestehen gerechtfertigte hygienische Bedenken gegen die Verwendung von Blausäure und blausäurehaltigen Mitteln (Zyklon) als Vernichtungsmittel für Ungeziefer im grossen (Entwesung)', *MMW* 67 (1920), 1517–20.

[62] G. Metzler, ' "Welch ein deutscher Sieg!". Die Nobelpreise von 1919 im Spannungsfeld von Wissenschaft, Politik und Gesellschaft', *Vierteljahreshefte für Zeitgeschichte*, 44 (1996), 173–200.

thereby remedying shortages of nitrogenous fertilizers; his concern for Germany's national survival resulted in taking a key role in the founding of the *Notgemeinschaft der deutschen Wissenschaft* (NDW, the Emergency Association for German Science) in 1920 as a national science funding body drawing on state and private funds. Haber's backing for research into pesticides was in the spirit of his commitment to a national science policy. In February 1919 he brought together at the Kaiser Wilhelm Institute for Physical Chemistry the two leading experts in hydrocyanic acid and pest control: Flury and Hase were drafted into a new pharmacological-zoological department, and the ever resourceful Haber found pest-infested woodland at Guben for gas experiments. Haber's pesticide research was a covert way of developing poison gases, as the presence of the inter-allied control commission from 1920 made it politic to disperse his research team. Haber found Hase a niche at the restructured Biologische Reichsanstalt; he arranged a field station for Hase's insect experiments and suggested that he devise gas bombs against insects. Haber secured funds for Hase from the Reich Ministry of Trade and DEGESCH, and from 1923 to 1924 arranged secret finance for Hase's laboratory from the War Ministry. Cooperation continued between DEGESCH, Flury (by then at the University of Würzburg), and Hase at the Biologische Reichsanstalt on chemical weapons and poison gas research.[63]

Several technical handicaps had to be overcome before the new version of HCN could be approved for distribution on a wide scale. Flury was concerned that the great defect in hydrocyanic acid was its lack of a smell; so that the gas could be detected by humans and animals before succumbing to its deadly poison, he suggested that an acrid smell be added. Such a warning agent marked a decisive break with the chemical warfare programme. Flury and Hase chose methyl ester of cyanoformic acid (Zyankohlensäure-methylester) which was itself poisonous. Their abbreviation for the new compound was 'Cyklon'. They showed that Cyklon was as toxic as hydrocyanic acid when tested on insects, but that it left the quality of grain and other foodstuffs unimpaired.[64] Although it was still stored in a fluid form and costly to produce, the modified gas was simple to use. Various mixtures were marketed under the brand names 'Zyklon' (the name was registered on 20 October 1920) and 'Ventox'; although Ventox contained less of the warning substance, the Allies permitted its use for disinfesting mills. In 1922 Heerdt patented the process by which the gas was soaked up by diatomite (a silicious quartz) and stored in crystalline form in tin cans rather than as a fluid. This patent meant that the gas was easy to transport, store, and use.[65] Heerdt proclaimed Zyklon as a scientific miracle, arising from teamwork between chemists, zoologists, and physicians.[66]

---

[63] Stoltzenberg, *Haber*, 346–7, 448, 458, 465–6; Szöllösi-Janze, 'Von der Mehlmotte zum Holocaust', 675–6; id., *Haber*, 453–67.

[64] F. Flury and A. Hase, 'Blausäurederivate zur Schädlingsbekämpfung', *MMW* 67 (1920), 779–80; Peters, *Blausäure*, 56–61. The formula of Cyclon A was CN COO CH₃.

[65] W. Heerdt, 'Die Anfänge der Zyklon-Fabrikation', *20 Jahre*, 18–19; *Sonne und Mond*, 146–7; STAB 4, 21–491 Durchgasung von Schiffen.

[66] W. Heerdt, 'Zyklon Verfahren', *Der Praktische Desinfektor*, 13/2 (1921), 9–11.

Medical officials imposed restrictions on HCN use for delousing, as occupational hygiene experts were concerned at the high number of fatalities. In November 1918 ten workers died in a recently gassed building, and children were killed after sleeping in a room where the bedding had not been properly aired; deaths resulted when the paper used to seal rooms was gas permeable; persons deemed to be suicidal had entered the buildings despite warning notices, and there were cases when inhabitants of neighbouring appartments had been found close to death. Some medical officials attacked Zyklon as so unsafe that it should be banned. Others defended Zyklon as a safety measure overcoming the risks of HCN which caused large numbers of fatal accidents.[67]

Although the Bavarian authorities in 1920 objected to DEGESCH having a national monopoly over HCN, both sides agreed that medical and biological experts should be in control. The Bavarians argued that there should be free competition with other firms, and accused DEGESCH of irresponsibly supplying highly dangerous cyanide compounds, resulting in fatal accidents. Sustained Bavarian sniping against the DEGESCH consortium as a single national monopoly forced a move to devolve regulation from the Reich to the various state authorities. Escherich's dispute with Haber encouraged the Bavarian government to defend its autonomy in the sphere of pest control. From 1920 the Bavarian authorities encouraged local firms to undertake gassings. Moreover, Bavarian officials claimed to be fully competent in evaluating hazards and in providing training. The Bavarian state looked to Escherich to supervise procedures and training. Representations by the southern states meant that by 1921 a Süddeutsche Gesellschaft für Schädlingsbekämpfung and a Württemberg company were granted the concession of using hydrocyanic acid on equivalent terms to DEGESCH.[68]

The Bavarian opposition to the Prussian monopoly of HCN through DEGESCH prompted the professor of hygiene K. B. Lehmann to examine the records of DEGESCH in 1920 concerning twenty-eight fatalities. He condemned the use of the gas by private individuals (as when a teacher killed himself attempting to disinfect his wardrobe) or when inadequately trained, equipped, or supervised personnel carried out gassings. Lehmann concluded that if Zyklon had been used instead of HCN, accidents and deaths would have been avoided.[69] Hahn pointed out that inadequately aired clothing could contain pockets of hydrocyanic acid. Because of the solubility of the gas in water, it could dissolve in damp environments, and so the fumes could be released some time after a gassing occurred. Flury, Hase, and Heerdt lobbied the Reich Health Office in favour of Zyklon, and the balance of

---

[67] BAP 15.01/9367 RGA memo 25 Nov. 1919; Führer, 'Die Blausäurevergiftung und ihre Behandlung', *DMW*, (1919), 847; 'Gerichtsentscheidung betreffend Blausäure', *Zeitschift für Desinfektions- und Gesundheitswesen*, 22 (1930), 69–70; BAK 168/262 betr. Blausäure; Vergiftungen, report by E. Gilbrecht, 'Gasvergiftungen bei den Ungezieferbekämpfung', *Tag* (11 Jan. 1922), no. 9.

[68] BHSTA ML 2149 Schädlingsbekämpfung mit hochgiftigen Stoffen 1920–9.

[69] K. B. Lehmann, 'Bestehen gerechtfertigte hygienische Bedenken gegen die Verwendung von Blausäure und blausäurehaltigen Mitteln (Zyklon) als Vernichtungsmittel für Ungeziefer im grossen (Entwesung)', *MMW* 67 (1920), 1517–20. The *MMW* was published by K. B. Lehmann's brother, the Freikorps activist and medical publisher, Julius Lehmann.

medical opinion began to favour the new gases.[70] By way of contrast, the British Ministry of Health in 1922 regarded HCN as dangerous and experimental.[71]

Although by June 1921 fifty deaths occurred from the use of hydrocyanic acid, DEGESCH officials and Flury argued that numbers would have been much higher if Zyklon had been made available to the despised rat-catching *Kammerjäger*.[72] Conflict erupted between independent rat-catchers and disinfectors, and disciples of a modern industrial approach to pest control. The *Kammerjäger* had cultivated a rather folkloric image as a 'free order', and now felt their livelihood was under threat. The availability of dangerous gases raised questions of whether this occupation should be subject to state control and examination, merged with state-examined disinfectors, or whether they should be banned from using poison gas. The disinfectors agitated against the *Kammerjäger*, and they contrasted the advanced regulations surrounding agricultural and forest pest control to the 'backward' control of human pests. The Reich authorities conceded that establishing a monopoly for the national pest control agency would harm the independent *Kammerjäger*, who were skilled in using poisons like arsenic and strychnine. These pest control workers, recognizing a threat to their occupation, agitated for training in the use of hydrocyanic acid. In 1921 the *Verband Deutscher Ungezieferbekämpfungsbetriebe*, backed by the German National Party (DVP) and by scientists, denounced the *Kammerjäger* as wasteful, quacks, and deceivers. Hase argued that pests inflicted immense financial damage on the nation, and that vast sums were expended on useless pest control measures. Zyklon was a catalyst in the drive to attain state-employed, and scientifically trained disinfectors.[73]

Disinfectors agitated for state certification in order to guarantee their status. At the same time they allied with academic experts in applied entomology and poison gas technology. The Reich Health Office considered restricting control of disease-carrying pests to state-examined disinfectors, who should only be allowed to handle Zyklon, hydrocyanic acid, and other poison gases. The medical authorities had much experience with the thorny question of regulating the occupations of physicians, apothecaries, and midwives, and saw the advantages of elevating the disinfector to the status of a state-regulated occupation.[74] The state thus took on a key role in supervising the use of pesticides.

The Reich Health Office debated whether hydrocyanic acid was too dangerous to include in its revised delousing regulations. While advocates of sulphur dioxide fumigation recommended that HCN be omitted, Hetsch (the medical official of the Prussian War Ministry) insisted that it was less damaging than sulphur dioxide.

[70] Only Freymuth advised against the gas. BAK R 168/266 RGA meeting of 15 June 1921.

[71] PRO FD1/1361 Fumigation with hydrocyanic gas, Ministry of Health note of 10 June 1922.

[72] BAP 15.01/9367 RGA betr. die Verwendung von Blausäure, Cyklon und schwefeliger Säure zur Schädlingsbekämpfung 16 June 1921.

[73] BAP 15.01/9160 Gottstein to Prussian Minister of Welfare 8 July 1921; W. Rimpau, 'Entstehung, Verhütung und Bekämpfung der Infektionskrankheiten im allgemeinen', Rimpau, Rapmund, Sannemann, and Bundt (eds.), *Die Infektionskrankheiten* (Berlin, 1928), 75–7.

[74] BAP 15.01/9160 betr Regelung des Kammerjägergewerben, 1921–8, President of the RGA 5 Apr. 1921. Meeting of 11 June 1923 betr. Einführung eines Befähigungsnachweises für Kammerjäger.

HCN was included in the regulations, with the proviso that special safety measures were required.[75] The next few years saw a battle fought over the merits of the two gases. A victory for hydrocyanic acid would guarantee the fortunes of DEGESCH, and be a blow against the *Kammerjäger*. In 1921 Hase pronounced that Zyklon far outstripped sulphur dioxide in its capacity to kill.[76] Opposition continued: the epidemic prevention unit of the Berlin Kommandatur favoured sulphur dioxide rather than the more dangerous HCN.[77] While the Reich medical authorities endorsed the use of both gases as legitimate, hydrocyanic acid was subject to tough Reich controls. There was a general prohibition on poison gases in January 1919, although exemptions for HCN were granted to the army, navy, state research institutes, and to the TASCH organization.[78] In January 1920 it was agreed that while it was too expensive for a doctor to attend all gassings, the district medical officer should be informed, and medical officials would examine all DEGESCH personnel.[79] State medical authorities thereby gained control over poison gas disinfestation.

State controls were tightened when hydrocyanic acid was one of eight approved delousing substances listed in the *Reichsgesetzblatt* of 1920. The gas was banned with the exception of use on Reich property, in scientific research in state institutes, or by DEGESCH. The prohibition meant that medical officers had the power to conduct examinations in the use of gas equipment, and to grant exemptions from the ban.[80] The Reich Health Office rejected demands from other pest control organizations, and condemned the craft skills of the rat-catchers as unscientific.[81] In July 1922 the Reich Ministry of Food and Agriculture confirmed the policy of prohibiting the use of Zyklon gas except by special licence, and these discretionary powers were devolved to the Prussian Ministry of Welfare which revised the regulations in October 1923. For commercial and safety reasons, the codes regulating the use of the gas were kept strictly secret.

Demilitarization and clandestine rearmament were in curious symbiosis. The chemist Hugo Stoltzenberg had from 1917 worked with Haber on explosives research, and, after researches into cancer, undertook at Haber's instigation in 1920 destruction of stockpiles of explosives. Stoltzenberg had obtained the contract from the Military Inter-Allied Control Commission to dismantle the German poison gas equipment. He was slow to carry out this task, and he saw (like Haber) the opportunities of agricultural pest control. He founded a firm based from 1923

[75] BAK R 86/1040 Bd 6 RGR Besprechung 30 May 1919.

[76] BAP 15.01/9367 RGA betr. die Verwendung von Blausäure, Cyklon und schwefeliger Säure zur Schädlingsbekämpfung 16 June 1921.

[77] BAP 15.01/9160 RGA betr. Schädlingsbekämpfung mit Blausäure und schwefeliger Säure 18 Mar. 1921.

[78] 'Reichsverordnung über die Schädlingsbekämpfung mit hochgiftigen Stoffen', *Reichsgesetzblatt*, 31 (29 Jan. 1919) 160, 165; (1920) 151.

[79] BAP 15.01/9160 Besprechung über Massnahmen gegen Vergiftung durch Blausäuredämpfe bei Durchgasungen 20 Jan. 1920.

[80] 'Anweisung zur Bekämpfung des Fleckfiebers (Flecktyphus). Amtliche Ausgabe', *Reichsgesetzblatt* (3 Mar. 1920), 46; *Reichsgesetzblatt* (10 June 1920), 1441.

[81] BAP 15.01/9367 RGA betr. Blausäure zur Schädlingsbekämpfung 23 Mar. 1921.

in Hamburg, the Chemische Fabrik Stoltzenberg, and circumvented the Versailles restrictions by claiming that he was producing pesticides, while continuing production of poison gas and gas protection equipment like gas masks and filters for military purposes.[82] As Haber appreciated, the manufacture of gases for hygienic uses could be a convenient cover for the covert manufacture of armaments and military training. The aerial spraying of crops and forests, pioneered by Escherich, was taken over by the army, which formed a special forest protection air squadron, and motorized sprays were introduced.[83] The German army continued to sponsor secret laboratory tests of an array of gases throughout the 1920s.[84] Despite the strong Allied post-war controls, military backing for poison gas continued.

By 1923 the reserves of Zyklon were exhausted. The military commission of the Entente prohibited DEGESCH from manufacturing Zyklon: Article 171 of the Treaty of Versailles banned 'the use of asphyxiating, poisonous and other gases and all analogous liquids' in Germany, and the chemicals added to make what later became known as Zyklon A were prohibited. Henkel, the washing powder manufacturer of Persil (for which Degussa produced perborate of sodium), was among those handicapped by the ban.[85] The Chemical Warfare Committee of the British War Office continued to monitor the development of various lachrymators added to HCN.[86] Cyanogen chloride was tried as an ingredient of Zyklon, although this damaged metals. In 1924 DEGESCH (thanks to the efforts of its chemist Bruno Tesch and Flury) introduced a new formula known as Zyklon B (distinguishing this gas from the banned original formula).[87] Chlorine and bromide were added as lachrymators, and a stabilizer prevented polymerization. An advantage was that the warning indicator which served as an irritant also stimulated the respiration of insects.[88] Different strengths for use against various parasites like rats and lice were tested at the Degussa laboratories, but problems remained with the warning agent.[89] As the gas did not destroy bacteria, experiments were carried out to combine Zyklon with a bactericidal disinfectant. German public health armed itself with a powerful but dangerous weapon against lice.

The Reich authorities claimed a national stake in the utilization of the gas. In September 1920 the Reich Commissioner for Import and Export licences refused

---

[82] Curriculum vitae compiled by D. Stoltzenberg, and letter of D. Stoltzenberg to the author 31 Dec. 1994; W. Steed, 'The Future of Warfare', *The Nineteenth Century and After*, 106 (1934), 129–40, 132–6.

[83] Escherich, *Leben und Forschen*, 305–6.

[84] I. Kästner, 'Die medizinische Diskussion über die Gaskriegsfolgen des Ersten Weltkrieges', '*Medizin für den Staat—Medizin für den Krieg*' (Husum, 1994), 45–53.

[85] BAP 15.01/9367 RGA betr. die Verwendung von Blausäure, Cyklon und schwefeliger Säure zur Schädlingsbekämpfung 16 June 1921.

[86] PRO FD 1/1361 Fumigation with Hydrocyanic Acid.

[87] IfZ, *Trial by a Military Court of Bruno Tesch, Joachim Drosihn and K. Weinbacher on Friday, 1st March, 1946*, 3rd day, p. 17, cross examination of Tesch (transcript also in PRO WO 235/83). The date given for the development of Zyklon B was 1923, but other sources suggest 1924, e.g. BAP 15.01/9368 DEGESCH to Reichministerium für Ernährung und Landwirtschaft 29 Apr. 1926.

[88] C. M. Hasselmann, 'Zwei Jahre Zyklon-B—die Entwesungsmethode', *MMW* (1925) 96–9; Pressac, *Auschwitz*, 18.

[89] Stoltzenberg, *Haber*, 462.

permission for the export of sodium cyanide for use by Hoover's American Relief Administration in Poland. The Polish public health official Rajchman was keen to use hydrocyanic acid to disinfest railway carriages. The Germans feared that this would benefit Poland, and run counter to their national interest. However, scientists at the Kaiser Wilhelm Institutes argued that effective delousing in Poland would protect Germany against typhus epidemics. On 30 April 1920 Hase demonstrated to an American Relief Administration delegation in Berlin the different gas delousing methods involved in using HCN and Zyklon gases.[90]

In the event hydrocyanic acid was used in Polish detention and refugee camps (including the Oświeçim camp for refugees from the partition of Teschen) under US supervision. The procedure was found to be expensive, dangerous, and (predictably) ineffective against bacteria. But Eastern Europe offered the prospect of a valuable market, especially after Zyklon was patented; Haber promoted the benefits of the new Zyklon gas in Eastern Europe during 1921.[91] The German famine relief expedition to Russia in 1921 came equipped to test Zyklon. By the mid-1920s, Tesch and Stabenow gained the concession for marketing the gas to Danzig and Poland. The Saratov Microbiological Institute in the Volga region endorsed the use of the gas against typhus.[92] Zyklon came to be regarded as an effective solution to diseases from the east.

iii. Zyklon Goes Global

The Allied powers like the Germans sealed their borders against diseased Eastern Europeans. In Britain the Aliens Act of 1919 permitted medical inspection, cleansing, and disinfection of aliens, and was applied to all arrivals from Poland.[93] The tightening of US immigration quotas intensified pressures on European borders to exclude undesirables. Senior officials of the US Public Health Service kept a vigilant eye on European epidemics. Hugh Cumming (soon to be appointed Surgeon General) raised the alarm of typhus epidemics in Russia and Poland in September 1919. That Cumming joined the interallied commission in Poland to control typhus was consistent with his role in enforcing immigration restrictions. US sanitary officials stepped up their interventive policies: Rupert Blue, after eight years as Surgeon General, took charge of Service operations in Europe from 1920 until 1924, maintaining an office in Paris, from where he inspected European port health installa-

---

[90] BAK R 86/1040 Bd 7 I. G. Bräumüller to RGA 2 Sept. 1920; Hase statement 31 Aug. 1920; Addison papers, box 61 file 532 *International Health Conference*, 66.

[91] Stoltzenberg, *Haber*, 460–1. Heerdt and Haber undertook this eastern tour.

[92] Cornebise, *Typhus and Doughboys*, 96–9, 115; STAB 4, 21–493 Tesch und Stabenow, B. Tesch, 'Ueber Blausäure Durchgasungen und über Reizstoffzusätze zur Blausäure', *Desinfektion*, 10 (Mar. 1925), 1–4 cited as offprint; STAB 4, 21–491 Deutsche Gesellschaft für Schädlingsbekämpfung, C. M. Hasselmann, 'Zur Frage der Ueberwachung von Blausäure und Zyklondurchgasungen durch den beamteten Arzt', *Zeitschrift für Medizinalbeamte* (1925), 921–46.

[93] PRO MH 55/366 Medical Inspection of Aliens, 'Distribution of Typhus Fever Throughout the World'. Policy notes of Newman and Reece.

tions and fumigation procedures. A US Public Health representative was to be drafted into Hamburg during 1923. British and French port health measures were tightened up for those coming from Eastern Europe. Returning American soldiers were thoroughly deloused to rid them of 'cooties' (the slang for lice)—a gigantic glass model of a louse demonstrated the European menace in the New York Museum of Natural History.[94]

The US Public Health Service was strongly in favour of hydrocyanic acid. It developed an air-jet hydrocyanic acid sprayer, and devised a rat-proofing strategy, which gave much attention to the behaviour of rats and the design of ships.[95] The United States received dwindling numbers of immigrants from Eastern Europe. Instead, the US supported economic and medical reconstruction programmes in the Central European successor states, hoping that these would become model democracies. By 1925 it was observed that the 5,000 migrants per day who once had passed through Hamburg had dwindled to an average of 330 per day. Whereas in 1913 93 per cent (of 192,700 migrants) were from Russia and Galicia, in 1924 67 per cent (of 50,100 migrants) were Germans. Consequently, medical controls were relaxed and facilities in Hamburg became more luxurious: the quarantine pavilions were thoroughly disinfected using Zyklon gas and converted into hotels.[96]

Zyklon was distributed under licence by Tesch and Stabenow, the 'International Company for Pest Extermination' in Hamburg. Bruno Tesch was until April 1920 an assistant at Haber's Kaiser Wilhelm Institute for Physical Chemistry.[97] After working with DEGESCH on the development of Zyklon, disputes over its patenting in 1923 led to a partnership with Paul Stabenow, and by 1927 Tesch was in effective control of the firm.[98] Tesch and Stabenow also marketed products of the 'T-Gas' Company for Pest Eradication, a Degussa offshoot which specialized in domestic fumigation.[99] Tesch and Stabenow thrived because the development of Zyklon B provided a powerful new means for fumigating ships—between 1922 and 1924 150 ships were disinfested by poison gas in Hamburg.[100] Here was an international market opportunity: between the first gassing of the cruiser *Bosnia* in June 1917 and 1932, 5,000 ships underwent hydrocyanic acid gassing in German ports.[101] The shipping companies which had profited from the human cargoes of transmigrants before the war became major backers of the new gas. In May 1923 the Reich Health Office compared the traditional approaches by ship *Kammerjäger* using sulphuric acid (which was less poisonous to humans) to the new total eradication

[94] NAW RG 90 Records of the Public Health Service Central File 1897–1923, file 2126; Cumming telegram 18 Sept. 1919 concerning typhus in Poland; newspaper clipping on 'New Discoveries about Cooties: the Soldiers Pest'; Rupert Blue, notes on Hamburg port health, Aug. 1922. File 3847 Heerdt to US Surgeon General 31 Oct. 1923, US Consulate Hamburg April 1923.
[95] Williams, *Public Health Service*, 359–63.
[96] STAH II F6 Bd III Bl 148. Hafenarzt 1: 213 Bd 4
[97] IfZ, *Trial by a Military Court of Bruno Tesch, Joachim Drosihn and K. Weinbacher on Friday, 1st March*, 1946, 3rd day, p. 9.
[98] The firm's trade name was TESTA, and the trademark was a wind-blown maritime flag.
[99] Kogon, *Giftgas*, 282.
[100] BAP 15.01/11696 Desinfektion der Schiffe 1910–27 memorandum of RGA President 29 May 1923.
[101] Peters, *Blausäure*, 29–31; Degussa Direktion DL 5/20 Bl. 15, 8 June 1917.

procedures using Zyklon.[102] The superiority of Zyklon needed to be demonstrated over sulphuric acid gas and the Nocht-Giemsa process using carbon monoxide gas. After some hesitation the North German Lloyd company persuaded Bremen's port medical officer that hydrocyanic acid was quick, cheap, effective, and damaged neither the cargoes nor the paintwork of ships. Reich Health Office and port medical officers were invited to observe an experimental gassing with Zyklon on the steamer *Hameln*.[103] In March 1924 Tesch and Stabenow announced that Zyklon was a new, fully effective, and scientific means of pest eradication. But the debate between carbon monoxide and other gases continued to rage: tests were carried out using combinations of carbon monoxide and aethyloxide on a variety of insect pests.[104]

The early publicity for Zyklon claimed that just a tin opener and a gas mask were needed, but controls turned disinfectors into an auxiliary sanitary police: from November 1924 the Hamburg medical authorities supervised the use of Zyklon, and issued certificates of personal reliability requiring a clean police record.[105] The certificates required that individuals were 'physically and mentally fit' for the use and detection of hydrocyanic acid.[106] A new working code was drawn up by Tesch and Stabenow in consultation with the Hamburg harbour doctor and the director of the disinfection station.[107] Clothing and furniture could be brought to municipally designated gas chambers.[108] Mobile gas chambers mounted on lorries aroused much interest, and the interiors of buses and furniture vans were gassed.[109] State-examined personnel and organizations for the deployment of Zyklon thrived in Weimar Germany.

Great claims were made for the improved version of Zyklon: it was devastatingly effective, eradicating not only lice but also louse eggs, and left clothing and possessions unharmed. Zyklon's advantages included that it was deadly for rats and insects, it did not damage goods, there was no fire risk, and it was cheap in comparison with sulphuric acid. Its development involved scientists from many disciplines: chemists, pharmacologists, biochemists, entomologists, and botanists were

---

[102]   BAP 15.01/11696 Desinfektion der Schiffe 1910–27 memorandum of RGA President 29 May 1923.

[103]   STAB 4,21–491 NDL to Tjaden, 17 Oct. 1923; Tjaden to Bumm of Reich Health Office 9 June 1924; Bumm to Tjaden 29 May 1923; Tjaden to Bumm 5 June 1923.

[104]   Bayer-Archiv, IG-Fremdfirmen 6.14 Bd 1, Verstärkung der Wirksamkeit des Nocht-Giemsa Gases bei der Schiffsentrattung, 14 Mar. 1933. DEGESCH to IG-Farbenindustrie Werk Elberfeld 2 Aug. 1933.

[105]   STAH II J 15a Bd 1 betr Schädlingsbekämpfung. Antrag auf Genehmigung der Verwendung vom Blausäure Bl 95, 113. Hafenarzt I Verordnung und Arbeitsvorschrift für die Anwendung von Blausäure.

[106]   'Verordnung zur Ausführung der Verordnung über Schädlingsbekämpfung mit hochgiftigen Stoffen vom 25. März 1931', *Reichsgesetzblatt* (1931) 83; STAH II J 15a Bd 2 Bl 34 certificate of the suitability of Bruno Tesch to use Zyklon gas, 10 Oct. 1931; STAB 4, 21–491 Deutsche Gesellschaft für Schädlingsbekämpfung.

[107]   Solbrig, 'Die Desinfektorenschulen in Deutschland', *Zeitschrift für Desinfektions- und Gesundheitswesen*, 22 (1930), 492–6.

[108]   Schwarz, 'Entwicklung', 396; Beusch, 'Blausäureentwesungen der städtischen Desinfektionsanstalt in Königsberg i. Pr.', *Zeitschrift für Desinfektions- und Gesundheitswesen*, 22 (1930), 721–6.

[109]   Id., 'Bekämpfung der Gesundheitsschädlinge durch Blausäure', *Zeitschrift für Desinfektion*, 21 (1929), 41; 'Berichte über Blausäure-Entwesungskammern', *Zeitschrift für Desinfektion*, 21 (1929), 111 for pictures; G. Peters, 'Begasungsanlagen', *Zeitschrift für hygienische Zoologie*, 30 (1938), 178–87.

mobilized to work with military, state, municipal, and commercial interests. An extensive network of companies and technical experts collaborated in refining and disseminating the new gas. The gas was formulated to take account of Allied restrictions on chemical products, and of German safety regulations. DEGESCH marketed the gas internationally, claiming the gas in its refined Zyklon form as an achievement for 'Deutsche Wertarbeit und technische Leistung'.[110]

The formula and legal status of the Flury-DEGESCH patent of Zyklon B remained unsettled during the mid-20s, because the Prussian and Reich authorities were concerned about the instability of the warning agent. Six fatalities had occurred using Zyklon and Ventox since 1921. In 1925 the Prussian Ministry of Welfare did not accept the new Zyklon B as a satisfactory substitute for the old Zyklon. A revised formula was suggested for the back-up warning agent—this was referred to as 'Zyklon C', and had the added advantage that it was available in crystallized form.[111] The Reich Health Office demanded experiments on the permeability of the additives, concerned that Zyklon might seep through walls, whereas the warning lachrymators might not. In return for meeting the requirements of the Reich Health Office, DEGESCH demanded a Reich monopoly for the gas as safer than pure HCN. Protracted negotiations and experiments involved Hase at the Biologische Reichsanstalt and at Degussa's 'Zyklon laboratory' for control of plant and chemical pests.[112] After fumigating mills with Zyklon, the suspicion arose that workers could suffer from intoxication and muscle fatigue. In 1925 a hundred workers regularly exposed to Zyklon were screened to determine changes to their blood haemoglobin and other constituents, although no lasting pathological effect was detected.[113]

The Reich Health Office was reluctant to ban pure HCN, as it was dissatisfied with the safety of the reformulated Zyklon, and it did not wish DEGESCH to have a monopoly. In April 1926 the Reich authorities finally endorsed the new formula Zyklon.[114] Zyklon rapidly overtook hydrocyanic acid in popularity, and the French withdrawal from the Rhineland provided opportunities for large-scale gassings (as well as racist tirades) in the wake of the occupation. By 1930 13 million cubic metres

---

[110] *DEGESCH. 20 Jahre Schädlingsbekämpfung 1917–1937* (Frankfurt/M., n.d.), 3–12.

[111] The warning agent consisted of 10% chloric picrin (Chlorpikrin) and 3% bromic acid methyl ester (Bromessigsäuremethylester).

[112] Degussa Direktion 5/28 Bl. 106 Besprechung mit RGA Berlin 7 Mar. 1925; 5/29 Bl. 35 Über die Besichtigung der Zyklon B-Station und die Versuchen mit Zyklon B in Dessau am 16. Januar 1925. Bl. 150 report of 23 July 1925 concerning the Zylon B department. IW i.11/3 Erweiterung des Versuchslaboratoriums, 9 Feb. 1923; BAK R 168/268 Zyklon, Hase to Biologische Reichsanstalt, 4 Feb. 1925.

[113] C. M. Hasselmann, 'Das Blutbild beim Arbeitern mit Blausäure und Zyklon-B. Eine gewerbehygienische Studie', *Archiv für experimentelle Pathologie und Pharmakologie*, 108 (1925), 106–20.

[114] BAP 15.01/9368 President of the Reich Health Office to the Minister of the Interior 30 Jan. 1925; Niederschrift über die vom 22. bis 24. Juni von den Referenten Geheimrat Professor Dr Spitta und Dr A. Müller angeführte Dienstreise nach Frankfurt am Main. DEGESCH to RMdI 4 May 1926; RMdI to Reichministerium für Ernährung und Landwirtschaft 16 Apr. 1926; BAP 15.01/9369 Abänderung der Bekanntmachung zur Ausführung der Verordnung über die Schädlingsbekämpfung mit hochgiftigen Stoffen vom 17. Juli 1922, 17 Sept. 1926; Prussian Ministry of Welfare, decree of 7 Apr. 1926.

of German space had been gassed with Zyklon, giving the impression of a thoroughly cleansed national *Lebensraum*.[115]

Zyklon had its competitors. With clandestine backing from the Reichswehr, Stoltzenberg sought to gain official approval as a manufacturer of hydrocyanic acid using the manufacture of pesticides as a smokescreen for his illegal activities. In April 1924 Stoltzenberg complained to the Hamburg authorities that he had not been granted the concession to manufacture hydrocyanic acid. He claimed that if a petroleum burner was used, this would burn the residual gas rendering it safe for personnel. A critic observed that his patent method for the 'destruction of swarms of noxious creatures' with the aid of aircraft and flame-throwers really meant human beings. When tested in 1926, the Hamburg port medical officer condemned Stoltzenberg's liquid gas as liable to explode.[116] On 28 May 1928 one of Stoltzenberg's phosgene storage tanks in Hamburg blew up—eleven people were killed and several hundred were injured. From December 1926 there were Western suspicions of German rearmament with the Reichswehr developing chemical warfare.[117]

The instability of Zyklon meant that the search for a new chemical stabilizer continued, and an IG-Farben-manufactured chemical, carbonic acid methylester, was used. Economic symbiosis with IG-Farben developed, as DEGESCH and IG-Farben scientists co-operated more generally on cyanide-based pesticides. The cartelization of the chemical industry with the formation of IG-Farben in 1925 led to this giant conglomerate taking a holding of 42.5 per cent of DEGESCH shares in exchange for vesting its pesticide interests in DEGESCH; a further 42.5 per cent of the shares were owned by Degussa and 15 per cent were owned by the Theo Goldschmidt company, based in Essen, which invented the ethelyn ester-based insecticides Etox and Cartox. Five out of eleven members of the board of DEGESCH were from IG-Farben.[118] In 1930 Degussa and IG agreed on parity in the arrangements for managing DEGESCH.[119] For its part DEGESCH supplied the manufacturing equipment, the patented odour additive (produced by IG-Farben's Uerdingen plant), and packing material to the licensed producers of Zyklon B: the Dessauer Werke für Zucker und chemische Industrie AG at Friedberg in Hessen and from 1936 to the Kali-Werke of Kolín in Czechoslovakia. There were personal links between these firms: Gerhard Peters, a chemist at the Dessau Works from 1924, transferred to DEGESCH in 1928, and eventually became its managing director during the Second World War.[120]

[115] Schwarz, 'Entwicklung', 307–8.

[116] STAH II J 15a Bd 1 Bl 180, 198–9, 214. BAP 15.01/9367 Bumm to RMdI 16 Mar. 1922; Stoltzenberg to Reichminister für Ernährung und Landwirtschaft 6 Feb. 1922; H. Liepmann, *Death from the Skies. A Study of Gas and Microbial Warfare* (London, 1937), 217.

[117] Liepmann, *Death from the Skies*, 215–19; Haber, *Poisonous Cloud*, 287, 305–6, and 316 for a 1979 explosion in Hamburg at Stoltzenberg's disused chemical dump.

[118] Borkin, *I. G. Farben*, 122; *Sonne und Mond*, 147.

[119] Bayer-Archiv, IG Fremdfirmen 6.14 Bd 1, Vertrag zwischen IG und der Scheideanstalt 30 June 1930.

[120] *Sonne und Mond*, 147; P. Hayes, *Industry and Ideology. IG-Farben in the Nazi Era* (Cambridge, 1987), 361. For the biography of Peters see Degussa Firmenarchiv, Rechtsabteilung, 'Tatsachen zum Thema Zyklon B'.

Although in 1925 Germany signed the Geneva protocol banning chemical, gas, and bacteriological warfare, poison gas for pest eradication assumed a new international importance.[121] DEGESCH's emergence as a holding company acting for powerful corporate interests was confirmed in 1925 when production and distribution were devolved. Heerdt, who patented the storage of Zyklon in crystalline form, joined with a DEGESCH manager, Johann Lingler, to establish a company, known as Heerdt-Lingler (or 'Heli') of Frankfurt. Heli was granted a concession in Southern Germany whereas Tesch and Stabenow ('Testa') handled Zyklon gassings in Northern Europe—the division between Heli and Testa was sustained until 1945.[122] DEGESCH took a 51 per cent share in Heli in 1931, and it became a holding company with both supplies and gassings being undertaken by associated companies in which DEGESCH had a controlling interest. DEGESCH was itself owned by a triumvirate of larger companies. In 1929 an agreement was reached between DEGESCH and Cyanamid, a US corporation, dividing the buoyant world market.[123] US maritime regulations required regular fumigation of ocean liners with HCN, thereby pressuring European states to permit the gas.

The use of hydrocyanic acid gassing for pest control became routine in the 1920s. Sinclair Lewis' Nobel-prizewinning novel *Arrowsmith* heroized an international crusader for wiping out diseases by 'an admirable method of killing rats with hydrocyanic gas'.[124] Degussa expanded into a world company: it established fumigation subsidiaries in Hungary and Spain, and links with US companies like Roessler and Hasslacher and with the British companies ICI, Cynamid Products Company, and the London Fumigation Co. Progressive municipalities proudly installed HCN fumigation machinery.[125] Medical officials became acquainted with the construction and improvization of secure gas chambers, took account of the porosity of materials and temperature fluctuations, and made sure that people in the vicinity would not be gassed. But HCN fumigation continued to result in deaths and trenchant criticisms: two children died in 1935 after Aldershot council arranged a gassing against bedbugs, and bedding was not properly aired.[126]

Despite such hazards, Rajchman's positive view of the gas for Polish typhus prevention prompted the LNHO to support its deployment on a global basis. Zyklon B became internationalized as a result of comparative study tours by port health officers, arranged by the LNHO in 1925 around the Mediterranean and in 1926 around the North Sea and Baltic.[127] In 1926 the Paris International Hygiene Con-

---

[121] W. Deckert, 'Die gesetzlichen Grundlagen der Schädlingsbekämpfung mit Blausäure in den meisten Kulturstaaten', *Zeitschrift für Desinfektions- und Gesundheitswesen*, 22 (1930), 115–31.

[122] *Sonne und Mond*, 147.   [123] Hilberg, *Destruction*, 887–9.

[124] S. Lewis, *Arrowsmith* (New York, 1980), 165.

[125] Degussa IW 57.14./6. IW 57.17./1. For example, Bermondsey filmed the operation of its HCN fumigation chambers.

[126] PRO MH 55/386 Fumigation. Cyanide Fatalities at Aldershot. Report by Dr P. G. Stock, 24 Apr. 1935.

[127] STAB 4, 21–491 Deutsche Gesellschaft für Schädlingsbekämpfung, C. M. Hasselmann, 'Zur Frage der Ueberwachung von Blausäure und Zyklondurchgasungen durch den beamteten Arzt', *Zeitschrift für Medizinalbeamte* (1925), 921–46; R. J. Reece, *English Port Sanitary Administration* (League of Nations Health Organization, n.p., 1924).

vention ratified hydrocyanic acid as a means of rat extermination on board ships. The Office international d'hygiène publique praised the gas as a means of more effective 'deratization' in German harbours.[128] Between 1928 and 1932 the League of Nations Hygiene Organization convened a committee for the experimental study of hydrocyanic acid gassing for the fumigation of ships so as to derive standard procedures.[129] The endorsement by the League of Nations meant that Zyklon gained acceptance on a worldwide basis.

iv. The Cremation Solution

Germany's world lead in sanitary technologies was accompanied by the conviction that cremation was the counterpart of *Lebensraum* ideology: because more space was demanded for the living, the dead were to be hygienically disposed of in a way that was cost-effective, hygienic, rapid, and occupying minimal space. Cremation represented a new type of 'death control', and was a macabre counterpart of the inter-war craze for birth-control, sexual reform, and the medicalization of reproduction with eugenic rationales for screening marriage partners, sterilization and abortion.

Cremationists launched a determined onslaught on the Reich authorities during the First World War. They argued that because of the risks of infectious diseases and pollution of water supplies on the battlefield it would be healthier to cremate rather than bury. The question arose whether mobile crematoria could cope with the mass carnage. The Berlin Cremation Society informed the Prussian War Ministry about a mobile incinerator that had been constructed in Warsaw. The possibility of burning more than one body at once was raised, as military efficiency was now more important than the sanctity of individual life. Another solution mooted was to build cavernous crematoria on the borders of Germany to cope with military casualties. The Prussian military authorities replied that they were concerned about the practicalities of transportation and of the time taken to burn a corpse.[130]

Towards the end of the war cremationists mounted a vigorous campaign for national legislation in order to remove disadvantages on cremation as opposed to burial. The dawn of republican equality aroused expectations that cremation would attain equal status to burial. By 1919 the larger cremation societies discussed

[128] GSTA Rep 76 VIII B Nr 3460, die allgemeine Vorschriften über die gesundheitliche Behandlung der Seeschiffe in den deutschen Häfen, 1906–30, OIHP to German ambassador, Paris, requesting reports on German harbours, 25 July 1928.
[129] 'Commission on the Fumigation of Ships. History and Preliminary Work—Report', *Quarterly Bulletin of the Health Organisation*, 1 (1932), 208–32.
[130] GSTA Rep 76 VIII B Nr 3391, Leichenverbrennung, 'Feuerbestattung im Kriege', *Vossische Zeitung* (8 Oct. 1914). *Deutsche Tageszeitung* (20 Jan. 1915); 'Die Feuerbestattung im Krieg. Eine gebieterische Forderung für die Wohlfahrt von Heer und Volk', *Die Flamme*, 31 (1914), 476–8, also 534–8, 575–81; 32 (1915), 1.

legislation with the Reich Ministries of Justice and of the Interior.[131] Public health officials gained control over cremation just as they took over poison gases, as in line with the trend towards state regulation and the extension of medical powers of intervention to all spheres of life. Economic difficulties forced health authorities to support the rationalization of the disposal of the dead: in 1923 the Prussian Health Council recommended a type of utilitarian coffin to prevent the body decomposing too rapidly, while favouring cremation as requiring even less elaborate coffins.[132] A national cremation bill was prepared by the Reich Ministry of the Interior in 1922, scrutinized by the Reich and Prussian medical authorities, and passed by the Reichstag in 1922. But the bill was not granted constitutional approval in 1925 because of opposition from states with a predominately Catholic population like Bavaria, and from the confessional Centre Party.[133]

Under the Weimar Republic cremation societies flourished. The Verband Feuerbestattungsvereine was middle class, whereas the Volksfeuerbestattungsverein, founded in 1911, was avowedly proletarian and materialist, with a mass membership of 650,000 in 1931. The image of cremation was primarily that of a liberal or left-wing, atheist, and materialist movement. In line with the new concerns with rational health planning, public health officials took a more positive interest in cremation as an economically efficient and hygienic procedure. Conferences and displays were mounted at the vast health and recreation exhibition, the GESOLEI, at Düsseldorf in 1926, and at Dresden in 1930. Models of crematoria and the film *Momento Mori* won converts to the cause.[134] Cremationists argued against burial during the Hannover typhoid epidemic of 1926, and they painted a terrifying vision of the effect of natural catastrophes like flooding on cemeteries. Cremation attained the status of an advanced technology for public health purposes. But protestors against the building of a municipal crematorium in Breslau argued that the money should have been spent on bacteriology and delousing.[135]

The favoured style for columbaria and ceremonial halls was a bizarre modernistic art deco. Decoration incorporated glass prisms, spirals, and frescos representing mankind's path to an unknown land. A building in the form of a spiral was to house an international archive of the cremation movement.[136] Cremationists sustained the ethos of a masonic fraternity with conference delegates addressing each other as 'brother'. Medical officers condemned cemeteries as wasteful of space

[131] 'Zur Frage der Reichsgesetzliche Regelung der Feuerbestattung', *Die Flamme*, 35 (1918), 129–31, also 82.

[132] BAP 15.01/11733 Landesgesundheitsrat 3 Mar. 1923.

[133] BAP 15.01 Nr 11732 and 11733 Leichenbestattung, 26277/1 Bl. 53 letter to Brüning 12 Mar. 1931; BHSTA Ministry of Justice Feuerbestattung Reichsgesetz vom 15 Mai 1934. The Bavarian authorities opposed the law in May 1922, Nov. 1925, and Jan. 1926. For Prussia see GSTA Rep 76 VIII B Nr 3391, e.g. *Abgeordneten Haus*, question no. 692 (1 Oct. 1920).

[134] *Internationale Hygiene-Ausstellung Dresden 1930 Amtlicher Führer*, 345, Inseratenanhang, p. 22.

[135] GSTA Rep 76 VIII B Nr 3075 'Unzulängliche Seuchenbekämpfung in Schlesien!' *Schlesisches Tageblatt* (20 Apr. 1922).

[136] G. Schlyter, 'Ein neuer Krematoriumtyp', *Die Flamme. Nachrichten-Blatt des Verbandes der Deutschen Feuerbestattungs-Vereine in der Tschechoslovakischen Republik*, 12/2 (1 Feb. 1937), 1–3.

in populous cities and unhygienic. There was concern in Britain, Germany, and Sweden—the international leaders in cremation, and incidentally in campaigns for eugenic sterilization—that degenerates, the mentally deficient, and habitual criminals were polluting the race, and that when they died they polluted the earth.[137]

Cremation and Zyklon gassing were components of a new state-regulated and technological approach to public health, which conserved natural and financial resources. The post-war traumas intensified measures to exclude racial undesirables from Germany, as nationalists lamented how the German body suffered the amputation of vital territorial parts. While eugenics developed in the context of welfare measures meant to restore the national fabric, it still remained necessary to be vigilant against any recrudesence of infectious diseases. Apart from influenza, Germany was spared any large-scale epidemic: but the post-war catastrophe meant that radical new techniques were favoured, whether sterilization to prevent the spread of hereditary abnormalities, or disinfection with Zyklon to eradicate invasive parasites. On the war-torn peripheries of the nation the medical strategy pursued measures to disinfect disease-carriers on the German borders and to locate and eradicate the sources of infection further to the east.

---

[137] e.g. Mrs Alec Tweedie in her address. See *First Joint Conference of Cemetery and Cremation Authorities* (1932), 27.

6

The Sanitary Iron Curtain: The Relief of Polish and Russian Typhus

i. Medical Militancy

German medical officials polarized into two political camps—those seeking co-existence with the post-Versailles constellation of new states and supporting the Weimar Republic, as opposed to a rival group of Weimar imperialists, who fulminated at the 'unnatural' Versailles settlement. Both groups clamoured for medical, scientific, and technical assistance for their eastern neighbours, but for very different motives.

Resenting the loss of colonies and parts of the Reich, the revanchists nurtured hopes of regaining *Lebensraum* in the east as the antidote to national ills.[1] Schemes to revive German racial vigour by securing ethnic German communities in the east were linked to ideas, stemming from the geographer Karl Haushofer of geo-politics encompassing disease and environment. Militant medical scientists rallied to nationalist plans to restore Germany as a world power. Rabidly nationalist medical officials fought a rearguard action against the Versailles Treaty: aggrieved at the loss of their medical installations, and concerned to defend the starving and war-exhausted nation from the epidemic menace of refugees from the east, they denounced the new international order as jeopardizing German health. Epidemic prevention became an extension of right-wing politics to resurrect a German racial state.

Excluded from international congresses, and academic and medical associations, German doctors, professors, and medical students responded with an intensified cultural militancy.[2] They agitated for a counter-boycott of international science, and demanded nationalist solidarity in medicine. The tract *Krieg nach dem Kriege* by Gerhard Rose, a medical student embarking on a career in tropical medicine, called for a rekindling of national cultural values, while repatriating prisoners of war. Rose turned words into actions by joining the Freikorps to fight for a German Upper Silesia—he was to end up in the dock at Nuremberg in 1946 accused of typhus experiments.[3] German doctors, ejected from the former colonies, Alsace-Lorraine or Poland, were among the most diehard nationalists. A German physician, expelled from the Vistula area of Poland in 1920, went north-eastwards with a

[1] Smith, *Ideological Origins*, 196–230.
[2] B. Schröder-Gudehus, *Deutsche Wissenschaft und internationale Zusammenarbeit 1914–1928* (Geneva, 1966).
[3] G. Rose, *Krieg nach dem Kriege* (Dortmund, 1920).

sense of mission to sustain the beleagured community of Baltic Germans in the district of Memel, and campaigned against the Lithuanian destruction of German medical installations.[4] In 1920 the German Foreign Office formed a department for cultural affairs, which coordinated scientific visits, research expeditions, and the support of hospitals and sanatoria overseas to back up diplomatic and strategic interests.[5] Government policy that Germany should regain international respect through technical and scientific achievements was balanced with indignation against the Treaty of Versailles.

Medical supporters of Weimar imperialist revanchism included doctors who had served in the colonies, notably Philalethes Kuhn who had been a medical officer with the African colonial troops and Max Taute, a Reich Ministry of the Interior official who had assisted Koch on the East African sleeping sickness expedition. Kuhn's nationalist indignation increased when he was ejected from Strassburg University along with the bacteriologist Paul Uhlenhuth when Alsace-Lorraine reverted to France. Kuhn argued that the German race was ageing due to the declining birth-rate and needed to be rejuvenated by rural settlement programmes. Assistance to the scattered German ethnic groups became a priority, as these were regarded as a nucleus for future settlement in the east.

The ultra-nationalist cohort among German bacteriologists fulminated against the 'loss' of the territories incorporated into the new Polish state. Poland became pivotal in Allied policies for epidemic control, and assumed a central role in emerging international health organizations. Despite conflicts over territorial demarcation and ethnic rights, Poland was praised as (in Winston Churchill's words) 'anti-Bosch and anti-Bolshevik'.[6] Epidemic control stations, and quarantine and detention camps, were to strengthen the ill-defined borders of the new state. Polish public health officials accused the retreating Germans of dismantling facilities for disinfection and laboratory diagnosis, and the Bolsheviks for destabilizing Poland by unleashing hordes of destitute sick and starving on a trek westwards.[7] The breakdown of the cordon of preventive delousing stations, erected during the German occupation of Russian-Poland, fuelled fears that a typhus epidemic was poised to race across Europe.

ii. The Polish Bastion

Allied medical assistance to Poland inflamed German bitterness. The post-Versailles political order established international health agencies which reinforced

[4] Huwe, 'Unter Franzosen und Litauern Kreisarzt in Memel', *Der Öffentliche Gesundheitsdienst*, 6/17 (1940–41), 513–523, 613–24.

[5] W. U. Eckart, 'Medizin und auswärtige Kulturpolitik der Republik von Weimar-Deutschland und die Sowjetunion 1920–1932', *Medizin in Geschichte und Gesellschaft*, 10 (1993), 105–42. Philaletes Kuhn returned from the tropics to establish eugenically oriented public health schemes in Dresden.

[6] M. Gilbert, *Winston S. Churchill*, iv, *1916–1922* (London, 1975), 345.

[7] M. A. Balińska, 'Assistance and Not Mere Relief: The Epidemic Commission of the League of Nations, 1920–1923', in P. J. Weindling (ed.), *International Health Organisations and Movements 1918–1939* (Cambridge, 1995), 81–108; League of Nations Archives (LNA) R 824/2B/26009x/15255 Haigh address 28 Mar. 23.

the position of the victorious Allies and consolidated the new belt of central European states. The marginalizing of German medicine helps to explain German tactics of providing medical assistance to the Soviet Union. The Paris Peace conference had been disrupted during late 1918 and early 1919 by a resurgence of the influenza pandemic that had been sweeping the world since spring 1918. The global explosion of this virus, killing many young adults, left a sense of foreboding that worse catastrophes could follow. As Thomas Woodrow Wilson's principles of reconciliation and justice were under fire, he came down with what was diagnosed as flu in April 1919 and capitulated to revanchist demands. The Treaty of Versailles, signed on 28 June 1919, imposed heavy penalties on Germany.[8] German bacteriologists suffered a sense of double defeat—by Wilson caving into demands for punitive terms which medical experts argued would cripple the nation's health, and at their sheer impotence in combating the ravages of the influenza virus since spring 1918. The Germans perceived Allied aid-organizations as strategically linked to post-Versailles diplomacy and military intervention on behalf of the Poles. The Germans determined to outmanœuvre the Allied medical presence in central Europe and to overthrow the whole system.

The Allied efforts to contain the spread of infections struck a blow at German medical prestige. The pouring of Allied personnel, equipment, and lavish funds into the Central European belt of successor states was meant to supplant German and Austrian medical influence and secure the Versailles settlement. The Allied health planners divided between those demanding punitive burdens be placed on Germany, and liberal-minded progressives who hoped that equitable provision of health and welfare would reduce social conflicts and, consequently, prevent another war. It was not enough to contain the spread of infections: positively healthy social arrangements were required. Ministries of health marked a shift away from a policing approach to infectious diseases: specialist ministries were to secure social cohesion, and—as the Polish Minister of Public Health wrote to the US President—to produce 'a new breed of men' and promote 'health in the widest sense of the word'.[9] The Polish Ministry of Public Health, Welfare, and Labour Protection established in April 1918 under the Austrian and German occupying authorities marked the start of a Polish medical system; public health was allocated to a separate ministry under Ignacy Paderewski, Poland's first president. The Austrian ministries for social welfare and public health were similarly replaced in March 1919 by a single authority for welfare, food, and health.[10]

The rival state and voluntary agencies, that vied with one another in the task of preventing epidemics from the east, had contrasting attitudes to the rehabilitation of Austria and Germany. The International Committee of the Red Cross (ICRC) in

[8] A. W. Crosby, *America's Forgotten Pandemic. The Influenza of 1918*, 2nd edn. (Cambridge, 1990), 171–200; N. G. Levin, *Woodrow Wilson and World Politics: Response to War and Revolution* (New York, 1968); A. S. Link, *Wilson the Diplomatist: A Look at his Major Foreign Policies* (New York, 1957); E. A. Weinstein, *Woodrow Wilson, a Medical and Psychological Biography* (Princeton, 1981) 336–8.

[9] T. Janiszewski, 'The Versailles Treaty and the Question of Public Health', *International Journal of Public Health*, 2 (1921), 140–51.

[10] K. Sablik, *Julius Tandler. Mediziner und Sozialreformer* (Vienna, 1983), 140–51.

Geneva promoted central European sanitary cooperation, whereas Allied schemes for sanitary reconstruction led to the launch of the rival League of Red Cross Societies (LRCS) in 1919. A crucial difference was that the ICRC admitted the Austrian and German Red Cross organizations while the LRCS barred them. On 13 March 1919 the ICRC convened a conference in Budapest on measures to combat typhus. In April 1919 the ICRC supported the creation of an international commission for combating epidemics. The 'German–Austrian' Health Office gave enthusiastic backing to the new International Commission for Epidemic Control and Sanitary Improvement for South and East Europe.[11]

Vienna, already a centre for international relief for starving children, was a fitting headquarters as the organization covered the Austro-Hungarian successor states and ethnic German minorities. Delegates came from the Ukrainian Republic, Poland, the Kingdom of Serbs, Croats and Slovenes, the Hungarian Soviet Republic, the German–Austrian Republic, Czechoslovakia, a Committee to Protect the Peoples in Italian Occupied Areas (i.e. the South Tyrol and Dalmatia), and from the National Council of Siebenbürgen (the ethnic German area of Romania), the Romanian administration of Bukovina and the Kingdom of Romania. The commission planned a sanitary cordon against typhus in Poland and the Ukraine, as well as assistance to returning prisoners from Russia, given the spread of Bolshevik control to areas where prisoners of war continued to be held such as in Turkestan and the Caucasus. When delegates from the Ukraine and Bukovina requested sanitary assistance, the Austrian Red Cross mounted a medical expedition to the Ukraine with eighty typhus-immune personnel, and mobile delousing and bacteriological equipment in June 1919.[12] This model of sanitary assistance to the Ukraine was to be replicated by rival organizations: by the explorer and international philanthropist Fridtjof Nansen, who joined forces with the ICRC when he confronted typhus epidemics in the Soviet Union; and by rival Allied diplomatic and military interests working through the LRCS.

The ICRC alerted the Red Cross societies of Britain, France, Italy, and the US to the typhus danger for Europe.[13] Military medical experts from the United States, Great Britain, France, Italy, and Japan met at the plush yacht club in Cannes in April 1919, where they floated a scheme for an International Council and Bureau of Public Health. Allied diplomats and politicians, notably Marshall Ferdinand Foch and Winston Churchill, campaigned for a political cordon sanitaire against communism and German imperialism. The activities of international organizations like the American Red Cross (ARC), the LRCS, and the League of Nations Epidemic Commission gave substance to the political metaphor of Bolshevism as a virulent

[11] ÖSA, AdR Staatsamt für soziale Verwaltung, Volksgesundheitsamt 1919 Desinfektion Faszikel Nr 71/2, Karton 1605 Konstituierung des Zentralbüros für Seuchenbekämpfung 5 June 1919 Ferrière to Volksgesundheitsamt. Protokoll der konstituierenden Sitzung 13 May 1919. 9. Sitzung 7 Aug. 1919. Protokoll 20. May 1919. Karton 1649 Desinfektion, 1920. For earlier schemes, see Goodman, *International Health*, 56, 59.

[12] ÖSA, AdR Staatsamt für soziale Verwaltung, Volksgesundheitsamt 1919 Desinfektion Faszikel Nr 71/2, Karton 1605 Sitzung 7 Aug. 1919; Protokoll 20 May 1919; Karton 1649 Desinfektion, 1920.

[13] O. Peiper, 'Das Fleckfieber in Preussen', 6.

fever. Military medical experts planned a sanitary buffer zone to ensure that Western European civilization should not perish as a result of a pandemic more lethal than the influenza epidemic, as epidemics of typhus and cholera flared in Russia and Poland. The LRCS hoped to contain infectious diseases by establishing 'a sanitary line of defence from the north to the south' between the Baltic and the Black Sea.[14] The LRCS denounced endemic typhus in Russia as 'a permanent focus which menaces the whole of Europe'.[15] The Cannes meeting represented a turning-point in imposing policies of exclusion and intervention to suppress epidemics in Poland and Russia. The gathering at the plush yacht club terminated the shiploads of refugees flowing from the east.

The ICRC and LRCS fought for control over the new international health authority. The ICRC (entirely Swiss since its foundation in 1863) opposed the LRCS as an upstart body. The LRCS enjoyed the patronage of President Wilson—his wife Edith was an ardent ARC supporter, and Allied experts on infectious diseases formulated plans for an LRCS-dominated Central Bureau of Health. They envisaged international public health laboratories to monitor the spread of infectious diseases in epidemic zones. The alarming news of epidemic typhus in Central Europe provided a timely emergency to accelerate the international scheme. The LRCS director, Henry Davison, telegraphed the Allied leaders at the Paris Peace Conference that typhus was raging in the area between the Baltic and the Black Sea as a consequence of war and political revolution, and that it threatened Western Europe. Georges Clemenceau, the French prime minister, as a physician had experienced cholera emergencies, and David Lloyd George, who saw medicine as an incessant war on disease, supported massive resources for a commission of international experts acting to safeguard 'the health and peace of the world'.[16]

A militarist aura lingered as emergency relief teams provided an outlet for otherwise redundant military doctors and nurses, and surplus army supplies were released for famine and medical work. American, British, and French medical expeditions scoured Poland for the vestiges of typhus. A British team from the Lister Institute was drafted into Warsaw, and the medical entomologist Bacot reinforced the ARC team.[17] The ARC had three anti-typhus units in eastern Poland by April 1919. An American medical officer, Colonel Harry L. Gilchrist, directed the American–Polish Typhus Relief Expedition with a staff of 500 officers and men to assist the fledgling Polish Ministry of Public Health; they deployed surplus

[14] 'Resolutions of the Medical Advisory Board [on July 5–8, 1920]', *International Journal of Public Health*, 1 (1920), 216–21.

[15] 'The Agony of Russia', *International Journal of Public Health*, 2 (1921), 221–3.

[16] *Proceedings of the Medical Conference Held at the Invitation of the Committee of Red Cross Societies, Cannes, France April 1 to 11 1919* (Geneva, 1919), 148–51, 161–4. 800 copies of this report were distributed, CLB Strong Papers, box 35. On Clemenceau see J. D. Ellis, *The Physician-legislators of France. Medicine and Politics in the Early Third Republic, 1870–1914* (Cambridge, 1990); D. Lloyd George, *War Memoirs* new edn. (London, 1938) ii. 2037.

[17] H. Chick, M. Hume, and M. Macfarlane, *War on Disease. A History of the Lister Institute* (London, 1971), 135.

delousing equipment, steam sterilizers, and mobile bathing tents, and distributed sets of underwear.

The LRCS sent an Inter-Allied Medical Commission to Poland on 6 August 1919 to survey the extent of typhus. Strong, the medical director of the LRCS, had extensive war experience in Serbia and in organizing US military hygiene.[18] He argued that it was best to support sanitary intervention in Poland because 'Nations are tightening, instead of relaxing the cordon of their frontiers'.[19] US medical detachments entered Vilna after it was seized by the Poles in October 1920, and provided a cover for and medical assistance to 'Haller's army', consisting of American–Polish military squadrons. Railway coaches, Ford touring cars and ambulances, lorries, and mules carried sanitary equipment, and hygiene pamphlets and posters.[20] The commission found that the Polish health minister lacked authority in the eastern sectors where typhus was at its worst, and that because most Polish doctors were in the army, medical relief was urgently needed to provide the soap, clothing, linen, and laundering facilities in the battle against lice. The commissioners praised the Poles as 'a gallant people', acting as military 'guardians of Europe'; but the tone was hostile to Polish Jews, attacking them for poor personal cleanliness, and pointing to the dangers of the transmission of lice at Jewish ritual baths.[21]

The Inter-Allied Sanitary commission considered whether Europe and America were best protected by a 'sanitary cordon'. Although a total sealing of Eastern Europe was deemed impractical, the commissioners prescribed disinfecting stations for refugees, and that 'sanitary passports' should be issued to the cleansed and disinfected.[22] The Polish health authorities remained staunchly independent, and the Gilchrist Commission to Poland was pronounced a failure. As a concession to foreign pressure (and following German wartime precedents), the Polish state launched an anti-typhus committee under Colonel Emil Godlewski, a professor of biology from Cracow, who from March 1920 was referred to as 'typhus dictator', 'Czar', or 'commissioner in chief'—echoing the German First World War appointment of such an epidemic supremo. He had power over the areas under military administration where typhus was worst, and subordinate commissioners were appointed at Lwów, Vilna, Łuck, and Polskrow.[23]

Sanitary measures in Poland were associated with coercive foreign intervention, and encountered general hostility. LRCS medical officers reported that: 'There is much indifference in Poland towards typhus. Interest in the disease and in its sup-

---

[18] The commissioners were H. S. Cumming, George Buchanan, Aldo Castellani, and F. Visbecq; CLB Strong papers, box 36c, Strong to Henrietta Ely 28 Aug. 1919; Strong, 'Anti-typhus Campaign', 201.

[19] Strong, 'Anti-typhus Campaign', 210.

[20] Cornebise, *Typhus and Doughboys*, 77–87, 101–3, 132. On Jozef Haller see N. Davis, *God's Playground. A History of Poland* (Oxford, 1981).

[21] RAC Rockefeller Foundation 1.1/789/2/11 Shaw to Williams 4 May 1920; Strong, 'Anti-typhus Campaign', 202.

[22] 'Report of the Medical Commission to Poland', *Bulletin of the League of Red Cross Societies*, 1/4 (1–17 Oct. 1919).

[23] RAC Rockefeller Foundation 1.1/789/2/11 letter of 4 May 1920 from Col. Henry A. Shaw (of LRCS in Poland) to L. R. Williams of the Rockefeller Foundation anti-TB campaign in Paris. Godlewski was professor of biology at Cracow. Fisher, *New Poland*, 246.

pression is much less than foreign press dispatches, and the concern of foreign public health authorities would lead one to expect.' Lousiness was found to be widespread. Colonel Henry Shaw lamented that

At present there is almost universal antagonism toward all instructions in regard to bathing and delousing and a general clean up programme. This is due first to the result of the Russian administration when the people learned to distrust and whenever possible evade or disobey all government rules and regulations directed toward their personal habits and mode of life. And second, particularly in regard to typhus, they had been through three years of German occupation where bathing and delousing measures were enforced with military thoroughness and severity.

The LRCS concluded that no campaign combating typhus could be effective and that in any case the spread of typhus from Poland to Western Europe had been greatly overestimated.[24]

The US strategy to suppress typhus was based on hair clippers and baths. Lack of fuel meant that baths were cold, and the delousing operation was harsh. Many Poles distrusted foreign medical assistance and, sceptical of scientific superstitions, preferred to fight disease by exorcism, religious procession, and prayers. Allied medical attempts to enlist the support of priests and rabbis were unsuccessful; Orthodox Jews were suspicious of isolation hospitals, while the US officers accused Jews of evasion and concealment of typhus cases.[25] US detachments lacked respect for religious customs of the long-ringleted Orthodox Jews. The cutting of hair and beards of Orthodox Jews became associated with vicious pogroms when Polish and Ukrainian anti-Semites assaulted Jewish 'vermin'.[26] The US officials echoed the complaints of their anti-Semitic German predecessors that delousing certificates were forged or traded.[27] The Rockefeller Foundation's verdict on the Polish programme was damning: its Director informed John D. Rockefeller Jnr. that 'The Red Cross campaign against typhus in Poland accomplished practically nothing'.[28]

The report of the Inter-Allied Medical Commission to Poland in November 1919 spurred on plans for an International Health Section of the League of Nations. The British and French used the Polish epidemic emergency to plan a League of Nations Epidemic Commission, which was expected to concentrate on disinfection and

[24] RAC Rockefeller Foundation 1.1/789/2/11 Health conditions in Poland, report by Col. F. F. Longley and Col. H. A. Shaw to H. Biggs, 8 Oct. 1920; Shaw to Williams 4 May 1920; Strong, 'Anti-typhus Campaign', 202; 1.1/789/2/11 G. B. Vincent to S. J. Murphy, 15 Sept. 1920; Rockefeller Foundation 1.1/789/2/11 letter of 4 May 1920 from Col Henry A. Shaw (of LRCS in Poland) to L. R. Williams of the Rockefeller Foundation anti-TB campaign in Paris; E. R. Embree, *Typhus in Poland*.

[25] Strong, 'Anti-typhus Campaign', 208; Cornebise, *Typhus and Doughboys*, 117.

[26] A. L. Goodhart, *Poland and the Minority Races* (London, 1920), 36, 125; M. Levene, 'Frontiers of Genocide: Jews in the Eastern War Zones, 1914–1920 and 1941', in P. Panayi (ed.), *Minorities in Wartime* (Oxford, 1996), 83–117.

[27] Cornebise, *Typhus and Doughboys*, 46, 73–4, 131.

[28] LNA R 816/8138 LRCS correspondence 13 Mar. 1922. RAC Rockefeller Foundation 1.1/785/2/15, George Vincent to John D. Rockefeller Jnr., 9 Aug. 1921.

epidemic prevention.[29] The Council of the League of Nations convened international sanitary conferences in London in July 1919 and in April 1920 to draw up plans for a campaign against typhus. The League of Nations Health Organization was intended to promote social stability and international cooperation between public health experts. Article 23 (f) of the Treaty of Versailles stated that 'The members of the League will endeavour to make international arrangements to the end of preventing or combating disease'.[30]

The British Ministry of Health was concerned with keeping typhus at bay and with propping up the post-Versailles European order. George Newman, Chief Medical Officer of the Ministry of Health in London, approached the Rockefeller Foundation (RF) in September 1920 just after the Polish reversal of the Red Army's advance. The Rockefeller Foundation turned down his request for sanitary assistance because of the tense military situation and US non-recognition of the League of Nations. The Rockefeller Foundation (at the time engaged in an anti-tuberculosis campaign in France) argued that Polish mortality from tuberculosis far exceeded that from typhus. The Foundation regarded improving overall levels of health in Central Europe as a long-term project, for which peace and democracy were necessary to supplant the militarist excesses of German medicine.[31]

Given that typhus was endemic in the territories seized from the Ukraine, Lithuania, and White Russia by the Poles, medical assistance meant in effect consolidating the Polish hold on its conquests. The LRCS representative observed that 'the Polish army is undoubtedly acting as the first barrier against the further invasion of the country by epidemic diseases'. The London conferences of 1919–20 used the threat of typhus in Poland 'as a social and national danger for the entire world' to promote plans for an international health bureau. Chodźko, Poland's first Minister of Health, and the bacteriologist Rajchman, a charismatically radical public health reformer, joined representatives of Britain, France, Italy, Japan, and the United States in convening a League of Nations Typhus Commission to assist Poland.[32] Rajchman persuaded the League of Nations (LN) to fund local Polish authorities rather than to support the LRCS, as he distrusted voluntary organizations as mere conscience-salving for governments not prepared to provide adequate aid. American observers praised Rajchman as 'the most competent public health worker we have met in this part of Europe', although they were concerned

[29] LNA R811–1 Doc. 1994 Doss 126 memorandum Health Scheme of the League of Nations 18 Nov. 1919; LNA R811–1 1920 Health Section Doc. 3943, note by the British Delegate to the Assembly 5 Nov. 1920.

[30] LNA R 816/7901 Typhus Commission of Inquiry in Poland, Crowdy to Buchanan; 816/7340 Rajchman to N. White 5 Oct. 1920; Herefordshire Record Office, Records of the Newman Family of Leominster M4/159 Autobiographical notes of George Newman, p. 19, 1920; M4/164 'Balfour' concerning Balfour's grasp of bacteriology.

[31] RAC Rockefeller Foundation 1.1/789/2/11 Newman to Vincent 23 Sept. 1920; Embree to Biggs 21 Sept. 1920.

[32] Bodleian Library, Oxford, Addison papers, box 61, file 532 *International Health Conference April 13–17th 1920* (London, 1920).

that as a Jew he might be lacking in influence, despite his technical flair in establishing the new central laboratory of public health in Warsaw.[33]

An alliance of military medical experts, administrators, and diplomats regarded an international health body as strategically important to consolidate the successor states.[34] The League of Nations Epidemic Commission aimed to construct a permanent system of 'sanitary defence' in Eastern Europe between Poland and Russia. In contrast to the emergency relief organizations, the emphasis was on prevention in the long term. It was agreed that no scheme of economic reconstruction for Eastern Europe was possible until effective measures against epidemics had been taken. The Commission defended 'the Public Health of Europe' against 'invasion by epidemics so severely prevalent in Russia'.[35] The League of Nations office in Warsaw strengthened the Polish cordon sanitaire, disinfecting refugees, rather than assisting them and according them rights. It planned to modernize bathing and disinfecting establishments, and construct epidemic hospitals and bacteriological institutes at Toruń, Warsaw, Lwów, and Sluzew. The Baltic states, Czechoslovakia, and Romania were also beneficiaries of League of Nations assistance. The aim was to develop autonomous systems of public health and medical education, replacing the old German, Austro-Hungarian, and Russian medical systems.[36]

To justify the injections of aid into Poland, the epidemic threat was magnified to excess. In June 1921 the League of Nations's epidemic commissioner pricked the illusory epidemic bubble by concluding that despite reports of cholera the epidemic never existed: there were only a few localized cases among Bolshevik prisoners of war. The commissioners' verdict was that typhus was in fact on the decline.[37] The localized outbreak of typhus was a cover for Allied military intervention in Eastern Europe. In May 1920 the Labour MP J. J. Lawson in the House of Commons asked sarcastically 'whether the Polish attack on Russia is the international action recommended for the suppression of the typhus epidemic.'[38] Neville Chamberlain (who took a keen interest in agriculture and insect pests) opposed aid to Poland while it was attacking Lithuania, and the Treasury blocked expenditure on a typhus relief campaign.[39] But the Ministry of Health insisted that the typhus question affected 'the welfare of many countries and of Europe as a whole'. Although the Poles were invading Soviet territory, British officials considered that if the invasion was to secure 'better conditions of government in the Ukraine, it will increase the

[33] RAC Rockefeller Foundation 1.1/789/2/11 Health conditions in Poland, report by Col. F. F. Longley and Col. H. A. Shaw to H. Biggs 8 Oct. 1920, p. 8; M. A. Balińska, *Une vie pour l'humanitaire. Ludwik Rajchman 1881–1965* (Paris, 1995), 87–8 on Rajchman's appointment.

[34] On the Epidemic Commission see C. W. Hutt, *International Hygiene* (London, 1927), 25–41; Balińska, 'Assistance'; CLB Strong papers, box 36c, Strong to H. Cushing 22 Apr. 1919, 9 Apr. 1920.

[35] LNA R 823 12B/25642/15002 George Buchanan, Report on the Recent Work and Present Position of the Epidemic Commission, 11 Jan. 1923.

[36] *Second Annual Report of the Epidemic Commission of the League of Nations* (August 1922), 3–6.

[37] LNA 12B Doc 13880, Epidemic Commissioner to N. White, 27 June 1921.

[38] House of Commons, 17 May 1920.

[39] D. Dilks, *Neville Chamberlain* (Cambridge, 1984), 23, 27, 75, 91, 100, 115, 122, 134, 232, 389 on entomology; pp. 273–5 on Addison's vulnerability.

opportunities of controlling epidemics'.[40] Epidemic prevention offered a pretext for political intervention.

The Polish delousing and disinfection installations, and a chain of hospital and quarantine facilities in the border areas, amounted to a 'zone sanitaire' which consolidated territorial acquisitions.[41] American officers were assigned to five Polish medical stations in an attempt to cordon off Poland's eastern and southern borders.[42] Difficulties in controlling the infested refugees and soldiers rendered any anti-typhus measures futile, although there had been hardly any importation of infections into the former German provinces. Rather than a major epidemic threat, typhus had merely 'advertising value' as a way of securing international funds: the hope was that anti-typhus measures would result in general health improvements and stable frontiers which would keep typhus carriers away from the European heartlands.[43] The Polish drive eastwards in April 1920 exacerbated an unstable medical situation: the Polish forces reached Minsk and Kiev by June 1920, and a counter-offensive by the Red Army thrust close to Warsaw and East Prussia in August 1920 arousing fears of epidemics. The military reversal in the summer of 1920 prompted the Poles to raise an international alarm at impending new epidemic shockwaves which could be as devastating as influenza. On 5 October 1920 Rajchman telegraphed Norman White, the League of Nations's typhus commissioner: 'Asiatic cholera introduced by Bolshevik Army in reoccupied areas spreading seriously among the civilian population.'[44] The politics of political stabilization and disease control relentlessly drew the Allies into Russia, while arousing German anxieties. The German Foreign Office insisted that the League of Nations was an alliance of great powers exploiting the system for their own ends.[45] German medical nationalists resented their international isolation and Allied medical assistance to Poland, which they perceived as wounding Germany's health and national interests. Outflanking the Allies by mounting relief in Russia, the Germans opened up a vast terrain to test their disinfection technologies.

iii. Containing Bolshevism

Typhus provided the Allies with a pretext for military intervention in Russia. In 1919 Winston Churchill denounced Bolshevism as a German-inspired disease, believing that 'Lenin was sent into Russia by the Germans in the same way that you might send a phial containing a culture of typhoid or of cholera to be poured into the water supply of a great city.' Churchill had declared war on lice on the western

---

[40] LNA R 812/4410/1719 Buchanan to Harold Nicholson 14 May 1920; Buchanan, 'League of Nations and Typhus in Poland'.

[41] Balinska, 'Assistance'.

[42] Cornebise, *Typhus and Doughboys*, 70, 87, 89, 96–7. The sites were Tarnopol, Brest-Litowsk, Dorohusk, Oswiecim, and Bialystok.

[43] RAC Rockefeller Foundation 1.1/789/2/11 Health conditions in Poland, report by Col. F. F. Longley and Col. H. A. Shaw to H. Biggs.

[44] Ibid., 8 Oct. 1920, p. 8.   [45] Kimmich, *Germany and the League*, 32–9.

front in 1916, and he depicted post-revolutionary Russia as 'devoured by vermin, racked by pestilence' and 'as marching back into the dark ages'. The Russian 'poison peril' was to be contained by a cordon sanitaire of buffer states, stretching from Finland to Romania. The Red Army's invasion of Poland in 1920 prompted Churchill to rally support for Poland as 'the lynch-pin of the Treaty of Versailles' as menaced by 'a poisoned Russia, an infected Russia, a plague-bearing Russia, a Russia of armed hordes smiting not only with bayonet and with cannon, but accompanied and preceded by the swarms of typhus bearing vermin which slay the bodies of men, and political doctrines which destroy the health and even the soul of nations'.[46] Such Churchillian rhetoric epitomized a widespread mood that the health of Europe was under attack. As long as borders were fluid, the Allies attempted to topple the Bolsheviks indirectly by supporting Polish forces and the White Russian armies, and directly by mounting military expeditions.

While German forces withdrew from Russia, the Allied anti-Bolshevik expeditionary forces faced cold, hunger, and vermin. The British government supplied the Russian Relief Fund with surplus lime juice, tinned beef, 'time-expired' drugs, and moth-eaten clothing from an Egyptian dump.[47] The British and American troops based in Archangel and Murmansk in North Russia, and the US forces in Siberia from July 1918 to spring 1920, commandeered local bathing, laundering, and disinfection apparatus, and adapted vodka barrels for disinfecting clothes and blankets. A train was equipped with a disinfecting chamber and steam baths.[48] In Southern Russia the British Military Mission to Denikin's army established a hospital at Taganrog on the Sea of Azov in September 1919. Innovative (but probably ineffective) serotherapy for typhus was tested, involving vaccination with blood serum from convalescing patients; other types of bacterial proteins, sera, and even a milk-based vaccine were devised.[49] Mirroring German medical support for hospitals, the British aid workers had a vision of resuscitating the Anglo-Russian hospitals which had operated until the Revolution. The formidable Lady Muriel Paget dreamt of a chain of British hospital units from the Gulf of Finland to the Black Sea. Her mother-and-baby clinics were dotted around the Baltic States, Poland, Slovakia, and ministered to refugees in the areas held by General Wrangel around the Crimea. She applied measures from the East End of London to Eastern Europe; the clinics issued sulphur soap for the verminous, while besieged by crowds who did not accept that infants should have priority.[50] On their return the expeditions were stringently disinfested and checked for venereal diseases, scabies, and lice.[51]

[46] Gilbert, *Churchill*, iv. 345 on pro-German fears; p. 355 on Lenin; p. 365 on Russian barbarism; p. 372 on the cordon sanitaire; p. 417 on typhus; p. 441 on Bolshevism as cancer. I wish to thank John F. M. Clark for the 1916 reference to lice taken from N. Rose, *Churchill: An Unruly Life* (London, 1994), 134.

[47] 'The Russian Famine', *Lancet* (4 Mar. 1922), 457.

[48] *Hygiene of the War*, ii. 377–82.

[49] J. M. Mitchell, I. N. Ashesov, and G. P. N. Richardson, *Typhus Fever with Special Reference to Russian Epidemics* (London, 1922), 9–14, 38–47.

[50] W. Blunt, *Lady Muriel. Lady Muriel Paget, Her Husband and Philanthropic Work in Central and Eastern Europe* (London, 1962), 174–8, 209.

[51] Ibid., 174–8, 209; M. W. Ireland (ed.), *The Medical Department of the United States Army in the World War*, Viii, *Field Operations* (Washington, 1925), 945–53.

Huge numbers of refugees during the Russian civil war of 1919–20 exacerbated the epidemic hazards. Despite sporadic isolation, shaving, and delousing of typhus patients, behind the White Russian lines there were chronic shortages of clean linen and medicines. Hospitals were overrun by patients, and when evacuated the sick were packed into cattle trucks. A hospital train was characterized as a 'train of death' as its passengers starved, infected one another, and were overwhelmed by vermin and filth. Patients in a White Russian typhus isolation ward swarmed with hordes of lice, so extensive that they could devour a person.[52]

The Anglo-American attack on typhus in Russia hardly differed from the German strategies of containment and disinfection. The German medical authorities feared Russian 'agitators' escaping from typhus-infested internment camps. After the defeat of the Red Army in Poland in 1920, nearly 3,000 Russian soldiers took refuge in East Prussia to escape the Polish army, and were moved westwards to a camp at Ahlenfalkenberger Moor, swelling the numbers of Russian prisoners. The bacteriologist Otto supervised health conditions in the Russian transit camps.[53] Batches of Russian prisoners were useful counters in repatriating prisoners of war from the east—a task which meant that the Germans and Austrians maintained relations with the Bolsheviks during the civil wars and Allied interventions of 1919–21.

In the autumn of 1921 harvest failure resulted in famine in the normally fertile Volga region, which contained many refugees from the German wartime advances. When these Poles, White Russians, Galicians, and ethnic Germans began to move westwards, the fear that they carried typhus prompted the borders to be sealed.[54] The Volga Germans encountered resistance from the Soviet, Polish, and German authorities as no state wanted to take responsibility for persons condemned as louse-ridden and diseased. About 500 Volga Germans who had crossed into Poland (along with other foreigners—particularly Ukrainians) were incarcerated to the east of Poznań in the former German border camp of Stralkowo.[55] German officials were concerned for the refugees' health as the camp lacked delousing facilities.

Reich and Prussian authorities debated whether Volga Germans should be allowed to re-enter Germany, which they regarded as already deluged by refugees from the partition of Silesia. The Reich Ministry of the Interior insisted that the Volga Germans had left Germany so long ago that they had forfeited all rights of re-entry. One solution was that these German 'colonists' should be treated as a group in transit to the United States. But as a health hazard they were closely guarded in a sealed-off camp. The Volga Germans, tainted by their semi-Asiatic environment, were treated like other Eastern European transmigrants. The Reich Ministry of the

---

[52] Mitchell, Ashesov, Richardson, *Typhus Fever*, 9–14. For the experience of a typhus isolation hospital see A. Rachmanowa, *Studenten, Liebe, Tscheka und Tod* (Salzburg, 1931), 326–49 and 373–80, 428 for an infested sanitary train.

[53] GSTA Rep 76 VIII B Nr 3567, RP Lüneberg 7 Oct. 1920; RP Stade 21 Oct. 1920; Report on a tour of inspection by Hendel and Otto, 28 Aug.–9 Sept. 1920.

[54] Marrus, *Unwanted*, 58, on the high mortality in trains.

[55] BAP 15.01 Nr 9398, Bl 538–9 'Die Lage der Wolgadeutschen im Lager Stralkowo' by Pfarrer Kammel, 11 Feb. 1921.

SPECIAL MAP 1

e epidemic situation in Eastern Europe and a
mparative study of Typhus and Relapsing Fever
cidence in the various Gouvernements of the Soviet
nion and in Poland in 1922 (after Epidemiol. Intell.
Rep., League of Nations, No. 3, 1922)

SONDERKARTE 1

Die epidemische Situation in Osteuropa mit einem
Vergleich der Fleckfieber- und Rückfallfieberhäufig-
keit in den einzelnen Gouvernements der Sowjetunion
und in Polen im Jahre 1922 (nach Epidemiol. Intell.
Rep., League of Nations, No. 3, 1922)

MAP 3. Typhus in Russia, 1921–4

Interior condemned the Volga Germans stranded in Poland as a threat to German internal security, suspecting that they might import communism.[56]

The German Foreign Office was more supportive. The German ambassador in Warsaw, Wilhelm Eduard von Schoen, felt the Volga German refugees should be granted assistance, as further German hesitation could prompt the Poles to close their borders to German citizens stranded in the east. The Warsaw embassy pronounced the Volga refugees to be proper Germans in their appearance and attitude.[57] The embassy opposed abandoning the Volga Germans to the mercy of the Poles, as this would undermine the ethnic German minority in Poland.[58] German anti-Semites believed that the Volga German refugees were being exploited by Jewish agents in Poland, who were doing a good business smuggling refugees over the German border. Moreover, the Poles were criticized by the Germans as incapable of organizing effective delousing, let alone proper feeding and accommodation.[59]

The closing of borders meant that national identity became a matter of individual expediency, and (as for a disease) definitions were more malleable than often assumed. Desperate German 'colonists' pretended that they were Polish in order to obtain a Polish passport and then switched back to German identity to gain entry into Germany. Others crossed the border on forest paths to evade quarantine. Although the Polish-Soviet Treaty of Riga of March 1921 stated that no more than 4,000 prisoners of war should cross the frontier, these arrangements broke down during the famine.[60] Attempts were made to reactivate the German-imposed system of epidemiological monitoring and delousing stations. A barrier of delousing stations was meant to seal Europe against lethal epidemics. The Reich Health Office announced to the Reichstag in April 1922 that 'an epidemic prevention wall' (*Seuchenschutzwall*) was in place running from East Prussia to Silesia with facilities for quarantine, disinfection, and observation.[61] This epidemiological 'iron curtain'—a phrase later popularized by Joseph Goebbels—demarcated the new European order from Soviet communism.[62] On the one hand, it was in the West's interest to eradicate epidemics at source; on the other, the prospect arose of epidemics destabilizing the fragile new structures of Bolshevism. The refugee camps on the German border rapidly became horrifically overcrowded.[63] The refugee crisis culminated early in 1922, when the Poles closed the borders to refugees from the devastating famine in Russia. By May 1922 the Reich officials insisted that

    [56] BAK R86/2401 Bd 1 Besprechung betr die Rückwanderung deutschstämmiger Wolgaflüchtlinge, 17 Dec. 1921.
    [57] GSTA Rep 76 VIII B Nr 3569, RMdI 10 Dec. 1921; Auswärtiges Amt, 14 Dec. 1921; Von Schoen, Warsaw embassy 18 Jan. 1922.
    [58] Ibid., German embassy, Warsaw, 14 Feb. 1922.
    [59] BAK 86/2401 Bd 1 RMdI conference on 20 Feb. 1922 comments by Hasbach, a German national representative to the Polish Sejm.
    [60] Hutt, *International Hygiene*, 26–7.
    [61] Carl Hamel to the Reichstag, *204. Sitzung*, 6 Apr. 1922, p. 6968.
    [62] A *Cholerarayon* was also established on the border with China: Rachmanowa, *Studenten*, 430.
    [63] BAK R 86/2401 Heimkehrer, Flüchtlinge und Kriegsgefangenelager.

Germany had reached the limits in terms of numbers of refugees who could be absorbed. The Reich Health Office asked the Polish authorities to prevent refugees crossing Polish territory—apart from the humanitarian exception of orphaned ethnic German children.[64] German officials feared that any concession would provoke another wave of attempted emigration by the Volga Germans.

Over 5,000 Volga 'colonists' were stranded in Minsk, where relief was hampered by Polish–Soviet hostilities. The Reich government refused them entry into Germany. Infested by lice, overcrowded, and lacking clean bedding, many had typhoid, typhus, or relapsing fever, which killed half their number. A further 2,000 destitute, sick and hungry ethnic German refugees congregated in Polotsk, helped only by a Jewish aid committee (a matter of disquiet to the German authorities).[65] In the event the German Red Cross provided emergency accommodation, a medical team, and food supplies. Coping with the refugees was all the more difficult, because they concealed their diseases so as not to be separated from their families and friends in much feared isolation hospitals.[66] The miserable conditions in Minsk were reported in a Volga German newspaper, produced by the German Red Cross. German 'colonists' were warned that all emigration was hopeless and would probably end in death from epidemic disease.[67] In response to such crisis situations, German officials resisted the impending influx from the east by mounting a belligerent strategy of intervention to quell epidemics at their source in Russia.

iv. 'Brothers in Need': The Politics of Aid to Russia

German bacteriologists characterized Russia as 'a land of hunger and famine', and as drenched in disease.[68] The left-wing artist Georg Grosz caricatured the new Russia as 'Locust Land' because of the despoliation arising from starvation.[69] The image might also be applied to the predatory political interests supporting many of the teams of foreign relief workers who descended on Russia to tackle famine and disease in 1921. Epidemics of typhus, cholera, typhoid, and malaria spread to Moscow and Petrograd during the post-revolutionary turmoils. The epidemiological statistics were alarming with nearly five million cases of typhus and 1.2 million cases of relapsing fever by 1920; when cholera erupted in 1921, 176,885 cases were notified. It was suggested that these figures had to be multiplied by two and a half

---

[64] BAP 15.01 Nr 9400, Bl 122 RMdI to AA 26 Aug. 1922 concerning arrangements for 300 orphaned children.

[65] STAH 352 8/9 Bernhard Nocht Institut 23 Bd 1 Mühlens report 36, Karstens, 'Bericht über die bisher den Wolgadeutschen in Minsk vom Deutschen Roten Kreuz geleistete Hilfe', 19 Apr. 1922; BAP 15.01 Nr 9399, Bl. 23 Bericht über die Lage der nach Minsk geflohenen Wolgakolonisten; BAP 15.01 Nr 9400 Bl. 68.

[66] Karstens, 'Die Lage der nach Minsk geflohenen deutschen Wolgakolonisten', *Blätter des Deutschen Roten Kreuzes* (= BDRK), Sonderheft (1922), 12–13.

[67] 'Warnung vor der Auswanderung', *Nachrichten*, 5/64 (24 Mar. 1922).

[68] GSTA Rep 76 VIII B Nr 3570, Verkehrungen im Inlande, RMdI Beratung betr Abwehr den Seuchengefahr aus dem Ostens, opinion of Frey on Russian epidemics.

[69] G. Grosz, *The Autobiography of George Grosz. A Small Yes and a Big No* (London, 1982), 130.

times in order to gauge the real incidence of the diseases. These staggering sums may have been used to disguise deaths from sheer starvation.[70] Death-rates remained obscure, but estimates were immense, ranging from between 3 and five million deaths from typhus in European Russia between 1917 and 1923.[71] In sheer numbers, the scale of the Russian famine and epidemics was collossal. A crucial issue is whether the German responses to this vast human tragedy in any way represented a hardening of commitments to defend Germany's racial mission in the east.

The Bolsheviks attributed the famine to foreign intervention, anti-communist forces, and speculative profiteering and hoarding. Their opponents blamed the famine on Bolshevik requisitioning and centralization of food supply.[72] The control of famine and disease became a test of Bolshevik authority. Soviet propaganda urged the people to rid themselves of lice as they had of 'counter-revolutionary parasites' like Admiral Alexander Kolchak, and attributed the famine to the devastation of the civil war.

By July 1921 Lenin, concerned that famine and disease accelerated erosion of rural support for Bolshevism, conceded the need for international food aid. Famously declaring to the Seventh Congress of Soviets that 'socialism must defeat the louse (the carrier of typhus) or the louse will defeat socialism', he gambled that assistance from the West would reinforce the Soviet administration in overcoming the epidemic crisis.[73] Realizing that an effective famine relief programme required mobilization of massive economic, technical, and medical resources, Lenin calculated that an appeal to Germany would pose a counterweight to aid from the belligerent and capitalist Allied powers intent on undermining the Bolshevik regime.

The lifting of the curtain of secrecy in order to publicize the need for relief was a delicate matter. The Soviet leaders were unable to appeal directly to antagonistic governments, which did not recognize their rule and might again intervene militarily if they perceived the Bolsheviks as weak. A dramatic gesture was needed to alert foreigners to the urgency of the situation. Lenin authorized an appeal to Western 'men of culture' by the author Maxim Gorky, renowned for portraying poverty in pre-Revolutionary Russia. Gorky depicted Russia as a cradle of European cultural leaders, while he warned that this intellectual fecundity was threatened by the grave crisis of famine and disease.

Gorky telegraphed the German dramatist Gerhart Hauptmann on 12 July 1921, and then the Norwegian explorer Fridtjof Nansen and the American Relief Administration (ARA) supremo Herbert Hoover for 'bread and medicines' from 'honest European and American people'. Gorky glowingly portrayed Russia as the land of Tolstoy, Dostoyevsky (especially fitting given the epidemic nightmare in *Crime and*

---

[70] *European Health Conference* (1922), 15.
[71] Zinsser, *Rats*, 213, 299.
[72] L. T. Lih, *Bread and Authority in Russia, 1914–1921* (Berkeley, Calif., 1990); D. Footman, *Civil War in Russia* (London, 1961).
[73] F. Le Gros Clark and N. L. Brinton, *Men, Medicine and Food in the USSR* (London, 1936), 19.

Punishment), Mendeleyev, Pavlov, Mussorgsky, and Glinka. Gorky acted on behalf of an All-Russian Famine Relief Committee of ten communists and fifty non-communists, which the authorities fleetingly condoned.[74] Gorky's telegram was publicized on 18 July in German liberal and socialist newspapers.[75]

The appeal was a coded message to the German government for technical assistance but also for support against the iniquities of the post-Versailles political order. At this juncture Hauptmann was at the height of his influence as a national cultural icon. He supported the new German Republic from a standpoint of moderate nationalism.[76] In February 1919 he appealed to the Allies to alleviate burdens of the Versailles Treaty; in 1920 he called for a wholly German-administered Upper Silesia, and he had to put an end to rumours that he was intending to stand for the office of *Reichspräsident*.[77] Hauptmann contacted the mercurial Walter Rathenau in his capacity as Minister of Reconstruction, for he was a kindred intellectual, an industrialist, and hopeful of an eastern shift in Germany's foreign policy. The German Foreign Office confirmed that Gorky's gesture had the stamp of Russian government approval, and the cabinet decided that a committee should work with the German Red Cross to provide medical relief.[78] Hauptmann, reflecting that Gorky's appeal sought intellectual assistance as well as material aid, hoped that Rathenau could release healing forces and 'cure the poison in the body of Europe'. He diagnosed a relief programme as a cure for the German trauma of defeat: aid from the German to the Russian people would reinvigorate the soul of the Germans, and benefit not only Russia and Germany, but also Europe and the world.[79] Here was a rhetoric of salvation which countered the devastation conjured up by Churchill and other implacable foes of the new Russia.

Despite the threat of a domestic communist revolution, there was a pragmatic sense of *Realpolitik* that coexistence with the Soviet Union was in Germany's interest. Moreover, amicable relations with the central Soviet authorities, while

[74] B. D. Wolfe, *The Bridge and the Abyss. The Troubled Friendship of Max Gorky and V. I. Lenin* (London, 1967), 108–114; B. M. Weissmann, 'The American Relief Administration in Famine, 1921–1923: A Case Study in the Interaction Between Opposing Political Systems', Ph.D. diss., Columbia University, 1968, 123–7; revised as *Herbert Hoover and Famine Relief to Soviet Russia, 1921–1923* (Stanford, Calif., 1974); H. H. Fisher, *The Famine in Soviet Russia, 1919–1923: The Operations of the American Relief Administration* (New York, 1927).

[75] 'Helft Sowjetrussland!', *Die Rote Fahne*, 321 (18 July 1921); 'Russlands Hungerkatastrophe', *Vorwärts*, 324 (18 July 1921); 'Maxim Gorki für das hungernde Russland. Ein Notruf an Gerhart Hauptmann', *Vossische Zeitung*, 333, evening edn. (18 July 1921); 'Entsendung Maxim Gorkis ins Ausland', *Berliner Tageblatt*, 338 (21 July 1921). For bibliography see E. Czikowsky, I. Idzikowski, and G. Schwarz, *Max Gorki in Deutschland. Bibliographie 1894 bis 1965* (Berlin, 1968).

[76] For Hauptmann and eugenics see Weindling, *Health, Race and German Politics*, 64–89.

[77] C. F. W. Behl and F. A. Voigt, *Chronik von Gerhart Hauptmanns Leben und Tod* (Munich, 1957), 80–5. Hauptmann's reply to Gorky ran: Vielleicht trägt der übergrelle Strahl Ihres Notrufs dazu bei, das weiderum aus der blutgetränkten Erde hervorzulocken, was Sie die schöpferische Kraft und die Menschlichkeit der Völker nennen. Die ganze zivilisierte Welt hat ihren erschütternden Ruf nicht nur mit den Ohren, sondern mit den Herzen gehört.

[78] Staatsbibliothek Preussischer Kulturbesitz Berlin, Gerhart Hauptmann papers, letters from Rathenau 21 and 28 July 1921; Foreign Office to Hauptmann 8 Aug. 1921.

[79] Hauptmann papers, letter to Rathenau 19 July 1921.

stopping short of diplomatic recognition, would allow support for the ethnic Germans, who could take a key role in the event of a collapse of the Soviet regime. German medical scientists had high hopes for building up relations with Russian doctors and officials as they were excluded from the international medical and scientific arena. Such motives underlay the concern to sustain the German hospital in Tiflis (which kept its German staff after the German army withdrew from the Caucasus in 1918) when the Soviet Union incorporated Georgia in 1921. With a hidden agenda of German national support for the ethnic Germans, a bilateral German–Soviet programme of medical cooperation took shape.

The new medical Ostpolitik was a rallying-point for public health officials, diplomats, scientists, industrialists, and nationalists. On 22 July 1921 the German government approved a relief expedition with the covert support of the Foreign Office and Reich Ministry of the Interior as responsible for domestic anti-epidemic measures.[80] A Hamburg pharmaceutical company, Queisser, planned shipments of medicines to Russia, and on 23 July it contacted Ludolf Brauer, a former associate of Behring and director of a privately financed Research Institute for Clinical Pharmacology at Hamburg's immense Eppendorf Hospital. Brauer explained to Hauptmann that he regarded medical assistance as a means of spreading German culture, and that this might prepare the ground for political change in Russia. He planned a Russian edition of a German medical journal, while supplying medicines to Russia.[81] A crucial link was forged between Hamburg medical researchers and the relief measures.

On 24 July Hauptmann replied to Gorky with the approval of the Foreign Office in an allegorical, apocalyptic tone: that the post-war world was in an unnatural, inhumane, and divided state and that the German people stood on the edge of an abyss 'after the earth has drunk the nation's blood'. He welcomed Gorky's plea as a noble mission, even if its final solution was beyond all human powers. He hoped that the German people, despite its own misery, could assist the Russian struggle against hunger and disease.[82] The positive response to the appeal meant that Gorky's committee had outlived its usefulness, and its non-communist members were imprisoned and many were deported. Gorky was outraged, and became a dissident critic spending much of the 1920s in exile.[83]

Gorky's appeal provided an opportunity for nurturing German relations with the Soviet government as a preliminary to the formal diplomacy culminating in the Treaty of Rapallo between Germany and the Soviet Union in 1922. The Reich government mobilized the German Red Cross as a non-governmental but official body, which had just been formed in 1921 from a range of voluntary welfare and

---

[80] 'Eine deutsche Hilfsaktion für Russland', *Tägliche Rundschau*, 338 (22 July 1921), also in *Vossische Zeitung*, 341 (22 July 1921).

[81] Hauptmann papers, Br NL B V: Russlandhilfe, letters of Queisser and Co. to Brauer 23 July 1921; Brauer to Hauptmann 24 July 1921.

[82] Hauptmann papers, Briefe, Telegramm Maxim Gorki and Gerhart Hauptmann (original and abbreviated typescript); 1921 Antwort Gerhart Hauptmanns auf das Telegramm Maxim Gorkis.

[83] B. D. Wolfe, *The Bridge and the Abyss. The Troubled Friendship of Max Gorky and V. I. Lenin* (London, 1967), 108–14; Weissman, 'Famine', 123–7.

nursing organizations.[84] The German Red Cross was administered by imperially minded military figures, and had a highly conservative ethos, exemplified by its propagandistic relief work in the disputed territory of Upper Silesia.[85] Organizing a Russian relief expedition demonstrated the national aims of the German Red Cross.

Further assistance came from the 'Billroth Foundation for German Medicine Overseas', commemorating a nationalist and anti-Semitic German surgeon from Vienna, and founded in 1921 with funds once earmarked for military hospitals in Belgium. This choice of a medical icon asserted a Greater German identity going beyond the political confines of the Reich. The Billroth Foundation used its resources to sustain ethnic German communities abroad. Those involved included Major General Friedrich Freiherr Kress von Kressenstein, a veteran of the attack on the Suez canal, and chief of operations in the Caucasus from May 1918; doctors with military experience like Brauer who had been on active service in Palestine and Turkey, His who had been in Russian Poland, and Nocht, the supremo of German tropical medicine. The secretary, Rudolf Fricke, who had accompanied a military expedition to Georgia, believed that German physicians could gain influence and build up good will for Germany in the 'Halbkulturländer' of Eastern Europe by sustaining their hospitals as cultural centres.[86]

On 30 July 1921 the German Red Cross informed the Russian Red Cross that it was preparing a hospital ship with medical, disinfection, and nursing staff. A steering committee was selected from a broad political spectrum—the women members ranged from the right-wing Elisabeth Förster-Nietzsche to the left-wing artist Käthe Kollwitz. Hauptmann, the president of the Reich Health Office, bankers, parliamentary representatives including two socialists—Otto Braun and the radical physician Julius Moses—and a trade unionist joined the committee. Public health and German Red Cross officials gave their support. But the public involvement of notables was a front, as the German Foreign Office skilfully managed the proceedings.[87]

Russian famine relief gave the Germans an opportunity of stemming the tide of eastern refugees under the pretext of anti-epidemic measures, as well as securing an eastern ally. The strict immigration controls of the United States and the closure of the Soviet Union's borders coincided with rising German hostility to Eastern European migrants. The German authorities combined anti-Semitism, anti-Bolshevism, and anti-epidemic measures, fearing that returning prisoners of war

---

[84] H. Böhme, *Die organisatorische Grundlagen des Roten Kreuz* (Berlin, 1925); F. W. Brekenburg, *Das deutsche Rote Kreuz* (Berlin, 1938); H. Seithe and F. Hagemann, *Das Deutsche Rote Kreuz im Dritten Reich (1933–1939). Mit einem Abriss seiner Geschichte in der Weimarer Republik* (Frankfurt/M., 1993).

[85] BAP 15.01 Nr 9398, Bl. 76 Winterfeldt memorandum 6 Oct. 1921. Joachim von Winterfeldt was President and Paul Draudt was Secretary-General.

[86] Eckart, 'Medizin und auswärtige Kulturpolitik'. For contemporary heroization of Billroth see R. Gersuny, *Theodor Billroth* (Vienna, 1922); for the military background see W. Baumgart, *Deutsche Ostpolitik 1918. Vom Brest-Litowsk bis zum Ende des Ersten Weltkrieges* (Vienna and Munich, 1966), 181.

[87] The meetings were on 3 and 8 Aug. 1921.

would convey the 'bacilli of Bolshevism' into Western Europe.[88] The Hamburg medical department stressed the need for strict political, police, and sanitary controls on migrants, who were condemned as politically suspect, diseased, and poten-·tial burdens on the nascent German welfare state.[89]

The increasing distaste for the filth and disease of *Ostjuden* contrasted with the idealization of the pure Germanic qualities of the ethnic Germans in Russia. The German Red Cross organized a collection for the 'colonists', who were a potential antidote to modernist decay in the German heartlands. In November 1921 the Reich Migration Office convened a conference of organizations for the welfare of 'overseas Germans'. The policy of preventing Russian Germans from returning to Germany was extended to assisting other German communities in Eastern Europe to ensure that they stayed put. The mammoth US aid enterprise similarly compensated for the United States' restrictions on entry of Eastern Europeans.

Initially, the Reich Foreign Office planned a large-scale public collection by the German Red Cross so that aid should be from 'the German people' to 'the Russian people', manifesting the solidarity of the brotherhood of nations.[90] The German Red Cross mission countered more radical initiatives by the International Workers Relief. Left-wing municipalities like Berlin, Suhl, and Nuremberg made grants for Russian famine relief, and the communist leader Ernst Thälmann agitated for funds in Hamburg. The avant-garde theatrical director, Erwin Piscator, led an appeal of left-leaning artists and intellectuals, for which Kollwitz contributed a striking poster of an emaciated worker surrounded by outstretched hands.[91] But by November 1921 officials opposed a public collection, fearing that this would jeopardize foreign aid to Germany. The German Red Cross and other German civic organizations like the Deutsche Städtetag were advised by the Reich not to compromise Germany's image as a victim of an unjust peace by launching a public appeal for funds, or doling out grants from municipal coffers for the Soviet famine victims. The Hamburg authorities were concerned that any publicizing of their involvement might result in withdrawal of Dutch children's relief teams.[92]

The Reich Ministry of the Interior granted ten million marks exclusively for anti-epidemic measures, and in November 1921 allocated a further five million marks for Russian medical assistance. Despite the domestic ills of inflation, the Germans were determined to keep the expedition going. The Foreign Office imposed the condition that its subsidy should be concealed under the budgetary category of 'prevention of epidemic threats from the East'. So that awkward ques-

[88] A. Krammer, 'Soviet Propaganda among German and Austrian Prisoners of War in Russia 1917–1921', in S. R. Williamson and P. Pastor, *Essays on World War I. Origins and Prisoners of War* (New York, 1983), 239–64, also 116.

[89] STAH II F6 Bd III Meeting of Feb. 1921 Bl 101, 107.

[90] BAP 15.01 Nr 9398, Bl 158–9.

[91] Gerhart Hauptmann papers, Flysheet 'An alle Künstler und Intellektuelle' (Hauptmann was absent from the list of supporters); K. Kollwitz, *Ich sah die Welt mit liebevollen Blicken* (Wiesbaden, n.d.), p. 200, diary entry for 12 Sept. 1921; O. Nagel (ed.), *Käthe Kollwitz. Die Handzeichnungen* (Berlin, 1980), 368–9, 380–1; K. Kollwitz, *Bekenntnisse* (Leipzig, 1981), plate 33.

[92] STAH Senat Cl VI Nr 11, Vol. 1 Fasc. 64, Mitteilung des Deutschen Städtetags, 8 Sept. 1921.

tions should not be raised in the Reichstag the leaders of all political parties—with the exception of the communists—were informed about the covert financial arrangements on condition that secrecy was maintained.[93]

Diplomatic plots lay behind the scenes of the public drama of the famine. The German authorities sought to undermine the Treaty of Versailles by promoting Ostpolitik while at the same time projecting an image of being a victim of extortionate Allied conditions. Although Volga Germans had joined the White Russian and peasant resistance to Bolshevik food requisitions, the German government adopted a covert pro-Bolshevik policy. On 29 August 1921 Gustav Hilger, who was the German delegate to Moscow for repatriating prisoners of war and interned civilians, signed an agreement with Lev Borisovich Kamenev for German medical aid for the Soviet Union. The Germans avoided working under Nansen's multilateral arrangements, so that they could gain the confidence of Grigori Chicherin (the Commissar for Foreign Affairs), his deputy Maxim Litvinov, and Trotsky.[94]

Hilger, who had lived most of his life in Russia and (like Hoover) was an engineer by training, succeeded in gaining Soviet support at a high political level.[95] The German medical relief mission demonstrated the mutual benefits of cooperation with the Soviet authorities. Hilger had good official contacts as the repatriation office came under the Reich Finance Ministry, and he had links to the International Committee of the Red Cross and the League of Nations.[96] As the official delegate of the German Red Cross in Moscow, Hilger promoted medical assistance to pursue Germany's strategic aims.

The medical agenda of the expedition involved providing drugs, vaccines, and disinfectants against infectious diseases to prevent their spread to Germany, and the gaining of reliable 'epidemic intelligence'. While ostensibly for humanitarian relief and diplomatic ends of peaceful coexistence, the German relief expedition covertly provided an opportunity for medical advocates of *Lebensraum* to be planted in the Soviet Union. Although the tropical medicine specialist Nocht condemned the use of German resources in Russia as wasteful, his colleague at the Hamburg Tropical Institute, Mühlens, battled against such scepticism. Mühlens had been in naval service until 1911 while training in bacteriology at the Robert Koch Institute Berlin and the Hamburg Tropical Institute. From 1912 to 1914 he directed malaria prevention in Jerusalem, and secondment to the Bulgarian and Turkish armies made him aware of the importance of the Eastern arena. Mühlens directed the Red Cross expedition on temporary release from the Hamburg Institute where he was in charge of the clinical department. He was a dedicated

---

[93] BAP 15.01 Nr 9398, Bl. 45–6 memo of 1 Oct. 1921; Bl. 136–7 letter of 25 Nov. 1921 from Maltzan of Foreign Office to Reich Ministry of the Interior; Bl. 140–3 meeting of 6 Dec. 1921 in Reich Ministry of the Interior; STAH 352–8/9 Nocht to Mühlens 10 Aug. 1921.

[94] STAH 352 8/9 BNI 23 Bd 1, Mühlens report no. 3, 3 Oct. 1921.

[95] GARF 3341/6/316/153–5 for the text of the agreement; 3341/6/316/152 ratification of treaty by DRK Berlin 8 Nov. 1921; BAP 15.01 Nr 9398, Bl. 96–7 letter from Hilger 5 Nov. 1921.

[96] G. Hilger and A. G. Meyer, *The Incompatible Allies. A Memoir History of German–Soviet Relations* (London, 1953), 40–8; Hauptmann papers, letter of Schlesinger to Hauptmann 19 July 1921.

imperialist, promoting the expedition as a cultural mission which would also assist ethnic Germans.[97]

The Germans aimed to restore the prestige of German culture with Russian doctors, and to counter French and Anglo-American relief work. Mühlens regarded the expedition as a 'political gesture' to impress the Russians that the Germans were the first to provide aid. He had the backing of a steering committee, seasoned by military epidemic prevention: Frey was previously in charge of the German health administration in occupied Poland, Otto was the former typhus commissioner in Vilna, and Viktor Schilling from the Prussian Institute for Infectious Diseases had served with the Ottoman forces. With the support of the Billroth Foundation, they equipped the expedition with medicines, sera, and laboratory apparatus. On 17 September 1921 a German hospital ship, the *Triton*, arrived in Petrograd. Their tasks were to reoccupy the German Hospital, run an outpatient clinic for children, inoculate against cholera and smallpox, establish a central laboratory, co-operate with public health authorities, and mount famine relief and medical assistance within the city. The next objectives were to plant similar installations in Moscow and to relieve starvation among German 'colonists'—Mühlens spoke of 'his long-desired aim of helping German brothers'.[98]

Sanitary conditions in Petrograd and Moscow were better than expected with no plague and less cholera than had been reported in Germany. The Germans attended to the plight of 23,000 Volga refugees in Petrograd in November 1921. Although an effort was made to disinfect them and their clothing on arrival, the freezing water and lack of soap and washing facilities meant that they remained in a sick and louse-infested condition.[99] The relief team included a chemist, a sanitary engineer, and twenty nurses from the Hamburg Tropical Institute.[100] They distributed pharmaceutical supplies and children's dietary supplements to Soviet medical institutions, and diagnosed and treated infectious and sexually transmitted diseases. The German-equipped train, consisting of twenty-four coaches with a bacteriological laboratory, a pharmacy, disinfection and delousing facilities, a kitchen, an office, an operating theatre, and sanitary engineering equipment, was dispatched to quell the epidemic.

In October 1921 the relief train reached Kazan in the Tartar Republic.[101] Without

---

[97] F. Weyer, 'Zum Gedächtnis von Professor Mühlens', *Zeitschrift für hygienische Zoologie*, 35 (1943), 153–7.

[98] STAH 352 8/9 Bernhard Nocht Institut 23 Bd 1 letter from Mühlens to Nocht 14 July 1921; Mühlens report 21.

[99] BAP 15.01 Nr 9398, Bl. 190–6 Bericht über Besichtigung von Unterkunftsstätten für Wolgaflüchtlinge in Petersburg, 17 Nov. 1921.

[100] The doctors included: Peter Mühlens, O. Fischer, Ernst Nauck, and Heinrich Zeiss from the Hamburg Tropical Institute; Sütterlin, a bacteriologist; Wolfgang Gärtner, Privatdozent in hygiene at Kiel; G. Hellmann, a Berlin neurologist; Dr H. Karstens; Sanitätsrat Dr Mertens, an ophthalmologist from Wiesbaden; Sauer, a surgeon from Hamburg. Martin Hahn also went to the Crimea where he had extensive experience in cholera prevention. Gärtner died in Kazan. The chemist was Josef Halberkann. See W. Güthoff, 'Zur Epidemiologie und Bekämpfung der Seuchengeschehens in Sowjetrussland von 1918–1924', med. diss., Humboldt-Universität, Berlin, 1986, p. 71.

[101] E. Nauck, 'Von der Tätigkeit in Kasan', *BDRK* (1922), Sonderheft, 14–15.

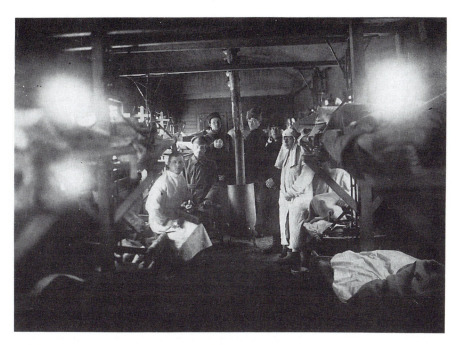

7. The German sanitary train, photographed by Peter Mühlens

food supplies apart from children's dietary supplements, the German doctors found that their medical equipment was of little use. Attempts to set up a hospital where the infectious might be diagnosed and then transferred to other hospitals failed. Bacteriological diagnosis ceased when Wolfgang Gärtner (a young bacteriologist) succumbed to typhus—a death that his colleagues hailed as a heroic sacrifice while on active service for the Fatherland. The Germans were appalled by excruciating poverty, filth, cramped, damp, and freezing living conditions, and hordes of starving refugees. Such distress exposed the impotence of the German mission, as well-equipped American and Workers Relief teams were able to dispense over two million meals a day to children.[102]

Hilger in Moscow and doctors on the expedition argued that expectations were running so high among the Volga Germans that for reasons of national prestige the German relief team had to have adequate food stocks. Moreover, without food the German aid would be eclipsed by Hoover's American Relief Administration and the (British) Save the Children Fund. Mühlens pronounced that the best medicine was food (echoing Virchow in 1848) but his plea fell on stony ground as German officials prefered a narrowly defined medical strategy giving priority to controlling

[102] BAP 15.01 Nr 9398, Mühlens report 14, 15 Dec. 1921; Wulf, *Tropeninstitut*, 15.

the spread of epidemic diseases.[103] The starving wanted bread rather than medical attention or laboratory analyses.[104] The German relief team argued that food and medical aid were vital: it was necessary to cure the sick as well as to feed them, and so prevent the spread of infectious diseases as improved diet enhanced immunity. Moreover, Russian support staff had to be paid with food packets—this took up 30 per cent of the rations.[105]

The Reich authorities refused to support a feeding programme, forcing Mühlens to cooperate with other relief agencies.[106] Achieving his priority of delivery of aid meant overcoming problems of transportation and distribution. The Germans used the railway network, but snow, ice, and floods impeded access to remote areas. Transport by sledge and horses consumed additional supplies, while demonstrating intrepid heroism of expedition members. The food stocks were donated by American Mennonites (a Baptist sect of German migrants with ancestral ties to the Volga Germans). The Germans also handed out semolina, patent dietary supplements, and clothing on behalf of the Swedes, the Nansen Relief Organization and the American Volga German Association.[107] The scale of American aid underlined the closure of the arteries of migration. With the prospect of conveying American donations of food to the Volga Germans, the time was ripe for the Germans to descend on Saratov (the main city in the Volga German area). Saratov was a focus of cholera and typhoid epidemics, and the German relief squad came equipped to combat an outbreak of plague. In June 1921 mortality in Saratov at the heart of the strategically important Volga grain growing region reached a crisis rate.[108] Bolshevik seizure of grain provoked violent resistance from the Volga German peasantry, and Saratov was crowded with destitute Germans.[109] The German relief train departed in March 1922 for the six-day journey to Saratov, and sledges drawn by camels and horses reached the outlying 'colonists'. Regular supplies were dispatched to the Volga German local committees for distribution on a weekly basis.

American Lutheran and Mennonite aid workers and the British Save the Children Fund were already active among the Volga Germans giving attention to the needs of children. The Germans' priority was feeding of the adult peasants in the remote outlying villages. They distributed flour, rice, oats, semolina, sugar, sauer-

---

[103] BAP 15.01 Nr 9398 Bl. 227 letter from Hilger 4 Dec. 1921.

[104] Mühlens, 'Hunger- und Seuchenkatastrophe', 19.

[105] STAH 352 8/9 Bernhard Nocht Institut 23 Bd 1, Mühlens report, no. 8, 29 Oct. 1921.

[106] BAP 15.01 Nr 9398, Bl. 140–8 meeting at Reich Ministry of the Interior of 6 Dec. 1921 concerning Russian relief.

[107] STAH 352 8/9 BNI 23 Bd 1 Mühlens report 14, 15 Dec. 1921; BAP 15.01 Nr 9398, Bl. 182 Agreement between Auslandskomitee zur Organisierung der Arbeiterhilfe für Hungernde and the German Red Cross 28 Nov. 1921.

[108] S. G. Wheatcroft, 'Famine and Factors Affecting Mortality in the USSR: The Demographic Crises of 1914–1922 and 1930–33', *Famine in History Newsletter. Alimentarium Colloquium* (1981). The Saratov death rates were 160 per 1,000 per annum.

[109] O. Figes, *Peasant Russia, Civil War. The Volga Countryside in Revolution 1917–1921* (Oxford, 1989), 272–3, 351; J. C. Long, 'The Volga Germans and the Famine of 1921', *The Russian Review*, 51 (1992), 510–25 for political background, attributing famine to excessive Bolshevik requisitions.

kraut, dried fruit, tea, miniscule amounts of meat extracts, dried milk, and soap. The expedition hoped to dissuade 'colonists' from desperate attempts at seeking provisions elsewhere in Russia or emigrating, but it could only do this with regular food consignments.[110]

The German relief teams took on an ever-widening sphere of operations. Between November 1921 and spring 1922 German teams went to the Crimea and the Ukraine, both areas with substantial German communities.[111] The bacteriologist Martin Hahn, who had last been in Odessa in spring 1918, returned there as German Red Cross representative.[112] In May 1922 a survey was made of the condition of the ethnic German settlers in the Ukraine and the Crimea. Famine and disease were intense, the main problems being typhus and relapsing fever arising from infestation by lice. Here 'colonists' had not received as much aid as the Volga Germans.[113] A German hospital was established at Simferopol, and a Red Cross expedition to the Ukraine and Crimea set out from Berlin in June 1922.[114] A German medical team at Minsk assisted thousands of refugees from the Volga-German Republic who intended to travel to Germany.[115] The Association of Volga Germans provided food aid and maintained fund-raising activities in Germany. The patriotic ideology of *Stammesbrüder* indicated the importance of racial motives in shaping German medical assistance.[116]

iv. International Intervention

The German relief effort projected domestic political animosities and nationalist grievances onto Russia. The distinctive profile of the German medical relief contrasted with the agendas of other international agencies. By 22 July 1921 Hoover (at that time Secretary of Commerce in Harding's Republican administration) was liaising with the US Secretary of State in order to gain clearance for an offer of massive aid; he contacted Gorky demanding absolute liberty in choice of area and independent local organization for American Relief Administration (ARA) relief

[110] P. Mühlens, 'Das Rote Kreuz bei den Wolgadeutschen', *BDRK* 1/4 (1922), 73–7; Gärtner, 'Die Hungersnot in den Wolgakolonien', *BDRK* 1/5 (1922), 113–14.

[111] Mühlens, 'Die Tätigkeit der Hilfsexpedition des Deutschen Roten Kreuzes in Russland', *BDRK* 2 (1921), 34–6.

[112] M. Hahn, 'Statistische Angaben über die Hungerleidenden im Gouvernement Odessa', *BDRK* 1/8 (1922), 197–8 dated 20 Apr. 1922.

[113] 'Reisebrief aus der Ukraine', *BDRK*, Sonderheft (1922), 15–16.

[114] BAP 0902/349 Bl. 59.

[115] W. Güthoff, *Zur Epidemiologie und Bekämpfung der Seuchengeschehens in Sowjetrussland von 1918–1924*, med. diss., Humboldt-Universität, Berlin, 1986, p. 68; LNA R 824 12B/26009X/15255 Haigh to Rajchman, 17 Feb. 1922; 'Visit to German Red Cross Sanitary Train'; R 825, 12B/29911X/15255 Zeiss to Zinsser, 30 July 1923; and Zeiss, 'Beobachtungen über die augenblicklich in den Wolgakolonien herrschende Malaria'.

[116] 'Gorki für die Wolgadeutschen', *Die Rote Fahne*, 53 (1 Feb. 1922), also in *Vossische Zeitung*, 53 (1 Feb. 1922), also in *Volk und Heimat. Zeitschrift des Vereins für das Deutschtum im Ausland*, 3 (1922), 44–5; *Helft Russland in Not* (Berlin: Auslandskomitee zur Organisierung der Arbeiterhilfe für Russland, 1922).

teams. Although the Soviets had previously refused entry to the ARA, which had started out as a US government agency for war relief and then to fight communism, they accepted the conditions by 26 July; conflicts then arose over what constituted unwarranted political intervention. The Germans had a head start over the ARA, which only agreed a treaty in Riga with Litvinov on 20 August 1921.[117] While the Bolsheviks hoped that aid would ultimately lead to economic and technical reconstruction, the Americans intended famine relief to boost the capacity of the population to resist the Bolshevik 'disease'. Lenin contrasted American subversion with German support.[118] The Germans accepted Soviet direction as a step towards subverting the post-Versailles European order.

The other lead role was taken by Fridtjof Nansen, whose heroic reputation as an arctic explorer and scientist gave him considerable personal authority, reinforced by Norwegian neutrality during the 1914–18 war. Early in 1919 Hoover persuaded Nansen to organize a medical relief commission for Russia backed by the Norwegians, Swedes, and other neutral countries but the scheme was wrecked by continuing hostilities, and by Hoover coming to regard Nansen as a rival.[119] From March 1920 Nansen supervised repatriation of prisoners of war for the League of Nations—there being somewhere near 200,000 Russians in Germany and France, and 300,000 German military and civilian detainees in Russia. During the First World War the tsarist government had forcibly evacuated ethnic Germans and Jews from frontline areas to the Volga region, from where after the Revolution came streams of demobilized and deserting soldiers and homeless and destitute civilians.[120]

Nansen and the League of Nations appealed for international aid for the repatriation of refugees and for famine relief.[121] Nansen's Comité international de secours à la Russie and the Nansen mission in Moscow from August 1921 had support from the International Committee of the Red Cross in Geneva. The Nansen Committee developed the ICRC's Central European strategy of epidemic assistance without involving the Allies. In a radio broadcast 'to the world' Nansen pleaded for surpluses of grain and livestock feed to be sent to the starving in Russia. He provided a coordinating structure for a plethora of international aid organizations, while resenting how Hoover's ARA monopolized famine relief.[122] The German relief teams forged close links with the Nansen organization and aid workers from countries which were not former German enemies; the Germans and Nansen shared a scientific outlook linked to a deeply held conservative nationalism. Nansen's assis-

---

[117] Weissman, 'Famine', 130–5.

[118] Ibid., 121; D. C. Engerman develops this argument in Engerman, 'Economic and Cultural Aspects of Early American-Soviet Relations', M.A. diss., Rutgers University, pp. 5–6. I am grateful to David Engerman for making sections of his dissertation available.

[119] Weissman, 'Famine', 41–6; E. E. Reynolds, *Nansen* (Harmondsworth, 1932), 216–23.

[120] Marrus, *The Unwanted*, 54–5.

[121] F. Nansen, *Russland und der Friede* (Leipzig, 1923); Nansen, *Russia and Peace* (London, 1923), 37, 146–55; 'Internationale Hilfskomittee für Russland', *MMW* (17 Feb. 1922), 259–60; Marrus, *Unwanted*, 86–91.

[122] Weissman, 'Famine', 152–3.

tant, Captain Vidkun Quisling (the future Norwegian fascist leader), was greatly liked by the Germans.[123] In June 1922 Hauptmann and Gorky praised Nansen for his self-sacrificing heroism and as a 'civilized European type on the verge of extinction' threatened by indifference and war.[124]

The various aid organizations exerted themselves to outdo one another. The Quaker 'Anglo-American Society of Friends', the Save the Children Fund, and the Mennonites competed with communist and trade union organizations. The International Workers' Commission for Aid to Starving Russia benefited from the vocal support of intellectuals like Kollwitz, Albert Einstein, and Bernard Shaw.[125] The combined European relief teams, grouped under Nansen's International Russian Relief Commission, fed two million persons per day. The Save the Children Fund fed 300,000 children and 250,000 adults from 1,450 kitchens in Saratov by July 1922, and supplied the kitchens of other relief agencies.[126] This far exceeded what the Germans were able to provide, but starving crowds besieged the feeding centres and increased the risk of typhus. The Quaker and the Save the Children Fund's strategy of concentrating on feeding children changed because of the increasing numbers of helpless orphans; mothers, transport workers, and finally whole communities were fed.[127]

Yet the whole relief enterprise was pervaded by suspicions of subversion. Trotsky denounced the American relief effort as a means of opening up the Soviet market, dumping US grain surpluses, and protecting counter-revolutionary bourgeois Russians; Stalin distrusted foreign philanthropy as spying and espionage agencies. The ARA accused the Soviet authorities of victimizing its Russian contacts.[128] The Germans were vulnerable to accusations of having a hidden capitalist agenda. Deals involving the export of furs reflected badly on the German mission.[129]

The German strategy was more scientific and racist when compared to that of

[123] Germany was the base for further international appeals by the Russian Red Cross, which issued bulletins (from an office at Unter den Linden 11) and organized two conferences in Berlin in 1922. *Bulletin der Auslandsvertretung der Hilfskommission für die Hungernden beim Allrussischen Zentral-Exekutiv-Komitee*, 4 (13 Jan. 1922); 'Zweite Internationale Konferenz für die Hungerhilfe in Russland am 9. Juli 1922', *Bulletin* (1 Aug. 1922).

[124] F. Nansen, M. Gorky, and C. Hauptmann, *Russland und die Welt* (Berlin, 1922); F. Mierau (ed.), *Russen in Berlin 1918–1933. Eine kulturelle Begegnung* (Weinheim and Berlin, 1988), 188–205.

[125] W. Duranty, *Russia Reported* (London, 1934), 23–43. For Soviet attempts to conceal deficiences from the ARA: A. Rachmanova, *Ehen im Roten Sturm* (Salzburg, n.d.), 193.

[126] *The Record*, 2 (1921–2), 19–21, 294, 298, 308; M. MacKenzie, *Medical Relief in Europe* (London, 1942), 16; R. Breen, 'Saving Enemy Children: Save the Children's Russian Relief Operation, 1921–23', *Disasters*, 18 (1994), 221–37.

[127] A. R. Fry, *A Quaker Adventure* (London, 1926), 175. The Quakers favoured soup kitchens with an emphasis on staple foods and cocoa-based items—a diet seriously deficient in calories, minerals, and vitamins.

[128] Weissman, 'Famine', 270.

[129] Güthoff, *Epidemiologie*, 65; Mackenzie, *Medical Relief*, 40. The SCF staff developed efficient supply routes: Charles Douglas Roberts served in the South Russia British [Military] Mission, and then joined the Nansen Organization and the Save the Children Fund in Russia. Gilbert, *Churchill*, iv. 306. Roberts was born in Odessa of British parents and was in the mining business in the Caucasus and Siberia 1924–30.

after relief agencies. The American agencies supplied medicines and food aid, whereas most bacteriological work was left to the Germans.[130] Many Russian physicians knew German and welcomed the presence of the Germans. The Soviet authorities preferred German doctors because of the diplomatic realignment with Germany.[131] The scale of ARA operations was vast when compared to that of the Germans: by August 1922 the ARA's 200 American personnel supervised feeding 10.5 million Russians from 18,073 kitchens, and sent food, linen, and medical supplies to 5,000 institutions and 1,837 hospitals, and to the Soviet Railway Sanitary Service. The most prominent ARA medical expert was Vernon Kellogg, a physiologist, nutritionist, and Hoover's special adviser on infant feeding. In marked contrast to the German bacteriologists, the emphasis of the ARA's director, Colonel William N. Haskell, was on the distribution of corn, milk, cocoa, wheat seed, soap, and clothing.[132] The American approach to hygiene was based on food, soap (2.4 million tons were sent), disinfectants (including 800,000 pounds of sulphur and 200,000 pounds of formaldehyde), and hair clippers, whereas the Germans deployed bacteriology, chemotherapeutic drugs, and sera as a means of restoring the health and productivity of the German 'colonists'.[133] The massive resources of the ARA, the Save the Children Fund, and the International Workers' Relief overshadowed the efforts of the German Red Cross. Mühlens conceded that in the Volga region the British agencies, the ARA, and American Mennonites saved thousands of children from death by starvation.[134] Neither the organization of relief, nor the choice of recipients was determined by disinterested humanitarianism.

v. The European Health Conference

The bad blood between the German and Allied medical experts impeded international dialogue and concerted assistance. German officials resented that they were not consulted over the founding of the League of Nations Health Organization. The German Foreign Ministry gained Dutch, Swedish, and Swiss support against British and French dominance over the new Health Organization.[135] In 1920 the President of the Reich Health Office regretted that only entente states were at the London health conference. There was public outrage that Germany, 'the land of Robert Koch and Behring', was not admitted to the new international sanitary authority.[136]

---

[130] Fry, *Quaker Adventure*, 190.

[131] Bod MSS Eng d 667 fo. 27: comment by Soloviev to E. Sharp.

[132] W. Duranty, *Russia Reported* (London, 1934), 23–43; Mackenzie, *Medical Relief*, 16; Engerman, 'Economic and Cultural Aspects', 19; Zinsser, *As I Remember Him*, 272–3.

[133] Mühlens, 'Hunger- und Seuchenkatastrophe', 44–5; H. H. Fisher, *The Famine in Soviet Russia 1919–1923. The Operation of the American Relief Administration* (New York, 1927), 427–43 for the Medical Division of the ARA.

[134] STAH 352 8/9 BNI 23 Bd 1 Mühlens report 21.

[135] BAP 15.01/ 11233 Akten betr internationales Gesundheitsamt beim Völkerbund Bd 1, July 1920.

[136] *Kreuzzeitung* (15 Dec. 1920) cutting in: GSTA Rep 76 VIII B Nr 3567.

Germany's exclusion from the League of Nations prompted the accusation that Allied dominance over international agencies suppressed German cultural and scientific influence. But the alarm over eastern epidemics provided a passport for Germany's entry to the League of Nations Health Organization. German bacteriologists reacted by dividing into hostile political camps. International idealists considered that here was an opportunity for Germany to cooperate in the pursuit of humane ends of peaceful coexistence. But nationalists fulminated at the loss of territories and colonies, and the burdens of reparations.

Many Allied health experts remained suspicious of German professors as representing an unrepentant militarism. The Rockefeller Foundation condemned German public health as backward in its clinging to laboratory-based methods, politically suspect, and dominated by authoritarian professors.[137] Revisionism of the Versailles territorial settlement and concern to protect ethnic German minorities in Eastern Europe shaped the general thrust of German diplomacy and its medical sub-plot. The Reich encouraged associations of German minorities to protest in Geneva against the oppressive central European states.[138]

German attitudes to international agencies for health and welfare were characterized by a complex pattern of ambivalence, hostility, and grudging cooperation. German resentment of the League of Nations can be seen as carrying on a pre-war tradition of distrusting French-sponsored medical schemes. The League's sponsorship of biological standardization outraged bacteriologists in Frankfurt am Main as this deprived the Institute for Experimental Therapy (established for Paul Ehrlich) of its international role as a standard setting authority. As a concession the League permitted the Germans to retain salvarsan standards in Frankfurt despite Belgian and French hostility.[139]

The League of Nations Epidemic Commission shifted its operations from Poland to Russia, so as to monitor the spread of the epidemic from its epicentre. The British and French commissioners were as alarmed at the activities of the German relief teams as at the disastrous health conditions. In September 1921 the League of Nations sent a special commission to Moscow and to tour the famine areas, the Ukraine, and the Caucasus to gauge the prevalence of typhus and malaria, and distribute laboratory equipment and supplies of quinine and other surplus British army drugs.[140] The American and League of Nations sanitary commissioners coordinated their efforts while being vehemently anti-communist and loathing the central authorities. The seconded British Ministry of Health medical officer W. E. Haigh wrote to Rajchman from Minsk in July 1922: 'the communist

---

[137] RAC Rockefeller Foundation Strode diary 19 Apr. 1928 concerning a visit to Berlin; E. Schnabel, *Soziale Hygiene zwischen Sozialer Reform und Sozialer Biologie. Fritz Rott (1878–1959) und die Säuglingsfürsorge in Deutschland* (Husum, 1995), 129–36.

[138] Kimmich, *Germany*, 136–7.

[139] RAC Rockefeller Foundation 6.1/1.1/38/468 H. H. Dale memo on standards.

[140] League of Nations, *Minutes of the Fifth Session of the Health Committee* (Geneva, 1923), 7–8. *Minutes of the Sixth Session of the Health Committee* (Geneva, 1923), 67–71. Reginald Farrar contracted typhus and died. Haigh established a Moscow office. In August 1922 a commissioner, M. Pantaleoni, was sent to Kharkov in the Ukraine, and took over the Moscow office from September 1922 until September 1923.

element is established fully so that no confidence can be placed in anything'.[141] Haigh resented that the Soviet authorities 'would not allow any distinction between the non-political, technical, epidemiological side, and the other League activities'.[142] He denounced the German Red Cross organization for supporting the communist authorities in the Ukraine: 'The German Red Cross introduction of literature, and the absence of all real contact with other parts of Europe must be balanced if any real international outlook is to be maintained in Russia in the future of medicine'.[143]

While the commissioners in the field were deeply hostile to the German medical alliance with the communists, Rajchman as director of the commission adopted a policy of building up good relations with these erstwhile foes. The Poles' alarm over invasion by infectious diseases from the east during the winter of 1921–2 prompted them to call on the League of Nations to hold an international conference. All European states were invited to a 'European International Health Conference' in Warsaw from 20 to 28 March 1922 to tackle Russian typhus. Its status was that of a Polish government conference held under League of Nations auspices. Non-member states like Germany, Ukraine, and Russia were invited, and their participation marked a turning-point in the efforts to rehabilitate German and Russian medical scientists internationally.[144] Russian typhus was depicted as a European problem. Supranational action was called for, but whether the resulting measures were to override or be accountable to the concerned states was left unresolved.

The Russians initially insisted that the conference should also deal with epidemics in the west, a symbolically interesting move against the stigmatization of the east (and understandable given typhus outbreaks in camps where Russian prisoners of war were held), but one that was deflated by the lack of epidemics in Western Europe. The French retained grave doubts concerning any cooperation with the Russians and Germans. However, German participation paved the way for representation on the Health Committee of the League of Nations: the appointment of the intensely nationalistic Nocht early in 1923 revived the flagging fortunes of German bacteriology.[145] The German delegates in Warsaw were Frey, Otto, and Mühlens, the head of the German Red Cross Relief expedition.[146] Brazenly nationalistic, German doctors condemned Polish public health as unreliable, and extolled their own achievements in combating epidemics. They welcomed the possibility of

---

[141] LNA R 824/12B/26009X/15255 Haigh to Rajchman letter of 7 July 1922.

[142] Ibid., Haigh to Rajchman 22 Apr. 1922.

[143] LNA R 824 12B/26009X/15255 Haigh to Rajchman, 17 Feb. 1922; R 824 12B/26009X/15255 Haigh to Rajchman, July 1922.

[144] Only Albania and Portugal did not send delegates. As a governmental conference, the LRCS had not been able to send a delegate but it contributed £5,000 to the conference costs. (*Minutes of the Third Session of the Health Committee* (May 1922), 64.) Although the Conference's report was published by the Health Secretariat of the League of Nations, the League's Secretariat could only take note of its recommendations rather than accept these as binding.

[145] Balińska, 'Assistance'.

[146] BAK R 86/3729 Report by Otto, 4 Mar. 1922. GSTA Rep 76 VIII B Nr 3401 RMdI conference with representatives from the Länder.

international support for intervention in Russia in order to eradicate the epidemic at its epicentre.

The conference delegates agreed that the epidemic posed a threat to Europe's health and stability. They inspected the Polish 'defence system' of quarantine stations and isolation hospitals, and heard about the distress of infested refugees carrying typhus and relapsing fever: Haigh reported that in White Russia and the Ukraine the refugee situation was out of control, with unknown numbers living wild in the forests.[147] The lack of disinfection procedures in Moscow was diagnosed as a major cause of infested refugees arriving in the west. In the Ukraine refugees crowding stations produced immense sanitary problems.[148] Mühlens warned of 'the terrible danger' of an exodus of starving and infected populations as the famine spread.[149] In view of the horrendous conditions, delegates concluded that the increase of cholera and mass-migration from famine-stricken areas 'combine to constitute an immediate danger to the rest of Europe'. While delousing was prescribed for all refugees, the priority was to prevent migration by eradicating the source of the epidemic.

The conference extended the policy of 'sanitary defence' to include most of European Russia—so that epidemics could be suppressed at their focal points. The Italian and German delegations modified the terms 'sanitary cordon' and 'quarantine', because quarantine required bacteriological examinations rather than just observation and isolation. A sanitary cordon was impractical given that a rigid line of demarcation along frontiers was not feasible, and so the concept of a 'sanitary zone' with 'stations of exchange' was mooted.[150] After cleansing and disinfection, all arrivals were to be vaccinated against smallpox and with typhoid–paratyphoid–cholera vaccine. The conference embarked on a macabre exercise of distributing non-existent funds. Latvia, Lithuania, and Poland were allocated aid to increase the capacity of quarantine and disinfection stations. The Poles requested funds for fifty hospitals, thirty mobile hospitals, ninety mobile delousing units, and fifty mobile delousing and shower bath units, five bacteriological laboratories, and sanitary improvements to internment camps at the immense cost of £700,000. But the Allies preferred to keep the starving in place rather than provide elaborate installations for transmigrants. This policy demonstrated that sanitary defence had become sanitary attack.

The Germans proposed an international campaign against the famine in Russia and the Ukraine as the chief sources of epidemics. The interventionist strategy was endorsed, despite Germany's status as an international outcast. Rajchman agreed that it was necessary to attack the epidemics at source rather than to rely on a double line of monitoring stations along the eastern frontier of Poland. The arteries of communication became channels of disease, as epidemics spread along railways and waterways.[151] The Railway Sanitary Service provided dispensaries, hospital beds (numbering 10,000 in 1923), baths, and medical supplies for railway

---

[147] *European Health Conference* (Geneva, 1922), 18–23.
[148] Ibid.   [149] Ibid., 24.   [150] Ibid., 12.   [151] Zinsser, *Rats*, 292.

workers and passengers, and the rolling stock and waiting-rooms had to be kept clean. What was in theory a well-planned system to control the spread of epidemics was overwhelmed by refugees. The strengthening of the public health service in Russia and the Ukraine was a general aim, as there were shortages of soap, disinfectants, disinfecting apparatus, vaccines, and drugs. Delegates planned a second line of delousing stations and feeding points further east to cleanse passengers in transit, and to protect Central Russia and the Ukraine. They targeted the Donets basin as an economically important centre of coal and iron-mining, which was affected by typhus, cholera, and famine. A priority was to combat childhood infections such as trachoma.[152] The cost of this grandiose programme was estimated to be one and a half million pounds. The League of Nations asked all European countries to support these measures, and to ratify them at the Genoa international conference in April 1922—somewhat ironic as the German diplomatic overtures to Russia secured the rival Treaty of Rapallo.

The Warsaw conference did little to suppress epidemics but it eased international tensions by paving the way for sanitary conventions. The Russian delegation insisted on bilateral sanitary agreements, rather than accepting the authority of the League of Nations, of which Russia was not a member, and consequently negotiated with Latvia, Estonia, and Finland; the Poles met the Russian and Ukrainian delegations; and the Czechoslovaks and Poles were prepared to deal with the Germans.[153] The Health Committee endorsed the plan 'to organise, on a broader basis, international co-operation in the campaign against epidemics in Eastern Europe'.[154]

The gloomy prognosis that financial support from respective governments would not materialize turned out to be correct, apart from a Czech contribution. After internal wrangles in the Cabinet, the British reluctantly offered £100,000 for anti-epidemic measures on both sides of the Polish–Russian frontier, providing that £200,000 would be raised from other governments. George Buchanan of the British Ministry of Health proposed that frontier sanitary measures be financed from a tax on trade with Russia.[155] The LRCS was willing to contribute to the costs of medical schools in Warsaw, Moscow, and Kiev, and it financed training courses in Kharkov and in Moscow on the prevention and control of epidemics for forty-nine medical officers between November 1922 and March 1923.[156] The financial shortfall meant that the League of Nations epidemic commissioners were restricted to the limited role of reporting on sanitary conditions in the frontier zone of Russia and White Russia.[157] Overall, the programme was a failure: in July 1923 the Poles conceded that it had not been possible to create a sanitary zone.[158] The scheme was

---

[152] *European Health Conference*, 38–41.
[153] *Minutes of the Third Session of the Health Committee*, 53.
[154] Ibid., 56.   [155] Ibid., 68.
[156] *Minutes of the Fifth Session of the Health Committee* (Geneva, 1923), 7–8; *Minutes of the Sixth Session of the Health Committee* (Geneva, 1923), 67–71; LNA R 816/8138 LRCS correspondence, Claude Hill to Rajchman 22 and 29 May 1922.
[157] 'Medical Provision in the Western Frontier Zone of Russia', *Second Annual Report* (1922), 24–7.
[158] *Sixth Report of the Health Committee*, 105.

redundant as by this time the epidemic was subsiding, and the frontiers had stabilized.

The Warsaw conference resulted in the Soviet Union and Germany being drawn into the League of Nations' international health schemes. Soviet medical experts favoured injections of aid to boost internal reconstruction; the energetic Commissar for Health, Nikolai Semashko, valued German medical expertise as crucial for the building up of a modern system of socialized medicine—and foreign relations. Semashko welcomed foreign technical assistance, whether from the Rockefeller Foundation which made periodic forays into the Soviet Union or from German medical scientists. Semashko attended the fifth session of the LNHO Hygiene Committee in Geneva on 11 January 1923 when he agreed to exchanges of experts and to an international survey of teaching in hygiene and social hygiene.[159] Semashko and Rajchman discussed arrangements for providing epidemiological information to the League, and decided to carry out a survey of typhoid immunization and endemic cholera.[160] The League of Nations Epidemic Commission drafted in the American bacteriologist Zinsser to investigate the spread of cholera, distribute medicines, and to collaborate with Russian immunologists under Lev Tarasevich. Pyjoff of the Ukrainian epidemiological service joined the international visit of medical personnel to Italy in December 1922, and Sergei Nikanorov, a plague expert from Saratov, visited Germany and the Pasteur Institute in 1922 and Germany in 1924 on the League of Nations exchange programme; from February to April 1923 three Soviet medical officers visited Britain.[161] Typhus prevention thus served to promote the interaction of professional élites, stabilize the post-war borders, and integrate Weimar German and Soviet medicine into international health schemes. But the disease control measures evoked a sense of fatalism and futility when it came to alleviating the sufferings of the sick.

vi. The Famine as Holocaust

The League of Nations sanitary commissioners reported on the epidemic 'holocaust'—the term conveyed their alarm at the mounting deaths and devastation. People were described as 'bravely carrying on under conditions whose horror we cannot picture', with agony, anguish, and lethargy from starvation and the inevitability of death, especially for small children.'[162] Zinsser's verdict on the famine was: 'It was a new experience of human misery, and more dreadful to see than battlefields or death from disease.'[163] Statistical efforts to convey the scale of the disaster invoked a sense of an overwhelming calamity rather than demographic

---

[159] League of Nations, *Minutes of the Fifth Session of the Health Committee* (1923), 12–15.

[160] Ibid., 23.

[161] Ibid, Annex 8. LNA R 823 12B/25642/15002 Epidemic Commission report 9 Jan. 1924; Zinsser, *As I Remember Him*, 278–9.

[162] LNA R 824 12B/26009x/15255, Haigh, 'Famine and Epidemics in the Ukraine', 30.

[163] Zinsser, *As I Remember Him*, 288.

precision. The Russian epidemiologist Tarasevich calculated that between 1917 and 1923 thirty million in European Russia contracted typhus, and three million died from the disease—others estimated forty million cases and five million deaths.[164] Local variations were extreme, with cities like Petrograd being relatively well supplied—despite three waves of famine between July 1918 and December 1921—but remote, drought-afflicted rural areas were devastated.[165]

Hunger caused a general indolence and fatalistic acceptance of death, often from an infectious disease.[166] The suffering was exacerbated by inflamed eyes, scabies, gaping mouth ulcers, stomach disorders, infections like diphtheria, scarlet fever, and typhus, and physical disfigurement of hunger oedema. The crowded hospitals were 'homes of death' without 'soap, no means of laundry, no water for baths, sometimes not enough for the drinks of the feverstricken, so that the condition of the wards was horrible, odours of every sort, and such linen as remained horribly dirty, lice everywhere, and disinfection impossible thro lack of fuel.' Corpses lay among the living in trains and hospitals, or piled up in ramshackle mortuaries; without the means of arranging burial, they were raided by starving dogs and people.[167] Stocks of cattle were exhausted and seed reserves consumed. Bread substitutes were concocted from tree bark, grass, acorns, oak or birch leaves, and dried dung. The British doctor Melville Mackenzie described this so-called bread as looking and smelling liked baked manure: 'The children cannot digest this food and they die.'[168]

Children were especially vulnerable. They were abandoned by parents at railway stations, food kitchens, and refugee camps. Babies and children were packed into institutions holding from forty to 4,000 without proper bedding, food, nursing, and medical supplies. A League of Nations commissioner reported: 'It is quite common to find dead children among the living. In one 'superior' home, the children actually had cots, but they had to be shared with two or three together, and I saw babies of two years fervently employed in picking off the lice off their younger bed fellows.'[169] Children were rounded up into ill-equipped Receiving Homes, before transfer after some weeks into a 'Distributing or Quarantine Home' where they were finally washed and disinfected, with the healthy segregated from the sick, pending often hazardous journeys, to permanent homes or hospitals.[170] A concentrated rather than dispersed system of relief meant overcrowding: a Quaker relief worker observed

---

[164] Id., *Rats*, 213, 299.

[165] On the problem of variation see C. Williams, 'International Relief Organisations and the 1921 Russian Famine' (unpub. paper, 1992).

[166] Long, 'Volga Germans', 510–25 for political background, attributing famine to excessive Bolshevik requisitions.

[167] LNA R 824/12B/26009x/15255 Haigh, 'Famine and Epidemics in the Ukraine', Sept. 1922, description of hospitals in the Cherson area.

[168] MacKenzie, *Medical Relief*, 19.

[169] LNA R 825 12b/27021x/15255 Report on the Medical Conditions in Russia.

[170] MacKenzie, *Medical Relief*, 21.

8. A Railway wagon with corpses of persons attempting to flee, photographed by Peter Mühlens

In each room normally intended for one or two adults, there were at least a hundred children packed like sardines on canvas beds—six on a bed and underneath the beds as well. The typhus cases, some of them completely naked, lay on straw in a separate room . . . They had neither bedding, medicines, nor disinfectants, though we had been able to give them a little soap and clothing. They had no doctor, but each morning the attendants picked out the dead from the living and put them in a shed for removal in a cart which every day makes its round of the Children's Homes.'[171]

Mortality among the impoverished and exhausted German 'colonists' was as high as 5 per cent per month, and German pastors reported that eating dead bodies—and cannibalistic murder—was on the increase.[172] Authorized by the Russian Red Cross to take photographs to elicit sympathy abroad, Mühlens documented mountains of corpses, and mothers eating the limbs of their dead children.[173] A German professor of hygiene, Rudolf Abel, who provided training

---

[171] M. Asquith, *Famine (Quaker Work in Russia, 1921–1923)* (New York, 1943), 21–3.

[172] P. Mühlens, 'Das Rote Kreuz bei den Wolgadeutschen', *Blätter des deutschen Roten Kreuzes* (= *BDRK*), 1/4 (1922), 73–77; W. Gärtner, 'Die Hungersnot in den Wolgakolonien', *BDRK* 1/5 (1922), 113–14.

[173] 'Das Rote Kreuz im hungernden Russland. Die Tätigkeit der deutschen Hilfsexpedition', *Berliner Lokal-Anzeiger* (21 Jan. 1922), evening edn. 'Das Grauen in Russland. Rückfall in den Kannibalismus'; GARF 3341/6/316/100 Russian Red Cross, Foreign Affairs Section to National Committee for Internal Affairs, Sept. 1921.

9. Bodies of famine victims, photographed by Peter Mühlens

courses for Soviet doctors in 1922, reported on staggering mortality rates and how
hunger led to theft, murder, and cannibalism, as when the inmates of a mental hospital at Samara were victims of barbaric practices.[174] Abel commented that the
robbers and cannibals were all native Russians: 'no German colonist, no Jew, no-
one from any other nation was among these.'[175] German pastors supplied Mühlens
with information about the selling of human flesh on market stalls.[176] The bacteriologist Ernst Nauck in Kazan reported on cases of murder within families, and on
the hospitalization of the killers.[177] Such images reinforced the sense of Russia as a
primitive Asiatic land with alien epidemiological condi-tions, and a backward sub-
sistence economy and culture. German newspapers ran horror stories on the barbarism arising from famine. Germans were confronted by photos of avalanches of
frozen corpses bursting out of goods trucks, with bones protruding through the
parched and famished skin.[178] Trains became death traps. Those crowding onto

[174] R. Abel, 'Von Hungersnot und Seuchen in Russland', *Münchener medizinische Wochenschrift*, 70
(1923), 485–7, 633–5.

[175] Abel, 'Hungersnot', 486; Fischer, 'Die Hungersnot in den deutschen Wolgakolonien', *BDRK* 1/5
(1922), 113–14.

[176] STAH 352 8/9 BNI 23 Bd 1, Mühlens report 21.

[177] Ibid., Nauck, 'Tätigkeitsbericht Kasan' in Mühlens report 25a.

[178] See the photographs taken by Mühlens (now in STAH), some of which were reprinted in the
Blätter des deutschen Roten Kreuzes.

trains risked infestation from lice in filthy conditions: yet only by clinging together was there any hope of surviving the freezing winter nights.[179]

There was a sense of impotence among the medical authorities. Many Russian doctors and nurses died tending the sick. Haigh, the League of Nations commissioner, commented 'in such conditions we wonder what we can do to help them'.[180] Mühlens described 'the racial catastrophe' as 'the most horrific yet to have occurred in world history' in that 'whole races will and must die if there is no immediate and effective help'.[181] Fervent nationalists staffed the German Red Cross expedition. Theodor Sütterlin, the bacteriologist at the Petrograd Hospital, had war experience in the navy, and then joined the Freikorps.[182] Other involved doctors moved rightwards in response to the plight of the Volga Germans. The German nursing personnel included notable enthusiasts for the welfare of the Volga Germans, Loresch and the budding agriculturalist Otto Aurich, who by February 1922 was the sole 'nurse' remaining and in a position of considerable authority.[183] Aurich and Loresch spent spring of 1922 in Saratov with the bacteriologists O. Fischer and Nauck, so fulfilling the expedition's primary hidden agenda of racial assistance.[184] Nauck, who was born and educated in St Petersburg but had just qualified in medicine in Germany, had valuable linguistic skills and patriotic enthusiasm for the mission.

Tensions between the ethnically blinkered Germans and the universalistic Save the Children Fund in Saratov arose from fundamentally contrasting approaches to famine relief.[185] The endeavour to place child welfare on an internationalist and anti-racist basis came under fire from eugenicists, as keeping alive the 'vicious, morally diseased or mentally defective'. A British Quaker relief worker took a more jaundiced view, as she prescribed 'a lethal chamber' as a solution for starving epileptic children.[186] The German intensification of racial nationalism was spurred by a sense that aid could only be distributed selectively.

German diplomats, Georg Otto von Maltzan of the Foreign Office's aristocratic Russian diplomats, and Hilger in Moscow, regarded the Volga Germans as a strategic priority.[187] There was alarm that ethnic Germans had sold their household goods in order to buy meagre amounts of food, and that the future of the German villages was in jeopardy. However, many heroically refused to consume their seeds and maintained a horse—thus testifying to the superior moral fibre of the hardy

---

[179] *European Health Conference* (1922), 18–23.

[180] LNA R 824/2B/26009x/15255 Haigh address 28 Mar. 1923.

[181] BAP 15.01 Nr 9398, Bl. 175 Mühlens report from Kazan.

[182] STAH 352 8/9 Bernhard Nocht Institut 23 Band 1 Sütterlin to DRK Berlin 31 Mar. 1923; M. Stürzbecher, 'Von den Berliner Stadtmedizinalräten, Stadtmedizinaldirektoren und Senatsdirektoren für das Gesundheitswesen', *Berliner Ärzteblatt*, 94 (1981), 937–9. Sütterlin joined the Stahlhelm and the Nazi Party in 1933 when he took a position as medical officer of Berlin.

[183] STAH 352 8/9 BNI 23 Bd 1, Mühlens report 16, 19 Feb. 1922.

[184] GARF 3341/6/334/94 Zeiss 4 Dec. 1923; STAH 352 8/9 BNI 23 Bd 1, Mühlens 19 Feb. 1922.

[185] *The World's Children*, 3 (1923); 161; 4 (1924), 32–5.

[186] M. Payne, *Plague, Pestilence and Famine* (London, 1922), 38, 71–2.

[187] BAP 15.01/9398 Maltzan to Reich Ministry of the Interior 25 Nov. 1921. For background see I. Sütterlin, *Die 'russische Abteilung' des Auswärtigen Amtes in der Weimarer Republik* (Berlin, 1994).

German peasant stock. The sharp distinction drawn between the valiant but starving Germans and savage Russians can be seen from Mühlens' description of men loading their sledges with supplies: 'Are these Germans—so ragged and scrawny. But their Swabian dialect sounds so familiar and attractive and yet their external appearance is repugnant. Are they really Germans? And yes they certainly are: our racial brothers so lacking in bread and money and any material to sustain their external appearance.'[188]

The notion of the Russian famine as a 'Holocaust' differs fundamentally from the planned Nazi genocide, in that the famine was an unforeseen natural and socio-political disaster. Yet the spectacle of millions of deaths and the distinctive political circumstances contributed to a sharpening of racial perceptions among public health officials and bacteriologists. The problem of ethnic Germans in Russia raised challenging questions concerning national identity. The Reich Ministry of the Interior drew the crucial distinction between *Reichsdeutsche*, or German citizens, and *deutschstämmige*, or ethnic Germans, about whom a debate erupted as to Germany's obligations.[189] The German bureaucrats distinguished between foreigners of German origin and the much-despised foreigners of alien origins (*fremdstämmigen Ausländer*). Racial propagandists legitimated the claims of ethnic Germans by calling them 'colonists'. As returning ethnic Germans placed burdens on the labour and housing markets, the solution was to intensify aid for *Auslandsdeutschen*, so that they could stay in their remote settlements.[190]

Nationalist rationales for medical activity intensified: as long as the bacteriologist Zeiss remained in the Soviet Union, he moved ever rightwards, and he became a key agent for German interests. He provides insight into the different phases of epidemic prevention from the First World War to the Nazi Holocaust. He came to the Soviet Union with a firmly fixed set of racial convictions. Born in 1888 into a Calvinist family, he qualified in medicine at Freiburg in 1913 where he encountered the eugenicists Eugen Fischer and Fritz Lenz, an advocate of Germany's need for *Lebensraum* in the East. From 1914 until 1921 Zeiss was assistant to the bacteriologist Martin Mayer at the Hamburg Tropical Institute. He followed Mühlens as medical adviser to the Fourth Turkish army from 1915 when he assisted Rodenwaldt, laying foundations for their leading role in Nazi public health and tropical medicine.[191] In 1919 he protested against the international boycott of German

[188] BAP 15.01 Nr 9399, Bl. 303 Bei den Deutschen in den Wolga-Kolonien.

[189] BAK R 86/2401 Bd 1 Besprechung betr. die Rückwanderung deutschstämmiger Wolgaflüchtlinge, 17 Dec. 1921.

[190] GSTA Rep 76 VIII B Nr 3571, 29 Jan. 1923 report on ethnic German refugees from Minsk and Połock in Frankfurt am Oder. RMdI betr. Verminderung weiteren Fremdenzustroms und zur Bekämpfung der aus der gegenwärtigen Misstände Überschwemmung Deutschlands mit Ausländern hervorgetretene Misstände.

[191] His, *Front der Ärzte*, 152–4 on Schilling in Aleppo, where he ran a bacteriological laboratory and undertook blood research. The Second Turkish Army fought the Russians in Armenia, and became implicated in the massacre of Armenians.

medical science.[192] He extolled the strategic value of the medical intervention in the Soviet Union as a means of lifting the 'iron curtain of war' which had separated the German and Russian people. The racism of Zeiss was channelled into the endeavour to save the lives of the million and a half ethnic Germans in Russia.[193] When Zeiss succeeded Mühlens as director of the expedition in May 1922, he ardently pursued his racial strategy.

Zeiss illustrates how the ideology of *Lebensraum* was a key motive for the German scientific approach to famine relief. He argued in terms of imperialist geopolitics: that just as the French had encircled the Mediterranean with Pasteur Institutes, so the German bacteriological station in Moscow served as an early warning station for epidemic threats to Europe, and could provide an entry-point for German cultural and trading interests with Afghanistan, Baluchistan, and Persia.[194] For not only did Germany share a common political destiny with Russia, Zeiss wanted to settle Germany's surplus population in areas where close contact with the homeland could be maintained.[195]

Such nationalist rationales spurred Zeiss into organizing a range of medical activities, going far beyond the task of epidemic prevention. In October 1921 he established a Central Bacteriological Laboratory in Moscow as 'a nursery of German science'. He gained an overview of medical conditions throughout the USSR, and dispatched mobile field laboratories (of a type developed by the Munich bacteriologist Wilhelm Rimpau in 1916) to discover the nature of epidemics. These laboratories went to Petrograd, Minsk, Saratov, and Astrakhan.[196] Medical inspections of Moscow school children were carried out, and a German medical reading-room was established to entice Russian physicians.

Experts in tropical medicine were dedicated supporters of the *Lebensraum* ideology. The loss of the colonies deprived them of facilities for clinical observations and experiments. The mass starvation and epidemics of the Soviet Union turned it into an *Ersatz*-territory for medical research, which became linked to racial priori-

---

[192] H. Zeiss, 'Der Kampf der feindlichen Wissenschaft gegen Deutschland', *Süddeutsche Monatshefte* (Nov. 1919), 157–62.

[193] J. Long, *The German-Russians. A Bibliography* (Santa Barbara and Oxford, 1979); J.-F. Bourret, *Les Allemands de la Volga* (Lyon, 1986), F. C. Koch, *The Volga Germans in Russia and the Americas, from 1763 to the Present* (University Park, 1977); I. Fleischhauer and B. Pinkus, *The Soviet Germans. Past and Present* (London, 1986). Among propagandistic studies are: R. Müller-Sternberg, *Deutsche-Ostsiedlung* (Bielefeld, 1971); K.-H. Ruffmann, *Die Russland-Deutsche. Schicksal und Erben* (Munich 1989); K.-D. Schulz-Vobach, *Die Deutschen in Osten. Von Balkan bis Siberien* (Hamburg, 1989).

[194] LNA R 825, 12B/29911X/15255, Zeiss on 29 Dec. 1921; BA P 15.01 Nr 9398, Bl. 307–9 Zeiss report 29 Dec. 1921. Cf. M. Burleigh, *Germany Turns Eastwards. A Study of Ostforschung in the Third Reich* (Cambridge, 1988).

[195] STAH 352 8/9 Berhard Nocht Institut 23 Bd 1 Billroth Stiftung to Nocht 13 Oct. 1921.

[196] GARF 3341/6/334/53 'Die Tätigkeit der Bakteriologischen Zentrale des Deutschen Roten Kreuzes in Moskau' 16 Nov. 1923; H. Zeiss, 'Die bakteriologische Zentrale des Deutschen Roten Kreuzes in Moskau', *BDRK*, Sonderheft (1922), 11–12. The Astrakhan laboratory was run by A. K. Reichardt under supervision of Zeiss, GARF No.3341/6/334/67 Zeiss 5 Oct. 1923.

ties. Experiments were carried out on typhoid victims. Teams tested rehydration therapy for cholera, and experimental injections of Novasanol and Argflovine against typhus (both drugs being probably useless against the disease).[197] The newly developed Zyklon gas was used to disinfect railway facilities and passengers' effects, exterminating lice and cockroaches.[198] The testing of experimental drugs was followed up by efforts to open up outlets for German pharmaceutical products. TheHamburg Tropical Institute was experimenting with malaria therapy for tertiary syphilis, a dangerous procedure resulting in fatalities.[199] Mühlens and Zeiss undertook clinical trials of the Bayer drugs Germanin (Bayer 205) for sleeping sickness and Naganal for the camel disease, trypanosomiasis. Russia provided an experimental arena for work begun by Koch in the German East African concentration camps for testing Atoxyl. The Moscow embassy relayed supplies of drugs, and funds flowed from the Notgemeinschaft der Deutschen Wissenschaft. The Bayer works financed Zeiss while at the Moscow bacteriological station until 1924. Semashko hoped that Zeiss would contribute to Soviet serum research.[200]

Although the German agreement of 29 August 1921 with the Russian famine relief committee had banned political activities, there were clear political and strategic aims.[201] From the outset one of the main tasks of the expedition was to 'conquer a permanent position in St Petersburg'. That financial shortages were forcing the Russians to close hospital laboratories provided the Germans with favourable opportunities.[202] In June 1922 the pathologist Paul Seifert took over a hundred beds in the Alexander Hospital (previously a German Hospital) in Petrograd on behalf of the German Red Cross, intending to restore its character as 'a purely German hospital'. The aims were supervision of the port medical facilities and of refugees leaving by sea, prevention of typhus, the organization of medical experiments for typhoid treatment, and outpatient treatment for sexually transmitted diseases.[203] Zeiss similarly developed a strategy for a permanent German presence. N. P. Gorbunov, an influential geographer and engineer, and Z. P. Solovyev of the Soviet Red Cross praised Zeiss's contributions to scientific and technical education of Russian physicians.[204] But, above all, Lenin endorsed the activities of Zeiss—documenting this became essential to Zeiss as he clung on to his position. When Zeiss was appointed director of the German Red Cross expedition, he explained to Gorbunov that he was ready to assume tasks as required by Lenin.[205] The German strategy of supporting the Soviet state was

[197] P. Mühlens, 'Die Hunger- und Seuchenkatastrophe in Russland', *MMW* (1922), 1444.

[198] See the illustration in *BDRK* 2 (1921), 31.

[199] Wess, 'Menschenversuche und Kolonialpolitik', 13–17.

[200] BAK R 73/221 Notgemeinschaft der Deutschen Wissenschaft.

[201] BAP 0902/350 Bl. 316.

[202] STAH 352 8/9 Bernhard Nocht Institut 23 Bd 1, Mühlens report no. 7, 23 Oct. 1921.

[203] BAP 15.01 Nr 9400, Bl. 255 concerning the Alexander-Spital. On Seifert see the unpublished paper by I. Kästner (Leipzig) presented to the fourth Berlin symposium on German–Soviet Medicine, July 1995.

[204] GARF 3341/6/336/4 Solovyev to Zeiss 13 Oct. 1923.

[205] GARF 5446/37/40/4 Zeiss to Gorbunov 6 June 1922.

much appreciated: Gorbunov urged Zeiss to stay and enter the Russian health service.[206]

Zeiss exploited his laboratory as an international cover for nationalist activities. In December 1921 he explained to Russian public health experts that his Moscow bacteriological laboratory was in a key position in a front opened up by the League of Nations against the great parasitic diseases from the East. Zeiss persuaded the League of Nations delegates Zinsser and Norman White that he would be the ideal plenipotentary to co-ordinate public health training in Russia.[207] The German central laboratories rapidly developed friendly relations with Russian doctors and medical scientists. By September 1921 Mühlens organized the supply of German medical literature to satiate the 'book hunger' of ethnic German and Russian doctors, and invited Nocht to preside over this scheme, stressing its urgency in order to combat the influence of other powers. The Reich Ministry of the Interior arranged a conference with German medical publishers on 22 October 1922, and the Billroth Foundation provided finance.[208] Semashko and Solovyev backed a scheme for a bilingual German-Russian journal, entitled *Folia medica*, to supplement the array of German medical journals supplied by Zeiss to Russian medical institutes.[209] At a Russian bacteriological congress in May 1922 Zeiss proclaimed that German–Russian scientific solidarity was fundamental for the reconstruction of Europe.[210] The German authorities reprimanded Zeiss for going beyond the brief of anti-epidemic measures, and for his plans to extend the role of the central bacteriological station. He hoped to study tuberculosis and sexually transmitted diseases, backed up by stocks of precious drugs like salvarsan. When Reich officials suggested that Zeiss should be stationed on Germany's eastern border in one of the new bacteriological institutes, Mühlens defended Zeiss that his activities in Moscow were important for German national prestige.[211] By February 1922 Zeiss saw his laboratory as the nucleus for a 'German research station' in Moscow, convinced that disease mapping had strategic relevance.[212]

---

[206] GARF 5446/37/40/10 Zeiss to Gorbunov 4 Mar. 1925.

[207] LNA R 825 12B/29922X/15255 Bernstein (physician at the German embassy Moscow) to Zinsser 30 July 1923, including Zeiss's report on meeting of Nov. 1921 with Solovyev and Tarasevich. LNA R 825 12B/34273X/15255 Zeiss to N. White 19 Jan. and 26 Feb. 1924.

[208] BAP 15.01 Nr 9398, Bl. 56 letter of Nocht 13 Oct. 1921, Bl. 86 meeting 22 Oct. 1921; STAH 352 8/9 Bernhard Nocht Institut 23 Band 1, Mühlens to Nocht 4 Oct. 1921.

[209] GARF 3341/6/334/88 2 Dec. 1923 on negotiations with Semashko and Bauer in June 1923. 3341/6/334/5300 'Die Tätigkeit der Bakteriologischen Zentrale des Deutschen Roten Kreuzes in Moskau' 16 Nov. 1923. The journal was due to appear 1 Jan. 1924: see GARF 3341/6/334/63. For the supply of medical journals see Zeiss to Semashko 17 Apr. 1925, 5446/37/40/14–13. The journal was the counterpart to the *Revista médica de Hamburgo* established in 1919. BNI Archivordner Tropeninstitut 1921–3, Zeiss to Nocht 29 Nov. 1922.

[210] STAH 352 8/9 Bernhard Nocht Institut 23 Bd 1, Mühlens report no. 25, 6 May 1922. Meetings were also held with Semashko in April 1922 and there was a beer evening with the Moscow and Petrograd medical faculties on 6 May 1922.

[211] BAP 15.01 Nr 3999, Bl. 327–32 meeting in RMdI 27 May 1922.

[212] STAH 352 8/9 Bernhard Nocht Institut 23 Bd 1 Mühlens report 16, 19 Feb. 1922.

The conflict over the scope of the expedition led to disagreement in October 1922 between the German Interior and Foreign Ministries over funding. By this time many of the survivors in Minsk were returning to the Volga region where the food situation had improved, and plans for German hospitals in Petrograd and Moscow were far advanced.[213] By January 1923 the Foreign Office declared that if it publicly took responsibility for German medical activities in Russia, then they would lose their non-political character. The Foreign Office proposed a system of secret subsidies, concealed under the category of the heating and lighting expenses of its Moscow embassy where the German Red Cross could have a representative. The German diplomats pressed the Ministry of the Interior to continue to finance the expedition as this guaranteed its humanitarian and medical status. The Finance Ministry proposed to transfer the budget to the Foreign Ministry for internal accounting purposes, while concealing this manœuvre from outside scrutiny.[214]

The build-up of German–Russian medical relations was the counterpart of military cooperation between the Red Army and Reichswehr. The medical exchanges provided camouflage to maintain secrecy as well as support. Zeiss's Moscow clinic catered for visiting Germans, and provided medical services for the Junkers aircraft factory at Fili near Moscow from 1923. He also established contacts with military medical officers in the Red Army.[215] The strategic thinking of General Hans von Seeckt that the German–Russian axis had to be restored was backed by the German medical cohort.[216] Just after Hilger engineered the sanitary agreement in August 1921 the Wehrmacht and the Red Army launched the Junkers aircraft factory.[217] Zeiss fantasized that his Moscow foothold was the first stage of a grandiose scheme to extend German influence to Afghanistan.[218] Oskar von Niedermayer, who had organized a military expedition to Afghanistan, headed (as 'Herr Neumann') the secret Moscow office of the German War Ministry's 'Special Group R'.[219] The Red Cross Expedition doctors saw medical activity in the southern USSR as a stepping-stone to German expansion in the east.

Ideologies of *Lebensraum* and geo-politics shaped the activities of a group of racially minded medical experts. But their right-wing nationalism stopped short of Nazism: when in the autumn of 1921 Ludendorff called for an anti-Bolshevik crusade in conjunction with Britain and France, this was profoundly embarrassing to the German Red Cross expedition. For Mühlens felt that Lenin's New Economic

[213] BAP 15.01 Nr 9400, Bl. 400–2, meeting in RMdI 5 Oct. 1922.

[214] BAP 15.01 Nr 9401, Bl. 70–3, meeting in RMdI 3 Jan. 1923.

[215] GARF 3341/6/334/5405 'Die Tätigkeit der Bakteriologischen Zentrale des Deutschen Roten Kreuzes in Moskau' 16 Nov. 1923; 3341/6/334/70. BAP 15.01 Nr 9398, Bl. 303 report by Zeiss 29 Dec. 1921; STAH CC VI No 11 Bd 1 Fasc. 64, Letter of G. Gerber, Hilger, and Zeiss in support of funding application of 29 July 1922.

[216] Hilger and Meyer, *Incompatible Allies*, 191; M. Kitchen, 'Militarism and the Development of Fascist Ideology: The Political Ideas of Colonel Max Bauer, 1916–1918', *Central European History*, 8 (1975), 199–220; O. Groehler, *Selbstmörderische Allianz. Deutsch-russische Militärbeziehungen 1920–1941* (Berlin, 1992), 36–7; M. Zeidler, *Reichswehr und Rote Armee 1920–1933* (Munich, 1993).

[217] Hilger and Meyer, *Incompatible Allies*, 194.

[218] BAP 0902/394 Bl. 10–14 Zeiss letter of 7 Sept. 1923.

[219] Hilger and Meyer, *Incompatible Allies*, 195–6.

Policy speech of 17 October 1921 signalled that Bolshevism had declared its own bankruptcy; he hoped that the expedition could achieve political change in Russia, and was consequently indignant at German ultra-nationalist hostility to any dealings with Russia.[220] When confronted by the horror of mass starvation, Mühlens pleaded for food in terms of saving racial collectivities from extermination, especially the Tartars and the German-Russian 'colonists'.[221] The political motives and tensions surrounding the German and other famine relief agencies suggest that it was all too easy for concern for the welfare of the starving to wither—from Hauptmann's initial literary circumlocutions to final racism.

Foreign relief teams began to withdraw from the spring of 1922, when infectious disease and deaths from famine subsided. The Dutch and Swedish Red Cross decided to leave in August 1922. By then the ARC, dominated by Republicans increasingly favouring isolationism, began to limit funding to the LRCS. Hoover decided in April 1922 to retreat from Russia, and operations began to be scaled down to a feeding programme for two million children, and the ARA finally left in the summer of 1923.

Only the Germans were keen to remain. A new spirit of reciprocity was kindled between the Soviets and Germans: in 1923 the Russian Red Cross made donations to alleviate the deprivation of the occupied Ruhr.[222] In January 1923 Semashko explained to the League of Nations Hygiene Organization, that he welcomed foreign medical aid provided that there was cooperation with Soviet sanitary authorities. He drew attention to shortages of medicines, laboratory equipment, anti-diphtheria serum, and soap, and that assistance was needed in the campaigns against infant mortality and malaria.[223] Typhus and relapsing fever remained endemic. However, the League's epidemic commissioners pointed out that the movement of refugees to the West had virtually ceased as the Soviet authorities had suppressed the repatriation service.[224]

The Germans met increased difficulties as they tried to maintain their foothold. In April 1924 the Saratov GPU (secret police) demanded closure of the German Red Cross office.[225] During July 1924 the German Red Cross representative in the Ukraine was accused of corruption because of speculating in grain trading and textiles, and was arrested by the GPU. The incident sent a message to the Germans that they might maintain a residual outpost providing that they complied with Soviet systems of administration.[226] The German Red Cross continued to channel aid for the Volga Germans, supplying them with seeds and motorized

---

[220] STAH 352 8/9 Bernhard Nocht Institut 23 Bd 1, Mühlens report no. 7, 23 Oct. 1921.

[221] Ibid., Mühlens report no. 9, appended letter to Hilger 8 Sept. 1921 from Kasan. Text of proposed international appeal for food.

[222] GARF 3341/6/334/73 DRK President to Russian Red Cross 27 Oct. 1923.

[223] 'La Situation en Russie: Exposé du Dr Siemashko', League of Nations, *Minutes of the Fifth Session of the Health Committee*, 31–3.

[224] STAH 352 8/9 Bernhard Nocht Institut 23 Bd 1, Mühlens 5th report (1923), 87.

[225] BAP 0902/349 Bl. 172, 17 Apr. 1924.

[226] Ibid., Bl. 23 report by consulate in Kharkov. On Breuer's arrest in February 1925 and trial see 0902/350 Bl. 124, 137, 189–93, 300. The Ukrainian expedition was separately organized from the main DRK expedition.

ploughs.[227] But the Soviet authorities exerted pressure to regain the hospitals in Simferopol and Georgia from the Germans: the resulting agreement of February 1923 placed the Tiflis hospital under the German Red Cross while ensuring substantial injections of funds from the militaristic Billroth Foundation.[228]

As the spectre of epidemic diseases evaporated, Zeiss defended the German laboratory in Moscow, intending to develop clinics and a small hospital, and if possible to retain the stations in Minsk and Saratov.[229] The normalization of conditions led to plans for German Red Cross involvement in an anti-malaria campaign on the Volga as well as efforts by the medical scientists Otto Fischer and Zeiss to strengthen German schools.[230] Although the German medical teams had been less effective than other contingents in providing famine relief, they established what they hoped would be a permanent base in Russia. The Russian adventure of a phalanx of ultra-nationalist bacteriologists deepened their sense of a racial mission.

[227] BAP 0902/350 Bl. 248 DRK letter 26 Sept. 1924 concerning the seizure of two German-owned motorized ploughs in the Ukraine.

[228] GARF No. 3341/6/336/15–19 'Das deutsche Krankenhaus Tiflis'. BAP 0902/350 Bl. 189, 265 letter 14 Sept. 1924 from German consul Tiflis; Eckart, 'Medizin und auswärtige Kulturpolitik'.

[229] STAH CC VI No. 11 Vol. 1 Fasc. 64, letter from Zeiss to Pfeiffer 29 July 1922. Denkschrift über das bakteriologische Zentrallaboratorium des Deutschen Roten Kreuzes in Moskau, 29 July 1922.

[230] BAP 15.01 Nr 9401, Bl. 38–9 O. Fischer, 'Die Verhältnisse in den deutschen Schulen an der Wolga'.

7

German–Soviet Medical Collaboration

i. The Seeds of Cooperation

By the mid-1920s scientific cooperation replaced German medical assistance to Russia: defending German racial stocks from the ravages of epidemics and famine gave way to futuristic schemes of advanced research in genetics and pathology. Nationally minded German scientists collaborated with Soviet medical planners on joint research projects and expeditions. The research into obscure illnesses from goitre to camel disease often in remote areas ostensibly demonstrated that two great nations were willing to cooperate in humanitarian medical research. But at the same time there were covert German national agendas: pathology, sero-anthropology, and genetics undermined the Treaty of Versailles by showing that it did not accord with the ethnic map of Europe, given the scattered German communities in the east. The Germans balanced the diplomatic and strategic aims of securing goodwill from the communist leadership with a racial agenda of assisting ethnic German 'colonists'.

Semashko, the Commissar for Health, encouraged contacts with German medical scientists and experts in social hygiene, eugenics, and genetics. The German connection reinforced his pragmatic support for the doggedly anti-Bolshevik physiologist Ivan Pavlov, and for the eugenic schemes of Nikolai Koltsov, who founded a Russian Eugenics Society in November 1920.[1] The eugenic organizations came under Semashko's centralized Commissariat of Public Health.[2] Links to German scientists were part of a policy of harnessing expertise in the biomedical sciences to advance socialism. This climate of medical optimism accounted for Soviet hospitality to nationally minded German scientists.[3]

Zeiss was crucial in sustaining German–Soviet medical cooperation. In 1923 he was under Soviet pressure to terminate the autonomous German Red Cross hospitals and networks of supply, and Reich medical officials no longer saw the need of an epidemic early-warning station located in Moscow.[4] Zeiss, who retained the

[1] M. B. Adams, 'Eugenics in Russia, 1900–1940', in id. (ed.), *The Wellborn Science*, 153–216; id., 'Eugenics as Social Medicine in Revolutionary Russia. Prophets, Patrons, and the Dialectics of Discipline-Building', in S. G. Solomon and J. F. Hutchinson (eds.), *Health and Society in Revolutionary Russia* (Bloomington, Ind. and Indianapolis, Ind., 1990), 200–23; D. Todes, 'Pavlov and the Bolsheviks', *History and Philosophy of the Life Sciences*, 17 (1995), 379–418.

[2] N. B. Weissman, 'Origins of Soviet Health Administration. Narkomzdrav, 1918–1928', in Solomon and Hutchinson (eds.), *Health and Society in Revolutionary Russia*, 97–120.

[3] S. G. Solomon, 'Social Hygiene and Soviet Public Health', in Solomon and Hutchinson, *Health and Society*, 175–99.

[4] STAH 352 8/9 Bernhard-Nocht-Institut 23 Band 1 Russland Hunger-Hilfe, letter of Hilger to Mühlens 6 Jan. 1923.

designation as professor of tropical medicine, hoped that the central bacteriological laboratory in Moscow could be continued after the German Red Cross had
withdrawn. He developed the laboratory into a policlinic for medical services,
offering Wassermann testing for syphilis. His medical activities provided a cover
for assisting German 'colonists' and for health care at the Junkers aircraft factory.
This German military and technological bridgehead ran into financial difficulties
as Soviet orders for aircraft did not materialize.[5]

Zeiss was to be disappointed in his hopes that the German medical research
institute in Russia could be financed by the pharmaceutical industry.[6] From September 1923 the German Red Cross tropical specialists, Otto Fischer, Mühlens,
Zeiss, and Nocht advocated a German medical information centre in Moscow, and
a joint Russian–German medical journal.[7] They expected funds from the *Billroth-
Stiftung* which supported the German hospitals in Leningrad until 1927 and in
Tiflis until 1928.[8] German pharmaceutical companies were prominent advertisers
in the bilingual *Deutsch-Russische Medizinische Zeitschrift*, edited by Semashko and
the Berlin clinician Friedrich Kraus from 1925 until 1928.[9] This journal paved the
way for IG-Farben to establish IGERUSSKO, a pharmaceutical concessionary
company, in 1927.[10]

When Zeiss failed to convince German pharmaceutical companies to support
the Moscow laboratory, Semashko arranged for him to enter into Soviet employment—a macabre situation for a right-wing nationalist. In October 1924 Zeiss outlined to Semashko a plan for an encyclopaedic collection of strains of human
pathogens, bacteria causing plant and animal diseases, and agriculturally important bacteria.[11] Zeiss cooperated with Russian scientists on projects relating to
therapy and control of diseases at the chemical and pharmaceutical institute of the
Supreme Economic Council and at the Moscow Pasteur Institute where he was in
charge of the microbiological collection.[12] The central bacteriological laboratory

[5] BAP 0902/349 Bl. 216, 227; Zeidler, *Reichswehr*, 54–7, 89–91.

[6] BAP 15.01/9398 Reichsministerium des Innern. Akten betreffend: das Hilfswerk des deutschen
Roten Kreuzes für Russland, Bd 1 vom 19. August 1921 bis 31. März 1922 Bl. 496–7 Zeiss, 'Die
Notwendigkeit eines deutschen medizinischen Forschungsinstitutes in Russland', Jan. 1922.

[7] BAP 0902/350 Bl. 222–3, Zeiss to Semashko 10 Oct. 1924.

[8] BAP 0902/394 Bl. 18, letter of 24 Sept. 1923, Bl. 23, 439 DRK letter 5 Nov. 1924.

[9] N. A. Semaschko, 'An die Leser', *Deutsch-Russische Medizinische Zeitschrift*, 1 (Oct. 1925) 1–2. Vol. 4
was published in 1928.

[10] Bayer-Archiv Leverkusen, Pharma Verkauf Länderberichte Signatur: 167/6 Vertretungsbezirk Russland. Signatur: 1/6.6.18.2 Russland. For Zeiss and IGERUSSKO see BAP 0902/420 Bl. 385 anti-worm
treatment. BAP 0902/419 Bl. 3, 4, 9 camel disease, Dec. 1930.

[11] Archiv der Humboldt-Universität zu Berlin (hereafter AHUB), Nachlass Zeiss, box 4 Zeiss to
Semashko 19 May 1925 offering services to the Red Army; GARF 5446/37/40/34–25; Zeiss, 'Die kriegshygienischen Aufgaben einer medizinischen Topographie in Russland in Verbindung mit der Allrussischen Mikrobiologischen Sammlung'; GARF 5446/37/40/18 and 45 Zeiss to Gorbunov 26 Apr. 1925 and 15
May 1925. See also GARF 5446/37/40/58 Zeiss to Gorbunov 24 Sept. 1925 for the sending of publications
on Russian epidemiology. I am grateful to Susan Solomon, Toronto, for making copies from the
Archives of the Russian Federation available to me.

[12] GARF 5446/37/40/10 Zeiss to Gorbunov 4 Mar. 1925; 5446/37/40/15–13 Zeiss to Semashko 17 Apr.
1925; BAK R 86/744 Bl. 25–30 Zeiss Lebenslauf.

was given an expanded role with the establishment of the All-Russian Microbiological Collection. Zeiss collected specimens from Russian colleagues and organized exchanges of bacteria cultures with other reference collections in Germany and the United States. He distributed the equipment of the German bacteriological laboratory to ethnic Germans at the medical faculty in Saratov, the German Volga Republic, the microbiological institute Saratov, and to the central bacteriological laboratory of the Red Army. Hilger and Department VI of the German Foreign Office supported his 'medical and cultural' activities, transforming Zeiss into an arm of the ministerial advocates of *Ostpolitik*. Once official contacts were ratified by the Berlin Treaty of neutrality and friendship, concluded between Germany and the Soviet Union in April 1926, a steady stream of funds flowed to Zeiss from the Notgemeinschaft der Deutschen Wissenschaft (NDW).[13] The President of the NDW, Friedrich Schmidt-Ott, was convinced of Germany's historical and cultural mission in the east, and was able to provide skilled and powerful backing to German–Soviet scientific ventures. Although Zeiss became fluent in Russian and was a Soviet employee, he maintained an ostentatiously German lifestyle and was unofficial medical attaché to the German embassy.[14] He had a wide network of Soviet contacts and greater freedom of movement than a diplomat. He reported to his embassy on health conditions, changes in Soviet medical education, the pernicious influence of French medical science, and on the medical implications of the Five-Year Plan.[15] Zeiss skilfully balanced the German national agenda by providing the Soviets with medical information and resources. He thereby laid the foundations for a wide-ranging programme of cooperation in medicine and the life sciences.

ii. Lenin's Brain and Medical Cooperation

The Soviet medical contacts had the blessing of a faction at the German Foreign Office, supporting cooperation with Moscow.[16] Lenin's sympathetic foreign policy towards Germany led to the Treaty of Rapallo of 16 April 1922, establishing a favourable climate for German–Soviet medical contacts.[17] Lenin's respect for

[13] Voigt, *Hoetzsch*, 321. letter of Hoetzsch to Schmidt-Ott 1 Nov. 1926 on Zeiss as 'wissenschaftlich und national so wertvoll'; BAK R 73/223 Bl. 104–8, Zeiss to German embassy Moscow 1 July 1931.

[14] H. Hamperl, *Werdegang und Lebensweg eines Pathologen* (Stuttgart and New York, 1972), 116.

[15] BAP 0902/420 Bl. 218–28 Zeiss on medical education, 3 Sept. 1931; Bl. 267 Zeiss on paratyphus; Bl. 276–83 Zeiss on maternal and infant welfare 4 June 1931; Bl. 286–301 Zeiss on prevention of epidemics; Bl. 303 Zeiss on history of medicine.

[16] For the high politics of the pro-Soviet faction see P. Krüger, *Die Aussenpolitik der Republik von Weimar* (Darmstadt, 1985), 151–83, 280–5.

[17] K.-D. Thomann, ' "Die medizinische Wissenschaft ist international". Zur Zusammenarbeit von deutschen und sowjetischen Ärzten während der Weimarer Republik', in W. Beck, G. Elsner, and H. Mausbach (eds.), *Pax Medica. Stationen ärztlichen Friedensengagements und Verirrungen ärztlichen Militarismus* (Hamburg, 1986); D. Tutzke, 'Alfred Grotjahn und die junge Sowjetunion', *Zeitschrift für die gesamte Hygiene*, 8 (1973), 596–9; D. Volkogonov, ed. D. Shukman, *Lenin: A New Biography* (Glencoe, 1995).

German medicine was so great that he placed his health in the hands of German doctors from March 1922. The first German doctors consulted in March 1922 were Georg Klemperer, noted for his skills in diagnostics in general medicine, and the neurologist Otfried Foerster. The surgeon Moritz Borchardt operated in April 1922 to remove two bullets from an assassination attempt in 1918.[18]

In May 1922 Lenin suffered a stroke, and when in December 1922 Lenin was partially paralysed from another stroke, Foerster was recalled from Germany and attended Lenin until his death in 1924. From March 1923 eight Soviet, German, and Swedish doctors deliberated on Lenin's deteriorating condition.[19] The small army of German physicians consisted of the neurologist Oswald Bumke, Max Nonne (a specialist for neuro-syphilis), and two specialists in internal medicine, Oskar Minkowski (originally from Kovno) and Adolf Strümpell, who had learned Russian as a child in Dorpat/Tartu. They suspected that Lenin suffered from neuro-syphilis. Oskar Vogt was at a neurological conference in Moscow in January 1923, when called on to give an opinion about Lenin's illness.[20]

Faced by an international scientific boycott, nationally minded German scientists welcomed Soviet invitations: Ludwig Aschoff (the Nestor of German pathologists) and Lubarsch attended a pathological congress in Petrograd in September 1923.[21] Aschoff had hopes of a German–Russian medical research institute as early as 1922.[22] Vogt, a neuro-anatomist, was active in building up contacts with the USSR from 1923, entering into discussions with Litvinov on German scientific assistance. Litvinov was exceptional in the Stalin circle, as he favoured close contacts with the outside world and, ultimately, compromise with Western democracies.[23] High-ranking Soviet politicians consulted the German doctors while they were in Moscow, and some continued to seek German medical advice: Trotsky visited a Berlin clinic in 1926, and Chicherin, the Commissar of Foreign Affairs, was treated by ambassador Ulrich Graf von Brockdorff-Rantzau's physician in Wiesbaden.[24] German doctors agreed on how both Germany and Russia needed to contain Poland and undermine the Treaty of Versailles. By the mid-1920s sporadic invitations to German medical scientists developed into a concerted programme, as the

---

[18] J. Richter, 'Medicine and Politics in Soviet–German Relations in the 1920s. A Contribution to Lenin's Pathobiography', *XXXIInd International Congress on the History of Medicine* (1990), 1–16; H. E. Müller-Dietz, 'Deutsche Ärzte bei V. I. Lenin', *Aus Dreissig Jahren Osteuropa-Forschung. Gedenkschrift für Dr. phil. Georg Kennert (1919–1984)* (Berlin, 1984), 161–70; id., *Ärzte zwischen Deutschland und Russland* (Stuttgart, 1995), 136–45; N. Tumarkin, *Lenin Lives! The Lenin Cult in Soviet Russia* (Cambridge, Mass., 1963), 112–33; ch. 4, 'illness and immortality'.

[19] BAP 0902/349 Bl. 242–3 Schmidt-Ott letter of 27 Mar. 1923.

[20] Lenin's death has now been attributed to arteriosclerosis of the brain arteries.

[21] *Ludwig Aschoff. Ein Gelehrtenleben in Briefe an die Familie* (Freiburg i. B., 1966), 309–7; O. Lubarsch, *Ein bewegtes Gelehrtenleben* (Berlin, 1931), 491–503; BAP 0902/393 Bl. 49 letter of Aschoff to Hilger, 5 Oct. 1923, confirming that he has contacted Zeiss; Bl. 189 Zeiss to Aschoff 24 Aug. 1923 concerning Aschoff's and Lubarsch's visit.

[22] AHUB NL Zeiss box 4 NDW, Aschoff to Zeiss 28 Dec. 1928. Aschoff's original scheme involved Hamperl.

[23] J. Haslam, *Soviet Foreign Policy 1930–1933. The Impact of the Depression* (London, 1983), 118–19.

[24] Hilger and Meyer, *Incompatible Allies*, 150–1; Fry, *Visits*, 28–9 on the friendship between Chicherin and Brockdorff-Rantzau.

NDW broadened its interests to the rebuilding of international academic relations. It argued that German science was 'spatially constricted', and would benefit from Soviet research.[25]

Vogt was a long-standing friend of the Krupp family of industrial magnates and a beneficiary of their patronage for his brain research institute, established as part of the Kaiser Wilhelm Society.[26] He belonged to the conservative and nationalist Eastern European studies grouping of the historian, Otto Hoetzsch, and Schmidt-Ott.[27] Why the invitation for the prestigious task of dissecting Lenin's brain should have fallen to Vogt is an interesting question. One of the involved researchers, Rudolf Rabl, considered that it was because Vogt was on cordial terms with the neurologist Foerster, but Vogt's diplomatic and economic contacts also counted. Gustav Krupp von Bohlen und Halbach was the first of the German armaments manufacturers to obtain Soviet concessions, signing an agreement in autumn of 1922.[28] In December 1924 Vogt was invited to undertake research on Lenin's brain.[29] In April 1925 Vogt accepted this task with the approval of the German Foreign Office, which was concerned to counter French medical influence in the Soviet Union.[30] Lenin's brain thus achieved a posthumous symbolism for continuity with Lenin's policies of coexistence with Germany—indeed, the Lenin brain research institute had the backing of Litvinov, as coinciding with his internationalist strategy. Although Vogt was nominally the director of the Lenin Institute for Brain Research, executive responsibility fell to Soviet researchers.[31]

Stalin set out to wrest control of the Institute from the health commissariat of Semashko, who was one of the old comrades of Lenin. This faction tried to establish that Lenin had been of sound mind after his second stroke of December 1922. On 4 January 1923 Lenin denounced Stalin in a postscript to his 'Testament' addressed to the Central Committee. Stalin arrogated the responsibility of

[25] *Siebenter Bericht der Notgemeinschaft der Deutschen Wissenschaft* (1928).

[26] W. Kirsche, *Oskar Vogt 1870–1959. Leben und Werk und dessen Beziehung zur Hirnforschung der Gegenwart. Ein Beitrag zur 25. Wiederkehr seines Todestages* (Berlin, 1986); J. Hallervorden, 'Der Berliner Kreis', *50 Jahre Neuropathologie in Deutschland 1885–1935* (Stuttgart, 1961), 112–23; R. Hassler, 'Oskar Vogt zum Gedächtnis', *Archiv Psychiatrie, Nervenkrankheiten*, 200 (1960), 239–56. Vogt has gained in notoriety with the novel by Tilman Spengler, *Lenins Hirn* (Hamburg, 1991).

[27] Voigt, Hoetzsch, 201–6, 221, 248, 320. For Ostforschung after 1925 see M. Burleigh, *Germany Turns Eastwards. A Study of Ostforschung in the Third Reich* (Cambridge, 1988), 32–9; J. Nötzold, 'Die deutsch-sowjetischen Wissenschaftsbeziehungen', in R. Vierhaus and B. Brocke (eds.), *Forschung im Spannungs-feld von Politik und Gesellschaft. Geschichte und Struktur der Kaiser-Wilhelm-/Max-Planck-Gesellschaft* (Stuttgart, 1990), 778–801.

[28] Hilger and Meyer, *Incompatible Allies*, 171.

[29] J. Richter and M. Lindemann, 'Die Berliner und die Moskauer Schule der Architektonischen Hirn-forschung', *Actes, Proceedings, XXX International Congress of the History of Medicine* (Düsseldorf, 1988), 923–36. The Lenin Institute for Brain Research is omitted from Tumarkin, *Lenin Lives!*.

[30] Historisches Archiv Friedrich Krupp FAH 4E 266 Bl. 245–7 Wallroth (Ministerial Director of the Foreign Ministry) to O. Hergt 26 May 1925. On Vogt's interview with the Kultusminister, Vogt papers Vogt to Bohlen 16 Dec. 1925.

[31] R. Rabl, 'Oskar Vogt, Gründer des Staatsinstitut für Hirnforschung in Moskau', *Die Waage*, 9 (1970), 65–73; J. Richter, 'Oskar Vogt, der Begründer des Moskower Staatsinstituts für Hirnforschung', *Psychia-trie, Neurologie und medizinische Psychologie*, 28 (1976), 385–95.

ensuring Lenin's compliance with the orders of his doctors, while preventing Lenin, held in seclusion at Gorky, from taking political initiatives. The historian of German–Soviet scientific relations, Jochen Richter, discovered that Stalin impeded the opening and work of the Institute through his secretary, I. P. Tovstukha, who was the Institute's deputy director.[32]

The Brain Research Institute became a central feature of a wide-ranging programme of scientific co-operation. Vogt was asked to take over a biological-genetic department in the Caucasus. Von Bohlen, who chaired the board of governors of the Kaiser Wilhelm Institute for Brain Research, approved of the research collaboration as in Germany's national interest. In June 1925 Vogt acted as intermediary between von Bohlen and the German ambassador in Moscow, Brockdorff-Rantzau. Vogt's indebtedness stretched to assisting von Bohlen's brother-in-law, Tilo Freiherr von Wilmowski, who visited the Soviet Union on commercial business for the Krupp concern and to pursue matters 'of general significance for German interests'.[33]

At the German embassy in Moscow Brockdorff-Rantzau established a special cultural department under Hilger to support Zeiss's medical activities.[34] Zeiss alerted the embassy to the 'terror' waged against the old guard of Russian intellectuals, and how they needed German scientific assistance.[35] He supported a vigorous bilateral programme of scientific cooperation to curb the excesses of Sovietization. In September 1925 the Germans participated in a liminological conference in Tiflis, and Vogt joined celebrations for the 200th anniversary of the Russian Academy of Sciences.[36] German–Soviet scientific cooperation was seen as a way of resisting the politicization of the Academy of Sciences. Vogt and Schmidt-Ott agreed with Anatoly Lunacharsky, the Commissar for Education, and the geographer, N. P. Gorbunov, an extensive programme of scientific exchanges and expeditions with genetics as a key element.[37] In 1925 the Soviet geneticist Nikolai Timoféef-Ressovsky came to Vogt's Kaiser Wilhelm Institute for Brain Research in Berlin (returning to the USSR only in 1945).[38] In 1927 Vogt, Hilger, and Zeiss arranged a Week of Soviet

---

[32] Richter, 'Medicine and Politics', 10–13.

[33] Historisches Archiv Friedrich Krupp FAH 4E 266 Bl 258 Aufzeichnung des Kuratoriums des Kaiser-Wilhelm-Instituts für Hirnforschung 16 Dec. 1924; FAH 4E 266 Bl. 241 letter of Vogt to von Bohlen 30 May 1925; Bl. 183 letter of von Bohlen to Vogt 15 Dec. 1925; Bl. 175 von Bohlen to Vogt 17 Dec. 1925; Vogt papers, Vogt to von Bohlen 14 and 16 Dec. 1925; Von Bohlen to Vogt 2 July 1926. Wilmowski subsequently pursued schemes for German commercial and political dominance in Southeast Europe; see W. Ruge, *Weimar—Republik auf Zeit* (Berlin, 1982), 182, 269–70.

[34] G. Rosenfeld, *Sowjetunion und Deutschland 1922–1933* (Cologne, 1984), 182–233 for an overview of cultural activities from an East German perspective. BAP 0902/414 Bl. 43–4 Brockdorff-Rantzau to Foreign Office, 30 Jan. 1925; 0902/349 Bl. 155–7 Brockdorff-Rantzau to Foreign Office 20 June 1924.

[35] BAP 0902/394 Bl. 369–70 Zeiss to German embassy, Moscow 10 July 1924.

[36] BAK R 73/291.

[37] BAP 0902/397 Bl. 152–8, protocol of meeting on 1 Oct. 1925 between Schmidt-Ott, Gorbunov, and Vogt. F. Schmidt-Ott, *Erlebtes und Erstrebtes 1860–1950* (Wiesbaden, 1952), 222; Voigt, *Hoetzsch*, 201; P. R. Josephson, 'Science Policy in the Soviet Union 1917–27', *Minerva*, 26 (1990), 21–58.

[38] D. Grainin, *Der Genetiker* (Cologne, 1988).

Science under the auspices of the Osteuropa Gesellschaft.[39] The Week led to joint ventures in archaeology, an alpine expedition to Pamir in 1930, and to polar and seismic research.[40]

Support for cooperative scientific ventures was linked to the conviction that biology was a pre-eminently German field of intellectual endeavour. The question arises to what extent the involved German scientists were motivated by eugenic and racial concerns, and whether these should be seen within the distinctive paradigm of strictly scientific approaches to human diseases and psychology, or whether the Russian ventures formed a crucial phase of the German racial *Ostpolitik*? Vogt examined Lenin's brain for its 'racial characteristics', as he detected enlarged pyramid cells, which he flatteringly portrayed as the intellectual equivalent to an athlete's enlarged muscles. The Moscow institute collected not only 'élite brains' of politicians, artists, and scientists, but also racial specimens.[41] Richard Goldschmidt and Erwin Baur, both geneticists with pronounced eugenic concerns, attended the Russian Genetics Congress of 1927, which marked the high point of Soviet support for what would soon be denounced as a bourgeois and reactionary science.[42] German medical researchers took great interest in Soviet serology as relevant to eugenics and infectious diseases. Ukrainian research on blood groups was publicized by the German Society for Blood Group Research from 1928 and by the *Ukrainische Zentralblatt für Blutgruppenforschung*—indicating how German remained a favoured language of scientific communication in Eastern Europe.[43] In 1928 Aschoff called for an International Society for Geographical Pathology, which was founded in Geneva in 1929. Strong support came from Aschoff and Zeiss and from the newly founded Russian Society for Racial Pathology and the Geographical Distribution of Disease, which involved the eugenicist Koltsov and Russian pathologists.[44] The most favoured of all the joint German–Soviet scientific ventures was the Institute for Racial Research. This was referred to by the influential Schmidt-Ott as 'unser besondere Lieblingsgedanke'.

---

[39] O. Vogt (ed.), *Die Naturwissenschaft in der Sowjet-Union, Vorträge ihrer Vertreter während der 'Russischen Naturforscherwoche' in Berlin 1927* (Königsberg and Berlin, 1929); GARF 5446/37/40/156 Zeiss to Gorbunov 15 July 1927.

[40] BAK R 73/234 The polar expedition of Wölken was to leave in July 1932 and return in autumn of 1933. GARF 5446/37/40/178, Zeiss to Gorbunov 30 Nov. 1928.

[41] O. Vogt, '1. Bericht über die Arbeiten des Moskauer Staatsinstituts für Hirnforschung', *Journal für Psychologie und Neurologie*, 40 (1929), 108–18. The neurologist Ludwig Spielmeyer pointed out that mental defectives also have enlarged brain cells, see *Handbuch der Geisteskrankheiten*.

[42] Nötzold, 'Wissenschaftsbeziehungen', 785.

[43] Among the honorary members of the German Society for Blood Group Research were V. Bunak (professor of anthropology, Moscow), W. Rubaschkin (protozoa research, Kharkov), W. Schamoff (surgery, Kharkov), Boris Wischnewski (office of blood group research, Anthropological Museum, Leningrad).

[44] M. Askanazy, 'Die Internationale Gesellschaft für geographische Pathologie', *Centralblatt für allgemeine Pathologie und pathologische Anatomie*, 42 (1928), 55–60; Nachlass Aschoff VIII/14 'Welche Aufgaben hat die medizinisch-geographische Forschung in SSSR? Ein Vorschlag von H. Zeiss' (MS presented on the founding of the Russian Society for Racial Pathology, 14 Dec. 1928).

iii. The German–Russian Institute for Racial Research

The establishment of a German–Russian Laboratory or Institute for Racial Research was the outcome of the anthropological and medical activities of Aschoff, Vogt, and Zeiss when German–Soviet cultural interchanges had reached a high point in 1927–8. The aims of this medical triumvirate diverged on matters of race. Aschoff reiterated in June 1926 his wish to found a laboratory for studying the geography of disease: in this sense the programme represented a renaissance of the localist approach to epidemiology, in sharp contrast to bacteriological emphasis on pathogenic micro-organisms. He hoped that the laboratory would be sited in Tiflis, where the German hospital had survived since 1918. The scheme was favoured by the Georgian health authority, with whom Vogt had been negotiating since 1925.[45] As the Soviet authorities decided to take over the German hospitals in Tiflis and in Leningrad, the proposed Forschungsstätte für Rassenforschung became a form of compensation. German and Soviet cultural diplomats agreed on the Institute's foundation by October 1927.[46] Although Aschoff pursued the Tiflis plan until the autumn of 1930, arrangements could not be finalized. Semashko discussed with Vogt a Moscow location at the Brain Research Institute. Zeiss continued to act as intermediary, and the resulting institute fulfilled his hope for a German medical research centre in Moscow. The original plan was for an institute modelled on the Naples Zoological Station (a private venture relying on academies and states renting research facilities), and on German medical initiatives at Shanghai and São Paulo. Zeiss suggested departments for pathological anatomy, microbiology, epidemiology, and medical geography. Aschoff responded enthusiastically to this scheme as coinciding with his original notion of such an institute in 1922.[47] The Institute represented a revised form of Vogt's Caucasian genetic research department, for which he hoped that the Reich Foreign Office would contribute 20,000 marks yearly.[48] In September 1927 Brockdorff-Rantzau endorsed the view of Zeiss that the Institute for Racial Research should be a permanent base for German scientific and cultural activities in the Soviet Union, and as such the Reich Foreign Office should contribute to its running costs.[49]

The finance was shared between the German Foreign Office and a rather more generous NDW, but the lack of a Soviet contribution created difficulties.[50] Because

---

[45] BAP 0902/423 Deutsches Krankenhaus in Tiflis 1923–31. 0902/350 Bl. 265, letter from the German consul Tiflis, 14 Sept. 1924; *Ludwig Aschoff*, 391. 0902/395 Bl. 148–50.

[46] BAP 0902/400 Bl. 198 Göppert to Brockdorff-Rantzau 8 Oct. 1927.

[47] AHUB NL Zeiss Nr 4 NDW 1925–8, letter of Aschoff to Zeiss 28 Dec. 1928; Nr 11 Medical Geography, correspondence with Rabl 22 June 1933; *Ludwig Aschoff*, 391.

[48] Historisches Archiv Friedrich Krupp FAH 4E 266 Bl. 187–9 Vogt to Brockdorff-Rantzau 14 Oct. 1925.

[49] BAP 0902/400 Bl. 199–200 Brockdorff-Rantzau to the Foreign Office, Berlin 29 Sept. 1927.

[50] BAK R 73/226 Finanzierung. Aktennotizen 4 June 1929; 73/228 Meeting of 8 Oct. 1932; S. G. Solomon and J. Richter, *Ludwig Aschoff Vergleichende Völkerpathologie oder Rassenpathologie. Tagebucheiner Reise durch Russland und Transkaukasien* (Pfaffenweiler, 1998), 192 for respective financial contributions.

of the sharp cuts in German public finances in 1931 the agricultural venture, DRUSAG, made up the financial shortfall, but in May 1933 the Soviet authorities rejected further DRUSAG funds but offered to finance the running costs of the laboratory and personnel, provided that the NDW could supply chemicals and pay for travel to and from the Soviet Union.[51] Funding remained precarious and well below the initial grandiose expectations. It suggests that the common ground initially identified regarding disease pathology was disintegrating, as the Russians increasingly distrusted the German political agenda.

A Soviet management committee included Semashko, the zoologist and eugenicist Koltsov, and the geneticist Sergei Chetverikov, and there was a parallel German committee including Schmidt-Ott and Vogt.[52] Yet the position of the Institute was ill-defined and shifting. In 1930 Aschoff was forced to yield to the control of Vogt. Similarly, the pathologist Alexei Ivanovich Abrikosov and the neurologist Semyon Alexandrovich Sarkisov clashed over administrative responsibility for the Institute, until Sarkisov, who had spent some months training in Berlin, was confirmed as deputy director. The whole political context was being restructured in 1930, as the charismatic and internationally minded Semashko was replaced as Commissar by the 'apparatchik' Mikhail Vladimirsky.[53] While nominally a collaborative venture under Aschoff and Abrikosov, no Soviet researcher was employed in a senior capacity.[54] The involved German (and in the case of Hamperl, Austrian) researchers were primarily interested in pathology and tropical medicine, and it was only after 1933 that the coherence of their concerns would be shattered.

That the Institute was to have facilities in both Moscow and the provinces meant that field studies could be made of ethnic factors in chronic diseases. In 1929 the Deutsche Gesellschaft zum Studium Osteuropas agreed with the Georgian Socialist Republic to establish a racial institute in Tiflis.[55] In August 1930 the geneticist Timoféef-Ressovsky acted as intermediary at a meeting of Georgian and Soviet representatives at Vogt's Neuro-Biological Institute in Berlin-Buch. Vogt and Koltsov negotiated with the Georgian Peoples' Commmissar Kudshaidze to establish a Transcaucasian Racial Institute with departments for anthropology and racial pathology. It was suggested that each of the Transcaucasian health commissariats should send a young doctor to Berlin for training in genetics. They were meant to return by spring 1931 and, accompanied by German researchers, to collect anthropological materials in the Caucasus. The NDW was to pay for equipment.[56] Vogt

---

[51] BAP 0902/421 Bl. 242–5 Nauck to NDW, Vogt, Aschoff, and the German embassy Moscow, 21 May 1933.

[52] Nachlass Vogt, Oskar-Vogt-Institut, Düsseldorf, 'Information f. d. Deutsche Mitglieder des deutsch-russischen Komitees f. Rassenforschung'.

[53] NL Vogt file no. 32, Sarkissov to Vogt 10 Jan. 1929 complaining that Arndt regarded Sarkissov as head; Vogt to Sarkissov 13 Apr. 1929.

[54] For an inventory of equipment in 1929 see BAP 0902/417 Bl. 37–44.

[55] Schmidt-Ott, *Erlebtes*, 226, 232, 234, 242 on Tiflis meeting and discussions with Semashko in 1928.

[56] BAK R 73/225 Protocol of meeting 13 Oct. 1930.

Containment

TABLE 7.1. The German-Soviet Institute for Racial Research

Researcher	Date	Interests	Politics after 1933
Arndt, Hans-Joachim	Aug. 1927–Mar. 1929	goitre	d.1932
Hamperl, Herwig	May 1929–Sept. 1930	stomach ulcers, malnutrition	NSDAP/1942
Rabl, Rudolf	Feb. 1930–Apr. 1933	pathology of liver	NSDAP/1937
Nauck, Ernst Georg	Apr.–June 1931	pathology of spleen, Caucasus expedition	NSDAP/1937
	Apr.–July 1933	pellagra	
Mayer, Martin	Apr.–June 1931	Caucasus expedition	emigration
Lührs, Paul Erich	Sept. 1932 Mar.–June 1935	veterinary pathology (research in Moscow)	—
Laas, Ernst	entry refused in 1934	pathology	NSDAP/1938

was also offered a research institute and a fifty-bed hospital in Tiflis for clinical researches.[57]

The scheme linked pathology, genetics, and serology to correlate the effects of disease and environment. Arndt researched on goitre, cretinism, and the effects of altitude in the Caucasus.[58] Hamperl investigated stomach ulcers and catarrh as related to malnutrition, following up the effects of the famine of 1921–3.[59] Nauck studied pellegra in the Caucasus.[60] Rabl examined liver diseases and choleliathis among ethnic groups such as the Ukrainian Jews and Volga Germans.[61] Russian researchers like Koltsov traced diseases among different races in similar geographical conditions; for example, Kirgiz, Uzbeks, and Tajiks in central Asia.[62]

The racial institute was an offshoot of earlier medical and veterinary ventures, arising from Zeiss's mission to establish a permanent German medical centre in

[57] BAK R 73/227 28 Oct. 1930; *Elfter Bericht der NDW* (1931–2). Aschoff-Archiv, VIII/14 Zeiss to Aschoff 29 July 1929.

[58] H.-J. Arndt, *Der Kropf in Russland. Morphogeographische Studie, Ergebnisse der deutsch-russischen Rassenforschungsarbeitsstelle* (Jena, 1931) (= *Veröffentlichungen aus der Kriegs-, Gewerbe und Konstitutionspathologie*, 7/3–4).

[59] H. Hamperl, 'Beiträge zur geographischen Pathologie unter besonderer Berücksichtigung der Verhältnisse in Sowjet-Russland und des runden Magengeschwürs', *Ergebnisse der allgemeinen pathologischen Anatomie*, 26 (1932), 353–422.

[60] E. G. Nauck, *Beiträge zu Pathologie und Epidemiologie der Pellegra. Nach Beobachtungen aus Transkaukasien* (Leipzig, 1933), (= *Archiv für Schiffs- und Tropenhygiene*, 37 (1933), Beiheft 2)).

[61] R. Rabl, *Untersuchungen über Ikterus, akute Leberatrophie, Leberzirrhosen und Choleliathis* (Leipzig, 1934) (= *Archiv für Schiffs- und Tropenhygiene*, 38 (1934), Beiheft 1 (Ergebnisse der deutsch-russischen Rassenforschungsarbeitsstelle)).

[62] NL Vogt no. 32 Koltsov to Vogt 9 May 1928 concerning racial pathology. When a Society for Racial Pathology was established in 1929, Zeiss criticized the superficiality of Koltsov's approach to racial questions; BAK R 73/226 Zeiss report on meeting of 22 Mar. 1929.

Moscow. Susan Solomon has shown how a German-Soviet syphilis expedition was planned in 1925; a pilot study was conducted in Buriat-Mongolia in 1926 as a preliminary to a major expedition in 1928. The expedition tackled the effects of syphilis on a 'primitive race', the Buriats whose religion prohibited bathing. The German specialists (a neuro-physiologist, a geneticist, serologists, and a pharmacologist) performed experimental research on an ethnic group that confirmed the stereotype of a filthy Asiatic race, ridden with syphilis.[63] The Racial Laboratory offered a launching pad for similar investigations of racial factors in disease.

The link with agricultural research was also prompted by racial concerns. The NDW financed veterinary studies of animal diseases, thereby assisting the German agricultural communities; drugs like Bayer 205 were tested for animal diseases in the hope of finding new uses. An agricultural and veterinary source can be traced back to 1923 when the Essen iron and steel manufacturers Krupps established the MANYTSCH company in the North Caucasus to promote animal breeding.[64] Assistance to the ethnic German 'colonists' led to agricultural ventures: the German concessionary organization for agricultural and veterinary research, DRUSAG (Deutsch-Russische Saatbau, i.e. seed nurseries), was launched in 1922 and taken over by the Reich and the East Prussian city of Königsberg in 1926; the DRUSAG maintained an experimental station in the North Caucasus. An agrarian venture, DRUAG (Deutsch-Russische Agrargesellschaft), supported German medical and veterinary research.[65] Two German veterinary researchers worked in the Caucasus, late in 1929.[66] Model farms bred German livestock, tested German seeds and agricultural machinery, and were intended to benefit the German 'colonists' in the surrounding areas.[67] Scientifically, they represented the counterpart of Soviet botanical endeavours to discover seed stocks which could resist the harsh climatic conditions. The involved medical interests tapped the DRUSAG's resources in support of the racial institute.

The agreement between Schmidt-Ott of the NDW with Kalinin, Lunacharsky, Semashko, and Gorbunov paved the way for Zeiss to lead a German-Russian expedition to Uralsk (east of Saratov in Kyrgyzstan) to test the new Behringwerke product Naganal for the camel trypanosomiasis, Su-auru in 1926. This launched a strategy of conquering the eastern pharmaceutical market, and inspired the admiration of Zeiss for Behring as a symbol of German medical genius. Zeiss followed up his camel disease experiments with investigations of tularemia in the Volga delta, a plague-like infection in rodents to which rural populations were vulnerable. An epidemic laboratory monitored conditions among the Cossacks and

---

[63] S. Gross Solomon, 'The Soviet-German Syphilis Expedition to Buriat Mongolia, 1928: Scientific Research on National Minorities', *Slavic Review*, 52 (1993), 204–32.

[64] For conditions on this estate see 0902/418 Bl. 81, report by Bederke, dated 13 Sept. 1929.

[65] BAK R 73/221; W. Beitel and J. Nötzold, *Deutsch-sowjetische Wirtschaftsbeziehungen in der Zeit der Weimarer Republik* (Baden-Baden, 1979), 121.

[66] Aschoff-Archiv Zeiss to Aschoff concerrning Bederke and Nöller researching in the Caucasus, 10 Feb. 1929.

[67] O. Bederke, 'Deutsche Zuchtvieh im Kaukasus', *Osteuropa*, 5 (1929–30), 782–98. Dirksen, *Moscow*, 123, 145.

worked in conjunction with the bacteriological institute of the plague and tularemia expert Sergei Nikanorov in Saratov. Uralsk was an ethnically complex focal point, straddling Europe and Asia and populated by Cossacks and Kyrgyz.[68] Zeiss attempted to secure NDW funds for a more permanent German laboratory in the Uralsk region during 1928 to monitor animal and human epidemics.[69]

Attempts were made to introduce breeding stock from Germany, notably Rotvieh cattle and Prussian merino sheep. German experts in veterinary medicine visited the Caucasus and the Volga German Republic to study cattle diseases, a manœuvre rendered more significant because collectivization of farms took off during 1929–30.[70] These ventures furthered German scientific, racial, and strategic interests, while monitoring the impact of collectivization on the surviving 1.2 million ethnic Germans.[71] The German Foreign Office financed academic visits: the Austrian Hamperl guided Aschoff and Vogt on an *Ostland* lecture tour to Baku, Tiflis, Yerevan, and Samarkand during 1930 when they visited persecuted academic colleagues and gathered information about the suppression of the churches among ethnic Germans.[72] Mayer and Nauck travelled to the Caucasus in spring 1931 where they triumphantly reported that the local approach to tropical medicine accorded with the teachings of the Hamburg Tropical Institute.[73] German scientists and officials celebrated such cultural triumphs.

The multiple aims of the German diplomats and scientists were mutually reinforcing and show how cultural and medical schemes were integral to Weimar *Ost-*

---

[68] GARF 5446/37/40/87–6 Zeiss to Semashko 21 Oct. 1926; 5446/37/40/90 Zeiss to Gorbunov 21 Oct. 1926; 5446/37/40/91 Gorbunov to Zeiss 28 Oct. 1926; 5446/37/40/101 Zeiss to Gorbunov 12 Nov. 1926; 5446/37/40/108 Zeiss to Gorbunov 22 Dec. 1926; 5446/37/40/120 Zeiss to Gorbunov 3 Feb. 1927; 5446/37/40/121 Zeiss to Gorbunov 13 Feb. 1927; 5446/37/40/174–3 Zeiss to Gorbunov 16 May 1928; 170–69 (undated letter); 5446/37/40/157, Zeiss to Gorbunov 7 Jan. 1927; in praise of Emelin; 172 Zeiss to Gorbunov 30 Dec. 1927 concerning the election of Zeiss as corresponding member of the Society for Kazakhstan Research, and research plans; 178, Zeiss to Gorbunov 30 Nov. 1928. On tularemia see: H. Zeiss, 'Die Pest in Russland. Pestähnliche Lymphdrüsenentzündungen im Wolga-delta 1926 (Tularämia?)', *MMW* (1929), 1137–8; A. Roubakine, 'Tularemia', *League of Nations. Monthly Epidemiological Report of the Health Section of the Secretariat*, 9/1 (1930), 3–21. On Nikanorov see Olpp, *Tropenmediziner*, 296.

[69] Aschoff-Archiv VIII/14 Zeiss to Notgemeinschaft der deutschen Wissenschaft 19 Oct. 1928.

[70] Schmidt-Ott, *Erlebtes*, 226; Aschoff papers, Zeiss to Aschoff 11 Oct. 1929; Aschoff to Zeiss 25 Oct. 1929; BAP 0902/419 Bl. 57 report on animal breeding in the Caucasus, Bl. 109 8.8.1930 report on the Volga German Republic. 0902/418 Bl. 81 Bederke 13 Nov. 1929, Bl. 158–238 report on Soviet veterinary research. The German veterinary scientists were Otto Bederke and Nöller.

[71] GARF 5446/37/40/169–70 Zeiss to Gorbunov, n.d., and 156 Zeiss to Gorbunov 15 July 1927; AHUB Hygiene Institute Nr 189 Bl. 179: in 1926 there were an estimated 1,237,900 ethnic Germans in the USSR, 379,600 lived in the Volga region.

[72] BAK R 73/225. Aschoff to Schmidt-Ott 22 Oct. 1930; *Ludwig Aschoff. Ein Gelehrtenleben*, 393–409; S. G. Solomon and J. Richter (eds.), *Ludwig Aschoff. Vergleichende Völkerpathologie oder Rassenpathologie. Tagebuch einer Reise durch Russland und Transkaukasien* (Pfaffenweiler, 1998); Aschoff visited the German colony of Helenendorf near Baku, where Professor Mühlmann and Dr Seemann (the father of a Leningrad pathologist) were contacted; Hamperl, *Werdegang und Lebensweg*, 126–35. For Schmidt-Ott's tour of 1928 and contacts with ethnic Germans, see Schmidt-Ott, *Erlebtes*, 228, 241–2.

[73] BAP 0902/420 Bl. 234–44 report by Mayer and Nauck: M. Mayer and E. G. Nauck: 'Von einer medizinischen Studienreise nach Transkaukasien', *Deutsche medizinische Wochenschrift*, 58 (1932), 631; Wulf, *Tropeninstitut*, 25–6, 160 concerning abortive plans for a visit by Mayer in 1929.

politik. The NDW was keen to restore the international prestige of German science, and the Moscow embassy and German Foreign Office were interested in information gathering, trade relations (as the stability of the Soviet economy was attractive to German industrialists[74]), and maintaining cultural ties with the Soviet Union. The Kaiser Wilhelm Gesellschaft and the lavish Rockefeller Foundation grant to Vogt for a new institute at Berlin-Buch provided resources for sociobiological studies of population groups.[75] Aschoff's support for geographical pathology was accompanied by hopes that the institute for comparative pathological research would rival the Pasteur and Rockefeller Institutes as a German cultural bequest to foreign countries. He planned that a new type of research centre—which he called a 'Virchow Institute'—would permit international and interdisciplinary scientific research on pathology, bacteriology, anthropology, and tropical medicine, and he envisaged that the German government could endow Virchow institutes in each continent. By 1930 he recognized that he could not realize his scheme in the increasingly repressive Russian context.[76] Vogt advocated the comparative study of brain structures, relating cultural backwardness to brain anatomy, and the application of hereditary biology to brain research; his work appealed to von Bohlen as offering a scientific basis for industrial psychology. Zeiss was concerned primarily with questions of race and disease, so as to rekindle a sense of historic mission of German science in the east, and promote the welfare of German 'colonists'. He was the crucial link person in developing racial studies and in sustaining a German presence in Russia for nationalist reasons.[77]

Although a 'racial institute' might have seemed the least likely basis for a political rapprochement between ideologically antagonistic states, during the 1920s the image of race could involve progressive concerns with the health of population groups. The German scientists kept quiet about their concerns for their ethnic brethren. They defined race in scientific terms as differentiating factors, and as the result of genetic mutations. A rationale linking clinical research to bacteriology and genetics derived from constitutional medicine as formulated by Kraus, Aschoff, and the Austrian anatomist and social reformer, Tandler (who died in exile in the Soviet Union in 1936). Hereditary, geographical, and constitutional medicine offered a multifactoral means of overcoming what was perceived as the narrowness of genetics and bacteriology, and provided a modern definition of race on a scientific basis, in sharp contrast to *völkisch* nationalism.

The scientific definition of race went with a broadly inclusive sense of German identity. Nauck, born in St Petersburg and a veteran of the DRK Russian expedition, emerged as a leading figure in Nazi racial medicine prescribing ghettoization

---

[74] H. Pogge von Strandmann, 'Industrial Primacy in German-Russian Relations at the End of the Weimar Republic', in R. J. Bessel and E. J. Feuchtwanger (eds.), *Social Change and Political Development in Weimar Germany* (London, 1981), 241–67.

[75] Weindling, *Health, Race and German Politics*, 464–9; Vogt papers, no. 32, letter 26 Feb. 1929 from the RF Paris office to Vogt concerning a grant of $250,000 to Vogt.

[76] *Ludwig Aschoff. Ein Gelehrtenleben in Briefen an die Familie* (Freiburg, 1966), 391–2; Solomon and Richter, *Aschoff*, 62. AHUB NL Zeiss, Nr 3 fo. 3. BAK R 73/227 Besprechung 8 Oct. 1932.

[77] Aschoff-Archiv, 5 Apr. 1929 Zeiss to Aschoff on nationalist motives for remaining in Russia.

for epidemic prevention in German-occupied Poland.[78] By way of contrast, Martin Mayer (under whom Zeiss had trained) had to emigrate as Jewish from the Hamburg Institute for Tropical Medicine to Venezuela in 1938.[79] The surveys of disease in remote regions had strategic significance for the Germans, particularly after 1933. Völkisch leanings can be seen in the editorial participation of Zeiss and the sero-anthropologist Otto Reche in the *Zeitschrift für Rassenphysiologie* from 1931, as they fused racial ideology with scientific advances.[80] Zeiss exemplifies how racial interests were multi-layered. While a biologically based medical science initially shaped the development of the Institute for Racial Research, other covert motives were at work which would gain prominence after the Nazi takeover.

Semashko's dismissal as Commissar of Health early in 1930 posed a threat to the Institute for Racial Research, and was symptomatic of a changing ideological climate linked to Stalin's consolidation of power.[81] Soviet authorities carefully referred to 'nations' rather than 'races', and in May 1933 it was decided to change the name to the 'Institute for Geographical Pathology' with the primary aim of mapping disease. Soviet scientists valued the scheme in the context of improving public health, the eradication and control of disease in peripheral regions, the acquisition of German scientific techniques, political centralization, and potential economic and military gains.[82] The mercurial Zeiss saw his bacteriological specimens as of military significance—supplying (as he informed the Soviet authorities) strategic information in the event of an invasion.[83]

The German medical presence in the Volga region provided a cover for linking medical, strategic, and racial motives to military interests. During 1925 and 1926 various companies ostensibly working on pest control concealed German and Soviet military collaboration on gas warfare. A poison gas manufacturing plant was set up by the chemist Stoltzenberg, who had impressed Haber and the German military authorities by using his contract to destroy the remnants of the poison gas supplies left over from the war as a gigantic experiment on the composition and effects of gases, and by supplying poison gas to the Spanish army for its campaigns in Morocco from spring 1921. He accompanied a German delegation to

---

[78] BDC Nauck NSDAP 4178797, joined 1 May 1937; Rabl NSDAP Nr 3982662, joined 1 May 1937. Hamperl joined the NSDAP in 1942. Arndt died in 1932.

[79] STAH 352 8/a Berhard Nocht Institut 10/2 Martin Mayer.

[80] Reche joined the NSDAP in 1937 and Zeiss in December 1931. O. Reche, 'Blutgruppenforschung und Anthropologie', *Volk und Rasse*, 3/1 (1928), 1–12. For Reche's racial interests in the East see Burleigh, *Germany Turns Eastwards*, 166–76; P. M. H. Mazumdar, 'Blood and Soil: The Serology of the Aryan Racial State', *Bulletin of the History of Medicine*, 64 (1990), 187–219.

[81] BAK R 73/226 memorandum of Vogt 2 Dec. 1929; BAK R 73/226 Hamperl to Vogt 22 Jan. 1930; C. Davis, 'Economics of Soviet Public Health, 1928–1932', in Solomon and Hutchinson, *Health and Society*, 156, 166; Solomon, 'Social Hygiene', ibid., 189–91.

[82] Solomon and Richter, *Aschoff*, 32–3, 36 for the position of Koltzov and other Russians. For the context of nationalism see: J. E. Mace, 'The Famine of 1932–1933: A Watershed in the History of Soviet Nationality Policy', in H. R. Huttenbach (ed.), *Soviet Nationality Policies* (London, 1990), 177–205.

[83] GARF 5446/37/40/34–25; Zeiss, 'Die kriegshygienischen Aufgaben einer medizinischen Topographie in Russland in Verbindung mit der Allrussischen Mikrobiologischen Sammlung'.

Moscow in 1923, and negotiated with the Russians for a secret gas weapons factory at Ivanashenkovo near Samara utilizing German equipment and technology. Stoltzenberg's running of the poison gas section became a costly economic, political, and technical failure. The publicity surrounding the massive explosion at Stoltzenberg's plant in Hamburg, leaks of information concerning the Russian installations, financial difficulties arising from the Soviet pressure to take control of the installation meant that the grandiose Volga scheme to replenish the Wehrmacht's reserves of poison gas collapsed.[84]

The Volga scheme also ran into difficulties, partly financial and partly because the Volga flooded. From 1927 Stoltzenberg was involved in German army tests for explosives and gas-filled shells near Saratov. The British journalist Wickham Steed accused him of devising the aerial spraying of deadly germs from aircraft.[85] Chemists, doctors (notably the gas warfare expert Otto Muntsch), biologists, and a meteorologist formed part of the German poison gas contingent, and IG-Farben also tested gases in the USSR. Between 1925 and 1933 the Reichswehr and Red Army exchanged officers and technical experts, so that 156 Russians were sent to Germany.[86]

An advantage of the Volga region was that German officers were inconspicuous given the prevalence of ethnic German 'colonists', with whom German medical scientists had established links. Zeiss made frequent visits to Saratov; he assisted its newly established institute for tropical medicine and microbiology by providing the drug Bayer 205 and arranging study visits by German-sponsored researchers.[87] In addition to the Agricultural Institute founded by Sergei Vavilov, there was a eugenics society in Saratov from December 1923 with a membership of forty-four local doctors.[88] Zeiss fostered German education and *Heimatkunde* in Saratov: he arranged for the German embassy in Moscow to supply books obtained from the

[84] Liepmann, *Death from the Skies*, 215–19; Haber, *Poisonous Cloud*, 287, 305–6, and 316 for a 1979 explosion in Hamburg at Stoltzenberg's disused chemical dump. Szöllösi-Janze, *Haber*, 468–80.

[85] On Stoltzenberg see Liepmann, *Death from the Skies*, 104–6, 215–20; W. Steed, 'The Future of Warfare', *The Nineteenth Century and After*, 106 (1934), 129–40, 132–6; L. F. Haber, *The Poisonous Cloud. Chemical Warfare in the First World War* (Oxford, 1986), 287, 305–6, 316. Szöllösi-Janze, *Haber*, 476–9.

[86] Castellan, 'Reichswehr et Armée Rouge', 185–7; M. Zeidler, *Reichswehr und Rote Armee 1920–1933* (Munich, 1993), 73–4, 80–1, 97–9, 123–6, 198, 348–51; Groehler, *Reichswehr*, 40–1, 46–9, 59. Personnel included the physicians Haller, Laun, and Muntsch, the chemists Viereck and Wirth. The departmental head was a Dr Bormann (possibly, Felix von Bormann, born in St Petersburg in 1901). M. Speidel, 'Reichswehr und Rote Armee', 7–45. Szöllösi-Janze, *Haber*, 466.

[87] H. Zeiss, 'Das Reichsinstitut für Epidemiologie und Mikrobiologie für den Südosten Russlands in Saratow an der Wolga', *Münchener Medizinische Wochenschrift* (1924), 1468–9; BAP 0908/351 Bl. 317 Brockdorff-Rantzau to Zeiss 1 Oct. 1925 concerning a visit to Saratov; BAP 0902/419 Bl. 268, Zeiss 11 Feb. 1930 concerning the German refusal to finance this post; AHUB Zeiss papers box 4 NDW, Zeiss to Schmidt-Ott 24 Sept. 1925; Aschoff to Zeiss on Saratov scheme 28 Dec. 1928.

[88] N. Koltzov, 'Die rassenhygienische Bewegung in Russland', *Archiv für Rassen- und Gesellschaftsbiologie*, 17 (1925–6), 96–9; Adams, 'Eugenics as Social Medicine', 208; id., 'Eugenics in Russia', 166. Among members with German names was the plant breeder G. K. Meister. The Society was independent until late 1925.

Munich eugenicist Fritz Lenz, and he was in close contact with the Saratov philologist Georg Dinges, who compiled a Volga German songbook.[89] From 1927 Zeiss studied the serological samples taken from Volga Germans in order to establish their ethnic origins from Hessen, and generally favoured studies of their racial characteristics.[90] The German Society for Blood Group Research and the Reich Ministry of the Interior supported this research, indicating official backing for assistance to ethnic German 'colonists', as well as an effort to demonstrate the distribution of German settlement in the east.[91] The Moscow Institute of Racial Pathology reinforced this strategy. Hamperl was aware of Muntsch's gas warfare tests in Russia during 1926.[92] Arndt researched on disease among the Volga Germans as part of the programme of comparative racial pathology.[93] But the strategic context favouring the build up of academic relations was to change fundamentally during the early 1930s.

The German–Soviet Racial Institute was established at a difficult juncture in German–Soviet relations, as forced industrialization and collectivization of agriculture coincided with a tightening of political authority over scientific élites from 1929. Stalin took power in 1929, and initially turned to Litvinov (a long-standing contact of Vogt) to ensure stability. The Institute represented continuity with policies of international coexistence, albeit in a changed power structure. From 1931 Stalinist centralization had draconian ramifications for the sciences in terms of tightening ideological and party political controls. The rise of Lysenkoist biology was in part a rejection of any pro-Western orientation. Contacts between Soviet and Western researchers became more difficult. Hamperl characterized the mentality of Soviet professors as radishes—red on the outside and white to the core, but he observed a rapid shift from deference towards German scientists to party political hostility during 1929.[94] Koltsov, whose eugenics society was under political pressure, cautiously objected to the proposed Tiflis Institute being called a 'Rasseninstitut', and other Soviet researchers insisted on practical utility.[95] Koltsov's

---

[89] Voigt, *Hoetzsch*, 188 concerning Schmidt-Ott's interest in Zeiss's visit to Saratov in March 1926; BAP 0902/401 Bl. 311–2 Zeiss, 7 Feb. 1928; 0902/402 Bl. 61 note of 31 Mar. 1932 on the disappearance of Dinges in 1931 and on the persecution of other Volga German academics, Bl. 69. Walter Kuhn, 'Die Russlanddeutschen', *Volk und Rasse*, 6/1 (1931), 1–12.

[90] BAP 15.01/9421 betr. menschliche Vererbungslehre und Bevölkerungskunde Bl. 172. BAK R 73/221. Nachlass Aschoff, VIII/14 Zeiss to Aschoff 27 Jan. 1928 and 15 Feb. 1929, forwarding a copy of W. Essen, 'Die Deutsche Kolonisten in Transkaukasien. Ihre Entwicklung, ein Problem für die menschliche Erblichkeitslehre und die Anthropologie'.

[91] BAK R 73/221 7 Oct. 1927, letter of Zeiss; BAP 15.01 Nr 9421, Bl. 172 14 Oct. 1927, H. Zeiss memorandum on 'Blutgruppenforschung in der Wolgadeutschen Republik'.

[92] Hamperl, *Werdegang und Lebensweg*, 101; I. Kästner and S. Hahn, 'Der Toxikologe Otto Muntsch (1890–1945) und die deutsche Kampfstoffforschung', *1999* (1994), 42–50.

[93] BAK 73/226 letter of Arndt 30 May 1928 concerning Volga German specimens. Arndt collaborated with the Kazan Veterinary Institute directed by the German-educated Karl Bohl. L. Z. Saunders, *Veterinary Pathology in Russia, 1860–1930* (Ithaca, NY and London, 1980), 123–49; BAP 0902/419 Bl. 237 letter of Zeiss of 11 Apr. 1930 that the researcher Skriabin had a German mother.

[94] H. Hamperl, *Werdegang und Lebensweg eines Pathologen*, (Stuttgart and New York, 1972), 212; BAK R 73/226.

[95] BAK R 73/225 Tiflis meeting of 13 Oct. 1930.

demands for a biological institute were part of his survival strategy for hereditary biology and medical genetics in a hostile Stalinist climate.[96] The Stalinist onslaught on eugenics and Mendelian genetics was a crucial difference to Hitler's Germany where racially oriented genetic research and health policies thrived.[97]

Whatever attempt there was to place Weimar and Soviet medicine on common biological foundations came to grief with the ideological polarization. Zeiss attempted to organize scientific resistance to the 'Bolshevizing' of the Academy of Sciences, denouncing the 'red scientists' Nikolai Bukharin and Lunacharsky.[98] Zeiss warned against recognition by Western academics of these party ideologists.[99] The Racial Research Institute's position was helped by Vogt's good relations with Litvinov, and in any case his arch-rival Viacheslav Molotov was pro-German.[100] An autonomous German research institution was increasingly an anomaly, and the possibilities of employing Russian researchers and technical staff receded. The integration of the racial laboratory with Soviet institutes for experimental biology, brain research, and pathology threatened to undermine the Institute.[101] The Soviet authorities insisted on a Russian director paid by the NDW.[102] In March 1931 Rabl was ordered to cease work; but intervention by Timoféef and Zeiss enabled him to continue in Moscow until October 1932. After Vogt's final visit to Moscow in January 1930, he argued that support should be withdrawn from the Brain Research Institute, deploring its metamorphosis into an anti-religious propaganda institute.[103] In 1931 the institute was amalgamated with an institute for neurology, and attention shifted away from Lenin's brain to other élite brains. When confronted by party political pressures in the institute during 1932, Vogt decided to resign.[104] The Reich Foreign Office decided on political grounds that subsidies for the Racial Laboratory should continue, while it considered transferring support to the planned Tiflis institute.[105] Between 28 November and 2 December 1932 the Germans tried to restore good relations by hosting a 'Week of Soviet Medicine' in Berlin—but

---

[96] Adams, 'Eugenics in Russia', 188–99.

[97] For the link between Mendelism and Nazism see K. H. Roth, 'Schöner neuer Mensch. Der Paradigmenwechsel der klassischen Genetik und seine Auswirkungen auf die Bevölkerungsbiologie des "Dritten Reiches"', in H. Kaupen-Haas (ed.), *Der Griff nach der Bevölkerung. Aktualität und Kontinuität nazistischer Bevölkerungspolitik* (Nördlingen, 1986), 41; B. Müller-Hill, *Tödliche Wissenschaft. Die Aussonderung von Juden, Zigeunern und Geisteskranken 1933–1945* (Reinbek bei Hamburg, 1984).

[98] For the background to the ideological commitments of Bukharin and Lunacharsky see C. Read, *Culture and Power in Revolutionary Russia. The Intelligentsia and the Transition from Tsarism to Communism* (London, 1990); D. Todes, 'Pavlov and the Bolsheviks'; R. Medvedev, *Nikolai Bukharin: The Last Years* (New York, 1980).

[99] BAK R 73/223 Bl. 104–8, Zeiss to German Embassy, Moscow 1 July 1931.

[100] BAK R 73/228, Vogt to Secretary of ZIK, Enuchize 10 May 1932.

[101] BAK R 73/226, Hamperl report during December 1929; BAK R 73/227 Bl. 55, on Soviet control.

[102] BAK R 73/227 Bl. 112, Grjasnow to Vogt 10 Jan. 1931.

[103] BAP 0902/420 Bl. 68–9, Vogt to Molotov 10 May 1932.

[104] BAK R 73/228 and 73/227, 29 Aug. 1932 Vogt to Schmidt-Ott.

[105] BAK R 73/227 Bl. 77.

disinterest among doctors and the public was symptomatic of the demise of an era of medical cooperation.[106]

iv. Geo-medicine and Racial History

While the Soviets hoped for technical 'know-how', and the Germans required a strategic ally, German–Soviet medical relations cannot be completely reduced to such functionalist terms. Zeiss and his diplomatic patrons had a sense of carrying out a historic mission in Russia, and his programme for geo-medicine reinforced a deep interest in the history of epidemic diseases. He saw history as demonstrating the German racial aptitude for science; medically, he considered it was important to chart the historical contours of diseases as they changed in time. Zeiss fused two currents in German history of medicine—applied epidemiology, and the heroizing of great doctors. His stance had well entrenched roots: in 1889 at the founding of the Prussian military medical training institute, August Hirsch, the professor of the history of medicine and epidemiologist in Berlin, fought a rearguard action against bacteriology. He argued that effective epidemic controls could only be implemented if bacteriology was supplemented by historical studies of the rise and fall of epidemics. History thus had to fill a gap between practice and medical science—in contrast to the heroizing of laboratory researchers undertaken by Zeiss.[107] His experience in the prevention of typhus and relapsing fever in Turkey during the world war had aroused his interest in the history of diseases. Zeiss had been encouraged by the leading medical historian Karl Sudhoff to take an interest in the history of typhus. Zeiss used his position in Russia to develop studies of the ebb and flow of epidemics.[108] Certain epidemiologists discussing typhus during the First World War—notably Friedrich Wolter—had drawn on Pettenkofer's interest in ground water and the soil as affecting disease transmission. Because typhus required an insect vector, it could confirm the theories of anticontagionist environmentalists.[109]

The attempts by Zeiss to blend environmentalism with bacteriology was permeated by a sense of nationalist mission and ultimately by racial theories. His office in the Pasteur Institute, Moscow, was adorned with icons of German bacteriology—Koch, Behring, and Ehrlich—and he supported the founding of a Mechnikov Museum as a historical archive and research centre. From 1926 Zeiss intensified his efforts to kindle interest in the history of medicine as a means of promoting cultural understanding between Germany and Russia. His protector Gorbunov rec-

---

[106] K.-H. Karbe, 'Die "Woche der Sowjet-Medizin" zu Berlin (28. November bis 2. Dezember 1932)', *Zeitschrift für die gesamte Hygiene*, 27 (1981), 784–8.

[107] A. Hirsch, *Über die historische Entwicklung der Öffentlichen Gesundheitspflege. Rede gehalten zur Feier des Stiftungstages der militärischen Bildungsanstalten am 2. August 1889* (Bad Reichenhall, 1967).

[108] AHUB Zeiss papers, file 8, Bl. 54–5 Sudhoff to Zeiss 7 Oct. 1919, 30 July 1919.

[109] Hansen, *Biologische Kriegsführung*, 69–75, 116.

ommended Zeiss's scheme to Semashko.[110] He envisaged an institute and a society for the history of science and medicine—following the German model of Sudhoff—that would investigate the relations of Russian and Western medicine, the history of Soviet medicine, medical biographies, relations with folk medicine, professionalization, military medicine, and historical epidemiology. By 1929 an Institute for the History of Natural Sciences was established, although the hoped-for Institute for the History of Medicine had not crystallized from the Mechnikov Museum.[111] Zeiss combated Soviet initiatives to gear history of science and medicine to changes in productive forces by offering an idealist antidote to dialectical materialism.

Zeiss's first step in developing his nationalist vision of medical history was to edit Otto Obermeier's seminal paper on the cause of relapsing fever, appearing in Sudhoff's series of medical classics: he portrayed German and Russian medical scientists as part of a harmonious tradition of mutual interaction.[112] In the spirit of this cooperative idealism, Zeiss translated the biography of the Russian immunologist Mechnikov, by his widow Olga, and added appendices and recollections by living scientists. Zeiss demonstrated the enduring persistence of intellectual creations, and the racial psychology of scientific genius. At the same time, he applied the philological virtues of Sudhoff's medical history to modern medicine, and assembled archival sources and conducted interviews. The NDW financed his visit to the archives of the Pasteur Institute in Paris.[113]

Although Mechnikov had been a leading figure in the Pasteur Institute, Zeiss emphasized German–Russian scientific contacts and debts to German scientists. Rather than chronicling Mechnikov's empirical research, Zeiss analysed his scientific achievements as generated by his philosophy of optimism, which he saw as inspired by the monist philosophy of evolution of the German Darwinist, Ernst Haeckel.[114] Zeiss demonstrated that Mechnikov's achievement in establishing the body's mechanisms of resistance to infections was basically German rather than French in inspiration.

Karl Haushofer's nationalist ideas of a politicized geography, or *Geopolitik*, inspired Zeiss to develop 'geo-medicine': he analysed epidemics as not simply due to infectious micro-organisms but to geographical and historical factors. In 1924 Zeiss extolled the significance of Russia for applying Haushofer's ideas to medical

[110] GARF 5446/37/40/123–9 Zeiss, 'Die Notwendigkeit der Gründung einer Russischen Gesellschaft für Geschichte der Medizin und Naturwissenschaften und eines Forschungsinstituts, 11 Dec. 1926'. This was sent to Gorbunov on 27 Jan. 1927, 5446/37/40/130. Also Gorbunov to Semashko 14 Feb. 1927; Gorbunov to Zeiss 11 Feb. 1927.

[111] H. Zeiss, 'Das neugegründete Forschungsinstitut für Geschichte der Naturwissenschaften in Moskau', *Archiv für Geschichte der Mathematik, der Naturwissenschaft und der Technik*, 11 (1929), 209–316.

[112] H. Zeiss (ed.), *Otto Obermeier. Die Entdeckung von fadenförmigen Gebilden im Blut von Rückfall-fieberkranken* (Leipzig, 1926), 9.

[113] BAK R 73/223 Bl. 172, Hahn on application for funds by Zeiss 10 Jan. 1930.

[114] BAK R 73/223 Bl. 175–80. Zeiss to NDW 27 Mar. 1929, to German Embassy, Moscow 3 Sept. 1931.

geography.[115] Zeiss astutely reformulated the programme in terms acceptable to the Soviets. He cited an observation of Trotsky on the characteristics of armies as determined by physical geography: Zeiss used communist insights to legitimate an environmentalist and historicist epidemiology. He noted how there were different diseases on the western and eastern fronts, and how the types of diseases had changed in step with military strategies. It was as important for an army to know which diseases were endemic in a theatre of operations as about physical geography. In an uncharacteristic burst of internationalism, Zeiss praised the League of Nations and Rockefeller Foundation as contributing to medical geography as a new international field of medical cooperation.[116]

Liberal and environmentalist concerns to root disease in the problems of modern civilization competed with approaches based on the nationalist ideology of *Lebensraum*: this can be seen by comparing the views of Max Kuczynski, a pathologist, with those of Zeiss. Kuczynski completed a doctorate in 1919 on *Rickettsia prowazeki* as the cause of typhus, and in 1921 was appointed professor of experimental pathology in Berlin. In 1923–4 he accepted a visiting professorship at the Siberian University of Omsk, and studied malaria and the incidence of typhus in Kazakhstan; in 1925 he held NDW grants to study syphilis and other endemic diseases in Soviet central Asia and Mongolia. His researches can be seen as complementing those of Zeiss on camel diseases. In contrast to the hereditary and racial determinism of Zeiss, Kuczynski developed an ecological analysis of social and sanitary conditions.[117] He applied his ecological approach to the study of the typhus 'virus' which he pursued in conjunction with Rudolf Weigl, the typhus expert in Lwów, and with the support of the Polish health services. This research involved altering the virulence of the virus by passing it through different classes of animals.[118] He emphasized adaptive change as opposed to a deterministic and uniform notion of the *Rickettsiae*. Kuczynski's liberal outlook (and Jewish background) contrasted with how Zeiss took the geographical approach in a nationalist and racist direction.

In 1931 Zeiss coined the term 'Geomedizin', providing medical rationales for the demands for *Lebensraum*. In a contribution to Haushofer's journal for geo-politics, he argued that there was a natural transition from geo-medicine's geographical and spatial aspects to geo-politics. Geo-medicine had a predictive and preventive function of strengthening ethnic groups and states. Rather than the urban and industrial perspectives of the Weimar mandarin of social hygiene, Alfred Grotjahn, Zeiss believed that the German village was the elementary

[115] H. Zeiss, 'Die Bedeutung Russlands für die medizinischen geographischen Forschung', *MMW* (1925), 1834–8. A note explains that article was completed in 1924.

[116] GARF 5446/37/40/34–25, Zeiss, 'Die kriegshygienischen Aufgaben einer medizinischen Topographie in Russland in Verbindung mit der Allrussischen Mikrobiologischen Sammlung'.

[117] The contrast was remarked on by Jochen Richter. This paragraph is largely drawn from his unpublished paper 'Max Kuczynski und Heinrich Zeiss—zwei deutsche Annäherungen an das Problem der geographischen Medizin'. It should be noted that Kuczynski was forced by the Nazis to emigrate after 1933.

[118] M. Kuczynski, *Fleck- und Felsenfieber* (Berlin, 1927), pp. i–v, 1–12.

category of public health. Geo-medical considerations supported German settlements in the east as a biological necessity, protecting Germany's open flank against the wave of eastern undesirables. There was a need to select hardy, weather-immune types for the variable epidemiological circumstances of life in the east, as climatic rather than social factors determined fluctuations in diseases. Arguing that Germany had a mission to dominate the 'Eurasian' space, he suggested that geo-medicine should function as a 'national social hygiene' renewing Germany's youthful vigour and expansive role in the east.[119] These environmentalist prescriptions for regeneration clashed with the racial hygienists' insistence on eugenic controls on reproduction.

The presence of German medical experts in the Soviet Union, particularly when they made much of contacts with Lenin and Trotsky, could be easily misinterpreted. Zeiss sought advice from Arnold Leese, a British veterinary expert, for medical literature on camel diseases. Leese was a notorious anti-Semite and denounced Zeiss as a Jewish Bolshevik:

> Professor Zeiss, You have addressed the wrong man—the international brotherhood of science does not extend to jou or jour jewish masters. British politicians may be fools; do not judge the average intelligent Briton by their example. I have all the information that jou require; but jou will not get it.[120]

Leese assumed that the only camel doctors active in the Soviet Union were 'Judaeo-Bolsheviks'.

Undaunted, Zeiss moved towards a more explicitly Nazi position. Soviet collectivization of agriculture provoked Germans to intensify their cultivation of racial research and geo-medicine. The Volga Germans were perceived as hard hit by collectivization and the expropriation of small landowners.[121] German nationalists were concerned that collectivization resulted in the 'liquidation' of ethnic Germans, equating resettlement with planned racial eradication.[122] In the autumn of 1929 thousands of ethnic Germans (largely Mennonites from Siberia) fled to

---

[119] H. Zeiss, 'Die Notwendigkeit einer deutschen Geomedizin', *Zeitschrift für Geopolitik*, 9 (1932), 474–64; id., 'Der augenblickliche Stand medizinisch-geographischer Forschungen in der Sowjet-Union', *MMW* 73 (1931), 1447–9.

[120] GARF 5445/37/40/109 A. S. Leese (Veterinary Infirmary, Stanford, and Chief Political Officer, Central Counties, British National Fascisti) to Zeiss 21 Jan. 1927; A. S. Leese, *A Treatise on the One-humped Camel in Health and Disease* (Stanford, Calif., 1927); C. Holmes, *Anti-semitism in British Society* (London, 1979), ch. 10; R. Thurlow, *Fascism in Britain* (Oxford, 1985) ch. 4; S. Cohen, 'In Step with Arnold Leese: The Case of Lady Birdwood', *Patterns of Prejudice*, 28 (1994), 61–75. My thanks to Tony Kushner for these references.

[121] M. Buchsweiler, *Volksdeutche in der Ukraine am Vorabend und Beginn des Zweiten Weltkriegs—ein Fall doppelter Loyalität* (Gerlingen, 1984), 222–3 based on H. Neusatz and D. Erka, *Ein deutscher Todesweg* (1930). Koch, *Volga Germans*, 278 argues that a far higher proportion of Volga German landholdings were collectivized (78%) in contrast to a rate of 24% throughout Russia. Fleischhauer and Pinkus, *The Soviet Germans*, 45 point out that German-owned land in Russia in 1914 was of enormous extent (14,750,000 hectares), and that the average holding was 28 hectares.

[122] S. Merl, '"Ausrottung" der Bourgeoisie und der Kulaken in Sowjetrussland? Anmerkungen zu einem fragwürdigen Vergleich mit Hitlers Judenvernichtung', *Geschichte und Gesellschaft*, 13 (1987) 368–81.

Moscow with the aim of emigration. German public opinion was alerted to their plight, and the German Red Cross asked the Foreign Ministry to intervene. The German ambassador, Herbert von Dirksen initially rejected these requests, but Hindenburg supported an appeal for funds to aid the distressed 'colonists'. Although German and international publicity was embarrassing to the German Foreign Office and the Soviet authorities, the 'colonists' were forcibly evicted and exiled.

Auhagen, the agricultural attaché, publicized the plight of the ethnic Germans. His consequent dismissal from the German embassy in Moscow demonstrated how a rift was opening between racial nationalists and official policies. German assistance for the starving 'colonists' was relaunched amidst much ultra-right-wing propaganda against Soviet collectivization as involving the deportations of Germans to concentration camps. The Nazis moved from outright hostility to anything to do with Russia, to support for the ethnic Germans, and attacked official indecision. German–Soviet relations were strained by press reports on the liquidation of the 'colonists'. German nationalists were insensed that the few who left the Soviet Union were detained in the former POW camps of Hammerstein and Eydtkuhen, where the German authorities subjected them to harsh disinfection procedures.[123]

Given that Auhagen and Hilger had links to Zeiss and the *Ostforscher*, the crisis over ethnic German demands to emigrate reveals how a racially motivated grouping had taken root at the German embassy. In October 1929 Auhagen, Hoetzsch, and Zeiss reported to the embassy on the condition of the refugees, and Zeiss stressed the potential hazard of typhus and other epidemics.[124] In 1931 Hilger attempted to gain information through the International Committee of the Red Cross about the Volga German deportation camp ('Verschicktenlager').[125] The German Red Cross again supervised border crossings by ethnic Germans returning, and relaunched its 'Brothers in Need Campaign'.[126] The crisis of collectivization fuelled Nazi propaganda against the Soviet Union with the accusation that brutal expropriation of the 'colonists' meant extermination of over a million Volga Germans.[127] At this juncture Zeiss left the German National People's Party (DNVP) and joined the Nazi Party in December 1931: what had been a fringe political group was rapidly attracting support from medical experts seeing *Lebens-*

---

[123] H. L. Dyck, *Weimar Germany and Soviet Russia 1926–1933. A Study in Diplomatic Instability* (London, 1966), 162–84. On Auhagen see Burleigh, *Germany Turns Eastwards*, 34; BAK R 86/2401 Heimkehrer-, Flüchtlings-und Kriegsgefangene Lager, report of Lentz on conditions in the camps of Hammerstein and Eydtkuhnen 10 Dec. 1929. O. Auhagen, *Die Schicksalswende des russlanddeutschen Bauerntums in den Jahren 1927–1930* (Leipzig, 1942). Id., 'Wirtschaftsumschau', *Osteuropa*, 6 (1930–1), 55.

[124] Auhagen, *Die Schicksalswende*, 55–7.

[125] BAP 0908/351 Bl. 87 note by Hilger of 6 Mar. 1931, Bl. 88 on attitude of Foreign Office.

[126] F. Grüneisen, *Das Deutsche Rote Kreuz in Vergangenheit und Gegenwart* (Berlin, 1939), 181.

[127] K.-H. Görbing, 'Das Deutschtum in der Sowjetunion', Verband Deutscher Vereine im Ausland, *Wir Deutsche in der Welt* (Berlin, 1937), 49–64. *Ein deutscher Todesweg. Authentische Dokumente der wirtschaftlichen, Kulturellen und seelischen 'Vernichtung des Deutschtums in der Sowjetunion* (Berlin, 1930).

raum in the east as an antidote to national ills. The defence of the German race from its impending extermination was set to become a central concern for German epidemiologists.

v. The Moscow Bridgehead

Despite their ideological antagonisms, Nazi–Soviet medical relations became strained rather than severed in 1933. German medical installations planted in the Soviet Union during the 1920s changed from being part of an international programme of scientific and technological cooperation to being viewed as bridgeheads for a future advance. Between 1933 and the Nazi–Soviet pact of 1938 German diplomats and scientists tried to salvage the Racial Research Institute in Moscow. The underlying aim was to gather strategic information about Soviet scientific expertise, institutions, and epidemic conditions.

The Nazi takeover did not dim German hopes that the Institute for Racial Pathology would survive. Initially the Politburo member Molotov gained ascendancy in Soviet foreign policy and maintained relations with Dirksen, the German ambassador in Moscow. In March 1933 the German Foreign Office remained determined that the Racial Institute be sustained 'aus kulturpolitischen Gründen'. In April 1933 the Foreign Department of the Soviet Health Commissariat authorized further German–Soviet ventures, but *Sturmabteilung* storm troopers harassed Vogt in March and June, preventing his return to the Moscow brain research institute. Vogt vehemently denied that his contacts with the USSR meant that he had socialist sympathies.[128] The Russian-speaking bacteriologist Nauck returned from the Hamburg Institute of Tropical Medicine to Moscow in April 1933, and exhumed the scheme to transfer the Institute for Racial Pathology to Tiflis. A sign of deteriorating relations was that Soviet pathologists declined an invitation to meet German colleagues in Rostock in June 1933.[129] By July (when relations between the Reichswehr and the Red Army were disintegrating) Nauck recommended terminating the Institute.[130] Yet in October 1933 the German authorities still hoped to sustain ties with Georgia and the Transcaucasus.[131]

In December 1933 Stalin endorsed Litvinov's anti-German position, which had scientific repercussions in the building-up of relations of Soviet with American

---

[128] Archiv zur Geschichte der Max-Planck-Gesellschaft, Berlin 1 Abt. Rep 0001A Gesetz zur Wiederherstellung des Berufsbeamtentums—KWI Hirnforschung 1933–4, Vogt to KWG 21 Mar. 1933, Aktennotiz 22 Apr. 1933. Historisches Archiv Friedrich Krupp 4E 1155, O. Vogt note of 30 Aug. 1937 concerning criticisms by the SS and 'Was hatte Lenin eigentlich im Kopfe?', *Das Schwarze Korps* (19 Aug. 1937); J. Richter, 'Oskar Vogt und die Gründung des Berliner Kaiser-Wilhelm-Instituts für Hirnforschung unter den Bedingungen imperialistischer Wissenschaftspolitik', *Psychiatrie, Neurologie und medizinische Psychologie*, 28 (1976), 449–457.

[129] BAP 0902/421 Bl. 284, 287–8.

[130] BAK R 73/228 letters of Aschoff, 16 June 1933 and 18 July 1933; Groehler, *Reichswehr*, 67–72.

[131] BAK R 73/231 9 Oct. 1933, letter to Donnevert.

and French medical scientists. The move of Hermann Muller, the American pioneer of radiation genetics, from Vogt's Berlin Institute to the USSR in September 1933 meant that Soviet geneticists had less intellectual need to maintain contact with German researchers. The United States' diplomatic recognition of the Soviet Union in 1933 reinforced the momentum to replace German with US scientific contacts.[132] Further Soviet–German scientific co-operation did not materialize owing to the tense diplomatic situation, the internal hostility of the Communist Party to scientific élites, and pressures for autarchy in pharmaceutical products.

There were disagreements over repatriation to Germany of scientific equipment of the syphilis expedition; faced with the embarrassment that some of the German researchers were Jews, the NDW withdrew support in January 1934.[133] By May 1933 the lack of a firm German reply about the Racial Research Institute prompted the Soviet request that the Emergency Fund withdraw its equipment.[134] Although nominally director of the laboratory, Nauck left in May 1933 owing to restrictions on his freedom to travel. The laboratory then had a phantom existence as the sole German medical institution to survive in Moscow, although it was not staffed. Indeed, when the NDW decided in August 1933 that the laboratory should be closed, Dirksen argued that it should be sustained as the last surviving outpost of German science in Moscow.[135] In February 1934 Schmidt-Ott reaffirmed the interest of the Emergency Fund in the Racial Research Laboratory. In 1935 Lührs, who had worked in Vogt's brain research institute, was sent to Moscow, but to no avail.

It was only in October 1935 that the Deutsche Forschungsgemeinschaft (the successor organization to the Emergency Fund) abandoned efforts to continue the Racial Laboratory.[136] Residual funds of over 10,000 marks were deposited in an account with the Berlin bankers Mendelssohn, originally under the name of the Deutsch-russische Abteilung für Rassenforschung; from 1934 the account name *Rassenbiologische Forschungen* reflected the Nazi takeover.[137] On 18 February 1937 the Reich Minister of Education banned academic contacts with the USSR. One consequence was that Timoféeff-Ressovsky, the Russian geneticist in Berlin, refused a Soviet order to return. He gained a protected and ideologically ambivalent niche when the Germans declared radiation biology a war priority.[138]

The Nazi authorities tried to maintain the internationalism of German research

---

[132] E. A. Carlson, *Genes, Radiation and Society. The Life and Work of H. J. Muller* (Ithaca, NY, 1981), 184–203. Litvinov preferred to align with the British and the French; D. A. Alexandrov, 'The Closure of International Contacts of Soviet Scientists: A Shift from Germany to Nowhere', unpub. paper at 4th Berlin symposium on German-Soviet Medicine, July 1995.

[133] BAK R 73/232, 22 Jan. 1934 NDW memorandum; Solomon, 'Soviet-German Expedition'.

[134] BAK R 73/227, Saluschki to NDW 16 Apr. 1933; NDW 22 Aug. 1933.

[135] BAK R 73/227, German embassy 14 Aug. 1933; BAK R 73/228 Dirksen to Foreign Office 14 Aug. 1933; 73/227, German embassy to Foreign Office 3 Oct. 1933, 16 Jan. 1934; BAP 0902/405, Notiz 16 Nov. 1933; 0902/421 Bl. 192–5, memorandum by Dirksen 14 Aug. 1933; Bl. 201–3, Nauck to NDW 25 June 1933.

[136] BAK R 73/229, 24 Feb. 1934 Schmidt-Ott, 14 Oct. 1935 and 6 Dec. 1935 NDW memoranda; BAP 0902/421 Schmidt-Ott 22 Aug. 1933.

[137] Vogt papers, 'Rassenforschung file', the last bank statement was issued in 1934.

[138] D. B. Paul and C. B. Krimbas, 'Nikolai V. Timoféeff- Ressovsky', *Scientific American*, 266/2 (1992), 64–70.

to offset mounting outrage abroad over the dismissal of Jewish and dissident academics. German tropical medicine specialists used foreign visits and congresses as opportunities to drum up support for the new Germany. Nuttall was honoured by the Hamburg Institute of Tropical Medicine, and Zeiss reported in triumph that on a visit to London he found that British tropical specialists agreed that Germany might one day have its colonies restored. Congress delegates were ordered to appear as closed units, and to secure German representation.[139] German racial hygienists dominated the International Federation of Eugenics Organizations, using its meetings to endorse Nazi racial policies. In 1935 maximum propaganda value was extracted from the International Congress for Population Science held in Berlin.[140] While these eugenic gatherings were primarily to promote Nazi policies of sterilization and hereditary health, racial ideologues and researchers on infectious diseases drew attention to the issue of *Lebensraum* in the east. The eugenicist Hans Harmsen became obsessed with the health and fertility of ethnic Germans in the east.[141] The military adventurer von Niedermayer, who had managed the clandestine affairs of the Wehrmacht in the Soviet Union, was rewarded with an academic post in military geography at Berlin in 1933, and (despite criticism of his pro-Russian opinions in 1935) a full chair in 1936.

Zeiss maintained an eastern orientation at the Berlin Hygiene Institute. So as to sustain his bacteriological contacts, he sent reprints in 1935 to the Institute for Microbiology in Saratov, the Tarasevitch Institute in Moscow, the Bacteriological Institute Tashkent, and to the Tropical Medical Institutes in Baku and Moscow.[142] Behind Zeiss's amicable gestures smouldered eastern ambitions, and Reiter of the Reich Health Office in 1936 asked him to conceal these by toning down laudatory comments about Niedermayer.[143]

In 1936 the German Foreign Office unleashed a wave of propaganda directed against the forthcoming Seventh International Genetics Congress that was planned for Moscow in 1939 (but ultimately transferred to Edinburgh owing to Lysenkoist opposition).[144] Positive German–Soviet scientific relations continued in less controversial fields: the medical entomologist Escherich was permitted to publish a Russian scientific paper in 1936, and German pest control experts welcomed reports on Russian forestry.[145] The ban on academic relations with the Soviet Union

[139] AHUB Hygienisches Institut Nr 188 Zeiss to Mühlens 2 Dec. 1937. Nr 205 concerning Zeiss and Phillip Manson-Bahr. L. Alexander, 'Methods of Influencing International Scientific Meetings as Laid Down by German Scientific Organisations', CIOS Item No. 24 File No. XXVIII-8, 1945.
[140] S. Kühl, *The Nazi Connection. Eugenics, American Racism and German National Socialism* (Oxford, 1994), 27–36; Kühl, *Die internationale der Rassisten. Aufstieg und Niedergang der internationalen Bewegung für Eugenik und Rassenhygiene im 20. Jahrhundert* (Frankfurt/M., 1997), 126–43.
[141] H. Harmsen, *Bestandsfragen der deutschen Volksgruppen im Osteuropäischen Raum* (Berlin, 1935).
[142] AHUB Hygienisches Institut Nr 1, Zeiss on 17 Jan. 1937 about exchanges with Russia.
[143] AHUB Hygienisches Institut Nr 205 Reiter to Zeiss 21 Nov. 1936.
[144] Kühl, *Nazi Connection*, 138–9.
[145] Munich University Archives, Akten des Akademischen Senats der Universität München betr Karl Escherich, Personalakte E II N, 11 Aug. 1936 Escherich to Rektor, reply of Reich and Prussian Minister 7 Oct. 1936.

in February 1937 temporarily interrupted academic contacts, while Nazi propaganda fulminated against 'world Bolshevism'. At this point the ideological clash between Soviet communism and Nazism severed their residual academic and medical ties.

8

The Demise of Internationalism

i. Collecting Pathogens

Realizing the dangers of an international conflagration, medical scientists sought to offset this by cooperating internationally in identifying strains of bacteria and other microbial pathogens, and in developing vaccines. Yet sinister nationalist undercurrents persisted with military concerns about epidemic control, the targeting of racial groups as disease carriers, and germ warfare. While international organizations facilitated international scientific cooperation, they became arenas of national and medical conflict. Research on the cause and spread of infectious and chronic diseases was part of broader international programmes sponsored by the League of Nations Health Organization (LNHO) and the Rockefeller Foundation. The Zeiss laboratory in Moscow and racial research schemes were offshoots of broader European programmes of disease control and medical anthropology, involving identifying different strains of pathogens as well as anthropological and medical studies of ethnic groups. The stages by which such pathogen-plotting programmes arose between the 1920s and 30s reveal mounting international tensions, and ultimately the emergence of military power blocs, which anticipated a major flare-up of typhus as Europe stood poised on the brink of war.

At first medical cooperation continued between the successor states. In 1922 the Prague bacteriologist Edmund Weil conducted research in the laboratory of the zoologist and typhus expert Rudolf Weigl in Lwów—both shared origins from Bohemia—until Weil fatally contracted typhus as a result of a laboratory accident. Weigl had started research on typhus during the First World War when he served with an Austrian field laboratory in Cracow and a typhus laboratory in Przemyśl. Ludwik Fleck remarked on how at international conferences on sero-diagnosis, scientists derived different results from similar tests. Fleck had assisted Weigl at Przemyśl and then at Lwów between 1920 and 1923 with studies of sero-diagnosis of typhus. Fleck visited Vienna in 1927, where he imbibed a heady mixture of medical and philosophical culture contributing to his view of scientific workers as thought collectives.[1] Weigl established Lwów as an international centre for typhus research during an era when the Rockefeller Foundation and League of Nations internationalized bacteriological research. The British entomologist Bacot learned from him how to inject a louse with rickettsiae and feed the louse with blood from a

---

[1] O. Klein and P. Svobodny, 'Die Prager Hygiene-Schule: Edmund Weil und andere im Dienste der Wissenschaft Verstorbene', in N. Goldenbogen, et al., *Hygiene und Judentum* (Dresden, 1995), 23–6. For Flect see p. 236, below.

pipette inserted into its minute rectum.[2] Lwów was recognized as at the forefront of typhus research.

The lavish funds contributed by the Rockefeller Foundation for Eastern European hygiene institutes and public health provision contrasted to its refusal of appeals from individual Russian institutions like the Bacteriological Institute of the Moscow School of Medicine. As an organization fuelled by US capitalism, the Rockefeller Foundation's belligerence to Russia was understandable; but as an organization promoting modern public health systems, the Foundation officers were fascinated by plans of the Commissariat of Public Health to centralize health care.[3] The Foundation denied aid for typhus and famine relief during 1921, and, despite the enthusiasm of the American typhus expert Zinsser for a Russian programme, rejected requests for a Rockefeller 'Plenipotentiary' to develop Soviet social hygiene in 1923. However, the Rockefeller Foundation did not rule out sending medical literature and making small grants and travelling fellowships available to Soviet scientists. The Rockefeller Foundation also supported the League of Nations anti-malaria programme in Russia and south-east Europe.[4]

Zeiss used his position at the All-Russian Microbiological Collection in Moscow to build up his international credentials. After the 1922 Warsaw typhus conference Nocht was invited to join the Health Committee of the League of Nations.[5] Nocht loathed the League because it transferred German colonies as mandated territories to the victorious Allies; and on the commission for sleeping sickness in equatorial Africa, a German representative was conspicuously lacking, despite the new Bayer drug Germanin. Nocht counter-attacked by asserting German scientific expertise on the League of Nations malaria committee from 1923, and he ventured into the heart of French microbiology when the standards committee met at the Pasteur Institute in 1924.[6] By 1924 Nocht sat on five out of a total of ten commissions. The German Foreign Office tried to prove that German medicine was under-represented: it insisted on acting as a channel for communications of a non-scientific nature with the Health Organization, and demanded reports on all League of Nations meetings.[7] By backing Zeiss in Moscow, Nocht resisted the Anglo-French predominance in the LNHO, as well as endorsing Zeiss's plan that Russia was to be an *Ersatz*-territory for German tropical research.

[2] M. Greenwood, 'Bacot', *The Medical Dictator* (London, 1936), 210.

[3] N. B. Weissman, 'Origins of Soviet Health Administration. Narkomzdrav, 1918–1928', in S. G. Solomon and J. F. Hutchinson, *Health and Society in Revolutionary Russia* (Bloomington and Indianapolis, Ind., 1990), 97–120; S. G. Solomon, 'Social Hygiene in Soviet Medical Education, 1922–30', *Journal of the History of Medicine and Allied Sciences*, 45 (1990), 607–43; N. A. Semashko, *Health Protection in the USSR* (London, 1934).

[4] RAC Rockefeller Foundation 1.1/100/20/166 letter of Gunn to Russell 12 Oct. 1923 concerning the League of Nations and malaria.

[5] On Nocht's hatred of the Versailles treaty see Wulf, *Tropeninstitut*, 6–7.

[6] BAP 15.01/11233 Internationale Gesundheitsamt beim Völkerbund Bd 1 report by Foreign Office Berlin to Bumm, 2 Jan. 1923 concerning Nocht.

[7] BAP 15.01/11235 Nocht report, 17 Mar. 1924; AA R 65751 vol. 3, 8 May 1927; AA R 96835 Terdenge to Hamel, 28 June 1929; Hamel to Terdenge, 12 July 1929.

Nocht recommended Zeiss for employment by the LNHO Secretariat when he addressed the League of Nations malaria commission on its visit to the Soviet Union in August 1924. Zeiss favourably impressed the League of Nations epidemic commissioner Norman White, and Rajchman asked Zeiss in March 1925 whether he would be interested in working for the LNHO secretariat. Zeiss submitted a research programme based on his microbiological collections, and he provided information on epidemics and health conditions in Russia. He argued that such technical work was essential in Russia. To avoid suspicions that he was a spy, Zeiss hoped to be the LNHO's agent in Russia with a role equivalent to the LNHO's Singapore Epidemiological Office. He was invited to Geneva, and offered a job with the Secretariat. Zeiss was supported by his mentor Nocht and by Max Taute, an ultra-nationalist medical official at the Reich Ministry of the Interior. Zeiss was by now committed to building up the collection of Russian bacteria strains at the Moscow Pasteur Institute, not least because this allowed him to study the variation of disease pathogens: he undermined his position with the LNHO by stressing his reluctance to abandon laboratory work in Russia. Rajchman did not have laboratory facilities in Geneva to support the bacteriological collections of Zeiss. Moreover, Zeiss was unwilling to betray his sense of a Germanic mission by working under a director who was a Polish Jew, even though Rajchman was pursuing policies to internationalize medical standards and promote cooperation in ways markedly different from those of the British and French delegates, who remained anti-German.[8]

Rajchman then attempted to recruit the liberal-minded Martin Hahn, the professor of hygiene in Berlin, who had extensive experience in Russia. In the event, Otto Olsen the assistant of Hahn was appointed, causing consternation among conservative German bacteriologists. The choice of Olsen marked an apparent victory for the centre-left of the German public health community. Olsen was ultimately to join the Nazi Party while in Geneva, and he was to channel information to Nazi diplomats; but his appointment in 1925 was supported by the SPD. Grotjahn, the Berlin professor of social hygiene, had discussed the nomination of a German candidate to the LNHO with the SPD politician Rudolf Bretscheid.[9] Grotjahn hoped that Olsen would move the LNHO towards social hygiene, so thwarting the laboratory-based approach of Zeiss. Rajchman's preference for Grotjahn over Nocht as adviser marked a crucial turning-point for the LNHO: Rajchman wished to develop the scope of international health from merely advance warning of impending epidemics and the biological standardization of sera. He hoped that international social medicine would tackle the economic causes of sickness as

[8] LNA R 826 12B/43198X/15255 Rajchman to Zeiss, 22 Mar. 1925; Rajchman to Cazeneuve, 20 March 1925; 12B/37789/15255 Zeiss to Cazeneuve, 17 Apr. 1925 including memorandum for LNHO; 12B/43198/15266 Zeiss to Rajchman, 6 Aug. 1925; 12B/43198X/15255 Rajchman to Zeiss, 22 June 1925; Zeiss to Rajchman, 31 July 1925; Rajchman to Zeiss, 13 Aug. 1925, Rajchman to Nocht n.d. (June/July 1925); 12B/43198X/16255 Rajchman to Zeiss, 18 Sept. 1925; *Münchener Medizinische Wochenschrift*, 72 (1925), 41 (9 Oct. 1925); AHUB NL Grotjahn, Olsen to Grotjahn, 18 Mar. 1925; BNI Archivordner Tropeninstitut 1924–5, Zeiss to Nocht, 30 Apr. 1924, 22 Apr. 1925, 11 Aug. 1925.
[9] AHUB NL Grotjahn, Grotjahn to Bretscheid 23 Jan. 1925.

embedded in the social infrastructure.[10] There was friction between the environmentalist social medicine of Rajchman, the eugenically oriented hygiene of Grotjahn focused on fertility control, and the bacteriological approach of Frey and Zeiss. Their approaches influenced Semashko's ill-fated attempt to harness biology and statistics to develop a broad-ranging programmme of social hygiene and preventive medicine.

German academic input was welcomed by Semashko because of international constraints. Although the Rockefeller Foundation turned to support scientific solutions to the problems of poverty and disease, it remained antagonistic to Soviet requests for grants. The German–Soviet cooperation was intensified by a sense of exclusion from international health organizations and academic activities. The Allies aimed to supplant the German and Austrian belt of eastern hygiene institutes, which had once stretched from the Bukovina to the Baltic. The Rockefeller Foundation established a belt of central state hygiene institutes from the Baltic to the Black Sea: it funded central state hygiene institutes in Prague, Warsaw, and then in Budapest between 1923 and 1925, a plethora of hygiene institutes and health centres were planted in Serbia and Croatia, and the Rockefeller Foundation embarked on highly contentious medical ventures in Bulgaria and Romania. The tasks of these institutes included monitoring the spread of infectious diseases, and research and production of new vaccines and sera. Intervention in the successor states was motivated by Rockefeller Foundation officers' vision of 'a middle Europe based upon a recognition of even justice with international team play substituted for German domination.'[11] They were to be conspicuously unsuccessful.

ii. The Vaccine Network

Genes, vitamins, and viruses set the tone of advanced medical cooperation between the wars, as science was a manifestly international and humane medical endeavour. Although the intensity of the bilateral German–Soviet medical relations arose from the two nations being outcasts from international society, there were during the 1920s attempts to integrate them into a collective international endeavour in the field of vaccines and epidemic control. But the rise of typhus vaccine research shows how this collapsed during the 1930s.

Zeiss built up an extensive network among Soviet researchers to compare different strains of plague cultures; among those with whom he collaborated were Tarasevich in Moscow and Nikanorov in Saratov. Undaunted by his failure to gain the backing of the LNHO, in 1926 Zeiss tried to obtain tularemia cultures from the US Public Health Department. The Director, G. W. McCoy, declined to send the speci-

---

[10] A. Grotjahn, *Erlebtes und Erstrebtes. Erinnerungen eines sozialistischen Arztes* (Berlin 1932), 259–61; AHUB NL Grotjahn, Olsen to Grotjahn, 3 May 1926, 7 July 1926; Rajchman to Grotjahn, 7 July 1926; Grotjahn to Olsen 2 Sept. 1927.

[11] RAC Rockefeller Foundation 1.1/712/3/16 Rose and Gunn report 'Public Health Situation in Czechoslovakia' (c. 1919).

mens partly on the grounds of safety, and partly for political reasons. However, in October 1926 an acquaintance of Aschoff in New York arranged to transfer the tularemia specimens to Nocht in Hamburg, who then forwarded them to Zeiss in Moscow, and in 1927 McCoy sent specimens to the veterinary scientist Noller in Berlin at the request of Zeiss.[12] In 1928 Zeiss mounted a more ambitious scheme to obtain 37 specimens from the American Type Culture Collection of the American Society of Bacteriologists so that these could be compared to Russian strains. For his part Zeiss sent batches of paratyphoid A and B, cholera—all mainly isolated in 1921 in Moscow, Leningrad, and Saratov, and a disease called Melitense isolated in Baku in 1925.[13] Zeiss became an international broker exchanging historically significant microbiological cultures between the United States and the Soviet Union.

Yet as typhus crept back onto the international medical agenda, German researchers were frozen out of international research networks. A rift grew between Zeiss as a campaigner for German medicine in the east, and the Nobel-prizewinning researcher Nicolle and his friend Zinsser who masterminded a grand medical strategy to defend Western civilization. At the Tunis Pasteur Institute, Nicolle characterized typhus as a viral disease (having pioneered work on the viral causes of influenza and pneumonia) and enthused Zinsser at Harvard to resume work on typhus from 1928. In 1930 Nicolle wrote a historical account of the birth, life, and death of infectious diseases, predicting the end of typhus through natural attenuation and new vaccines.[14] His strategy was to produce a vaccine whose virulence would be attenuated by passages through animal organisms but whose powers of generating immunity would be considerable. Such a vaccine would draw on the symbiotic and cooperative potential of man, animal, and micro-organism. Zinsser was convinced that he stood on the brink of the final chapter of the history of the impact of typhus on human civilization and economic life.[15]

Typhus studies in the United States and Mexico undermined the *idée fixe* of 'no lice, no typhus': observations of mild forms of typhus led to notions that it was transmitted by mice or rats harbouring fleas, lice, or ticks.[16] Zinsser was advised by Henry Sigerist, the radical medical historian newly arrived at Johns Hopkins University from Leipzig, and advocate of the international programme for the history and geography of diseases.[17] Zinsser presented a vivid overview of the new 'multiple persona' of the disease in his eloquent 'biography' of the disease, *Rats, Lice and History* of 1935. Dedicated to Nicolle, not only discoverer of the role of lice as

[12] AHUB NL Zeiss box 17 fo. 16 Zeiss to Nocht, 15 Oct. 1926, fo. 13 Nocht to Zeiss, 24 Jan. 1927, fo. 25 McCoy to Rhodenburg, 17 Oct. 1925, fo. 7 McCoy to Noller, 15 Mar. 1927.

[13] AHUB NL Zeiss box 17 fos. 31–7 Zeiss to American Type Culture Collection, 8 Mar. 1929.

[14] K. A. Pelis, 'Pasteur's Imperial Missionary: Charles Nicolle (1866–1936) and the Pasteur Institute of Tunis', PhD thesis, Johns Hopkins, 1995.

[15] CLB Zinsser papers, Zinsser to Edsall, 26 Oct. 1932. The Commonwealth Fund awarded $2,500 for typhus serum production, 18 June 1937; RAC Rockefeller Foundation 1/100/32/259 Typhus fever 1938–40 on Snyder as IHB fellow with Zinsser.

[16] Williams, *Public Health Service*, 206–9.

[17] CLB Zinsser papers, Sigerist to Zinsser, 21 Sept. 1932; Zinsser to Sigerist 8 Aug. 1932, 23 May 1933.

the vector of typhus but also a celebrated author, the book was a manifesto for international collaboration opposing the dictatorship of a single central institution, and—at a scientific level—the reduction of all the diverse manifestations of a disease to the effects of a single species of microbial pathogen. As the international situation meant that German and Soviet researchers were excluded from the collaborative networks, scientific studies of variability went with defence of liberal values.

Zinsser exploited research opportunities in New York, testing blood specimens from immigrant Russian Jews for a Weil-Felix reaction to see if the disease was still latent. He concluded: 'I do not believe that there is a racial difference, either in resistance or in susceptibility in the Jews, but I think that it is not at all impossible that all of us who have had typhus retain the virus for many years . . .' His reasoning that the mild form of typhus identified in New York by Nathan Brill in 1910 was a recrudesence of typhus among 'Russian Jews' underlined his interest in different forms of the disease and in producing immunity from mild forms of typhus.[18]

Zinsser and Nicolle built up a Polish–French–US axis for international collaboration in typhus research, with offshoots in Chile, Bolivia, Mexico, and China. Germans were pointedly absent from this network. Zinsser mobilized support from the Commonwealth and Rockefeller Foundations to finance the international vaccine strategy. Both researchers were fascinated by Mooser's discovery of a new form of typhus in Mexico with rat fleas as vectors. At Lwów Weigl infected rats with European typhus rickettsiae and lice with the Mexican strains.[19] After meeting in Mexico during 1931, Nicolle and Zinsser fervently believed that typhus studies required radical revision, and that comparative and collaborative research marked the way forward.

Zinsser hoped to defeat 'the European disease' with a serum produced from the Mexican strain of typhus. The team of Nicolle and Zinsser persuaded the Mexican government to take on production of their murine (i.e. rat-blood based) serum. In November 1931 Nicolle envisaged a mobile League of Nations laboratory for typhus studies, and Zinsser mobilized the Rockefeller Foundation to support this enterprise. In 1932 he hoped to test a new serum-based vaccine in cooperation with the State Institute of Hygiene, Warsaw, and with the Pasteur Institute in Paris. Both Nicolle and Zinsser despaired of the political and institutional decay that they encountered—Nicolle's obsession was the ailing Pasteur Institute in Paris, which he feared was seeking to exert central control of the network of Pasteur Institutes. Nicolle and Zinsser believed that in science as in politics leadership from dynamic and humane intellectual leaders was required.[20] They shared a sense of foreboding that the world order was disintegrating, and they agreed on the urgency of produc-

---

[18] CLB Zinsser papers, Zinsser to Edsall, 19 Dec. 1933.

[19] Ibid., Weigl to Mooser, 18 Nov. 1932, 30 Jan. 1933. The presence of the papers in the Zinsser collection indicates Zinsser's interest in these findings.

[20] Ibid., Zinsser to Giroud, 20 Feb. 1939; Nicolle to Zinsser, 4 Mar. 1931, 10 Nov. 1931, 18 Jan. 1934, 2 Apr. 1934.

ing an antidote to what looked like terminal social ills: an idealistic energy infused their research, which was tempered by personal struggle with their own severe and ultimately fatal illnesses—Nicolle died in 1936 after completing a visionary book on the future of mankind, and Zinsser struggled on despite cancer.[21] Their vision of a multi-centered research network found a counterpart in their political views that world civilization rested on cooperation and coexistence between states, and the cultivation of humane values, rather than the dominance of a great imperial—or fascist—power.

During 1937 Zinsser produced a vaccine for field trials; he interested researchers in China, and this aroused the enthusiasm of Rajchman, who convened a major conference on typhus vaccines. Zinsser was anxious to test his vaccine in Spain during 1937 with LNHO backing, having gained support from the Minister of Health of the Spanish Republic. Other locations for trials were Algeria and Morocco, Romania, Turkey, and China. While Zinsser retreated from the Spanish project, he fought to establish a European field laboratory to test his new vaccine and to train young researchers from Romania, France, and Poland under League of Nations auspices: 'I am entirely willing to put everything that we have and are doing at the disposal of European laboratories and governments for thorough trial . . . This typhus business has become a sort of obsession with me and I would like to help bring it to a successful conclusion in Europe, where the problem is much more important than here.'[22] Once this possibility evaporated, not least because of Franco's victory, Zinsser hoped that the Pasteur Institute in Paris would become the centre for vaccine production for the Near East and Eastern Europe.[23]

Zinsser drew on field-work in Mexico on rat-borne typhus. He sent consignments of sera for testing to the Romanian Ciuca (who had close contacts with the LNHO secretariat) and to Édmond Sergent at the Pasteur Institute Algiers. In 1937 Sergent agreed with the LNHO that he would compare Zinsser's murine serum to the more dangerous type of live vaccine, pioneered in Morocco by Georges Blanc, and to Weigl's louse gut vaccine, sent by the Polish government. Helena Sparrow, a Pole who had worked both in Mexico and the US, acted as intermediary between Nicolle and Weigl.[24] Sparrow had left the Warsaw Institute of Hygiene in 1931 to work under Nicolle: they set off for Mexico where they discovered with Mooser a rat-based form of typhus, and established that this was widespread in the Mediterranean area. The rat cultures provided a form of typhus which was low in virulence, and in 1937 25,000 persons were vaccinated in a single day. Sergent spent two

---

[21] C. Nicolle, *La Destinée humaine* (Paris, 1936).

[22] CLB Zinsser papers, letter of Zinsser to Rajchman, 25 Jan. 1937, 20 Oct. 1937, 13 Apr. 1937, 22 Jan. 1938; Zinsser to Plotz, 22 Sept. 1937, 22 Dec. 1937; Zinsser, *As I Remember Him*, 368–9; Zinsser to Giroud 21 Sept. 1937 for vaccine batches for Sergent in Algiers.

[23] CLB Zinsser papers, Zinsser to Plotz, 21 Nov. 1938.

[24] Ibid., Sergent to Zinsser 25 Mar. 1937, 9 Oct. 1937, 25 Feb. 1938; Zinsser to Sergent 3 Mar. 1937, 17 Mar. 1937, 8 Apr. 1937, 21 Sept. 1937, 4 Feb. 1938, 27 June 1938, 27 July 1938; Zinsser to Sparrow, 9 Jan. 1937; G. Blanc, 'La Vaccination contre le typhus', *Archives de l'Institut Pasteur du Maroc*, 1/4 (1937), 869–918.

years comparing the Weigl and Blanc vaccines to a non-vaccinated control group in areas of Algeria where typhus was endemic.[25]

By 1937 the Rockefeller Foundation recognized typhus as 'the greatest lurking danger' in endemic foci in parts of Poland, Czechoslovakia, Romania, Yugoslavia, and Bulgaria, particularly among such migrants as gypsies, and that its epidemic potential could cause a chaotic shift of populations. Delousing was pronounced a failure, and vaccination offered the best means of control. The Rockefeller fellow, Snyder, eventually developed Zinsser's Spanish scheme into a comprehensive plan for control and investigation of typhus. In 1936 Ludwik Anigstein, a typhus expert from the Warsaw Hygiene Institute, wished to conduct a trial of Zinsser's vaccine in Poland. However, Weigl objected to Zinsser's tissue culture method as reducing virulence of *Rickettsiae*, and Anigstein attempted to culture rickettsiae without tissue. In June 1939 the Rockefeller Foundation was concerned that the Warsaw Hygiene Institute dismissed Anigstein as Jewish. The hygiene institutes, founded as part of the Rockefeller Foundation's scheme for stabilizing Europe, were falling prey to militarism and nationalist xenophobia.[26]

Zinsser was concerned that nationalist impulses to support vaccines jeopardized his internationalist strategy. He objected when Nicolle advocated research with live 'viruses', as the French military medical authorities backed a potentially dangerous live vaccine of Blanc. Zinsser also clashed with the Poles over the merits of Weigl's louse gut vaccine. Weigl had expressed scepticism that louse-borne *Rickettsiae prowazeki* was the sole cause of typhus at a speech at the newly opened Warsaw Hygiene Institute in 1926. From 1930 Weigl intensified work on the vaccine from louse intestines. The vaccine was successfully used in areas of Poland with endemic typhus, in Egypt in 1933, in Manchuria by Belgian medical missionaries, and during 1939 in Ethiopia where the Duke of Aosta established an institute for the study of rickettsiae. Weigl had set up louse farms in Poland staffed by immune volunteers who had recovered from typhus. The Polish government supported production of Weigl's vaccine from 1936, and Anigstein attempted to gain Rockefeller Foundation finance. 67,893 Poles were inoculated with the Weigl vaccine by 1938. In November 1939 Sergent requested that the League of Nations secure the release of Weigl from Poland for research in Algiers on his typhus vaccine.[27]

[25] C. Nicolle and H. Sparrow, 'Application au cobaye et à l'homme de la méthode de vaccination contre le typhus exanthématique par l'emploi d'intestins phénique de poux (méthode de Weigl)', *Archives de l'Institut Pasteur de Tunis*, 21 (1932), 25–31; OIHP, *Procès-Verbaux* (1936), 101, 129; (1937) 67–8; *Notice sur l'Institut Pasteur d'Algérie* (Algiers, 1949), ii. 240–2.

[26] Zinsser papers, Zinsser to Rajchman, 25 Jan. 1937, 13 Apr. 1937, 25 May 1937, 26 May 1937, 20 Oct. 1937, 22 Jan. 1938; Zinsser to Anigstein, 5 Jan. 1932, 16 Sept. 1936, 6 Oct. 1936; Anigstein to Zinsser 3 Sept. 1936, Oct. 1936, 18 Dec. 1936. For Zinsser's disapproval of Anigstein see Zinsser to R. M. Taylor, 13 Sept. 1939; Szulc to Zinsser 5 Jan. 1937, 27 Jan. 1937; RAC Rockefeller Foundation 1/100/32/261 JHJ to WAS on typhus 19 Dec. 1941; Rockefeller Foundation 6.1/1.1/31/379 Taylor to Strode, 7 Sept. 1937; Gunn to Grant, 29 June 1939; R. M. Taylor to G. K. Strode 1 Oct. 1936.

[27] On Weigl see Eyer, *Zentralblatt für Bakteriologie*, 1 Abt., vol. 171 (1958), 377–9, 'Weigl', *Słownik biologów polskich* (Warsaw, 1987), 567–8; Chodzko, in *Procès verbaux* (May 1933), 142–4; (Oct. 1934), 129; Reis, 79; RAC Rockefeller Foundation 6.1/1.1/31/379, R. M. Taylor to G. K. Strode, 1 Oct. 1936; R. Weigl, 'Über das Wesen und Form des Fleckfiebererregers', *Bull. Acad. Pol. des Sciences* (1930), 1–27; Weigl, 'Die

The legacy of the Nicolle–Zinsser international strategy continued to shape developments during the Second World War. Zinsser's historical popularization, *Rats, Lice and History*, predicted that while a massive epidemic of typhus would erupt during the war, vaccines could be deployed. Since the early 1930s US researchers pioneered the use of embryonated eggs as a culture medium for viruses: Zinsser encouraged Herald Cox in 1936 to plunge into typhus vaccine work, resulting in a breakthrough when in December 1938 Cox tested his egg yolk culture technique on various strains of typhus rickettsiae.[28]

In September 1939 Wilbur Sawyer of the Rockefeller Foundation's International Health Division abandoned hostility to typhus research, convinced that typhus was to be a major wartime hazard. The Rockefeller Foundation's International Health Board favoured laboratory-based strategies. As the United States war-machine boosted vaccine research, it integrated advanced research in virology with new approaches to immunology and biochemistry; Erwin Chargaff (formerly of the Berlin Institute of Hygiene and the Pasteur Institute) researched into the purification of typhus vaccine as a step towards molecular biology.[29] Research was to have priority over relief.[30]

Zinsser kept in close touch with the beleagured Pastorians like Paul Giroud ('mon cher copain') once the war erupted. Having tested Zinsser's serum at the Pasteur Institute, Paris, Giroud set about developing the Tunis serum as a strategic priority.[31] Zinsser's enthusiasm for the Pasteur Institutes as the international focus of typhus vaccine research stood in marked contrast to his alienation from Germany. He courteously responded to questions of the German bacteriologist Otto, and offered hospitality in his laboratory to a young German researcher.[32] But he reflected on 'a pitiful sight' of this Nazi specimen in his Harvard laboratory, and the Germans did not figure in his international programme.[33] The Rockefeller Foundation supported a select number of German refugee scientists like Max Delbrück who appeared able to contribute to the new molecular biology. The Rockefeller laboratories hosted visits by researchers from the Robert Koch Institute,

Methode der aktiven Fleckfieber-Immunisierung', *Bull. Acad. Pol. des Sciences* (1930); J. Rutten, 'La Mortalité des missionaires avant et après l'emploi du vaccin de Weigl', *Dossiers de la commission synodale (Peking)* (Feb. 1936), 183–91; H. Eyer, 'Das Problem der Fleckfieberschutzimpfung und ihre Bedeutung für die Praxis', *Der Öffentliche Gesundheitsdienst*, 7 (1941), 97–106. RAC Rockefeller Foundation 1.1/100/22/181 Gautier to Gunn 15 Nov. 1939. For further references see Ch. 12 n. 53.

[28] CLB Zinsser papers, Zinsser to Herald Cox, 23 Apr. 1936, 20 Aug. 1937, 7 and 12 Dec. 1938, 12 Apr. 1940, 15 Apr. 1940; S. S. Hughes, *The Virus: A History of the Concept* (New York and London, 1977).

[29] NAW RG 227/27/Box 83 Records of the OSRCD, Contractors Reports No. 228 Chargaff, Studies on the Chemical and Immunological Properties of Fractions from Rickettsia Prowazecki. RG 227/163 Box 9 for resulting papers. On Chargaff see P. Abir-Am, 'From Biochemistry to Molecular Biology: DNA and the Acculturated Journey of the Critic of Science Erwin Chargaff', *History and Philosophy of Life Sciences*, 2 (1980), 3–60.

[30] RAC Rockefeller Foundation 1.1/700/14/104, memo by Fosdick, 7 Sept. 1939.

[31] CLB Zinsser papers, Zinsser to Plotz, 28 May 1938 on Giroud's potential; Zinsser to Giroud, 20 Feb. 1939; Giroud to Zinsser, 3 Sept. 1940.

[32] Ibid., Otto to Zinsser, 13 Mar. 1934, 14 Feb. 1934, 17 June 1939; Zinsser to Otto 28 June 1939.

[33] Ibid., Zinsser to Mooser, 4 Sept. 1934.

notably Gildemeister for research on viral infections and Eugen Haagen from 1930 to 1933 for work on a yellow fever vaccine. Haagen returned to Germany to work on virological problems of myxomatosis in rabbits and isolated the first influenza strain in Germany. In 1935 the Foundation opposed futher injections of funds for Gildemeister and Haagen. An outburst of colonialist pan-Germanic rhetoric by Claus Schilling (a former associate of Koch and member of the League of Nations malaria commission, and subsequently executed for human experiments on chemotherapy for malaria in Dachau) disqualified him from Rockefeller Foundation funding.[34] Werner Fischer, who was from 1932 to 1933 a fellow at the National Institute for Medical Research in London, rose from 1938 to be departmental head of serology at the RKI and as an SS officer undertook experiments in the concentration camp of Sachsenhausen in 1942. Fischer collaborated with the Hygiene Institute of the Waffen-SS on serological research on human races, particularly gypsies.[35]

Zinsser regretted how nationalism drove the Poles to support the costly Weigl vaccine and the French a potentially more hazardous live vaccine. Zinsser's schemes were linked to new understanding of virology—boosted by the conviction that vaccines would be effective against viral diseases. He was well aware that typhus was of primary relevance to the French army, and he hoped that he could train French army physicians at Harvard.[36] On the dark side the Rockefeller Foundation diagnosed that interest in typhus was symptomatic of a militarist malaise, as Europe plunged into the abyss of world war. By September 1939 Zinsser redoubled his efforts to place vaccine production on a cooperative large-scale basis, as the impending war meant that a typhus vaccine was a strategic priority in the fight for human liberty.[37]

iii. Nazifying International Health

The Germans and the Soviets initially shared the distinction of being excluded from the League of Nations, and despite Rajchman's efforts to integrate formally the Germans and informally the Soviets the situation remained strained. In 1927 Zeiss drew the attention of the Soviet authorities to German medical attacks on the LNHO.[38] Rimpau, a Munich bacteriologist, denounced the LNHO as a pernicious

---

[34] RAC Rockefeller Foundation 1.1/717/11/68 and 69, Robert Koch Institute Berlin, 1.1/717/350/2369. Cf Weindling, 'The Rockefeller Foundation, 136; Fischer and Haagen were not formally Rockefeller Foundation fellows although their visits derived from funds granted by the Rockefeller Foundation to the host institutions. For this distinction see Rockefeller Foundation, *Directory of Fellowship Awards for the Years 1917–1950* (New York, n.d.), p. xiii.

[35] BDC SS-HO 651–743 Grawitz to Himmler, 20 July 1943, 2786–977 concerning W. Fischer and Mrugowsky; Hubenstorf, 'Aber es kommt', 411.

[36] CLB Zinsser papers, Zinsser to Plotz, 3 Dec. 1938.

[37] Ibid., box 2, Zinsser to P. Lépine, 14 Sept. 1939; Lépine to Zinsser, 12 Oct. 1939.

[38] GARF 5446/37/40/169–70 Zeiss to Gorbunov, n.d., and 156 Zeiss to Gorbunov 15 July 1927; Zeiss submitted his publication in the *Süddeutsche Monatshefte* 'as a warning for German doctors' requesting Gorbunov's opinion.

organization of Francophile cultural imperialism.[39] LNHO personnel and policies were criticized for being in the pockets of the British and French. An example was the development of a quarantine station at the Latvian port of Libau/Liepāja, which the British subsidized. The appointment of Olsen was derided by nationalist critics of social hygiene. Mussolini was criticized for having snubbed German delegates at an LNHO malaria congress in Rome. The LNHO pavilion at the massive GESOLEI hygiene exhibition in Düsseldorf in 1926 aroused resentment because of its positive presentation of Polish public health. 'A German doctor' argued that relations should be cool with Geneva, 'for instead there is another flame which will illuminate the East'.[40] This oblique reference to the rising tide of medical cooperation between Weimar Germany and the Soviet Union in the later 1920s hinted that the eastern axis would provide the antidote to the affliction of the post-Versailles medical system.

Although Nazi Germany set great store on continuing to take a prominent role in international health, hostility to the League of Nations meant that relations with the LNHO were abruptly severed. When Germany joined the League of Nations, Carl Hamel, president of the Reich Health Office, was elected as second member of the health council in 1927. He overcame long-standing German hostility to membership of the International Office of Public Health in Paris from 1926. Hamel was politically moderate, and cautious over eugenics.[41] When the imperialist Nocht was replaced by the venereologist Josef Jadassohn in 1930, the liberal internationalists were in the ascendant.

Visits by LNHO committees confirmed German integration into the post-Versailles political order, while opening the LNHO to accusations of sponsoring frenetic academic tourism and bureaucratic pomposity. By the later 1920s Germany was invaded by a sequence of LNHO commissions: the commission on smallpox met in January 1927 at the Robert Koch Institute in Berlin, and during May the League of Nations convened a course on tropical medicine at Nocht's Hamburg Institute.[42] The commission for biological standards met in Frankfurt in 1928, and the commission on rural hygiene inspected German rural health schemes; the commission on social medicine toured Germany in 1929; the commission on health education visited the Dresden Hygiene Museum in 1930. The commission on nutrition met in Berlin in December 1932, but the visit of the commission to study the psychological effects of unemployment was postponed in February 1933.[43] Whether such élite commissions could really safeguard European

---

[39] W. Rimpau, 'Der geistige Krieg gegen Deutschland und wir', *MMW* 72 (1925), 1889–90; Rimpau, 'Aerzte als internationale Politiker', ibid., 1524–6.

[40] 'Die Hygienesektion des Völkerbundes', in BAP 15.01/ 11241.

[41] BAK R 86/929 Hygiene-Kommission des Völkerbundes. BAP 15.01 Nr 11228 die Errichtung eines internationalen Gesundheitsamt in Paris 1907–13; GSTA Dahlem Rep 76 VIII B Nr 3460 die allgemeine Vorschriften über die gesundheitliche Behandlung der Seeschiffe in den deutschen Häfen, 1906–30, RMdI to Pr. Landesregierungen concerning the OIHP, 16 Apr. 1927.

[42] LNA R 65750. The visit took place on 13–14 Jan. 1927 and involved Gildemeister, Gins, Groth, and Paschen.

[43] BAP 15.01/ 26348 Bl. 320 Hamel to Olsen 1 Feb. 1933.

health and social stability was a somewhat vain hope. Internationalists supportive of League work (notably Carl Prausnitz, the professor of hygiene in Breslau) clashed with nationalists like Taute who sat on the LNHO trypanosome committee.[44] Nationalist critics accused the LNHO of working solely for Britain and France. Moreover, there were fundamental contrasts in the overall aims of German and LNHO public health strategies. The LNHO made a heroic effort to investigate the socio-economic bases of disease—in terms of employment, diet, and housing. Its prescriptions for dietary supplements and social medicine were in stark contrast to the German public health establishment which was obsessed with eugenic controls, infectious diseases, disinfection, and the burdens of hereditary defects.

Hitler's marching orders to withdraw from the League of Nations meant that German medical representatives rapidly disengaged from the League's international health system. The Germans left in October 1933, and formal resignation followed in 1935. The medical delegates to LNHO committees were commanded to resign, and the liberal internationalist camp of public health experts were purged from office in Germany. Hamel resigned from the presidency of the Reich Health Office in June 1933. He was replaced by the Nazi professor of hygiene, Hans Reiter, who was a vociferous advocate of compulsory sterilization as well as a highly competent bacteriologist.

The LNHO responded to the Nazi onslaught by considering a scheme to appoint a dismissed German professor, Carl Prausnitz, as director of a new international standards laboratory in London. Rajchman commissioned Stampar, an exiled Croatian health reformer, to study the medical profession in Nazi Germany with the idea that the League of Nations might assist with the ousted doctors. Other medical refugees who found a haven with Rajchman included the Spanish Republicans Gustavo Pittaluga and Marcellino Pascual. The LNHO's initiatives in physical culture, the redistribution of the population to the countryside, and nutritional standards were developed from social rather than racial perspectives. The LNHO work on vitamin standardization was extended in 1934 to Czechoslovakia, Poland, Hungary, and Yugoslavia—and was symptomatic of the League's wish to retain its influence in central Europe.[45] Despite Russian membership of the LNHO from 1934, the Soviet medical delegates kept a low profile until their expulsion in 1939 for the Soviet attack on Finland.

German cooperation with other international health agencies and institutions continued as public health officials did not wish Germany to be isolated internationally. Reiter keenly took a prominent role in international health, and in October 1933 became the German representative to the Office international

---

[44] Other public health experts involved in LNHO work included the professor of hygiene, Carl Prausnitz, Paul Wolff on the Opium Commission, Martin Hahn on the syphilis committee; AHUB Hygienisches Institut 165 for details of the syphilis committee.

[45] RAC Rockefeller Foundation 6.1/1.1/38/468 H. H. Dale memo on standards; note of 12 May 1934 on standards, Rockefeller Foundation 6.1/1.1/38/464 Crowell diary extract on Stampar, 8 Aug. 1933.

d'hygiène publique in Paris.[46] Former German delegates to the LNHO were encouraged to take a lead in medical associations in Central Europe, and the bacteriologists courted medical contacts in Bulgaria. Public health experts like the paediatrician Fritz Rott represented Nazified organizations in child health conferences—tackling the high infant mortality in the Balkans.[47] The Nazi assertion of medical leadership in eastern and southern Europe rivalled the Nicolle–Zinsser attempt to build an international network of liberal-minded scientists during the 1930s. As the French and US gained increasing scientific influence in the Soviet Union, the Germans sought to regain medical influence in increasingly authoritarian Central European states, notably Hungary and Bulgaria.

German contacts with the LNHO did not altogether cease. Olsen, a German national who remained on the Health Organization's staff, leaked information to the German consul in Geneva.[48] When Olsen attempted to rehabilitate himself in Berlin from 1939, Zeiss settled an old score against the rival who had been appointed in his stead in 1925. Zeiss accused Olsen of being an unpatriotic internationalist, and had him struck off the university lecture list. Yet while Olsen remained in Geneva as a staff member of the LRCS, he found support from the Overseas Organization of the NSDAP and from Reiter of the Reich Health Office who opened a department for international health.[49]

International concern for the welfare of civilians diminished. In 1934 a draft convention on the responsibility of the International Committee of the Red Cross (ICRC) for civilians interned by occupying forces was not ratified—a momentous lapse. The ICRC restricted its efforts to protect the health and well-being of prisoners of war of states which had (unlike the Soviet Union) signed the Geneva Convention. At a national level the German Red Cross (DRK) was Nazified and militarized, while maintaining links to the ICRC to which it had affiliated in 1927–8. The militarism was underlined by the Nazi medical activist Kurt Blome becoming president of the DRK, succeeded in 1938 by the Reichsarzt-SS Ernst Grawitz. Grawitz visited Geneva in 1939, and DRK officials maintained contacts with the ICRC. In July 1940 Hitler affirmed the international character of the DRK as a non-Party and non-military organization.[50] The DRK—once the channel for German medical assistance to Russia—became a front for Nazi militarism and genocide, as the German propaganda machinery depicted Red Cross nurses as caring for, washing, and disinfecting war victims and Jews.[51] At a more mundane

[46] BAP 15.01/26349 President of RGA (draft by Breger) to RMdI, 9 Oct. 1933; RMdI memo (draft by Taute) 25 Oct. 1933.

[47] Schabel, *Soziale Hygiene*, 136–9.

[48] BAP 15.01/26349 letter from German consul Geneva, 21 June 1934.

[49] AHUB Personalakten Nr 30 Otto Olsen.

[50] J.-C. Favez with G. Billeter, *Das Internationale Rote Kreuz und das Dritte Reich. War der Holocaust aufzuhalten?* (Zurich, 1989), 56–60; H. Seithe and F. Hagemann, *Das Deutsche Rote Kreuz im Dritten Reich (1933–1939)* (Frankfurt/M., 1993).

[51] R. L. Braham, *The Politics of Genocide. The Holocaust in Hungary* (New York, 1994), 679–80, for the example of a German propaganda film.

level the DRK opened a gas protection and explosives training school in Oranienburg.[52] This was where the SS would establish a training school for disinfectors, central offices, as well as the concentration camp of Sachsenhausen. The German onslaught on international health ended in a vast scheme of racial engineering and population resettlement in the east, requiring genocidal disease eradication measures.[53]

[52] F. Grüneisen, *Das Deutsche Rote Kreuz in Vergangenheit und Gegenwart* (Berlin, 1939), 170–1.

[53] M. Dworzecki, 'The International Red Cross and Its Policy vis-à-vis the Jews in Ghettos and Concentration Camps in Nazi-Occipied Europe', *Rescue Attempts During the Holocaust* (Jerusalem, 1977).

III
ERADICATION

9

From Geo-medicine to Genocide

i. Nazifying Geo-medicine

Nazi medical propaganda characterized the enemy in the east as 'fundamentally Asiatic', and typhus as historically a Central Asian disease spread by nomadic types like Jews and gypsies.[1] Typhus prevention was a key component of the Nazi geo-medical masterplan, as control of insect parasites and disease vectors became intertwined with military operations and genocide. A 'New German Art of Healing' provided a spiritual antidote to the mechanistic materialism which debased medicine in the communist east and capitalist west. This found its counterpart in geo-medicine with ideas of environmental, psychological, and racial factors in infection. Geo-medical enthusiasts supported military conquest and racial resettlement: Poland was to disappear, Russia was to be relegated to its Asiatic heartland, and eastern peoples were to be brutally subjugated and exterminated as 'parasites'.[2] An enlarged Germany was to dominate Europe while directing dependent vassal states. Preventing epidemics from the east came to involve genocide.

Zeiss and a new breed of geomedical experts in the SS personify the Nazification of epidemiology. The German-Soviet programme of medical cooperation was under severe strain due to the polarities of Nazism and the Stalinist demands that the Soviet Union be 'decontaminated' and 'sterilized' of foreigners.[3] Cooperation gave way to an anti-Bolshevik crusade, as the public health and hygiene experts with prior experience of the east joined the ranks of Baltic Germans, émigrés, and nationalists in planning the seizure of *Lebensraum*.[4]

Zeiss's expulsion from Moscow on 23 February 1932 was to his advantage: by November 1933 he took charge of the Institute of Hygiene in Berlin. His responsibilities encompassed epidemic prevention, and gas fumigation and cremation as disinfection technologies. Zeiss as a geo-medical agent underwent a remarkable political metamorphosis, in passing from service under the Soviets to becoming the watchdog (*Vertrauensmann*) of the NSDAP in the Berlin medical faculty, and Personalreferent in the Kultusministerium, allowing him influence over medical appointments. In December 1931 Zeiss abandoned the ultra-conservative

---

[1] H. Unger, *Helfer und Soldaten. Ein Buch vom Kriege* (Berlin and Vienna, 1943), 61, quoted by Thom, 'Wandlungen', 453; H. Eyer, 'Fleckfieber', in S. Handloser and W. Hoffmann (eds.), *Wehrhygiene* (Berlin, 1944), 49–57.

[2] H. Zeiss, 'Geomedizin und Seuchenbekämpfung', Handloser and Hoffmann, *Wehrhygiene*, 9–11.

[3] For these expressions see U. Pope-Henessey, *The Closed City. Impressions of a Visit to Leningrad* (London, 1938), 63.

[4] Dallin, *German Rule* emphasizes the role of Baltic Germans and émigrés while overlooking the ties with ethnic German communities.

DNVP for the Nazi Party out of concern over the fate of the ethnic German 'colonists'. Others from tropical medicine also rallied to the NSDAP: Mühlens (the first director of the German Red Cross famine relief expedition) attempted a similar move from the Deutsche Volkspartei although to his annoyance he was not admitted to the NSDAP until 1937—when Nauck (another Russian relief veteran) also joined.[5]

Zeiss's arrival in Berlin coincided with a renaissance of German military medicine. When the Academy for Military Medicine, closed since 1919, was reopened in the buildings of the old Kaiser Wilhelm-Akademie for military medical training, it provided Zeiss and his geo-medical cronies in tropical medicine with an influential power-base straddling state, military, and academic hygiene.[6] The Academy's Institutes for Hygiene and Bacteriology, and for Tropical Medicine and Parasitology launched a programme of medical geography for strategic purposes, correlating the incidence of disease with environmental conditions. By 1940 Rodenwaldt and Helmut Jusatz (a bacteriologist and hygiene expert, who deputized for Zeiss in Berlin), commanded military departments for malaria research, parasitology, zoology, entomology, pathology, and experimental field stations for testing pesticides, and for health technology. In May 1941 Rodenwaldt added a laboratory train which provided back-up for the Barbarossa campaign, as well as for anti-malarial campaigns in the Balkans and Greece.[7] Geo-medicine and tropical medicine assisted military operations in eastern and south-eastern Europe and throughout the Mediterranean.[8] Muntsch, the gas warfare expert, ran an institute for gas therapy under the auspices of the Academy. The chief military medical officer Anton Waldmann supported geo-medicine as crucial for his programme of military hygiene. The Academy's strategic medical tasks included determining blood groups and storage of blood and sera; these tasks were carried out by an SS Unit under Hans Delmotte who was seconded from the Hygiene Institute of the Waffen-SS.[9] Zeiss used military and SS contacts to improve the academic standing of hygiene in order to give it parity with other clinical specialisms, and to increase its range of strategic functions.[10]

In June 1934 Zeiss was appointed to the Scientific Senate for Military Medicine,

[5] BDC personal files Zeiss and Mühlens, No. 4349786, 1. May 1937. For Zeiss and the DNVP see *Das Deutsche Führer Lexikon 1934/1935* (Berlin, n.d.); Wolf, *Tropeninstitut*, 81. Gotschlich was DNVP member from 1920 to 1925; although he did not join the NSDAP he provided information on who among his colleagues were pure Aryans, see Nöske, *Gotschlich*, 355, 377.

[6] H. Fischer, *Der deutsche Sanitätsdienst 1921–1945. Organisation, Dokumente und persönliche Erfahrungen* (Osnabrück, 1982–91), iv. 3212–16; Kersting, 'Die Leistung des deutschen Sanitätsdienstes im Weltkriege', *Deutscher Militärarzt*, i (1936), 369–74; H. Fischer, *Die militärärztliche Akademie 1934–1945* (Osnabrück, 1975).

[7] BA-MA 20/70 Sammelbericht des Beratenden Hygienikers 1942, 1943; Hubert Fischer, *Die militärärztliche Akademie 1934–1945* (Osnabrück, 1975); W. Fricke and J. Schweikart, *Krankheit und Raum. Dem Pionier der Geomedizin Helmut Jusatz zum Gedenken* (Stuttgart, 1995); Rodenwaldt, *Tropenmedizin*, 406–10, 417.

[8] Waldmann, 'Einführung', Waldmann and Handloser, *Lehrbuch der Militärhygiene*, p. xv.

[9] YVA 068/586 BDC Hans Delmotte file, Mrugowsky note of 19 Feb. 1943.

[10] BDC Zeiss, to de Crinis 31 Aug. 1942, to Handloser 26 Aug. 1942.

and enthused about the past glories of German military doctors. Nazi war medicine celebrated the sanitary measures of the First World War as the basis of military hygiene.[11] The Reich Health Führer and SS officer Leonardo Conti drew inspiration from the German sanitary struggle for survival during the First World War in planning medical defences against eastern epidemics.[12] Rodenwaldt lectured military doctors about his First World War experiences concerning sanitation and delousing. The medical entomologist, former assistant to Koch and fervent Nazi, Erich Martini, regaled disinfectors with the heroic German victory over the 'Asiatic epidemics' spread by tsarist troops in the Great War. Martini was soon under Rodenwaldt's command, so that he could deploy his experiences in the Balkans, the Middle East, and Russia for strategic ends.[13] A celebratory history of military hygiene in the First World War endorsed the reliance on vaccination, disinfection, and personal hygiene.[14] Medical researchers used typhus cultures that had been kept alive in generations of guinea-pigs since the war.[15] The mimicry of sanitary procedures from the First World War led to a consciously archaic and heroizing style. Yet at the same time a fundamentally novel spirit of genocidal extermination pervaded epidemic prevention.

Having gained control of the hygiene institute with the support of Rudolf Hess, who was a geo-political enthusiast, Zeiss was penalized by a delay until 1937 in the university conferring the status of a full professor.[16] This was largely due to the Medical Faculty's suspicion of the academic credentials of geo-medicine. Zeiss viewed hygiene in dual scientific and practical terms—as a scientific discipline encompassing bacteriology, eugenics, and environmental health studies, and as a means to advance settlement programmes.[17] He praised the hygienic virtues of *Auslandsdeutschen*—especially in the scattered German communities in the east—as having sustained traditional racial virtues and not succumbing to rootless, urban decadence.[18] Zeiss regarded the science of hygiene as a weapon of total war. In 1935 the Deutsche Forschungsgemeinschaft (the successor to the NDW) supported his research into 'iron rations' on behalf of the

---

[11] *Sanitätsbericht über das deutsche Heer (Deutsche- Feld- und Besatzungsheer) im Weltkriege 1914/18*, 3 vols. (Berlin, 1935–8); A. Waldmann, 'Einführung', in id. and W. Hoffmann (eds.), *Lehrbuch der Militärhygiene* (Berlin, 1936), pp. xv–xix.

[12] Conti film in *Filmarchiv der Persönlichkeiten*, BA Berlin.

[13] E. Martini, 'Läuse und Flecktyphus', *Der praktische Desinfektor*, 31 (1939), 43–5, 54–7; Rodenwaldt, *Tropenhygiene*, 405, 409.

[14] *Sanitätsbericht über das deutsche Heer (Deutsche- Feld- und Besatzungsheer) im Weltkriege 1914/18* (Berlin, 1935–8), 3 vols.

[15] *Der Fall Rose*, pp. 89–90.

[16] AHUB NL Zeiss 12/a Zeiss personal file Bl. 42; also letter of Waldmann 5 June 1934 for military contacts; AHUB Hygienisches Institut file 138, Bl. 140 concerning the appointment of Zeiss; AHUB Medizinische Fakultät 12/a Zeiss file concerning the appointment authorized by Rudolf Hess and the Stellvertreter des Führers (i.e. Martin Bormann); K. D. Bracher, *The German Dictatorship* (Harmondsworth, 1973), 352–3 for Hess and geo-politics.

[17] AHUB Hygienisches Institut file 138, Zeiss to Schultze, Staatskommissar für das Gesundheitswesen 4 Dec. 1934.

[18] H. Zeiss, 'Entwurzelung und Wurzellosigkeit. Beobachtungen und Gedanken zum Problem der Verstädterung', *Zeitschrift für Geopolitik*, 10 (1933), 310–19.

army.[19] His sense of a geo-medical mission meant that he continued to cultivate historical studies, comparing the history of cholera in Germany and Russia since the 1830s, and he investigated Pettenkofer's thesis that certain localities were immune.[20] This project typified how history, medical geography, and preventive medicine were combined to combat epidemics from the east. The Germans invoked medical history to legitimate a bloody crusade in the name of 'securing Europe'.[21]

The war enabled Zeiss to embark on a new phase of medical activities in Eastern Europe. He was convinced that Germany was waging a defensive war, so that ruthless deportation, ghettoization, and killings could be legitimated as preventive medicine. Ruthless policing measures to control epidemics became genocidal, as typhus was magnified into a European threat. In December 1939 Zeiss was in Łódź in the newly annexed Warthegau, from where Jews were rounded up and expelled eastwards.[22] He saw active service in the Balkans until the conquest of Crete in June 1941. He visited Kiev in German-occupied Ukraine in 1941, and made occasional forays to the Generalgouvernement. In 1942 Zeiss was promoted to the rank of Generalarzt, when he correlated reports on epidemics and prepared an epidemiological atlas.[23] He advised the army on sanitary measures in the east, accusing civilians of causing the spread of typhus.[24] An action-oriented geo-medicine was geared to eastern conquest and genocide.

ii. Rekindling Russian Contacts

The Nazi–Soviet pact of 1938 paved the way for reactivating German–Soviet medical relations. After the invasion of Poland in 1939, the German and Soviet occupying authorities cooperated to repatriate German ethnic groups from the Soviet Union and the Baltic states into German-occupied Poland. Himmler as Reich commissar for defending German blood directed the resettlement programme. German doctors and Red Cross nurses were drafted into the Soviet-controlled areas to supervise the evacuation. Ethnic German medical personnel

---

[19] BDC Reichsforschungsrat card 1 Aug. 1935. For differing views of DFG funding see U. Deichmann, *Biologists under Hitler* (Cambridge, Mass., 1996) and P. J. Weindling, 'A Biological Sonderweg', *Nature*, 340 (1996), 399–400.

[20] BAK R 74/ 15922, Zeiss to DFG 4 Feb. 1936; R. Olzscha, 'Die Epidemiologie und Epidemiographie der Cholera in Russland', *Veröffentlichungen aus dem Gebiete des Volksgesundheitswesens*, 54/1 (1940). Zeiss also examined the effects of manganese on reproductive capacity and heredity.

[21] Dallin, *German Rule*, 56.

[22] AHUB Zeiss papers, Box 7 Bl. 232, letter of Dec. 1939. For background see M. Gilbert, *Atlas of the Holocaust*, 2nd edn. (Oxford, 1988), 41–3, 50–1. The Lódź ghetto was established only in May 1940.

[23] Sammelberichte des Beratenden Hygienikers, no. 1 (1 July 1942) in BA/ MA H20/59; no. 3 (23 Jan. 1944) in H20/123. On Zeiss in the Balkans see H.-G. Sonntag and A. Bauer, *100 Jahre Hygiene-Institut der Universität Heidelberg 1892–1992* (Heidelberg, 1992), 99.

[24] Leven, 'Fleckfieber', 132, 154 n. 42 citing Zeiss, 1. Sammelbericht ü. Kriegsärztliche Erfahrungen. 1. Halbjahr 1942, H 20/59. For genocidal massacres in the wake of the German advance see Gilbert, *Atlas of the Holocaust*, 67–9.

were brought 'home' from Soviet territory to the Reich: it was claimed that 300 doctors were 'repatriated' from the Baltic states. Tropical medicine experts prevented malaria and typhus from being imported, and the first doses of typhus vaccine were acquired from Soviet-occupied Lemberg/Lwów.[25]

In February 1940 Commissar Sergei Kaftanov, head of the Soviet Committee for Higher Education, contacted the Reich Minister for Science and Education, Bernhard Rust. They reactivated German–Soviet scientific contacts on 21 October 1940. A special office coordinated exchanges of literature, and leading academics evaluated Russian research: Zeiss reported on hygiene, the anthropologist Eugen Fischer was allocated anthropology and human genetics; zoological genetics fell to Karl Henke, biological genetics to Fritz von Wettstein of the Kaiser Wilhelm Institute for Biology, and racial hygiene to Fritz Lenz.[26] The exercise was a means of obtaining strategic information for the impending invasion. The Soviets for their part delegated the plant geneticist Vavilov early in 1940 to survey their newly acquired territories in Poland and Finland.[27]

The Barbarossa campaign launched on 22 June 1941 involved the capture of key scientific installations. The SS recruited experts in anthropology, entomology, and botany as part of its strategy for the Nazi reordering of Europe, promoting German settlement, and Germanizing science. The SS sought 'primitive races' of plants to reinvigorate agricultural stocks so as to make them frost resistant. The Kaiser Wilhelm Institute for Biology cooperated with the Ostministerium of Alfred Rosenberg, and the SS organized an estate in Styria to collect and maintain wild varieties of plants. In 1941 a botanical expedition evaluated Russian research stations. Wettstein planned a network of research stations in Russia stretching from Murmansk in the north to Baku in the Caucasus, to exploit the work of Russian plant geneticists. Biologists took a hand in extending *Lebensraum*, as the scientific counterpart of the Generalplan Ost formulated in 1941–2. In macabre imitation of Soviet Lysenkoist botanists, the German 'botanical research troops' set to work in the Balkans, Greece, and the East to find plants resistant to disease and drought.[28] The SS botanist, Heinz Brücher, who had philosophical pretensions and had just completed a biography Nazifying the Darwinian Haeckel, plundered Vavilov's collections with his SS unit in 1943.[29] Vavilov had strenuously built up an internationally renowned reference collection of plant seeds during the 1920s and 30s. Arrested by Stalin in 1940 as a British spy because of his international contacts, he died in prison in 1943. The tragic fate of Vavilov and his collections showed how internationalism had been replaced by nationalist xenophobia, plunder, and persecution.

[25] Thom, 'Wandlungen', 431–3.
[26] AHUB Hygienisches Institut Nr 11 circular of 21 Oct. 1940. For Henke, see Deichmann, *Biologen*, 112.
[27] Krementsov, *Stalinist Science*, 78.
[28] Deichmann, *Biologen*, 158–65, 176; S. Schleiermacher, 'Begleitende Forschung zum "Generalplan Ost"', in M. Rössler and Schleiermacher (eds.), *Der 'Generalplan Ost'. Hauptlinien der nationalsozialistischen Planungs- und Vernichtungspolitik* (Berlin, 1993), 339–45.
[29] Deichmann, *Biologen*, 178; Schleiermacher, 'Begleitende Forschung'. BAK R 73/ 10497 Heinz Brücher.

The Kaiser Wilhelm Institute (KWI) for Brain Research supported the planned takeover of academic facilities in Moscow. In October 1941 its Director (Julius Hallervorden who displaced Vogt) set as a strategic target the capture of Lenin's brain from the Moscow Brain Research Institute. If the Germans could prove that the Soviet leader had been syphilitic, this could be of immense propaganda value.[30] By this time the KWI was involved in obtaining brains of patients, who were victims of the euthanasia killings.

The demise of cooperation with the east was not total. A Zentrale für Ostforschung was established in December 1942 as an offshoot of the Ostministerium to look after Russian scientists in Germany. These scientific 'patriots' were the equivalent of the anti-communist forces of the turncoat General Vlasov. The office, which was run by the Baltic German geologist Leo von zur Mühlen, also cared for young scientists from Estonia, Latvia, and Lithuania, and 450 Russian students in Germany.[31] Joint projects involving German and local academics were initiated. The idea was to integrate the east into the new Nordic-Germanic Europe, by reviving research after 'racial political selection' of the academic personnel.[32] There was even a camp for Russian scientists working for IG-Farben in Upper Silesia.[33]

Public health experts promoted academic cooperation between the Axis powers. Hans Hoske of the Ostministerium cultivated links with Bulgarian and Romanian medical researchers. At the Berlin Hygiene Institute, visiting foreign researchers were mostly military and naval doctors from Bulgaria, Greece, and Turkey.[34] In May 1939 Zeiss was awarded an honorary doctorate at Sofia University, and he also visited Hungary that year.[35] Each contact with doctors from the Axis client-states advanced geomedical research, while hammering a nail in the coffin of the Rockefeller-sponsored central European public health programme. Berlin Hygiene Institute members on active service supplied material on infectious diseases and nutrition.[36] Karl Pesch moved from Zeiss's institute to the chair of hygiene at German-occupied Prague. Military action intensified contacts with other devotees of geo-medicine, including several veterans of the German typhus relief expedition.[37]

Military medicine continued to be a highly academic affair, involving many university and state hygiene institutes. Generaloberstabsarzt Siegfried Handloser was honorary professor in Vienna from 1939 and, when appointed supreme military medical officer, in Berlin from 1941.[38] Each medical specialism had a special adviser,

[30] BAK R 21/ 101 Bl. 144, Physiological dept, KWI Hirnforschung to de Crinis, 11. Oct. 1941.

[31] BAB R6/ 605 Bl. 1. R 6/33 Bl. 1–3, Satzung der Zentrale für Ostforschung 23 Dec. 1942.

[32] BAB R 6/ 238 Bl. 89. R 6/ 233 Bl. 13–14.

[33] BAB R 6/ 33 Bl. 10–13.

[34] *Chronik der Universität Berlin*, Hygienisches Institut Berlin (Apr. 1937-Mar. 1938). AHUB, Hygienisches Institut Nr 11, letter of 8 Dec. 1941 on Dr Tschakmatoff from Bulgaria and geo-medicine.

[35] AHUB Medical Faculty Zeiss personal file, Bl. 64.

[36] AHUB Hygienisches Institut Nr 11 Bl. 82, letter of 26 July 1940; Bl. 138 letter of 8 Dec. 1941.

[37] AHUB Hygienisches Institut Nr 42 Bl. 48–9, letters from Pesch 8 and 19 June 1940. AHUB Zeiss papers, box 7 Bl. 118, Zeiss to Bosneff of the Bulgarian War Ministry July 1941.

[38] *MMW* 89 (1942), 900 for the composition of the Scientific Senate for Military Medicine in Aug. 1942. Zeiss was ausserordentliches Mitglied.

conferences, and dedicated research groups.[39] The research-ethos led to reckless human experiments, as military doctors tried to gain the university research qualification of the Habilitation.[40] The military medical connections of Zeiss reinforced Nazi vaccine research in the East.[41] Zeiss and other experts in tropical medicine participated at the military medical conferences on medical problems on the Eastern Front.[42] Zeiss's assistant, Dötzer, became deputy director of Joachim Mrugowsky's Hygiene Institute of the Waffen-SS, and (Ding-)Schuler (notorious for human experiments at Buchenwald) also trained under Zeiss. The military hygienist stationed in Cracow, Eyer, was granted an associate chair at the Berlin Hygiene Institute in 1943—a sign of the interest of Zeiss in building up links with military medical researchers. Zeiss conducted joint research with institutes in Vienna, with the SS in Oranienburg, and until 1945 with the Institute for Public Health in Stockholm on conservation of typhus vaccines using ultraviolet light. His project on the biological effects of sauna baths in increasing resistance to infections had Nordic racial overtones.[43]

Zeiss maintained links with former associates from the German Red Cross expedition to Russia of 1921–3. He was on comradely terms with Otto Fischer, who had aided the Volga colonists. After contacts with Albert Schweitzer while conducting research in Africa, Fischer became involved with the missionary medicine school in Tübingen—this also attracted the conscience-stricken poison gas expert Kurt Gerstein. Fischer joined the NSDAP in 1937 and the SS in 1938, which backed his appointment as head of tropical medicine in Vienna. From November 1939 to January 1940 he worked on 'racial biological questions' on the Western Front. He visited the Ukraine in August 1943 on behalf of the Hygiene Institute of the Waffen-SS, reporting on which German settlements were fever free.[44] German bacteriologists again confronted mass starvation and piled corpses, which deepened a sense of ethnic German identity as the German forces thrust eastwards. Fischer typified how tropical specialists were in the occupied east, assessing health conditions, assisting with repatriation and resettlement, and combatting epidemics.[45]

Echoes of the past glories of German bacteriology shaped activities at the Hamburg Institute of Tropical Diseases. Its director from 1934, Mühlens, a veteran of the German Red Cross expedition to Russia, was initially distrusted by the Nazis

---

[39] R. Valentin, *Die Krankenbataillone. Sonderformationen der deutschen Wehrmacht im Zweiten Weltkrieg* (Düsseldorf, 1981) for the specialism of gastro-enterology.

[40] BA MA H 20/480 letter of 10 June 1939 by Waldmann, Heeressanitäts-Inspekteur.

[41] BA-MA H 20/70 Sammelbericht des beratenden Hygienikers.

[42] BA-MA H 20/481 2. Arbeitstagung Ost der Beratenden Ärzte.

[43] BAK R 86/4164.

[44] BDC O. Fischer files. AHUB Hygienisches Institut Nr 189 Bl. 67–9, report of Fischer dated 31 Aug. 1943; Letter of Fischer to Zeiss 24 Aug. 1943. Fischer held the rank of Oberstabsarzt and in 1943 was Unterstumführer in the SS.

[45] O. Fischer, 'Der Untergang der deutschen Volksgruppen an der Volga', *Deutsches Archiv für Landes- und Volksforschung* (1942), 17–33; id., 'Die Kollektivierung in der Sowjetunion und ihre Auswirkung auf die Siedlungsgebiete in der Ukraine', *Deutsches Archiv für Landes- und Volksforschung* (1944), 85–94.

as a diehard imperialist associated with tropical medicine under Nocht. The Nazi Party—and Zeiss—favoured appointing Rodenwaldt as '*völkisch*' and 'a dedicated anti-Semite' even though he had resigned from the Nazi Party in 1933 over the treatment of ethnic Germans abroad.[46] Zeiss and Rodenwaldt, who had first met in Aleppo during the First World War, formed a *völkisch* Axis in academic hygiene, as they collaborated on a textbook, an epidemiological atlas, and geo-medical schemes to correlate disease and pathology: determining the incidence of parasites and climatic factors was to establish health risks for the German invasion forces.

The Hamburg Tropical Institute's standing steadily rose, as bacteriologists fantasized about the restoration of Germany as a colonial power.[47] In 1939 Mühlens was Dean of the Hamburg Medical Faculty; he then took over responsibility for organizing sanitary services in the Bulgarian army (as in the First World War); as tropical medical adviser to the German navy, he promoted schemes for a German dominated Africa, organized according to principles of racial segregation.[48] The war provided an opportunity for deploying the experiences gathered on the German Red Cross famine relief expedition—O. Fischer, Mühlens, Nauck, and Zeiss all rallied to support epidemic prevention. The former agricultural attaché at the Moscow embassy and German Red Cross expedition nurse, Auhagen, favoured the Nazi programme of population transfers.[49]

Since his period at the All-Russian Microbiological Laboratory, Zeiss had been collecting data on the history and geography of epidemics. He joined forces with Mrugowsky and Rodenwaldt in evaluating Russian medical topographies. A large number of Russian medical studies were 'collected' (many were captured) for the strategically important Caucasus area. The mapping of diseases in the east provided the basis for the epidemiological atlas edited by Zeiss, who collated the surveys carried out by fellow supporters of geo-medicine.[50] Specialists in public health charted the epidemic hazards which could threaten strategic operations. The atlas was meant to assist the German invasion forces; yet it also had a broader academic agenda, as the geographical approach to the ebb and flow of disease vindicated the environmentalist critique of bacterial uniformity.[51] Scientific skirmishing over the causes of infectious diseases continued despite the military upheavals.

[46] K-H. Roth, 'Von der Tropenheilkunde zur "Kolonialmedizin"', in A. Ebbinghaus, H. Kaupen-Haas, and K. H. Roth (eds.), *Heilen und Vernichten im Mustergau Hamburg. Bevölkerungs- und Gesundheitspolitik im Dritten Reich* (Hamburg, 1984), 123–30.

[47] Roth, 'Von der Tropenheilkunde zur "Kolonialmedizin"' in Wulf, *Tropeninstitut*, 83–6.

[48] Roth, 'Tropenheilkunde', 124–5.

[49] R.-D. Müller, *Hitlers Ostkrieg und die deutsche Siedlungspolitik* (Frankfurt/M., 1991), 104.

[50] H. Zeiss, 'Medizinische Kartographie und Seuchenbekämpfung', in id. (ed.), *Seuchen-Atlas* (Gotha, 1942–5).

[51] Id., *Seuchen-Atlas*; id., 'Geomedizin und Seuchenbekämpfung', in S. Handloser and W. Hoffmann (eds.), *Wehrhygiene* (Berlin, 1944), 9–10; id., 'Medizinische Kartographie und Seuchenbekämpfung', *Petermanns Geographische Mitteilungen*, 90 (1944), 41–3; BA-MA H 20/70 Sammelbericht des beratenden Hygienikers, report by Zeiss; H 20/481 notes by Zeiss on Medizinische Kartographie der Seuchenbekämpfung; Fricke, Schweikart, *Krankheit*, 28–9.

iii. Recasting the Historical Legacy

Historians of medicine glorified the programme of disease prevention for conquest and settlement by providing an academic pedigree. The historical publications by Zeiss on Obermeier, Mechnikov, and Behring reinforced the image of the bacteriologist as a heroic warrior against disease. Zeiss glorified German national contributions to science, portraying scientific genius as a *völkisch* racial type of Nietzschean *Übermensch*. The vision of medical innovation as a spiritual and creative process was set against Marxist interpretations of medical advance based on economic materialism. In 1933 Zeiss had prospects of the chair in medical history at Leipzig, but preferred the Berlin Hygiene Institute where he could cultivate history as a means to promote the Nazification of public health and his vision of German medicine's destiny in the east.[52]

Zeiss campaigned for a properly German history of hygiene, based on racial consciousness to inspire a demoralized medical profession. He condemned the history of hygiene published by Alfons Fischer, who was liberal and of part-Jewish descent.[53] He became interested in the psychology of scientific creativity, as he plunged into work on the biography of the German bacteriologist, von Behring, with the aim of portraying the racial psychology of the German medical genius. Pasteur symbolized the hated Versailles system, whereas Behring stood for the restoration of German scientific leadership.

A biography of Behring was originally planned in conjunction with Behring's widow Else (daughter of Spinola, the director of the Charité Hospital in Berlin) and two favoured former students, Wernicke (the Posen bacteriologist) and Alfred Goldscheider, who was honorary professor in Berlin. The project did not develop fruitfully; Wernicke became embroiled in proving that he had priority over Behring in administering serum therapy in 1892.[54] Zeiss's Russian schemes brought him into contact with Else von Behring in 1928, when he obtained copies of Behring's extensive correspondence with Mechnikov for deposit in the proposed Mechnikov Museum. In 1931 Zeiss suggested that he should publish the letters between Behring and Mechnikov, having located archives in Marburg and Moscow, to assist Mechnikov's widow Olga in revising her biographical memoir. When Zeiss returned from the Soviet Union Else von Behring brought him into contact with Richard Bieling, an IG-Farben researcher at its sero-bacteriological department in Hoechst and professor at the University of Frankfurt; Bieling had been organizing Behring's papers,

---

[52] V. Roelcke, ' "Zivilisationsschäden am Menschen" und ihre Behandlung: Das Projekt einer "Seelischen Gesundheitsführung" im Nationalsozialismus', *Medizinhistorisches Journal*, 31 (1996), 3–48. For the background to the multifaceted interpretations of Nietzsche see S. E. Aschheim, *The Nietzsche Legacy in Germany 1890–1990* (Berkeley, Calif., 1992).

[53] H. Zeiss, 'Die nationalen Aufgaben der deutschen Hygiene', *Reichs-Gesundheitsblatt*, 52 (1936), 965; A. Fischer, *Geschichte des deutschen Gesundheitswesens* (1933), vol. i.

[54] C. Oedingen and J. Staerck, 'First Cure for Diphtheria as Early as 1891', *Annals of Science*, 54 (1997), 607–10.

and together they gathered recollections from former colleagues. In June 1932 they agreed with Else von Behring that the elderly Goldscheider should focus on Behring's biography in a separate book, whereas they should assist Frau von Behring in a study of Behring's discoveries and ideas in a co-authored biography.[55] The scheme reflected the ethos of the later Weimar Republic with an emphasis on the role of the great doctor as an international scientific leader.

The project became a means of Germanizing Behring as symbolic of past and present achievements of German bacteriology. In April 1933 Bieling raised the problem that it did not seem right that Behring's sons were dismissed for having Jewish blood. That Else von Behring's maternal grandparents converted from Judaism to Christianity, and that Goldscheider was a baptized Jew, became a profound embarrassment to the Nazi medical fanatics. For if Behring was to be a Germanic hero of science, his apparent lack of concern with anti-Semitism was unfortunate, a lapse which Behring shared with Koch. Bieling persuaded Zeiss to join him in a campaign to Aryanize Behring's sons. Else von Behring was harassed by the SA, and was forced to resign from the Patriotic Women's League. Bieling and Zeiss stressed how Behring's ancestors were German 'cultural pioneers' in the east since the time of Frederick II, and that their copious German hereditary gifts far outweighed the few drops of Jewish blood. Bieling said it would be absurd to portray Behring's achievements as German, while his sons were being excluded from society as un-German. Their efforts failed to persuade the experts for racial research in the Reich Interior Ministry to make an exception of the Behring family, even though Behring's ancestry was favourably evaluated by Ernst Rüdin's Kaiser Wilhelm Institute for Psychiatry project on 300 great German geniuses. But Else von Behring's tenacity prevailed, and in July 1935 Hitler agreed to 'Aryanize' Behring's five surviving sons (one had been killed in the First World War) so that they should not be disadvantaged as *Mischlinge*.[56]

When, in 1940 history of medicine became a compulsory part of the medical curriculum, so as to inspire young physicians with a sense of their racial duties, Zeiss stressed the need to give the Behring biography status as an academic and ideological work. Bieling as an IG-Farben employee was prepared to go along with his firm's views that there were sound commercial reasons for the book to appear as soon as possible, and for the Behringwerke to issue the biography.[57] Zeiss rejected such an arrangement as he feared that this would commercialize the image of Behring—as though it were an IG-Farben monopoly product.[58] But at the same

[55] AHUB, NL Zeiss Nr 7 Bl. 594, Besprechung am 18 June 1932 mit Frau von Behring, Geheimrat Goldscheider, Prof. Bieling und mir; Bl. 591, Else Behring to Zeiss 31 Jan. 1931, 29 Apr. 1932. Bieling to Zeiss 13 June 1932; Bl. 537, Bieling to Zeiss 5 Dec. 1932; Bl. 560, Else von Behring to Zeiss 28 Aug. 1932; Bl. 533, Zeiss to Akademische Verlagsgesellschaft 31 Dec. 1932.

[56] AHUB NL Zeiss, Nr 7 Behring Biographie Bl. 423, on Behring's children as non-Aryan; Bl. 524, Bieling to Zeiss 14 Apr. 1933, 8 Aug. 1933; Bl. 490, Bieling to Zeiss 3 Dec. 1933; Bl. 510, Zeiss to Fritz von Behring 9 Oct. 1933; Bl. 519, Fritz von Behring to Zeiss 13 Oct. 1933; and Bl. 58, memo by Fritz von Behring; Bl. 423, Bieling to Zeiss 13 July 1935.

[57] AHUB NL Zeiss Nr 7 Bl. 480, Bieling to Zeiss 31 Jan. 1934.

[58] Ibid., Bl. 394, Zeiss to Bieling 23 Dec. 1937.

time he felt that a 'Jewish' aura still lingered with the Weimar publishing arrangements. In 1937 he had denounced the contract with the Akademische Verlagsgesellschaft (which had originally proposed a Behring biography in 1917), fulminating against these publishers as being in Jewish ownership. In 1932 the Akademische Verlagsgesellschaft had included in its series 'Great Men. Studies in the Biology of Genius' the first volume of a meticulously researched biography of Robert Koch written by Bruno Heymann, the pioneer of hydrocyanic acid delousing. Zeiss had in August 1932 approached the publishers with the scheme for a joint biography with Goldscheider and Bieling. Indeed, Heymann had high praise for the publishers when Zeiss approached him on the matter. The publishers had found that the Koch biography hardly sold, but they were willing to include a Behring biography in their series 'Grosse Männer' for idealistic reasons because of Behring's great achievements.[59] Dismissed from the Berlin Hygiene Institute in 1935, Heymann found a refuge preparing the second volume.[60]

Zeiss took a lead in Nazifying the historical image of Behring. He carried out his task with subtlety and sophistication, as he heroized Behring's character, and projected him as an inspirational figure in German medical research.[61] Behring's achievements countered the excessive French emphasis on Roux and other Pastorians.[62] The monumental Behring biography was a classic of Nazi history of medicine. Zeiss demonstrated the interaction of cultural, psychological, philosophical and local influences, developing a geo-political approach to scientific innovation. Keen to analyse irrational factors in creativity, Zeiss contacted the Secretary of the British Cremation Society in order to find out about Lytton Strachey's approach as to how a political context shaped personality.[63] Far from Strachey's debunking of hero figures, Zeiss achieved the reverse in heroizing the mundane. He depicted the interaction with the eastern borderlands as crucial to the origins of Behring's genius.[64] Zeiss emphasized how Behring's discovery of serum therapy drew on his ability to think in terms of images and analogies. He regarded the demonic ideas of Schopenhauer and Nietzsche as correctives to the superficialities of Kantian rationalism.[65] Beneath the surface of the cool, objective scientist, there were deeper emotions. Zeiss commented on an entry in Behring's diary demanding personal self-sacrifice: 'Los von sich selbst—Symbolisch: Aufräumen, Verbrennen.' This placed Behring in a tradition stretching from Paracelsus to Schopenhauer—that of 'enthusiasm'; medical research was thereby infused with the status of a spiritual mission. Such a

[59] Ibid., Bl. 584, Zeiss to Bieling n.d. [July 1932]. Zeiss to Akademische Verlagsgesellschaft 10 Aug. 1932; Verlagsgesellschaft to Zeiss 17 Sept. 1932; B. Heymann, *Robert Koch I. Teil 1843–1882* (Leipzig, 1932).

[60] G. Henneberg, K. Janitschke, M. Stürzbecher, and R. Winau (eds.), *Robert Koch II. Teil 1882–1908. Nach Fragmenten von Bruno Heymann* (Berlin, 1997).

[61] AHUB NL Zeiss, Nr 7 Behring-Biographie Bl. 412, Zeiss to Bieling 20 July 1937; Bl. 414. Wernicke Papers, Box 2, Akademische Verlagsgesellschaft to Wernicke 18 June 1917; E. von Behring to Meta Wernicke 29 Aug. 1932; A. von Engelhardt to Johanna Wernicke 12 Aug. 1940; Heymann, *Robert Koch*, vol. i.

[62] AHUB NL Zeiss Nr 7 Bl. 479, Bieling to Zeiss 15 Feb. 1934; Bl. 484, Bieling to Zeiss 28 Dec. 1933; Bl. 482, Bieling to Zeiss; Bl. 484, 3 Jan. 1934, Bieling to Zeiss.

[63] AHUB Hygienisches Institut Nr 44, Zeiss to Reginald Perkins 17 June 1938; Perkins to Zeiss 24 June 1938.

[64] H. Zeiss and R. Bieling, *Behring. Gestalt und Werk* (Berlin, 1941).   [65] Ibid., 146–7, 481–4.

German ideology legitimated mass destruction as heroic and creative. The inspirational quality of their historical portrait was in keeping with the authors' careers, as Bieling became involved in vaccine production in the Caucasus and Ukraine, and Zeiss saw active service in the Balkans and also in the Ukraine in pursuit of his geomedical crusade.[66] Fire and ideas of racial cleansing scarred the occupied east: to give just an example of the welter of atrocities, on 29 April 1943 3,000 typhus patients at the isolation camp of Doroschitz were burned alive in a barn.[67]

The geo-political and Gestalt approach to scientific innovation countered Marxist and Soviet history of science as based on dialectical materialism and on economic determinants. The Nazi stress on the racial character of leading individuals was in striking contrast to the sociology of science as pioneered by the Polish immunologist, Ludwik Fleck, who emphasized thought-collectives of collaborating groups. Fleck's study of the sociology of a scientific fact of 1935 focused on Behring's Jewish contemporaries, Paul Ehrlich and August von Wassermann, and their relations to the Prussian state. It has been suggested that 'In Germany the Nazis could have no interest in the Polish Jew Fleck'. Yet as a German-language work published in Basle in 1935 (and abstracted in the *Klinische Wochenschrift*), Fleck's work received a substantial number of reviews in Germany, and was acquired by German medical libraries. One reviewer pointed out that Fleck's term *Denkkollektiv* was derived from the Soviet concept of a collective, and inferred that science was a materialist product, whereas the appropriate German term *Gemeinschaft* had fitting psychological and philosophical dimensions.[68]

The conceptual parallels are striking between the collectivist ideas of Fleck and the Gestalt approach to the history of bacteriology. Fleck's concept of an epistemic community was more sociological when compared to the historicist and hero-worshipping Zeiss. Yet both approaches drew attention to non-rational factors in scientific innovation. Fleck's subsequent persecution by a historically minded Nazi medical élite was a cruel irony as leading SS bacteriologists had pronounced historical interests—although Fleck was contemptuous of their brutal experiments.[69] Fleck's fate as a bacteriologist became entangled with German typhus research. He had been under pressure from Polish anti-Semites, and so sought recognition by publishing in German. After Weigl's departure from Lwów to Cracow in 1939, the Soviet authorities appointed Fleck director of the bacteriological laboratory in the Lwów medical school.[70] Under Soviet occupation the renamed 'Iwan Franko' University of Lwów became linked to Ukrainian academic institutions. The Pasteur

[66] Zeiss and Bieling, *Behring*, pp. 13, 146–7, 481–4.

[67] Yad Vashem Archives (YVA) 03/2434 testimony of Dawid Zwi Stauber.

[68] Hans Petersen, 'Ludwik Flecks Lehre vom Denkstil und dem Denkkollektiv', *Klinische Wochenschrift*, 15 (1936), 239–42. Favourable reviews include: M. H. B. in *Natur und Geist. Monatshefte für Wissenschaft, Weltanschauung und Lebensgestaltung*, 5 (1937), 380–1; W. Caspari, in *Die Umschau*, 40 (1936), 338.

[69] YVA 033/17, 0/650 Fleck testimony.

[70] L. Fleck, *Entstehung und Entwicklung einer wissenschaftlichen Tatsache. Einführung in die Lehre vom Denkstil und Denkkollektiv* (Basle, 1935); new edn. (Frankfurt, 1980), tr. as *Genesis and Development of a Scientific Fact* (Chicago, 1979). See p. 191 for early reviews. T. Schnelle, *Ludwik Fleck—Leben und Denken* (Freiburg, 1982); R. S. Cohen and T. Schnelle (eds.), *Cognition and Fact. Materials on Ludwik Fleck* (Boston, 1986), 13 for quotation on Fleck and Nazism.

Institute in Lwów was oriented to the Mechnikov Institute at Kharkov—so named because Mechnikov had studied there.

This realignment under the Soviet secularizing and de-Polonizing occupation was in marked contrast to the brutal liquidation of Polish academic institutions under Nazism. After arresting and murdering many university teachers, the Germans only allowed a few medical institutes to remain. The Lemberg 'Institute for Hygiene and the Institute for Typhus and Virus Research (Behring Institute)' was ceremonially opened in December 1942, when the Jewish ghetto was being savagely annihilated.[71] The change of name meant Behring displaced Pasteur as a scientific symbol of German power.[72] The Behring cult provided a medical icon for the Nazi mobilizing of medical research for the war in the east.

In December 1940 the University of Marburg hosted an elaborate ceremony marking fifty years since Behring's pioneering of serum therapy for diphtheria—at a time when this disease was on the increase in Nazi Germany. Behring was honoured as a physician and researcher, and more generally the celebrations glorified German scientific and medical research. Freiherr Alexander von Engelhardt, who had established the Behring archive in Marburg, organized a vast rally, mobilizing the university, the Behring Factory, and the town which cultivated its medieval looks and Nazi cadres.[73] The Marburg professor of hygiene, Wilhelm Pfannenstiel, made sure that the leading SS doctors Ernst Robert Grawitz, Genzken, and Mrugowsky, and the pharmacist Blumenreuther, were invited to the celebrations.[74] The orations by Bernhard Rust, the Minister of Education, by Reichsgesundheitsführer Conti, by Reiter as president of the Reich Health Office, and by the military medical supremo, Handloser signalled the strategic value placed by the Nazi state on medical research. Brauer, formerly associated with Behring in Marburg, praised Behring as fusing national ideals with far-sighted research, while himself under attack from Nazis as having supported Semites and socialists. The racially minded immunologist Uhlenhuth (who liaised with Japanese medical scientists) presided over a scientific conference. The celebrations took on an eastern profile: Robert Kudicke of the Warsaw health office was invited. The organizers even hoped for a Soviet delegation to attend.[75]

[71] The Soviet occupation of Lwów dated from 22 September 1939, eastern Galicia was incorporated in the Ukraine from 1 November 1939, and the Nazi occupation began 29–30 June 1941. The address of the Institut für Fleckfieber- und Virusforschung (Behring-Institut) was Grüne Strasse 10–12. It was housed in the former social insurance building, which had been renovated by the Russians for Weigl. K. Baedeker, *Das Generalgouvernement* (Leipzig, 1943). For the slaughter of university academics see Z. Albert, 'Mord an den Professoren Lwów (Lemberg) Juli 1941', Albert, *Kaźń Profesorów Lwówskich Lipiec 1941* (Wrocław, 1989), 137–75. For the Holocaust at Lemberg see T. Held, 'Vom Pogrom zum Massenmord', in P. Fässler, T. Held, and D. Sawitzki, *Lemberg—Lwów—Lviv* (Cologne, 1995), 113–66.

[72] For connections between Mechnikov and Kharkov see O. Metschnikoff, *Life of Elie Metchnikoff 1845–1916* (London, 1921); A. I. Tauber and L. Chernyak, *Metchnikoff and the Origins of Immunology. From Metaphor to Theory* (New York, 1991), 6–7.

[73] R. Koshar, *Social Life, Local Politics and Nazism. Marburg 1880–1933* (Chapel Hill, NC, 1986), 47.

[74] BDC Pfannenstiel file, Pfannenstiel to de Crinis 2 Jan. 1943. Behring-Archiv, Behring-Feier, Pfannenstiel to Dean of Medical Faculty 18 Nov. 1940; *Marburger Geschichte*, 628. BA R6/33 Bl. 27.

[75] Behring-Archiv, Behring-Feier, Reichsminister für Wissenschaft, Erziehung und Volksbildung to Rector Marburg, 2 Nov. 1940, Bl. 2. H. van den Bussche (ed.), *Medizinische Wissenschaft im 'Dritten Reich'* (Hamburg, 1989), 56–7.

10. German mothers honour Behring, Marburg 1940

A Behring memorial was placed by the ruins of a castle of the Teutonic Knights, which fortuitously was adjacent to Behring's former Hygiene Institute. Vaccine researchers considered themselves scientific Teutonic Knights on a crusade against eastern barbarism, as they looked back to the departure of the Teutonic order from Marburg in 1231 to colonize the east.[76] Such ideals reinforced Hitler's mission to resurrect the spirit of the 'German Order' for a crusade against Russia.[77] The sense of a Teutonic mission infused academic dealings with the east: von Engelhardt was joined by the SS bacteriologist Joachim Mrugowsky in manning a section of the Zentrale für Ostforschung, the agency to support pro-German academics in the east. Moreover, the presence of Conti, Handloser, and Reiter indicated the importance of Behring for the ruthless pursuit of the Germanic medical mission; they initiated human experiments in concentration camps so as to produce vaccines for the troops in the east.

The Marburg historical fanfare for German vaccine research was silent about crucial features of Behring's life and science. Members of the Behring family were absent, despite their Aryanization to conceal their 'quarter-Jewish' ancestry. Indeed, Behring's widow had been so harassed after the Nazi takeover that she

---

[76] BA Berlin R 6/ 33; M. Lemberg and G. Oberlik, *Die Wandgemälde von Peter Janssen in der Alten Aula der Philipps-Universität zu Marburg* (Marburg, 1985); W. Wippermann, *Der Ordenstaat als Ideologie. Das Bild des Deutschen Ordens in der deutschen Geschichtsschreibung und Publizistik* (Berlin, 1979); M. Burleigh, 'The Knights, Nationalists and the Historians', *Ethics and Extermination. Reflections on Nazi Genocide* (Cambridge, 1997), 9–24.

[77] W. Wippermann, *Der konsequente Wahn*, 64–75.

11. The Behring Memorial

reputedly committed suicide in 1936—this was not long after the 'unexpected' death of one of her sons.[78] Stress was placed on the intrinsically Germanic nature of Behring's achievements. Although 'men of science' had been mustered from twenty states to pay homage to the superiority of German medicine, there was no French representative despite Behring's cordial relations with researchers at the Pasteur Institute; moreover, Madsen, the former Chairman of the League of Nations Health Assembly, from occupied Denmark courageously mentioned Paul Ehrlich's

[78] AHUB NL Zeiss Nr 7, Bl. 422 death notice of Kurt von Behring. Bl. 420 death notice of Else von Behring.

12. The Guard of Honour at the tomb of Behring

contribution to the discovery of serum therapy, as well as the internationalism of the LNHO standards commission. But the Germans did not acknowledge Ehrlich without whom the anti-toxin serum could not have been clinically applied or manufactured, and there were only muted references to other Jewish researchers like Wassermann. Behring's bust was unveiled to Nazi salutes given by university dignitaries, and by 'child rich' bearers of the *Mutterkreuz* hailing this scientific saviour of their children. As a finale, Hitler Youth brandished flaming torches, as they mounted a guard of honour in Behring's mausoleum.[79]

Nazi propaganda machinery projected a heroized portrait of Behring in newspapers, medical and technical journals, and, after lobbying by Bieling and Zeiss, on a postage stamp. Mrugowsky hailed Behring for combining the skills of a physician and medical researcher, and Behring was celebrated in the journal for disinfectors. Zeiss hoped that the Behring celebrations would mean that this 'pioneer of European medicine' and saviour of German children and soldiers would enter German popular culture. Rectifying the French absence in Marburg, he proclaimed Behring as a figure whose friendship with French researchers presaged the Führer's

[79] *Bildbericht für die Teilnehmer der Behring-Erinnerungsfeier vom 4. bis 6. Dezember 1940 in Marburg-Lahn* (Marburg, n.d.); *Behring zum Gedächtnis* (Berlin, 1942). The eradication of Ehrlich from the historical record should be contrasted with: *Hundertjahrfeier der Geburtstage von Paul Ehrlich und Emil von Behring. Verleihung der Emil von Behring-Preise 1948, 1952 und 1954* (Marburg, 1954) (= *Behringwerk-Mitteilungen*, no. 29).

demand that Franco–German hostility be buried as long as the Pétain regime remained an ally. Moreover, Behring had forged links with (and some would have said, ruthlessly exploited) Japanese bacteriologists.[80]

The Nazi calculation was that freeing humanity from disease could only be achieved by the death of racial undesirables. That Behring was romanticized in a popular biography by the euthanasia propagandist and poet-physician Hellmuth Unger underlined the link between Behring and extermination. Renowned for his *Kerndeutsch* outlook, Unger ignored Behring's racially tainted family and the contributions of Ehrlich, and instead portrayed Behring as a great German scientist indebted to Koch and other national scientific heroes.[81] An even cruder vulgarizer, Oswald Gerhardt injected virulent anti-Semitism in his Behring biography through the device of giving a leading role to Behring's sister Emma (and making no reference to Behring's fiancée Else, who had assisted in the serum experiments); in this version Emma and Behring's father were anti-Semites, supporting Behring's struggle with a Jewish rival, Hans Aronson, a protégé of the despised liberal Virchow.[82] The Nazified image of Behring accompanied eastern medical schemes, and Unger portrayed Prowazek's heroic engagement with typhus. The Behring Institute, Lemberg was well stocked with such ideological resources: when eventually evacuated in March 1944, among the repatriated remnants were seven volumes of the Zeiss/Bieling biography, thirty-three volumes of Unger's populist biography, and thirty-four volumes of Gerhardt's vulgarization.[83]

As Zeiss feared, the Behring cult was manipulated for commercial ends. IG-Farben, which had taken over the Behringwerke, transferred serum production from Hoechst to Marburg, and so initiated an upswing in production during the 1930s. The Behring name was retained for a sales division.[84] The celebrations at Marburg in 1940 served to launch a research venture by IG-Farben which had acquired the Behring Works in 1929: the 'Behring Institute for Experimental Therapy' was initially for typhus vaccine production, but was intended to become a central state serum institute. IG-Farben's aim was to oust the Pasteur Institute and Rockefeller Foundation from their leading role in the new European states of the Versailles system, to establish the primacy of German pharmacy overseas, and to found a major institute for infectious diseases. By 1943 among the eleven Behring Institutes were those in Agram (i.e. Lubljiana), Budapest, Sofia, Lemberg, Berlin, and Neuhausen in East Prussia. Also, the Behringwerke had substantial interests at the serotherapeutic institute in Vienna, and in captured serum and veterinary

[80] H. Zeiss, 'Leben und Wirken Behrings', *Deutsche Medizinische Wochenschrift*, (3 Jan. 1941), 16–10. Zeiss was invited to the celebrations, although it is not clear whether he attended.

[81] H. Unger, *Unvergängliches Erbe. Das Lebensweg Emil von Behrings* (Oldenburg i. O, 1941); J. Mrugowsky, 'Behring und die Serumtherapie', *Der Öffentliche Gesundheitsdienst*, 6 (1940), 523–6; 'Emil von Behring zum 25. Todestag', *Der praktische Desinfektor*, 34 (1942), 23; Klare, 'Hellmuth Unger zum 50. Geburtstag', *Deutsche Medizinische Wochenschrift*, 67 (1941), 16–19.

[82] O. Gerhardt, *Stationen einer Idee. Behrings schicksalsvoller Weg* (Berlin, 1941), 11, 54, 56.

[83] Behring-Archiv, Lemberg buff folder, inventory, p. 12; H. Unger, 'Prowazeck der Erforscher des Fleckfiebers', *Die Gesundheitsführung. Ziel und Weg* (1942), 256–9.

[84] J. W. Staerck, *90 Jahre Behringwerke 1904–1994* (Marburg, 1994).

institutes in the Ukraine.[85] The military victory was an opportunity to establish Germany's scientific and economic leadership in research, production, and marketing of sera. IG-Farben welcomed the collapse of the Polish autarchy in serum production as a state monopoly centred on the Warsaw Hygiene Institute. The Behringwerke subsidiary hoped to gain control of pharmaceutical supply in the Generalgouvernement, reinforced by the Behring Institute Lemberg, and the Behringwerke hoped to establish production centres in Russia. IG-Farben's strategy was to impose lucrative agreements so that it could dominate European markets.[86]

The rise of Behring's ideological stock was matched by equivalent attempts to portray Koch as a *Vorkämpfer* of Nazism. In April 1942 the Prussian Institute for Infectious Diseases became a Reich Institution, bearing the name 'Robert Koch Institute' (RKI). This marked the culmination of the RKI's role as a central state institute for epidemic prevention, along with an increased military role. Colonization, conquest, and combating epidemics from the east became part of the RKI's medical agenda, as bacteriologists had the mission to sanitize the newly acquired *Lebensraum* in Eastern Europe and Africa. Its president, Eugen Gildemeister, a veteran of the Hygiene Institute in Posen, rekindled the spirit of a bacteriological war, as he energetically backed typhus vaccine research as a military priority in the 1940s.[87]

Researchers seasoned by field-work overseas directed new RKI laboratories for 'cell and virus research' and for biochemistry. Gerhard Rose became RKI vice-president in 1942, researching into the transmission and prevention of insect-borne diseases. Born in Danzig, after the First World War Rose rallied to the German defence of Upper Silesia, and (like Zeiss) composed nationalist tirades against the Versailles Treaty. Rose first joined the Nazi Party and SA in 1922, and rejoined the foreign section of the Nazi Party while in China in November 1930.[88] Between 1929 and 1936 he directed the provincial medical department of Chekiang and the Chinese national schistosomiasis programme set up by the LNHO; Rose took over from the veteran bacteriologist Claus Schilling as head of the tropical

---

[85] *Idee und Tat. E. v. Behring und die Behringwerke* (n.d., n.p.); BAK R 21/11061 Bl. 1–2, Rektor der Universität Marburg to Mentzel, Reichserziehungsministerium 19 Nov. 1940; Bl. 6 I.-G. Farben Wirtschaftspol. Abt. 4 to Klingelhöfer, Reichsministerium für Wissenschaft, Erziehung und Volksbildung 14 Oct. 1940; Bl. 7–11 memorandum by W. R. Mann 'Vorschlag zur Neuordnung des Serumgeschäftes', 29 July 1940; Homburger, *Behringwerke*, 84, 144–9; Bayer-Archiv, 6.14 'Neuordnung des Serumgeschäftes' 1 Aug. 1942; Behring-Archiv, *Bericht über die Tätigkeit der Behring-Institute im Jahre 1943*. The Buenos Aires Institute was run by Karel F. Wenckebach from 1938, after he was dismissed from the Robert Koch Institute Berlin, see Hubenstorf, 'Aber es kommt', 419.

[86] BAK R 21/11061 'Neuordnung des Serumgeschäftes', esp. Bl. 25–7, 33. Also BAK R 86/ 4164 Bl. 161.

[87] Hubenstorf, 'Aber es kommt mir doch so vor . . .', 357–80, 409–10; E. Gildemeister, 'Bericht über die Tätigkeit des Instituts für Infektionskrankheiten "Robert Koch" in Berlin in der Zeit vom 1. April 1936 bis 31. März 1937', 39; Gildemeister, 'Bericht über die Tätigkeit des Robert-Koch-Instituts', 143–200; Liepmann, *Death from the Skies*, 267–8.

[88] BDC Rose file, Personalblatt Kameradschaftliche Vereinigung der Offiziere des Beurlaubtenstandes, 16 Dec. 1937; H. Vondra, 'Malariaexperimente in Konzentrationslagern und Heilanstalten während der Zeit des Nationalsozialismus', med. diss., Hannover, 1989, 73.

department at the RKI in 1936 and became the RKI vice-president as well as medical consultant to the German Luftwaffe.[89]

Rose's *Heim ins Reich* move from the peripheries to the centre typified how Nazi experts on infectious diseases returned from remote outposts. Notable cases included Zeiss (from the Soviet Union) teaming up with Rodenwaldt (from New Guinea); Kudicke (dean of the medical faculty of the Sun-Yat-Sen University, Canton) and Jost Walbaum (also on the Canton faculty, where they were incensed at the arrival of Jewish refugee physicians from 1933[90]) moved to the Generalgouvernement; Herbert Kunert had worked in Tanganyka during 1930 and from 1937 to 1939 as well as at the Robert Koch Institute, and in 1940 moved to the Institute of Hygiene in Litzmannstadt (the Germanized city of Łódź).[91] During the 1930s Hamburg Tropical Institute personnel focused on former German colonies in Africa: the entomologist and Nazi activist Fritz Zumpt was in the Cameroons, also visited by Mühlens in 1938, while war service took Zumpt to southern Russia.[92] At a more mundane level, a German doctor, Ernst Thennard-Neumann, who had been an NSDAP member since 1933 and had worked in the Panama Canal Zone, was assigned the task of making sure that repatriated Germans from the Black Sea area did not import malaria.[93] While these doctors varied in their commitment to the NSDAP (not joined by Kudicke or Wohlrab), the SA, and SS (from which Rose kept aloof), a sense of restoring Germany's imperial greatness and racial vigour infused their medical work. Indeed, Rose returned to Germany in 1936 assuming that Germany's colonies would soon be restored.[94]

The eastern hygiene institutes were in the vanguard of the bacteriological struggle with Asiatic epidemics. A Baltic German, Harald Waegner, born in the Ukrainian city of Kharkov in 1908, having fled Russia in 1925 (when he quickly joined the ultra-right Wehrwolf), drew on his Russian background in his career as an SS medical officer; from September 1941 he directed the medical department in Rosenberg's ministry for the occupied eastern territories.[95] Hans Grossmann, a Nazi Party member since 1933, joined the Hygiene Institute at Landsberg on the ill-fated Polish border in 1938; in 1940 he transferred to the State Hygiene Institute at Litzmannstadt, and in 1941 he became professor at the Reich University of Posen thereby restoring German bacteriology to this eastern outpost.[96] Rudolf Wohlrab, the youthful commander of the Warsaw Hygiene Institute, had lived in Russia as a child, as had Ernst Nauck, who made periodic forays to the east before becoming director of the Hamburg Tropical Institute. Certain biographical traits were appar-

[89] Eckart, *Deutsche Ärzte*, 195; Hubenstorf, 'Aber es kommt', 414–17; Vondra, 'Malariaexperimente', append., pp. i–xxxi; Wulf, *Tropeninstitut*, 81.
[90] Eckart, *Deutsche Ärzte*, 192–4; R. Kudicke, 'Beobachtungen und Erfahrungen an einer chinesischen Universität', *Deutsche medizinische Wochenschrift*, 61 (1935), 350–2; Wulf, *Tropeninstitut*, 80; Walbaum on return to Germany was appointed medical officer in the Berlin-Tiergarten district.
[91] Hubenstorf, 'Aber es kommt', 419.   [92] Wolf, *Tropeninstitut*, 87–91.   [93] BNI, Paket 4.
[94] Vondra, 'Malariaexperimente', 74.
[95] NAW microfilm B 0214 SS officers, Harald Waegner Lebenslauf.
[96] BDC Hans Grossmann files, containing materials on the new medical faculty at Posen. *Kürschners Deutscher Gelehrten-Kalender* (Berlin, 1970), 905.

ent among the bacteriological and tropical researchers of the Third Reich: birth on the eastern fringes of Germany or Russia, experience in the frontline fight against diseases in remote destinations like German East Africa or Aleppo, and a commitment to sustaining ethnic German communities.

Yet enthusiasm for Germany's racial mission did not elicit ideological uniformity. Although the military, colonialist, and eastern racial strands in hygiene fused under Nazism, infighting remained rife among the ranks of the bacteriologists. Such differences can be illustrated by divisions among those celebrating Koch's achievements. Medical leaders gathered on 1 April 1942 to hear Reich Health Führer Conti celebrate Koch as a bacteriological warrior who forged the medical weapons to combat infectious diseases.[97] While Conti represented Nazi orthodoxy, the notion of medicine as embodying racial struggle could arouse protest. As an act of muted defiance against medicine as a racial and cultural mission, Marburg witnessed a counter celebration to the Behring cult in December 1943, when the medical faculty marked the centenary of Koch's birth. The new Rector of Marburg University, Rudolf Reinhardt, emphasized how science transcended political constraints, as part of a policy of distancing the university from Nazi militarism. The fanatically Nazi professor of hygiene, Pfannenstiel, furiously denounced the proceedings. The Robert Koch Institute stressed the beleagured heroism of Koch as a rugged individualist overcoming adversity, so as to exhort the Institute to continue work despite bomb damage to the crypt in Berlin where his ashes were interred.[98] Koch's image seemed to have a higher, and more purely scientific status than that of the more nationally oriented Behring: Rose admired Koch for not having undertaken human medical experiments—overlooking the testing of Atoxyl as a therapy for sleeping sickness.[99]

The counter-image of Koch as an objective experimentalist meant that he was celebrated by Jewish physicians. Although expelled by Zeiss from the Berlin Hygiene Institute, Heymann doggedly drafted substantial parts of a biography which covered the sleeping sickness expedition in East Africa. The Reich Health Office retained a discrete interest in the project, possibly with a view to its exploitation in an altered guise. Heymann died in May 1943 in the Jewish Hospital, Berlin with his manuscript unfinished.[100] On 26 August 1943 Hermann Strauss, a deported Berlin physician who directed the medical committee in Theresienstadt, marked the anniversary of Koch's birth with celebratory lectures on 'Medical Berlin at the Turn of the Century' and on the 'The Great Medical Discoveries and how Jews Contributed to Them'.[101]

---

[97] Gildemeister, 'Bericht', 143–7.

[98] BDC Pfannenstiel file, Pfannenstiel to de Crinis 2 Jan. 1943; *Marburger Geschichte*, 648–9; E. Boecker, 'Robert Koch zu seinem 100. Geburtstag am 11 Dezember 1943', *Deutsche medizinische Wochenschrift*, 69 (1943), 829–30.

[99] *Der Fall Rose*, 89.

[100] G. Henneberg, K. Janitschke, M. Stürzbecher, and R. Winau (eds.), *Robert Koch, ii, Teil 1882–1908. Nach Fragmenten von Bruno Heymann* (Berlin, 1997).

[101] Elena Makarova Tcheznichovski, Project Theresienstadt. The List of the Cultural Programs in Terezin. H. G. Adler, *Theresienstadt 1941–1945. Das Antlitz einer Zwangsgemeinschaft* (Tübingen, 1955), 504–5.

How German doctors martialled historical precedents to support the idea of their European mission to eradicate Jewish Bolshevism can be seen in their programme for international health.[102] War meant that cooperation between nations was supplanted by the vision of Germany as the master-power of the 'New Europe'. In the spheres of hygiene and population policy, the Nazi authorities encouraged conferences, and plans for cooperation and integrating medical services among the Axis powers under German leadership. In 1941 a conference at the Reich Education Ministry promoted a new European scientific order under German control. Doctors involved in typhus prevention and research rallied to support such schemes. A plan for a European health organization was formulated by Hellmut Haubold of the health office of the NSDAP. He drew inspiration from a historical study of Johann Peter Frank, the originator of the concept of medical police in the late eighteenth century, whose career took him to Vilna in 1804, and St Petersburg from 1805 to 1808. Zeiss also identified his mission with the achievements of Frank as a powerfully Germanic organizer of health care, who was thwarted by political intrigues at the tsarist court.[103] In 1942 Reiter, as Director of the Reich Health Office, considered that Germany had to take the lead in international health work, and found cooperation with Olsen (formerly on the staff of the LNHO) in Geneva of great value. Olsen joined the NSDAP in May 1942, and by 1943 Olsen was employed by the Reich Health Office, while remaining in Geneva as a medical adviser to the League of Red Cross Societies.[104]

The Nazi scheme of international health cooperation was developed by Hellmut Haubold, a Nazi Party member since 1933 and of the Reich Health Office since 1935. Haubold's international credentials were based on studies of cancer treatment in France, and since May 1936 he directed the foreign department of the Reich Chamber of Physicians. He built up links with Hungary, Bulgaria, and Romania in the belief that German coordination of scientific exchanges would facilitate the emergence of a 'new' (and racially purified) Europe. He took charge of the health of repatriated ethnic Germans at the Volksdeutsche Mittelstelle. He was convinced that Germany was defending Western culture against Bolshevism.[105]

---

[102] STAN KV-Prozesse Interrogations, M 104 J. Mrugowsky, 'Zur psychiatrischen und psychologischen Beurteilung Hitlers und seine Lehre', 19 Sept. 1946. Although a post-war text, Mrugowsky draws on observations and opinions made before the capitulation of Germany.

[103] H. Haubold, *Johann Peter Frank der Gesundheits- und Rassenpolitiker* (Munich, 1939); H. Zeiss, 'Johann Peter Franks Tätigkeit in St Petersburg', *Klinische Wochenschrift*, 12 (1933), 353–6; Zeiss, 'Deutsche Ärzte in Russland. 1. Johann Peter Frank. 2. Christian Wilhelm Schmid', *Sudhoffs Archiv*, 31 (1938), 219–346. The sequel, Zeiss, 'Deutsche Ärzte in Russland. 3. Johann Peter Brinckmann', ibid., 35 (1942–3), 261–93 was more pessimistic given Brinckmann's succumbing to dysentery in St Petersburg in 1785. A. Labisch, 'Einführung', in J. P. Brinckmann, *Patriotische Vorschläge* (Düsseldorf, 1997), 50–4.

[104] AHUB Personalakten Nr 30, a.O. Prof Olsen NSDAP Auslands-Organisation 14 July 1942 to Gaudozenten Führer Berlin; note of Dekan on visit from Olsen 12 May 1942; Zeiss to Rektor concerning discussions with Reiter 7 May 1943; DRK Führungsstab to Dekan of Medical Faculty Berlin 9 Oct. 1944; BDC file on Olsen.

[105] BDC party registration files; H. Haubold, *Krebs und Krebsbekämpfung in Frankreich* (Leipzig, 1936); H. Haubold, 'Zwischenstaatliche Zusammenarbeit. Wirken für die Gesundheit und den Aufbau des neuen Europa', *Die Gesundheitsführung. Ziel und Weg* (1942), 31–2; BAK R 86/ 4153 Bl. 53, 255. The address of the Auslandsabteilung was Berlin-Grunewald, Königsallee 62. Thom, 'Wandlungen', 429 for the disappearance of its archives.

From November 1939 Haubold was an SS officer, and from April 1940 served in the Waffen-SS, and from July 1941 in combat squads in the Balkans, Russia, and Finland; in April 1942 he became the doctor in charge of the Sonderkommando Gruppe Künsberg.[106] Haubold resumed administrative work for the foreign affairs department, attempting to win over peripheral states like Finland for the Nazi medical sphere. Haubold's scheme to regenerate European medicine demonstrates how the Nazi ideology of international health linked German medical science to the expansion of *Lebensraum* while subjugating French medical culture.[107]

Even amidst the disintegration towards the end of the war, Haubold clung onto his sense of a historical mission for German medicine, and in so doing was by no means untypical. He opened a final chapter on the attempt to assert the superiority of the German medical genius, when he took the anti-Semitic French author Céline under his wing in Berlin during 1944, so becoming a target of Céline's mordant satire. Haubold recruited Céline to assist in producing a propagandistic history of medical and scientific collaboration between France and Germany. Haubold saw the conquest of epidemics as a major achievement of this collaboration over many centuries, using the image of reducing the terror of the rider of the apocalypse who symbolized epidemics. Céline's heart sank at the futility of the task, rendered all the more absurd because diseases like typhus were all around. He nostalgically derided Haubold's work when compared to the intellectual calibre of the League of Nations, and vented his spleen on Haubold's project which showed which 'professeur fritz' was where and when, and what had been achieved.[108] Eventually, Haubold sent Céline as doctor in chief to the puppet French government in exile, when this was farcically detained at the Hohenzollern fortress of Sigmaringen—condemned by the acerbic Céline as a suburb of Katyń—they were prey to lice, fleas, and scabies, which were immune to all such ideological antidotes.

iv. From Hygiene to Racial Extermination: Joachim Mrugowsky and the Hygiene Institute of the Waffen-SS

How the SS fused medicine with ideas of race, history, and Germanic mythology raises crucial issues concerning the ideology, organization, and techniques of genocide. The SS developed a distinct medical organization to service its agenda. As a step towards tightening its stranglehold on military and civilian medicine, the Waffen-SS instituted a medical academy in 1936. Its cadets underwent eighteen months' training as SS officers, having completed their medical education at the University of Berlin. The SS provided military hospital facilities in Munich in 1937 and in Berlin in 1938, and a sanitary depot under a pharmacist and a food chemist. In 1938 the military medical officer in Berlin supported the founding of an SS

---

[106] BDC Haubold files. The Gruppe Künsberg undertook special operations and intelligence work in the Balkans and Greece.

[107] F. Vitoux, *Céline. A Biography* (New York, 1992), 406–12, 415–29.

[108] L. Céline, *Nord* (Paris, 1960), 142–5, 199. Céline (*alias* Destouches) had worked for the LNHO.

Hygiene Institute. SS doctors were stationed in university clinics for further training, special courses for SS sanitary personnel were provided, and the SS opened a
medical academy in Graz. These institutions gave SS medicine coherence in terms
of organization and tasks. SS doctors were responsible for heredity and reproduction, all aspects of health and medical care of the storm troopers, and were to disseminate a distinctive new style of medicine: the SS doctor was to strengthen both
the body and soul of the patient.

Since its origins the SS had given prominence to the racial health of recruits. The
Reich Peasant Leader Richard Walther Darré, advised by the eugenicist Lenz, established a racial office in 1931. Recruitment to the SS as a Nordic élite required medical
checks on height, weight, intelligence, ancestry, character, the qualities of the
spouse, and political attitudes; dental decay and poor eyesight were among dis-
qualifying factors.[109] SS hospitals and convalescent homes (including the notorious
Lebensborn homes for single mothers), and a department for psychology and neurology were part of the expanding web of special health care and medical institutes.
The blood group was tatooed on all SS troops from 1939, although Grawitz, the
powerful but dissipated Reichsarzt SS, was concerned about possible errors in mass
screening for the blood type. The SS waged a 'war of extermination' against micro-
organisms and disease vectors like rats, house flies, mosquitoes, and lice. Military
and racial activities became entwined as the sanitary experts of the Waffen-SS took
charge of the public health side of concentration camps, by attending to water supply,
sewerage, and control of insect and animal pests. War and genocide meant SS doctors
undertook periodic 'selections' of the sick and infirm, and in Auschwitz selected the
trainloads of human 'parasites', who were to go directly to the gas chambers.

Special sanitary regulations shielded the SS and police against the threats of
infection. The SS had their own rubbish dumps and latrines, and a battery of products and sanitary procedures protected them against flies, lice, and other insect
pests. The SS regulations favoured less toxic patent products like Morel's Rusla
powder, Lauseto, or the DDT-derivatives Gix and Gesarol which were non-
poisonous. Bedbugs received more radical treatment: they were gassed with Zyklon
B. For this the permission of the SS chief of hygiene was necessary, as—sinisterly—
the SS controlled the deployment of Zyklon. Only trained SS personnel were
allowed to disinfect SS and police premises.[110] The SS was continually extending its
powers in the medical sphere. For example, in July 1943 a 'hygienic-bacteriological
diagnostic laboratory for the SS and police' opened in Pfannenstiel's Hygiene Institute in Marburg.[111] The SS sustained its expansion by recruiting scientific experts
whose outlook was at times unorthodox on race and disease.

Mrugowsky, the head of the Hygiene Institute of the Waffen-SS, took a key role
in providing sanitary and bacteriological services for the SS. Mrugowsky's academic ties to Zeiss reinforced theories of the role of geographical factors in the

---

[109] Weindling, *Health, Race and German Politics*, 476–7; H. F. Ziegler, *Nazi Germany's New Aristocracy.
The SS Leadership, 1925–1939* (Princeton, NJ, 1989), 52–8 points out that the biological sifting of recruits
functioned very incompletely, and standards were rapidly diluted.

[110] *Die grössten Moskitos der Welt* (n.d., n.p.).   [111] Fischer, *Sanitätsdienst*, iv. 2222.

variation of diseases. He applied geo-medical theories to suppress the medical hazards in the occupied territories. The image of the convicted (and many untried) Nazi human vivisectors has been that of crude abusers of science. In overlooking their academic rationales, crucial links with public health and epidemiological research have been obscured.[112]

Mrugowsky fits into the pattern of a Nazi medical activist of the younger generation. He was born in 1905 and was a Protestant; his father, a physician, had been killed in the First World War. The early years after the war were tough, as at first he lacked the means to study. In 1930 he joined the Nazi Party and SA, but he transferred to the more disciplined and organized SS in 1931 which offered better career prospects. In 1932 he was dismissed for political reasons from his assistantship in the hospital at Küstrin—so qualifying him for rapid promotion in the SS after 1933. As assistant at the Hygiene Institute, Halle, he conducted bacteriological examinations and directed a state school for disinfectors, gaining expertise in disinfection techniques.[113] From 1935 until the end of 1936 he served as a political security officer for the SS. He encountered a range of solidaristic theories of the state including the Catholic conservative ideas of Othmar Spann.[114] Mrugowsky's task in rooting out political heresies contaminated him with a strain of unorthodoxy. His underlings included such ambivalent spirits as the sanitary engineer Kurt Gerstein and the Auschwitz physician Hans Münch. The prisoners recruited to work in the concentration camp research stations had a curious affinity with some of Mrugowsky's ideas—for example, Eugen Kogon, the convict-secretary at the Buchenwald experimental station was also influenced by Spann.

Mrugowsky's sense of closeness to nature aroused his interest in botany; he armed himself with doctorates in botany and medicine. His medical dissertation pointed to the dangers in contracting infections when handling corpses, despite the use of disinfectants, and (significantly given his lethal role in human experiments) he infected himself with Bang's disease to study its effects.[115] As a medical student in Halle between 1925 and 1931, Mrugowsky had the same botanical teacher as Himmler and Darré, Valentin Haecker, a geneticist, and conducted ecological field-work on the Kyffhäuser mountain, which was renowned as the burial place of a mythical German Emperor.[116]

[112] Bayle, *Croix gammée*, 246–58, 283–4 for a psychological analysis. S. Sterkowicz, 'Lekarz ludobójaca, Joachim Mrugowsky', *Przegląd Lekarski*, 44 (1987), 126–7 differentiates Mrugowsky from the norms of extreme cruelty of SS doctors. P. J. Weindling, 'Die weltanschaulichen Hintergründe der Fleckfieberbekämpfung im Zweiten Weltkrieg', in C. Meinel and P. Voswinckel (eds.), *Medizin, Naturwissenschaft, Technik und Nationalsozialismus—Kontinuitäten und Diskontinuitäten* (Stuttgart, 1994), 129–35; Hansen, 'Biologische Kriegsführung', 72–3.

[113] J. Mrugowsky, 'Über die Desinfektion bei Infektionskrankheiten in der täglichen Praxis', *Der Öffentliche Gesundheitsdienst*, 1 (1936), 817–23; W. Kaiser and A. Völker, 'Die faschistischen Strömungen an der Medizinischen Fakultät der Universität Halle', A. Thom and H. Spaar (eds.), *Medizin im Faschismus* (Berlin, 1983), 53–67; W. Kaiser, K. Renker, and K. Werner, 'Die territoriale Früh- und Vorgeschichte der Aufgaben des halleschen Hygiene-Instituts', *Zeitschrift für die gesamte Hygiene*, 24 (1978), 708–22.

[114] NAW Microfilm Publication 1019 roll 47 Mrugowsky interrogation, first session. Kogon, prisoner-secretary of Ding in Buchenwald, had completed a doctorate under Spann.

[115] J. Mrugowsky, *Über den Bakteriengehalt von Anatomie-Leichen* (Halle, 1933).

[116] On the Kyffhäuser myth see N. Cohn, *The Pursuit of the Millennium* (London, 1957).

Mrugowsky applied his botanical studies of the ecology and sociology of plant communities to teaching racial hygiene. He was an enthusiastic convert to geo-medicine, and saw that by modernizing Pettenkofer's environmentalism he could provide a critique of Koch's bacteriology: he argued that hygiene involved study of the interactions of the living with their environmental *Umwelt*.[117] His bio-geographical approach to the social problems of the Mansfeld miners who lived in villages to the east of the Harz mountains was geared to the Nazi policy of moving industry to rural areas. In line with Nazi views of dynamic and holistic science, he constantly criticized Koch's bacteriology as narrow in its concern with infectious pathogens rather than with the totality of physical, social, cultural, historical, and geographical factors shaping health. Reichsarzt SS Grawitz introduced Mrugowsky's exercise in holistic health care, praising this rising star among SS doctors.[118]

From 1937 a new chapter opened in Mrugowsky's life, as he qualified as a military doctor, and joined the sanitary division of the SS. The Waffen-SS opened a disinfection training establishment in the Oranienburg complex of offices, prisons, and the concentration camp, where the DRK already provided training in disinfection and gas protection. Mrugowsky was appointed head of the Office for Bacteriology and Hygiene of the Waffen-SS in 1938, and from 1940 achieved a full-scale Institute.[119] That the training in tropical medicine provided by the Waffen-SS included a period at the nearby concentration camp of Sachsenhausen indicates how such camps were regarded as routine training facilities.[120]

Mrugowsky gained a foothold at the Institute of Hygiene at Berlin University, while Zeiss acquired a powerful ally in the SS.[121] In January 1939 Zeiss secured the Privatdozent title for Mrugowsky.[122] Although Zeiss was not an SS member—and indeed had some difficulties with the NSDAP over cremation, Mrugowsky's arrival provided Zeiss with a useful ally. Mrugowsky's qualifying lecture on 'Race and Disease in the German South-East' focused on the Sudetenland.[123] This topic marked a transition from domestic sanitary measures targeted at a grouping with a socially radical reputation—the Mansfeld miners—to issues associated with the

[117] J. Mrugowsky, 'Die Formation der Gipspflanzen. Beiträge zu ihrer Ökologie und Soziologie', Dr Sc nat. diss. Halle, 26 Feb. 1930. The work focused on limestone areas; Mrugowsky, 'Hygienische Untersuchungen in einem Mansfeldischen Bergmannsdorf', Greifswald, 1938. This was Mrugowsky's Habilitation thesis, Kater, *Doctors*, 131.

[118] J. Mrugowsky, *Biologie eines Mansfeldschen Bergmannsdorfes* (Berlin, n.d. [1938]); id., 'Zur Hygiene ländlicher Arbeiterwohnungen', *Zeitschrift für Hygiene*, 120 (1938), 402–504. For a similar exchange see E. Martini, 'Bemerkungen zu Friedrich Wolters Schrift: Über das Fleckfieber als Kriegsseuche', *Zeitschrift für hygienische Zoologie*, 35 (1943), 105–19.

[119] The address in 1940 was Berlin W 15, Knesebeckstrasse 43–4, where the main sanitary office of the SS was located until at least May 1943. The Institute then moved to Berlin-Zehlendorf 6, Spanische Allee 10–12.

[120] AHUB Hygienisches Institut Nr 3 Bl. 99–117. There was also a period at the Institute of Tropical Medicine, Amsterdam.

[121] AHUB Universitätskurator Personalakten Joachim Mrugowsky UK-Pers. G 259 Bd III.

[122] AHUB Hygienisches Institut Nr 42 Bl. 207 Zeiss to Mrugowsky 9 June 1939; Zeiss to Dean of the Medical Faculty 9 Jan. and 12 Jan. 1939.

[123] 'Volkstämme und Krankheiten im deutschen Südostraum', AHUB Hygienisches Institut Nr 42 Bl. 230 Zeiss to Mrugowsky 5 May 1939.

expansion of German *Lebensraum*. Mrugowsky's immunology was linked to living conditions, according with the Nazi medical dictate that hygiene was to be geared to practice.

Racialized concepts of *Lebensraum* shaped technologies of disinfection and pest control, as well as academic theories of medical geography. Mrugowsky, Rodenwaldt, and Zeiss drew on the geo-political ideas of Haushofer, and the dynamic spatial concepts of Nazi geographers and environmentalists in developing concepts of 'geo-medicine' and 'geo-epidemiology'.[124] Zeiss linked geo-medicine to the Nazi ideology of 'blood and soil', while arguing that the new science should predict epidemics and diseases. Great epidemics like cholera had an individual life history (a view akin to that developed by Zinsser for the history of typhus). Heroic medical researchers grappled with demonic diseases, which meant that the 'east' (or *Ostraum*) opened up extensive prospects for geo-medical research.[125]

Geo-medicine replaced individualistic health care with notions of the interaction of mankind and the environment: the raising of the body's physical capacities (*Leistungsfähigkeit*) would prevent diseases.[126] The reverse side of positive health measures was the elimination of disease-producing threats: geo-medical studies pointed to Eastern Europe and Asia as the origins for infectious diseases threatening the rest of Europe.[127] The linkage between military strategy and medicine can be seen in the Institute of Medical Zoology at Riga, which was supported by Mrugowsky. Here Fritz Steiniger pursued a geographical and environmentalist approach to disease control.[128] Rodenwaldt's research on acclimatization of Europeans to the tropics and on the geo-medicine of a locality, and Rose's studies of mosquito distribution provide other environmentalist examples.[129]

Mrugowsky ambitiously expanded the functions of his institute and gained promotion. Reichsarzt SS Grawitz had ultimate responsibility for sanitary and health matters within the SS, as well as for directing medical research and planning. The medical cadres of the Waffen-SS steadily assumed greater powers within the SS and more broadly in public health. The organizational complexity and conflict within the SS triggered off power struggles between key medical officers and associated cliques. Grawitz had no technical staff or laboratories, and he relied on subordinate organizations and services in the SS directorate. The Hygiene Institute of the Waffen-SS, nominally under Carl Genzken's medical office, provided technical services: Mrugowsky's Hygiene Institute and an associated Sanitary Office

---

[124] H. Zeiss, 'Die Notwendigkeit einer deutschen Geomedizin', *Zeitschrift für Geopolitik*, vol. 9 (1932), 474–84; AHUB Hygienisches Institut Nr 189, Bl. 33, 35, 36 on Zeiss maintaining contacts with Haushofer in 1944.

[125] H. Zeiss, 'Die Geomedizin des Ostraumes', *Grenzmärkische Forschungen*, 1 (1939), 42–57.

[126] BAK NS 31/ 183 statement made in 1937 concerning SS medicine at Hohenlychen, etc.

[127] BAK R6/ 387 Dr Waegner, memorandum on the Ostgebieten and Jewish doctors, 1941.

[128] BAK R 90/ 352 Report of Institute of Medical Zoology, 11 Mar. 1944. Steiniger edited a *Zeitschrift für medizinische Geographie*.

[129] BAK R 73/14064 Rose, 73/14014 Rodenwaldt.

serviced the SS as a whole, and reinforced the military medical services of the Wehrmacht.[130]

As 'leading hygienist' in the SS, Mrugowsky was responsible to Grawitz, and from September 1943 the medical organization in the SS became more tightly organized. Mrugowsky—having elbowed Genzken aside—was transferred from the central directorate of the SS to the staff of Grawitz with the title of 'chief hygienist'. Mrugowsky went on to challenge the position of Grawitz as chief SS doctor, while retaining dual military links to the sanitary services of the army.[131] These organizational complexities remained difficult to unravel, when Mrugowsky was interrogated after the war at Nuremberg.

The SS accelerated the deaths of concentration camp prisoners from starvation, harsh work regimes, and overcrowding: but SS hygienists feared that the atrocious conditions would generate epidemic infections, which could be lethal to the camp staff and could spread beyond the camps. The expanding responsibilities of Mrugowsky's Hygiene Institute of the Waffen-SS illustrate how energetic medical figures extended their power. Mrugowsky's Hygiene Institute had a staff of 200 and several departments, providing a vast range of services and research skills: his academic armoury included bacteriology and serology, sanitation, pest eradication and medical zoology, chemistry, geology and hydrology, climatology, statistics, and hereditary or constitutional medicine.[132]In order to determine the range of factors affecting the spread of epidemics, among the ranks of the Institute's staff was an engineer to devise delousing equipment (this was Gerstein), a geographer (Kurt Scharlau who headed the section for climatology and cultural geography), a geologist, several zoologists, a botanist, a mathematician, and protein chemists.[133] In 1941 the Institute supplied the SS with three field laboratories and a contingent of forty SS doctors for deployment in the east. By 1942 the Institute spread its academic tentacles by setting up outposts: a department of blood conservation in Frankfurt am Main; an institute for virology and typhus in Buchenwald and a hygiene institute for serological testing in Auschwitz (subsequently relocated to Raisko, just outside the camp); hygiene and vaccine production institutes in Dorpat, Kauen, and Minsk; and a mobile delousing unit in a specially equipped train.[134] Mrugowsky secured a permanent site for the Middle Ukraine laboratory in the bacteriological institute of the Ukrainian Academy of Sciences, and established another laboratory as the Bacteriological-Hygiene Institute for the *Ostland*, based at the Technical

---

[130] NAW, M887 Nuremberg Medical Trial (hereafter NMT) roll 30, frame 658, evidence of Erwin Filling who in 1944 was successor to Murthum as in charge of hygiene in the Sanitary Office of the Waffen SS; frames 664–8 evidence of Adolf Murthum.

[131] NMT roll 30 Blumenreuther testimony, Mrugowsky defence file.

[132] AHUB Personal file of Mrugowsky. NMT roll 38, frame 876.

[133] NMT roll 30, frame 691 testimony of Scharlau, frame 723–7 testimony of Fritz Krantz the geologist. K. Scharlau, 'Bioklimatische Beobachtungen aus den südrussischen Steppen', *Archiv für Hygiene und Bakteriologie*, 128 (1942), 260–80.

[134] AHUB Hygienisches Institut Nr 192 Bl. 244–7 Arbeitsberichts des Hygiene-Institutes 1941; BAK R 21/11061 Bl. 21 Zahn to RMdI 1 Aug. 1942 on serum institutes in the east, Bl. 24–25 memorandum 'Neuordnung des Serumgeschäfts', listing serum institutes in the east.

University of Riga.[135] These acted as centres for suppressing mosquitoes and other insect foes. He gained control of the captured anti-malaria stations in the Ukraine. The Ahnenerbe research organization of the SS and the Hygiene Institute of the Waffen-SS supported an Institute for Medical Entomology under Eduard May at Riga in 1942.[136] Mrugowsky's research organization steadily increased his powers, responsibilities, and spheres of influence.

The Hygiene Institute carried out a variety of tasks for the military forces and the concentration camps. Mrugowsky drew up practical manuals for sanitary provision for combat units, regarding whether water might be safe to drink, and tested the water supply at Buchenwald, Dachau, Auschwitz, and Neuengamme concentration camps. He also supervised medical conditions in armaments factories sited in mines, and staffed by forced labour. Mrugowsky was at the Auschwitz concentration camp in 1943 and 1944 to advise on typhus and water supply problems.[137] Although each concentration camp had its own medical and sanitary service under the SS physician Enno Lolling, Mrugowsky advised on special health problems in the camps. This was a crucial task, for it was important that infections did not spread to the SS, camp guards, or to surrounding areas. Mrugowsky's Hygiene Institute liaised with the Waffen-SS Buildings Division, which was responsible for delousing and sanitary installations in the concentration and extermination camps.[138] Mrugowsky dealt with a paratyphoid epidemic in Buchenwald early in 1939, when it was alleged that he executed those whom he considered could not recover.[139] His Institute undertook blood-group testing and serological research into syphilis, and stressed prevention of epidemics and isolation to break the cycle of infection by insect vectors for malaria, typhus, and 'Wolhynian fever'.[140] Geo-medical ideology underpinned Mrugowky's practical work on pest eradication, as on the combating of disease carrying midges in the Ukraine.[141]

Settlement by German stock was to come in the wake of mass 'clearance' of those deemed racial undesirables. The Generalplan Ost and racial resettlement schemes provided a major theatre of operations for biologically minded population experts in the German programme of conquest and genocide.[142] Maintaining the health of German settlers in the Ukraine and other eastern areas required support of the German Hygiene Institute in Kiev. Mrugowsky's staff drew up plans for the repatriation of the estimated 350,000 Volga Germans, as their hardy Germanic character

---

[135] NAW M 1019/roll 47 Mrugowsky interrogation 27 Aug. 1946; The Kiev Institute was under Andreas Schuller. Mrugowsky testified to having visited the Institute at least three times, when inspecting sanitary conditions in the Ukraine.

[136] BDC 468–625 Ahnenerbe to Mrugowsky 23 Nov. 1942.

[137] J. Mrugowsky, *Untersuchung und Beurteilung von Wasser und Brunnen an Ort und Stelle* (Berlin, 1941); NAW, M 1019 roll 47, Mrugowsky interrogation, 25 July 1946; Letter from Hans Münch to the author, 25 Apr. 1997.

[138] Pressac, *Auschwitz*, 71.   [139] Bayle, *Croix gammée*, 279–80.

[140] AHUB Hygienisches Institut Nr 192, Bl. 244–57 Report of the Hygiene Institut d. Waffen SS, dated 1941. NMT Mrugowsky defence pp. 35–6, microfilm 30 evidence of Oswald Pohl.

[141] BDC SS-HO 1–217 Report of 12 Sept. 1944 Mrugowsky to Grawitz.

[142] G. Aly, *'Endlösung'. Völkerverschiebung und der Mord an den europäischen Juden* (Frankfurt/M., 1995).

and fertility were a potential asset to the Reich.[143] He examined 200,000 repatriated ethnic Germans from the east for syphilis and infectious diseases under the 'Heim ins Reich' scheme. Conti stressed how Mrugowsky's rigorous medical controls and delousing prevented an epidemic catastrophe arising from the resettlement of over 600,000 ethnic Germans.[144]

The disinfection expert Gerstein joined the entomologist May in Riga to supervise disinfection squads. Technically innovative but tormented by his complicity in genocide, Gerstein equipped a delousing train for emergencies arising from the shifting tides of population transfers and epidemic flare-ups. Gerstein was praised for his technological ingenuity, which meant that the Waffen-SS had its own sanitary equipment unlike the Wehrmacht which depended on private firms. Gerstein's dynamism was consistent with Mrugowsky's plans to expand his institute so that it should become central for all military hygiene.[145]

That the ranks of this key SS installation contained the ambivalent Gerstein and the convoluted Hans Münch (of whom more in chapter 11) suggests that Mrugowsky's geo-epidemiology cannot be seen as simply an extension of SS Nordic racism. The bacteriologist Münch claimed that he attenuated the excesses of genocidal bacteriology while at the Raisko branch of the Hygiene Institute of the Waffen-SS near Auschwitz. Under Mrugowsky's command, this Institute had routine functions for the surrounding area, including the concentration camp at Gross-Rosen. The primary role of the Raisko Institute was to assist with the control of infectious diseases in Auschwitz and to serve as a camp experimental centre. Although situated five kilometres outside Auschwitz, it was an integral part of the regime of forced labour and extermination. The director of the institute, Bruno Weber, collected human tissue from executed persons to make bacterial cultures, while profiting from his allocation of laboratory animals. His assistant, Münch, visited the Auschwitz prisoner hospital, where being diagnosed as a typhus case could mean dispatch to the gas chambers. Revolted by brutal X-ray sterilization experiments and operations on the uterus by Clauberg and Schumann, Münch established a benign experimental programme, which was life-saving rather than destroying. Yet he also conducted more hazardous and probably lethal experiments in malaria and tetanus, and examined body parts sent by Mengele. His case well illustrates the ambiguities of hygiene as central to the Holocaust, but also as

[143] AHUB Hygienisches Institut Nr 189, Bl. 67–9 Fischer, 'Kurzer Bericht über meine Reise in die Ukraine, im Auftrag des Hygiene Instituts der Waffen-SS', 16 June–July 1943; Bl. 162–78 'Zur Frage der Rücksiedlung der deutschen Bauern an der Wolga'; Thom, 'Wandlungen', 445; Dallin, *German Rule*, 52, 94, 251, 288–9. For German surveys of the Russian Germans in 1941–2 in occupied districts see R. H. Walth, *Strandgut der Weltgeschichte. Die Russlanddeutschen zwischen Stalin und Hitler* (Essen, 1994). How the Kiev hygiene institute related to the genocidal pathological institute in Kiev is not clear; see Breitman, *Himmler*, 181.

[144] NAW T 175 roll 69 14 Aug. 1942, Conti memo to Himmler (also BAK NS 19/ 1591). Also Conti in *Filmarchiv der Persönlichkeiten*, BA Berlin.

[145] AHUB Hygienisches Institut Nr 192 Report of the Hygiene Institut der Waffen-SS 1941 Bl. 252. BAP 11.03 Reichsministerium für die besetzten Ostgebieten II.2 K45 19 Nov. 1942 concerning delousing ovens in Tauroggen und Wirballen. EKvW 5,2 NS Nr 246 Hygiene Institut der Waffen-SS Beurteilung 19 Feb. 1943.

sporadically detached and differentiated. He refused at one stage to undertake selections in Auschwitz, and gained Mrugowsky's backing for his stance to resist the directives of Lolling as the medical superintendent of the camps. Yet he has recently confessed to then carrying out selections for the gas chamber. While the Hygiene Institute of the Waffen-SS shows how preventive medicine and genocide were inextricably linked, there were deviant counter-currents.[146]

While a case can be made for interpreting Mrugowsky's activities within a distinctively medical set of rationales, there is no worthwhile evidence for him as a dissident. His military and SS identity, and demonic sense of duty to the Nazi cause were overwhelming. Yet he stubbornly kept his Polish name (to Himmler's annoyance), had his children baptized, and was known to distribute minor goodies like cigarettes to prisoners.[147] He argued that he sited the hygiene institutes in Buchenwald and Raisko so as to make use of 'the first-class specialists among the prisoners', although he did not go so far as to say that the Institutes could take on a life-sustaining role.[148] Academic distinction and redeemingly humane gestures should not obscure genocidal complicity: dedication to medical research supported and at times increased the scientized slaughter. Mrugowsky's Hygiene Institute supplied cultures of infections like gas oedema to Ravensbrück where they were used to infect wounds deliberately inflicted on prisoners to test whether sulpha drugs had any therapeutic effect. This programme was supported by Himmler, concerned that Reinhard Heydrich had died from wound infections resulting from the bomb blast. Mrugowsky was to deny personal knowledge of supplying the cultures for the Ravensbrück experiments.[149] But he was compromised by having overall responsibility for typhus research in Buchenwald, where human experiments were conducted on different types of vaccines. He evaluated the 'experimental' use of bullets poisoned with acontine (a highly toxic substance similar in composition to nerve gases).[150] While he was condemned to death for complicity in acts of hands-on murder at the Nuremberg Medical Trial, it is important not to lose sight of Mrugowsky's medical priorities and dedication to the strategic aims of the SS.

Mrugowsky took a key role in supervising the control of epidemics in concentration camps and in the eastern campaign. From 1942 (according to the evidence of Gerstein and the Auschwitz commandant Höss), Mrugowsky's Hygiene Institute allocated supplies of Zyklon. In his post-war history of typhus prevention, he wrote that only once did he delouse a *Barrackenlager* with Zyklon.[151] Early in 1942 Gerhard Peters, the managing director of DEGESCH, solicited Mrugowsky's

---

[146] L. Shelley, *Criminal Experiments on Human Beings in Auschwitz and War Research Laboratories. Twenty Women Prisoners' Accounts* (San Francisco, Calif., 1991), 139, 275–316. Bruno Schirra personal communications. Claude Romney, personal communications.

[147] Sterkowicz, 'Lekarz ludobójca', 126–7.

[148] NAW M 1019/roll 47 Mrugowsky interrogation 17 Oct. 1946, p. 3.   [149] Ibid.

[150] R. Harris and J. Paxman, *A Higher Form of Killing: The Secret Story of Chemical and Biological Warfare* (New York, 1982), 60–1.

[151] Mrugowsky denied the supply of Zyklon to Auschwitz for genocide. See NMT roll 38, frames 1156–9; NAW M 1019/roll 47 Mrugowsky interrogation, 23 Sept. 1946. Mrugowsky, MS history of typhus in the Second World War. I am grateful to Dr Gertraud Rudat for allowing me to consult this important source. A full evaluation will be possible once Dr Rudat has completed transcription.

support for a wider use of Zyklon for delousing. Peters had marketed a new form of gas chamber using a circulatory system, which Mrugowsky endorsed.[152] Tins of Zyklon in crystalline form were more convenient to handle and to store than carbon monoxide used in liquid form in the T4 euthanasia killings, and more efficient than diesel engine fumes in the gas chambers of the Sobibor and Treblinka extermination camps. Mrugowsky later testified that the supplies were solely for delousing and epidemic prevention, that he personally did not calculate the Zyklon allocations for the camps, and that the threat of typhus was the main factor in determining the amount supplied. Set against such protestations of innocence was the case that his Institute took the key role in seeking the removal of the warning agent from Zyklon, apparently received some dental gold of murdered victims, spawned a network of satellite institutions in the conquered eastern territories, and carried out 'experimental' research in concentration camps.[153] Preventive medicine, research, and extermination were intertwined.

In addition to inspecting concentration camps, Mrugowsky was on the Eastern Front in June 1941 as well as during the flare-up of typhus from December 1941 to January 1942. From October 1941 he was medical adviser to Rosenberg's Ministry for the Occupied Eastern Territories.[154] He took the lead in combating typhus in the winter of 1941, claiming to have defeated its advance in Lithuania and Belarus. His strategic powers were ratified on 15 January 1942 when he was appointed 'Seuchenkommissar für das Ostland'. Although other officials dealt with typhus prevention in Germany and occupied Poland, Mrugowsky's disease-eradication measures were hailed as saving Germany from a catastrophic typhus epidemic.[155]

The genocidal viciousness of epidemiology intensified in the second half of 1941, when typhus was perceived as a threat to German racial health. The invasion of the Soviet Union brought not only increasing military difficulties, but also a range of epidemic hazards. By the winter of 1941–2 the typhus epidemic was a major problem in Russia and the Generalgouvernement, and there were isolated outbreaks in Germany. With Hitler frustrated at the lack of a military knockout blow against the Soviet Union, the resurgence of typhus added to the difficulties of maintaining supplies and equipment.[156] Prediction and prevention were the leitmotif of Mrugowsky, as he issued quarterly bulletins forecasting epidemics in the half-year to come.[157] Sanitary codes for SS units show the genocidal role of preventive medicine with the warning that all civilians were potential typhus carriers—thus justifying their extermination.[158] The military medical officer, Felix von Bormann, considered that

[152] Gerhard Peters deposition, defence testimonies Mrugowsky, 16–18, NMT roll 30.

[153] NAW M 1019/roll 47 Mrugowsky interrogation, summary; also 17 Oct. 1946, 17–18.

[154] AHUB Mrugowsky personal file, Mrugowsky to Dean 25 June 1941 concerning his transfer to the Eastern Front.

[155] AHUB Personal file Mrugowsky, Reich Ministerium für Wissenschaft, Erziehung und Volksbildung to Dekan 18 June 1942.

[156] For the military context of the Holocaust see Burrin, *Hitler and the Jews*.

[157] AHUB Personal file Mrugowsky, Bl. 57 bibliography, p. 4.

[158] BAK R NS 33/ 167 Bl. 23 Merkblatt für Absonderungsmassnahmen und Behandlung von Dauerausscheiden und Keimträgern bei den wichtigsten ansteckenden Krankheiten im Kriege; AHUB Hygienisches Institut Nr 42, Bl. 232–4 Report on Prevention of Infectious Diseases by Hygienisches Institut der Waffen-SS.

eradication of typhus among the civilian population in Russia was fundamental to prevention of typhus among the troops.[159] Despite such crude prescriptions, Mrugowsky's epidemiological studies and clinical observations on typhus among German, Polish, and Jewish patients deployed sophisticated medical, statistical, and geographical methods for racial ends. He characterized Jewish patients as often having few of the normal symptoms of typhus; this explained the vulnerability of the more civilized German to the Jewish and Slav carriers of lethal parasites.[160] Epidemiology and immunology fused with racial stereotypes.

Mrugowsky advised the Ostministerium chief medical officer, Harald Waegner: again, Mrugowsky stood on the margins of the Holocaust as Waegner had a key role in working on epidemic control and racial welfare with chief military medical officer Handloser, Reich Health Führer Conti, and Hitler's accompanying surgeon, Karl Brandt. Tough anti-epidemic measures in the east were to protect the racial health of ethnic Germans. By early 1943, although Himmler was convinced that Waegner was unsuited to further work in disease suppression, attempts to move him to frontline service in a death's head division of the Waffen-SS were countered by arguments over the strategic importance of Waegner's position. Mrugowsky contrasted with the action-oriented crudeness of a frontline medical officer. After the war Mrugowsky pointed out to his interrogators that Waegner, who had seen frontline service in France, the Netherlands, and the Balkans, was involved in the killing of Poles, Jews, and Ukrainians.[161]

Mrugowsky saw typhus prevention in the context of a vast system of geographical epidemiology. The border with the east was a cultural divide: he correlated the racial threat of the Slavs with high rates of typhus, typhoid, and dysentery in Russia and Lithuania, but argued that Latvia and Estonia had epidemiological similarities to the Reich. He considered that control of the cities of Warsaw, Lublin, and Lemberg, which were crucial for communications to Ukraine and Belarus, was essential for preventing epidemic threats from the east. Natural features like Lake Peipus between Estonia and Russia were strategic bulwarks against epidemics. He argued that European Russia between the Baltic and the Black Sea constituted a distinctive medical and geographical entity; its cultural, ethnic, and epidemiological characteristics coincided. He concluded that typhus was a *Gemeinschaftskrankheit*, in which all racial inferiors were germ carriers.[162] A geographically oriented epidemiology took a key role in combating 'Asiatic threats' of epidemic infections by condemning Jews, slavs, and gypsies as disease carriers.

[159] BA-MA H 20/ 518 von Bormann report on the period 31 Dec. 1943–15 May 1944.

[160] J. Mrugowsky, 'Typischer und atypischer Krankheitsverlauf beim Fleckfieber', *Medizinische Klinik*, 38 (1942), 192–6, 221–3.

[161] NAW Captured German documents, SS membership, Harald Waegner, note of SS-Richter beim Reichsführer-SS, 8 Feb. 1943. Mrugowsky to SS-Führungshauptamt 23 Nov. 1943. NAW M1019 roll 47 Mrugowsky Vernehmung 27 Aug. 1946, 8.

[162] J. Mrugowsky, 'Die Seuchenlage in europäischen Russland', *Medizinische Klinik*, 38 (1942), 625–9, summarized in *Bulletin of War Medicine*, 1 (1942), 212–13. For germ warfare implications see Hansen, *Biologische Kriegsführung*, 159.

While providing medical support for eastern combat units, and facilitating the deployment of Zyklon in the extermination camps, Mrugowsky's practices drew on heterodox ideas. Rather than seeking slavishly to conform to conventional Nazi rhetoric, he sought alternative biological and philosophical rationales in national scientific and intellectual traditions. He supported an environmentalist approach to disease derived from historical accounts of pre-bacteriological medical literature such as those by the nineteenth-century medical authorities Wilhelm Griesinger and Charles Murchison, who emphasized clinical observation. Mrugowsky did not restrict his focus to micro-organisms and vaccines, but he carefully observed the clinical course of typhus. He rejected notions of new diseases like 'Bessarabian fever' or 'Ukrainian fever' named according to geographic locality. On the other hand, he was sceptical of laboratory evidence, considering that negative results of a bacteriological or serological test or the lack of an expected agent of transmission were insufficient to explain disease outbreaks. He observed how 'our soldiers in the Russian arena react differently from the indigenous populations.' He publicized notions of prevention based on prediction with the periodicity of epidemics due to seasonality and changing virulence. Mrugowsky's wide-ranging knowledge of the environmental, geographical, and biological aspects of disease bore fruit in a treatise on the control of epidemics; the book was left unpublished because of his post-war arrest, trial, and execution.[163]

Mrugowsky perceived typhus as a complex constellation, or *Gestalt*. This invocation of *Gestalt* theory went with an emphasis on vitalism and the holistic thought of the Hamburg philosopher Adolf Meyer-Abich, who testified that scientific principles meant more to Mrugowsky than those of the NSDAP. Mrugowsky's holism was developed in studies of the romantic thought and literature of Friedrich Hölderlin and August Wilhelm von Schlegel, and in an edition of an ethical work, *Das ärztliche Ethos*, by the eighteenth-century German physician C. W. Hufeland. He admired Hufeland's concept of a *Lebenskraft* and of healing by supporting nature, and he applied these to the notion of an epidemic constitution. He was fascinated by the nineteenth-century romantic bio-geographer Alexander von Humboldt, and endorsed a renaissance of neo-Hippocratic environmentalist notions in the form of geo-medicine. He considered that bacteriologists should ally with physicians in a mission to promote a larger healing process of the *Volk*. Although Mrugowsky and his heterogeneous group of subordinates drew on distinctive medical rationales, they ultimately conformed to Hitler's vision of the bacteriologist as engaged in a racial struggle.[164]

Instead of the expected icons of Hitler and Himmler, in his office hung a picture of Virchow, venerated as a critic of bacteriology and as a sanitary reformer rather

---

[163] J. Mrugowsky, 'Impfschaden nach Fleckfieberschutzimpfung', *Deutsche medizinische Wochenschrift*, 69 (1943), 447–8; NMT roll 34, frame 80 for Mrugowsky's publications; id., *Zeitschrift für Hygiene*, 123 (1941), 361. Mrugowsky's ideas of epidemic prediction were publicized at the opening ceremony of the Behring Institute Lemberg, and widely reported in the German press; see Behring-Archiv, Lemberg red file.

[164] Lifton, *Nazi Doctors*, 31–3.

than as a noted liberal.[165] Race and its medical extensions were neither administratively nor ideologically monolithic. The eugenicist Fritz Lenz criticized
Mrugowsky for advocating Meyer-Abich's Lamarckian holism by arguing that
infections were an environmental cause of mutations. Critics in the SS denounced
holism as crypto-Roman Catholicism (much importance was attached to the
middle syllable of 'CatHOLic').[166] In June 1942 Lenz resisted Mrugowsky's promotion at the Berlin university to the rank of professor, arguing that his services in
combating typhus on the eastern front were insufficient for an academic honour.
Lenz opposed Mrugowsky's vitalism and *Umwelt* theory as inconsistent with a
genetically based racial hygiene. He denounced Mrugowsky's version of racial
hygiene—the extermination of sick genes (*Anlagen*)—as much too narrow.[167] Zeiss
(from his more environmentalist perspective) proclaimed that Mrugowsky's geo-
medicine approach to epidemiology was the best way forward for the future
science of hygiene.[168] Although the prevention of sick genes came into conflict with
the hygienic ideology of clearance and disinfection, both racial and environmental
hygiene could serve Nazi ends.

While SS academics forced their way into controlling positions in universities
and in the German Research Council, the ranks of SS doctors included racial
mystics, genetic reductionists, advocates of herbal medicines, and sponsors of
industrially produced drugs and vaccines. The coexistence of diverse strands
within the SS strengthened its power. Mrugowsky claimed that he 'never was the
"typical SS man"', and became able to view Hitler from a critical distance.[169] Yet he
believed in the concept of a racial parasite, and he applied this to the biological
basis of psychology. In 1936 Mrugowsky attacked what he characterized as the cal-
culating rationalism of Jewish frontline soldiers in the First World War. He tore
into a recently published collection of Jewish soldiers' patriotic letters, denouncing
them for their ideals of fraternity, equality, and individualism, and as lacking a
racial sense of German national identity. During the war Mrugowsky targeted Jews
as carriers of lethal germs, indicating that he sustained his medicalized view of the
Jew as pathological.[170]

Capable of anti-Semitic outbursts, the question arises whether Mrugowsky supported the elimination of the Jewish race. On the one hand, Mrugowsky did not
launch (at least in print) into ideological tirades against the extermination of
Jewish racial parasites. On the other, his notions of preventive medicine legiti-

[165] NMT roll 30, frame 601 for Mrugowsky's studies of romanticism; frames 633–9 testimony of
Meyer-Abich on behalf of Mrugowsky; frames 724–30 testimony of Fritz Krantz.

[166] NMT roll 30, 642–9 Mitteilungen zur weltanschaulichen Lage. Der Beauftragte des Führers für die
Überwachung der gesamten geistigen und weltanschaulichen Erziehung der NSDAP, 27 Nov. 1936.

[167] AHUB Personalakt Mrugowsky, Lenz to Dekan 6 July 1942. The professor title was conferred in
1944.

[168] AHUB Personalakt Mrugowsky, Zeiss to Dekan 13 July 1942.

[169] NMT roll 46, frame 601 Clemency plea Mrugowsky.

[170] J. Mrugowsky, 'Jüdisches und deutsches Soldatentum. Ein Beitrag zur Rassenseelenforschung', *NS
Monatshefte*, 7/76 (1936), 635–8. After the German defeat in 1945, Mrugowsky analysed Hitler's messianic
beliefs and why Hitler demonized the Jews: STAN KV Ankl. Interrrogations Nr M 104 'Zur psychiatrischen und psychologischen Beurteilung Hitlers und seiner Lehre'.

mated genocide as he inspected the concentration camps of Auschwitz and Buchenwald, and toured installations in the east. Gerstein's tormented conscience well shows how such tours of duty brought full awareness of the Holocaust. Mrugowsky was well aware of genocide as he assisted Münch in evading duty on the selections at Auschwitz. As Mrugowsky had some sympathy with the stress on a physician involved in such a task, he cannot have been blind to the atrocious conditions of the camps. Mrugowsky later defended himself by clinging to a strictly defined sanitary brief that his medical activities were solely in support of the Waffen-SS; he concealed that his anti-epidemic measures against typhus had racial implications.[171]

Mrugowsky's sanitary institute was part of a network providing materials and assistance to the extermination camps and squads. The conventional view that the 'technical' implementation of the Final Solution was carried out by very small staffs, implies that Nazi genocide was a mere working out of the logic of genocidal policies. It is assumed that the techniques of mass killing were easy to organize. While the historian Hans Mommsen has recognized that 'Technocratic and subordinate attitudes could be as important as blind racialism or the mere parroting of national socialist anti-Jewish cliches', there remains a gulf between the anti-epidemic measures and their harnessing to the machinery of extermination. Race and its medical extensions were neither administratively nor ideologically monolithic. How distinctive ideologies motivated the technocrats, and the diversity of technical expertise and methods, have to be considered.[172]

v. Between Disinfection and the Holocaust

By the 1930s extensive regulatory mechanisms surrounded the utilization of HCN and Zyklon. Their use by certified experts was regarded as routine, providing there was proper medical supervision. Studies were made of the effects of the gas on the animal and human metabolism in terms of quantities needed to have different physiological effects, and an intricate understanding of the stages of death was acquired. Elaborate procedures for fumigating and airing buildings, special training, and state licensing continued in force in Nazi Germany.[173] But circumstances began to change: T-Gas, or aethyloxide was introduced for domestic fumigation, having great advantages as far less poisonous.[174] The maritime and international

[171] Lifton, *Nazi Doctors*, 308–9.

[172] H. Mommsen, 'The Realization of the Unthinkable: The "Final Solution of the Jewish Question" in the Third Reich', in id. *From Weimar to Auschwitz. Essays in German History* (Oxford, 1991), 224–53.

[173] L. Gassner, 'Wie schützt man sich vor Schädigungen durch die in der Schädlingsbekämpfung gebräuchlichen Giftgase?', *Zeitschrift für hygienische Zoologie und Schädlingsbekämpfung*, 380? (1938/9), 297–300. 'Directives for the Use of Prussic Acid for the Destruction of Vermin', Hygiene Institute Prague (Nuremberg Document No NI-9912) in Pressac, *Auschwitz*, 19–20.

[174] STAH II J 15a Bd. 2 *Der T-Gas-Kammerjäger. Hausmitteilungen der T-Gas-Gesellschaft für Schädlingsvernichtung m.b.H. Frankfurt a.M. Weissfrauenstr.* 9 Nr 1 (1938).

markets declined, and the military market for Zyklon and other pesticides increased. A British War Office manual warned regarding hydrocyanic acid in March 1939 that 'a study of the gas is essential as it may be used again in different circumstances'.[175]

Can the German predeliction for such powerful gases be explained in ideological terms? That ultra-conservative forces condemned modernism as degenerate and corrupting meant that whatever the technical brilliance of chemists like Haber, their rationalism laid them open to being branded as part of the degenerating process. For the German right, technology required a spiritual reverence as a means of recreating the Germanic vision of the past. Escherich, as rector from 1933 until 1935 of the University of Munich, condemned mechanistic views enshrined in communism as exterminatory.[176] Harnessing science for nationalist ends meant a transposition from a gas designed to eradicate threats to human existence. Instead of defending the German forest against insect predators, the task became defence of the German race against Judaeo-Bolshevik parasites. Destruction became revered as a regenerative process in a nation attributing its ills to the burdens of human parasites.[177]

Ideology was reinforced by organizational factors: the ranks of disinfectors suggest that these were a type of epidemic police battalion. The Nazification of pest control and the instilling of a special sense of mission for action in the east meant that the squads of disinfectors became an auxiliary to the 'ethnic cleansing' by the Einsatzgruppen. Historians have examined atrocities committed by police units in order to show how ordinary men could follow commands to kill civilians, particularly women and children, in the occupied east. As Christopher Browning points out, some refused to comply with the orders, but this did not stop most obeying.[178] Unfortunately, few disinfectors were tried after the war, although their expertise in the use of poison gas and skill in improvising gas chambers was to be crucial in constructing and operating the human gas chambers. Such a low-grade technical occupation did not attract historians' attention, unlike the railway administration or SS building departments. What one can readily document is how an exterminatory epidemiology was used to mobilize disinfectors for their work, and also how occupational disputes reinforced the alliance between pest control workers and medical experts.

The notion of the parasite or *Schädling* had become axiomatic to Nazi racial demonology; in 1937 a law was passed to round-up 'good-for-nothings and parasites', targeting vagrants and alcoholics with contagious diseases in concentration camps for preventive custody for a 'labour training cure'. Social and racial identities fused as the Nazi theorists constructed an image of the human parasite. The drive towards a 'cleaner Germany' and purifying the body politic were preconditions for

---

[175] War Office, *Medical Manual of Chemical Warfare* (London, 1939), 60–1.

[176] K. Escherich, *Termitenwahn. Rede gehalten beim Antritts des Rektorats der Ludwig Maximilian-Universität am 25. November 1933* (Munich, 1934).

[177] cf. Eksteins, *Rites*, 328.

[178] C. Browning, 'One Day in Józefów: Initiation to Mass Murder', in id., *Path*, 169–83.

genocidal deployment of disinfection technologies.[179] Anti-Semitic rationales for the technology of disinfection and preventive microbiology meant that Jews were referred to as 'lice', and gas chambers disguised as delousing showers perverted the novel delousing routines introduced in the course of the First World War.

It was necessary to train a compliant and effective corps of disinfectors and pest control officers to eradicate epidemic hazards. By 1935 there were (it was claimed with exaggerated precision) 5,134 German disinfectors and pest exterminators, of whom over 3,000 had state certificates.[180] Disinfectors campaigned for incorporation into a unified Nazi occupational structure under the new health offices, which united hitherto disparate state and municipal public health.[181] Experts in bacteriology organized training as well as inculcating Nazi racial values into this crucial tier of otherwise 'ordinary men'.

In 1934 the journal *Der praktische Desinfektor* adopted a militaristic tone in its sections on the science of disinfection, gas and air defence, and racial hygiene and practice.[182] Mrugowsky wrote on virology and control of infectious diseases, stressing the crucial exterminatory mission of the disinfector.[183] From 1938 the journal highlighted epidemic prevention and pest extermination as tasks which were part of the military build-up. The war demanded effective service in the struggle against Germany's enemies which were depicted as intent on exterminating the nation: professionally, the war meant greater official recognition could be attained for disinfectors and pest control. Job advertisements began to appear for experienced personnel to work in the east.[184] The change of journal title to *Desinfektion und Schädlingsbekämpfung* signified how central the concept of the parasite had become. The Hauptamt für Volksgesundheit of the Nazi Party and the self-employed occupations section of the Deutsche Arbeitsfront backed the journal. The editorial board swarmed with medical and biological scientists. The contributions of Albrecht Hase, the louse expert, Heinrich Kliewe, who was to take a crucial role in biological warfare, Gerhard Peters of DEGESCH, Theodor Sütterlin, the former German Red Cross bacteriologist in Petrograd and now medical officer in Berlin augmented the status of disinfection and pest control.

War was waged by the disinfectors and their scientific patrons on empirical, self-employed *Kammerjäger*; corporate organization and industrially produced chemicals were weapons in a struggle for economic survival and status. By 1933 the *Kammerjäger* consolidated their position by aligning with Nazi ideology, although they had no access to modern pesticides. The attack on the *Kammerjäger* was supported by scientific figures with commercial interests, like the managing director of

[179] Burleigh and Wippermann, *The Racial State*, 169–70, 178.

[180] Solbrig, 'Das Desinfektionswesen und die Arbeiten eines staatlich geprüften Desinfektors vor 30 Jahren bis zur Jetztzeit', *Der praktische Desinfektor*, 30 (1938), 3–5.

[181] E. Deleiter, 'Entseuchungsdienst im Dritten Reich', *Der praktische Desinfektor*, 29 (1937), 349–50.

[182] 'Zum Geleit!', *Der praktische Desinfektor*, 26/1 (1934), 1.

[183] J. Mrugowsky, 'Die Bekämpfung der ansteckenden Krankheiten durch Desinfektion', *Der praktische Desinfektor*, 29 (1937), 235–44, 322–8, 352–8; Mrugowsky, 'Die Seuchenlage im europäischen Teil der UdSSR', *Der praktische Desinfektor*, 34 (1942), 115–21.

[184] K. Demmer, '1940–1941', *Der praktische Desinfektor*, 32/12 (Dec. 1940).

DEGESCH, Peters, who had joined the Nazi Party in 1937. Working with gas transformed a haphazard craft into the modern, technically expert *Schädlingsbekämpfer*.[185] In return for state recognition, pest control officers took on new responsibilities in civil defence against poison gas attacks. This occupation was a useful resource in a militarizing state, that foresaw a crucial role for poison gas. The link between science and practice echoed Nazi ideology of dynamic action: pest control was infused by Nazi social, racial, and military values.

In 1941 'reliable' pest control workers formed a Reichsarbeitsgemeinschaft für Schädlingsbekämpfung, which was supported by Peters as necessary for waging total war. By 1943 demands for increased professional status won official backing.[186] The inter-occupational feud against the *Kammerjäger* was accompanied by opposition to 'wild' pest control in agriculture and forestry. Given the strategic role of delousing in the east as well as its perversion in the Holocaust, the close ties of Peters with pest control workers suggest that commercial interests, scientists, and the authorities were keen to ingratiate themselves with this key occupational group.

The Reichsarbeitsgemeinschaft für Schädlingsbekämpfung ensured that the role of disinfectors in the Nazi combat forces achieved due recognition. Nazi Germany proliferated all sorts of *Lager*—for youth, work, sports, the military, and for numerous categories of detainees—while increasing the hazards of vermin and infection.[187] The *Entwesungsfachmann* from Linz, Anton Slupetzky, typified the new breed of technical entrepreneur: his firm was wholly dependent on distributing Zyklon B, and he was a Nazi Party member briefly in 1933 and again from 1938. Peters supported the development of Slupetzky's firm, which obtained advantageous marketing concessions in 1940 for Zyklon. Slupetzky was disturbed by witnessing human gassings at Mauthausen, but after joining a military disinfection squad in the Balkans and Greece, he resumed exterminatory duties, instructed by Peters that Zyklon caused less suffering than carbon monoxide.[188]

The Nazified concept of the parasite demanded vast resources for control and organized extermination. A vision of the model German city was based on Fallersleben, where the Volkswagen beetle was to be produced: all incoming traffic would be automatically gassed so as to ensure dwellings free from parasites.[189] Hase, while not an NSDAP member, argued obsessively that it was necessary to undertake a comprehensive census of the prevalence of domestic insects in order to facil-

[185] G. Peters, 'Materialkunde für Kammerjäger', *Der praktische Desinfektor*, 30 (1938), 166–7; Peters, 'Die Durchgasungsberechtigung als Massstab für die Leistungshöhe eines Schädlingsbekämpfungsbetriebes', *Der praktische Desinfektor*, 32 (1940), 90–1; BDC party membership no. 4376678, dated 1 May 1937 for Gerhard Peters, chemist, Frankfurt/M.

[186] K. Demmer, 'Die Reichsvereinigung der Schädlingsbekämpfer (RDS) e.V.', *Desinfektion und Schädlingsbekämpfung*, 35 (1943), 31; G. Peters, 'Was wurde erreicht? Eine Stellungnahme zur Gründung der Reichsvereinigung der Schädlingsbekämpfer (RDS) e.V.', *Desinfektion und Schädlingsbekämpfung*, 35 (1943), 32–3; 'Tagung der Beauftragten der RDS', *Desinfektion und Schädlingsbekämpfung*, 35 (1943), 54–6.

[187] G. Peters, 'Ungezieferfreie Arbeitslager?', *Desinfektion und Schädlingsbekämpfung*, 35 (1943), 77–8; BAK 168/ 62 Biologische Reichsanstalt, Gewerbsmässige Schädlingsbekämpfung.

[188] STAN KV-Anklage Interrogations S 235 Anton Slupetzky.

[189] H. Mertens, 'Die hygienische Musterstadt', *Der praktische Desinfektor*, 30 (1938), 198–9.

itate their control.[190] A travelling exhibition on *Schädlingsbekämpfung* was mounted in 1935. In 1938 a film, *Kleinkrieg*, depicting the war against pests, mobilized the public to exterminate all the varied species of parasites. With the outbreak of war disinfectors had racial convictions drummed into them by training films with such titles as *Feind Fliege*, *Kampf dem Fleckfieber*, and *Kampf den Schädlingen*; these reinforced their enthusiasm for exterminating parasites.[191] Delousing in the east invoked the Nazi stereotypes of Jews as typhus carriers, while the disinfector was to remove 'Jewish filth'.[192]

Ironically, pest control experts recognized an increase in irrational fears concerning imagined parasites—patients were obsessed by itching and demanded that their homes be gassed. Others attributed illness and disabilities to innocuous animals. All sorts of human pathologies like obsessive cleaning accompanied such neuroses.[193] Yet the idea that people might also fall victim to being denigrated as parasites did not strike observers. The Nazis' frenzied delusions of human parasites meant they mobilized vast medical resources for their eradication. The campaign against parasites intensified with war, as the biological and racial concepts of the parasite fused.

vi. The Cremation Movement between Internationalism and Nazism

Public health experts regarded cremation as an effective weapon in their armoury of disinfectants. Cremation could also be combined with ideologies ranging from freethinking materialism to Nordic idealism. Once the public health establishment succumbed to Nazism, then these two technologies were available for racial engineering. The medical lobby supporting cremation had to fight a series of administrative and political battles internationally and in Nazi Germany: for the swift victory providing absolute medical control was wrested away by party ideologues. Initially cremation was portrayed as a heroic Nordic rite for the master race while adhering to strict sanitary precepts.

Zeiss was the pivotal figure, having already won a battle for cremation in the Soviet Union, when he campaigned for a crematorium to be opened in Moscow in 1927. He secured a German oven for the Moscow crematorium, cooperating on this project from 1925 with Guido Bartel of the State Institute of Social Hygiene.[194] At

[190] A. Hase, 'Ueber die Notwendigkeit einer Statistik betreffend Verbreitung des Hausungeziefers', *Der praktische Desinfektor*, 30 (1938), 291–8.

[191] BA-MA H20/554 Lehrplan: Mannschaftslehrgang der Entseuchung und Entwesung, 6–18 Mar. 1944; H 20/763 31 Jan.–9 Feb. 1945 Sanitätslehrgang Berlin Reinickendorf. 'Schädlingsbekämpfung im Film', *Der praktische Desinfektor*, 30 (1938), 183–4.

[192] A. Benthin, 'Etwas von der Tätigkeit des Gesundheitsaufsehers im Warthegau', *Der praktische Desinfektor*, 34 (1942), 82–3.

[193] A. Hase, 'Pseudoparasitismus und Pseudparasitismus', *Zeitschrift für hygienische Zoologie und Schädlingsbekämpfung*, 30 (1938), 353–9; J. Wilhelmi, 'Ungezieferwahn', *Die medizinische Welt* (1935), 351–2.

[194] S. Lichtgang, 'Die Feuerbestattungsbewegung und die Wahrheit', *Die Flamme*, 12 (1937), 4–5.

the Cremation Society founded in Saratov in 1929 doctors and professors composed nearly a third of its total membership of 3,310 members in 1934.[195] Saratov had the only provincial Soviet eugenics society, as well as being Zeiss's favourite scientific centre. Here, an immense, cylindrical crematorium with a ramp, spiralling upwards, was designed to serve the east on the banks of the Volga.[196] The Volga Germans would have been accorded funeral rites appropriate to their heroic status as being in the vanguard of German settlement. The scheme represented a symbolic assertion of Germanic sanitary technology in the east.

Paul Mühling, a German physician and cremationist in East Prussian Königsberg, was an ardent nationalist, who regarded his location on the Prussian frontier as a bastion for the defence of German values. He disseminated cremation propaganda in Russia, and persuaded Zeiss to join the German Association of Cremation Societies in January 1928. Zeiss regularly reported on the progress of cremation in the Soviet Union; from 1929 he was on the editorial board of the journal *Zentralblatt für Feuerbestattung* and from October 1932 he was on the committee of a national association.[197] He saw his role in the cremation movement—as in other spheres of medicine—as combating materialism by rekindling the flames of Nordic idealism. The linking of cremation to a transcendent creed of racial ideals was the antithesis of the embalming of Lenin's body to convey his eternal inspiration in the world struggle for communist revolution.

Germany had in the 1920s and 30s the highest percentage of cremations, giving German cremationists a special sense of leadership in the international movement. The 1936 anniversary meeting of the Greater German Cremation Society celebrated fifty years of the crematorium at Gotha in Thuringia, a state which was a hotbed of cremationist and racial ideology, and where the Topf works manufactured furnaces in Erfurt.[198] The meeting marked the attempt by the Nazified Greater German Association of Cremation Societies to secure international influence. Zeiss welcomed the Sudeten German, Austrian, and Saar delegations with nationalistic fervour. The Scandinavian delegations represented a pristine Nordic vigour, and he proclaimed comradeship with the French and British delegations as headed by former *Frontkämpfer.*[199]

The International Cremation Congress in Prague, held in 1936, was traumatic for Zeiss, as opposition erupted to a German-led cremation movement. In Czechoslo-

---

[195] Juri Krupenikow, 'On the Way Towards Cremation', *Pharos*, 1/1 (1934), 27–9.

[196] G. Schlyter, 'Ein neuer Krematoriumtyp', *Die Flamme. Nachrichten-Blatt des Verbandes der Deutschen Feuerbestattungs-Vereine in der Tschechoslovakischen Republik*, 12/2 (1937), 1–3.

[197] There were articles by Zeiss from 1926 in *Deutsche Flamme*, 2/1 (1926); 45/46 (15 Mar. 1927); 4/3 (1928), 363; id., 'Die Fortschritte der Feuerbestattung in Sowjet-Russland im Jahre 1928', *Zentralblatt für Feuerbestattung*, 1 (1929), 59–64; id., Brief aus der Sowjetrussland. 'Die Feuerbestattung (1927 bis 1931)', *MMW*, 79 (1932), 1776–7; id., 'Die Fortschritte der Feuerbestattung in Sowjetrussland im Jahre 1930 u. 1931', *Zentralblatt für Feuerbestattung*, 4 (1932), 75–8; AHUB Medical Faculty 12/a Zeiss personal file, letter of 14 May 1937 from Zeiss to Kurator outlining his prior activities as a cremationist.

[198] Pressac, *Auschwitz*, p. 2, ch. 1 provides a detailed analysis of the history of the Topf works and of its cremation furnaces.

[199] H. Zeiss, *Die 50-Jahr-Feier (zugleich 31. Tagung) des Grossdeutschen Verbandes der Feuerbestattungsvereine in Gotha, 26–28. 1936* (Berlin, 1937), 13, 32.

vakia there was an active but renegade German cremation society, which retained the materialist ethos so loathed by the Nazis. Zeiss, a vice-president of the Congress, proclaimed: 'We are no international horde with countless ties both within and without but a consolidated army for cremation which rallies round the ideal of universal cremation . . .'. The Nazi delegation denounced the Czechs as in league with the French, socialists, Freemasons, and Jews. The Czech organizers baited the Germans by putting the wrong type of swastika on the German flag. Zeiss demanded vigorous renewed German efforts to curb these dissidents by promoting an alliance with British cremationists.[200]

Zeiss drew up plans for an international cremation federation.[201] This terminated an earlier free-thinking *Weltbund* for cremation which had organized conferences at the hygiene exhibitions of Dresden in 1911 and of Düsseldorf in 1926. Zeiss argued that the new federation was based on national variations in race, religion, and politics, and retained the militant spirit of the Great War. Moreover, the federation excluded all forms of 'culture-destroying Marxism' to the annoyance of the German-Czech cremationists.[202]

German leadership was shown when in February 1937 an international agreement for the transport of bodies—and ashes—was ratified in Berlin in February 1937.[203] When a second international congress was held in London from 24 September to 2 October 1937 under the presidency of the eugenically minded Lord Horder, Zeiss intended to assert the leadership of German cremation.[204] On this occasion the International Cremation Federation was formally established.[205] Zeiss failed in his campaign to be elected president (a Dutchman secured more votes).[206] In June 1939 Zeiss was again in London ostensibly concerning cremation, just before the flames of war ended the international movement.[207]

From 1934 there was a steady increase in the numbers of German crematoria:

Year	Place of New Crematorium
1934	Fürstenberg
1934	Lauscha
1934	Naumburg

---

[200] AHUB Hygienisches Institut Nr 1 Behörden Bl. 385–98, Bericht über den Internationalen Kongress für Feuerbestattung, Prag 1936; AHUB Hygienisches Institut Nr 201 Perkins to Zeiss 3 Dec. 1938.

[201] *The International Cremation Congress at Prague 1936* (Prague, n.d.). For German-Czech criticisms of this commission see *Die Flamme*, 11/12 (Dec. 1936) and 12/2 (Feb. 1937), 2–5; also the counter declaration in *Pharos*, 3/3 (Apr. 1937), 5.

[202] H. Zeiss, 'Was lehrt uns Prag?', *Die Feuerbestattung* (Jan. 1937), 2–3.

[203] *Office internationale d'hygiène publique. Session extraordinaire du comité permanent* (10 Feb. 1937).

[204] AHUB Medical Faculty 12/a Zeiss personal file Bl. 40 Zeiss 1 Mar. 1937 requesting permission to attend.

[205] *Pharos*, 4/1 (Nov. 1937), 4, 10.

[206] *International Cremation Congress London. September 24th to October 2nd. Report* (London, n.d.).

[207] AHUB Hygienisches Institut Nr 201, letter of Reg Perkins of the Cremation Society to Zeiss 3 Dec. 1938; ibid., 205 concerning his 1939 visit to London and contact with Manson-Bahr; Medical Faculty 12/a Bl. 67, letter by Zeiss of 24 June 1939.

1935	Celle
1935	Essen
1936	Düsseldorf
1937	Cologne
1937	Schneidemühl
1938	Flensburg
1938	Gleiwitz
1938	Döbeln

By 1938 121 German crematoria conducted 86,147 cremations, and in the Greater Germany of 1939 numbers swelled to 131 crematoria. (This can be compared with Britain where there were 29 crematoria which dealt with 9,614 bodies in 1935; by 1945 the number of crematoria rose to 58 where 42,963 cremations took place.[208]) The expanding market for crematorium equipment was the salvation of engineering firms and their employees, like the engineer Karl Prüfer of Topf who was nearly made redundant in the Depression. The Topf brothers joined the NSDAP in 1933, along with Prüfer, whose crucial links with the SS opened up market opportunities in the concentration camps.[209]

Cremation was transformed from a secularizing and pantheistic creed to a Nazified Nordic cult. In 1919 the Darwinist biologist and veteran campaigner for a biologically based ethics, Ernst Haeckel, was cremated at a ceremony including readings from Goethe and wreaths of pine and laurel.[210] Fritz Haber's wishes that his ashes be buried in Dahlem were not to be fulfilled in 1934, denying a symbolic significance to this patriotic pioneer of nitrogen fixation and HCN gassing, who had been forced to emigrate.[211] Zeiss believed that ashes should be returned to nature, having a dual ecological and national significance, while reviving the primeval Germanic sense of nature piety. He revelled in the forest as a Germanic sanctuary. Cremationists could adapt the Nazi blood and soil ideology by arguing that burial in the earth defiled and polluted what was sacrosanct. Nationalists regarded cremation as antithetical to Roman Catholicism and Judaism, and Jewish cremationists who had drafted proposals for national legislation were ejected from the Grossdeutsche Verband. Cremationists declared that they were in the vanguard of the struggle for a new Germanic faith.[212]

The ideological impetus to cremation remained fraught with controversy under Nazism. Ever more elaborate attempts to legitimate cremation linked it to a romantic movement for the revival of ancient Germanic values. Zeiss argued that cremation was consistent with beliefs that were deeply rooted in German cultural

---

[208] C. Polson (ed.), *The Disposal of the Dead* (London, 1953), 89, 131, 135.

[209] Pressac, *Auschwitz*, 94–5; id., *Crématoires*, 136–7.

[210] 'Ernst Haeckels Bestattung', newspaper cutting of 17 Aug. 1919 in possession of author.

[211] Stoltzenberg, *Haber*, 630.

[212] H. Zeiss, 'Feuerbestattung und Nationalsozialismus', *Zentralblatt für Feuerbestattung*, 6 (1934), 1–5; also published in *Mitteilungs-Blatt für die Mitglieder des Feuerbestattungs-Verein 'Flamme' München*, 38 (Oct. 1934), 1–4.

traditions.[213] He led the Nazification of the cremation movement's ideology and organization. In the summer of 1932 the Nazi Party had condemned cremation because of its left-wing and materialist connotations. A cremationist, Oberingenieur Peters from Dessau, went to the Brown House (the Nazi Party headquarters) in Munich and put the case for cremation to Walter Gross of the Racial Political Office and Leonardo Conti.[214] A forensic scientist from Munich, Merkel, attempted to overcome entrenched police opposition to any liberalizing of the law. At the time there were divisions between the Nazi Party in Bavaria and Prussia, as the Nazi group in the Prussian Assembly in November 1932 tabled a bill to facilitate cremation and protested against the legal restrictions.[215]

In April 1933 Conti granted Zeiss full powers to Nazify the cremation movement; Zeiss helped to draw up national statutes for the Grossdeutsche Verband and appointed Mühling to implement the Nazification and *Gleichschaltung* of the association.[216] In line with the Nazi attack on materialism, Zeiss called for crematoria to resound to 'German blood and customs'.[217] In April 1933 Zeiss telegraphed Hitler that Jews and Marxists were ousted from the cremation movement now reorganized into a single national society.[218] Gleichschaltung killed off the independence of cremation societies which were coerced into a Nazified Grossdeutscher Verband der Feuerbestattungsvereine. By June 1933 the Reich Ministry of the Interior under Wilhelm Frick planned to implement the national cremation law that had failed to be enacted during the Wilhelmine or Weimar eras.[219]

Although the new Greater German Association was designated by the Reich Ministry of the Interior as the sole organization of the cremation movement, it was beset by problems.[220] Freethinking elements were purged from the cremation movement, as *Gleichschaltung* required that cremation societies should be a member of a 'national organization' consistent with the Nazi Party.[221] This led to problems when Nazi cremationists attacked the leadership of the national society as still polluted by bourgeois, Marxist, and masonic elements. In 1934 the Grossdeutsche Verband was again purged when its chairman, the physician Mühling from Königsberg, was criticized for calling himself the Führer of the society, as this

[213] H. Zeiss in *Zentralblatt für Feuerbestattung*, 5/3 (Sept. 1933), 65.

[214] It is possible that this was the poison gas expert Gerhard Peters who had worked in Dessau until 1928. This would provide an interesting link between Zyklon gassings and cremation. Against this are the facts that Gerhard Peters only joined the NSDAP in 1937 and that he had the 'Dr' title rather than that of 'Oberingenieur'.

[215] BAP 15.01/ 2621 Bl. 265, Beratung von 30 June 1933.

[216] P. Mühling, 'Der Grossdeutsche Verband und Deutschlands Erwachen', *Zentralblatt für die Feuerbestattung*, 5/3 (May 1933), 33–8; Also 'Das Schicksalstunde des Grossdeutschen Verbandes am 23. April 1933', ibid., 39–42; AHUB Medical Faculty 12/a Zeiss to Kurator, 14 May 1937.

[217] H. Zeiss, 'Feuerbestattung und Nationalsozialismus', *Zentralblatt für Feuerbestattung*, 6/1 (1933), 1–5.

[218] BAP 15.01 Nr 26277/1, Bl. 157 telegram from Zeiss to Hitler.

[219] BAP 15.01 Nr 26277/1, Bl. 47, 171–3.

[220] RMdI to Zeiss, 26 Jan. 1934 in *Zentralblatt für Feuerbestattung*, 6/2 (1934), 17.

[221] BAP 15.01/ 2621 Bl. 223, Zeiss to Mühling 2 May 1933.

term was a prerogative of the Nazi Party. An NSDAP tribunal established that Mühling had applied to join the Nazi Party on 25 April 1933 having only resigned from a masonic lodge the previous day. Despite protesting that he belonged to one of the nationalist Prussian lodges, and that since 1926 he had led the cremation movement in a nationalist struggle against political Catholicism, Mühling was deposed and replaced by Zeiss.[222]

Burial remained the preferred option for many Germanic heroes. Hindenburg was laid to rest at the Tannenberg National Monument in 1935, commemorating his victory of August 1914 which swept back the Russian army and reversed the ignominy of the defeat of the Teutonic Knights by the Poles in 1410.[223] Opposition to cremation continued as the Reich Ministry of the Interior drafted legislation. Criminologists were concerned that cremation could increase the incidence of poisoning and other foul play as incriminating evidence would be destroyed.[224] The Nazi Party's committee on public health and the Reich Ministry of the Interior consulted Zeiss over the drafting of a cremation law.[225] Frick, the Minister of the Interior, and Reiter of the Reich Health Office heralded cremation as a modern technology to serve racial ends.[226]

On 15 May 1934 the state legislation removed restrictions on cremation, which was declared a 'primeval Germanic custom'. Vestiges of the liberal demands of the 1920s survived, such as the principles of the equality of cremation to burial and that the wishes of the deceased were paramount. The Nazi cremation law imposed elaborate formalities, ensuring that cremation remained more costly and bureaucratic than burial, with police and public health officials taking key roles. Urns were standardized in size, and had to be buried or laid in special columbaria. Most importantly, urns were not to be returned to relatives.[227] Freedom of choice in death was not acceptable under Nazism.

The Gotha anniversary meeting of 1936 marked the high point of the fusion of cremation and Nazism, and of Zeiss's power in the Nazi and international cremation movement. The oration by Reiter, the president of the Reich Health Office, which had settled the technical and medical aspects of the new cremation law, linked biological and Nordic values to modern medical technologies. He glorified cremation as appropriate for those who died heroically in the service of the Fatherland—indeed, soldiers in the Wehrmacht could now be cremated.[228]

Zeiss, who presided over the meeting, combined Nordic racism with medical

---

[222] BAP 15.01 Nr 26277, Bl. 94, 139, 148, 150, for dismissal of Mühling on 28 June 1934; Nr 26278 Bl. 34–7 Mühling to RMdI 16 Feb. 1934 and to Zeiss 9 and 16 Feb. 1934; Bl. 42 Volks-Feuerbestattungsverein Halle to RMdI 20 Feb. 1934.

[223] J. W. Baird, *To Die for Germany. Heroes in the Nazi Pantheon* (Bloomington Indiana, 1990), 5; A. Bucholz, 'Germany and the Death Paradigm', *Central European History*, 24 (1991), 187–94.

[224] AHUB Hygienisches Institut Nr 188, Zeiss to Popp 12 Feb. 1934, Popp to Zeiss 16 Feb. 1934.

[225] AHUB Hygienisches Institut Nr 188, NSDAP Reichsleitung Sachverständigen Beirat für Volksgesundheit to Zeiss 19 Jan. 1937.

[226] BAP 15.01/ 26278 Bl. 265–9 Beratung von 30 June 1933; Bl. 364–78 Beratung von 7 Feb. 1934.

[227] W. Kahler, *Das Reichsgesetz über die Feuerbestattung vom 15. Mai 1934* (Berlin, 1935).

[228] Zeiss, *50-Jahr-Feier*, 13–15.

fervour. The doctor had to fuse modern technical procedures with the customs of *Blut und Boden*: at every stage of cremation the body and its remains could be handled both hygienically and in accordance with the spirit of Germanic ship burials and funeral pyres. Zeiss saw cremation as a type of Nordic 'fire veneration'.[229] He ardently proselytized among the medical profession for converts, and was keen that the health authorities should sponsor a documentary film about cremation. Nordic ideals and public health interests opposed the culture of secular modernity. Just as medical experts and manufacturing interests joined forces against the individualistic *Kammerjäger*, so the funereal pomp of undertakers and burial rites were denounced as primitive, inefficient, expensive, unhygienic, and un-German.

Despite the passing of the Reich law, cremation remained controversial. The Bavarian authorities placed administrative obstacles in the way of cremation. Moreover, Nazi leaders were divided. In May 1933 Zeiss presided over the Bavarian Cremation Association, but from 1936 Zeiss found himself in the midst of a furious row. The cremation insurance organization led by the Munich cremationist Max Harbauer, which had over a million subscribers, resigned from the Greater German Cremation League, leaving its finances utterly crippled. Harbauer had good NSDAP connections in Munich and used these to dislodge Zeiss from his leadership of the German cremationists in Berlin. As a result of the dispute Zeiss was investigated by the SS, and resigned in November 1937.[230]

Nazi cremation offered far more than a crude technology of concealment for Holocaust and euthanasia victims. Public health interests persuaded Party ideologists to overcome, albeit reservedly, their hostility to cremation. Although Germany was the world-leader in cremation, associations with free thought and materialism made cremation highly suspect to the Nazis, whose leadership in the early 1930s had denounced cremation. Physicians took the lead in the Nazi Gleichschaltung and purging of cremationist organizations. Ideological links between medical notions of a pathogen-free earth were combined with Nordic beliefs in fire as eternal life. Zeiss fused his interest in the holistic roots of German medicine with medical support for the cremation movement. His historical work emphasized the ideology of clearance, and of a purging fire with the flames of destruction necessary for a momentous scientific discovery. Such ideas went with training cohorts of medical experts to support the military onslaught on the East as well as control of epidemics in concentration camps. Doctors can be seen as supplying the methods and ideological rationales for the realization of the Nazi racial Utopia.

The Nazification of the cremation movement is revealing of the rationales of a technology that was to become essential in the 'disposal' of 'surplus' populations, initially in German psychiatric hospitals and then in the east. It was a cruel irony that the notion of the purifying flame—the Nordic ideal of the fire of eternal

---

[229] Ibid., 33–8; Zeiss and Rodenwaldt, *Hygiene und Seuchenlehre*, 95–100.
[230] Zeiss was replaced by Max Warsow from Berlin. *Akten der Partei-Kanzlei der NSDAP*, microfiche no 12403697 NSDAP Reichsleitung to Adjutantur des Führer, 17 Nov. 1937; Harbauer, 'An alle Mitglieder der "Flamme"!', *Mitteilungs-Blatt*, 33 (July 1933).

life—sealed the fate of millions branded as *Untermenschen*. For with the onset of war and genocide, cremation—its stigma never fully removed—was deemed to be most appropriate not for the Germanic élite but for the degenerate. Ideals of international cooperation, of sanitary improvement, and the clearance of insect pests gave way to notions of the disinfection and clearance of alien peoples as parasites.

10

Delousing and the Holocaust

i. Epidemic Racism

Typhus was virtually extinct in pre-Second World War Germany; but during the war it rocketed to levels at least as high as during the First World War. Ominously, it was again denounced as a *Judenfieber*, as draconian counter-measures were ruthlessly imposed. It is hard to know whether the initially low rates of typhus in German-occupied Poland were due to energetic implementation of delousing and vaccination or because the disease was an inherently trivial problem before the German attack on the Soviet Union. Yet once disease rates began to spiral, typhus became caught up in genocide.[1]

Soon after the German attack on Poland was unleashed, the Reich Ministry of the Interior decreed on 13 September 1939 procedures for thorough and repeated delousing to combat typhus.[2] Epidemiologists were relieved that the German army occupied areas of eastern Poland only briefly, and that the border between the German and Soviet zones coincided with the westerly extent of endemic typhus.[3] The Race Political Office observed that 'medical care from the German side has only to prevent epidemics spreading to the Reich. We can stay indifferent to the health conditions of the Jews'.[4] Ghettoization of Jews was justified as a 'sanitary precaution', and resettlement of ethnic Germans from the Balkans and the Soviet zone of occupation magnified the fear of typhus among the German authorities. Although less prevalent than other diseases like gut infections or tuberculosis, it was typhus which shaped coercive and exterminatory measures.[5] The importation of Polish forced labour and the presence of Polish prisoners of war in Germany raised the spectre of a typhus epidemic spreading to the hitherto typhus-free Reich. Sporadic typhus outbreaks occurred in the winter of 1940–1 in Leipzig, Nuremberg, and Breslau. German public health officials became alarmed as typhus mortality crept up, accusing prisoners of war and labourers from the east of importing infections. In 1940 Reich Health Führer Conti appointed an epi-

---

[1] C. G. Roland, *Courage under Siege. Starvation, Disease and Death in the Warsaw Ghetto* (New York and Oxford, 1992), 124–30. Glass, '*Life Unworthy of Life*', xiv–xix.

[2] 'Runderlass des Reichsministers des Innern, betr Anweisung zur Bekämpfung des Fleckfiebers. Vom 13. September 1939', *Reichs-Gesundheitsblatt*, 14 (1939), 815–19.

[3] G. Rose, 'Fleckfieberfragen der Heimat', *Die Gesundheitsführung. Ziel und Weg* (1942), 96.

[4] L. Wess, 'Menschenversuche und Seuchenpolitik—Zwei unbekannte Kapitel aus der Geschichte der deutschen Tropenmedizin', *1999*, 9/2 (1993), 11.

[5] Guth, 'Militärärzte', 180; Hagen, Das Gesundheitswesen der Stadt Warschau September 1939 bis März 1942, Archives of National Institute of Hygiene Warsaw.

demic commissioner to ensure that all German districts and towns had delousing installations.[6]

Such was the alarm, distortion, and racial prejudice surrounding the disease that the statistics for the civilian population were in many ways unreliable, not least because the disease was one of the fictitious causes of death used to conceal euthanasia of psychiatric patients. Registration procedures were also faked in Auschwitz. One of the earliest victims of an Auschwitz gassing, Count Mieczysław Nałęcz-Sobieszczański, had a falsified time (4 p.m. on 4 September 1941) and cause of death—Herzmuskelschwäche nach Fleckfieberverdacht; the student Mieczysław Rowiński was certified as dead at 3.30 p.m. on 4 September 1941 with the cause as Bronchialkatarrh nach Fleckfieberverdacht.[7] Given the experimental use of Zyklon, suspected typhus might have seemed appropriate.

German bacteriologists proudly looked back to the preventive measures of the First World War when delousing showed how typhus could be eradicated.[8] Jost Walbaum, the chief medical officer of the Generalgouvernement, pointed out that Polish legislation on infectious diseases was virtually word for word derived from German precedents: what was needed was German thoroughness in its implementation.[9] Western areas of Poland were incorporated into 'Greater Germany', while the remnants of the Polish state were placed under the Generalgouvernement, exhuming the puppet state of the First World War. Frey had characterized typhus as a *Judenfieber* but his sanitary measures were more medically than racially motivated. The relatively benign sanitary regime of Frey in the First World War was replaced by brutality, malice, and genocide, as typhus became a racial ideology. Doctors rallied to the tasks of racial classification, delousing the German troops and Polish prisoners, and screening for infections.[10] Racial and sanitary science intertwined: the discovery that louse faeces could remain infectious while deposited on clothes and in dust for long after lice had died meant that renewed emphasis was given to disinfection of possessions and dwellings. A dispute erupted between traditionalists advocating concentration on louse eradication and those experts stressing dust control.[11]

In October 1939 the serologist, Otto Reche, who had promoted blood group surveys in the Soviet Union during the 1920s, offered his services to the SS as a racial expert, declaring his mission as clearing 'Polish lice' to make way for a new warrior caste of German settlers.[12] Population transfers involved screening for carriers of

---

[6] STAN KV-Anklage Interrogations C 10 Werner Friedrich Christiansen, 6 Feb. 1947.

[7] State Museum of Auschwitz-Birkenau, *Death Books from Auschwitz. Remnants* (Munich, 1995), i. 54–7.

[8] Rose, 'Fleckfieberfragen', 100.

[9] J. Walbaum, 'Gesundheitswesen', in M. du Prel (ed.), *Das Generalgouvernement* (Würzburg, 1942), 191.

[10] Rodenwaldt, *Tropenarzt*, 405.

[11] Braemer, 'Die amtliche Bekämpfungsvorschriften im Wandel der epidemiologischen Erkenntnesse', *Zeitschrift ges. Krankenhauswesen*, 38 (1943), 357–61; Rose, 'Fleckfieberfragen', 99–100; Roland, *Courage*, 150.

[12] BDC Reche file, Reche to Pancke Oct. 1939; Weindling, *Health, Race and German Politics*, 539–41; R. D. Müller, *Hitlers Ostkrieg und die deutsche Siedlungspolitik* (Frankfurt/M., 1991), 26–7.

infectious diseases and maintaining sanitary conditions. Posen became a centre for population transfers and 'racial sifting'; here Mengele assessed the applications of ethnic Germans for their racial qualities.[13] The Germans struck agreements with the Soviets and Romanians to transfer ethnic Germans from Galicia, Volhynia, the Ukraine, the Banat, and Bukovina.[14] The idea of an eastern barrage or *Ostwall* defending Europe against Slavic hordes required rigorous delousing schemes to regulate the flow of persons from east to west.

Degrading racial violence flared, as street cleaning and the cutting of the hair and beards of orthodox Jews became part of the brutal regime of persecution. The Polish physician Zygmunt Klukowski recorded the following on 14 October 1939 in Zamość under temporary German occupation: 'Today is Saturday but the Germans required that all Jews work at cleaning the streets even though it is a Jewish holy day. The Germans are treating the Jews very brutally. They cut their beards; sometimes they pull the hair out.' Rabbi Oshry in Kovno responded to the German attack on beards by allowing observant Jews to shave.[15] In the Lemberg ghetto the Nazis used street cleaning and ragged clothing as a pretext for vicious killings. The Swiss Red Cross motorcyclist Franz Blättler recorded how German soldiers contemptuously referred to Jews and Poles as carriers of filth and disease.[16]

Medical science underpinned calculated policies of genocide.[17] In November 1939 the Germans forced the Judenrat in Warsaw to place signs that the area under its authority was a 'quarantined area'—*Seuchensperrbezirk*.[18] The Germans exploited the typhus cases that their discriminatory measures caused with crude propaganda linking typhus, lice, urban filth, and Jews.[19] The poster 'Jews, Lice and Typhus' and German film propaganda blamed parasitic Jewish exploitation as the cause of the mass misery that allowed the disease to spread, while praising invasive disinfection squads for clearing overcrowded ghetto housing.[20] No large-scale epidemics occurred at the time, and when the ghetto was established, the notices were removed. But later the Nazi prophecy came to be self-fulfilling given the starvation and deprivation.[21]

The fear of infection was a pretext for isolating Jews. In March 1940 the Germans ordered Polish doctors not to treat Jews as 'infectious diseases are mainly among

---

[13] N. Gutschow, 'Stadtplanung im Warthegau 1939–1944', in Rössler and Schleiermacher, *'Generalplan Ost'*, 232–58; Aly, *Endlösung*, 60–92, 103–5.

[14] Aly, *Endlösung*, 72–92, 152–60.

[15] Z. Klukowski, *Diary from the Years of Occupation 1939–44* (Urbana, Ill., 1993), 40. E. Oshry, *Responsa from the Holocaust* (New York, 1983).

[16] F. Blättler, *Warschau 1942. Tatsachenbericht eines Motorfahrers der zweiten schweizerischen Aerztemission 1942 in Polen* (Zurich, 1945), 52, 64, 121.

[17] Trunk, 'Epidemics', 84–5.

[18] Roland, *Courage*, 22, 126, 132–4; I. Gutman (ed.), *Im Warschauer Getto. Das Tagebuch des Adam Czerniakow 1939–1942* (Munich, 1986), 25.

[19] Roland, *Courage*, 132–3.

[20] An unfinished propaganda film about the Warsaw ghetto is in the Stephen Spielberg archive, Jerusalem.

[21] YIVO, 'Walka z tyfusem', 39.1, p. 1.

the Jewish population.'[22] The Generalgouvernement medical authorities under 'Gebietsgesundheitsführer' Walbaum, an SA Brigadeführer and former colleague of Kudicke in Canton, demanded that the quarantine zone be cordoned off by an 'epidemic wall'.[23] Quarantine accelerated racial segregation, as yellow signs warning of typhus were placed by buildings where persons were incarcerated for fourteen days.[24] In May 1940 Walbaum pointed out that typhus diminished in western Poland, coinciding with the deportation of Jews, proving that typhus was 'a purely Jewish disease'. He extended his argument that Jews were a focus of infection everywhere and that the Jewish problem required 'a fundamental solution'.[25] Statistics of typhus cases in September 1940 were a convenient pretext for Gauleiter Frank to set up ghettos in Cracow and other Polish cities.[26] Horrific overcrowding, lack of facilities for washing, and shortages of basic essentials like clothing and soap increased the risks of typhus in the ghettos.

The ghettos, camps, and prisons for the forcibly evacuated contributed to the spread of typhus. The Germans blamed the disease on Jews—often portrayed as louse infested—and on Poles—for example, on Polish doctors misdiagnosing typhus as influenza (echoing a complaint against German doctors after the First World War). The German medical officers organized 'cleanliness weeks' with a barrage of pamphlets, posters, films, and lectures: the slogan 'only one louse' stressed the necessity of maintaining louse-free domestic environments.[27] Rigorous delousing was necessary for the repatriation programmes of ethnic Germans, as well as for Poles sent as forced labour to Germany.[28] The medical authorities planned a network of delousing stations—there were forty-four in the Generalgouvernement by 1942, thereby reinstating the epidemic wall to protect the Reich from typhus.[29]

German self-interest was paramount: it was agreed that delousing facilities be established not only on the border between Germany (now expanded to include

---

[22] Klukowski, *Diary*, 82–3. Klukowski protested against the order not to treat Jews. References to lice suggest a mistranslation for typhus rather than typhoid.

[23] J. Walbaum, 'Gesundheitswesen', in M. du Prel (ed.), *Das Generalgouvernement* (Würzburg, 1942), 190–4; J. Bühler, *Das Generalgouvernement. Seine Verwaltung und seine Wirtschaft* (Cracow, 1943), 85–6. On 20 Jan. 1943 the health department became a Hauptabteilung of the administration.

[24] M. Edelman, *The Ghetto Fights* (London, 1990; 1st edn., 1946), 42.

[25] The phrase used was 'eine grundlegende Lösung'; J. Walbaum (Gebietsgesundheitsführer Krakau), 'Fleckfieber und Volkszugehörigkeit in Polen', *MMW* 87 (1940), 567–8; BDC Walbaum file, NSDAP member since August 1930; R. Kudicke, 'Ausbreitung und Bekämpfung des Fleckfiebers', *Schriftenreihe für Seuchenbekämpfung*, 1 (1944), 5–21; Rose, 'Fleckfieberfragen', 106.

[26] Jost Walbaum, *Kampf den Seuchen! Deutscher Ärzte-Einsatz im Osten. Die Aufarbeit im Gesundheitswesen des Generalgouvernements* (Cracow, 1941); C. R. Browning, 'Genozid und Gesundheitswesen. Deutsche Ärzte und polnische Juden 1939–1941', *Der Wert der Menschen*, 316–28; Roland, *Courage under Siege*, 22–3.

[27] Kudicke, 'Ausbreitung und Bekämpfung des Fleckfiebers', *Schriftenreihe für Seuchenbekämpfung*, 1 (1944), 5–21; Rose, 'Fleckfieberfragen', 98; 'Nur eine Laus' is the slogan in the film *Kampf dem Fleckfieber*.

[28] G. Rose, 'Fleckfieberfragen bei der Umsiedlung der Volksdeutschen aus dem Ostraum 1939', *Deutsche Medizinische Wochenschrift* (1941), 1262–5.

[29] J. Walbaum, 'Gesundheitswesen', in M. du Prel (ed.), *Das Generalgouvernement* (Würzburg, 1942), 190–4.

'lost' areas of western Poland) and the Generalgouvernement, but also along the old Reich borders, so reviving the border delousing station of Eydtkuhnen which first served the transmigrants of the 1890s.[30] The deportation of Jews from the newly incorporated Warthegau from October 1939 into ghettos lacking adequate sanitary amenities prompted concern over possible typhus. Reich Interior Ministry officials inspected the delousing facilities in the ghettos of Neuhof and Plöhnen. The Germans felt that energetic typhus prevention methods in Poland meant that typhus outbreaks were confined to the ghettos until the spring of 1941. Medical rationales reinforced racial stereotypes: it was claimed that troops at the front had a lower rate of infection than those behind the lines who were in contact with the civilian population.[31]

The attack on the Soviet Union (and Soviet-occupied territories) in June 1941 heightened expectations of an epidemic. The Germans blamed Soviet prisoners of war for causing epidemic flare-ups in concentration camps close to German cities like Sachsenhausen near Berlin and Neuengamme near Hamburg.[32] The Germans were concerned that typhus was spreading from the ghettos: by July 1941 there were 1,800 recorded cases of typhus in Warsaw, and by September 3,000 cases. Systematic delousing of Jews was enforced: it was claimed that 331,528 persons in the Warsaw ghetto were deloused in 1941: the result was horrific situations when hundreds of people were left without food in freezing conditions. Officially, 15,780 persons died that year from typhus in the Warsaw ghetto.[33]

The combination of overcrowding, forced labour, severe food shortages—and finally the murderous 'selections'—meant that the ghettos were death traps. In October 1941 the medical department of the Generalgouvernement called a meeting on prevention of epidemics, ostensibly because of the medical hazards of the eastern advance, and the onset of winter when typhus could be expected to increase. No sooner had an epidemic been brought under control in the Warsaw ghetto, then more persons were herded into the cramped conditions, so undermining anti-typhus measures.

The German medical officials agreed that the epicentre of the typhus epidemics was located in the ghettos. Blame was heaped on the Jews for their lack of discipline and for spreading typhus by escaping. But the Germans disagreed over preventive measures. Kudicke, the former assistant of Robert Koch, who was in command of the Warsaw Hygiene Institute, and Wilhelm Hagen, the municipal medical officer of Warsaw from January 1941, attributed the epidemics to the lack of soap, fuel, and clothing exacerbating louse infestation.

Hagen and Kudicke argued that merely sealing the ghettos was inadequate, and

---

[30] BAK R 86/4164 Bl. 71–8 RMdI meeting of 14–16 Oct. 1941. For RMdI meeting of 29 Dec. 1941 see NMT roll 30, frames 272–4.

[31] Leven, 'Fleckfieber', 132; M. Gilbert, *Atlas of the Holocaust* (Oxford, 1988), 50.

[32] Kaienberg, *Der Fall Neuengamme*, 177.

[33] Hagen, 'Das Gesundheitswesen der Stadt Warschau', 10; L. Wulman and J. Tenenbaum, *The Martyrdom of Jewish Physicians in Poland* (New York, 1963), 194–9, 227–30; J. J. Heydecker, *The Warsaw Ghetto. A Photographic Record 1941–1944* (London, 1990), 4; Gutman (ed.), *Das Tagebuch des Adam Czerniakow*, 181–2 (31 Aug. 1941).

that improved delousing and washing facilities, and rapid isolation of typhus cases were needed. Kudicke pointed out that only adequate food supplies could prevent Jews from breaking out of the ghettos, and Hagen demanded bread, coal, and soap for the ghetto (here were distinct echoes of Virchow's protestations in 1848 that medical police measures of quarantine needed to be replaced by economic assistance).[34] Hagen regarded the rise of infections in the ghetto as a threat to Warsaw's population: he had restored the water and sewage systems, and inoculated feverishly against typhoid. He imposed registration, isolation, and delousing of whole apartment blocks and streets in the ghetto. Hagen aimed to protect Germans and Poles from the spread of typhus, while stopping short of accelerating genocide within the ghetto. Hagen was aware of the exterminatory measures of the increasingly powerful SS, which from July 1942 began the round-ups for the gas chambers of Treblinka. He was eventually dismissed when he complained to Hitler in December 1942 about plans to liquidate 70,000 Poles on the pretext of tuberculosis to make way for settlement by armed German peasants.[35]

The question arises to what extent epidemic control measures in the Warsaw ghetto were genocidal? The German medical officials were varied in their commitments to Nazism. Hagen had joined the NSDAP in 1938, although Kudicke was not a member. Hagen and Kudicke did not indulge in anti-Semitic notions of the Jew as a parasite, or urge brutality. But what they called 'energetic and extensive' measures to suppress the sources of the epidemic involved coercive delousing and disinfection. The sanitary assault stigmatized Jews as indolent and any Jew found in bed was assumed to be a typhus case. Hagen's house-to-house searches to find 'concealed cases' of typhus—he claimed there were 14,000 such cases—meant measures for extermination of lice were life-threatening for anyone assumed to be infested.[36] Hagen's abrupt stop to medical intervention in the ghetto can be interpreted in a number of ways. He might be seen as accepting that the Jews were not only inherent typhus carriers but doomed to extinction whatever he did. Trunk and later Browning have gone further by arguing that he accelerated the destruction of the ghetto.[37] Even though derived from the traditional arsenal of anti-epidemic control measures of quarantine and cleansing, the genocidal circumstances meant that—as Ludwik Hirszfeld, the bacteriologist, argued—delousing was coercive, destructive, and largely ineffectual.[38]

At a meeting of German medical officials at the Carpathian resort of Bad Krynica in October 1941, Hagen and Kudicke were attacked by rabidly Nazi public health officials. Walbaum poured scorn on Hagen's optimistic faith in traditional

---

[34] YVA 053/195 Arbeitstagung der Abteilung Gesundheitswesen i. d. Regierung des Generalgouvernements in Bad Krynica vom 13–16 Oktober 1941, pp. 11, 13–17, 31; Roland, *Courage*, 132–7 for typhus epidemics.

[35] W. Hagen, 'Krieg, Hunger und Pestilenz in Warschau 1939–1943', *Gesundheitswesen und Desinfektion*, 8/9 (1973), 115–43, 139–43; YVA copy of BDC Conti file, Hagen to Hitler 7 Dec. 1942.

[36] Trunk, 'Epidemics', 96.

[37] Ibid.; Browning, 'Genocide and Public Health', 160; M. G. Esch and U. Caumann, 'Fleckfieber und Fleckfieberbekämpfung im Warschauer Ghetto und die Tätigkeit der deutschen Gesundheitsverwaltung 1941/42', 9.   [38] L. Hirszfeld, *The Story of One Life* (Fort Knox, Ky., n.d.).

delousing and disinfection procedures, instead prescribing extermination as a solution to the problem of epidemic control: either the Jews should starve to death in the ghetto or be shot—for 'our sole aim is to see that the German Volk is not infected and endangered by these parasites, and so any means is justified'.[39] Since the summer of 1941 large-scale massacres of Jews had been in progress in the Soviet Union, so that the genocide endorsed by this meeting reflected the reality that the Holocaust was underway.[40] By October 1941 reports on the famished, parched, and overcrowded deportees and on the high rates of typhus in the Warsaw ghetto were circulating among the allies.[41]

Kudicke was typhus plenipotentiary ('Sonderbeauftragte für die Fleckfieber-bekämpfung in die Generalgouvernement'—a position in keeping with Prussian disease commissars of the nineteenth century); he supervised sanitary squads and district doctors, and deployed physical and chemical methods of delousing on a vast scale. Delousing methods included hot air disinfection and ironing, boiling, and washing of clothes with creosol detergents. Rudolf Wohlrab, head of the typhus department of the Warsaw Hygiene Institute, supported in May 1940 an elaborate system of medical screening, hygiene squads, registration, isolation, and disinfection of the sick and of their housing. He prescribed warm showers with cuprex and cevadilla seed preparations, petroleum soaps, and prepared chalk for the disinfection of human bodies.[42] By September 1940 Warsaw had twenty new delousing stations with a capacity of 7,000 persons per day.[43] The Hygiene Institute (once the centre of Rajchman's internationalist activities but now under German direction) approved the use of various chemicals and gases, including carbon monoxide and sulphur compounds after rooms were sealed. While Wohlrab regarded other gases as suitable for disinfecting dwellings, he recommended hydrocyanic acid gases as most effective when used in special gas chambers with good heating and ventilation facilities—this typified German support for Zyklon delousing. For its part, DEGESCH was delighted at the profits in supplying Zyklon for large-scale gassings in occupied territories.[44] Gas chambers and delousing installations became a priority as medical conditions deteriorated under the German occupation.

ii. Resistance

The German use of typhus as a weapon of oppression met with ingenious and staunch resistance. In Radom, two ingenious Polish doctors faked Weil–Felix

---

[39] Arbeitstagung, 19–20. [40] Burrin, *Hitler and the Jews*, 6–7, 93–113.
[41] Gilbert, *Auschwitz*, 15.
[42] R. Wohlrab, 'Flecktyphusbekämpfung im Generalgouvernement. Vortrag gehalten vor der Academia Real, Madrid und der Universität Valladolid', *MMW* 89/22 (29 May 1942), 483–8.
[43] Hagen, 'Krieg', 117.
[44] Bayer Archiv, IG Fremdfirmen DEGUSSA 6.14 Bd 1, Geschäftsbericht der DEGESCH für das Jahr 1939 (dated 16 Apr. 1940); ibid., 1940 (dated 29 May 1941).

13. German propaganda poster: 'Typhus the Scourge of the East'

14. German propaganda poster: 'The Path of Horror', depicting how a Jewish beggar-woman reputedly infected forty-two persons with typhus

reactions so that Poles would not be sent as forced labourers to Germany. German military doctors came to the conclusion that typhus was endemic in the district.[45] The director of Zamość County Hospital, Klukowski, prayed 'Glory be to the louse', as the need to attend typhus cases secured his release from German custody. For as long as possible he admitted Jewish typhus patients partly to save them from deportation and partly so that the Germans should keep their distance and not impose Germanization measures. Klukowski erected warning signs *Achtung! Fleck-fieber* to ward off the Gestapo and to prevent his hospital from being evacuated. Donning a white coat could provide immunity from arrest, and a medical consultation could conceal a meeting with a member of the resistance.[46] Klukowski came under intense pressure as Zamość was designated a priority area for German settlement in the genocidal *Generalplan Ost*.[47]

Similar ploys worked in concentration camps. In the early days of Auschwitz as a punishment camp for Polish dissidents, Wiesław Kielar found it worthwhile enduring the torture of infested clothing: 'Dear old lice! Thanks to them the Kapos and SS men avoid our cell. Grub comes regularly, and it even seems that the portions are larger than usual. We laze about for days while outside the heat, 'sport' and blows continue. Life is beautiful. On our door is a warning notice: BEWARE LICE! And from the other side of the glass door the envious glances of our mates, tired out by 'sport' and work. They implore us to let them have at least one louse.' Facetious and exaggerated, the passage confirms the immense dread that the Germans had of lice and typhus.[48] Dissidents realized that a sign warning of typhus might keep the SS out. At Dachau prisoners used a sign 'Beware of Contagion from Dead Bodies' to keep the SS at bay, as they listened to foreign broadcasts, compiled records of German medical abuses, and planned resistance among piles of bodies in the mortuary.[49] The fear of disease could be exploited in innumerable ways: a radio in Auschwitz was wrapped in a bundle warning of infectious material, and work detachments were quarantined at Dora because of a false report about typhus.[50]

Although the Germans relentlessly murdered Jewish physicians, medical skills might facilitate survival. A prisoner in Auschwitz, condemned as a decrepit *Muselman*, had been an assistant of Weigl, and became a prisoner doctor when a typhus epidemic erupted in April 1941, because the German doctors were too

---

[45] One of the doctors was Lasczkovski. Information from Michael Thaler, San Francisco, and U. Caumann, Warsaw.

[46] Klukowski, *Diary*, 97 (21 June 1940—'typhoid' may possibly be typhus), 103 (23 July 1940), 148 (8 May 1941), 172 (30 July 1941), 191 (8, 10 Apr. 1996), 196 (8 May 1942), by this date Klukowski was forced to cease admitting Jews to his hospital, 264 (2 July 1943), 268 (10 July 1943). For the ideological significance of Zamość see Breitman, *Himmler*, 185.

[47] Dwork and van Pelt, *Auschwitz*, 315.

[48] W. Kielar, *Anus Mundi. Five Years in Auschwitz* (London, 1991), 14 (1st Polish edn., 1972). Note that 'sport' was an ironic term for punitive exercises.

[49] F. Blaha, 'Medical Science Run Amok', *Medical Science Abused. German Medical Science as Practised in Concentration Camps and in the so-called Protectorate. Reported by Czechoslovak Doctors* (Prague, 1946), 33. On resistance in the infectious diseases block see Langbein, *Menschen*, 252.

[50] Langbein, *Against All Hope*, 200–1, 250.

inexperienced in handling the disease.[51] Leon and Mina Deutsch, both doctors, moved east from Lwów and survived because they assisted in fighting typhus in Ukrainian villages under German occupation.[52] The development of ghetto medical services marked resistance to the genocidal regime of starvation, overcrowding, and deprivation inflicted by the Germans.

In 1940 Hirszfeld unmasked the whole horror of typhus: he diagnosed that typhus was created by the Germans, precipitated by the lack of food, soap, and water—'when one concentrates 400,000 wretches in one district, takes everything away from them, and gives them nothing, then one creates typhus.' Hirszfeld (who although confined to the ghetto, had a Polish Catholic identity) denounced German doctors' hyprocrisy for making Jews responsible for the epidemic.[53] Adam Czerniakow, who kept records of life in the Warsaw ghetto, echoed Hirszfeld in rejecting lice as a sole cause of typhus, and instead attributed the disease to overcrowding and starvation.[54]

Dvorjetski, who survived the Vilna ghetto, praised the physicians in the ghettos of Kovno, Białystok, Grodno, Cracow, and Łódź as guardians of life, thwarting Nazi intentions of exterminating ghetto inhabitants by means of epidemics.[55] When the Director of the Jewish Hospital in Warsaw requested supplies, the German response was that the Jews should perish in their filth.[56] The medical resistance defied such deadly policies. Incarcerated physicians organized medical services and hospitals in all the ghettos, and medical and nursing schools in the Warsaw ghetto. Despite the overcrowding the deprivations, and the German satisfaction at high Jewish mortality as long as typhus did not spread, it was possible to control typhus: self-organization sustained a relatively typhus-free ghetto at Cracow.[57] At Litzmannstadt (Łódź) the ghetto saw only isolated typhus cases, whereas epidemics occurred at neighbouring camps for gypsies and juvenile delinquents.[58] At Theresienstadt louse infestation was held in check and, typhus erupted (at least officially) only in April 1945 during the last chaotic period of German control, when Jewish medical officials feared that disclosure of typhus would give the Germans a pretext for further killings.[59] To protect those sick from typhus being killed in the camp of

---

[51] Id., *Der Auschwitz Prozess*, ii. 587–9; Klee, *Auschwitz*, 399–400.
[52] M. Deutsch, *Mina's Story. A Doctor's Memoir of the Holocaust* (Toronto, 1994), 38–9.
[53] Roland, *Courage*, 141, 266 n. 148; L. Hirszfeld, *The Story of One Life* (Fort Knox, Ky., n.d.), 217.
[54] Gutman, *Tagebuch des Adam Czerniakow*, 198 (23 Oct. 1941).
[55] M. Dvorjetski, 'The Jewish Medical Resistance and Nazi Criminal Medicine During Disastrous Period' (A Lecture at the World Jewish Medical Congress in Jerusalem on 19 August 1952), copy in Yad Vashem library.
[56] 'Die jüdischen Kranken sollen in ihrem Mistnest verrecken', cited in YIVO 39.8 reports by the director of Czyste Hospital, 12 Mar. 1941.
[57] M. A. Balinska, 'La Pologne face à ses crises médicales du XXème siècle', DEA diss., Institut d'Etudes Politiques, 1989, 44–5, citing from L. Hirszfeld, *Historia jednego życia* (Warsaw, 1946), 219. Also id., *Story*, 223.
[58] L. Dobroszycki, tr. R. Lourie, *et al.*, *The Chronicle of the Łódź Ghetto 1941–1944* (New Haven, Conn., 1984), 217, 420–1.
[59] H. G. Adler, *Theresienstadt. Das Antlitz einer Zwangsgemeinschaft* (Tübingen, 1955), 516, 695–6. Cases of typhus amounted to 2,100 whereas 50–60,000 suffered from dysentery.

Koureme in Estonia, Dvorjetski produced false medical records and concealed the distinctive rash with a solution of iodine, 'sepsa', and ichytol.[60]

In the Kovno ghetto the head of the delousing sanitation department Rabbi Ephraim Oshry secretly looked after Torah students and officiated at religious ceremonies. Although the water supply was sporadic and fuel for heating was often in short supply, Oshry hoped that suffering could be made more bearable by alleviating the filth and the stench; in any case delousing meant a day free from forced labour. Oshry defied German pressure to delouse on the sabbath. After a failed attempt to disguise the entrance to a hideout for children as a drain, Oshry and others decided to build a bunker deep below the delousing bath, where thirty-four survived fire, heat, and lack of air during the final annihilation of the ghetto.[61]

In the Vilna ghetto an exemplary health service was organized from September 1941 with district clinics allocated to a physician and a team of nurses. They supervised sanitary brigades, rubbish disposal, and sewerage teams; each district, courtyard, and room had sanitary delegates to ensure that rooms were swept and aired, and that dishes and linen were thoroughly washed. Communal baths were replaced by two 'Sanitary transit posts' with twenty showers, cement floors, benches and a changing room where clothes were disinfected. The ghetto Sanitary and Epidemiological Service fought the invasion of lice by compulsory and repeated delousing, and by insisting that food ration cards required a monthly bathhouse stamp. Typhus was successfully controlled in the ghetto, whereas it was endemic in the concentration camps.[62]

Preventing typhus was an act of resistance to maintain human life, dignity, and rights, defying the Germans' destructive intentions. Given that key German officials regarded Jews as inherently sick, a ghetto was meant to be a sick society containing invalids and the diseased. Much effort was made to combat lice as spreading infections and as a symptom of deprivation and demoralization. A play called 'The Public Trial of the Louse' was staged during the Vilna ghetto's 'hygiene week' to alert the inhabitants to the dangers of typhus—the medical evidence on how lice spread typhus was pitted against the defence that the ghetto conditions caused disease; the judgement was the death penalty on the louse. Public health education lectures were held, and eighteen issues appeared of a health popularization journal, *Folksgesunt*.[63]

---

[60] Dvorjetski, *Vilna*, 18.

[61] A. Tory, *Surviving the Holocaust. The Kovno Ghetto Diary* (London, 1991), 368–70, illustration. E. Oshry, *The Annihilation of Lithuanian Jewry* (New York, 1996), 93–4. Author's interview with Rabbi Oshry 6 Dec. 1998.

[62] M. Dvorjetski, *Le Ghetto de Vilna (Rapport Sanitaire)* (Geneva, 1946), 43–50, 82–3; L. Wulman and J. Tenenbaum, *The Martyrdom of Jewish Physicians in Poland* (New York, 1963), 225–7; A. Wajnryb, 'Medizin im Ghetto Wilna', *Dachauer Hefte*, iv (1993), 78–115. This German translation confuses typhoid and typhus. A. Sedlis, paper at YIVO/New School conference on Jewish Medical Resistance. S. Beinfield, 'Health Care in the Vilna Ghetto', *Holocaust and Genocide Studies*, 12 (1998), 68–98.

[63] Dvorjetski, *Le Ghetto de Vilna (Rapport Sanitaire)*, 43–50, 82–3; Wajnryb, 'Medizin im Ghetto Wilna', 78–115; A. Sedlis, paper at Yivo/New School conference on Jewish Medical Resistance; Beinfield, 'Health Care', 79.

In Theresienstadt over 4,000 prisoners (i.e. 9 per cent of the total imprisoned) were employed on health-related tasks in a vast medical service. They coped with a situation when a quarter of the ghetto population registered as sick in 1943. There were elaborate public health regulations—a survivor characterized these as dictatorial—line inspections to hunt out head and clothes lice, accompanied by commandments to avoid lice, bugs, and fleas, and a delousing installation which, when fully functioning, could shower a thousand persons in a day. There were eight gas chambers, using Zyklon gas, for clothes.[64] Hospital and bacteriological equipment were improvised, and an extensive laboratory was equipped, although animal experiments and bacterial cultures were forbidden. Considerable clinical research was conducted, and medical conferences and public health lectures were held: for example, in 1942 the incarcerated Berlin physician Hermann Strauss spoke on the distinction between typhus and typhoid, and in July 1943 an ambitious cycle of medical lectures dealt with the theory and practice of skin diseases and the transmission of disease by insects.[65]

Abraham Wajnryb, who was in charge of the infectious diseases department in the Vilna ghetto hospital, regarded infectious diseases as synonymous with resistance. The hospital became a refuge for all sorts of illegal activities and persons. The physicians concealed the incidence of typhus as they fought the spread of lice between September 1941 and April 1943, fearing that Germans would use the pretext of an epidemic and destroy the ghetto community. The Germans found a few cases of leprosy in the Kovno ghetto as an excuse to destroy the Jewish hospital with most of its patients in October 1941, and a few cases of typhus in the village of Nowo-Swienciany resulted in the burning down of a clinic and the shooting of the staff. Such incidents meant that Kovno ghetto doctors refused to report any cases of typhus to the increasingly suspicious Lithuanian Board of Health, while allocating extra soap, food, and firewood to the sick.[66] In Vilna fictitious statistics were kept, as each patient had a real case history which was concealed, and a fictional history which was displayed at the foot of the bed, and patients were coached to present false symptoms.[67] The sick could be provided with food, often at great personal risk. While persons suffering from typhus at the isolation camp at Doroschitz were left by the Germans without medical attention, internees in a collecting camp for forced labourers risked bringing food across to the isolation camp.[68]

Hagen's vigorous measures in the Warsaw Ghetto encountered resistance and medical objections. Hirszfeld observed that quarantine and delousing meant economic and personal ruin. He considered the stringent isolation procedures realistic for a localized outbreak in Germany but counter-productive amidst the mass deprivation of the ghetto. People did not comply with Hagen's elaborate sanitary routines until forced to do so by hefty coercion from German, Polish, and ghetto

---

[64] Adler, *Theresienstadt*, 503, 507–8, 516, 657, 691.   [65] Ibid., 504–5, 529.

[66] A. Tory, *Surviving the Holocaust. The Kovno Ghetto Diary* (London, 1991), 141. Oshry, *Annihilation*, 48–9.

[67] Dvorjetski, *Le Ghetto de Vilna*, 43–50, 82–3; Wajnryb, 'Medizin im Ghetto Wilna'.

[68] YVA 03/2434 testimony of David Zwi Stauber.

police, for only 10 per cent of those ordered to, appeared voluntarily for delousing baths. Hagen's sporadic forced delousing 'actions' caused confusion, terror, mass misery, and death from exposure to the cold or from contracting an infection in the overcrowded conditions. Clean and dirty possessions were disinfected together, and Hirszfeld found that lice survived exposure to the disinfectant. The disinfectors, doctors, and police took bribes in exchange for issuing delousing certificates.[69]

Disinfecting squads caused havoc and misery in the densely packed Warsaw ghetto. Hirszfeld took charge of the Warsaw ghetto epidemic committee from September 1941 with the aim of a more decentralized approach.[70] He modified the Germans' severe orders and converted delousing columns into household service teams to ensure that linen was changed and laundered as far as possible. He denounced quarantine of three weeks for typhus cases as causing death by starvation, and disinfection as being more dangerous than contracting the disease. In any case, overcrowding spread the disease.[71] That Hirszfeld was a leading international expert on sero-anthropology meant that he was in a strong position to attack German racial epidemiology. In February 1942 he lectured—presumably to the Ghetto medical school—on 'Blood and races'.[72] Although typhus was manipulated by the Germans to ensure compliance with genocidal measures, these met evasion and resistance.

Yet Hirszfeld's methods were not without their problems. The system of 'block' and district doctors who conducted regular inspections meant that there were considerable incentives for concealing cases. Hospital conditions were atrocious—a nurse at the children's hospital observed the 'shaven heads covered with sores swarming with lice' compounded by overcrowding, cold, and hunger. If a case was treated at home the whole household was quarantined and bathed and had their belongings disinfected. Such local medical inspections varied between the negligent and the corrupt. Thus the sick preferred a covert arrangement with a physician, rather than undergo the ordeals that ensued after notification. A medical observer noted: 'One cannot say that Jewish doctors failed the test of medical ethics or the principles of honesty, but they played on patients' fears of the hospital.'[73]

Realizing the great incentives to evade German and Polish police disinfection squads, Hagen urged a switch to Jewish self-help disinfection brigades. In the

---

[69] Hirszfeld, *Story*; Trunk, 'Epidemics', 111–13. Examples of the elaborate ghetto health regulations of the Department of Health of the Jewish Council are in YIVO Institute, 39.7 concerning Department of Health of the Jewish Council instructions for cleaning, washing and disinfecting communal staircases, March 1941.

[70] Gutman, *Tagebuch des Adam Czerniakow*, 178, 186 (15 Sept. 1941).

[71] Hagen, 'Erfahrungen über Seuchenbekämpfung in der Stadt Warschau', in *Arbeitstagung*, 22–35. For the chaos of a ghetto delousing action see Roland, *Courage*, 138–47; Hirszfeld, *Story*, 218–23.

[72] Gutman (ed.), *Das Tagebuch des Adam Czerniakow*, 231 (25 Feb. 1942).

[73] YIVO 39.1 'Walka z tyfusem', 9; 39.6 Jewish Council in Warsaw Department of Health, 'Directions in the Fight against Infectious Disease', 29 Jan. 1942; 39.5 concerning the decree of 26 Sept. 1941 permitting treatment of typhus cases in their own homes; Trunk, 'Epidemics', 104.

autumn of 1940 the Warsaw Institute of Hygiene trained fifty Jewish disinfectors. Quarantine of two weeks, and rigorous delousing which could result in wreckage and theft were enforced. The disinfection measures caused especial hardship for the persecuted, starved ghetto inhabitants who were more likely to be suffering from tuberculosis and a range of chronic ailments. Hirszfeld condoned bribery as a means of evading a medically harmful regime, and conceded that laundering and ironing of clothes, and local showers would be more effective.[74] A group of rabbis suggested a religious ceremony to halt the epidemic.[75] Rituals, self-help, and personal hygiene offered alternatives to coercive and ultimately genocidal routines of delousing and disinfection. German propaganda was scathing about primitive self-delousing as opposed to scientifically based mass delousing.[76] Survivors testified how they deloused themselves without the perils of German-imposed regimentation. Ghetto dwellers sterilized clothing, killed nits by ironing and tried to wash thoroughly despite the lack of privacy.[77] Mina Deutsch deloused her children's clothes and hair while concealed in a Ukrainian farmer's bunker.[78] Prisoners would cooperate in delousing each other—for example, Joseph Wargon and his fellow prisoners shared a razor blade for shaving their arms, chest, and between their legs to eliminate habitats where lice lurked. Or as Auschwitz women prisoners, they could impress the SS by organizing their own sanitary improvements.[79] At Sachsenhausen prisoners organized delousing and disinfection in the autumn of 1941.[80] One must be cautious in approaching typhus as a means of ensuring compliance on the part of victims. For the disease prompted significant resistance against delousing as oppressive and dehumanizing, while organized Jewish medical assistance fought conditions designed to accelerate death.

iii. Operation 'Barbarossa'

The German army claimed that it was free of typhus until it invaded Russia. The military medical authorities anticipated the disease as a problem in April 1941: when the military epidemiologists analysed Soviet morbidity statistics, the observation that typhus was endemic among poor Jews was ominous.[81] Military doctors spoke of cures and preventive measures as 'weapons' in the combat against hostile diseases. Troops were vaccinated against smallpox, typhoid, paratyphoid, cholera,

[74] Roland, *Courage*, 140–7.   [75] Ibid., 152.   [76] e.g. in the film *Kampf dem Fleckfieber*.
[77] P. Friedman, *Roads to Extinction: Essays on the Holocaust* (New York, 1980), 283. Wojdowsky, *Bread*, 196–8.
[78] Deutsch, *Mina's Story*, 72–3.
[79] 'Revue de poux', drawing by internee Marius Favier, *Konzentrationslager Buchenwald. Post Weimar/Thür.* (Buchenwald, 1990), 98; YVA 033/3271; M. Greselot (ed.), *La Force de l'espoir. Les Frères Wargon. Souvenirs de Joseph Wargon*, 52; Magda Blau in L. Shelley (ed.), *Criminal Experiments on Human Beings in Auschwitz and in War Research Laboratories* (San Francisco, Calif., 1991), 64–6.
[80] H. Naujoks, *Mein Leben im KZ Sachsenhausen* (Cologne, 1987), 280.
[81] Leven, 'Fleckfieber', 129; K.-H. Leven, 'Die bakterielle Ruhr im deutschen Heer während des Krieges gegen die Sowjetunion, 1941–1945,' '*Medizin für den Staat—Medizin für den Krieg'. Aspekte zwischen 1914 und 1945* (Husum, 1994), 82–97.

15. German propaganda poster. Inscribed in Ukrainian: 'Beware of Typhus. Do Not Come Near to Jews'

E-Schein

Entlausungsschein

Der Inhaber dieser Bescheinigung

....

(Dienstgrad)   (Name)   (Feldpost-Nummer)

....

(Leserliche, eigenhändige Unterschrift des Inhabers)

ist heute hier entlaust worden.

Er ist frei von ansteckenden Krankheiten und Ungeziefer und somit zur Benutzung der vorgesehenen Beförderungsmittel zur Erreichung seines Bestimmungsortes zugelassen.

Die Bescheinigung ist in das Soldbuch einzulegen und auf Verlangen den Überwachungsorganen der Wehrmacht vorzuzeigen.

Tagesstempel   Stempel der Entlausungs-Anstalt

1 9. OKT. 1943

2111   Maximilian-Verlag, Berlin SW 68, Ritterstr. 33   (4. 43) WCo.

---

16. Military delousing certificate, 1943

dysentery, and—very much a novelty—against typhus. But Hitler and his generals banked on a swift victory in Russia: sanitary measures only became a priority when disease and the hostile climate jeopardized the faltering attack with the onset of winter in 1941.[82]

Medical experts feared that the German troops—originating from areas where typhus had died out—would succumb to typhus whereas local populations had accumulated natural resistance from the 1921 epidemic. Reichsleiter Martin Bormann was dismayed to discover that the Ukrainians had acquired immunity against typhus and malaria whereas the German occupation forces had to be dosed with Atebrin. The anxieties surrounding an epidemic flare-up of typhus intensified

---

[82] 'OKH Deployment Directive of 31.I.41. Barbarossa', Leach, *Strategy*, 263–9. For reports on hygienic conditions see Fischer, *Sanitätsdienst*, iv. 3482–92.

among the invading forces entering into a pathogenic environment with climatic extremes of heat and cold, and insect and racial predators. The lack of sanitary facilities and shortage of vaccines contributed to the sense of demoralization and fatigue. Typhus spread during the winter when there were fewer opportunities to wash and when there was overcrowding in heated billets. In the summer the eugenicist Harmsen reported from the Ukraine how typhus stubbornly refused to disappear. The authorities were petrified that civilians and prisoners of war would infect the troops, and that soldiers returning on leave or wounded would infect the *Heimat*.[83] The elaborate ritual of delousing was often impossible during military combat. During the much-publicized German attempt to reach the Volga area at Stalingrad—to which Hitler attached much symbolic significance—in the winter of 1942–3, the surrounded German–Romanian forces were crawling with lice, and the soldiers' skins were bitten, inflamed, and itching.[84]

The Führer decreed that the Reich Ministry for the Occupied Eastern Territories should have responsibility for health and welfare.[85] Despite the exterminatory intent of the decree, its savagery varied in different zones of occupation, and Hitler's Minister, Rosenberg (who was originally from Estonia), supported this differential policy.[86] Although the German authorities gave orders to close all institutions of higher learning in the Reichskommissariat Ukraine in January 1942, they allowed the medical, veterinary, and forestry faculties to continue.[87] Medical schools were permitted in Dnieprpetrovsk, Kiev, Minsk, and Vinnitsa for a time during 1942, until the Germans opted to deploy students as labour conscripts. The Germans tolerated medical institutions to a greater extent in the occupied (and not reconstituted) Baltic states, because they conceded that effective epidemic control required local medical support. In the Reichskommissariat Ostland, the Estonian university of Tartu (the former 'German university' of Dorpat) and the Latvian University of Riga were reopened for training medical personnel and disinfectors. Once Jewish academics and those who had cooperated with the Soviet occupation of the Baltics had been removed, the Germans attempted to draw on the skills and compliance of local doctors, academics, and technical staff in organizing disinfection. For large-scale delousing required local assistance.[88]

Military hygienists comandeered sanitary facilities and baths. Troops were instructed 'to search for public and private bathing and delousing equipment in every location', and to redeploy existing sanitary facilities. Brigade doctors were trained to operate delousing apparatus.[89] Early in 1942 Hitler ordered that rather

---

[83] BA-MA H 20/59 Sammelbericht über Kriegserfahrungen des beratenden Hygieniker, 1 July 1942 Bl. 11–13 and 1943, Bl. 1–3, 14 (includes Harmsen report). H 20/518 Assmann, 'Fleckfieberprophylaxe'; Dallin, *German Rule*, 455–6.

[84] K. Schneider-Janessen, *Arzt im Krieg* (Frankfurt/M., 1993), 175–6; Weinberg, *World at Arms*, 454.

[85] BAK R 90/351, decree of 17 July 1941.

[86] BAK R 6/387 Dr Waegner, memorandum of 1941.   [87] Dallin, *German Rule*, 463.

[88] Thom, 'Wandlungen', 437–43. On Tartu see I. Käbin, *Die medizinische Forschung und Lehre an der Universität Dorpat/Tartu 1802–1940* (Lüneburg, 1986).

[89] For the commandeering of Soviet disinfection apparatus see P. Kern, 'Erfahrungen aus dem Ostfeldzug', *MMW* 89 (1942), 1005–7. For anti-typhus measures in general see H. Hartleben and G. Schad, *Innere Medizin und Hygiene* (= Taschenbücher des Truppenarztes, vol. i) (Munich, 1936), 88–9, 154–9.

than disseminate medical innovations (as during the First World War), these must be restricted to Germans: 'No vaccination for the Russians, and no soap to get the dirt off them. But let them have all the tobacco and vodka they want.' When in July 1942 Bormann (head of the Parteikanzlei and contemptuous of Slavs as subhumans) reported that Ukrainians did not suffer from malaria or typhus and remained healthy despite drinking polluted water, Hitler insisted that all types of preventive medicine were out of the question for non-Germans, and he ordered that the rumour should be spread that vaccinations were dangerous.[90]

The extremism of Hitler and the SS set a dichotomy of raising sanitary standards for the German soldiers and settlers whilst inflicting exterminatory measures for populations under occupation. German soldiers were instructed that contact with civilians could result in contracting typhus. Troops were to bath as often as possible and at least once a week. Underwear was to be changed weekly and boiled; and uniforms were to be regularly deloused. Troops were to search for all sick people in villages and towns, and civilian patients were to be 'treated' as for those with tuberculosis. Soldiers were urged that, 'Foci of disease should be suppressed by every means'.[91] These Waffen-SS orders were an incitement to kill on medical pretexts.[92] The killing of the sick and infirm was integral to the German campaign—care and treatment of the sick and wounded were the exceptions.[93] Blättler recorded how German soldiers allowed Russian prisoners of war to freeze and starve to death, believing that they carried typhus.[94] German military doctors justified killings in prisoner of war camps and psychiatric hospitals on the basis of potential epidemic danger.[95] Exterminatory medical procedures were a component of the genocidal activities of the military, *Einsatztruppen*, and SS invading forces.

The Reich Ministry for the Occupied Eastern Territories took charge of delousing installations and disinfection squads, for the practice was chaotically inefficient. Lice and nits might survive a single delousing, and hot air might not be evenly distributed if a chamber was overfilled.[96] One official, Fritz Steiniger, who assisted with racial policy and anthropology for the Reich Commissariat in Riga, was a racially-minded ornithologist and entomologist, expert on the insect-feeding habits of birds as well as in genetics: as a biologist, he could not solve technical problems in running delousing units on a mass scale, but he applied what he

[90] Dallin, *German Rule*, 454–7, quoting H. Picker (ed.), *Hitlers Tischgespräche* (Bonn, 1951), 50–1 (19 Feb. 1942), 71–4, 425 (11 Apr. 1942), 575 (9 July 1942).

[91] AHUB Hygienisches Institut Nr 42, Bl. 232–4, Report on Prevention of Infectious Diseases by Hygienisches Institut der Waffen-SS. Blättler, *Warschau 1942*, 12, 43.

[92] A copy of the regulations is in the personal papers of Zeiss—presumably as drafted for the Waffen-SS.

[93] F. Kudlien, 'Begingen Wehrmachtsärzte in Russlandkrieg Verbrechen gegen die Menschlichkeit?', *Der Wert des Menschen*, 333–52, esp. 337–8. On the conduct of the German army see H. Jeer and K. Naumann (eds.), *Vernichtungskrieg. Verbrechen der Wehrmacht 1941 bis 1944* (Hamburg, 1995).

[94] Blättler, *Warschau 1942*, 52–3.

[95] F. Kudlien, 'Begingen Wehrmachtärzte im Russlandkrieg Verbrechen gegen die Menschlichkeit', *Der Wert des Menschen*, 333–52, 336–8.

[96] Rose, 'Fleckfieberfragen', 103.

knew of the biology of lice to their eradication.[97] In 1942/3 Steiniger assumed command of an Institute for Medical Zoology at Riga-Kleisthof in Latvia, where he trained local disinfection squads. In desperation at the poor functioning of conventional delousing installations, Steiniger opted for sauna baths for delousing, and he tried to destroy lice by freezing and starving them, in preference to damaging clothes by overheating or using highly toxic hydrocyanic acid. Steiniger's biological methods were condemned by the Reich Ministry for the Occupied Territories, insisting on the orthodoxy of hydrocyanic acid.[98]

The further east that the Germans advanced, the more difficulties with mass delousing became apparent. Delousing facilities were inadequate and prone to breakdown. Disinfection ovens caught fire in the Warsaw ghetto and at Kovno, which was a delousing centre for wounded troops returning from the front.[99] The Wehrmacht experienced immense problems with strategically positioned delousing stations at the border stations of Tauroggen (between Lithuania and East Prussia) and Wirballen. These took a year to build, resulting in complaints that the Reich was demanding foreign labour from the Baltic states, while it was not prepared to release raw materials for border delousing stations. In July 1942 the Reich Ministry for the Eastern Territories ordered four mobile and 200 fixed hot-air delousing ovens. At Riga and Dünaburg hydrocyanic delousing equipment was for ethnic Germans migrating back to the Reich or to new settlements. But once built, the installations failed to function: carbon monoxide escaped causing widespread nausea among the troops in neighbouring barracks, and ashes were scattered over a wide area, some ovens could not be heated to an adequate temperature. Even when delousing installations were functioning, they became hazardous when overused. The quality of fuel was often poor, and disruptions in the electrical power supply caused the ventilation equipment to overheat and malfunction; in any case, the installations needed to be cooled down for checking on at least two nights a week. The stupidity of locally trained disinfectors and stokers was blamed.[100] Yet such work could facilitate survival: Jewish workers from the ghetto

[97] BDC Steiniger file, Steiniger studied zoology in Greifswald where he was assistant to Günther Just in the department of genetics from 1932–7, was SA member from 1933, NSDAP member from 1935, worked for the Racial-Political Office Berlin from 1936, the RGA from 1939. In January 1943 Steiniger lectured on 'Vererbung und Infektionskrankheiten' for a teaching position to succeed Just at Greifswald.

[98] BAK R 90/455 Reichskommissar für das Ostland. Abteilung Gesundheits- und Volkspflege, Steiniger MS of 3 Feb. 1943 on the sauna. Steiniger's articles included: 'Das "Ausstreuen" der Läuse', 77–80; 'Dorfbäder als behelfsmässige Entlausunganlagen', *Zeitschrift für hygienische Zoologie*, 35 (1943), 57–62; 'Soll man bestehende Badeanstalten in Entlausunganlagen umbauen?', *Zeitschrift für hygienische Zoologie*, 35 (1943), 93–6 (with A. Schlote); 'Nicht brennbare Stoffe als Verbrennungszusätze zum Rohschwefel für die Schwefeldioxydentwicklung', 173–8; Steiniger and K. Losse, 'Über bewegliche Luftstromführung beim Einsatz von Lufthitzern in der Entlausung', ibid., 36 (1944), 42–9; Steiniger, 'Zweiwöchige Quarantäne Entlausung bei Temperaturen +10 C', ibid., 36 (1944), 106–11; Steiniger 'Der Läusebefall in den baltischen Ländern und in Weissruthenien', 128–30; BAK R 90/455, Dr Waegner of RM für die besetzten Ostgebieten to Reichskommissar für das Ostland 1 Sept. 1943.

[99] Gutmann, *Tagebuch des Adam Czerniakow*, 41 (12 Feb. 1940); Tory, *Kovno*, 142; A. Sedlis, paper at YIVO/ New School conference on Jewish Medical Resistance.

[100] BAP 11.03 Reichsministerium für die besetzten Ostgebieten, Bl. 76 Reichskommisar für das Ostland, Abt IV Hoch to Abt IIe and I, Riga 4 June 1942.

shaved and disinfected the wounded German soldiers at Kovno; a Jewish electrician at the Riga delousing station from March 1942 found that he could work unsupervised, could barter, and was able to collect useful articles from soldiers while they were deloused.[101]

Delousing facilities were improvised by municipalities and employers of forced labour when typhus epidemics flared in the Reich. In the province of Pomerania between November 1941 and mid-January 1942, the epidemic of typhus was variously blamed on Russians in prisoner of war camps, Russian forced labour, and Jews escaping from the Generalgouvernement. At the same time the authorities concealed the epidemic by not alerting the general public to the hazard of typhus.[102] Delousing policies differed in the sectors of the occupied east, partly because the severity of typhus varied (for example, its spread was low in Estonia and high in Lithuania), and partly because of administrative autonomy. Race was also a factor: delousing for troops and ethnic Germans was meant to be a regimented but not unpleasant operation. Disagreement arose on the incidence of typhus and of louse infestation. Conti announced a final triumph over typhus in March 1942, but this turned out to be premature. Soviet propaganda claimed that typhus epidemics were raging in occupied areas, whereas the Germans insisted that infectious disease rates were favourable, particularly in the Baltic region.[103] According to one view of the situation in Lithuania the statistics on louse infestation were inflated because the presence of lice was a qualification for an extra soap ration. Another view was that the local Lithuanian doctors could not be trusted and well over 50 per cent of the population were infested with lice.[104] Waegner, the SS officer responsible for health and welfare in the Ost-Ministerium from 1942, gave priority to the health of his fellow ethnic Germans, of the occupying troops, and of the German heartlands. No mercy was shown to Jewish doctors or to patients in hospitals and psychiatric asylums.[105]

For those lower down the racial hierarchy, delousing was punitive and generally unpleasant. Delousing was a routine part of camp procedures, and is ubiquitous in Holocaust survivors' accounts. A distinction has to be drawn between the procedures for the racial élite and those entering and enduring the hell of the camps. David Rousset, a former Buchenwald prisoner, described the bureaucrats noting down names of those newly admitted to the camp as 'fresh from a Kafka universe'.[106] Leo Kok's transport from France to Buchenwald revelled in the hilarity of the metamorphosis involving showers, shaving, and donning prisoners' uniforms, although the enjoyment was soon dissipated by the filth and overcrowding of the 'small'

[101] A. Faikelson, *Heroism and Bravery in Lithuania 1941–1945* (Jerusalem, 1996), 105; Tory, *Kovno*, 142.
[102] Information from Gabriele Moser, Rostock.
[103] BAK R 90/351 2 July 1943; R 90/352 on typhus incidence in the East in 1943; L. Conti, 'Dank des Reichsgesundheitsführers an alle Mitarbeiter im Kampfe gegen das Fleckfieber', *Die Gesundheitsführung. Ziel und Weg* (1942), 105.
[104] BAK R 90/455 Reichsministerium für die besetzten Ostgebieten, Generalkommissar in Kauen to Reichskommissar für das Ostland Riga 17 Mar. 1943; reply by Dr Bernsdorff to Generalkommissar, 12 Apr. 1943.
[105] Thom, 'Wandlungen', 437–43.   [106] Rousset, *Other Kingdom*, 30, 240.

quarantine camp.[107] A procedure designed to protect health was absurd given the murderous regime of the camps. Generally punitive and dehumanizing, delousing involved excruciating chemicals, but at times some relief from the daily struggle against insects, dirt, and excrement into which prisoners were plunged: Kay Gundel, an eighteen year old deported from Berlin, recollected that:

[We] were handed thick, awful smelling liquid shampoo which burned my scalp to the roots and the open sores I had scratched raw from lice. I rubbed and rubbed the sticky stuff down to my hair roots, into my scalp, determined that I would kill the awful bugs, according to our instructions. I even sat for a short while, despite the stinging wrapped up in a towel around my hair, waiting for the foul stuff to kill the live lice and the tiny eggs. It was exhilarating to walk out a while later, felling well scrubbed and absolutely shiny clean: But it couldn't last long. I was always wearing the same piece of clothing.[108]

The standard circuit for the delousing of clothes and showers was inflicted as a punitive and dehumanizing regime of admittance into hell—involving registration, tattooing, being stripped of clothes and personal effects, a bath in a burning mixture of water and Zyklon to disinfest body hair, a shower or sauna with alternately burning and freezing water, a medical examination, the cutting and shaving of head and public hair, and the issue of ill-fitting striped prison uniforms and footwear which lacerated the feet. The prisoners passed wholly naked from the 'dirty' to 'clean' sides of the operation—before being plunged into the filth of the camp. The feeling of being nothing was pervasive. Primo Levi spoke for the many who experienced these routines as profoundly depersonalizing: delousing was intended to kill the individual soul if not the body.[109]

The terror was increased by the vicious whims of *Kapos* or SS, and undressing might reveal a deformity resulting in execution. Clothes remained dirty if only deloused using Zyklon, whereas hot air disinfestation provided rough cleaning.[110] Kielar described how naked and shivering Russian prisoners were plunged into a vat of freezing disinfectant:

Everyone had to immerse himself in this old, smelly liquid, which in time came to be as thick as a mudpack. Anyone who recoiled was made to suffer worse than the rest. The SDG [*SS doctor*] in attendance and an SS-man who assisted him watched carefully to see that 'disinfection' took place according to regulations. With his boot he held the prisoner's head under water until there was a gurgling sound from inside the vat and air bubbles rose to the surface. After such a procedure the prisoner, frightened and choking, would jump out of the vat, always assuming that he was still strong enough to do so.[111]

---

[107] *Konzentrationslager Buchenwald. Post Weimar/Thür.* (Buchenwald, 1990), 97–8; NAW RG 153 War Crimes Case Number 12–390 The Buchenwald Case, microfilm reel 6, frame 1802 Richet evidence.

[108] Holocaust Museum, Washington, DC, Survivors' Testimonies, RG-02.004*1, pp. 75–6, testimony of Kay Gundel.

[109] P. Levi, *If This is a Man* and *The Truce* (London, 1987; 1st edn., 1958 and 1963); D. Rousset, *The Other Kingdom* (New York, 1947), 30; L. J. Micheels, *Doctor #117641. A Holocaust Memoir* (New Haven, Conn., 1989), 68 for the sense of metamorphosis.

[110] Pressac, *Auschwitz*, 53; Kafka, *Weg*, 45–7.

[111] W. Kielar, *Anus mundi* (Harmondsworth, 1982), 72; Smolen, 'Soviet Prisoners', 122. The disinfectant may have been lysoform.

Dr Aharon Beilin, a specialist in infectious diseases who had worked at a ghetto hospital, observed that on arriving in Auschwitz the cold shower, followed by much running about when still naked, meant that 70 per cent of his transport soon died from pneumonia and from other diseases due to exposure to cold.[112]

Mass delousing routines for camp prisoners were a humiliating ordeal, compounded by the loss of vital personal effects; standing for hours in the cold resulted in infections, although at Mauthausen a long wait provided Spanish Civil War veterans the opportunity to form a resistance group. At the end of the operation clothes were returned wet, soiled, and still crawling with lice.[113] Lice were widespread, and their temporary removal hardly alleviated the atrocious conditions: the *Muselman*, described as a 'dirty being, dressed in rags, often with lice, usually with severe diarrhea and an accordingly dirty uniform, with fallen in or bulging eyes, was a true picture of misery, of weakness, hopelessness and horror'.[114] Falling ill with a contagious disease meant removal to the camp hospital infested with lice, rats, and fleas, starvation rations, and generally resulted in being killed rather than being treated. Delousing was an ordeal, which was more punitive than effective.

The ordeal of delousing was as much a psychological as a physical torment. At the Czarnieckiego prison in the Litzmannstadt ghetto Sala Pawłowicz experienced the shaving of hair as robbing her and her companions of their self-esteem and as de-sexualizing, 'their faces were shrunken, their eyes seemed larger and deeper, and they looked like a new sex neither masculine nor feminine. They were no longer girls but something less.' The verdict of Eugen Kogon at Buchenwald was that 'This so-called induction ceremony was a thorough and complete indignity to human personality.' Guards took sadistic pleasure in shaving female hair, lacerating skin, conducting body searches for valuables and inflicting showers for their sexual gratification.[115] The Auschwitz commandant, Rudolf Höss, gloated over the naked bodies of the first batch of French women prisoners.[116] Kay Gundel's experience epitomized the stripping of identity on entering Auschwitz: 'in a few moments all hair and body hair was gone. Tears fell in that room as the last precious thing was stripped from us . . . [and] turned me into this sexless, nameless creature.'[117]

iv. Death as 'Disinfection'

While genuine delousing involved much physical and psychological torture, the question arises as a to how it came about that the abuse of Zyklon gas chambers for

---

[112] *Eichmann Trial Proceedings*, 1256, 1258.

[113] Pressac, *Auschwitz*, 54, testimony concerning delousing in Birkenau (women's camp) in July 1943; I. Strzelecka, 'Women', Gutman and Berenbaum, *Auschwitz*, 405; Langbein, *Against All Hope*, 79–80.

[114] Description by Vilo Jurkovic, quoted by D. Czech, 'The Auschwitz Prisoner Administration', in Gutman and Berenbaum (eds.), *Auschwitz*, 371.

[115] Pressac, *Auschwitz*, 31–5, 72–9; Pawłowicz, *I Will Survive*, 90–1, 108–9, 146–7; S. Weale, 'Lest They Remember, Lest We Forget', *Guardian* (14 Jan. 1995), 23. NAW RG 153 War Crimes Case Number 12–390 The Buchenwald Case, microfilm 5, Kogon cross examination, 241.

[116] National Sound Archives, London, interview with Claudette Kennedy.

[117] Holocaust Museum, Washington, DC, Survivors' Testimonies, RG-02.004*1, pp. 75–6, 108, testimony of Kay Gundel. For further accounts see Dwork and van Pelt, *Auschwitz*, 222–5.

genocide became a crucial phase of the Holocaust. Within the Reich the 'euthanasia' of the mentally ill perverted normal medical routines—of clinical inspection, diagnosis, bedside care, and personal hygiene. The basic disguise of the fake shower was used to cleanse the German gene pool of 'incurables', the mentally ill, and other chronically ill persons. Although the contexts and scale of the euthanasia gas chambers differed from that of delousing and of the fiction of deportation to the east, there were crucial links as gas chamber technology and personnel were transferred from euthanasia installations to running gas chambers in the east. The horrors of euthanasia, and the history of the extermination camps in Poland have been extensively reconstructed by historians; this brief section compares Nazi 'euthanasia' with the killing procedures in the extermination camps, so as to clarify how a lethal fusion arose of gas chamber technology and epidemic control methods.

The idea of coercive euthanasia arose among the radical Nazis close to Hitler, notably the Reich Physicians' Führer Gerhard Wagner, Brandt and Unger (the biographer of Behring). Exactly who convinced Hitler to authorize euthanasia and exactly when this occurred is not known, other than that it was sometime before July 1939; but how its implementation was left to the Führer's Chancellery has been documented. So that secrecy should be maintained, planning and administration was devolved to 'T4' bureaucrats (= Tiergartenstrasse, number 4, a villa confiscated from a Jewish welfare organization) who gave medical personnel key functions in selecting and overseeing the killing of disabled children, the incurably mentally ill, the infirm, the querulous, and other misfits who had fallen foul of doctors in charge.[118] 'Euthanasia' was motivated by medical concerns to eradicate the degenerate, economic concerns to save money, notions of racial purity, and by strategic requirements of gaining space in hospital accommodation for military casualties and for repatriated ethnic Germans. These aims brought together Nazi functionaries, doctors, and experts in poison gas technology.

A police chemist, Albert Widmann of the Kriminaltechnisches Institut (KTI) of the Reich Criminal Police Office advised that carbon monoxide gas (CO) was the most suitable poison. Widmann's new task coincided with his joining the SS in December 1939. His chemistry section produced poisons for the T4 killings.[119] The leading surgeon agitating for euthanasia, Karl Brandt, discussed the killing methods with Hitler, and they agreed that poison gas would be more 'humane' than injections. Conti, state secretary for health at the Reich Ministry of the Interior, also preferred poison gas. Other methods of hospitalized killing included injections of morphium, curare, or the barbiturates luminal (a sedative) or veronal (sleeping tablets); starvation diets were used especially for children. Widmann devised a method of releasing gas into hospital dormitories. As Henry Friedlander observes, 'The technology for gassing people had to be invented.' Gassings were compared with injections when a trial gassing of fifteen to twenty persons was conducted in the former prison of Brandenburg in December 1939 or January 1940; it was shown

---

[118] M. Burleigh, *Death and Deliverance. 'Euthanasia' in Germany 1900–1945* (Cambridge, 1995), 93–113 for the complex origins of euthanasia, p. 130 for ethnic cleansing.

[119] Friedlander, *Origins*, 53–6, 209.

that lethal injections took longer to kill. This prototype gas chamber was constructed to resemble showers. From May 1940 until the official 'stop' to euthanasia in August 1941, carbon monoxide gas was used on a regular basis at Brandenburg and at five psychiatric hospitals, where rooms were converted into gas chambers. The T4 bureaucrats proudly recorded that 70,273 persons were killed in this phase of the euthanasia programme.[120]

The T4 organization ordered supplies of carbon monoxide gas through the KTI in order to disguise its activities. A chemist of the KTI, August Becker, who was an SS officer from 1935, developed valves and specifications for the steel bottles, which were supplied by a subsidiary of Mannesmann. The bottles were filled at the Ludwigshafen works of BASF, an IG-Farben subsidiary, and the CO gas containers were transported to the T4 institutions.[121] The loss of export markets with the declaration of war in 1939 caused consternation among IG and DEGESCH. But the firms took heart that the war compensated by providing new spheres for application of poison gases.[122] The industrial tentacles of IG-Farben included CO gas, Zyklon, and (through its control of the Behringwerke) typhus vaccines: the conglomerate profited from whatever method of disease eradication or killing was adopted.

Nurses herded the patients into a changing room. A doctor examined the naked patients, doing little more than checking that the patient's identity coincided with the medical records. The medical examination served to pacify patients, and to enable a plausible fictitious cause of death to be made. The patients were given soap and a towel and forced in groups of forty to fifty into what was disguised at Brandenburg as an inhalation chamber, patients being told that they were to inhale a therapeutic substance; elsewhere the disguise was as a shower room with showerheads and wooden benches.[123] The doctor—assigned a symbolic role of overall control—turned the gas stopcock on and then off after about twenty minutes. After a further thirty minutes the doctor ordered the nursing staff to open the door so that the corpses could be removed by the crematorium staff known as 'stokers' (*Brenner*) or 'disinfectors' (*Desinfekteure*). A few bodies were reserved for autopsies providing specimens for brain and anatomical research. Doctors faked death certificates, with a false date and cause of death, frequently attributing death to a plausible infectious disease. Tuberculosis was a preferred cause as not subject to the notification procedures required for typhus; indeed, one institution director simply shot suspected typhus patients to avoid the bureaucratic repercussions. Rapid cremation without the permission of the next of kin could be justified as a precautionary hygienic measure. The officials of the T4 transport section used the euphemism *desinfiziert* for the

[120] Ibid., 86–91; Kogon, *Giftgas*, 46–7, 60–2; Burleigh, *Death and Deliverance*, 119.

[121] Friedlander, *Origins*, 210–11; Kogon, *Giftgas*, 52–3. On IG links to DEGESCH concerning manufacture of 'Calcid' see DEGUSSA Firmenarchiv, Bonath 2 'Geschichte der DEGESCH'.

[122] Bayer-Archiv, IG Fremdfirmen DEGUSSA 6.14 Bd 1, Geschäftsbericht der DEGESCH für das Jahr 1939 (dated 16 Apr. 1940).

[123] Friedlander, *Origins*, 88–93, 96; Kogon, *Giftgas*, 47; Burleigh, *Death and Deliverance*, 147.

gassings.[124] The killing procedures and technologies were devised to dispose of hospitalized populations.

Friedlander's careful analysis of the origins of the T4 programme establishes that the lethal carbon monoxide gas chamber derived not from the widely used hydrocyanic acid (HCN) delousing chambers but was a new invention. The police and involved doctors had experience of carbon monoxide poisoning, and did not draw any connections with HCN as a pesticide, nor with the Nevada HCN gas chamber used for executions since 1930. The French immunologist Alexis Carrel presumably had the Nevada chamber in mind when he demanded 'small euthanasic institutions supplied with proper gases' for criminals and the criminal insane.[125] It is possible that the SS buildings department might have drawn on gas chamber technology in its work for T4, but otherwise the HCN human gas chambers and the T4 killings represented separate strands of development.

With the invasion of Poland, an SS unit used vans equipped with carbon monoxide canisters (one disguised as a delivery lorry for 'Kaisers-Kaffee-Geschäft') to kill Polish mental patients between May and June 1940. As the mass extermination of Jews was unleashed in the summer of 1941, the vans (sometimes referred to as delousing vans or special vans) were used to gas Jewish women and children in Poland, Serbia, and the Soviet Union. The vans suited the mobility of the *Blitzkrieg*, and were supplied to the killing squads unleashed behind the front in the Barbarossa campaign, and they were used to kill Jews, the mentally ill, and sick children in the Ukraine, Crimea, and Caucasus until at least 1943.[126] Technical personnel from the T4 euthanasia programme were involved: at Mogilev near Minsk in September 1941 Widmann experimented with CO exhaust fumes, showing the superiority of gas vans to blowing up patients with explosives. Becker in late 1941 and early 1942 evaluated and repaired the gas vans used by the Einsatzgruppen in Russia. Hellmut Kallmeyer, a T4 chemist, was dispatched to Riga in the autumn of 1941 to assist with the vans; he was in Lublin early in 1942 to work on the new fixed killing installations.[127] Prior to the invasion of the Soviet Union, Walther Heess (the chief of the KTI) and Widmann discussed the development of a mobile gas chamber using exhaust fumes, because of the strategic problem of delivering gas containers at a distance from the Reich.[128] Parts of the vans were supplied from Switzerland, although whether the Swiss manfacturers knew of the use of the vans is uncertain. At the concentration camp of Zemun, near Belgrade, Jews from Serbia

---

[124] Friedlander, *Origins*, 96–102, 104–6 on fake causes of death; Kogon, *Giftgas*, 50–1; Burleigh, *Death and Deliverance*, 150–2.

[125] The suggestion was made in A. Carrel, *Man, the Unknown* (Harmondsworth, 1948), 291, first published in 1935. Carrel returned from the Rockefeller University, New York to Vichy France where he founded an institute to harness science to advance the nation. Id., 'Les Premiers Mois de Travail de la Fondation Française pour l'Etude des Problèmes Humains', *Bulletin OIHP*, 36 (1944), 127–33.

[126] Kogon, *Nazi Mass Murder*, 52–72; Friedlander, *Origins*, 286–7.

[127] Friedlander, *Origins*, 141–2, 210–15, 296 on the T4 chemists; Hilberg, 333, 875; Kogon, *Nazi Mass Murder*, 52–3; Burleigh, *Death and Deliverance*, 133, 180; Aly, *Endlösung*, 342–3; M. Beer. 'Die Entwicklung der Gaswagen beim Mord an den Juden', *Vierteljahreshefte für Zeitgeschichte*, 35 (1987), 403–17.

[128] Friedlander, *Origins*, 208–15, 286; Kogon, *Giftgas*, 63–4; Beer, 'Gaswagen', 403–17.

were gassed in vans disguised as Red Cross vehicles; the vans were then transferred
to Riga. Reports of the mobile gas chambers reached the Warsaw ghetto, and by
May 1942 filtered through to the west.[129]

The faltering war in the east spurred the launching of a genocidal campaign to
eradicate the Jewish race. Whether the shift to genocide in the late summer of 1941
was to compensate for the failure to eradicate Bolshevism, or to extend the eastern
campaign at a time of Allied weakness remains a matter of debate. The Einsatzgruppen broadened their murderous agenda from the killing of the Bolshevik élite
to wholesale destruction of Jewish communities. The vast scale of atrocities raised
problems as to how the enlarged programme of genocide should be realized.
Shooting, burning, and beatings were effective in killing a probable 1.3 million
persons, but such mass butchery could not be imposed on the European heartlands
without profoundly destabilizing consequences. Himmler wished to avoid the
spectacle of mass killings like shootings or setting fire to men, women, and children
locked into barns. He demanded a more clinical approach from his SS generals and
troops:

Anti-semitism is exactly the same as delousing. Getting rid of lice is not a question of
ideology, it is a matter of cleanliness. In just the same way, anti-semitism for us had not
been a question of ideology but a matter of cleanliness which now will soon have been
dealt with. We shall soon be deloused.[130]

The first fixed killing installation at the village of Kulmhof (Chełmno) in the
annexed Wartheland used the gas vans when it began operations on 7 December
1941. The perpetrators had experience in killing Polish mental patients. The
victims were mainly Jews from the provinces of Posen and Litzmannstadt. A
former camp staff member later testified that 'The victims were usually induced to
take off their clothes by being told that they had to take a bath before starting work
. . . were naked and given a towel.'[131] The fiction of a shower or steam bath meant
that clothing was conveniently left by the victim, so that it could be collected by the
Germans.

Despite the vast scale of the genocide in the east, the impatience of the Holocaust
planners was such that they condemned mobile gas vans as inefficient, in that they
could 'only' cope with small numbers (of thirty or sixty persons depending on the
type of van), and they were prone to breakdowns. The frustration of Nazi leaders at
the slow pace of the killing created the demand for mass extermination technology
to kill the Jews of the Generalgouvernement. Possibly in the summer of 1941 the
Reich SS physician Grawitz advised Hitler that the gas chamber was the most effec-

[129] Gilbert, *Holocaust*, 239–40; Gilbert, *Atlas of the Holocaust*, 83.
[130] R. W. Cooper, *The Nuremberg Trial* (Harmondsworth, 1947), 140; Himmler added 'We have only 20,000 lice left, and then the matter is finished off within the whole of Germany'; C. Streit, 'Wehrmacht and Anti-Bolshevism', Cesarani, *Final Solution*, 107, 116. Goebbels also denounced Jews as 'the lice of civilized mankind' on 2 Nov. 1941, see R. G. Routh, *Joseph Goebbels' Tagebücher 1924–1945* (Munich, 1992), 1695.
[131] Kogon, *Nazi Mass Murder*, 73–90; Burleigh, *Death*, 131–3; Dwork and van Pelt, *Auschwitz*, 293–5.

tive method for genocide. However, the type of gas was not specified. Improvised and then purpose-built gas chambers increased the scale of the killing.[132]

The euthanasia 'stop' of August 1941 in reality signalled a broadening out of the Nazi killing programmes. While 'wild' euthanasia was ferociously pursued on a decentralized basis in hospitals, the T4 staff required alternative employment. The most compelling evidence for a direct link between 'euthanasia' and the Holocaust is that ninety-two former T4 personnel were transferred to the SS under the command of Christian Wirth, an SS officer and inspector of the euthanasia institutions, while continuing on the T4 payroll. This T4 contingent helped to construct a gas chamber at Bełżec in December 1941; it became the prototype of the carbon monoxide type of chamber in the extermination camps of what became called the 'Aktion Reinhard', commemorating the assassination of the SS officer entrusted with accelerating genocide, Reinhard Heydrich, in May 1942.[133] The carbon monoxide gas was supplied by the T4 euthanasia organization.

The Bełżec camp commander (and from August 1942 in overall charge of Bełżec, Sobibor, and Treblinka), Wirth, disguised the gas chamber as a shower, and the victims were told they were to bathe and be disinfected. The false shower room—taken over from the T4 killing of mental patients—now changed its meaning from the routines of personal hygiene to disinfestation as an anti-typhus measure. The victims were to be deceived into believing that they were entering a camp for a temporary stay prior to permanent resettlement. The delousing fiction involved segregation of the 'dirty' from a fictitious 'clean' side, and the expectation that clothes and personal belongings would be removed for delousing. A chain of extermination camps of the 'Aktion Reinhard' ran along Poland's former eastern border, where once there had been delousing installations. Wirth rejected the use of Zyklon as an expensive product from private firms, and as difficult to requisition; he devised a lethal cocktail of petrol and diesel fuel with the gas produced by an engine.[134] In mid-April 1942 the extermination camp of Sobibor (commanded by another T4 veteran, Franz Stangl of the Hartheim euthanasia centre) became operational using carbon monoxide gas from diesel motors. Treblinka near Warsaw replaced mass shootings with carbon monoxide gas chambers, built with advice from a T4 expert, and initially supervised by the T4 doctor, Irmfried Eberl. Again, the gas chambers had false shower heads, and fake water pipes were used as gas outlets. The camp operated from July 1942: arrivals were directed by a sign 'to the baths'; they were instructed that a bath was required 'for physical cleanliness', while baggage was to be handed over 'for disinfection' to prevent epidemics.[135] The disinfection rituals for migrants were exploited to attain compliance, although in practice high levels of coercion were needed.

[132] Hilberg, *Destruction*, 863–4.

[133] Burleigh, *Death and Deliverance*, 126 for Wirth, and 232–5 for further connections; Kogon, *Nazi Mass Murder*, 105–7.

[134] Kogon, *Giftgas*, 153–4; Burleigh, *Death and Deliverance*, 126.

[135] Kogon, *Giftgas*, 162–3; Kogon, *Nazi Mass Murder*, 115, 125; Hackett, *Buchenwald*, 352–4, testimony of Oscar Berger.

A catastrophic typhus epidemic in the winter of 1941–2 coincided with the search for a mass killing method for human undesirables. Zyklon was stockpiled for anti-epidemic measures in the camps. Although T-gas (aethyl oxide) for fumigation, and dry heat for clothes and personal effects were safer alternatives, the SS remained fixated on the highly poisonous Zyklon for disinfestation. How Zyklon was deployed to kill humans was left to a devolved and informal process of trial and error, expediency, and improvisation within the camps. There is no evidence for systematic experiments having been undertaken by a group like the KTI or for guidelines on human gas chambers having been issued. But Eichmann's activities, and the observations by Gerstein and Pfannenstiel at Bełżec do suggest a concerted plan to replace carbon monoxide. The Hygiene Institute of the Waffen-SS was drawn into supplying Zyklon and came to have a decisive role in its formulation, but it did not initiate the Zyklon killings. A British investigator later commented that it appeared 'that no controlled experiments were carried out on a scientific basis'. For the size of gas chambers and other circumstances such as numbers of victims, amounts used, and temperature constantly varied.[136] As so often in Holocaust history, events were shaped by the expediency of zealots on the sites of killing.

The murderous gas chambers at Auschwitz marked the apotheosis of all the varied types of gas chambers. They consumed perhaps 10 per cent of the overall numbers of Holocaust victims, and yet, thousands could be killed daily in these chambers. A sharp line demarcates the Zyklon gas chambers at Auschwitz, assigned a special role in the plans to eradicate European Jews shunted in trains from western and southern Europe, from the carbon monoxide gas chambers of Bełżec, Sobibor, and Treblinka, which were part of the Aktion Reinhard programme with Polish Jewry as the main target. Racialized anti-typhus measures accelerated and extended the Nazi genocide.

The period from July 1941 saw the gestation of new methods of mass killing using Zyklon: it is worthwhile going over the shreds of evidence in order to see whether any linkage between the implementation of typhus control methods and the use of Zyklon for genocidal purposes emerges. Hydrocyanic acid in the form of Zyklon had become a standard weapon in the armoury of hygiene for disinfestation purposes, and was subject to complex medical and administrative controls. The HCN regulations of March 1931 remained in force after 1933 and were extended to cover the newly acquired territories like the Ostmark and Sudetenland in 1941. On 3 April 1941 the Waffen-SS became authorized to use Zyklon, a sign of their increasing military role and in supervising sanitation in the concentration camps, and it is possible that this decree increased the stockpiles of the gas canisters in concentration camps.

Mass training courses in louse eradication became a priority: in the summer of 1940 Hase and a team of applied zoologists trained 2,000 disinfectors and health

---

[136] J. C. Evans, 'German CW Experiments on Human Beings', report dated 12 Jan. 1948 for Ministry of Supply, Advisory Council on Scientific Research and Technical Development, Chemical Defence Advisory Board, 4, copy in Wiener Library Kh (1). PRO WO 195/9678.

inspectors in louse control methods. Tesch trained SS disinfectors at Oranienburg, some of whom later carried out human killings. Did the suppliers of the gas like Tesch and Peters, who also advised on the design of gas chambers in the camps, suggest or at least facilitate the fatal transfer to human gassings?[137] By 1936 Peters, the DEGESCH manager, was working on more efficient designs for gas chambers to ensure that the Zyklon circulated rapidly and evenly. Peters was triumphant concerning his carefully devised system, comparing his scientific approach to the empirical bravado during the First World War. The cold winters endured on the Russian fronts provided an opportunity for Peters to test the gas in freezing temperatures. Peters became deputy managing director of DEGESCH in 1939, and, when Heerdt was ousted in 1941, its general director. The supply of gas chambers in the east meant useful contacts were forged with the military.[138] But the increased use of Zyklon during the war led to a rise in fatal accidents. For example, after fumigation of a family's furniture, bedding, and clothes in the Königsberg disinfection office in January 1941, the family was found dead the next day. Officials concluded that more safety procedures should be included in the regulations and that only DEGESCH, Heerdt-Lingler, and Tesch and Stabenow should be allowed to train disinfectors.[139]

The gigantic scale and atrocious conditions at Auschwitz meant that the camp administration was on the lookout for improving the fumigation system of Zyklon delousing. In July 1941 the director of the Auschwitz building department showed Höss an article on HCN delousing by Peters and Wüstinger of DEGESCH using a new ventilation technology; this had been developed at DEGESCH using a Swiss patent system acquired by DEGESCH and Heli. The technology could replace the rather slapdash system of piling prisoners' clothes in an improvised sealed room and then opening the tins of Zyklon and emptying them, before the prisoner-disinfectors sealed the door with paper strips.[140]

The adoption of Zyklon for genocide at Auschwitz was a mixture of expediency and murderous intent. In July 1941 Horst Schumann selected 575 prisoners from

[137] 'Verordnungen über die Einführung von Vorschriften über die Schädlingsbekämpfung. Vom 2. Februar 1941', *Reichsgesetzblatt* (1941), i. 69; 'Anwendung von hochgiftigen Stoffen zur Schädlingsbekämpfung durch die Waffen-SS', *Zeitschrift für Schädlingsbekämpfung*, 33 (1941), 120 H. Kemper, 'Ueber Läusebekämpfungs-Lehrgänge', ibid., 32 (1940), 138–43. PRO WO 235/83 f. 219, 262, 390.

[138] G. Peters, 'Ein neues Verfahren zur Kammerdurchgasung', *Zeitschrift für Schädlingsbekämpfung*, 28 (1936), 106–12; G. Peters and W. Rasch, 'Die Einsatzfähigkeit der Blausäure bei tiefen Temperaturen (Praktische Erfahrungen des Kriegswinters 1940/41 und ihre exakte Nachprüfung.)', *Zeitschrift für Schädlingsbekämpfung*, 33 (1941), 148–53; Bayer-Archiv, IG Fremdfirmen DEGUSSA 6.14 Bd 1, Geschäftsbericht der DEGESCH für das Jahr 1939 (dated 16 Apr. 1940), 6–7.

[139] BAK R 168/259 Blausäure; Aenderungen zum Runderlass 1927–44; Report 27 Mar. 1942 to Reichsministerium für Ernährung und Landwirtschaft; Ministry report on accident to Parteikanzlei, 27 June 1942.

[140] G. Peters and E. Wüstinger, 'Sach-Entlausung in Blausäure-Kammern', *Zeitschrift für hygienische Zoologie und Schädlingsbekämpfung*, 32 (1940), 191–6; Peters and Wüstinger, *Entlausung mit Zyklon-Blausäure in Kreislaufbegasungskammern* (Berlin, 1940). On Wüstinger see STAN KV Ankl. Interrogations Nr P25, Bl. 22; Bayer-Archiv IG Fremdfirmen Degussa 6.14 Bd 1/2, E. Wüstinger, 'Die spontane Entwicklung der Kammerbegasung', 4 Sept. 1942. Dwork and van Pelt, *Auschwitz*, 219–22. See n. 197 for Peters' innovations.

Auschwitz for gassing at the T4 installation at Sonnenstein. These killings by a veteran of the first euthanasia institution, Grafeneck, who in June 1940 was made director of the killing institution at Sonnenstein bei Pirna in Saxony, link Auschwitz to the euthanasia gas chambers. Although this was the first selection for gassing in Auschwitz, the operation did not lead to routine carbon monoxide gassings.[141] When Russian prisoners earmarked for immediate liquidation (described by Höss as political commissars 'combed out' by the German invaders) arrived in Auschwitz, they and 300 'incurably sick' prisoners were 'experimentally' killed with Zyklon B by one of Höss's underlings—either Schutzhaftlagerführer Karl Fritzsch (or Fritsch), or Höfle. One or other of these subordinates has in all probability the distinction of having invented the method of killing with Zyklon. The victims were pacified with the instruction that they were to be deloused.[142] Dwork and van Pelt date this first trial gassing as occurring on 3 September 1941; this would nearly coincide with the faked death book entries. A second gassing took place on 16 September in a mortuary, where there was a convenient ventilation system and a flat roof from which the Zyklon could be poured through improvised hatches.[143] Zyklon was available in large quantities in the camp for epidemic control since July 1940 as death rates from typhus soared: but the concern over the spread of typhus in the winter of 1941 provided an incentive for killing by Zyklon gas.[144] Anti-typhus measures precipitated this lethal furthering of the Holocaust.

Höss was triumphant—'now we had the gas and we had the procedure', he later reflected. He repeated what he later claimed was an 'experiment' that confirmed the superiority of Zyklon B over carbon monoxide. In January and June 1942 two bunkers were converted into gas chambers; later a peasant's cottage in the Auschwitz complex used established techniques of sealing windows and adding gas-tight doors.[145] The SS's priority was to increase the capacity of the gas chambers.

The victims of the first gassings at Auschwitz were Poles and Russians, and it took several months before the function of the camp changed to that of an exter-

[141] Schumann was on the hereditary health tribunal for sterilization cases at Halle, and an NSDAP member since 1930. From July 1941 until 1944 Schumann was in Auschwitz where he conducted X-ray castration experiments. H. Schumann, *Zur Frage der Jodresorption und der therapeutischen Wirkung sogenannter Jodbäder* (Halle, 1933); W. Kaiser and A. Völker, 'Die faschistischen Strömungen an der Medizinischen Fakultät der Universität Halle', in A. Thom and H. Spaar (eds.), *Medizin im Faschismus* (Berlin, 1983), 53–67; E. Klee, *Was sie taten—was sie wurden* (Frankfurt/M., 1986), 98–107; D. Czech, *Auschwitz Chronicles* (London, 1990), 821.

[142] Höss, *Autobiography*, 91–3, 112–13; State Museum of Auschwitz-Birkenau, *Death Books from Auschwitz. Remnants* (Munich, 1995), i. 54–7; K. Smolen, 'Soviet Prisoners of War in KL Auschwitz', *Death Books*, 113–31, 117–20; *The Trial of Adolf Eichmann*, 2252 for confusion over the name of the responsible underling and the invention of Zyklon B.

[143] Dwork and van Pelt, *Auschwitz*, 192–3; Wojciech Barcz, 'Die erste Vergasung', in H. G. Adler, H. Langbein, and E. Lingens-Reiner, *Auschwitz: Zeugnisse und Berichte* (Frankfurt/M., 1988), 18.

[144] For the dating of this see Pressac, *Crématoires*, 112–13; Aly, *Endlösung*, 361; Gilbert, *Holocaust*, 239; Borkin, *Crime*, 122; Kogon, *Giftgas*, 194, 204–5 for a data in September. Kogon suggests that 15 Aug. 1941 (a date mentioned by another witness) was erroneous. Pressac with van Pelt, 'Machinery', 209, 214.

[145] For a recollection of the early gassings, see Kielar, *Anus mundi*, 61–5, 79–80.

mination centre for Jews. Dwork and van Pelt have carefully argued that when in June 1941 Himmler ordered Höss to undertake preparatory measures for the 'final solution of the Jewish question', only limited facilities to dispose of Jews incapable of surviving transport to some intended eastern reservation may have been envisaged. It was after the Wannsee Conference of 20 January 1942 that Himmler gained authority over the fate of the Jews, and Auschwitz was deemed a suitable location for mass murder. By June 1942 the camp had improvised gas chambers, one with false shower heads, a large incinerating capacity, and had begun to annihilate sick and elderly Jews from Upper Silesia and Slovakia.[146]

Eichmann instructed Höss (at least according to the latter) that the carbon monoxide gas chambers were inadequate for the intended scale of killing. The chain of command ran down from Himmler to the Reich Main Security Office where the zealous Eichmann was in charge of the Jewish section; Eichmann signalled the intention to kill by poison gas, and underlings devised a procedure, which was then given backing from their superiors. Acting on orders from Eichmann, Höss inspected the Kulmhof gas chamber with the intention of setting up a similar installation at the Birkenau site in Auschwitz. He found carbon monoxide slow and insufficiently poisonous.[147] Höss realized that the carbon monoxide chambers were too small, and that some other type of gas would be necessary.[148] Höss pointed out that Treblinka (which began operation in July 1942) required ten times as many smaller gas chambers (each with a capacity of 200) to equal the cavernous Auschwitz chambers.[149] Diesel oil froze in cold weather, thereby paralyzing operation of carbon monoxide chambers. The endorsement of the efficacy of Zyklon by Höss led to bitter rivalry with Wirth (the Bełżec commandant), who correctly surmised that the method of carbon monoxide gassing would be replaced.[150] Here, the initiative came from Eichmann's office, when the SS officer Günther ordered the disinfection officer Gerstein to deliver a consignment of Zyklon to the extermination camp director Odilo Globocnik in June 1942.[151]

The Peters and Wüstinger ventilation technology pointed to how human killings could be accelerated. The initial gassings at Auschwitz had been crude affairs, leaving some prisoners alive after a day, and the building had to be aired to get rid of the pungent acrid smell before the corpse bearers could remove something like a thousand bodies. The significance of the Peters article is that it showed how temperature control, correct quantities of the gas, and improvements in ventilation could render the killing process far more efficient. The technological transfer from epidemic prevention led to new gas chambers being disguised as shower rooms—sometimes with fake shower heads, but at times with the simple device of a sign 'zum Baden' and another sign on the fictitious exit 'zur Desinfektion'. The

[146] Höss, *Autobiography*, 108–9; Pressac and van Pelt, 'The Machinery of Mass Murder at Auschwitz', in Gutman and Berenbaum, *Auschwitz*, 213; Dwork and van Pelt, *Auschwitz*, 276–87, 298–304.
[147] Höss, *Autobiography*, 116–17; *The Trial of Adolf Eichmann*, 2004–5, 2176–8.
[148] Höss, *Autobiography*, 109–13; Piper, 'Gas Chambers', 157.
[149] *Trial of German Major War Criminals*, ii. 360.   [150] Hilberg, *Destruction*, 892–3.
[151] *The Trial of Adolf Eichmann*, 2004–5; YVA Gerstein file, testimony 6 May 1945.

SS guards gave repeated assurances that prisoners were to have baths and be deloused as an epidemic control measure, and sometimes victims were issued with a piece of soap and a towel. SS doctors supervised and were ready in case an SS man accidentally inhaled the gas. SS disinfectors poured the gas into the chambers, and prisoners were ordered to remove the convulsed corpses under medical supervision.[152]

The first transports of Jews were told that the chambers were for delousing, but sensed that they were to meet their death by some form of asphyxiation. Mothers expressed fear that the delousing fluid would harm young children and had to be reassured.[153] The killing generally took from three to fifteen minutes, depending on climatic conditions. Peters calculated that Zyklon B was six times more poisonous than chlorine, thirty-four times more poisonous than carbon monoxide, and 750 times more poisonous than chloroform.[154]

While the initial testing of Zyklon at Auschwitz was the product of expediency, a number of predisposing factors facilitated its genocidal use. Zyklon B had immense advantages for the SS over carbon monoxide, being faster acting and technically simpler; Zyklon was simply poured from tins through an opening in the roof of the gas chamber by SS men wearing gas masks. Disinfectors could double up as killers, as was the case with the Auschwitz disinfectors Klehr and Theuer, who poured in the Zyklon crystals while under medical supervision.[155] Trainloads of victims could be gassed rather than bus and truckloads as with the T4 killings. Given that Zyklon B was used to delouse clothing without damage, victims' hair was salvaged for reuse, and clothing and possessions of the victims were separately disinfected. As a temperature of 25.7 degrees centigrade was necessary, the SS added cruelty to calculation by waiting to allow natural human warmth to attain this. Tins of Zyklon in crystalline form were convenient to handle and to store when compared with carbon monoxide used in liquid form in the T4 euthanasia killings, and more efficient than diesel engine fumes in the gas chambers of the Sobibor extermination camp. The disadvantage of Zyklon was that it could not be stored more than three months, and thus regular supplies needed to be maintained.[156] The pain induced by the warning agent in Zyklon B—intended to be a life-saving device, designed to make it unbearable for a person to remain in a room before hydrocyanic acid could fatally act—would have been excrutiating. The agonized convulsed bodies made their removal all the harder.[157]

[152] Pressac, *Auschwitz*, 172; Piper, 'Gas Chambers', 162, 169–70; Smolen, 'Soviet Prisoners', 119.
[153] Höss, *Autobiography*, 94–7; Kogon, *Giftgas*, 206–7. The first chamber was demolished late in 1942 to make way for the new crematoria and the second was demolished at the beginning of 1945; Pressac, *Auschwitz*, 174.
[154] G. Wellers, 'The Two Poison Gases', in Kogon (ed.), *Nazi Mass Murder*, 205–9; Bayer-Archiv IG Fremdfirmen Degussa 6.14 Bd 1/2, DEGESCH 1 Jan. 1939.
[155] H. Langbein, *Der Auschwitz Prozess. Eine Dokumentation* (Vienna, 1965), ii. 568–9.
[156] BA-MA H 20/929 OKW to Arbeitsausschuss für Raumentwesung 9 Nov. 1944. The army reported in 1944 that tins of Zyklon which were over two years old were still in good condition; Hilberg, *Destruction*, 885–9. Hilberg suggests that from 1944 there was reference to Zyklon C for cockroaches and the fumigation of wooden buildings, D for lice, mice, and rats in buildings, E, F, and B for humans. These categories seem dubious.
[157] Kielar, *Anus mundi*, 65.

Despite the initiating role of the upper echelons of the SS, there is no extant evidence for a central body of scientists developing ever more lethal killing procedures in any research institute like the KTI. Yet disinfection experts inspected the gas chambers in the camps. First, it seems that subordinates devised expedients so as to execute the genocidal intentions communicated from above. While Höss solved the problems of gassing at Auschwitz, others were not so pliable. Secondly, Gerstein, the chief disinfection officer of Mrugowsky's Hygiene Institute of the Waffen-SS, illustrates how expertise in delousing led to on-site evaluation of gassings, followed by his idiosyncratic involvement in human extermination. Gerstein's testimony on the chain of command involved in the supply of Zyklon and on gassing procedures furnished crucial evidence at the Nuremberg Trial of major German war criminals, and at the trial of Eichmann.[158] His 'normal' role of providing technical support for delousing, and devising new facilities, throws additional light on the links between typhus control and the Holocaust. He developed mobile delousing equipment for use in motorized transport, and equipped a train for delousing which made up some of the defects in stationary facilities during 1943.[159] He advised on water purity and on pest control in concentration camps—for example, on the plagues of rats and flies attracted by the mounting heaps of corpses.

Although a member of the Nazi Party from 1933 to 1936, Gerstein had been in trouble with the Nazi authorities because he was a member of the dissident church of Pastor Niemöller, and protested against the anti-Christian views of the Nazis. He was imprisoned and expelled from the NSDAP. After studying medicine at Tübingen in association with the Protestant Missionary Institute for Tropical Medicine, he was again in custody at the Welzheim concentration camp in 1938. Disquiet over the killing of mental patients, culminating in finding out that his sister-in-law was a victim, spurred him to gain insight into the killing process. Gerstein joined the SS in March 1941, convinced that the SS was to take a crucial role in mass murder. He believed that just as Nazi informers had infiltrated dissident religious circles so he could infiltrate the organizations responsible for mass killing to alert the public. His dual technical and medical qualifications led to his selection for training in preventive medicine; he attended courses in hygiene and disinfection at the Disinfectors School of the Waffen-SS in Oranienburg while attached to the Hygiene Institute of the Waffen-SS from June 1941.[160]

In January 1942 Gerstein was appointed head of 'technical disinfection services' at Mrugowsky's Institute. Gerstein supervised the medical engineering section of the institute, giving it the edge over the army which relied on contracts with private firms.[161] He constructed mobile and fixed disinfection apparatus for use in barracks, prisons, and concentration camps, gaining a reputation as innovative in the

---

[158] *The Trial of Adolf Eichmann*, 2176–7.

[159] LkA EKvW Gerstein Papers 5,2 Nr 198 Hygiene Institute of the Waffen-SS to Gerstein 7 Aug. 1941 concerning his work in developing mobile disinfection equipment. For a delousing train see the film *Kampf dem Fleckfieber* (copy in BAK); BAK R 90/455 Request to Stubf. Bludau to send the sanitary train to the Flüchtlingslager Olita, Lithuania 3 June 1943.

[160] LkA EKvW Gerstein Papers 5, 2/246.

[161] LkA EKvW Gerstein Papers 5,2 AS Nr 246 Beurteilung!, 19 Feb. 1943.

use of Zyklon for delousing. When ordered by an official of the Reich Security Office (the chain of command was to be furiously contested at the post-war trials) in June 1942 to deliver Zyklon to the SS in Lublin, he sabotaged the consignment by faking an accident. Gerstein joined a select group of high-ranking observers in August 1942, because the appropriate technology of mass destruction was being evaluated. The group included Wilhelm Pfannenstiel (professor of hygiene at Marburg, SS-Obersturmbannführer, and hygienic advisor to the Waffen-SS), Linden of the T4 euthanasia organization, Christian Wirth, a former euthanasia administrator, and Globocnik, in charge of the Aktion Reinhard extermination camps: they witnessed the horrors of a 'trial' gassing with carbon monoxide at the new extermination camp of Bełżec when the diesel motor failed to function, and inspected the sites of Treblinka and Maijdanek. The circumstances of the Bełżec gassing were subject to dispute after the war. Gerstein accused Pfannenstiel of declaring the killing process to be humane and noble, whereas Pfannenstiel claimed that he actually suggested Zyklon gas would be more humane as faster-acting. Gerstein testified that Globocnik was interested in using HCN not only to disinfect clothes and possessions of the murdered, but also to develop a faster method of killing than carbon monoxide.[162] It was through this group of observers that disinfection experts became directly involved in shaping the implementation of poison gas procedures.

Shortly after this traumatic gassing, the disturbed Gerstein informed a Swedish diplomat Göran van Otter in late August 1942, although Gerstein's wishes that the information about mass extermination be passed to the Allies were not respected. Otter recollected after the war—there is no extant report made at the time, even though Gerstein called on him again—that Gerstein showed him a camp comman-dant's instructions concerning supply of prussic acid. Given that the gassing he had witnessed used CO, the HCN instructions may have been just an order for the gas for fumigation purposes, or may have concerned converting the human gas cham-bers to HCN.[163] Globocnik gave Gerstein assignments regarding the disinfection of clothing of the victims, and to evaluate changing the gas chambers over from carbon monoxide from diesel exhausts to Zyklon.[164] Gerstein continued to take people into his confidence about the extermination procedures—for example, a Luftwaffe disinfection expert Armin Peters.[165] Despite his spiritual tortures over the

[162] LkA EKvW 5,2 NS Nr 192 for a vivid description by Gerstein. Nr 22,1 Fasc 2 for Pfannenstiel's testimony. YVA 9/30 (6a) 460 Gerstein file, Gerstein testimony 6 May 1945; Rottweil 26 Apr. 1945, indications personnelles; Klee, *'Euthanasie'*, 377–8; BDC Pfannenstiel file, joined NSDAP May 1933, the SS in 1934.

[163] P. A. Levine, 'Anti-Semitism in Sweden's Foreign Office: How Important was it?', *Historisk Tidskrift* (1996), 8–27; Levine, *From Indifference to Activism. Swedish Diplomacy and the Holocaust* (Uppsala, 1996), 126–9; S. Friedländer, *Kurt Gerstein ou l'ambiguité du bien* (Paris, 1967), 114–124. YVA Gerstein files Swedish Embassy London 7 Aug. 1945.

[164] LkA EKvW 5,2 NS Nr 191 file concerning Gerstein's role in resisting Nazi ideology, pp. 39–49; Nr 192 curriculum vitae and testimony about his role in delivering Zyklon; Nr 22,1 Fasc 1 on Mrugowsky, Fasc. 2 on Pfannenstiel. The explanation that he joined the SS to gain insight into euthanasia of mental patients is problematic in that the SS was only marginally involved in the T4 organization which came under the Führer's Chancellery.

[165] Friedländer, *Gerstein*, 118.

clash between his deep Christian piety and the anti-Christian ethos of the SS, Gerstein found both a refuge and a mission in his identity as technical expert, as he hovered on the fringes of the extermination process.

In the post-war trials of war criminals, there were elaborate attempts to evade responsibility for the supply of Zyklon to the camps. While it is clear which authorities were involved, the individual officials disclaimed responsibility. Whoever in the office dealing with Jewish affairs and emigration (under Eichmann) or the Reich Security Office (under the Police Chief Heinrich Müller) gave the order to supply Zyklon, it was communicated to the Hygiene Institute of the Waffen-SS by Eichmann's deputy, Rolf Günther. Given that this Institute had a legitimate role in using the gas for delousing, exploiting the Institute as a cover for supplying such a lethal substance for genocidal ends made sense. Günther's orders went to Gerstein as Mrugowsky's subordinate.[166] Gerstein's role indicates how Mrugowsky's sanitary institute provided materials and assistance to the extermination camps and squads. The Hygiene Institute of the Waffen-SS trained sanitary personnel and from 1942 (according to the evidence of Gerstein and the Auschwitz commandant Höss) allocated supplies of Zyklon.[167] Early in 1942 Peters gained Mrugowsky's support for a wider use of Zyklon for delousing; and Mrugowsky endorsed the gas chamber using the circulatory system, which Peters had publicized.[168]

Mrugowsky asked Peters to supply Zyklon directly to the SS. As the SS requirements were classified as a top secret *Geheime Reichssache*, this indicated that Zyklon might be used for purposes other than delousing. Peters circumvented the agreement with the distributing company TESTA about its Zyklon monopoly in the east, thereby cutting out the increasingly cantankerous Tesch. Mrugowsky delegated the orders to Gerstein and a subordinate, Lange, who purchased and allocated Zyklon B. Consignments went to the Waffen-SS disinfectors school, which trained and equipped disinfectors to use Zyklon; that this was without the warning agent indicates that the disinfectors were murder squads. At the Sachsenhausen concentration camp at Oranienburg, DEGESCH installed delousing installations using its new ventilation system. The SS office in Oranienburg gave orders on behalf of the disinfection service in Auschwitz to collect supplies of Zyklon B directly from the Dessau molasses factory, initially for pest control and then for 'special treatment' of humans.[169]

Gerstein communicated to Peters on behalf of the SS in June 1943 the order to

---

[166] *The Trial of Adolf Eichmann*, 2368.

[167] Mrugowsky denied this role. See NMT roll 38, frames 1156–9. NAW Microfilm Publication M 1019/roll 47 Mrugowsky interrogation, 23 Sept. 1946.

[168] NMT roll 30 Gerhard Peters deposition, defence testimonies: Mrugowsky, 16–18.

[169] Kogon, *Giftgas*, 222–4 dates the 'special treatment' order as August 1942; NAW Microfilm Publication M 1019/roll 47 Mrugowsky interrogation 17 Oct. 1946, pp. 21–2; STAN KV-Anklage Interrogations P 25, Gerhard Peters, 26 Oct. 1947, pp. 9–10; R. Queisner, 'Erfahrungen mit Filtereinsätzen und Gasmasken für hochgiftige Gase zur Schädlingsbekämpfung', *Zeitschrift für hygienische Zoologie*, 35 (1943), 190–4; Queisner, 'Erfahrungen mit Blausäure bei Grossraumentwesungen' [Aus der Desinfektorenschule der Waffen-SS, Oranienburg (Leiter: SS-Hauptsturmführer H. Gundlach)], *Zeitschrift für hygienische Zoologie*, 36 (1944), 130–7; Brillot, 'L'argent', 78–9.

omit the warning agent, because of the odour and because the added irritant induced painful retching and vomiting. Initially, DEGESCH officials were unwilling to comply because the SS's request could endanger the company's monopoly position, as the additive was the basis of the patent. They claimed that the gas would decompose more rapidly as the warning agent also stabilized it. The SS informed DEGESCH that it needed Zyklon to kill criminals, the mentally ill, and the feeble-minded—executing persons falling into these categories being regarded as legitimate, and indicating that knowledge of euthanasia was widespread.[170] Peters later asserted that he had only been informed by Gerstein of the use of Zyklon in the death camps in 1943; until then he was told that condemned criminals were to be killed.[171] The motives for removing the warning agent are open to different interpretations: on the one hand, Gerstein may have wished that death should come as swiftly and as painlessly as possible. On the other hand, the pungent additive may have left a residual smell, warning the victims of their fate; bodies may have been more difficult to remove from the gas chamber, after suffering the violent contortions of pain endured before death. Ludwik Fleck observed the corpses used by SS medical researchers for bacterial cultures: their twisted state suggested that the victims suffered great pain which he attributed to excessively weak doses of the gas.[172]

The production of Zyklon B trebled between 1937 and its peak in 1943, when turnover increased by 22 per cent and production rose from 133 to 411 tons. A tenth of this went to the SS. Eighty tons were supplied to the Wehrmacht for use in occupied territories. Although in a war economy supply could be expected to fall short of demand, since Zyklon was in short supply as a *Mangelprodukt*, hydrocyanic acid production fulfilled 80 per cent of its calculated demand in 1943. The profit per kilo for DEGESCH was 1.29 marks. Auschwitz was supplied 23.8 tonnes of which an estimated 5.6 tonnes were for actual fumigation.[173]

The rapid increase in production of a substance that was crucial for both genocide and epidemic prevention was highly profitable. DEGUSSA retained its share of 42.5 per cent in DEGESCH, equaling that of the IG conglomerate.[174] There were three IG-Farben representatives on the board of DEGESCH, and the extent to which they were informed about the use of poison gas for genocide was a matter of critical legal importance after the war. In 1947 a Nuremberg defence lawyer obtained documents which showed that members of the supervisory board were

[170] LkA EKvW, Nr 5, 2 Gerstein Papers AS 6, Blausäure; Borkin, *I. G. Farben*, 123.
[171] STAN KV Ankl. Interrogations Nr P 25, Bl. 20–1, 24; Kogon, *Giftgas*, 284.
[172] YVA 033/17, 3.
[173] Hayes, *Industry and Ideology*, 362 citing Hilberg, *Destruction*, 570. 70; BAK R3/361 Arbeitsausschuss für Raumentwesung, 28 for the 1943 production targets for poison gases. Degussa. Bon 010002, Unterlagen Dr. Bonath zur Degesch 1930–61: Degesch Umsätze 1936–47. Anlagen zum Geschäftsbericht der 'Degesch' für 1943. For production statistics as calculated by US investigators see STAN KV-Anklage P 35, p. 17 stating that the SS received 40,000 kg. out of a total production of 250–300,000 kg. Geschäftsbericht der DEGESCH für das Jahr 1943 (dated 27 Sept. 1944). For amounts supplied to Auschwitz see NAW 1019 roll 47 Mrugowsky interrogation of 3 Dec. 1946.
[174] DEGUSSA Rechtsabteilung, 'Tatsachen zum Thema Zyklon B'.

kept informed about DEGESCH activities until at least October 1942, including the technical work of Peters on gas chambers.[175] In February 1941 the IG manager Otto Ambros, an expert on synthetic fuel and rubber, engineered the agreement with the SS concerning the opening of IG-Auschwitz for the manufacture of synthetic rubber and oil.[176] IG established its private concentration camp at Monowitz, opening in September 1942.[177] Close attention was given to elaborate delousing, disinfection, and laundry arrangements, using the Zyklon to fumigate prisoners' clothing—although only partially implemented, this plant meant that news of the Auschwitz crematoria filtered up the IG-Farben managerial hierarchy.[178]

DEGUSSA had a partnership agreement with the French chemical concern of Ugine to manufacture Zyklon for German requirements since 1940, and turned out 37 tonnes alone in May 1944. Pharmaceuticals loomed large in the widespread collaboration between Vichy French and German industry.[179] It is not known whether any of this French-produced Zyklon was sent to the extermination camps, although given the overall shortfall in Zyklon an additional source of supply would have been of indirect assistance.

DEGUSSA had an interest in profiting from refining gold and silver of Jewish origin. The company offered its services in processing loot from the east; one instance was a bid to smelt gold and silver taken from the Litzmannstadt ghetto.[180] The gold and other precious objects taken from Jews in the concentration camps were sent to the Deutsche Reichsbank, for whom DEGUSSA undertook the smelting. The historian Karl-Heinz Roth has suggested that DEGUSSA produced gold bars from the dental gold extracted in the concentration camps.[181] Dental gold was assiduously harvested from the living as well as from the dead. While much remains to be clarified as to how the gold was processed, DEGUSSA was involved in the processing of looted gold transfered by the SS to the Reichsbank.[182]

DEGUSSA and its part-owned subsidiary DEGESCH were drawn to the brink of the Holocaust. Peters attained a position of national influence, claiming credit for establishing a committee in the Ministry of Weapons and Munitions to supervise the allocation of supplies, production, and standardization of disinfectants and pesticides for epidemic prevention. The launch of the Arbeitsausschuss für Raumentwesungs- und Seuchenabwehrmittel in May 1942 coincided with Peters' agreement to increase supplies to Mrugowsky for distribution to the SS. The com-

---

[175] Bayer-Archiv IG Fremdfirmen Degussa 6.14 Bd 1–2, I.G.W.-Elberfeld to O. Nelte, n.d. (1947–8); Inhaltsverzeichnis zum Akt 'Aufsichtsrat Degesch'.

[176] Borkin, *I. G. Farben*, 115. On Ambros see Harris and Paxman, *A Higher Form*, 64; Dwork and van Pelt, *Auschwitz*, 197–235.

[177] Borkin, *I. G. Farben*, 121.   [178] Hayes, *Industry and Ideology*, 363–76.

[179] A. Lacroix-Riz, 'Les Élites Françaises et la collaboration économique. La banque, l'industrie, Vichy, et le Reich', *Revue de l'histoire de la Shoah*, 159 (1997), 8–123.

[180] I. Traynor, 'Nazi Shame of Germany's Boardrooms', *Guardian* (28 June 1997), p. 26, citing evidence discovered by Hersch Fischler.

[181] Roth, 'Degussa', 35–6.

[182] H. Fischler, 'Das Totengold der europäischen Juden und die europäischen Grossbanken', *1999*, 13/1 (1998), 146–73.

mittee's rationale was ostensibly to secure adequate amounts for typhus prevention, but its responsibilities expanded to include all aspects of pest control and disinfection. Given that the priority was to remedy the shortage of supplies, particularly to the SS, in effect this committee accelerated the Holocaust. Other remits included notification of fatal accidents using hydrocyanic acid—there had been seventeen during the war by February 1943, mainly in the occupied territories—showing how concern for German operatives contrasted to the silence surrounding genocidal gassings.[183] Peters chaired the committee as well as a subcommittee on highly poisonous gases.[184] He complained that the committee often had to battle against the view that pest eradication was unimportant.[185] Peters pursued centralized administration for the production and distribution of insecticides, so as to meet production targets; he also ensured that DEGESCH was dominant among pest control firms. He justified his role in terms of fending off the malign powers of the state and SS, claiming that had not DEGESCH cooperated with Albert Speer's Ministry for Munitions, the state could have nationalized poison gas production, and that Himmler was also a predator.[186]

The committee included representatives from the nine German disinfestation and chemical firms (including Bruno Tesch who was informed about the gas chambers from August 1942, if not earlier), the Reich Ministry of the Interior, the Reich Health Office, and the Wehrmacht. Rose, deputy director of the Robert Koch Institute, represented Reich Health Führer Conti, and the entomologist Hase was frequently present. Not a member of the NSDAP, Hase reinforces the sense of heterodox political ideas among the experts, as he was reprimanded by the Gestapo in 1942 for denouncing the Nazi state and because his wife was said to be half Jewish.[187] When Zyklon was on the agenda, at first Mrugowsky and then a deputy (König or Gerstein) attended. Peters argued that the alternative to cooperation with the SS was that the firm would have been nationalized or subjected to direct control by the SS. Guntram Pflaum, who headed an SS department for pest destruction, was regarded as an opponent of the committee, not least because Pflaum advocated biological rather than chemical means of pest control.[188] When interrogated

---

[183] BAK R3/361 for an overview of activities of the Arbeitsausschuss until 1 June 1943; BA-MA H 20/929 Entseuchung, Entwesung und Desinfektionsmittel for reports on meetings. NMT microfilm 30, Testimony by Gerhard Peters 24 Feb. 1947, Mrugowsky defence document, pp. 16–30. Blausäure-Tagung 27–8 Jan. 1944 frames, 578–83; W. Reichmuth, 'Neuere Ergebnisse und Probleme der Schädlingsbekämpfung', in Rodenwaldt, *et al.*, *FIAT Review of German Science 1939–1946. Hygiene Part II Preventive and Industrial Medicine* (Wiesbaden, 1948), 24 on the Arbeitsausschuss; W. Christiansen, H. Kemper, G. Peters, *et al.*, *Richtlinien für die zweckentsprechende Auswahl von Mitteln, Apparaten und Verfahren zur Entwesung* (Frankfurt, 1943); Hilberg, *Destruction*, 889–91.

[184] Hayes, *Industry and Ideology*, 363.

[185] BAK R3/361, G. Peters, report on activities of the Arbeitsausschuss until 1 June 1943, dated 6 June 1943.

[186] Bayer-Archiv, IG Fremdfirmen, Degussa 6.14 Bd 1/2 Peters, 'Neue Zielsetzungen der Degesch', 4 Sept. 1942.

[187] BAK R 168/293 Personalakt Hase, Anzeige wegen ORR Hase 27 Feb. 1942; Reichsministerium für Ernährung und Landwirtschaft note of 11 July 1942 regarding the Gestapo reprimand of 26 June 1942.

[188] On Pflaum see NAW microfilm A 0377, SS officers, Guntram Pflaum. PMOA, SS Wirtschafts-Verwaltungshauptamt, Berlin 18 Apr. 1944 on transfer of Stubaf. Pflaum Auschwitz. I deal with Pflaum more fully in chapter 13.

by the Allies, Peters blamed Pflaum for applying the notion of a parasite to Jews.[189]

By 1944 key government committees for pest control were chaired by DEGESCH management; Peters and Gassner claimed that they had responsibility for an array of 'comprehensive and war-related tasks'.[190] The *Arbeitsausschuss* was to ensure that industry had enough raw materials to manufacture the required quantities of pesticides. Meetings of producers and suppliers took place regularly in Frankfurt am Main, involving representatives of DEGESCH, the distributing companies Tesch und Stabenow (based in Hamburg) and Heerdt-Lingler (based in Frankfurt), the Dessau Sugar Refining Works, the IG management, Slupetzky, and the SS.[191] By 1944 Wüstinger proudly proclaimed to the committee that 552 Zyklon chambers using his patent circulation system carried out 25 million delousings.[192] Maintaining the supply of Zyklon B was the essential task of the committee. How many on the committee would have known of the genocidal gas chambers in addition to Peters, Gerstein, Slupetzky, and Tesch is difficult to assess. Overall, the committee indirectly facilitated the murderous use of Zyklon, but there is no evidence to suggest that it instigated the human gas chambers or conducted systematic tests about quantities of Zyklon required to kill people in varying circumstances.

Coordination between producers and distributors was only attained at the cost of cut-throat machinations on the part of DEGESCH and its managing director, Peters. In autumn 1941 Peters replaced Heerdt as managing director of HELI (the acronym of the Heerdt-Lingler distributing company), after considerable pressure from the Gestapo. Heerdt had developed the crystalline form of Zyklon, enabling its storage in tins. In August 1941 local Nazi officials launched a campaign against Heerdt, accusing him and his wife of anti-Nazi sentiments, and he was ejected from the board of DEGESCH. Whether the reasons for Heerdt's removal were purely local, possibly with Peters exploiting links with the NSDAP to undermine Heerdt, or were related to strategic (or indeed genocidal) attempts to secure the supply of Zyklon is unclear. One benefit for Peters was that control of HELI by DEGESCH meant influence over training and practice of disinfectors. Given that HELI had obtained the concession for supply of non-hydrocyanic acid delousing chemicals for the new product Tritox (introduced in 1940) in the Reich and the eastern territories, this furthered the leading position of DEGESCH.[193]

Peters was daggers drawn with the other distributing company, Testa (i.e. Tesch und Stabenow), finding co-operation with Tesch very difficult. It is necessary to revise historians' assumptions that the different elements of the DEGESCH and its distributing partners functioned in a state of amicable cooperation. DEGESCH

[189] STAN KV-Anklage Interrogations P 35, p. 15.

[190] IG Fremdfirmen DEGUSSA 6.14 Bd 1–2, G. Peters and L. Gassner, 'Nach 25 Jahren DEGESCH-Arbeit—zu neuem Anfang!'.

[191] Kogon, *Giftgas*, 248, concerning a meeting of 27–8 Jan. 1944.

[192] E. Wüstinger in *Gesundheits-Ingenieur*, 67 (1944), 179–80.

[193] DEGUSSA Firmenarchiv, DEGESCH Geschäftsberichte, Peters, lecture 'Neue Zielsetzung der DEGESCH', 2, 4; IW 57.14./2 file 'Ausscheiden von Dr. Heerdt als Geschäftsführer'. Nachfolger Dr Peters; NSDAP Gauwirtschaftsberater to DEGESCH, 13 Aug. 1941; Bericht über eine Ausprache beim Gauwirtschaftsberater in Sachen Dr Walter Heerdt, 18 Aug. 1941; Bayer Archiv, IG Fremdfirmen DEGUSSA 6.14 Bd 1, Heerdt-Lingler memorandum Sept. 1941.

and its Kali subsidiary won a case in May 1941 preventing Testa from marketing Zyklon in the Protectorate of Bohemia and Moravia, the Sudetengau, and Slovakia.[194] In 1942 Degussa sold its shares in TESTA to Tesch, who became its sole owner. TESTA was forced to accept that it could only supply DEGESCH products in Europe (hardly a loss at the time) and undertook to buy 24,000 kg of Zyklon each year, for which it was allotted territories to the east of the Elbe and the Sudetenland, and Scandinavia. HELI's outlets included the rest of Germany (with the exception of the free harbours) as well as the Netherlands, Croatia, Serbia, Romania, Bulgaria, Greece, and Turkey.[195] But Tesch continued to wage war against DEGESCH for directly supplying the army and SS.[196]

DEGESCH consolidated its position under Peters. The army commissioned DEGESCH to carry out pest control in the east and south-east, as did Speer's armaments ministry and the DAF conscript labour organization. DEGESCH secured a share in developing new products like Tritox and Ventox, which were produced by IG-Farben, and were in combined usage by 1942. It still meant that Zyklon as a product was under threat, unless its effectiveness could be enhanced. One way forward was by technical innovation: DEGESCH supplied gas chambers with the circulation system to speed up gassing procedures. During the war DEGESCH installed 340 gas chambers, of which 105 were taken by the Waffen-SS at Mrugowsky's instigation. Special gas chambers for cleansing railway waggons were dispatched to Budapest, Belgrade, Kishinev, and Sarajevo.[197]

Zyklon gas not only had to compete against newer products, but it had many critics. Just at the time that the Final Solution was being decided on, the Reich Ministry of the Interior agreed in October 1941 that hydrocyanic acid was too dangerous and ineffective at low temperatures, and so recommended hot air ovens for disinfestation.[198] Rose stressed the merits of steam over hydrocyanic acid for delousing repatriated ethnic Germans.[199] Peters of DEGESCH lobbied hard to preserve the key role for Zyklon in delousing—so successfully that by 1944 there was increased use of hydrocyanic acid in all sectors apart from the Wehrmacht.[200]

SS medical and sanitary personnel were trained in the use of Zyklon, steam, and

---

[194]   DEGUSSA Firmenarchiv, IW 57.14.3, legal decision of 25 Jan. 1941.

[195]   Ibid., Rechtsabteilung 'Tatsachen zum Thema Zyklon B'. IW57.14.3 file on relations with Testa, agreement between DEGESCH and Tesch 27 June 1942.

[196]   BA-MA H20/929 Tesch on 9 Mar. 1943.

[197]   Degussa Firmenarchiv, DEGESCH Geschäftsberichte, Peters, lecture, 4 Sept. 1942 'Neue Zielsetzungen der DEGESCH'; H. G. Sossenheimer, 'Entwicklung des Tritox- u. Ventox-Verfahrens'; Wüstinger lecture 'Die spontane Entwicklung der Kammerbegasung'; Memoranda of Herbert Rauscher, 18 June 1947; NMT deposition of Peters concerning Mrugowsky; BA/MA H 20/705 Reichmuth patent of Tritox and Ventox in combined usage, 1942. See n. 140 for references table Peters-Wüstinger patent.

[198]   BAK R 86/4164 Bl. 71–8 RMdI meeting of 14–16 Oct. 1941.

[199]   G. Rose, 'Fleckfieberfragen bei der Umsiedlung der Volksdeutschen aus dem Ostraum 1939', *Deutsche Medizinische Wochenschrift* (1941), 1262–5. By 1942 he advocated HCN; see 'Fleckfieberfragen der Heimat', 103.

[200]   Wüstinger, 'Vermehrte Einsatz von Blausäure Entlausungskammern', paper for the Blausäure committee in January 1944 in NMT microfilm 0582–3, frame 30.

hot air disinfestation procedures for delousing. The expertise of the German Red Cross (DRK) in sanitary technology was an important resource: in 1931 the DRK established a 'Gas Protection School' in Oranienburg with the support of the Auergesellschaft, which was a subsidiary of DEGUSSA. The medical training provided an ostensibly defensive role in protecting against air and gas attack.[201] The transfer of expertise to the SS was made all the easier as Oranienburg became the administrative headquarters of the SS, and Grawitz was for a time a German Red Cross functionary and chief SS physician. Courses were held in Oranienburg to train SS disinfectors. Model Zyklon gas chambers for disinfesting clothing were installed in the nearby concentration camp of Sachsenhausen, where a building for pathological autopsies and for a 'research' mortuary provided a location for gruesome medical experimentation and specimen collecting. In April 1941 the Sachsenhausen gas chambers were inspected by Tesch and officials from the RMdI and the zoological department of the Reich Institute for Air and Water. Tesch also trained SS disinfectors sent by Höss from Auschwitz, as well as from other concentration camps. Enno Lolling (the chief physician of the concentration camps) informed disinfection squads by 1943 that they would have to obey orders when required to use the gas on humans. SS personnel, routinely trained in handling Zyklon, were equipped with gas masks.[202] Significantly, the Oranienburg school provided training in the use of Zyklon without the warning agent, noting that there were no technical disadvantages in its removal.[203] Given the additional hazards in using the gas in this form, the purpose could only be for killing people.

The sanitary services of the SS deployed the conventional terminology and methods of 'delousing' using Zyklon B for prisoners' effects (particularly for the furs and valuables deriving from those killed), of 'disinfestation' for destroying lice by means of dry heat in hot air chambers, and 'disinfection' for the use of steam autoclaves (comparable to giant pressure cookers) or hot air to destroy pests and germs. The literature on delousing with Zyklon proliferated after 1941.[204] The textbook of hygiene published by Zeiss and Rodenwaldt in 1942 proclaimed Zyklon as the most effective means of disinfestation, and that it had advantages over mixtures of carbon dioxide produced from a generator (a finding which paralleled the switch away from carbon monoxide in the extermination camps). Zeiss and Rodenwaldt emphasized that the use of Zyklon should only be in accordance with state regulations and that it required 'disciplined and trained personnel'. The climate of medical opinion endorsed the superiority of the gas.[205] The evidence martialled here suggests that the structures of technical expertise and state

[201] Seithe and Hagemann, *Deutsche Rote Kreuz*, 150–61; F. Grüneisen, *Das deutsche Rote Kreuz in Vergangenheit und Gegenwart* (Berlin, 1939), 170–1.

[202] Kogon, *Giftgas*, 264, 268; Konrich, 'Bericht der Reichsanstalt für Wasser- und Luftgüte', 205.

[203] R. Queisner, 'Erfahrungen mit Blausäure bei Grossraumentwesungen' [Aus der Desinfektorenschule der Waffen-SS, Oranienburg (Leiter: SS-Hauptsturmführer H. Gundlach)], *Zeitschrift für hygienische Zoologie*, 36 (1944), 134, 137.

[204] e.g. F. Puntigam, H. Breymesser, and E. Bernfuss, *Blausäurekammern zur Fleckfieberabwehr* (Berlin, 1943).

[205] H. Zeiss and E. Rodenwaldt, *Hygiene und Seuchenlehre*, 4 edn. (Stuttgart, 1942), 104.

regulation concerning the controls on Zyklon facilitated the use of the gas for mass murder, and the racialized understanding of typhus provided an additional rationale for the killing of the 'human vectors' of the disease. The excruciating suffering during the final minutes of life was caused by the warning agent. Overall, the institutions, technologies, and experts for pest control, once mobilized to combat typhus and other epidemics as racial threats, accelerated the 'final solution'.

Genuine delousing facilities in concentration and extermination camps helped to conceal the gas chambers used for mass murder.[206] The varieties of gas chambers at Auschwitz have been studied in meticulous detail to distinguish the human gas chambers from the routine sanitary procedures and installations for the reception of camp prisoners, human delousing, and the disinfestation of their clothes. Only a few medical aspects will be considered here in order to place the camp within the broader perspective of typhus prevention. Zyklon gassing was used to fumigate the former Polish military barracks and migrant labourers' settlement, when a camp for Polish dissidents opened in June 1950.[207] The techniques of delousing, routine for the SS disinfection squads, made it easier to devise killing installations. At first delousing facilities for clothing were improvised at Auschwitz by sealing rooms with strips of paper, bricking up windows, and fitting gas-tight doors. Boilers were required for heating water for delousing showers.[208] When there was a typhus epidemic in August 1942 additional buildings were adapted for use as gas and delousing chambers.[209]

Typhus remained endemic in the atrocious camp conditions. Beilin observed about typhus, 'This plague was never suppressed. There were merely chance fluctuations as manifested in the decline or increase in the numbers of those stricken.'[210] SS 'selections' of prisoners with typhus left blankets and bunks infested with lice. When typhus spead to the SS guards and the civilian population, two camp doctors, Friedrich Entress and Kurt Uhlenbroock arranged for 746 sick, convalescents, and prisoner nurses from Block 20 to be murdered in the gas chambers on 29 August 1942.[211] Mengele arrived at Auschwitz in May 1943, and his favoured means of epidemic control was to send typhus suspects to the gas chambers. He was a noted exponent of SS-style *Epidemiebekämpfung*, as when he ordered the killing of 1,035 gypsies suspected of harbouring a peculiar type of lethal chicken pox and typhus. He condemned 600 women in a complete block to the gas chambers so that other blocks could be emptied, disinfected, and their inmates deloused. Although hereditary degeneracy was the rationale for sending the gypsies to Auschwitz, the atrocious conditions of deportation and incarceration meant that typhus provided a pretext for their being killed.[212]

---

[206]   Pressac, *Auschwitz*, 22, 67.   [207]   Dwork and van Pelt, *Auschwitz*, 166–70.

[208]   Pressac, *Auschwitz*, 24–5.   [209]   Ibid., 26–7, 65.

[210]   *The Trial of Adolf Eichmann*, 1257.

[211]   Langbein, 'SS Physicians', *Death Books*, 62–3; Langbein, *Der Auschwitz Prozess*, ii. 590–1.

[212]   BDC Mengele file; G. L. Posner and J. Ware, *Mengele. The Complete Story* (London, 1986), 24–5; J. S. Hohmann, *Robert Ritter und die Erben der Kriminalbiologie. 'Zigeunerforschung' im Nationalsozialismus und in Westdeutschland im Zeichen des Rassismus* (Frankfurt/M., 1991), 117–18, 126–7, 128–9; H. Kubica, 'The Crimes of Josef Mengele', in Gutman and Berenbaum, *Auschwitz*, 328; Czech, 'Prisoner Administra-

Delousing procedures shaped the design and operation of the most 'efficient' gas chambers, installed at Auschwitz-Birkenau, and beginning operation between March and June 1943. Höss devised a compact layout with the room for undressing, the gas chamber, and the crematorium within a single building. From autumn 1943 these gas chambers were disguised as showers with false shower heads along the walls. Victims were told that they were first to have a shower bath and then be disinfected. At this time wooden benches were installed, and each person had a numbered hook for clothes. The tins of gas labelled *Zyklon für Schädlingsbekämpfung* were kept in a car marked with a Red Cross.[213] The capacity of the four new gas chambers was far larger than any carbon monoxide gas chamber, or the first improvised Zyklon gas chamber in Auschwitz, which had space for 340 victims. The 'crematoria' were immense with an incinerating capacity of 1,440, 1,440, 768, and 786 bodies per 24 hours. Equipment was ordered from the firm of Topf as specializing in crematorium ovens and from civil engineering firms, the SS specifying 'mortuary items'.[214]

'We know all of that'[215]; that the Germans exploited delousing both as a technology and as a deception to ensure compliance has been meticulously documented by Holocaust historians, so that commemoration rather than historical analysis might be more appropriate. Detailed studies by Pressac and van Pelt on the technology and circumstances of the gassings, the construction of gas chambers, and the surrounding built environment document the steps by which improvised gas chambers were replaced by purpose-built crematoria equipped to kill trainloads of people. Many issues remain unresolved in the broader medical context of typhus, concerning those involved in supplying and using Zyklon, their rationales, and social interests. Were the first two gassings conducted by Fritsch carried out by an SS-trained disinfector, using routine techniques? Here the complex background of disinfectors' training and medical supervision comes into play. Despite the receipts and documents for Zyklon supply, the intentional ambiguity between real delousing and genocide continues to create problems. Thus the role of the Hygiene Institute of the Waffen-SS remains hazy; the lack of a coherent archival deposit suggests that an attempt was made to erase the historical record, for the Institute clearly handled consignments of Zyklon. What remains unclear is the transition from normal delousing to mass killing. Gerstein represents here a figure of considerable ambiguity—did he aim to disrupt the lethal procedures, or to allow them to function more effectively, and was the removal of the warning agent an act of mercy or to increase the efficiency of an operation which was prone to all sorts of malfunctions? Despite all documenting of the rationales, techniques, and economy of this technological genocide, too many critical problems remain unresolved. It is also important to lay aside the assumption of the passivity of victims, and of the image of efficiently functioning death machinery. Warnings whispered when trains were

tion', 367; I. Strzelecka, 'Hospitals', in Gutman and Berenbaum, *Auschwitz*, 379–92; K. Smolen and M. Zimmermann, 'The Gypsies in KL Auschwitz', *Death Books*, 133–44; *The Trial of Adolf Eichmann*, 1259, 1261.

[213] Kogon, *Giftgas*, 224–32.   [214] Ibid., 219–22.   [215] Dwork and van Pelt, *Auschwitz*, 352.

unloaded, the hiding of children in bundles of clothes, continuous force and terror, protests, screams, struggle, and attempts at evasion disrupted the gassings.[216]

Despite the visit by Gerstein to Bełżec and Treblinka, these camps continued to use carbon monoxide gas until the winding down of the Aktion Reinhard by November 1943. But the extermination technology using Zyklon was rapidly applied in other concentration camps, marking a distinctive phase of the Final Solution. Sanitary experts and disinfectors having been trained to improvise gas chambers, readily innovated to increase the numbers being killed. Two Zyklon chambers in Majdanek were built between September and October 1942, while a third gas chamber used carbon monoxide. The entrance carried the inscription *Bad und Desinfektion*. The Majdanek administration was in contact with the firm Tesch and Stabenow, at one stage ordering 7,711 kg of Zyklon B, although the quantities for human killings is not clear. Here an estimated 40,000 persons were killed in the gas chambers.[217]

In Mauthausen and Gusen around 10,000 gassings took place.[218] A mobile gas van plied between the two camps; prisoners were also sent to the nearby euthanasia centre of Hartheim. From December 1941 Mauthausen had a permanent gas chamber with the capacity of 120 victims, and where both carbon monoxide and Zyklon B were used. Zyklon B was delivered by the Linz firm of Anton Slupetzky, who in May 1942 saw how SS officers forced prisoners suffering from typhus and tuberculosis into one of the huts which was being fumigated. The camp commandant told Slupetzky to support such killings 'as a hygienic measure'—after all, troops were dying on the eastern front.[219]

From autumn 1941 the SS had an execution chamber for shootings in Sachsenhausen disguised as a medical bloc, and an experimental gassing had taken place on 3 November 1941. In March 1943 Chefarzt Baumkötter prescribed that a Zyklon gas chamber be installed in Sachsenhausen using the shower disguise. At Stutthof Zyklon gassings were carried out from at least 1944 using the pretext of delousing. A railway carriage was also used as a disguise. At Neuengamme near Hamburg there were two gassings of Soviet prisoners of war in September and November 1942. According to the testimony of SS Sanitätsdienstgrad Willi Bahr, it was there that Dr von Bothmann improvised a gas chamber, which used the pretence of delousing showers. Bahr had been trained by Tesch in the use of the gas and readily complied.[220] In August 1943 120 prisoners from Auschwitz were transferred to the

---

[216] Dwork and van Pelt, *Auschwitz*, 351. For the image of an efficiently functioning system see W. Sofsky, *The Order of Terror. The Concentration Camp* (Princeton, NJ, 1997), 259–75, 'the death factory'.

[217] Friedlander, *Origins*, 287; Kogon, *Giftgas*, 241–5; Hilberg, *Destruction*, 879. E. Gryń, *Majdanek* (Lublin, 1984), 92–9.

[218] Abzug, *Vicious Heart*, 107; Holocaust Museum, Washington DC, RG-O2.002*22, p. 4.

[219] Kogon, *Nazi Mass Murder*, 177–83; STAN KV-Anklage-Interrogations S 235 Anton Slupetzky. E. Le Chêne, *Mauthausen: The History of a Death Camp* (Bath, 1987), 81, 85–6.

[220] Kogon, *Giftgas*, 266–73; Kaienburg, *Der Fall Neuengamme*, 371. For the Sachsenhausen 'experiment' see Aly, *Endlösung*, 361; H. Kuhn, *Stutthof. Ein Konzentrationslager vor den Toren Danzigs* (Bremen, 1951), 65–6. Dvorjetski recollected that von Bothmann selected him to be killed, and later flogged him; Dvorjetski, *Vilna*, 13, 19. For Bahr's testimony see PRO WO 235/83 fos. 219, 390.

Natzweiler concentration camp in Alsace, where they were killed in an improvised gas chamber. August Hirt, the professor of anatomy at Strassburg University, used their skeletons for 'medical research'. Zyklon B and mustard gas were used, and in August 1944 gypsies were killed by testing different doses of phosgene gas. The Natzweiler gas chamber was for purely 'experimental' purposes.[221] In Dachau Sigmund Rascher initiated experiments for gas warfare purposes in 1942. A gas chamber marked '*Brausenbad*' was installed in a new crematorium building, where there were also four smaller disinfestation chambers.[222] At the women's camp of Ravensbrück a gas chamber was improvised early in 1945 when personnel and prisoners from Auschwitz were transferred. In the camp by the Abbey of Melk a large gas chamber, which was camouflaged and soundproofed, indicated the intention to shift exterminations westwards as the third Reich crumbled.[223] Eichmann planned releasing Zyklon in the open air to wipe out the final Jews at Theresienstadt—Gerstein being consulted about this absurd plan.[224] It was said that Buchenwald was a 'good' camp, because of the absence of gas chambers.[225]

The Germans were successful in using typhus to conceal the extent of the mass killing from the Allies. In July 1942 a British consular official in Bern was asked to transmit to London news of the plan to exterminate 'all the Jews of Europe and a great part of the Russian prisoners-of-war' by extermination in gas ovens; in July 1944 the British Foreign Office received a report on Auschwitz compiled from information gathered by the Czech underground: this described with chilling accuracy how typhus was a pretext for wholesale killing and a gas *megacyklon* supplied from Hamburg to kill up to 2,000 persons at a time was used in gas chambers disguised as delousing baths.[226]

'One louse your death' (*Eine Laus dein Tod*) was the macabre exhortation to prisoners in Auschwitz. Reality and deception became intertwined in the extermination camps. The vocabulary and methods of hygiene were part of a lethal disguise of the killing process, and indeed shaped the lethal operation. Disinfection, cleansing and disinfestation were not only euphemisms for the disguise of mass murder, but also generated technical procedures and rationales for the perpetrators.[227]

---

[221] Kogon, *Giftgas*, 271–7, 286–7; Harris and Paxman, *Higher Form of Killing*, 60. For the use of HCN see Klee, *Auschwitz*, 373–4.

[222] Kogon, *Giftgas*, 277–80. Survivors' evidence varies as to the extent that the gas chamber was used; see R. H. Abzug, *Inside the Vicious Heart. Americans and the Liberation of Nazi Concentration Camps* (New York, 1985), 100, 185–6.

[223] A. K. Mant, 'The Medical Services in the Concentration Camp of Ravensbruck', *Medico-Legal Journal*, 17 (1949), 99–111. Le Chêne, *Mauthausen*, 246–7.

[224] *The Trial of Adolf Eichmann*, 109, 2177; YVA Gerstein file, Gerstein testimony 26 Apr. 1945, p. 12.

[225] C. Richet, 'Experiences of a Medical Prisoner at Buchenwald', in H. L. Tidy (ed.), *Inter-allied Conferences on War Medicine 1942–1945. Convened by the Royal Society of Medicine* (London, 1947), 453–5.

[226] Gilbert, *Auschwitz*, 56 for a report of July 1942 on extermination by poison gas; pp. 262–3 for a comprehensive report of July 1944.

[227] The concept of cleansing was used by the Auschwitz camp doctor Heinz Thilo; see Czech, *Auschwitz Chronicles*, 823.

v. The Fatal Flame: Crematoria and Genocide

The ideal of a death fit for Nordic heroes helped overcome the initial Nazi hostility to cremation. But the outbreak of war resulted in cremation being demoted to disposing of the accumulating bodies of the degenerate. The criminological arguments against cremation as destroying evidence of murder rendered cremation attractive for the instigators of the Holocaust. The concerns with economy, efficiency, and hygiene, as well as with concealment, were given new significance by the killings in concentration camps and psychiatric hospitals. When the ground was frozen in winter, and the risks of certain infectious diseases like typhus were high, cremation was valued as a technology of disinfection. That corpses polluted the groundwater provided an incentive for installing cremation furnaces. The authorities used the concealment that they had once condemned to their advantage, so as to annihilate totally the bodies of the feared and hated subhuman parasites.

In November 1941 the status of cremation as a Nordic rite was undermined when Hitler expressed a preference for burial as more natural. Hitler conceded that both cremation and burial had established Germanic roots, but the coincidence with the formulating of grandiose genocidal policies should be noted. By this time the Munich cremationist Harbauer was Leiter of the Cremation League, and he was keen to modify the law so as to take account of the diversity of opinion within the Nazi Party on cremation and burial. Hitler seems to have found cremation distasteful: did he order that his body be set ablaze to avoid humiliating public exposure or did he envisage a 'Viking funeral' amidst the burning ruins of Berlin?[228]

The principles of one body per oven and separation of the ashes, so elaborately sustained by officials in Weimar Germany, were abandoned for the 'racially inferior'. The administrative procedures surrounding cremation meant that it could readily be used for concealment. The families of euthanasia and concentration camp victims were required to pay for the return of victims' ashes. But the urns were filled with ashes from any corpse, and the families had by law to place their urn in a cemetery. Normal practices of laying out, washing, and storage of the corpse were replaced by rapid disposal of bodies. Cremationists became concerned with the economics of procedures which indicated a shift from selective heroization to mass disposal of the degenerate. In 1937 there were objections that corpses were being burned in serviceable clothes. The question of salvaging gold teeth was also discussed, in view of Germany's economic difficulties. Zeiss was of the opinion that the salvage of gold inlays was difficult given the small amounts involved but he favoured a petition to the Reich Ministry of the Interior that the dead should not be burned in usable clothing.[229] When the killing of psychiatric patients became

---

[228] *Akten der Partei-Kanzlei der NSDAP*, microfiche no. 12602928, Rosenberg's office to Bormann 20 Oct. 1941; microfiche no. 12602924, Bormann to Rosenberg 14 Nov. 1941. H. R. Trevor-Roper, *The Last Days of Hitler* new edn. (London, 1962), 231–2. E. G. Schenck, *Patient Hitler* (Dusseldorf, 1989), 440–5.

[229] AHUB Hygiene Institute Nr 188 Hey (of Institut für gerichtliche Medizin Frankfurt) to Zeiss 2 Dec. 1937; Zeiss to Hey 16 Dec. 1937.

routine, their gold teeth were in fact removed. The disguise of gas chambers as showers meant that clothing was conveniently taken off by the deceived victims, and when force had to be used showers provided a pretext. In the case of psychiatric patients clothing and personal effects were returned to their original institutions, and if relatives did not claim private property this was donated to the National Socialist Welfare organization, NSV.[230]

At Auschwitz, jewellery, dental gold, and hair were systematically removed prior to cremation, and dental crowns were extracted in vast quantities from the living. Gold and jewellery fuelled the war economy. The stockpiles of clothes and luggage were destined after disinfection for the ethnic Germans, and the heaps of spectacles and surgical belts were to make good those physical incapacities afflicting the master race. Mengele collected body parts such as eyes and internal organs for racial research. Bodies were transmuted from racial parasites into economic and medical resources. Medical procedures were meant to erase the polluting racial characteristics while leaving a usable residue.[231]

Expediency played a role in the development of lethal cremation technology. After the SS experimented with cremation in 1937, a crematorium was installed by the Topf works in Dachau in 1939, at Buchenwald (near to Topf's factory at Erfurt in Thuringia, and consequently a testing ground for new designs) late in 1939, in Mauthausen in 1940, in Sachsenhausen, at Auschwitz-Birkenau in November 1940, and at Natzweiler. A gigantic battery of four four-muffle furnaces was installed in the Mogilev prisoner of war camp in the Soviet Union at the site of a possible eastern extermination camp.[232] (Muffles or retorts were the chambers in the cremation ovens.) At this stage mass cremation furnaces (violating the Reich law specifying one body per chamber) were not yet in use; they were planned by Topf for use in the east only in 1943. The Berlin firm H. Kori (Topf's main competitor) supplied numerous other camps. After the order that bodies previously buried were to be exhumed and cremated, in September 1942 Höss inspected the Kulmhof crematoria where different methods of cremation had been tried.[233] In a massive deal for Auschwitz-Birkenau, Pressac has calculated that Topf supplied sixty-six cremation muffles with forty-six of these being sited at Auschwitz, whereas Kori built twenty to thirty muffles in the camps. Mobile furnaces were also produced.[234]

Himmler spoke of a 'crematorium–delousing unit' when discussing facilities at the Buchenwald concentration camp with his deputy Oswald Pohl in December 1939. But it would be premature to see what was only a hot air delousing oven as the birth of a euphemism to hide the murderous reality of human gas chambers. While the killing hospitals and camps were equipped with gas chambers disguised as showers and cremation furnaces, the linking of the two functions was only attained once killing with Zyklon produced otherwise unmanageable

---

[230] Klee, '*Euthanasie*', 150, 156.

[231] A. Strzelecki, 'The Plunder of Victims and their Corpses', in Gutman and Berenblum, *Auschwitz*, 246–66.

[232] Pressac with van Pelt, 'Machinery', 186–8; Aly, *Endlösung*, 342–6, 351, 359, 361.

[233] Höss, *Autobiography*, 116–17.   [234] Pressac, *Auschwitz*, 94–6, 100–1.

numbers of bodies.[235] The SS was not centrally involved in the T4 programme, although in December 1939 SS units killed mental patients using carbon monoxide in vans. Given that crematoria and delousing units both required fuel and logistically were sited adjacent to each other, it is most likely that Himmler had confused autoclaves (steam sterilization units, produced by firms like Topf) with cremation furnaces. A 'crematorium–delousing unit' might have consisted of disinfestation facilities for humans, and louse disinfestation chambers for clothing and personal effects using poison gas or steam. The technology of furnaces was valuable in producing hot air disinfestation chambers (Topf also devised autoclaves); and the hot water was used for the autoclaves as well as for showers and saunas.

Cremation became integral to the T4 programme of medical killing. Viktor Brack in charge of 'euthanasia' in the Führer's Chancellery had formerly been an engineer, and he favoured technical solutions to the killing of racial undesirables, and disposal of their bodies. Crematoria were installed in the T4 psychiatric killing institutions. At Hadamar there was a macabre celebration in 1941 when the 10,000th body was cremated.[236] The impossibility of an autopsy meant that causes of death on the death certificates could readily be falsified. But the very aim of secrecy was undermined by the overloading of the ovens: smoke, smell, and sporadic flames from the chimneys alerted the local inhabitants to the mass killing. At Brandenburg chimney fires and the pungent smell meant that ovens had to be moved to nearby woodland.[237]

Cremation changed from being a spiritually idealized form of death to a medicalized technology for concealing the mass disposal of the murdered. The impulse to conceal prompted Himmler in 1943 to order that all those executed by the SS should if possible be either cremated or sent to a department of anatomy.[238] The T4 body burners, drafted into the concentration camps, facilitated genocide. Cremation asserted German supremacy and control over Catholic and Jewish populations, as for the orthodox of both faiths cremation was anathema. Hermann Voss, professor of anatomy in the Nazified 'Reich' University of Posen in June 1941 gloated over the cremation furnace in the anatomical institute originally intended for disposing of the remnants of the dissecting course for the students, but then used by the SS to incinerate executed Poles. He rejoiced over how: 'The Poles recently have become increasingly impudent and thus our furnace is very busy. How nice it would be to chase the whole population through such furnaces! Then the German people would finally get some rest in the East.'[239]

---

[235] R. Breitman, *The Architect of Genocide. Himmler and the Final Solution* (London, 1991), 87–9.

[236] Friedlander, *Origins*, 98; B. Winter, 'Hadamar als T4 Anstalt', *Euthanasie in Hadamar* (Kassel, 1991), 98; *Trial of Adolf Eichmann*, 2252.

[237] Friedlander, *Origins*, 90; Klee, 'Euthanasie', 149–59.

[238] NMT roll 30, frame 719 Durchführungsbestimmung für Exekutionen 6.I.43.

[239] G. Aly, 'Das Posener Tagebuch des Anatomen Hermann Voss', *Biedermann und Schreibtischtäter, Beiträge zur nationalsozialistischen Gesundheits- und Sozialpolitik*, 4 (Berlin, 1987), 43–4, entry of Sunday 15 June 1941; tr. (but omitting the Ney quotation) by C. Pross, 'Nazi Doctors, German Medicine and Historical Truth', Annas and Grodin (eds.), *Nazi Doctors*, 34; also in *Cleansing the Fatherland*, 130. On Posen see B. Piotrowski, *W Słuzbie Rasizmu i Bezprawia. 'Uniwersytet Rzeszy' w Poznaniu 1941–1945* (Poznań, 1984).

Cremation became integral to genocide, once gas chambers were sited in the same buildings as the crematoria. The delousing circuit, involving absolute separation between the infested and the cleansed, was transformed into a lethal transit, which required as short a passage as possible for the final removal of valuables and the feeding of bodies into the battery of cremation furnaces. The suppliers of the crematoria ovens were the same firms which had profited from the expansion of the crematoria in the 1930s. A major factor in determining the pace of killing at Auschwitz was the capacity of cremation ovens.

By May 1941 the Polish government-in-exile in London circulated information on the cremation of prisoners held at 'the Oswiecim camps'.[240] The crematoria at Auschwitz, initially part of the normal facilities of the detention camp, were adapted by the Waffen-SS for mass murder, providing a cover for the lethal gas chambers. The morgue at the first crematorium to be built was used for shooting prisoners, for experimental gassings of Russian and sick prisoners in September 1941, and when adapted into a gas chamber (possibly at the end of 1941), it was sporadically in operation until 1943.[241] In the interim a bunker was used as a gas chamber, improvised in what had been a peasant's house, and those gassed had been buried in pits—a sight that Himmler found repugnant. After an inspection visit by Himmler in July 1942, the commandant of Auschwitz, Höss, went in September 1942 to Kulmhof to study the crematorium. From the end of October 1941 the Buildings Department of the Waffen-SS and Prüfer of the Topf firm cooperated in designing a purpose-built 'crematorium' for mass incineration of bodies, soiled clothes, and other waste. The bodies buried in mass graves were subsequently cremated.[242]

In October 1941 Prüfer negotiated with the SS for supplying a crematorium with economically designed furnaces with multiple openings fed by two underground morgues. The capacity was to be sixty corpses per hour, with a throughput of 1,440 bodies in twenty-four hours.[243] The technology of cremation was changed by the voracious demands of the SS from the individualized methods of the 1920s, to continuous burning of bodies on a mass scale. Pressac dates the involvement of Topf in the human extermination from April–June 1942, when plans for a five-furnace crematorium were modified so as to produce an extermination installation at Birkenau. A crucial feature was the two-floor arrangement, with the gas chambers underground; bodies were taken by elevator to the furnaces on the floor above. Typhus was a pretext for concealment of the 'special treatment', but human gassings also allowed the camp administration to siphon off substantial quantitites of Zyklon to tackle the typhus epidemic of August 1942. In July 1942 Himmler ordered the cremation of the vast numbers of corpses filling immense trenches. Hygiene was a factor: corpses in mass graves attracted vermin. Rats were potential vectors in the spread of epidemics that threatened the German concentration camp personnel, and indeed might spread to major centres of population. Moreover,

---

[240] Gilbert, *Auschwitz*, 15.   [241] Pressac, *Auschwitz*, 131–3.   [242] Ibid., 161–5.
[243] Ibid., 95–6. See G. Fleming, *Hitler and the Final Solution*, revised edn. (Berkeley, 1994), appendix on Prüfer.

corpses polluted the groundwater.[244] Topf managers must have known about the lethal links between killing and cremation for some time, as the supply of cremation equipment to the euthanasia institutions meant that there would have been clear indications of the lethal source of the bodies.[245]

Gas chambers were referred to as 'crematoria' under SS Hauptscharführer Erich Muhsfeldt, a sometime baker who attained the inflated title of Chef für die Gaskammer und Crematorien.[246] He had served as crematoria chief in the Lublin concentration camp before transfer to Auschwitz in May 1944. The larger Birkenau crematoria could incinerate—in theory at least—1,500 bodies each per day. These crematoria had fifteen ovens with openings for four to five bodies which would take ninety minutes to incinerate. The two smaller crematoria had eight ovens, each with nine openings for three bodies and a capacity of 1,000 bodies a day.[247]

Lindner (a Ministry of Interior official who had been involved in drafting the cremation law and in initiating euthanasia) was reported by Gerstein to have asked Globocnik in August 1942 whether it would not have been better to cremate rather than bury corpses in order to remove traces of the Final Solution. Globocnik replied that the grandiose mass killing deserved to be commemorated by memorials to honour the heroism of the involved National Socialists. But in practice cremation like delousing and human gassings involved chaotic inefficiency as the ovens broke down. The inadequacies of the furnaces meant that arguments arose when homespun ideas about physics and other stratagems were discussed to solve the horrendous problem of how best to burn the mountains of corpses: one solution was to douse bodies with petrol on improvised stands constructed out of railway sleepers.[248]

Although Auschwitz has come to symbolize the technical perfection of scientific genocide, the technical systems were overstrained and vulnerable to sabotage. The construction materials were so poor that some of the ovens could not stand up to continuous use. Repairs had to be made to the overheated flues and chimneys. Breakdowns meant that bodies were burned in pits behind the crematoria.[249] By late 1943 no more furnaces were ordered from Topf (possibly because of technical difficulties), while small, mobile single-muffle units were ordered from Kori.[250] By 1945 supplies of Zyklon were disrupted, and victims (sometimes alive, sometimes after being shot) were pushed into mass open pits for burning.[251] Without the lethal technology, the system of mass murder continued to be implemented.

Throwing living persons directly into the ovens was gratuitously brutal, given all the available killing techniques. Trudi Birger wrote that at the Stutthof camp: 'They grabbed the women any which way and shoved them in headfirst. Sometimes, if a

[244] Pressac, *Auschwitz*, 131; Dwork and van Pelt, *Auschwitz*, plates, especially plate 16, pp. 320–1, 324.

[245] Pressac, *Auschwitz*, 71–3.

[246] Lasik, 'Biographies of SS-men', in *Death Books*, 266.   [247] Kogon, *Giftgas*, 226.

[248] LkA EKvW Gerstein Papers 5,2 NS Nr 192, p. 4; Testimony of Ernst B, in Lifton, *Nazi Doctors*, 177–9.

[249] Kogon, *Giftgas*, 224–5.   [250] Pressac, *Auschwitz*, 103.

[251] Ibid., 171, 177; Nyiszli, *Auschwitz*, ch. 13.

woman was too tall to fit into the oven, only the top part of her body was burned, and they had to push her feet in after her . . .'[252]

Delousing and cremation were sanitary technologies which when aligned produced voracious killing installations for populations stigmatized as vermin. The master race lacked a masterplan in how the genocide was to be implemented, and the methods of genocide were shaped by expediency. Technical experts realized that the use of new technologies of extermination boosted their individual prestige. Bitter skirmishes erupted between advocates of carbon monoxide and Zyklon, or between the technically trained and autodidacts: the pesticide chemist Peters fought the dry cleaner and SS pest supremo Pflaum, and the cremation furnace engineer Prüfer vied with the baker and SS crematorium chief Muhsfeldt. The experts were undeterred by technical breakdowns, whether of delousing equipment, gas chambers, or cremation furnaces, as they pushed for ever more gigantic and powerful installations. Meanwhile, medical experts stoked the mental furnaces of a psychological fear of typhus, demanding ever larger consignments of the contaminated for the consuming flames.

---

[252] Birger, *Gift of Love*, 131.

11

'Victory with Vaccines': Human Guinea-pigs and Louse-feeders

i. 'The War of the Laboratories'

Developing a typhus vaccine was to boost Germany's medical and racial defences. Given that typhus was a primitive 'Asiatic' disease spread by racial vermin, an effective vaccine was required to protect the German invasion forces, and to prevent the disease spilling over from ghettos and concentration camps. German research teams raced against those of the Allies to produce an anti-typhus vaccine, which had to be effective on remote fronts, safe, and available in vast quantities.[1] Typhus vaccines supplemented Zyklon delousing, and their production involved human experiments in concentration camps and establishing vaccine factories with louse-feeders in the occupied east. Vaccines became caught up in medical genocide, and a complex international web of vaccine research has to be disentangled. Rather than a selective account of German medical achievements—or atrocities—the broader context merits scrutiny, so as to provide an explanation for the barbarous turn taken by vaccine production and research.

The strategic development of vaccines was achieved at much human cost. There were disastrous anaphylactic reactions and contaminated batches of vaccines. Rival groups competed to develop ever stronger vaccines with high-risk attempts to formulate a live vaccine. The competition intensified as all sides encountered shortages in supplies. The Germans acquired information about production methods and batches of vaccines by conquest and coercion. The internationalism of typhus vaccine research was sustained despite military offensives, harsh occupation policies, and experimental human butchery. The British and the US for their part consulted the Russians about the incidence and control of typhus in Eastern Europe, not least because, as Anthony Eden, the foreign secretary, reported to the House of Commons in January 1942, the Germans were trying to keep typhus outbreaks secret.[2]

The impact of the Nazi racial agenda on vaccine production is by no means clear-cut. Typhus vaccine experiments figured prominently at the post-war Nuremberg Medical Trial, when the prosecution case rested on proving that the SS organized deadly experiments. German pharmaceutical and medical researchers were accused of instigating experiments involving the deliberate infection and

---

[1] 'La Guerre des laboratoires', *La France Libre*, 1/5 (1941), 423–32.

[2] RAC Rockefeller Foundation 1.1/700/14/99 Rockefeller Foundation to ARC Aug. 1941; Folder 102 WAS diary 25 Nov. 1941; NLM Bayne Jones Papers, 'Typhus Control, Russian'; Bayne-Jones, 'Typhus Fevers', 255–6; *Parliamentary Debates*, 377 (1942), cols. 235, 327.

death of several hundred prisoners. The defence sought to establish that German research and production were decentralized and conformed with international norms for clinical trials. Cross-examinations and interrogations focused on knowledge of human experiments in concentration camps. While the linkage between Nazism and human experiments was the key issue, it is necessary to reconstruct scientific and strategic rationales, and to take account of deep conflicts among German scientists. Although an apparently value-neutral and technical sphere, the development and deployment of vaccines is riddled with ideology and sectional interests.

ii. Crossing Fronts

Cooperation and exchanges of information were facilitated by the permeable divide between Vichy and occupied France, and by US neutrality until 1941. German and US relief teams competed to test vaccines in neutral Spain. The Spanish typhus epidemic of 1941 provided the opportunity for Giroud of the Pasteur Institute and André Lemierre of the Paris Faculty of Medicine to meet US military medical personnel. The Rockefeller Foundation backed US epidemiologists conducting trials of the new vaccine, as well as comparing delousing methods. The German medical teams worked to lever French and American medical advisers out of Spain, which they achieved in December 1941 once the US entered the war.[3] Spanish–German contacts were backed up by researchers from the Hamburg Tropical Institute and the Frankfurt Institute for Experimental Therapy: Nauck lectured on typhus in Spain in December 1941, where he reported on delousing programmes in Poland, and on contacts with Giroud in preparing a vaccine. He arranged for a Spanish researcher to be sent to Warsaw to study German methods of vaccine production. Wohlrab lectured on conditions in Warsaw, and urged intensification of medical policing methods. Otto published in Spanish and English on new typhus vaccines.[4] Other neutral countries like Sweden and Switzerland enabled transfer of medical data between the Axis and Allied researchers.

After the US researchers were expelled from Spain, it was French North Africa—under Vichy government control—which provided an international testing ground for comparing new vaccines. Given US neutrality until December 1941 and

---

[3] NAW RG 112 Typhus Commission Box 33 Prisoners of War, memo 18 Nov. 1944; RAC Rockefeller Foundation 1.1/700/14/101 Spain; On the Rockefeller Foundation team see CMAC RAMC 466–46.

[4] BAK R 86/4164 Bl. 208–18 report by Nauck on a visit of 11 Dec.–22 Dec. 1941; R. Wohlrab, 'Flecktyphusbekämpfung im Generalgouvernement. Vortrag gehalten vor der Academia Real, Madrid und der Universität Valladolid', *MMW* 89/22 (29 May 1942), 483–8, tr. as Wohlrab, 'La lucha contra el tifus exantemático en el Gobierno general de Polonia', *Gaceta Médica Española*, 16/2 (1942), 51; R. Otto, 'New Vaccines for Prophylactic Inoculation against Typhus Fever (typhus exanthematicus)', *Research and Progress*, 8 (1942), 67–72; I. Jimenez Lucena, 'El tifus exantemático de la posguerra española (1939–1943). El uso de una enfermedad colectiva en la legitimación del "Nuevo Estado"', *Dynamis*, 14 (1994), 185–98; id., *El Tifus en la Málaga de la Postguerra* (Malaga, 1990).

US relations with the Vichy state until 8 November 1942, the United States could keep in touch with French medical research. The allied landing in Algiers in November 1942 and capture of Tunis in May 1943 meant that the innovative French anti-typhus measures and production of vaccines became once again accessible to the Americans and British, who rapidly evaluated French research. Allied cooperation and support of civilian health services in North Africa enabled vaccine trials, and the British army obtained over a million doses of typhus vaccines from the Pasteur Institute, Algiers.[5]

The Pasteur Institute in Paris was faced with the problem of keeping the German occupation forces and rapacious pharmaceutical manufacturers at bay. With its traditional links to Poland and Russia, its contingent of Eastern European researchers was vulnerable. Eugène Wollman, who was one of a cohort of Pastorians with Russian origins, was arrested at the Institute in December 1943; his wife and faithful collaborator Elizabeth was imprisoned, and they died in Auschwitz.[6] The Russian-born entomologist Alfred Balachowsky was arrested in July 1943 as leader of the resistance group Buckmaster-Prosper—he was involved in supplying weapons and radio receivers, and assisting Allied agents and aviators; but he survived Buchenwald where he was incarcerated in January 1944 along with many French medical supporters of the resistance. Among other Institute members supporting clandestine activities was Louis Pasteur. Valery-Radot, the chair of the Pasteur Institute's governing body, who from January 1943 distributed tetanus and gangrene sera to the resistance.[7]

Set against such individual heroism, Annie Lacroix-Riz has uncovered a web of collaboration in the chemical and pharmaceutical industry between the Germans and leaders of French industry who believed that the long-term future was a Europe under German domination.[8] The question arises whether the Pasteur Institute should be seen in such a collaborationist context? The Pasteur Institute's expertise in typhus vaccines made it vulnerable to the predatory Germans, suggesting that it was forced to make limited concessions to them. In 1940 Durand and Sparrow jointly worked on new culture methods for typhus rickettsiae. Durand travelled from Tunis to Paris, where he and Giroud cooperated on vaccine production, taking the legacy of the Zinsser–Nicolle collaboration back to the Pasteur

---

[5] CMAC RAMC 651/1 Rapport à Monsieur le Gouverneur Géneral de l'Algérie sur l'évolution de l'épidemie de typhus de 1941–1942 en Algérie et sur les résultats obtenus par les vaccinations au virus vaccin de BLANC et BALTAZARD et aux vaccins morts, copy of H. D. Chalke, 19 Dec. 1943 Algiers; 'Congrès Médical Interallié. Alger du 21 au 24 Février 1944', file 17 'Typhus Fever', Zinsser reprints, Countway Library, Boston; *Notice sur l'Institut Pasteur d'Algérie* (Algiers, 1949), ii. 243; S. Friedlander, *Prelude to Downfall, Hitler and the United States 1939–1941* (London, 1967), 180–6, 285–90 (on Vichy and Africa); *Parliamentary Debates*, vol. 377 (1942), 1919 comment to the House of Commons on 19 Feb. 1942.

[6] 'Hommage à la mémoire d'Eugène et Elizabeth Wollman', *La Lettre de l'Institut Pasteur* (June 1994), 29–32.

[7] AIP, 'L'Institut Pasteur, Centre de Résistance', Agence France Presse, 13 Dec. 1944; Fonds Balachowsky, A. Balachowsky, 'Déposition au sujet des expériences et recherches faites sur le typhus exanthèmatique au camp de Buchenwald'. P. Burrin, *France under the Germans* (New York, 1996), 355.

[8] A. Lacroix-Riz, 'Les Élites Françaises et la collaboration économique. La banque, l'industrie, Vichy, et le Reich', *Revue de l'histoire de la Shoah*, 159 (1997), 8–123.

Institute.[9] By 1940 the Institute possessed a vaccine of formolized rickettsiae obtained from mice and rabbits. On 22 October 1941 the German authorities demanded that the Institute provide a range of vaccines and sera as part of a new scheme of European vaccine supply. The French raised various economic, political, and technical objections, and although the Behringwerke attempted to secure an agreement with the Pasteur Institute in May 1942, the Institute evaded this by insisting that any agreement required the support of the French state and army.[10] The Pasteur Institute did not rush headlong into collaboration, but prevaricated and made only limited concessions to preserve its autonomy.

The Germans made some headway in obtaining the French typhus vaccines. Prompted by the concerns of the Vichy government about possible health threats to French prisoners of war and French civilian workers in Germany, the Pasteur Institute was asked by the French Ministry of Public Health in December 1941 to expand production of an anti-typhus vaccine.[11] Lemierre, having just been in touch with the Americans in Spain, set off to inspect the medical conditions of French conscripts in the German labour camps, observing that however hard the Germans tried to suppress typhus by enforcing quarantine and keeping French and Russian workers separate, the German systems of louse control could never be fully effective. The French medical authorities thought that there were 400 French typhus cases in Germany by 1942, and that delousing repatriated French workers was difficult—Lemierre had observed how some escaped over a wall on arrival at the delousing station of Compiègnes. The French knew that the Germans lacked adequate supplies of vaccine, and they suspected that a massive typhus epidemic was raging in Russia. They expected from the start that the Germans would requisition a share of their vaccine.[12]

In January 1942 the Vichy government authorized production of the 'Durand–Giroud' vaccine (Sparrow's name being omitted possibly for patriotic reasons), hoping that the vaccine would boost French national prestige and that the surplus would provide valuable foreign exchange.[13] Epidemics in North Africa and Spain early in 1942 provided opportunities for clinical trials. At a meeting of French research scientists in February 1942, Alexis Carrel, having returned from the Rockefeller laboratories to assist the Vichy war effort, asked impatiently, 'What

[9] P. Durand and H. Sparrow, 'Innoculation pulmonaire des virus typhiques et boutonneux', *Compte rendu Académie de Sciences*, 210 (1940), 420–2, séance du 11 Mar. 1940; 'Développement dans le poumon des virus typhiques et boutonneux instillés par voie respiratoire', *Archives de l'Institut Pasteur de Tunis*, 29 (Mar. 1940), 1–4; P. Durand, P. Giroud, and H. Sparrow, 'Innoculation pulmonaire du virus pourpré (fièvre des montagnes rocheuses)', *Archives de l'Institut Pasteur de Tunis*, 29 (Sept. 1940), 1–6, cited as off-print; AIP Fonds H. Sparrow, letter from Bogna Seiler, 29 Nov. 1970 concerning the claim that the vaccine should have been called 'Durand-Giroud-Sparrow'; J. Fribourg-Blanc, *La Vaccination contre le typhus exanthèmatique par la méthode de P. Durand et P. Giroud* (Paris, 1942).

[10] Bayer-Archiv, 'Neuordnung des Serumgeschäftes' 1 Aug. 1942, pp. 8–9.

[11] P. Giroud, 'Vaccination against Typhus', in J. Hamburger (ed.), *Medical Research in France during the War (1939–1945)* (Paris, 1947), 33–7. See also AIP, dossier Giroud.

[12] AIP Fonds Direction, Réunion du 27 Février 1942 sur le typhus exanthèmatique.

[13] AIP dossier Giroud, MS 'Notions de bactériologie et d'immunologie concernant le typhus exanthèmatique'.

obstacle has to be overcome?'. Giroud and Lemierre explained that they had to train large numbers of personnel for precise, delicate, and highly dangerous work, and that scarce refrigerators and rabbits had to be obtained. The strains used derived from Tunis and from the Warsaw epidemic of 1941. Large-scale production was underway by February 1943. French Newspapers took patriotic pride in the rapidity of the development of the vaccine.[14] Vaccine was produced at a specially built centre at Laroche-Beaulieu near Périgeux in the 'unoccupied zone' of Vichy France—where the Pasteur Institute planned to produce three million doses per year, at the Pasteur Institute in Paris, and at the Pasteur Institutes of Algiers and Tunis which at the time remained under Vichy control.[15] The decentralization of production meant that the Germans could not take control of a single source of supply.[16]

A German airforce doctor in Casablanca passed Durand's note publicizing the new typhus vaccine in the *Archives de l'Institut Pasteur de Tunis* to the director of the Robert Koch Institute (RKI) in Berlin.[17] The RKI opposed appropriating the Pasteur Institute's rabbit lung vaccine because Gildemeister and Haagen were developing a chick-egg-based vaccine on the US model.[18] The SS used its authority to elicit an invitation from the Vichy Ministry of Health in order to force the Pasteur Institute to impart its expertise. Mrugowsky was too embroiled in epidemic control in the east to visit Paris, but arranged with Haubold's foreign department of the Reich Medical Chamber for Doetzer (the director of the department of bacteriology at the Hygiene Institute of the Waffen-SS) to study at the Pasteur Institute in July 1942. Erwin Ding (a subordinate of Mrugowsky) was sent from Buchenwald to study typhus vaccine production at the Pasteur Institute with Giroud.[19] Thus, to use Céline's derogatory term, the Pasteur Institute had to concede to periodic visits by

[14] *France Soir* (zone libre), (19 Apr. 1943); AIP Fonds Direction, Réunion du 27 Février 1942 sur le typhus exanthèmatique.

[15] AIP Fonds, 'Instituts Pasteur d'outre-mer', Aujaleu, 'Vaccination contre le typhus exanthèmatique (Comité permanent d'hygiène et d'épidémiologie d'Afrique du Nord.—Juin 1942)', 11; AIP, Institut Pasteur d'Alger 1941–4, Sergent to Tréfouel 13 and 16 Jan. 1942 concerning experimentation with typhus vaccines and the obtaining of Giroud vaccine; AIP Fonds, 'Direction de l'Institut 1941–1965', letter to minister 29 June 1942 concerning Laroche-Beaulieu, Périgeux.

[16] NAW USATC Box 35 13 Oct. 1944 Memo on Typhus Vaccine Production at Pasteur Institute, Paris. Box 36 Typhus Vaccine OSS report 6 Feb. 1944.

[17] The note in the *Archives* was published in 1940; BAK R 86/ 4164 Chef der Luftwehr to Gildemeister 10 Feb. 1942 Bl. 130–1; AIP Ministère de la Santé Publique Divers, authorization for Durand-Giroud vaccine preparation, 19 Jan. 1942.

[18] BDC SS-HO 2041 Haubold to Gildemeister 27 Feb. 1943.

[19] AIP Fonds Direction, Dr Knapp, Auslandsabteilung Reichsärztekammer to Fourneau 8 July 1942 concerning visit by Doetzer. There were probably three visits of Ding to Paris: according to NMT roll 16, frame 866 on official trips by Ding, it was twice between Feb. and May 1943; according to the Buchenwald 'diary' it was from 10 Sept.–10 Oct. 1942; see NMT roll, 16 frame 888, and 28 Feb.–6 Mar. 1943 (frame 893), and 27 Apr.–1 May 1943 (frame 895). These visits were omitted from the text of the diary in Bayle, *Croix gammée*, but the visit of 27 Apr.–1 May 1943 appears in a photographic reproduction on p. 1140. E. Ding, 'Über die Schutzwirkung verschiedener Fleckfieberimpfstoffe beim Menschen und den Fleckfieberverlauf nach Schutzimpfung', *Zeitschrift für Hygiene*, 124 (1943), 670–82. For Mrugowsky and French science see Bayle, *Croix gammée*, 255, letter of 16 May 1947.

one or another 'Professor Fritz' in response to German demands for access to technical know-how.

The Germans sanctioned medical research in occupied France, the Netherlands, and Denmark, partly because of an overall strategy of securing compliant puppet regimes, and partly to exploit foreign medical innovations. Prior to the war Ernest Fourneau, the director of the therapeutic chemistry laboratory at the Pasteur Institute, had advocated amicable Franco-German relations. Yet the Germans wavered between deference and resentment when it came to French medicine: a dispute had erupted between the Hamburg Institute for Tropical Medicine, which honoured Fourneau with its Bernhard Nocht medal in 1937, and Zeiss who denounced the French for having stolen the Bayer sleeping sickness drug, Germanin, by producing a similar product.[20] IG-Farben in 1940 formulated a strategy for the return of confiscated pharmaceutical products, the opening up of French markets, and establishing the dominance of the German pharmaceutical industry in Europe: the firm pressed for a cooperative agreement between the Behringwerke and the Pasteur Institute concerning delivery and distribution of sera and vaccines. The Pasteur Institute managed to deflect demands to supply the Behringwerke with unpackaged vaccine despite an agreement reached in June 1942; the Vichy government conceded that once French needs had been met, it might be possible to supply the German government or Behringwerke with ampules clearly marked as manufactured by the Pasteur Institute. Jacques Tréfouel, director of the Pasteur Institute, prevaricated by pointing out that there were problems with the purity and efficacy of large flasks of vaccine; German laws differed from the French in requiring an antiseptic in the vaccine. Yet the German military authorities failed to support these negotiations, not least because the Wehrmacht had its own vaccine production plants.[21]

The Pasteur Institute was inspected by high-ranking German health officials, notably by the Reich Health Führer Leonardo Conti in September 1941, who then backed extended vaccine production in the east.[22] German demands for vaccine from the Pasteur Institute began in November 1941, and in February 1942 the German military medical authorities demanded bulk supplies of the typhus vaccine, as it was by now clear that there was a shortfall in what their own plants could produce. In October 1942 Tréfouel offered as a concession to allow a Behring employee to study vaccine production at the Paris Institute. In January 1943 Richard Haas, the Director of the Behring Institute for Typhus Research at Lemberg (sponsored by IG-Farben's Behringwerke subsidiary in association with Mrugowsky) was

---

[20] AHUB Hygienisches Institut Nr 188 Zeiss to Mühlens 2 Dec. 1937; Mühlens to Reiter 13 Jan., 7 Feb. 1938.
[21] AIP Fonds Direction, Tréfouel to Ministre de la Santé Publique, 12 Oct. 1942; BAK R 21/11061 Bl. 27 'Neuordnung des Serumgeschäftes', 1 Aug. 1942; U. Schneider and H. Stein, *IG-Farben—Buchenwald—Menschenversuche* (Buchenwald, 1986), 13.
[22] AIP Ministère de la Santé Publique Divers, 12 Sept. 1941 concerning Conti's visit on 14 Sept. 1941.

sent to Paris to learn about Giroud's rabbit lung culture method.[23] French medical experts went to Germany: Lemierre (having been in touch with US typhus experts a few months previously) inspected German anti-typhus measures in 1942.[24] The Pasteur Institute remained an international crossroads with its simultaneous links to German and US medical research.

In the coercive context of the German occupation, a bargain appears to have been struck between the Pasteur Institute and the Germans, so that the Pasteur Institute—in any case a private foundation rather than a state institute—remained free from direct control by the Germans. The Pasteur Institute provided vaccine to immunize French prisoners of war and foreign workers in Germany, and the Germans took a share of the vaccine for their own use, and were granted access to learn about production methods. The Institute delivered ninety-two batches of vaccine from April 1942 to the German army. US intelligence officers in September 1944 reported that 10 per cent of the monthly production was supplied to the Germans. By 1944 the Paris production was 60,000 ampules per week, of which the Germans requisitioned up to 10,000 ampules. At the same time the Pasteur Institute disseminated the vaccine internationally: small amounts were sent to Denmark, Italy, Greece, Spain, Poland, Afghanistan, and Jersey, to Mooser in Zurich, as well as to the Red Cross and the Scapini agency for French prisoners of war.[25] The Pasteur Institute retained its dignity under strained circumstances by offering the Germans only limited concessions, thereby avoiding wholesale seizure of its products and resources. By way of contrast, German vaccine research in the occupied east was ruthlessly exploitative.

iii. Allied Advances

The Allies no less than the Germans had to cross the inherently problematic bridge between laboratory experiments and clinical trials of the typhus vaccine. It is worthwhile comparing Allied research with the notorious German work in concentration camps, not least to determine how much of a scientific impulse there was to undertake risky human experiments. The US ran trials to test vaccines and insecticides among conscientious objectors, and although they suffered severe privations over long periods, these were volunteers who under the duress of war

---

[23] AIP Ministère de la Santé Publique—Divers, 1941–1948, Militärbefehlshaber to Pasteur Institute 12 Sept. 1941 concerning visit by Conti; Oberstabsapotheker und Parkführer to Pasteur Institute 2 Feb. 1942; Tréfouel to Jurewitch 10 Feb. 1942 and to Secretary of State for Family and Health; Reichsärztekammer, Verbindungsstelle Paris, 8 July 1942 concerning Doetzer; Tréfouel to Ministère de la Santé Publique, 12 Oct. 1942; Folder typhus—pharmacie allemands containing German orders of vaccine; AHUB Hygienisches Institut Nr 189, Haas to Zeiss 5 Jan., 8 Feb. 1943 concerning visiting Paris; STA N KV Anklage Interrogations H2, p. 3.

[24] AIP Ministère de la Santé Publique Divers, Tréfouel to Ministère de la Santé, 12 Oct. 1942; NAW Typhus Commission Box 33 Prisoners of War, memo 18 Nov. 1944.

[25] AIP Fonds Direction, Institut Pasteur 10 Oct. 1944, 'Vaccin anti-rickettsiae délivré gratuitement. Depuis 1942 jusqu'au 25 Août 1944'; NAW RG 112 USATC Box 35 13 Oct. 1944 Memo on Typhus Vaccine Production at Pasteur Institute, Paris. Box 36 Typhus Vaccine OSS report 6 Feb. 1944; CIOS, *Medical Research in Paris* (London, 1944), 4.

had consented to their role as experimental guinea-pigs. Some researchers pre-fered to test the vaccine under naturally occurring epidemic conditions in Spain and Egypt. As British troops had embarked for North Africa before supplies of vaccines arrived, they were treated in effect as experimental subjects. The much higher incidence of typhus and fatalities among the non-vaccinated British troops as opposed to vaccinated US soldiers (who suffered no deaths and only sixty-five cases of louse-born typhus fever) confirmed the efficacy of the Cox vaccine.[26]

Developments in the scientific study of viruses boosted the academic status of typhus research and raised expectations of medically useful outcomes. Rick-ettsiae were shifted from being classed as bacteria to the still mysterious but scientifically exciting class of viruses, which some scientists considered held the keys to the ultimate secret of life. The rise of academic interest in virology meant that international academic links provided the basis for exchanges of informa-tion and personnel. Channels of scientific communication were opened despite the war: the *Archiv für die gesamte Virusforschung*, first published in Vienna in 1940, had a Swiss editor and an editorial board with members in Britain, Germany, and the United States.[27] The United States restricted the circulation of research papers only from March 1942, when a notional date of publication was assigned to papers to be released after the war.[28] A series of handbooks on viruses app-eared in Germany. The virus remained difficult to define: a favoured German view was that the virus was a cellular parasite. German medical researchers ranked typhus as a viral disease: its causal micro-organism and the means of transmission reinforced the racial concept of a lethal parasite.[29] While the German research effort in virology at one level shared international scientific concerns, it was financed by a state requiring remedies against viral diseases so as to protect German penetration into Russia and Africa. The mobilized medical researchers justified human experiments by the doublethink of facilitating eventual victory and of benefits to humanity from a more efficacious evidence-based medical science.

The take-off of virology increased the medical interest of typhus, as basic research had practical spin-offs. There was an international array of competing vaccines and research groups (see Appendix II) with British, Canadian, Danish,

---

[26] NAW RG 112 box 1109, S. Bayne-Jones, 'Commentary on Typhus Control in World War II', 3; USATC J. P. Fox, 'Immunization against Epidemic Typhus', offprint in USATC files. PRO FDI/6632 Anglo-American Typhus Commission, Alex Wood (War Office) to E. Mellanby 14 June 1943; Report by J. Burn on USATC.

[27] The editor was R. Doerr, and the editorial board consisted of S. P. Bedson (London), J. Craigie (Toronto), A. Gratia (Liège), C. Hallauer (Bern), R. E. Shope (Princeton), K. M. Smith (Cambridge), W. M. Stanley (Princeton), W. J. Tulloch (Dundee), O. Waldmann (Insel Riems—a veterinary research centre).

[28] USATC N. H. Topping, *et al.*, 'Studies of Typhus Fever', *National Institute of Health Bulletin*, 183 (1945).

[29] R. Bieling, *Viruskrankheiten* (Leipzig, 1941), 2nd edn. (Leipzig, 1944); R. Doerr and Hallauer, *Hand-buch der Virusforschung*, 2 vols. (Vienna, 1938); Gildemeister, Hagen, and Waldmann, *Handbuch der Viruskrankheiten*, 2 vols. (Jena, 1939).

French, German, Italian, Latvian, Polish, Romanian, Soviet, and US products. Opposing sides monitored research results in journals: summaries of German papers appeared in the MRC's *Bulletin of War Medicine*.[30] The Germans appeared to be better informed about what the Allies were doing than about the medical work of the Japanese. The International Committee of the Red Cross (ICRC) and the League of Nations spread information across frontiers and fronts—indeed, the Allies suspected twenty-eight Red Cross officials were German agents.[31] Rose (professor at the RKI) sent his Swiss lecture on typhus and malaria prevention to the ICRC.[32] The League of Nations Health Organization produced a substantial bibliography on typhus research and epidemiology in 1943, containing data on Spain, Germany, parts of occupied Poland, Lithuania, Romania, Bulgaria, and Turkey.[33] But when the British Army Pathology Advisory Committee reported in 1943 that there had been 3,786 cases of typhus in Poland, the statistic was meaningless in its precision.[34] In 1944 the League of Nations stressed the unreliability of the available statistical data due to the German extermination policies: 'The effects of a heightened epidemic level have been comparatively trifling when compared with these other causes of enfeeblement of the nation'—the discriminatory rationing system, deportation, forced labour, and 'eradication' of 'the Jewish elements'.[35] Allied intelligence concluded in 1944 that despite the number of vaccine-producing institutes in occupied Europe, quantities of typhus vaccine remained insufficient.[36] Intelligence reports were compiled on epidemics, and German prisoners were interrogated regarding the incidence of typhus.[37] Overall, the multiplicity of channels of exchange of medical data suggests that military strategists had an avid interest in vaccines and prevailing epidemic conditions. The lack of curiosity on the part of the Allied leaders to reports of the mass killing of Jews and of hospital patients in mobile gas vans, and about the extermination camps was in marked contrast to the high alert for information on epidemics.[38] While medical information was disseminated internationally, knowledge of the Holocaust spread with difficulty.

[30] P. S. Richards, 'Great Britain and Allied Scientific Information: 1939–1943', *Minerva*, 26 (1988), 177–98; Richards, 'The Movement of Scientific Knowledge from Germany under National Socialism', ibid., 28 (1990), 426–45; e.g. R. Wohlrab, 'Immunisierungen gegen Flecktyphus', *Medizinische Klinik*, 37 (1941), 532–5 was summarized in *Bulletin of War Medicine*, 1 (Sept. 1942), 179–80.

[31] T. Bower, *Blood Money. The Swiss, the Nazis and the Looted Billions* (London, 1997), 40.

[32] NMT roll 38, frame 1543. BA/MA H 20/1026 series of lectures on vaccines by Rose.

[33] The data covered the period from October 1941 until the end of March 1942; Y. Biraud, 'The Present Menace of Typhus Fever and the Means of Combating It', *Bulletin of the Health Organisation*, 10/1 (1943), 1–64.

[34] NAW RG 112 USATC Box 37 C. H. Stuart-Harris, Army Pathology Advisory Committee, July 1943; Report on typhus research from the Emergency Vaccine Committee, May 1943.

[35] Y. M. Biraud, 'Health in Europe. A Survey of the Epidemic and Nutritional Situation', *Bulletin of the Health Organisation*, 10 (1943–4), 559–699 (on Poland, pp. 648–51).

[36] PRO WO 188/681 BW reports WWII, Military Medical Problems in Occupied Europe, 14 Feb. 1944.

[37] CMAC RAMC 651/1 interrogation report on Dr Walter Huffstaat, 3 Feb. 1944; 20/5 extracts from European Medical Intelligence Summaries, n.d. PRO/FDI/6632 Anglo-American Typhus commission, meeting of 10 Sept. 1943 at the Ministry of Production; USATC report to Mellanby 19 Mar. 1944; PRO/FDI/661 2 Typhus Committee, Constitution and members, Oct. 1941.

[38] Gilbert, *Auschwitz and the Allies*, 56 for the plan to gas Jews; 149 for reports on the mobile gas vans in July 1943; 263–4, 275 for delousing as a deception; 340 for conclusions.

German experimental atrocities at Buchenwald involved deliberate infection of prisoners. By way of contrast, Durand combined human vaccination (a benign act) with infecting animals when he tested six French vaccines (three with killed typhus *rickettsiae* and three live vaccines) on 175 prisoners in Algiers around June 1942. Durand took serum from the vaccinated prisoners, mixing it with typhus cultures from the lungs of infected mice, injecting the mixture in rabbits and then counting the antibodies. The idea was to compare the neutralizing power of the different vaccines. Here was a method of evaluating the strength of the different vaccines on the basis of animal rather than human vivisection.[39]

The fluid military situation in North Africa meant that the Pasteur Institutes exchanged information while undertaking mass immunization campaigns to reduce epidemic prevalence, and after liberation the North African Pasteur Institutes contributed to Allied clinical research.[40] Sergent at Algiers experimented with British military volunteers in the winter of 1943 when he compared the Durand-Giroud mouse and rabbit lung vaccine and the Cox type egg vaccine: French researchers regarded their vaccine as more effective.[41] The Americans conducted comparative tests during 1943 on vaccines by Cox (achieving best results), a variant produced at the Canadian Craigie laboratories, the Mexican Castenada vaccine, and the French mouse lung vaccine. The vaccine obtained directly from France was described as the same vaccine that 'is being prepared for the Germans'.[42]

The fragmented German research effort contrasted to a much more coordinated Allied research structure. Under an Office of Scientific Research and Development, a US Committee on Medical Research was established in June 1941.[43] Inter-allied Conferences on War Medicine from December 1942 involved 6,500 officers of the Allied Medical Services meeting twenty-four times, to evaluate medical innovations.[44] The United States of America Typhus Commission (USATC) controlled the supply of typhus vaccines from 1942, becoming by the end of the war a global distribution agency.[45] An Anglo-American typhus committee, established in 1943, pooled information on research and field experience of the USATC and the

[39] AIP Fonds 'Instituts Pasteur d'outre-mer', Aujaleu, 'Vaccination contre le typhus exanthèmatique (Comité permanent d'hygiène et d'épidemiologie d'Afrique du Nord)—Juin 1942', pp. 5–7.

[40] H. D. Chalke, 'Typhus'; Hansen, *Biologische Kriegsführung*, 107–9.

[41] NAW RG 112 USATC Box 36 Experiments, Plotz and Bennett memo 4 Feb. 1944 'A Comparative Study Concerning the Antibody Response in Man Following the Administration of the Durand-Giroud Lung Vaccine and the Cox Type Egg Vaccine', using the evidence of complement fixing titres.

[42] NAW RG 112 USATC Typhus vaccines, box 36, folder 5, Bayne-Jones to Forbes 8 Dec. 1943 concerning 'Report on the Testing of Four Different Vaccines to Determine their Immunising Properties' by Dyer and Topping.

[43] NAW RG 227 Inventory of the Office of Scientific Research and Development. James Phinney Baxter III, *Scientists Against Time* (1946); *Science in World War II*, 7 vols. See also *Army Medical Bulletin* (1922–49) and *Bulletin of the US Army Medical Department* (1943–).

[44] H. L. Tidy (ed.), *Inter-allied Conferences on War Medicine 1942–1945. Convened by the Royal Society of Medicine* (London, 1947), 11.

[45] NAW RG 112 Records of the Office of the Surgeon General (Army). The USA Typhus Commission 1942–6, Technical and Administrative Records, Boxes 33–40; USATC chronology on British equivocation on dominant role of USATC 30 May 1944; A. E. Cowdrey, *Stanhope Bayne-Jones and the Maturing of American Medicine* (Baton Rouge, La., 1992), 153.

Medical Research Council's Typhus Research Committee.[46] The Germans failed to develop such coordinating structures either within the Reich or to liaise with their allies.

The USATC supplied vaccines throughout North Africa and the Middle East, as part of a strategy to gain commercial and diplomatic goodwill—for example, to areas where the Arabian-American Oil Company was active.[47] Between January and June 1943 the USATC distributed 41,000 cc of typhus vaccine; from July 1943 to June 1944 1,916,410 cc; and from July 1944 to May 1945 2,053,520 cc. Substantial quantities were out of date, but were redesignated under an 'extended' dating system for civilians. In any case it was felt that the US code of commercial and professional ethics was so high that some latitude could be allowed when it came to non-European civilians.[48] One might see the differential between what was suitable for soldiers and non-Europeans as racist, but this was a highly attenuated form of racism in comparison to the genocidal German vaccine policy.

There were significant national variations. Whereas the French were vaccine obsessed, and the Germans were divided over the value of vaccines, the British gave much less priority to vaccine-based strategies, preferring insecticidal powders. A mixed preventive and vaccine-based strategy was deemed prudent when in September 1941 British medical experts feared a major outbreak of typhus infection, arising from refugees, prisoners of war, and returning troops from North Africa. Among the experts consulted was Felix, the former Austrian medical officer who during the First World War discovered with Weil the classic diagnostic test for typhus. He was critical of the Cox vaccine, and developed a diagnostic and therapeutic typhus serum designed to stimulate the production of OX19 agglutinins to resist infection. Felix drew on a range of international work dating from the mid-1930s, as well as on results published in German journals like the *Klinische Wochenschrift*. However, the serum did not enjoy the same success as the Cox vaccine, although it was widely distributed to medical officers of health for testing on volunteers from the staff of fever hospitals. Felix had greatest faith in the Lwów louse-based vaccine, regretting that it was unobtainable for the allies.[49]

The USATC triumphantly pointed out that German production of vaccine lagged behind needs, and that there was rank discrimination about whom was vaccinated. It tested captured batches of vaccine from June 1943 until the end of the war, when they were found to be highly variable but often low in potency giving only partial or no protection; the bullish USATC director from September 1943, Stanhope Bayne-Jones (a former Zinsser student), dismissed a batch of rival

[46] NAW RG 112 USATC Typhus Vaccines, Box 36, folder 5 Bayne-Jones to T. R. Forbes, 8 Dec. 1943 concerning the forwarding of Topping's report, 'Epidemic Typhus Fever a Summary of Recent Work'. The USATC passed on information concerning vaccine tests to the Medical Research Council in December 1943.

[47] Ibid., concerning distribution of typhus vaccine; letter of L. A. Fox to SBJ 9 May 1945.

[48] Ibid., Leon A. Fox to Bayne-Jones, 9 May 1945.

[49] A. Felix, 'The Typhus Group of Fevers', *BMJ* (21 Nov. 1942), 597–601; Typhus Commission Box 35 Felix to Bayne-Jones 13 Sept. 1943; Report of 24 Feb. 1944; PRO FD1/6232 Typhus Fever, G. S. Wilson to A. Felix 12 Sept. 1941, Felix to Wilson, 15 Sept. 1941.

German vaccine: 'this egg yolk vaccine was no good.' US army potency tests after the war suggested that Bieling's egg yolk and mouse lung vaccine were not more than half as strong as the US Cox vaccine.[50] Confusion between different agencies was resolved, when the USATC was given prime authority over coordinating supply and distribution of the vaccine on a global scale.[51] The Allied coordination stands in contrast to the far greater fragmentation and rivalries among German vaccine researchers.

iv. Conquest and Production

Combating typhus was one of the *Sonderaufgaben* entrusted to German scientists. Although the Nuremberg Medical Trial drew attention to the immense scale of the German typhus vaccine production, and to the ruthless cruelty of the SS, the prosecution underestimated the vicious infighting between the production centres. Nazi typhus research was never centrally coordinated according to a masterplan. Although propagandists linked the past achievements of German medical research to the national ability to organize, medical research was bedevilled by conflict, overlapping powers, and competing interests.[52] The need to exploit foreign expertise and to carry out the hazardous research either outside Germany or in the security of concentration camps accelerated fragmentation. Typhus vaccine researchers clashed over the merits of the different vaccines as well as over human experimentation and biological warfare. Comparison with the relatively more integrated Allied medical research programmes suggests that the power struggles which were endemic under Nazism crippled medical research and preventive medicine.

German vaccine research was parasitic on international cooperation, and drew increasingly on Polish expertise. In October 1938 Otto of the Frankfurt Institute for Experimental Therapy obtained from Warsaw specimens of a typhus 'virus' cultured in a mouse; he developed a serum at the Behringwerke, keeping the army and the Reich authorities informed about his progress.[53] German bacteriologists contacted typhus researchers in the Soviet zone of Poland to obtain vaccine until their own production was ready. In the winter of 1939–40 the Lwów authorities exchanged 5,000 doses of Weigl vaccine for five German microscopes. Was the exchange organized by Weigl, or by Ludwik Fleck who had been

[50] NAW RG 112 USATC, Rose interrogation 25–26 June 1943; Report on Potency Tests of German Typhus Vaccine, 30 Nov. 1945; Greeley to SBJ, 5 Sept. 1945; Cowdrey, *Bayne-Jones*.

[51] Ibid., file 'General 1943', memo 21 June 43, file 'German Typhus Vaccine', memo by SBJ 17 Aug. 1945 and 22 Mar. 1946; USATC gains co-ordinating powers for the Middle East, 16 July 1943; Veldee to SBJ 22 Dec. 1944 re Weigl vaccines; Captured German Typhus Biologicals, 20 Jan. 1945; SBJ to Veldee 21 Dec. 1944 and 17 Jan. 1945 referring to ASID produced sera.

[52] 'Emil von Behring. Der Retter der Kinder', *Neues Volk*, 8/19 (1940), 6–7; L. E. Simon, *German Research in World War II. An Analysis of the Conduct of Research* (New York and London, 1947), although focusing on air force research provides a general analysis of the Nazi research 'experiment'.

[53] Bayer-Archiv, Marburg Protokolle, B.B. 25–28 Niederschrift über die 25. Sero-bakteriologische Betriebs-Besprechung in Marburg, am 25. Oktober 1938, p. 7.

appointed director of the bacteriological institute in Lvov, as a member of a newly formed Ukrainian Medical Institute? The exchange, proudly reported by Conti to Himmler, was prompted by the need to ensure that the resettlement programme of ethnic Germans from the east did not result in the importation of typhus; that Rose of the RKI took a key role in supervising the ethnic German repatriation, shows how bacteriologists were involved in schemes for racial resettlement.[54]

The invasion meant that the protectionist barriers against foreign imports of vaccines into Poland were swept aside. The Behringwerke (which under IG-Farben became Germany's leading producer of sera and vaccines) sought control of the Polish state serum production; IG managed to take over veterinary sera, but its efforts to comandeer the vaccines of the Warsaw Hygiene Institute were not successful.[55] Because of the lack of immune personnel, the Reich Ministry of the Interior (RMdI) agreed that the German army should supervise production in occupied Poland. The RMdI considered that if it placed vaccine production in the hands of the pharmaceutical industry, cases of infection within Germany would result. The army promptly established a laboratory at the University of Cracow in November 1939, and early in 1940 this was expanded into an Institute for Typhus and Virology. The Institut für Virologie, Oberstes Kommando der Heeresleitung (IFV/OKH) was under the command of a military medical officer, Hermann Eyer, who collaborated with Weigl in the manufacture of the louse-gut typhus vaccine. Weigl had advised the USSR Commissariat of Health in Moscow, Leningrad, and Kiev during 1940. He had declined evacuation with the Polish army to Romania, reckoning that his expertise in vaccine production rendered him indispensable in wartime. But he disliked working under the Soviet occupation in Lvov, and registered as an ethnic German. In Weigl's vaccine the *rickettsia* were killed by phenol; the antigens remained, so providing a dead vaccine suitable for active immunization.[56]

With the Barbarossa onslaught, Eyer opened an outpost in Lemberg in July 1941, where Weigl became co-director. Eyer also established satellite stations at Tschenstochau and for the mouse-lung vaccine from December 1942 at Rabka in the Tatra mountains under R. Bickhardt, who was transferred from Otto's Frankfurt Institute.[57] Overall, Eyer commanded a staff of over 1,500. His Cracow Institute was an international centre providing training for foreign doctors from Japan, Italy, Romania, Hungary, Slovakia, Finland, Bulgaria, Spain, Turkey, Switzerland, and Sweden, and he visited Amsterdam, Bucharest, and the Pasteur Institute, Paris

---

[54] NAW 175, roll 69 report by Rose. BA NS 19/ 1591 Bl. 3 L. Conti to Himmler 14 Aug. 1942, cited by Hansen, *Biologische Kriegsführung*, 120 and Thom, 'Wandlungen', 434. Hansen and Thom overlook the role of Fleck in this pragmatic exchange. For the Soviet administration of Lwów see Fässler, *Lemberg*, 118–20.

[55] Homburger, *Behringwerke*, 137.

[56] BDC Hermann Eyer files; M. Kordas, 'Working Conditions of Louse Feeders for Typhus Vaccine Production in Lvov during World War II'.

[57] R. Otto, *Bericht über die Tätigkeit des Staatl. Instituts für experimentelle Therapie in Frankfurt a. M. in der Zeit vom 1. April 1941 bis 31. Dezember 1943* (Wiesbaden, 1947), 17–19.

to acquire foreign expertise in vaccine production.[58] International cooperation was to continue within the German sphere of influence: in September 1942 and August 1943 German–Italian conferences of immunologists in Naples focused on typhus vaccines, and in May 1943 a German–Hungarian Serum Commission met.[59] The Behring Institute Lemberg proclaimed itself as open to all European researchers, despite its strategic role and the displacement of Jewish vaccine researchers in the nearby ghetto.[60]

Eyer had qualified in hygiene and medical microbiology at Erlangen, and had joined the Nazi Party in 1935. As a military doctor he was seconded in 1937–8 to the Virus Department of Haagen at the RKI Berlin, and from 1938 served at the Military Medical Academy, Berlin, absorbing the geo-medical ideas of Zeiss and Rodenwaldt, and gaining a position in the Hygiene Institute of the University of Berlin.[61] He drew inspiration from the historical classic on medical police by Johann Peter Frank to produce in 1937 a medical topography and eugenic study of a strategic border area, the Oberpfalz. He cooperated with the Behringwerke in research on an influenza vaccine, and during 1939 he served with the Italian army in Ethiopia, where he became acquainted with Weigl's vaccine. He organized mass production of the Weigl louse-gut vaccine 'as a weapon' which would give effective immunity against typhus. He admired Weigl's vaccine innovations and adopted his arduous methods while introducing more mechanized procedures on a vast scale.[62] Eyer applied racial theory to argue for the superiority of the Weigl vaccine as 'natural', whereas cultivated *rickettsiae* in other animal tissues were 'degenerate'.[63]

---

[58] The address of Eyer's Institute in Cracow was Czystastrasse 18, and Siegfriedstrasse 45, Lemberg. The Lemberg address of the Institut für Fleckfieber- und Virusforschung (Behring-Institut) was Grüne Strasse 12. There was also an Institut für Hygiene at Kopernikusstrasse 14 and a Medizinisches Institut at Glawiniskistrasse 12. See K. Baedeker, *Das Generalgouvernement. Reisehandbuch* (Leipzig, 1943). For German mapping of Lemberg/ Lwów as a stategic centre see Generalstab des Heeres, *Verkehrsplan Lemberg (Lwów)*, 1931 (marking hospitals); also Generalstab des Heeres, *Militärgeographische Angaben über das Europäische Russland. Ukraine (einschliesslich Moldaurepublik und Krim)* (Berlin, 1941). Both maps identify the university hospital complex at ul. Piekarska.

[59] R. Otto, *Bericht über die Tätigkeit des Staatl. Instituts für experimentelle Therapie in Frankfurt a. M. in der Zeit vom 1. April 1941 bis 31. Dezember 1943* (Wiesbaden, 1947), 19, 26–7.

[60] Behring-Archiv, Behring-Institut Lemberg, photo no. 54.

[61] BDC Hermann Eyer files. After the war he denied Nazi affiliations, see CIOS report on 'Institut für Fleckfieber- und Virusforschung des Oberkommandos des Heeres at Roth Bavaria, 27–30 April 1945, 16–17 May 1945, p. 5; E. Gildemeister, 'Bericht über die Tätigkeit des Instituts für Infektionskrankheiten 'Robert Koch' in Berlin für die Zeit vom 1. April 1938 bis 31. März 1939', *Veröffentlichungen aus dem Volksgesundheitsdienstes*, li. 604.

[62] G. Schierz, *Gesammelte Beiträge zur Hygiene und Mikrobiologie. Eine Festschrift für Hermann Eyer* (Munich, 1975), 2–9; H. Eyer, 'Rudolf Weigl und die ätiologische Fleckfieberbekämpfung', *MMW* 109 (1967), 2185–91; Eyer, '50 Jahre Fleckfieberschutzimpfung. In memoriam Rudolf Weigl', *Zentralblatt für Bakteriologie und Parasitenkunde*, 1 Abt., vol. 205 (1967), 268–76; H. Eyer, 'Die Fleckfieberprophylaxe der deutschen Wehrmacht im 2. Weltkrieg', *Wehrmedizin und Wehrpharmazie* (1979) 56–60; H. Eyer, *Gesundheitspflege und Bevölkerungspolitik in der Ostmark. Eine medizinische Topographie eines ausgewählten Landbezirks im Bereich der oberpfälzischen Grenzmark* (Erlangen, 1937); Bayer-Archiv, Marburg Prokolle, B.B. 25–28 Niederschrift über die 25. Sero-bakteriologische Betriebs-Besprechung in Marburg, am 25. Oktober 1938, p. 7.

[63] Hansen, *Biologische Kriegsführung*, 123; Kordas and Weindling, 'Working Conditions'; CIOS, *Tropical Medicines and Other Medical Subjects in Germany* (London, n.d.), 13.

The sense that his vaccine was racially superior prompted Eyer to attack the US Cox embryo and the French Durand-Giroud vaccine derivatives.

From April 1940 the Cracow institute supplied the army with ampules of vaccine, and the Generalgouvernement gave it authority over the distribution of vaccines from all sources—a monopoly which the SS was to challenge. The vaccine was restricted to military personnel liable to come into contact with typhus. By the end of the war three million ampoules were produced.[64] One million lice were maintained in Cracow, and American intelligence calculated that despite the immense resources involved, Eyer could have only provided enough vaccine for 180,000 men per year.[65] A black market flourished in what was called the *weiglowki*.[66]

A major concern during the typhus epidemic in 1941 was the insufficiency of supplies for the German army. IG-Farben and its Behringwerke subsidiary saw that here was an immense market opportunity to add to its already buoyant business supplying the army with plague, gas oedema, and diphtheria sera for the east and North Africa. The Behringwerke drew up a strategy in 1940 for German domination of serum products through the national *Arbeitsgemeinschaft* between the German vaccine-producing companies. The plan involved securing international agreements between foreign serum works and the German companies.[67] The Behringwerke set about building up the capacity to produce 12 million cc of typhus vaccine per year by 1945 (in theory enough to vaccinate four million persons), so that military needs were covered only when the army was on the verge of disintegration. The strength of the vaccine was reduced to a third or even a quarter of the pre-war level, using twenty-five or thirty instead of a 100 louse intestines. From 1943 Eyer produced a version of the French mouse-lung vaccine. The lungs of 100–200 mice were harvested daily, providing enough serum for the vaccination of 50,000 persons a year. The Cracow Institute also produced yellow fever and rabies vaccines, researched into trench fever, and developed a diagnostic test for typhus suitable for a field laboratory. Even after evacuation in the summer of 1944, a staff of fifty-four was maintained.[68]

The resources poured by the Germans into vaccine research reflected a situation that the incidence of typhus in the German army was far higher than among the Allies—with estimates varying from 70,000 to 180,000 German soldiers afflicted by the disease. The onslaught on the east brought the Germans into areas where typhus was endemic. That the Kiev–Kharkov sector seems to have been the hardest

---

[64] Eyer, 'Fleckfieberprophlaxe', 56; BAK R 86/ 4164 Bl. 49. Leven, 'Fleckfieber' Guth, 130; Fischer, iv, 3200–1; BDC SS-HO 2051 RMdI to OKH and to Regierung des Generalgouvernements 9 Dec. 1941.

[65] Combined Intelligence Objectives Sub-committee (CIOS) Target Number 24/241 Medical, Institut für Fleckfieber- und Virusforschung des Oberkommandos des Heeres at Roth, Bavaria 27–30 April 1945, 16–17 May 1945, 4.

[66] Roland, *Courage*, 147–9.

[67] BAK R 21/11061, Bl. 6 I.G. Farben Wirtschaftspol. Abt 4 to Klingelhöfer, Reichsministerium für Wissenschaft, Erziehung und Volksbildung 14 Oct. 1940; Bl. 7–11 memorandum by W. R. Mann 'Vorschlag zur Neuordnung des Serumgeschäftes', 29 July 1940; Bl. 22–35 'Neuordung des Serumgeschäftes' 1 Aug. 1942; Homburger, *Behringwerke*, 113–15.

[68] CIOS, *Institut für Fleckfieber- und Virusforschung des O.K.H.*, 1945.

hit during the winter and spring of 1941–2, and again in 1942–3, helps to explain why the Germans regarded typhus control as crucial in their racial war.[69] As the German army, the SS, and IG-Farben exercised increasing control over vaccine production, the efforts to produce sufficient and effective vaccines became caught up in policies of conquest and genocide.

Mühlens mobilized the Hamburg Tropical Institute for typhus work from October 1939, and looked for research opportunities in Cracow and Warsaw in July 1940. The pathologist Nauck, assisted by Fritz Weyer, was responsible for the Institute's Fleckfieberforschungsstelle in Warsaw from May until September 1940. The department was then integrated into the Warsaw Hygiene Institute under Wohlrab who was seconded from the Frankfurt Institute for Experimental Therapy.[70] The Hamburg Institute increased its prestige at a time when not only Germany was reasserting its claim to be a colonial power, but when the population was being racially cleansed: Eichmann consulted the Hamburg Tropical Institute in 1940 for advice on the suitability of Madagascar as a dumping ground for European Jews.[71] Nauck was was convinced that Jews were the main carriers of typhus. While Walbaum pressed for a *Seuchenmauer* in Warsaw, taking advice from the Tropical Institute on the suitability of Madagascar held out prospects of transfering Jewish bacilli carriers to a colonial ghetto.[72]

Nauck recommended that in order to produce the Weigl vaccine, there should be an institute in an area where typhus was endemic; for staff had to have acquired immunity from typhus.[73] In March 1940 Nauck explained to the director of public health in Cracow that to obtain fresh cultures of typhus *rickettsiae*, a research station in Poland was necessary, and that the Tropical Institute and Zeiss in Berlin wished to send research workers to Poland.[74] Instead of merely augmenting resources for the Weigl vaccine, other vaccines were contemplated. The State Institute for Hygiene in Warsaw (under German administration) cooperated with the Health Office (staffed by Poles) in November and December 1941 to test the Behring vaccine in the Warsaw ghetto: 238 Jews were inoculated with the new vaccine, and of these twenty-four suffered adverse reactions.[75]

The priority was to keep the occupying troops free from typhus, and to prevent

---

[69] A. Weiss, *Le Typhus exanthématique pendant la deuxième guerre mondiale en particulier dans les camps de concentration* (Paris, 1954), 21 citing Bieling and Heinlein in: *Naturforschung und Medizin in Deutschland 1939–1946* (Wiesbaden, 1947).

[70] Wulf, *Tropeninstitut*, 118–23, 231 for photograph of the department with a staff of twelve; Roland, *Courage*, 124. Weyer then researched on the Crimea with the support of Mühlens from Hamburg, F. Weyer, 'Zum Gedächtnis von Professor Mühlens', *Zeitschrift für hygienische Zoologie*, 35 (1943), 153–7.

[71] *Eichmann Interrogated* (London, 1983), 67.

[72] Browning, 'Genocide and Public Health', 148–51; Roth, 'Von der Tropenheilkunde zur "Kolonialmedizin"'.

[73] AHUB Hygienisches Institut Nr 203 Bl. 29, Nauck to Zeiss 14 Mar. 1940.

[74] Ibid., Bl. 33, Nauck to Leiter, Abteilung Gesundheitswesens Krakau 27 Mar. 1940.

[75] BAK R 86/ 4164, Bl. 134 Kudicke to Gildemeister of RKI 9 Feb. 1942; Bl. 135 T. Ganc (Kommissar für Seuchenbekämpfung) and I. Milejkowski (Vorsitzender des Gesundheitsamtes) to Kudicke 1 Feb. 1942; L. Hirszfeld and M. Szejnman, 'W sprawie szczepién przeciwko durowi plasmistemu', *Polski Tygodnik Lekarski*, 1/5 (1946), 137–44.

its introduction into Germany: high Jewish mortality was a matter of indifference as long as the epidemic could be contained. Researchers tested susceptibility of animals to diverse typhus strains, and forced the staff of the Jewish hospital of Czyste to test sulphonamide drugs for IG-Farben. Nauck even carried out autopsies at the hospital. He supported the ghettoization of Jews as a 'sanitary precaution', arguing that while Jews were resistant to typhus they could infect non-Jewish populations.[76] Nauck's idea that typhus was a Jewish disease was supported by a theory that Jews expelled from Spain at the end of the fifteenth century spread typhus throughout Europe.[77]

Military requirements shaped the research agenda in the Berlin Institute of Hygiene. In February 1940 Zeiss applied to the Deutsche Forschungsgemeinschaft (DFG) for funds to support an alternative to the costly and laborious louse vaccine of Weigl. Zeiss's assistant, Hilda Sikora, had considerable expertise in medical entomology derived from her pioneering studies on louse breeding during the First World War.[78] The aim of the research was to find an insect in the same class as lice (i.e. another arthropod) from which it would be simpler and cheaper to produce an anti-typhus vaccine. Zeiss and Sikora attempted to cultivate typhus rickettsiae in an artificial medium, given that it 'was inappropriate for large numbers of lice to be kept in civilised lands'.[79]

Cutting across the traditional alliance between the army and experts in hygiene came the dynamic force of the-SS. The ascendant status of the Hygiene Institute of the Waffen-SS was indicative of the tightening grasp of the SS on the academic, medical, and the military spheres. The SS promoted its Ahnenerbe research organization, which built up links to the DFG through overlapping personnel; from 1935 the DFG president, Rudolf Mentzel, was an SS officer, veteran of the 1923 Kapp Putsch, and a specialist in the physical chemistry of gas warfare. Himmler wrote to Reichsarzt-SS Ernst Grawitz in April 1941 that medicine should not keep the sick alive, but reduce their numbers; he complained 'that doctors were such bureaucrats, that this would cause a dog to cry'. Himmler supported Grawitz's extensive human experiments in concentration camps, including the sterilization of homosexuals. In June 1941 Himmler arranged for eight Polish Jews to be transferred from Auschwitz to Sachsenhausen for medical research (conveniently situated close to Berlin for sending skeletons to metropolitan scientific institutes) and for human experiments on hepatitis, which he justified as relevant to 'our troops' in Southern Russia.[80] On 2 August 1943 Himmler insisted that he personally authorize all experiments in concentration camps.[81]

---

[76] AHUB Hygienisches Institut Nr 203, letter of Nauck to the Abteilung Gesundheitswesen of the Generalgouvernement, dated 27 Mar. 1940; Wess, 'Menschenversuche und Seuchenpolitik', 32–6.

[77] H. H. Ries, 'Über die geschichtliche, insbesondere die kriegsgeschichtliche Bedeutung des Fleckfiebers, Aus dem Hamburger Tropeninstitut Direktor: Professor Dr Nauck', med. diss. Hamburg, 1944, p. 5.

[78] BAK R 86/ 4164 Bl 16 The RKI refused to employ her because of her unreliable personality, memo of 21 Jan. 1940.

[79] BAK R 73/15922 Zeiss to Wilhelm Richter, Leiter der Fachgliederung Wehrmedizin, DFG 20 Mar. 1941; H. Sikora, 'Meine Erfahrungen bei der Läusezucht', *Zeitschrift für Hygiene*, 125 (1944), 541–52.

[80] BDC Grawitz SS record. Letter to Himmler 1 June 1943.

[81] BDC SS-HO 2049–156 Order of 2 Aug. 1943 signed by Brandt.

German hygiene institutes established research stations in occupied areas for typhus studies, because of the risks of infection if such research were to be carried out in Germany. The High Command established a Typhus and Viral Disease Research Centre for vaccine production early in 1940 at the microbiological institute of the savagely Nazified Cracow University: the Polish staff of the university was deported to the concentration camp of Sachsenhausen and equipment removed to Germany. Hamburg bacteriologists comandeered the Warsaw Hygiene Institute, previously a symbol of the renaissance of Poland. The new 'Reich Universities' of Posen and Strassburg included typhus research as part of their mission to act as bastions of German culture. At the Reich University of Strassburg, founded in November 1941 for carrying out 'special tasks', virologists tested typhus vaccines on prisoners shipped over from Auschwitz. After deporting the staff and students of the 'Uniwersytet Zachodni' at Posen, the Reich University became a major centre for 'research' into infectious diseases—no fewer than 4,500 Polish and Jewish victims were cremated in the ovens of the Anatomy Institute, and a centre for biological warfare research was launched.[82]

The Barbarossa campaign unleashed in June 1941 boosted Mrugowsky's bacteriological empire. The Hygiene Institute of the Waffen-SS and Police was established at Auschwitz; preparation began in the autumn of 1942 and it became operational in spring 1943 and it then was expanded on being relocated to Raisko.[83] Its counterpart was the Institute for Virus and Typhus Research at Buchenwald (its origins in January 1942), and Mrugowsky established links between the Behring Institute Lemberg and the Hygiene Institute of the Waffen-SS. Mrugowsky exploited the military situation to establish eastern outposts: a German Hygiene Institute in Kiev initiated research on patient blood samples as well as bacteriological and serological tests,[84] and a German Hygiene Institute for the East in Riga was responsible for epidemic control and serum production in the Baltics. These were supplemented by a sub-station at Kothla-Jaerwe in a mining area of Estonia, and a bacteriological station at Minsk.[85] Mrugowsky supported the Landesanstalt für medizinische Zoologie in den besetzten Ostgebieten, founded in February 1943 by the Reichsministerium Ost to oversee anti-malaria stations in the Southern Ukraine. Zumpt of the Hamburg Tropical Institute took charge; he directed the anti-malarial stations of Grünwaldt at Cherson, of Hundertmark at Dnjepropetrowsk, and of the Nazi veterinary scientist Ernst Liebsch at Melitopol. Mrugowsky suggested that they test Thiodiphenylamin, an insecticide captured from the Soviets.[86]

[82] For Posen see BDC Grossman file.

[83] M. Kieta, 'Das Hygiene-Institut der Waffen-SS und Polizei in Auschwitz', *Die Auschwitz-Hefte* (Weinheim, 1987), 213–17.

[84] BA-MA H 20/ 70 Sammelbericht des beratenden Hygienikers. Bieling's expertise on paratyphoid was of importance.

[85] NAW microfilm 1019/roll 47 Mrugowsky interrogation 11 Oct. 1946; H. Waegner, 'Ärzteeinsatz für die Seuchenbekämpfung in den besetzten Ostgebieten', *Deutsches Ärzteblatt*, 28 (1942), 314–15.

[86] F. Zumpt, 'Thiodiphenylamin und Dinitro-o-kresole in der Stechmückenbekämpfung (vorläufige Mitteilung)', *Zeitschrift für hygienische Zoologie*, 35 (1943), 186–90; F. Zumpt and N. Dinissowa, 'Versuche mit neuen Anopheles-Bekämpfungsmitteln', *Zeitschrift für hygienische Zoologie*, 36 (1944), 82–95.

17. Behring Institute, Lemberg

18. Celebrating the Behring Institute: Richard Haas explaining the work of the Behring Institute to Reichsminister Hans Frank

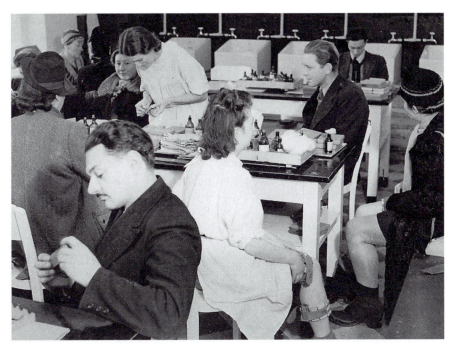

19. Louse-feeders at the Behring Institute, Lemberg

Vaccine research attracted vast resources of manpower and materials. While Mrugowsky worked with the Ostministerium on epidemic prevention, it was Reichsmarschall Hermann Göring who nominally had power over the economy in Russia. Mrugowsky joined forces with the Behringwerke and its IG-Farben managers Zahn and Demnitz, and with Göring's deputy Heinrich Neumann to develop a predatory strategy for serum and bacteriological institutes. Tellingly, the British confused the Behringwerke as a 'Göringwerke.[87] Neumann, retaining strong ties to IG-Farben for whom he worked as a chemist, surveyed captured Soviet vaccine institutes for strategic and economic purposes. Among the booty were serum institutes at (to use the German forms of place names) Dorpat in Estonia, Kauen in Lithuania, Riga (where IG-Farben agreed to license manufacture of its pharmaceutical products), Kiev, and Dolschi near Vitebsk in Belarus. The IG-Farben manager, Demnitz, enthused in June 1942 over the commercial possibilities of Galeschtschina, and the Metschnikov Bacteriological Institute at Kharkov was earmarked for the Behringwerke. Woroschilowsk was captured intact in the Caucasus, where the bacteriologists Bieling and Felix von Bormann drew up plans. Other institutes included Simferopol in the Crimea; veterinary institutes at Armawir, Cherson, and Dnjepropetrowsk; a serobacteriological institute at Dnjepropetrowsk; and two *Biofabrike* at Cherson and Krasnodar. Holding a military

[87] PRO WO 188/683.

commission while remaining in close contact with the Behringwerke, Bieling liaised with IG-Farben, planning to take charge of a Behring Institute at Tiflis, and from April 1943 he was given overall command of the IG institutes in the Ukraine.

These captured installations provided the Germans with over 20 million cc of sera and vaccines, and raised tantalizing economic opportunities. German pharmacaeutical companies planned to divide the spoils: in August 1942 IG-Farben wished to retain serum institutes at Riga and Galeschtschina, and for swine plague serum at Dnjepropetrowsk, but conceded that Dorpat was to go to the Hamburger Serumwerk and Kauen to the Sächsische Serumwerk. Neumann was given powers by Göring to boost vaccine production at Lemberg and to establish vaccine and sera production plants in the Ukraine, Don-Donets, and Caucasus in January 1943. The Behringwerke set up a company called Behringwerke Ukraine GmbH, and undertook to rebuild the Serum Institute in Pomerki near Kharkov. Although the plans were disrupted by the German retreat, the Behringwerke gained massive amounts of equipment and sera worth over 400,000 marks. Mrugowsky was represented on the council of German serum institutes in the Ukraine which drew up a production and research strategy at the serum institutes.[88] Given that many of these serum works were located in the midst of epidemic danger areas, Mrugowsky regarded their rehabilitation as a high priority, while the Behringwerke valued them as a great opportunity to be rapidly exploited. The upshot was the establishing of a company Pharm-Ost to supply the needs of the German administration in the east.[89]

Mrugowsky's position in the Ost-Ministerium served to expand his scientific empire. His clients included the Director of the German Hygiene Institute for the Eastern Territories in Riga, Heinrich Bludau,[90] and Adolf Murthum, the departmental head of the Medical Office of the Reich Commissar for the Eastern Territories. Murthum was seconded to the Hygiene Institute of the Waffen-SS in May 1942 after active service with a Waffen-SS Unit, and acquired some of Mrugowsky's responsibilities when the sanitary office of the Waffen SS was reorga-

[88] BAK R 21/11061 Bl. 25, Behringwerke to Reichsministerium für Wissenschaft 1 Aug. 1942; NLM Bayne Jones Papers, 'Health in Axis Europe', 25; Bayle, *Croix Gammée*, 201; Thom, 'Wandlungen', 443–5, 448; Bayer-Archiv, 6/14 Bericht über die Tätigkeit der Behring-Institute im Jahre 1942, pp. 4–5; Bericht über die Tätigkeit der Behring-Institute im Jahre 1943; Homburger, *Behringwerke*, 139; Behring-Archiv, Lemberg pink folder, Reichsmarshall Persönliche Referent Görnnert 30 May 1942, Reichsmarschall 25 Aug. 1942, Bayer-Ostbüro 3 June 1942 betr. Sonderausweis vom Stabsamt des Reichsmarschalls, Reichsmarschall 16 Jan. 1943, Karl Brandt to Neumann 15 July 1943. Bayer-Archiv, B.B. 25–28 Marburg Protokolle, Aktennotiz Demnitz 19 Jan. 1942 concerning Riga. Besprechung Zahn am 10 July 1942, Besprechung Zahn 29 Dec. 1942, Ost-Aufgaben. Besprechung Zahn 17 Nov. 1942 concerning Worschilowsk, and Besprechung Zahn 29 Dec. 1942 concerning the release of veterinary and medical staff from the army to serve in the eastern institutes. On their evacuation see Bayer-Archiv Leverkusen, 169/17 Besprechung in Marburg am 18. und 19.8.44. IG placed Dnjepropetrowsk under the command of Dr von Mendel, Besprechung Zahn in Marburg am 7 Sept. 1943. For Bieling's role see Besprechung am 11 September 1942, 2/3. Juni 1943; also BAK R 86/ 4164 Bieling to Otto Bl. 261.
[89] BAK R6/605 Bl. 86 Tätigkeitsbericht der Hauptabteilung II (Verwaltung) 23 Dec. 1944. For background see R. J. Overy, *Goering. The 'Iron Man'* (London, 1984), 130–8.
[90] BDC file. b. 22 Aug. 1913, Passenheim, East Prussia. Joined NSDAP 1 May 1937, SA member from 1 July 1933.

nized in 1943.[91] With satellite institutes in two concentration camps and outposts in captured hygiene institutes in the east, Mrugowsky commanded an eastern belt of bacteriological and vaccine-producing stations.

German efforts to coordinate research and production rapidly dissolved into competition and recrimination. Senior military medical staff defended the louse-based Weigl vaccine as of proven efficacy. Its disadvantage was that production was costly and laborious: breeding millions of lice required a small army of immune human feeders, and technicians to inject the anal orifice of each louse (pinned down in a gallows construction) with typhus *rickettsia*, and to dissect every louse to obtain the *rickettsia*-rich gut. The delicate work of injecting 2,000 lice a day strained the eyes and nerves. The harvested guts were centrifuged, and neutralized with phenol. The Military Medical Academy commissioned a film—*Kampf dem Fleckfieber*—in 1941 to publicize the intricate procedures as the way to win the war on typhus—and thus the war in the east.

Demand exceeded supply: not all troops could be immunized, and given an annual booster. Amounts produced were limited, and the different producers argued over standardization in the strength of the vaccine, which would have simplified its use.[92] The RKI was under contract to produce vaccine for the Luftwaffe, and not much was left for German public health authorities in occupied Poland.[93] There were complaints of a *Fleckfieberpsychose* as organizations deploying Russian forced labour agitated for vaccine.[94] In any case the new vaccines were a *Hilfswaffe* with delousing held to be the *Hauptwaffe*, in that they only reduced the severity of infections rather than providing total immunity. That troops on leave could introduce the infection into Germany increased the demand for vaccine.[95] These concerns meant that German pharmaceutical companies, public health authorities, and the SS established rival vaccine-producing plants in the occupied east.

Just at this time efforts were made to obtain the US Cox vaccine for comparison with its German counterpart. Hermann Mooser, while in Mexico had established the distinction between rat-borne 'murine' and louse-borne typhus. Now professor of hygiene at Zürich, he joined the Swiss Red Cross relief teams assisting the German army in Poland and Russia.[96] Mooser caused consternation when he telegraphed from Warsaw to the Rockefeller Foundation in New York a request for

---

[91] NMT roll 30, frame 667–70 testimony of Murthum 12 Apr. 1947; BDC Murthum files.

[92] CIOS report, 'Institut für Fleckfieber', 6–7; Bayer-Archiv B.B. 25–8, Fleckfieber-Impfstoff-Besprechung in Marburg am 4.5.42.

[93] BAK R 86/ 4164 Bl. 82 Kudicke to Gildemeister 20 Oct. 1941; Bl. 84 Gildemeister to Kudicke 29 Oct. 1941.

[94] Ibid., Bl. 234 Gesundheitsamt Neustadt to RKI 5 Sept. 1942.

[95] Gildemeister, 'Bericht', 153 for the weapons metaphor; Leven, 'Fleckfieber', 140–1. For a review of the available vaccines see H. Hetsch, 'Die Schutzimpfung gegen Flecktyphus und die zu ihr verwendeten Impfstoffe', *Medizinische Klinik*, 15 (1942), 341–2.

[96] F. Blättler, *Warschau 1942. Tatsachenbericht eines Motorfahrers der zweiten schweizerischen Aerzte-mission 1942 in Polen* (Zurich, 1945); Rudolf Bucher, *Zwischen Verrat und Menschlichkeit. Erlebnisse eines Schweizer Arztes an der deutsch-russischen Front 1941/1942* (Frauenfeld, Stuttgart, 1967); D. Bourgeois, 'Operation 'Barbarossa' and Switzerland', in B. Wegner (ed.), *From Peace to War* (Providence, 1967), 593–610; R. B. Marti, *Hermann Mooser 1891–1971. Der Entdecker des murinen Fleckfiebers* (Zurich, 1978).

the US Cox vaccine. The Rockefeller Foundation felt that given the Swiss policy of cooperating with the highly suspect German Red Cross, the situation was 'delicate and difficult'. The request was referred to the American Red Cross and US government, and turned down in November 1941 because of fears that the Germans would appropriate the consignment.[97] This was just at the time that the Germans were testing their vaccine in the Warsaw Ghetto. The question arises whether Mooser was attempting to aid the ghetto, or whether he supported the Swiss medical detachments which were active on the eastern front, providing covert support to the Germans. In 1943 the Swiss Serum and Vaccine Institute, Bern generously offered its mouse-lung vaccine to the Germans.[98]

Behringwerke employees exerted pressure that they should be given the opportunity to produce the Cox vaccine on a large scale: Albert Demnitz (director of the Behringwerke) gained Mrugowsky's support for his scheme. He pointed out that the louse vaccine of Eyer and Weigl was solely for military use and quantities remained insufficient. Demnitz and Gerhard Zahn of IG-Farben were keen to exploit the expanding market for typhus vaccines by developing a distinctive Behring product, derived from Cox's method. Kudicke tested the German version of the Cox vaccine on 'especially vulnerable Jews' in the Warsaw ghetto on behalf of the Behringwerke. Mrugowsky (then in Kiev) had agreed to test the various vaccines—he later affirmed he intended field trials rather than human experiments. The Behringwerke requested that its vaccines be included in the trials, while undertaking to open a serum institute in Lemberg.[99]

The massive typhus outbreak in Russia and rising rates of typhus in the ghettos and prisoner of war camps spurred Reich Health Führer Conti to convene a crucial conference on 29 December 1941, involving key officials from the state, military, research institutes, and pharmaceutical production plants. Those present included: Walter Bieber of the RMdI (responsible for epidemic prevention within Germany), a representative of the army medical chief of staff, Eugen Gildemeister (director of the RKI), Gerhard Zahn of IG-Farben, Albert Demnitz (director of the Behringwerke), and Neumann; the Generalgouvernement was represented by Kudicke—in charge of typhus prevention in Warsaw, and Otto Buurmann who supervised epidemic control in Cracow.[100] This meeting represented a high point of coordination in the launching of human experiments, as conflicts soon arose.

Reich Health Führer Conti discussed human experiments with the bacteriologist Reiter, who claimed to have expressed doubts as to their worth. The infuriated Conti declared that he would from then on only deal with Gildemeister of the RKI.[101] It appears that Reiter lost out in a power struggle with the SS bacteriologists.

---

[97] RAC Rockefeller Foundation 1.1/700/14/99 Rockefeller Foundation to ARC 14 Nov. 1941; Folder 102 WAS diary 25 Nov. 1941; Roland, *Courage*, 149.

[98] BAK R 86/ 5143 Bl. 222 Sächsisches Serumwerk to Gildemeister concerning military interest in this 14 Dec. 1943.

[99] STAN KV-Anklage Interrogations D 24 Albert Demnitz 17 Jan. 1947.

[100] NMT roll 30 Dokumente Mrugowsky, pp. 102–7 Besprechung im RMdI 29 Dec. 1941. Also, account by Demnitz frames 330–4; Baader, 'Humanexperiment', 60 on the Leipzig physiologist Martin Gildemeister. Behring-Archiv, Lemberg green file RMdI 5 Jan. 1942.

[101] Maitra, *Hans Reiter*, 198–9.

Although the Reich Health Office became marginalized, it still took a key role in the anthropological investigations and the incarceration of thousands of gypsies, as spreading infections was a supposed attribute of racial inferiority.[102]

Conti intended these conferences to produce a grand strategy for vaccine production, involving the state, the SS, bacteriologists, and manufacturers. But the proliferation of research groups resulted in competition and recrimination. Researchers formed alliances with the Wehrmacht, the Luftwaffe, and groupings in the SS; the competing research and production departments triggered off rivalries in the east and in concentration camp research stations. Research teams (Haagen and Gildemeister of the RKI, Otto and Wohlrab, the Behringwerke at Marburg, and the State Institute for Hygiene at Warsaw) raced to develop a chick embryo-based vaccine adapting Cox's methods. The resulting vaccines had the advantages of not involving human exposure to lice, and were thus far easier to produce.[103] But Eyer distrusted the continuous egg culture of *rickettsiae* (yielding *rickettsiae* in abundance) because he feared a loss of virulence, and he insisted on a laborious egg–louse–egg passage when he came to be involved in producing a variant of the Cox vaccine.[104] Americans evaluating Eyer's work after the war found his procedures most peculiar and doubted the value of the resulting vaccine.[105]

Overall, the Hygiene Institute of the Waffen-SS gained in power. Mrugowsky supported schemes of the Behringwerke, and oversaw the establishing of a testing and production station at the Buchenwald concentration camp. As adviser to the Ministry for the Occupied Eastern Territories, he was able to secure resources for production as well as having a commanding position in the deployment of vaccines. The military links of the Waffen-SS meant that Mrugowsky served the army (reporting also to the chief military medical officer, Handloser) as well as the SS. The components of his sprawling medical research Reich merit closer inspection.

v. The Behring Institute Lemberg and the Louse-feeders

The Behring Institute at Lemberg consumed immense economic, technical, and ideological resources. It was the linchpin of the eastern network of vaccine stations, and was the most fully developed as it remained in German hands for a longer period than the Russian vaccine plants. The idea of vaccine production at Lemberg

[102] Ibid., 248–9; J. S. Hohmann, *Robert Ritter und die Erben der Kriminalbiologie* (Frankfurt/M., 1991), 50–1.

[103] BAK R 86/ 4164 Bl. 82 Kudicke to Gildemeister 20 Oct. 1941; Bl. 84 Gildemeister to Kudicke 29 Oct. 1941; BDC SS-HO 228, 13 January 1942 Reiter to RMdI concerning vaccine production of 2,000 ccm per month at the RKI; BDC SS-HO 2040 E. Gildemeister, Arbeitsanweisung des Robert Koch-Instituts zur Herstellung von Fleckfieberimpfstoff aus Eikulturen der Rickettsia prowazecki. E. Gildemeister and E. Haagen, 'Fleckfieberstudien. II. Mitteilung: Ueber die Züchtung der Rickettsia mooseri und der Rickettsia prowazecki im Dottersack des Hühnereies und über die Herstellung von Kulturimpfstoffen', *Zentralblatt für Bakteriologie*, 1. Abt. Originale, 148 (1942), 257-64.

[104] BDC SS-HO 2049–156 Report by the Robert Koch Institute 18 Jan. 1943.

[105] CIOS, 'Institut für Fleckfieber', 7.

originated with the IG-Farben salesman Neumann, who was called up in 1940 to serve with the chemical group of the army economic staff. Noting that typhus vaccine was in short supply, by early 1941 he was in contact with Weigl in Cracow. Neumann alerted his former boss and managing director of the Behringwerke, Zahn, who established that scientists at the Behringwerke thought highly of the Cox vaccine and that this was also the opinion of Mrugowsky. Neumann secured the political support of Conti and Göring in December 1941, when counter-measures against the typhus epidemic in the east were a priority.[106] By January 1942 Neumann was making arrangements in Lemberg, and he negotiated with the Wehrmacht to secure Weigl's deployment. His aim was to cover civilian needs in the Generalgouvernement, the Reich, and the remainder of occupied Eastern Europe, as well as to establish a 'European centre' for typhus research.[107] In the event most production went to the German army, although the residual amounts supplied to the Bayer concession in Warsaw proved more profitable.[108]

Conti supported the Lemberg scheme at the seminal meeting of 29 December 1941 as a means to remedy the shortage of vaccines. Gauleiter Hans Frank of the Generalgouvernement, who was fanatical in his hatred of 'Jewish vermin', provided resources, not least slave labour. Richard Haas, a medically qualified chemist from the Institute for Experimental Therapy 'Emil von Behring', was appointed director of the Lemberg Institute on 1 January 1942. He had in 1940 proved his organizational skills by establishing a diagnostic institute in Posen. Neumann obtained local resources and backing from the Generalgouvernement medical officer Buurman. IG-Farben's Behringwerke gained commercial backing from another IG-Farben concession, the Bayer-Pharma Warschau, which injected a third of the million-złoty capital; the Generalgouvernement health authorities provided a large modern office block to house the Institute. The Institute was administered by IG-Farben from Leverkusen, and its scientific agenda was dictated by scientists from the Marburg Behringwerke. Weigl (Fleck's former superior) supervised the initial arrangements and staff training in addition to co-directing a military vaccine institute at Lemberg.[109] The new Behring Institute drew on Weigl's expertise and contacts to secure Polish staff, and to organize vaccine production.[110]

Yet absent from all these multifarious links was the army, which refused to sponsor a joint scheme at Lemberg with the Behringwerke, being already com-

[106] STAN KV-Anklage Interrogations Heinrich Neumann N 13 3 Feb. 1948; Behring Archive, Görnnert 30 May 1942.

[107] Heinrich Neumann, Bericht über die Reise vom 4.1 bis 16.1.1942 nach Berlin, Königsberg, Warschau, Krakau und zurück, dated Leverkusen 16 Jan. 1942, copy made available by Behringwerke archives. WAB 169/ 17 Aktennotiz Demnitz 19 Jan. 1942.

[108] Behring-Archiv, *Bericht über die Tätigkeit der Behring-Institute im Jahre 1943*, 72–3.

[109] BDC SS-HO 2036 protocol of RMdI meeting of 23 Dec. 1941, dated 4 Jan. 1942; Behring-Archiv, Zeugnis Dr Richard Haas, 31 May 1949; Lemberg pink file, Besprechung Neumann und Buurman 19 Feb. 1942.

[110] Behring Archiv, Lemberg green file, Haas and Golz to Weigl 10 Sept. 1942; Weigl to Behring Institut Lemberg 18 Sept. 1942.

mitted to building up a military plant under Eyer at Cracow. Mrugowsky was keen to test the Behringwerke version of the Cox vaccine, and Bieling, who was the Behringwerke's link to serum institutes in the east, kept Mrugowsky informed about developments at Lemberg.[111] Mrugowsky was enthusiastic at what appeared to be a way of outflanking his military rivals: he agreed that Haas could be given immunity from military call-up and continue to be stationed at the Lemberg Institute, providing that he joined the Waffen-SS. Haas was a member of the NSDAP and Nazi Physicians League since 1937, but he later insisted that his membership of the Waffen-SS was purely nominal, so that he could undertake vaccine research, and that he never appeared in uniform. Yet Haas was not immune from having to attend courses at the Waffen-SS Medical Academy in Graz, and in April 1943 production at Lemberg was disrupted when Haas was called to fulfil military obligations in the Waffen-SS.[112]

Haas and Neumann rushed to Lemberg to launch the scheme in January 1942, IG-Farben injected finance of one million marks, Göring continued support, and in March 1942 a contract was signed in Warsaw by Zahn. Haas trained with Eyer in Cracow and at the Pasteur Institute—his mission was first to produce the Weigl vaccine as rapidly as possible, and then to develop the more experimental egg yolk vaccine of Otto and Wohlrab, and the rabbit- and mouse-lung vaccines.[113] Vaccine was produced in small batches from August 1942.[114] The scheme encountered the problems of shortage of materials, bureaucratic complexities, and scientific rigidities which meant that production was never as high as required, and that the research activity did not lead to momentous discoveries.

While most Allied war research was shrouded in secrecy, German newspapers broadcast news of vaccine production with a fanfare of publicity. The official opening by Generalgouverneur Frank of what was variously known as the *Behring-Institut GmbH Lemberg* or *Fleckfieberforschungs-Institut Lemberg* on 10 December 1942 was an opportunity to inject a dose of Germanic ideology into vaccine production. The NSDAP and SS medical administrators joined with vaccine researchers to admire this new 'German Defensive Wall against Epidemics', which as Kurt Blome (the Deputy Physicians' Führer) proclaimed, would defend Western civilization against Eastern barbarism. Kudicke and Wohlrab were decorated for their achievements in vaccine production in Warsaw, and Lemberg was characterized as a miniature Vienna where German medical science was to be revitalized

---

[111] BDC SS-HO 1945–2048 Reich Ministry of the Interior notice of January 1942. Also in BAK 86/ 4164 Bl. 161. On Bieling see NAW M 1019/36 interrogation of Kogon; Hessisches Staatsarchiv Wiesbaden Abt. 507 Nr 656, Fragebogen der amerikanischen Militärbehörde; Homburger, *Behringwerke*, 92.

[112] Bayer-Archiv, 169/17 Besprechung Zahn in Marburg am 29. Dezember 1942, p. 2; am 16. u. 17. April 1943, p. 8.

[113] STAN KV-Anklage Interrogations H 2, Haas 30 Jan. 1948; NAW microfilm F 0025 SS-Enlisted Men, Richard Haas; Waffen-SS card, Marburg 14 Aug. 1942; Behring-Archiv, Spruchkammerangelegenheiten 1945–8, Haas documents; E. Oldenburg. Privat, Haas to Oldenburg 28 Jan. 1945, Graz. Bayer-Archiv, B.B. 25–8 Marburg Protokolle, Aktennotiz Zahn 29 Dec. 1942, Berufung Dr Haas durch die Waffen-SS. On Göring's support see Homburger, *Behringwerke*, 117.

[114] Homburger, *Behringwerke*, 117.

(ignoring the distinguished role of Lemberg as a medical centre until 1941).[115] Zeiss stressed the significance of the Institute in the context of 'Geo-medicine in the East'. Although he acclaimed the Behring Institute as 'a great achievement in the annals of German research', he overlooked that the Institute was intended to apply vaccine production techniques developed in the United States, France, and Poland.[116] The Lemberg Institute conducted joint research with Zeiss in Berlin, on cat distemper as a rickettsial infection, and on typhus vaccines.[117]

The collossal Behring Institute overshadowed the Pasteur Institute in Lemberg— which survived to produce rabies vaccine during the war when taken over by Eyer and Weigl. The Behringwerke pointed out that a military institute was ser- vicing the civilian sector, so encroaching on its territory.[118] The Behring Institute Lemberg was a massive and well-equipped production and research installation with a large scientific and technical staff, including the virologist Adam Deinart, the veterinary scientist Hans Sedlmeier from Munich and the biologists Rudolf Gönnert and Ilse Schuster. The administration was handled by Bruno Golz, a chemical engineer born in Łódź. Neumann and Zahn, key supporters of the venture, were born in the 'lost' city of Bromberg, and its surrounds. Most of the German employees were females in ancillary posts. Six of the twenty-four female technical assistants who volunteered to go to Lemberg came from the 'lost' eastern territories: they were born in Posen and Oppeln in 1918, in Danzig in 1919, in Riskusritz (Upper Silesia) in 1917, in Beuthen in 1913, and in Tilsit in 1912. The work was dangerous in that staff were at risk from typhus, and the Germans preferred administrative and security work at the institutes, leaving the dangerous handling of lice to Poles. Among the Polish and Ukrainian technical staff employed was Ivan Hach, a former professor of bacteriology from Kiev with an extensive record of publications on typhus: he had been translating Russian scientific papers in Marburg, and it was hoped that he could avoid discrimination as an *Ostarbeiter* by moving to Lemberg. By 1944 the Behring Institute employed fifty Germans and 1,050 Poles and Ukrainians, even acquiring a chicken farm and an estate where animals were kept.[119] Haas had considerable resources in the enclave under his command.

[115] Behring-Archiv, Lemberg red file, 'Deutsche Kulturtat im Osten. Fleckfieber-Forschungsinstitut in Lemberg eröffnet', *Völkischer Beobachter München* (11 Dec. 1942) typifies the reports in numerous national and local papers. Ironically, the celebratory brochure to mark the opening was only ready when the Institute was evacuated, Bayer-Archiv Leverkusen, 169/17 Besprechung in Marburg am 18. und 19.8.44. See also 6/14 Behring-Werke, *Eröffnung der Fleckfieberforschungsstätte Lemberg am 10. und 11. Dezember 1942*. BAK R 86/ 5143 Bl. 165–6 'Fleckfieber-Schutzimpfung. Eine Grosstat deutscher Forschung'.

[116] BAK 86/ 4164 Bl. 161; R 86/ 5143 Bl. 165–6 'Fleckfieber-Schutzimpfung. Eine Grosstat deutscher Forschung'. AHUB Hygieneisches Institut Nr 189, Walbaum to Zeiss 25 Nov. 1942; Invitation to Zeiss from Walbaum 9 Nov. 1942. For Rose's speech see *Reichsgesundheitsblatt*, 5 (5 Feb. 1943).

[117] AHUB Hygieneisches Institut Nr 190 Zeiss to DFG 22 Feb. 1943 Bl. 148, Zeiss to Haas 16 Dec. 1942.

[118] CIOS 'Institut für Fleckfieber', 5, 8–9; Behring Archive, Lemberg pink file, Besprechung 27/28 Aug. 1942.

[119] A. Terstappen, '1,000 Polen für Versuche mit Läusen missbraucht. Behringwerke und Zwangsar- beiter—ein düsteres Kapitel', *Frankfurter Rundschau*, 115 (19 May 1993); Behring-Archiv, *Bericht über die*

Haas intended to test vaccines on soldiers who had spontaneously contracted typhus—confirming Mrugowsky's plea that field research was an alternative to human experiments. That Haas came under Mrugowsky's patronage opened up the link between the Lemberg Institute and Buchenwald. The Behring Works sent Mrugowsky batches of trial vaccines for scarlet fever, dysentery, typhoid, and TB, and dispatched yellow fever vaccine directly to Buchenwald. Mrugowsky cultivated contacts with the IG-Farben vaccine production executives, Bieling, Alexander von Engelhardt, Demnitz, and Zahn. The Behring Institute cooperated with Mrugowsky's satellite institutes in the east, notably the Institute for Medical Zoology in Riga. The most compromised associate was the Buchenwald typhus specialist Ding, who was among the SS officers attending the pompous opening ceremony and who remained in contact with Haas. Ding offered to undertake trial vaccinations of his 'personnel', and explained that he was establishing a Buchenwald institute for vaccine production. Haas's Institute in Lemberg sent a batch of Weigl vaccine to Ding for testing in Buchenwald in October 1942. Gönnert, who directed the department of infectious diseases at the Behring Institute, took infected lice to Buchenwald on behalf of Haas, but fearing that these could escape, the lice were destroyed. Haas was thus fully informed that Buchenwald was a concentration camp. A trial with vaccines from Lemberg took place in Buchenwald from December 1942 until March 1943.[120]

Confusion arose from the mixing of varying doses of vaccines that happened to be allocated. In June 1942 Ernst Hirschfeld, a Jewish doctor attached to a forced labour camp, was so perplexed that he addressed his problems concerning the different vaccines to the RKI.[121] Diverse dosages caused tensions between the Cracow and Lemberg Institutes, giving rise to complaints about lack of standardization, exacerbated by the absence of state-administered quality controls that were the norm for vaccines. Once standardization procedures were introduced, then many batches of vaccine were found to be ineffective. But a chronic shortage of guinea-pigs hampered testing.[122] Typhus rickettsiae were in any case difficult to culture in

Tätigkeit der Behring-Institute im Jahre 1942, 58–9; *Bericht über die Tätigkeit der Behring-Institute im Jahre 1943*, 71; Lemberg Personal, Demnitz and Oldenburg to Landratsamt Marburg Betr.: Prof. Hach und Frau aus Woroschilowsk 28 Apr. 1943, Demnitz and Oldenburg to Behring-Institut Lemberg 5 Apr. 1943, Else Gallinat from Tilsit contracted typhus in July 1942, Vorläufige Ausweise für Techn. Ass. Lemberg. Hach returned to Marburg in 1944, and then served as a military doctor, see Bayer-Archiv, Nr 169/17, Besprechung Marburg 14 Nov. 1944; H. G. Schwick, 'Prof. Dr. Haas, sein Wirken in den Behringwerken', in F. Deinhardt, G. Maas, and H. Spiess (eds.), *Neues in der Virusdiagnostik* (Marburg, 1991), 175–86.

[120] NMT roll 38, frame 626, 932. NAW M 1019/ roll 47, Mrugowsky interrogation, p. 22, 11 Oct. 1946; NMT roll 16, frame 889 Ding's Buchenwald 'diary' gives the date of the opening ceremony as 15–18 Dec. 1942, instead of 10 Dec. 1942; Schneider, Stein, *IG-Farben*, 45–6; STAN KV-Anlage Interrogations H 2, Haas on 30 Jan. 1948, and 31 Jan. 1948. G 47 Rudolf Gönnert 3 Feb. 1948; E 34 Alexander von Engelhardt 29 Jan. 1948; B 81 Bieling 17 Jan., 3 Apr. 1947 concerning meeting Mrugowsky and Ding. D 24 Demnitz 17 Jan. 1947; A. Schlote, 'Die Einwirkung von Schwefeldioxid auf Fleckfiebererreger', *Zeitschrift für hygienische Zoologie*, 36 (1944), 74–6.

[121] BAK R 86/ 4164 Bl. 193, Ernst Hirschfeld, Reichsautobahnlager Lagower See to RKI 11 June 1942.

[122] Ibid., Bl. 238, Behringwerke to RMdI 25 July 1942; Bieling to Otto, Staatliches Institut für experimentelle Therapie 11 Jan. 1942; R 86/ 5143 Bl. 149–51, Otto to RMdI 8 May 1943; Bl. 264, Otto to RMdI 5 Sept. 1944.

most animal tissues. The shortage of laboratory animals contrasted to the ready supply of Poles and Jews. Vaccine-production took virologists to the brink of the Holocaust.

The deadly tentacles of typhus vaccine research touched numerous categories of victims: the coerced medical researchers, louse-feeders, experimental subjects, and those who having contracted typhus in ghettos or concentration camps were used to test vaccines or drugs. Typhus research and vaccine production was hazardous for the non-immune: Gildemeister of the RKI, Ding, and the researchers at the State Institute for Serum Therapy in Copenhagen contracted typhus.[123] Weigl experienced two bouts of typhus, and Eyer's staff regarded catching typhus as inevitable, believing that they inhaled rickettsiae-laden louse faeces.[124] The question arises to what extent vaccine production exploited Russian prisoners and Jews, or whether it provided a protective niche.

Production of the Weigl vaccine required a small army of louse-feeders. In Lemberg a feeder had to nourish about 5,000 lice twice a day for about thirty minutes. Whereas Allied researchers carried lice canisters with some thousand lice strapped to their limbs, or asked for conscientious objectors to volunteer, the Germans generally regarded louse-feeding as a task for racial inferiors. German soldiers and technicians fed lice for extra rations when the Lemberg Institute was evacuated to Cracow (where production facilities for the louse vaccine were obtained at the Buiwid Institute), Marburg, and Dillenburg in February 1944, and when Eyer's Cracow Institute arrived in Roth in Bavaria in August 1944. At the 'louse station' in Marburg about fifty Polish and Russian foreign workers served as feeders until their liberation by the US army.[125] Hase sustained louse colonies on Russian prisoners of war. That medical researchers tried to avoid infection, increased the exploitation of prisoners and racial inferiors. An estimated thousand prisoners were supplied by the Generalgouvernement as louse-feeders in Lemberg, although the evidence suggests that Poles were also keen to act in this capacity. The RKI pointed out that since they were typhus-immune, Red Army soldiers were suited for the care and feeding of lice.[126]

There is little documentation and only a few testimonies about how the louse-feeders were recruited and treated. Eyer's technicians (who lied about his NSDAP membership) gave the Americans a positive picture of louse-feeding in Cracow: 'Civilians were given one mark daily and some extra rations for louse feeding. According to the German women technicians there were always plenty of towns-people willing to carry lice (in boxes) for this recompense.'[127] If correct, there would be a contrast between voluntary arrangements in Eyer's military institutes and a

---

[123] BAK R 86/ 5143 Bl. 81, Statens Seruminstitut to Gildemeister 8 Feb. 1943.

[124] CIOS, 'Institut für Fleckfieber', 6–7.

[125] Homburger, *Behringwerke*, 126–7; Bayer-Archiv, Nr 169/17, Aktennotiz über Besprechung in Marburg am 18–19 Aug. 1944.

[126] BAK R 86/ 4164 Bl. 111 letter of RKI to Rose and RGA 27 Nov. 1941; J. R. Busvine, 'On Rearing Human Lice', *Antenna*, 3 (July 1979), 89–91. For the testimony of a German feeder, see Schwick, 'Haas', 181.

[127] CIOS, 'Institut für Fleckfieber', 6.

coercive regime in the Behring Institute, Lemberg. Eyer claimed to have employed 2,000 feeders, of which fifty were Germans and the rest Poles.[128] Haas initially hoped to recruit between 300 and 500 louse-feeders as employees. Either a shortage of applicants, or the temptation to employ feeders at minimal cost prompted Haas to ask Mrugowsky to arrange the drafting in of labour. Hans Frank, the head of the Generalgouvernement, authorized the exploitation of captive louse-feeders. Many hundreds of louse-feeders worked as forced labourers for the Behring Institute, Lemberg.

After the war it was claimed that reliance on Polish expertise facilitated survival and resistance. Weigl adopted a more benign and protective policy, and recruited many Poles from the academic élite, including dismissed professors, the relatives of murdered academics, and students. Among the beneficiaries was the mathematician Stefan Banach, whom Weigl employed as a feeder. Polish scientists and students also served in this capacity, and testimonies confirm that feeding brought material benefits of a labour permit, an identity card (helpful during round-ups of hostages and deportations to labour camps) and extra food rations. On occasions Weigl persuaded German supervisors to intervene when arrests were made.[129] Weigl claimed that he was able to employ Jews threatened with arrest as louse-feeders, although their Jewish identity was concealed. Eyer maintained after the war that the feeders were volunteers and rewarded by extra rations.[130] Germans claimed that they took Jews, but they fed them well, and that . . . they also tried to keep them out of the concentration camp for as long as possible.[131] Post-war self-justification may mean that the scientists and their underlings magnified their magnanimity.

German assistants of Haas testified that he treated his Polish and Ukrainian staff well, providing them with extra rations, that he allowed three Jewish staff—an opera tenor Artur Big, his friend Friedmann, and a number of others—to spend some nights in his institute to avoid arrest, and that Haas attempted to retrieve staff from the Lemberg ghetto (established in June 1942 and ferociously destroyed in June 1943). Haas sheltered some relatives of Polish diplomats and of Stroński (a member of the Polish government in exile), and claimed to have saved the life of a 'half Jewish' chicken farm worker who accompanied his family when evacuated to Germany, as well as of a Jewish female physician on his staff and of her husband by transporting them in one of his official cars.[132] These small-scale acts of mercy leave

---

[128] CIOS, *Tropical Medicines and Other Medical Subjects in Germany* (London, n.d.), 14.

[129] R. Haftmann, 'Zum 100. Geburtstag von Stefan Banach', *Wissenschaftliche Zeitschrift der TU Chemnitz*, 34 (1992), 1–18. Jan Kostrzewski, currently director of the Warsaw Institute of Hygiene, served in this capacity from May 1941; Homburger, *Behringwerke*, 118; Schneider and Stein, *IG-Farben*, 45; Kordas and Weindling, 'Working Conditions'; interviews by Maria Kordas of Boleslaw Bros (student of engineering), Tomasz Cieszynski (lab asssistant and medical student), Jan Reutt (lab assistant and medical student), and Irena Stuchly, Zbigniew Stuchly (supervisor of vaccine production and assistant of Weigl).

[130] Eyer, 'Fleckfieberprophylaxe', 56.

[131] Klaus Munck, producer of parts of *Kampf den Fleckfieber* has given this impression.

[132] Behring-Archiv, Spruchkammerangelegenheiten: Richard Haas, Heinz Lange to H. Schmidt 11 Jan.

the question open as regards the fate and treatment of the many hundreds of louse-feeders, not least because the work could make one sick from anemia or typhus.[133] Given that the harassed Jews of Lemberg regarded work in a German factory as a sanctuary from persecution, louse-feeding might have been regarded as relatively benign.[134] Other cases of using Jews for vaccine production can be documented: three Jews were blood donors for feeding lice at the Riga Institute for Medical Zoology from November 1942.[135] Recent interviews with former Polish louse-feeders suggest that the work was attractive as providing security, money, and food, and that Poles rather than Jews predominated in the Eyer's military institute.[136] The ethnic composition, and final fate of the louse-feeders from the Behring Institute remains uncertain, especially what happened to them during the continuous selections and when the vaccine plants were evacuated.

vi. Human Experiments

Many German researchers considered that the concentration camps were a vast human reservoir of 'experimental material'. The Nazi human experiments—at least as formal programmes—began only after the start of the war, indicating military priorities, and were often carried out either in euthanasia centres or concentration camps. The SS exerted tight control over what went on in the camps with most experiments approved by Himmler. The difficulty in testing typhus vaccines was that researchers like Mrugowsky insisted that the physical condition of victims was to be like that of the German soldier, even though prisoners were starved, exhausted, freezing, suffering from incessant dysentery, and were incapacitated by abrasions, cuts, and sores. He may have calculated that among the more recently detained political prisoners there were a few whose physical condition had not yet been ground down by starvation and forced labour.[137]

The obsession of the SS with biological experimentation and the need to test the efficacy of the different vaccines provided researchers with lethal opportunities. A crucial issue is whether the experiments were initiated from 'the top down' by leading Nazis such as Himmler and his entourage, or whether the experiments arose from scientists unscrupulously exploiting the genocidal conditions. The origins of the Buchenwald experiments were disputed at the Nuremberg Medical Trial, as interrogators tried to make sense of the bewildering hierarchy of 'Ober-',

1946; testimonies of Maria Ross, Ulrike Brückner, Genia Szczygiel, Albert Demnitz, Peter Naumann, C. Thomé.

[133] Behring-Archiv, Lemberg Personal, testimony of Janina Zyck, Zabrze, 18 June 1992.

[134] T. Held, 'Vom Pogrom zum Massenmord', *Lemberg-Lwów-Lviv*, 134.

[135] D. Rousset, *Le Pitre ne rit pas* (Paris, 1948), 223 and plate 8; Bayle, *Croix gammée*, 1156.

[136] Communication from Maria Kordas, Wrocław 11 June 1997; M. Kordas and P. J. Weindling, 'Warunki pracy i wynagrodzenia personalu zatrudnionego przy produkcji szczepioniki przeciw tyfusowi plamistemu metoda Weigla we Lwówie podczas II wojny swiatowej', paper presented in Gdańsk 27 Sept. 1997.

[137] NAW RG 153 War Crimes Case Number 12–390, The Buchenwald Case, microfilm 5, Kogon evidence, pp. 246, 269; microfilm 6, Richet evidence, p. 1802; Lifton, *Nazi Doctors*, 308–9.

'Über-', and 'Unter-' SS medical officers, who later used the cut-throat competition between them to disclaim responsibility.[138]

Mrugowsky testified that he had suggested a comparative epidemiological survey of vaccinated officials of the Ministry for the Occupied Eastern Territories, but that his superior Grawitz advocated human experiments. Mrugowsky claimed that he dissented, and the matter was taken to Himmler, who insisted on human experiments. Adding to these mitigating circumstances, Mrugowsky pleaded that his superiors undermined his authority by commissioning Ding to undertake the murderous experiments.[139] However, the Buchenwald station was part of Mrugowsky's Institute: Ding reported to Mrugowsky, and Mrugowsky to Eduard Genzken, who was the head of the SS sanitary office from 1940 and a former naval medical officer whose interests lay more in soldiers' health than in research.[140]

That Genzken was loath to initiate the human experiments meant that he could be outdone by his rival Mrugowsky or by Ding as his less competent but unscrupulous underling. Genzken supervised the sanitary facilities in the concentration camps, and had launched Ding's career as camp physician at Buchenwald until 1939; Ding then became his adjutant until 1940. Ding retained contacts throughout the SS medical élite rather than slavishly working under Mrugowsky as his immediate superior.

SS Sturmbannführer Erwin Ding was typical of the young physician imbued with Nazi ideals—as a student he had joined the NSDAP and SA in 1932, the SS in 1936, and after qualifying in medicine in 1937 was by 1938 camp physician at Buchenwald. Ding underwent bacteriological training at the hygiene institutes of Zeiss and Mrugowsky, and in 1941 he joined the Hygiene Institute of the Waffen-SS. On his return to Buchenwald he headed what was designated as a department of Mrugowsky's Institute. Although Mrugowsky sporadically descended on Buchenwald, he was also away for long periods in the east, and later argued that Ding took orders from others in the SS in mounting numerous experiments.[141] As more a creature of the SS than an accomplished research scientist, Ding had to cover for his lack of scientific competence by relying on prisoner researchers. He sought experimental commissions from a wide range of persons and organizations, and exploited the power struggles between senior SS medical officers.[142]

---

[138] STAN KV-Anklage Interrogations G 28, Genzken.

[139] NMT roll 38, frame 951; affidavit of Mrugowsky, frame 1,000.

[140] AHUB Hygienisches Institut Nr 192 Bl. 247, Report of the Hygiene Institute of the Waffen SS. It should be noted that at the NMT, Mrugowsky argued that Ding's experimental work was directly ordered by Genzken and Grawitz. However, Ding certainly sent written reports to Mrugowsky. See affidavit of Mrugowsky, roll 16, frame 848. STAN KV-Anklage Interrogations G 28, Genzken who joined the NSDAP in 1926 and the Waffen SS in 1936. *Konzentrationslager Buchenwald Post Weimar/Thür* (Buchenwald, 1990), 118–21; Bayer-Archiv, B.B. 25–8 Marburg Protokolle, Aktennotiz Demnitz 19 Jan. 1942 concerning Lemberg: the note indicates that Mrugowsky was responsible for comparing the efficacy of different vaccines.

[141] NMT microfilm 30, frame 726 evidence of Krantz.

[142] NAW RG 153 War Crimes Case Number 12–390, The Buchenwald Case, microfilm (copy in Gedenkstätte Buchenwald archives Sign. 503–8), Ding-Schuler interrogation June 1945, p. 8; Film 5, Kogon Affidavit, frames 105–7.

In determining who had prime responsibility for human experiments much hinged on Ding's diary of the experiments, which was contested by Mrugowsky at the Nuremberg Trial. While giving the impression that Mrugowsky closely supervised Ding's work, factual errors in the diary suggested that it might have been written by Ding in cooperation with his prisoner-secretary Eugen Kogon during the days before liberation. Kogon was anxious to make good the loss of incriminating documents which the SS had destroyed, and Ding was keen to shift the burden of responsibility on to his superiors. Kogon, secretary to Ding since April 1943, exercised considerable powers of persuasion over Ding whose world was collapsing. Kogon was accustomed to producing documents which appeared to have been written by Ding, and in any case the diary was typed.[143] A change of names by Ding may have indicated a wish to conceal his record of human experiments. By 1944 Ding assumed the name Schuler (he was the natural son of a physician, von Schuler, but on adoption was given the name Ding).[144]

Ding's good terms with Genzken, Mrugowsky's superior until 1943, may explain why he was drafted into Mrugowsky's Hygiene Institute of the Waffen-SS. Ding then studied production of the Giroud vaccine at the Robert Koch and Pasteur Institutes. An array of typhus experts visited the Buchenwald research station—including Gildemeister and Rose of the RKI, the SS doctors Genzken and Mrugowsky, and the military researchers Bieling, and Eyer, and Karl Brandt, whose expanding powers included supervision of medical research. Ding maintained contacts with the Academy of Military Medicine in Berlin, the Military Hygiene Institute at Cracow under Eyer and Weigl, the Behring Institute, Lemberg, the Behringwerke, and other branches of IG-Farben—indicating that far from detached and isolated the Buchenwald research station was of key strategic importance.[145]

Ding's experimental facilities were promoted from a research station (*Fleckfieberversuchsstation*), to a department ('Abteilung für Fleckfieber und Virusforschung') from January 1943. On 12 August 1943 he attained a fully fledged Hygiene Institute. Its address—'Hygiene-Institut der Waffen-SS, Weimar-Buchenwald'—concealed that it was located in the heart of the concentration camp. Ding often gave the impression that he was stationed in Berlin.[146] The first experiments took place on 5 January 1942 when five prisoners were injected with typhus *rickettsiae* deriving from the RKI; this was to establish the best means of

---

[143] Diary of Ding-Schuler cited in Bayle, *Croix gammée*, 1134. The veracity of the diary was contested at the Nuremberg Doctors Trial and thereafter. It may have been typed by Kogon and counter-signed by Ding. See also Bayle, loc. cit., 1171–3; Buchenwald Trial, Ciepolowski testimony, microfilm 5, frame 1,227; Kogon Affidavit, 5, frame 109.

[144] BDC files, Erwin Ding; Bayle, *Croix gammée*, 1146, 1171.

[145] Bayle, *Croix gammée*, 1133–46, 1171, 1198–1210; NAW RG 153 War Crimes Case Number 12–390, microfilm 5, The Buchenwald Case, Kogon Affidavit, p. 11, frame 116.

[146] STAN KV-Anklage Interrogations S 131 Hans Schmidt, p. 3; AIP Fonds Balachowsky, Carnet de Buchenwald, entry of 12 Aug. 1944: '1 an de la néation de Hygiene Institut de Buchenwald—réunion intime'.

experimental infection. The Buchenwald station sustained several types of typhus cultures in humans (rather than in lice feeding off humans as at Cracow); three to five 'passage persons' were infected each month. Kogon estimated that at least 120 'passage persons' were killed, but Balachowsky reckoned 600 prisoners died at Buchenwald who were used for establishing reservoirs of different types of typhus germs. Instead of breeding generations of infected lice, infected blood was taken from prisoners at the high point of infection, and then injected in order to infect (generally fatally) another prisoner: these 'passage persons' were treated as if they were lice.[147]

Ding kept away from the typhus block to minimize the risks of becoming infected. He delegated the organization of the procedures to a clique of communists privileged by the SS and to a brutal convict, Arthur Dietzsch, who used his powers as 'Kapo' over life and death to considerable personal advantage. The victims were meant to be well nourished so as to correspond to the German soldier, but tensions between prisoners meant that the physically and morally exhausted were liable to be pressed into becoming experimental victims. From August 1942 the experiments were carried out in the specially equipped Block 46, which was isolated from the rest of the camp to maintain secrecy and to prevent the spread of infections. Twenty-four series of experiments were conducted until the end of 1944. For most of the ca. 450 to 600 prisoners their use as human guinea-pigs meant death.

The Buchenwald experiments were intended to prove which of the different vaccines was best. In 1942 the Reich Ministry of the Interior informed the Behringwerke that its serum was under-strength, and in 1943 many batches were found to be ineffective; a dispute erupted between the SS and the RKI over whether the Pasteur Institute rabbit-lung vaccine was weaker than the RKI vaccine.[148] Comparative tests of vaccines continued during 1944.[149] Not only did many die in the course of such experiments, but survivors were left horribly maimed or were executed by injections of prussic acid or phenol.[150] Here was a medical island in the midst of barbarism, but one in which humane values were reversed with deliberate infection, disabling, and killing.

The human experiments carried out by Ding in 1942 involved infecting four groups of prisoners of war originating from areas where typhus was not endemic. Some were vaccinated and others were left unvaccinated as a control group. The vaccines tested were the Cox vaccine as modified by Richard Otto and Wohlrab of the Frankfurt Institute for Experimental Therapy, and then put in production by

[147] Balachowsky calculated 600 prisoners were sacrificed to maintain twelve strains of infection over four years, NMT roll 16, frame 916; NAW RG 153 War Crimes Case Number 12–390, The Buchenwald Case, microfilm 5, Kogon cross examination, p. 276.

[148] BAK R 86/ 4164 Bl. 161 RMdI memo by Bieber on a meeting of 29 Dec. 1941; R 86/ 5143 Bl. 105 RKI to RMdI 13 Mar. 1943; BDC SS-HO 2032 Bieber (RMdI) to Behringwerke 17 Apr. 1942; SS-HO 2035 Gildemeister to RMdI 7 Apr. 1942; SS-HO 2041 Haubold to Gildemeister 27 Feb. 1943.

[149] NMT roll 16, frame 916.

[150] Bayle, *Croix gammée*, 1159–61; Schneider and Stein, *IG-Farben*, 28–30 for prisoners' testimonies.

Gildemeister and Haagen of the RKI; two further types of Cox vaccine produced by the Behringwerke from April 1941; and the Weigl vaccine derived from louse guts.[151] Mrugowsky drafted a bland report on human experiments, stating that each group of prisoners was vaccinated with one of the four available vaccines during an epidemic when the mortality of non-vaccinated persons was 30 per cent. Only two deaths occurred among those vaccinated (no figure was given of how many were in each group).[152]

Mrugowsky used the fiction of an 'epidemic' to conceal the deliberate infecting of the experimental victims, and the deaths of the non-vaccinated. While the Behring vaccine was pronounced to be the most satisfactory, the others were also deemed to be good. Ding's published paper describing the treatment of the experimental groups made it easy to infer that human experiments were involved.[153] In January 1943 a German report compared the Pasteur Institute's rabbit-based antityphus vaccine, the louse vaccine of Weigl, and the chick embryo vaccine of the RKI. All were found to have equivalent value, although a dispute erupted with Haubold (the international health official), who claimed that the French lung-based rabbit vaccine was superior. While Mrugowsky agreed that Weigl's vaccine was reliable, he set out to manufacture a vaccine according to the Pasteur Institute's methods. For this he relied on Ding's much overvalued skills.[154]

Ding's publications on vaccine tests prompted muted debate among German medical researchers, and were a target of international criticism. In December 1943 an editorial in the *Lancet* condemned Ding's paper: it noted that the Allied yolk-sac vaccine was at least as good as its rivals but deduced that human experiments on large groups of persons had been carried out by Ding, and that the age of the victims suggested that they were prisoners of war.[155] Both inferences were correct, as the prisoners were Soviet soldiers.[156]

New sera proliferated. Chick embryo typhus vaccine came to Buchenwald from Italy, and the Copenhagen Serum Institute sent mouse-liver vaccine. Mrugowsky encouraged Rose to obtain a new vaccine developed by Cantacuzène based on

---

[151] E. Ding, 'Über die Schutzwirkung verschiedener Fleckfieberimpfstoffe beim Menschen und den Fleckfieberverlauf nach Schutzimpfung', *Zeitschrift für Hygiene*, 124 (1943), 670–82; Report by Mrugowsky to Conti, Genzken, Grawitz, Eyer, Gildemeister, and the Behring-Werke, dated 5 May 1942, in NMT microfilm 30; Behring-Archiv, Demnitz, and Schmidt, 'Stellungnahme zu den Ausführungen im Buch von EGON (sic) KOGON: "Der SS-Staat" ', 15 Jan. 1947.

[152] BAK R 86/ 4160 Mrugowsky to Conti, Grawitz, Genzken, Gildemeister, Eyer, and Demnitz 5 May 1942 Bl. 177–9.

[153] E. Ding, 'Über die Schutzwirkung verschiedener Fleckfieberimpfstoffe beim Menschen und den Fleckfieberverlauf nach Schutzimpfung', *Zeitschrift für Hygiene*, 124 (1943), 670–82; BAK R 86/ 4160 Mrugowsky to Conti, Grawitz, Genzken, Eyer, and Demnitz 5 May 1942 Bl. 177–9; Behring-Archiv, report by Demnitz and Schmidt.

[154] BAK R 86/ 4153 report by Haubold 11 Dec. 1942 (see also BDC SS-HO 982 Haubold Aktennotiz); BDC SS-HO 2060, Bieber (RMdI) to Haubold 3 Feb. 1943; J. Mrugowsky, 'Typischer und atypischer Krankheitsverlauf beim Fleckfieber', *Medizinische Klinik*, 38/9 (1942), 193–7.

[155] *Lancet*, ii (18 Dec. 1943), 770, concerning Ding in *Zeitschrift für Hygiene*, 124 (1943), 670. Noted in NAW RG 112/ 295A/ Box 10 Current Intelligence.

[156] Balachowsky testified that survivors of Buchenwald typhus experiments were then killed: NMT roll 16, frame 913.

dog lungs from Bucharest in 1942, and then had it tested at Buchenwald.[157]
Under German occupation, the Laboratory for Immunology of the Institute
for Experimental Medicine at Kiev undertook typhus research in conjunction
with ASID (Anhaltische Serum-Institut Dessau).[158] Mrugowsky hoped that
serum could be produced in Riga, in Dorpat under Petersen, an Estonian, and
in Kiev.[159] Although the Behringwerke supported serum work at Riga in Latvia,
the SS became alarmed at the claims made by the Serum Institute of the University
of Riga under a Latvian professor, Darsin. Mrugowsky dispatched Ding
from Buchenwald who condemned Darsin's rudimentary research facilities and
findings. Ding compared Darsin's cultures with those of his own research station.
Ironically, Fleck (transferred to Buchenwald from Auschwitz) demonstrated that
Ding's cultures did not consist of typhus *rickettsiae*. The medical officer of
the Reich Commissar for the Eastern Territories, Bernsdorff, proposed to take over
the Riga institute and to delegate the SS serologist Erik Wheeler-Hill to produce
a vaccine.[160]

Researchers were keen to exploit outbreaks of typhus in concentration camps,
particularly when sited close to their institutes. The camps of Buchenwald,
Natzweiler, Neuengamme, and Sachsenhausen all served local scientific interests.
In December 1941 typhus erupted in the Neuengamme concentration camp near
Hamburg. The combination of starvation and typhus among the Soviet prisoners
of war transformed Neuengamme into a convenient laboratory for the Russian
front. Researchers from the Hamburg Tropical Institute preferred using the
facilities of their nearest concentration camp. In January 1942 Mühlens requested
cooperation of the Tropical Institute with Mrugowsky and Genzken of the SS
Sanitätsamt to tackle the outbreak of typhus. Mühlens considered that in concentration camps clinical practices could be developed from laboratory experiments
on animals. He mobilized the facilities of the Hamburg Tropical Institute for
typhus prevention and research. Mühlens also cooperated with DEGESCH and
the Hamburg firm of poison gas agents Tesch und Stabenow.[161] Sievers of the
Ahnenerbe organization of the SS supported a programme of medical entomology.

[157] NMT roll 38, frame 1,596.

[158] BAK R 86/5143 Bl. 199 Schütz of Hauptamt für Volksgesundheit, NSDAP to Gildemeister 10 Sept.
1943; NMT roll 30, Mrugowsky defence, evidence of Karl Ludwig Wolters, pp. 92–5. Asid had a typhus
serum production station at Forst in the Lausitz under Dr Uthe Rokohl.

[159] NAW M 1019/roll 47, Mrugowsky interrogation, summary.

[160] BAK R 90/ 361 report by Ding, 16 Nov. 1943; memo by Bernsdorff 15 Jan. 1944. According to NMT
roll 16, frame 866 'Work Report for the Year 1943' from 25 October to 15 November 1943 Ding was with
the 'German Hygiene Institute for the Eastern Territories' Riga; BDC Wheeler-Hill file, Erik Wheeler-
Hill was born in Libau in 1898, and joined the NSDAP in May 1933, and was serologist in Riga from June
1943 until October 1944.

[161] BDC SS-HO 1519–639 Mühlens to Sievers 10 Jan. 1942; Sievers to Mühlens 22 Jan. 1942; Sievers
to Genzken 22 Jan. 1942; Note of conversation with Mühlens 3 Jan. 1942. Also in BAK NS 21/ 789. Roth,
'Der Hamburger Weg zur "Endlösung der Judenfrage" ', *Mustergau Hamburg*, 56, 74–5 (reproducing
Nauck, 'Die Geissel "Fleckfieber". Die Fleckfieberforschungsstelle des Hamburger Tropeninstituts im
Staatlichen Institut für Hygiene in Warschau'); 'Grosshungern und Grosshorchen. Das Universitäts-
krankenhaus Eppendorf', *Mustergau Hamburg*, 125–9; Wulf, *Tropeninstitut*, 122–4.

A special relationship was established between the SS camp physician and the Tropical Institute for the testing of pharmaceuticals.

Eugen Haagen's typhus experiments at the concentration camp of Natzweiler conformed to the pattern of securing approval from the SS to research in a concentration camp conveniently situated close to a medical institute. The president of the RKI, Gildemeister, collaborated with Haagen on replicating the Cox vaccine, but they became bitter enemies after Haagen's move to Strassburg in 1941. When Rose was appointed vice-president of the RKI against Gildemeister's wishes in 1942, tensions flared between them.[162] In 1941 Haagen was appointed professor of hygiene at the Reich University of Strassburg (also inciting Gildemeister's enmity), and in 1943 he became consultant in hygiene for a Luftwaffe squadron. The Strassburg anatomist August Hirt was building up a collection of skeletons from concentration camps, and Hirt became Haagen's intermediary with the SS. Haagen requested that his institute be given the status of a military installation, while he sought the support of the Ahnenerbe organization of the SS for production of a typhus vaccine for use on the Eastern Front. Haagen attempted to develop a more powerful live vaccine (the other typhus vaccines were derived from killed pathogens), based on a trial vaccine developed by Sparrow in Tunis, and by Georges Blanc and Jean Laigret at the Pasteur Institute in Casablanca, using an asymptomatic form of *rickettsia* taken from rats. Giroud supplied Haagen with a dried *rickettsia* culture from rabbit lungs.[163] Just as Eyer and Haas exploited Polish vaccine research, so Haagen in Strassburg drew on French work, but in a highly lethal form.

Haagen hoped to diminish the dangers by first vaccinating with a killed vaccine and then with the live vaccine. In October 1943 Himmler authorized Haagen to undertake experiments on 100 prisoners at the Natzweiler concentration camp. Haagen rejected a transport of gypsies from Auschwitz because of their pitiful physical condition, so condemning them to death. He experimented on a further ninety gypsies and 200 prisoners in May 1944, as he attempted to develop a dry vaccine with improved storage properties. The vaccine remained problematic—continuous modification meant further lethal experiments. Haagen used a 'control group' of deliberately infected but unvaccinated prisoners. Himmler sustained a personal interest in the new vaccine. Indeed, Haagen was commanded to acknowledge Himmler's support as well as that of the Waffen-SS Institute for Military Science in a research paper on the vaccine, and as late as November 1944 Haagen requested equipment in the hope that his results would impress Himmler. By this time he was also engaged on biological warfare research at Fort Ney.[164]

---

[162] Bayle, *Croix gammée*, 1241–7.

[163] G. Blanc and M. Baltazard, 'Vaccination contre le typhus exanthématique par virus vivant de typhus murin', *Archives de l'Institut Pasteur du Maroc*, 2 (1941), 445–86.

[164] *Trials of Major German War Criminals*, xxi, 9–10; NMT roll 16, frame 919, testimony of Rudolf Brandt; frame 924, letter of Sievers to Haagen, 30 Sept. 1943; frame 930, letter of Haagen to Hauptamt SS 9 May 1944; frame 941, Brandt to Sievers 27 June 1944, Hirt to Haagen 10 June 1944; Haagen to Rohde (camp physician Natzweiler) 16 Nov. 1944; NAW, Biological Warfare, file Strasbourg, CIOS Report, Black List item 24, Medical (9 Apr. 1945); Bayle, *Croix gammée*, 1148 for Rose to Haagen, 13 Dec. 1943; pp. 1149–54 for Haagen's correspondence with the SS; pp. 1179–81 for testimony concerning experiments

The typhus menace became a topic for widespread and reckless experimentation at the concentration camps of Mauthausen and Ravensbrück, where sulpho-namide drug therapies were tested.[165] As there was no specific therapy for typhus, the Germans tested a wide range of drugs, and many of these were obtained from various branches of the IG-Farben conglomerate.[166] The Buchenwald station under Ding tested therapeutic and preventive effects of the drugs Acridin and Rutenol[167] on behalf of the Bayer and Hoechst branches of IG-Farben in 1943. Such activities were regarded as not only scientifically useful but also a way of cementing relations with the SS. Hellmuth Vetter, a concentration camp physician, was paid a retainer by the Bayer branch of IG-Farben. Vetter tested Rutenol on deliberately infected patients in Dachau, Auschwitz, and Gusen (a camp dependent on Mauthausen). Vetter's links to IG-Farben may be compared with Bieling and Neumann who similarly continued to work for IG-Farben while on active service.[168] Ding admin-istered Acridin, methylene blue, and Rutenol in Buchenwald, reporting to Lauten-schläger, a director of IG-Farben, on the 'doses of infection', implying that the infection was deliberate. The results of the 'experiments' were catastrophic: most of a group of sixty persons, infected with typhus, died. Balachowsky and Fleck reviewed the results, which Ding wrote up in 1944, pretending that observations were carried out at a 'clinic attached to the Department of Typhus and Virus Research of the Hygiene Institute of the Waffen-SS'. Other experimental treat-ments were benign: urine from pregnant women was used on typhus patients in Ravensbrück in the hope that this might contain special antibodies against typhus. Curiously, Mrugowsky devised a honey-based therapy for typhus, but Eugen Kogon suggested that this was merely a device to obtain large stocks of honey for Mrugowsky's personal consumption.[169] The Germans in Warsaw forced medical staff in the Cyszte ghetto hospital to administer a newly discovered sulphonamide drug, Uliron, that turned the body blue and cold, and resulted in many deaths.[170]

The pattern of human experiments on typhus was repeated for other infectious diseases, notably for malaria and hepatitis because of their high incidence among army and Waffen-SS troops in southern Russia. The elderly Claus Schilling, having

in 1943; pp. 1182–97 for Rose's views; pp. 1256–60 for Haagen to Rose, 29 Nov. 1943 concerning con-centration camp experiments; pp. 1269, 1275, Mrugowsky to Rose, 16 May 1942 requesting vaccines for trial; p. 1276, Rose to Mrugowsky, 2 Dec. 1943 concerning a trial of the Copenhagen murine vaccine; E. Haagen and B. Crodel, 'Versuche mit einem neuen getrockneten Fleckfieberimpfstoff', *Zentralblatt für Bakteriologie*, 151 (1944), 369–73 (dated 20 Dec. 1944); PRO WO 188/689 report on Haagen's institute 7 Dec. 1944, and subsequent intelligence report on Fort Ney.

[165] See the table in Wuttke-Groneberg, *Medizin im Nationalsozialismus*, 324–5.

[166] G. Baader, 'Das Humanexperiment in den Konzentrationslagern. Konzeption und Durch-führung', *Menschenversuche* (Cologne, 1988), 48–69.

[167] Rutenol was a combination of a nitro-acridin derivative and arsinic acid.

[168] On Vetter see Lifton, *Nazi Doctors*, 291–2; Klee, *Auschwitz*, 284–6.

[169] Bayle, *Croix gammée*, 1136–40 (Ding Diary, 10 Jan.–1 June 1943), 1154–6 concerning Ding's report of 20 Aug. 1944; NAW 1019/36, frame 1,811, Interrogation of Kogon, 28 Nov. 1946; Schneider and Stein, *IG-Farben*, 51–4; STAN KV-Anklage Interrogations K 127 Eugen Kogon 28 Nov. 1946; Czech, *Auschwitz Chronicle*, 824 concerning Vetter who was tried and condemned to death for these experiments.

[170] Trunk, 'Epidemics and Mortality', 83; Roland, *Courage*, 124.

retired from the Tropical Department of the RKI, gained the support of Conti and Himmler to conduct experiments to produce immunity against malaria. He experimented on about 1,100 prisoners, some deliberately infected in the Dachau concentration camp (situated in a swampy district) from February 1942 until March 1945, injecting a cocktail of malaria parasites, quinine, and other drugs.[171] The military medical authorities supported hepatitis experiments in association with the RKI; by June 1943 these established that the disease was spread by a virus rather than a bacterium. The hepatitis virus was to be injected into prisoners at the Sachsenhausen concentration camp, where Himmler, Grawitz, and Sievers of the SS Ahnenerbe organization authorized experiments.[172]

A range of vaccines was tested: the Behringwerke sent to Buchenwald for testing batches of yellow fever vaccine, a triple typhoid–paratyphoid–cholera vaccine, and controversial gas gangrene vaccines. However, evidence was lacking that those vaccinated were then deliberately infected with these diseases—indeed, during 1944 Mrugowsky withheld permission for the testing of the gas gangrene vaccine.[173] The human experiments could encounter ethical and scientific objections. One researcher at the Hoechst branch of IG-Farben refused to undertake human experiments. Rose had protested about the human experiments in March 1942, and had visited the Buchenwald typhus barracks where he was disturbed at the sufferings of the non-vaccinated typhus victims. In May 1943 military medical experts met to hear papers on medical problems on the eastern front; they were informed of results from human experiments, so that the nation's medical élite became accomplices. But any hoped-for consensus was shattered when Rose attacked Ding for needlessly experimenting on problems about which there was already considerable clinical experience. He castigated Ding for proving what was already self-evident, that the vaccines were not as effective as a naturally acquired immunity. In any case Rose doubted the validity of concentrating on a vaccine-based strategy, rather than deploying a number of weapons against the louse. Rose took his complaints to Reich Health Führer Conti, who retorted that the emergency of typhus in the east justified the testing of a vaccine on 'condemned criminals' (a frequently used pretext for human experiments, assuming that everyone in a German concentration camp or prison was under a death sentence), and that in the end more lives would be saved once the vaccines were fully tested. Rose's relations with Mrugowsky were already strained, and this attack was a rebuff to the SS medical researchers.[174]

But Rose capitulated to the idea of human experiments: he changed his opinion

---

[171] E. Ost, 'Die Malaria-Versuchsstation im Konzentrationslager Dachau', *Dachauer Hefte*, 4 (1993), 174–89; H. Vondra, 'Malariaexperimente in Konzentrationslager und Heilanstalten während der Zeit des Nationalsozialismus', diss. Hannover, 1989.

[172] *Trial of German Major War Criminals*, xxi. 8–9; YVA copy of BDC Karl Brandt file, letter to Himmler 1 June 1943.

[173] Behring-Archiv, memorandum by Demnitz, 20 May 1947; Schneider and Stein, *IG-Farben*, 47–8.

[174] *Bericht über die 3. Arbeitstagung Ost der Beratenden Fachärzte vom 24.–26. Mai 1943 in der Militärärztlichen Akademie Berlin*, 108–11; Klee, *Auschwitz*, 127–8 for Klee's opinion that there was no questioning of human experiments.

on the value of Ding's typhus experiments. Rose then recommended in December 1943 that a new Danish vaccine based on mouse and rat liver be tested in Buchenwald, and contacted Mrugowsky and Haagen (who was experimenting in Natzweiler) to suggest trials. In March 1944 the vaccine was tested in Buchenwald killing six out of the twenty persons injected and the ten uninjected control persons (who were gypsies transfered from Auschwitz). Rose's complicity was contested in the courts and press until he died in 1992.[175]

Despite his earlier reservations concerning Ding's human experiments, Rose carried out malaria experiments. He directed experiments on mentally ill *Ostarbeiter*. By 1943 480 patients had been infected with a Greek strain of mosquito. From August 1942 Rose and other doctors working in association with the Bayer branch of IG-Farben tested the antimalarial drug Sontochin on patients at the Arnsdorf asylum. Backed by the Air Force, Rose established clinical and entomological departments at a hospital (which doubled as a euthanasia institution) at Pfafferode in Thuringia where he carried out clinical trials on fever therapy for schizophrenia and tested DDT derivatives.[176] The fate of Rose's patients is controversial. Rose's sister had been killed at the Grafeneck asylum, and it is possible that experimental treatment for schizophrenia provided a legitimation for sustaining the lives of those who would have otherwise been killed.

The Germans conducted ruthless human experiments on a colossal scale. Experimentation was part of an exterminatory regime of starvation, disease, and violence; their brutalizing effects confirmed the German image of the eastern *Untermensch* to which 'there was no parallel in any zoological text in the world'.[177] As part of its strategy to dominate biological and medical research, the SS provided research facilities in concentration camps. On the one hand, concentration camp prisoners were starved in atrociously cramped and filthy conditions, that were ideal for the spread of infectious disease—death by starvation and disease was in-built into the camp routines. On the other, the SS had an immediate interest in making sure that any epidemic did not infect their own personnel, as well as surrounding populations. The concentration camps offered a ready supply of experimental victims. As camp routines involved many preventive medical procedures, prisoners at times did not realize that they were about to be experimented on. Accounts were contradictory: a witness at the Nuremberg Medical Trial testified that there was no distinction between Germans or other nationals; criminals, homosexuals, and Jews of other nationalities were often used, and experiments took place in psychiatric

---

[175] NMT roll 38, frame 1,598, Mrugowsky doc. no. 48, testimony by Rose 29 Jan. 1947; Bayle, *Croix gammée*, 1237–8, 1243–5; Leven, 'Fleckfieber', in Guth, 131; NAW USATC interrogation by J. B. Rice and George Rosen, 25–6 June 1945 does not refer to these experiments; Rose, 'Fortschritte in der Bekämpfung der Kleiderlaus', reported in *Desinfektion und Schädlingsbekämpfung*, 35 (1942), 24–5; Vondra, 'Malaria-experimente', interview with Rose, pp. xii–xvi; STAN KV Interrogations Nr R 132 Bl. 26–8. For evidence that the victims were gypsies see Klee, *Auschwitz*, 337.

[176] Vondra, 'Malariaexperimente', 83–6; Tennoe, 'Human Experimentation', 29; cf. Klee, *Auschwitz*, 130–1.

[177] Dallin, *German Rule*, 415 quoting from Karl Schwarz, 'Das Gesicht des bolshewistischen Feindes', *Geist der Zeit* (Berlin, 1942), 265–70.

asylums. It was only necessary to have a residual glimmer of health, and additions to the meagre rations were meant to render victims comparable with soldiers. But another testimony insisted that racial distinctions were made, as an experimenter on typhus based in Strassburg declared 'One uses only Poles and no Alsatians and the Poles are not human beings.'[178] Similarly, Soviet prisoners of war were treated as experimental animals: although racially classified as *Untermenschen*, medically they were regarded as having a greater capacity of physical resistance to infections.

Experimentation was carried out on the initiative of military doctors in the field, who submitted their findings for evaluation by the hygiene expert of the chief of staff—none other than Heinz Zeiss.[179] This responsibility establishes a crucial link between his notions of a racial crusade, military medicine, and genocide. Similarly, his historical collaborator Bieling took a key role: having frontline duties from 1939, he was retained while on active service by the Behringwerke, for whom he tested vaccines and drugs; he reported back to Demnitz, and kept in touch with Mrugowsky.[180] Although the most benign investigations could be clinical analyses, the taking of blood specimens could run to dangerously large quantities, and be gratuitously cruel. In March 1942 Bieling analysed the blood of patients in the Jewish typhus hospital at Radom. He was fascinated by the varying incidence of fatalities in differing locations, periods, and infected ethnic groups. Jews, Serbs, and Croats were all reported as having only a mild incidence of typhus. Lethality rates for (the racially superior) German soldiers might vary between 8.45 per cent and 16.75 per cent—whereas in 1915 fatalities in the Balkans reached 60 per cent. Bieling compared diverse strains of rickettsia.[181] His next step was to undertake clinical trials of medication and vaccines on prisoners, and to calculate the numbers who became sick after a Behringwerke vaccine was tested.[182]

Impromptu field experiments indicate the drive to experiment came from opportunistic doctors rather than being necessarily dictated by SS high-ups. Experiments were carried out on hospitalized Soviet prisoners of war by an assistant doctor, Schmitz-Formes, and autopsies were conducted on those that died. Between February and March 1943 von Bormann, a bacteriologist originating from St Petersburg and attached to the ninth army, carried out a comparative study between convalescent blood and serum therapy on fifty-nine 'condemned Russians'. Infecting the prisoners with blood from convalescent patients, forty-six became ill; the duration of the illness was compared for those who had received serum or convalescent blood as opposed to those who had no treatment at all. Well over a thousand Soviet prisoners were used for experimental purposes.[183]

Military medical officers on the Eastern Front experimented on prisoners with a

---

[178] NMT roll 16, frame 904; frame 924 Haagen to Hirt; frame 953 testimony of Olga Eyer (Secretary to Haagen).

[179] BA-MA H20/518.

[180] STAN KV-Anklage Interrogations B 81 Bieling; D 24 Albert Demnitz 17 Jan. 1947, p. 21.

[181] BA-MA H20/518 Bl. 113, Bieling was attached to Panzerarmee 2.

[182] BA-MA H20/518 Bieling, 18 July 1944 trial of Impfstoff M.

[183] Ibid. Bormann, 31 Dec. 1943–15 May 1944; Leven, 'Quellen', 29–30, 33; id., 'Fleckfieber', 138–9; NMT microfilm, roll 30, frame 743–4, testimony of Kogon; roll 38, frames 1,144–6.

vast battery of drugs and therapies, including dangerous medications such as scopolamin or the anti-malarial drugs atebrin, prontosil, or neosalvarsan; or with convalescent blood, or blood from the recently immunized. 'Wild' experiments were condemned as 'statistically ill-disciplined'.[184] Experimental medicine led to misery, pain, and death, and scientifically the results of this medical butchery were at best sparse.

vii. Survival and Resistance

The strategy to kill ethnic undesirables by hunger, cold, and disease encountered relentless and often ingenious resistance. There was an incalculable amount of sabotage and illicit manufacture and use of vaccines. Batches of vaccine from Eyer's Institute were contaminated. Secret vaccine production was organized at the State Institute for Hygiene by the Polish resistance. By means of various acts of subterfuge like double registration of batches, some was siphoned off by Eyer's Polish staff. Even if the quantities were small and the efficacy of the vaccine difficult to assess, the symbolism of such acts of medical resistance was significant.[185] The ghetto health services had to manufacture their own vaccines (as achieved by Fleck at Lemberg), diagnostic tests (as devised by Hirszfeld in the Warsaw ghetto combining typhus serum and urine), and medicines (as successfully managed for vitamin preparations at the Vilna ghetto), or obtain these by bribery and smuggling. If the Germans offered drugs and vaccines to a ghetto, these were tested on dogs in case they were poisoned.[186] Eyer sent some units of vaccine to Hirszfeld in the Warsaw ghetto, and Weigl conducted trials in which 8,000 civilians were vaccinated.[187] But such direct acts of assistance (in this case tempered with the need to carry out a clinical trial) were rare.

   In concentration camps, the prisoner sick wards were avoided as far as possible because of the risks of murderous selections, human experiments, and medical tests. Yet prisoners managed to improvise medical assistance, 'organize' stolen drugs, and conduct illicit operations. One prisoner-physician, Milolasz Korn, refused to administer lethal injections of phenol, and another, Adélaïde Hautval, objected to removing uteruses of women experimental victims. The underground in Auschwitz secured supplies of typhus vaccines, when the typhus epidemic of the winter of 1941–2 raged. In stark contrast the Waffen-SS doctor Friedrich Entress ordered executions of typhus patients by phenol injections, while in charge of the infectious diseases block. Experiments were sabotaged by prisoners—X-ray machinery for sterilization experiments was not repaired, only one ovary rather

---

[184] BA-MA H20/518 Büttner 3 Mar., 6 July 1942; Atebrin was developed in 1932, and first tested on canaries infected with avian malaria.

[185] Kordas, 'Working Conditions'; K. Barbarski, 'Sabotaz w Ampułce', *Przekroj*, 99 (1947), 16.

[186] L. Fleck, 'Specific Antigenic Substances in the Urine of Typhus Patients', *Texas Reports on Biology and Medicine*, 6 (1947), 168–72; Roland, *Courage*, 152; Sedlis paper, YIVO conference on Jewish Medical Resistance.

[187] Roland, *Courage*, 146.

than two was removed (so as not to impair fertility), and smears were substituted.[188] Faced by brutally disabling sulphonamide experiments, the protests by the experimental 'rabbits' in Ravensbrück—mainly Polish resistance activists—became well organized and internationally publicized. These young women, whose limbs were infected, lacerated, and crippled by the German camp doctors, justified their resistance by arguing that medical experiments violated human rights under international law.[189]

In the Lwów/Lemberg ghetto the sanitary conditions were atrocious: once the ghetto was moved to a small area on the fringes of the city, Ludwik Fleck reckoned that 70 per cent of the population became ill with typhus. By now in charge of a laboratory in the Jewish hospital, Fleck demonstrated a very different ethic to that of the SS in first vaccinating himself and his relatives with an experimental vaccine, and then a group of thirty-two volunteers. Fleck and his colleagues Olga Elsterowa, Bernard Umschweif, Anna Seeman, Anhalt and Owseij Abramowicz developed a diagnostic test and vaccine for typhus, based on human urine from patients who had contracted typhus as a source of rickettsial antigen. They vaccinated 500 persons in the Lemberg ghetto; survivors of the ghetto testified that the vaccine successfully reduced the severity of the disease.

Striking features of the Fleck–Elster urine vaccine were the adherence to normal scientific procedures in sheer defiance of the atrocious circumstances, and the success in rapidly scaling up from the laboratory to industrial manufacture. The discovery was announced to a meeting of Lemberg doctors on 27 May 1942, and communicated to Hirszfeld in the Warsaw ghetto. The patent for the new vaccine was offered to a German, Dr Schwanenberger, in return for production facilities and raw materials like chloroform. The ordeal of explaining the project to the Gestapo resulted in specimens being provided for Otto in Frankfurt. The Germans installed Fleck in a factory with nine Jewish assistants. Fleck and his colleagues realized that the larger the production group, the more lives might be saved as factory workers had a protected position. Fleck used the opportunity to employ his son and wife as lab technicians. Moreover, the scheme meant that convalescents from typhus were also protected as they were needed to produce large amounts of urine. Fleck cunningly persuaded the Germans that Jews' urine should be used for the ghetto vaccine.[190]

The urine was collected in sterile flasks of fifty litres, to which chloroform was added. After dialysis, the aim was to precipitate the urine and extract the antigen. One batch—'K14'—produced an especially powerful antigen, and this was then used for clinical trials. Large-scale production followed, and the vaccine was used in the main Lemberg ghetto, and then the small Janowska Street camp. Lists of

[188] Shelley, *Criminal Experiments*, 22–3, 39–40, 66, 82–3 for sabotage and clandestine abortions, 167, 266–7. For illegal typhus vaccines, phenol injections, and gassing of typhus patients in Auschwitz see Langbein, *Auschwitz-Prozess*, 583–91; for Entress see *Death Books*, i. 251.
[189] W. Poltawska, *Und ich fürchte meine Träume* (Abensberg, 1994), 118.
[190] YVA P10/52 Fleck to Dvorjetzky 13 Dec. 1958; Fleck, 'Badania nad tyfusam palmistym w getcie lwowskim w latach 1941–1942'. My thanks to Ilana Lowy for translating this testimony.

those vaccinated were carefully compiled. But the brutal liquidation of these meant that Fleck was unable to gauge the overall efficacy of the new vaccine.[191]

The work drew Fleck to the attention of the German bacteriological establishment. Fleck demonstrated his vaccine to Kudicke, the bacteriological commandant of the Warsaw Hygiene Institute. A German bacteriologist was drafted in from Berlin to oversee the production process, but he turned out to be not very competent.[192] Fleck—described by Hautval as 'homme silencieux, lucide'—was deported with his medical colleagues from the 'Weigl Institute' in Lemberg to Auschwitz in February 1943 where he survived, despite contracting typhus and pleurisy after violence from an SS guard. His medical skills having been brought to the attention of the SS, he conducted routine serological tests (for which he had immense skill and insight) diagnosing illnesses like syphilis and typhus in the 'Hygiene Institute of the Waffen-SS and Police', opened in April 1943. His wife, Ernestina Fleck, along with Nusia Umschweif and Anna Seeman worked as laboratory assistants; the families of Fleck, Seeman, and Umschweif were moved with their children to Block 10, an experimental block in Auschwitz used by the Hygiene Institute. 'The Polish bacteriologists' were an unusual feature of this block of human guinea-pigs, prisoner nurses, and vivisectors. Despite this unusually fortuitous arrangement, Fleck remained deeply pessimistic: he was convinced that they would all end as smoke from the cremation ovens in the form of their initials.[193]

The Auschwitz Hygiene Institute used bacteriological equipment looted from Cracow University, and its prisoner-scientists were shocked by the SS substituting human flesh for that of animals for bacterial cultures. The Institute had a staff of biologists, bacteriologists, and pathologists assembled from the prisoners, including the distinguished French haematologist Jakob Lewin and others from France, the Netherlands, and Greece. They were an international grouping very similar to the Buchenwald prisoner-scientists. They carried out tests and provided services for the camp resistance. The prisoners held their German masters in contempt: Léon Landau characterized the SS bacteriologist Hans Münch as a scientific nonentity, but blessed him for the supply of rabbits.[194]

The director of the Auschwitz Institute, Bruno Weber, had worked with

[191] YVA P10/52 Fleck to Dvorjetzky 13 Dec. 1958; Fleck, 'Badania nad tyfusam palmistym w getcie lwowskim w latach 1941–1942'.

[192] YVA P10/52 Fleck to Dvorjetzky 13 Dec. 1958; Fleck, 'Badania nad tyfusam plamistym w getcie lwowskim w latach 1941–1942'; Fella Rosengarten-Singer testimony; Hackett, *Buchenwald Report*, 357–61; J. Schoenfeld, *Jews in the Lwów Ghetto, the Janowski Concentration Camp, and as Deportees in Siberia* (Hoboken, 1985), 72; Kordas, 'Working Conditions'.

[193] YVA 033/17, 0/650 (3 Feb. 1958) testimonies of Ludwik Fleck; 033/2250 A. Hautval to B. Klibanski, 8 Dec. 1987 and p. 64; T. Schnelle, 'Microbiology and Philosophy of Science, Lwów and the German Holocaust: Stations of a Life—Ludwik Fleck 1896–1961', R. S. Cohen and T. Schnelle (eds.), *Cognition and Fact. Materials on Ludwik Fleck* (Dordrecht, 1986), 20–3; L. Fleck, 'Kilka spostrzeżeń i doświadczeń z dziedziny duru plamistego', *Polski Tygodik Lekarski*, 1 (1946), 307–9. For the capture of Lwów see Dallin, 119–22; Shelley, *Criminal Experiments*, 8, 57–8, 69, 182; D. Czech, *Auschwitz Chronicle. 1939–1945* (London, 1990), 325, 328.

[194] PRO WO 309/468 German medical experiments, Landau deposition of 27 August 1946. L. Landau and R. P. Truck, *Réquisitoire* (Paris, 1946).

Mrugowsky on serology at the SS Hygiene Institute in Berlin. In May 1943 the Institute moved from the main camp to Raisko, a few kilometres outside the camp complex: having 'cleansed' Poles from the surrounding areas, this was where Himmler was developing an agricultural research station. The SS Hygiene Institute gained a degree of autonomy, as it also serviced the concentration camp of Gross-Rosen near Breslau, and the police and SS hospitals in the area from Posen and Prague to Kiev. But close links with the Auschwitz camps were maintained: for example, the SS serologist Hans Delmotte carried out dual 'medical duties' in Auschwitz, by which was meant in all probability selections for the gas chambers. Weber tried to keep control over Block 10 at Birkenau, where the gynaecologist Carl Clauberg and Horst Schumann performed excruciating sterilization experiments. Weber and SS colleagues sent prisoners to collect corpses from the crematoria, using body parts for bacteriological cultures. Weber profited from supplies of meat allocated for bacteriological purposes, while the shocked prisoner laboratory-workers secretly provided a token funeral. Weber stored specimens of the mutilated gypsy corpses, and his laboratories serviced disease and epidemic control within the camp. He conducted human experiments, injecting opposite blood groups to study the serological reactions; he also tested the psychological effects of mescalin. Landau characterized Weber as 'ce diable d'homme', who felt driven to place the Raisko Institute at the pinnacle of European medicine by means of subservience to superiors and ruthless exploitation of inferiors.[195]

Mrugowsky insisted on the autonomy of the Raisko Hygiene Institute and on the employment of Jewish medical staff—the prisoners were in a good position to provide false results in the hope that these might save lives. The Raisko Institute grew rapidly, acquiring over 100 workers in rivalry with the brutal Clauberg in the main camp. Hans Münch, an SS physician and NSDAP member since 1937, obstinately presented himself as a physician who used his position to save lives. But recently Münch has described how he fought epidemics by sealing huts and gassing those inside, taking part in selections for the gas chambers, and being involved in lethal experiments as well as inhumane practices. He was involved in malaria and tetanus vaccine experiments, and injected prisoners with streptococci. But he saved his conscience and, when it came to being placed on trial after the war, his skin, by having obtained Himmler's permission to carry out experiments in Block 10. These were protracted but benign experiments on skin allergies as a possible cause of rheumatism. The experiments, which involved injections, entitled the human

---

[195] Kieta, 'Hygiene-Institut'. This article records the names and nationalities of the prisoners who worked at Weber's Institute, and establishes its integration into the camps. Czech, *Auschwitz Chronicles*, p. 823; Lifton, *Nazi Doctors*, 289; Wuttke-Groneberg, *Medizin*, 322; Shelley, *Criminal Experiments*, 8–27, 255–72, testimony of Pola Plotnicka, and 275–316 correspondence with Hans Münch. For the neighbouring agricultural research station see A. Zieba, 'Das Nebenlager Rajsko', *Hefte von Auschwitz*, 9 (1966), 75–105; author's interview with Claudette Bloch Kennedy, Mar. and Apr. 1997; YVA 033/2250 testimomy of Adélaïde Hautval; YVA copy of Hans Delmotte BDC file; L. J. Micheels, *Doctor #117641. A Holocaust Memoir* (New Haven Conn., 1989), 111 on the human bouillon for bacteriological cultures. C. Romney, 'Les Témoignages écrits des médecins déportés à Auschwitz', A. Goldschläger and J. Lemaire (eds.) *Le Shoah: témoignage impossible?* (Brussels, 1998), 95–111 (*La Pensée et les hommes*, 39). PRO WO 309/469, 472 and WO 309/652 on Bruno Weber and British suspicions of Münch.

guinea pigs to extra rations. Münch claimed that they saved the life of Ernestina Fleck, among many others. It looks as though Münch devised a cunning survival strategy for himself. The French internee Claudette Bloch staged—with appropriate irony given the extent of duplicity and sabotage—a production of Molière's *Malade Imaginaire* at a New Year's celebration.[196] Even when Auschwitz was dissolved, the laboratory and its prisoner staff were evacuated to Dachau: a Dutch prisoner-technician reflected on the relative luxury: 'It was unreal, like a dream. I lived in a neat and tidy enclave, surrounded by horror. Only a hundred feet away people were starving and dying of typhus.'[197]

The Polish prisoner-bacteriologists owed their salvation to the privileged status of the hygiene laboratories. Weber approved Fleck's transfer in December 1943 to the Hygiene Institute of the Waffen SS in Buchenwald—as Mrugowsky's Berlin Hygiene Institute was responsible for both the Buchenwald and Auschwitz Hygiene Institutes. Fleck was eventually able to secure the transfer of his son to Buchenwald, and Ernestina Fleck survived Auschwitz.[198] Although Mrugowsky planned to produce an equivalent of the Pasteur Institute Durand-Giroud vaccine at Buchenwald in the autumn of 1942, he relied on Ding's much overrated medical skills. Ding gathered together a group of prisoner-bacteriologists, so that vaccine production finally began during August 1943 in block 50.[199] Vaccines were meant to be produced using the method of the Pasteur Institute, but Ding was at the mercy of his prisoners who made much show of their scientific expertise while pursuing an agenda of survival and resistance.[200]

The Buchenwald research station was somewhat detached from the deprivations, beatings, and executions in the camp.[201] The importance attached to the production of typhus vaccines meant that prisoners working on vaccine production were granted special privileges in a camp with conditions otherwise described by the French medical scientist Charles Richet as an overcrowded rabbit coop.[202] Prisoner-researchers were exempted from the normal shaved head, and they could

---

[196] NAW M 1019/roll 47, Mrugowsky interrogation; Lifton, *Nazi Doctors*, 303–36; Shelley, *Criminal Experiments*, 31 (for the children of other prisoner-scientists), 265 and 296 (for Weber and Fleck), 281–316 (recollections of Dr Hans Münch); interviews with Claudette Bloch Kennedy, Oxford, March and May 1997; YVA copy of BDC file on Hans Münch. BAK Sammlung Pross, Leo Alexander diary 21 Mar. 1947.

[197] Micheels, *Doctor #117641*, 140.

[198] Personal communication Hans Münch to the author 25 July 1997 (actually 27 May 1997) concerning Fleck; YVA, testimony of Arye Fleck. Klee, *Auschwitz*, 314–15 wrongly suggests that Fleck was at Buchenwald in August 1943.

[199] On the origins of the experimental station see S. Zimmermann, 'Behührungspunkte zwischen dem Konzentrationslager Buchenwald und der Medizinischen Fakultät der Universität Jena', Meinel and Voswinckel, *Medizin*, 54–61. On Erwin Ding(-Schuler) see W. Poller, *Medical Block Buchenwald* (London, 1988), 90, 99–106, 126, 130–6, 169–71, 177, 179, 182, 185–90, 193, 222–4, 226–30; on typhus disinfection, pp. 236–7; on typhus experiments at Buchenwald see J. Rousset, *Chez les barbares* (Lyon, 1946).

[200] BAK R 86/ 4153 Bl. 53 Haubold report 11 Dec. 1942; NAW microfilm 1019/roll 47 Mrugowsky interrogation 3 Dec. 1946 a.m. p. 12.

[201] Rousset, *Chez les barbares*, 15; C. Richet, *Trois bagnes* (Paris, 1945); Richet, 'La Médecine au Bagne (Buchenwald, janvier 1944)', *La Presse médicale* (14 July 1945) 389.

[202] Richet, 'Experiences', 453–4. Richet worked at the *Krankenrevier*.

receive Red Cross parcels and correspondence; Kogon (a journalist) learned biology and immunology from a substantial scientific library supplied by the University of Jena, indeed the Dutch prisoner Jan Robert used the university library, and prisoners had access to a camp literary library. Balachowsky recorded that on 11 January 1945 he worked on 'bibliography and writing about lice and fleas'. He compiled obsessive lists: the books he read—ranging from works by Proust and H. G. Wells to Michelet's *Le Moyen Âge*, the letters and parcels received, medical notes, tables of arthropods transmitting rickettsiae and on his work to develop 'the Lice Laboratory' from January 1945, when comrades visited, and (here the routine horror of camp punctures the scientific idyll) when they were executed or otherwise died. Among the benefits of Block 50 was that prisoners secretly used the centrifuge to mash the remains of dead laboratory rabbits, and cooked these in a soup. The Germans, fearful of typhus, did not rigorously check the disposal of dead laboratory animals.[203]

Scientific innovation was not to be held back by humane considerations. Any new observation—for example, concerning serological reactions—would prompt Ding to organize a series of murderous experiments. Balachowsky noted that the research team resisted Ding's demands for such information.[204] That Ludwik Fleck came to work (albeit indirectly) under Mrugowsky was ironic given that both had historical and philosophical interests in holistic ideas. Fleck owed his survival to his skills as a microbiologist and serologist. He was not only experienced in discerning microbiological phenonemena, but he also found examples of thought-collectives among his co-workers, as they mis-identified typhus rickettsiae.

Ding worked with two subordinate SS officers, otherwise the vaccine team consisted of prisoners.[205] The brutal Kapo Arthur Dietzsch supervised a medical team of fifty-nine prisoners, many being veterans in resistance. The Buchenwald captives produced about thirty to fifty litres of vaccine each month from late in 1943. In the privileged scientific enclave of Block 50, this large group was a remarkable example of an international and interdisciplinary research team.[206] It was directed by a Polish bacteriologist Marian Ciepielowsky, whom Ding had saved from execution in Block 46; but far from being compliant Ciepielowsky organized clandestine resistance to limit the executions, falsify results, and sabotage vaccine

[203] AIP, Fonds Balachowsky, Ausweis, dated 15 June 1944 providing exemption from haircuts and the privilege of receiving post. His camp diary and notebook were fruits of the privileges enjoyed by the typhus research prisoners. He compiled a 'Bibliographie scientifique allemande': NAW RG 153, War Crimes Case Number 12–390, The Buchenwald Case, microfilm 5; Kogon cross-examination, p. 272; Hackett, *Buchenwald*, 265 for the library; Langbein, *Against All Hope*, 229.

[204] AIP Fonds Balachowsky, 'Déposition au sujet des expériences et recherches faites sur le typhus exanthèmatique au camp de Buchenwald', 12; NMT roll 16, frame 916; R. Waitz and M. Ciepelowsky, in *La Presse médicale* (1946); Schnelle, 'Microbiology and Philosophy of Science', 23–9; NAW M 1019, roll 47 Mrugowsky interrogation 17 Oct. 1946, p. 6. In July 1944 Fleck reported a modification in the vaccine, and Balachowsky maintained that Ding initiated a series of experiments resulting in twenty deaths. Fleck strenuously rejected this accusation.

[205] NAW M 1019/roll 47 Mrugowsky interrogation, 17 Oct. 1946, p. 3.

[206] NAW RG 153 War Crimes Case Number 12–390, The Buchenwald Case, microfilm (copy in Gedenkstätte Buchenwald archives Sign 503–8), Ding-Schuler interrogation June 1945.

production. Balachowsky's register of the Buchenwald vaccine researchers shows that Germans and Russians were the largest contingents among the fifty-nine convicts.

The group was under orders to manufacture the rabbit-lung vaccine according to Giroud's methods. They retained about 60 litres of effective vaccine for use among prisoners while supplying the SS with ineffective batches—Balachowsky commented: 'I realised the almost complete inefficiency of the SS doctors, and how easy it was to sabotage the vaccine for the German army.'[207] As the military situation deteriorated, the vaccine producing stations in Poland had to be evacuated. In order to make up supplies the Buchenwald station was to produce Weigl's louse vaccine, which required louse-feeders.[208]

Balachowsky gave a vivid description of experimental 'research' in Buchenwald from May 1944 until April 1945, and later testified at the Nuremberg Trials. Deported to Buchenwald in January 1944, he nearly died in a slave labour battalion building rocket launching-sites. After friends made known his scientific pedigree to Ding, Balachowsky was transferred to the medical research block where he saved the lives of SOE prisoners and undermined the Nazi vaccine production.[209] On the one hand, here was a rapacious SS enterprise: Balachowsky testified that the research was continually directed by the Supreme Command of the Waffen-SS.[210] Mrugowsky was recorded as having visited the extermination Block 61 as late as 20 March 1945.[211] But on the other hand, this was a medical research establishment exploiting the scientific expertise and resources of the conquered. Ding was keen to have a luminary from the Pasteur Institute to reinforce the prisoner-researcher contingent. Balachowsky requested that Tréfouel as Director of the Pasteur Institute send to Buchenwald scientific publications about Giroud's vaccine.[212] The formal exchange of letters between two Pastorians under conditions of immense strain indicates how the SS was concerned to harness effective, 'normal' science to serve exterminatory ends.

Ultimately, scientific faith in the efficacy of vaccines intermingled with a strong dose of ideology combining militarism and medical triumphalism. The slogan of 'Victory with Vaccines' summed up the confident mood of researchers on all sides; but no clear victor emerged.[213] The German version of the Cox vaccine differed

---

[207] *Trials of the Major German War Criminals*, v. 257; Bayle, *Croix gammée*, 1177–9, 1227–9 for Mrugowsky's belief in the efficacy of the vaccine; NAW RG 153 Buchenwald Case, Ciepielowsky testimony, frames 1,230–1; K. Barbarski, 'Sabotaz w Ampulce', *Przekroj*, 99 (1947), 16.

[208] AIP, Balachowsky papers, diary entry of 3 Feb. 1945.

[209] Alfred-Serge Balachowsky, *Titres et travaux scientifiques (1925–1967)* (Paris, 1967); M. R. D. Foot, *SOE in France* (London, 1966), 257, 317, 337, 426–7; AIP Fonds Balachowsky for biographical articles and Carnet de Buchenwald.

[210] *Trials of the Major German War Criminals*, v. 248–61.

[211] AIP, Balachowsky papers, note on leaf inserted in notebook gives 22 Feb. 1945; NMT roll 16, frame 910 gives a March date.

[212] AIP, Balachowsky papers, Buchenwald notebook, list of correspondence, entry of 22 May 1944; Fonds Direction, Balachowsky to Tréfouel 5 May 1944; Tréfouel to Balachowsky 11 May 1944.

[213] For this slogan see H. J. Parish, *Victory with Vaccines. The Story of Immunization* (Edinburgh and London, 1968), 173–4.

considerably from what was produced in the United States, and it may well have
been weaker. By 1945 US medical experts regarded typhus as a vanquished enemy.
One official history proclaimed 'the preventive, clinical and laboratory events concerned with the typhus fevers represent a brilliant chapter in the history of medicine'.[214] But problems of trials, production, and assessing efficacy posed barriers to
the application of laboratory research. The Allied research effort also raises ethical
and methodological issues. But these pale before the gargantuan scale of the deliberate infection and killing of experimental victims on the German side.

TABLE 11.1. Buchenwald Prisoner Vaccine Researchers: 'Kommandoliste Block 50'

Name	Date of birth	Nation-ality	Home town	Date joined block 50	Occupation
Balachowsky, Alfred	15 Aug. 1901	French	Paris	11 Apr. 1944	Parasitologe
Baumeister, Hans	7 Feb. 1902	German	Dortmund	7 May 1944	Schr. u. Zeichn.
Bijen, Wilfried	7 Feb. 1920	Dutch	—	1 Sept. 1943	Laborant
Böhle, Hans	—	German	—	9 May 1944	Friseur
Ciepielowsky, Marian	30 Aug. 1907	Polish	Cracow	1 Sept. 1943	Leit. Arzt
Cohn, August	10 May 1910	Jewish	—	9 May 1944	Schreiber
Cyran, Henryk	12 Oct. 1918	Polish	—	1 Sept. 1943	Zahnarzt
van Dalen, Hendryk	4 Aug. 1919	Dutch	—	1 Sept. 1943	Glasbläser
Danilienko, Boris	30 Oct. 1919	Russian	—	9 July 1944	Türhüter
Dikunez, Dimitro	10 Feb. 1914	Russian	—	1 Sept. 1943	Tierpfleger
Escales, Erich	7 Apr. 1907	German	Wiesbaden	31 Mar. 1944	Chemiker
Fleck, Josef	14 July 1902	Czech	—	20 Dec. 1943	Gerber
Fleck, Ludwig	10 July 1896	Polish	Lwów	7 Jan. 1944	Serologe
Fundak, Ivan	23 Oct. 1923	Russian	—	7 Dec. 1943	Laborant
Grossman, Felix	22 Feb. 1897	Polish	—	1 Sept. 1943	Physiker
Grzedzczuk, Bronislas	26 Aug. 1920	Polish	—	20 Dec. 1943	Buchbinder
Dr Her[r]ing	—	French	Strasbourg	—	[Chemist]
Holper, Victor	20 July 1908	Luxemburg	Ettelbrück	7 Oct. 1943	Apotheker

[214] J. B. Coates (ed.), *Internal Medicine in World War II,* ii, *Infectious Diseases* (Washington, DC, 1963), 223.

TABLE 11.1. (*Continued*)

Name	Date of birth	Nation-ality	Home town	Date joined block 50	Occupation
Holzen, Ernst	15 Oct. 1920	German	—	12 June 1944	Chemiker
Hummelsheim, Walter	—	German	—	—	Arztschreiber
Jellinek, Wilhelm	28 Apr. 1916	Jewish	—	1 Sept. 1943	Bakteriologe
Jentsch, Wilhelm	22 Apr. 1892	German	—	1 Sept. 1943	Schriftenm.
Kirchheimer, Fritz	10 Mar. 1911	Jewish	—	1 Sept. 1943	Kalfaktor (orderly)
Kirrman, Albert	28 June 1900	French	Strasbourg	11 July 1944	Chemiker
Kogon, Eugen	2 Feb. 1903	German	Vienna	1 Sept. 1943	Arztschreiber
Kolotow, Nikolai	1903	Russian	—	17 May 1944	Bakteriologe
Korel, Iwan	21 Jan. 1924	Russian	—	16 April 1944	Kalfaktor
Labaziewicz, Thedor	20 Dec. 1909	Polish	—	7 Oct. 1943	Kalfaktor
van Lingen, Derk	6 Feb. 1895	Dutch	Amsterdam	1 Sept. 1943	Physiker
Makovicka, Karl	6 Sept. 1913	Czech	Prague	1 Sept. 1943	Bakteriologe
Markus, Alfred	19 Sept. 1924	German	—	5 June 1944	Kalfaktor
Mautner, Fritz	12 Nov. 1916	Jewish	—	1 Sept. 1943	Biologe
Meyer, Bernard	27 Apr. 1920	Dutch	—	1 Sept. 1943	Läufer
Meyer, Edgar	30 Dec. 1924	German	—	16 Dec. 1924	Kalfaktor
Michailuk, Feodor	23 Dec. 1926	Russian	—	1 June 1944	Türhüter
Millak, Andreas	18 Dec. 1919	Polish	—	26 Jan. 1944	Laborant
Morat, René	12 June 1914	French	—	4 Mar. 1944	Bakteriologe
Müller, Alfred	20 Sept. 1907	German	—	1 Sept. 1943	Sterilisator
Müller, Jacob	17 June 1886	German	—	19 Jan. 1944	Laborant
Neubauer, Franz	18 Sept. 1918	German	—	—	Tischler
Novy, Bohodan	10 Aug. 1914	Czech	—	1 May 1944	Kalfaktor
Odriensky, Alexej	8 Sept. 1925	Russian	—	15 Sept. 1943	Kalfaktor
Pankowicz, Zbiegnew	6 Sept. 1922	Polish	—	19 Nov. 1943	Laborant

TABLE 11.1. (*Continued*)

Name	Date of birth	Nation-ality	Home town	Date joined block 50	Occupation
Peirnew, Iwan	21 Nov. 1911	Russian	Cracow	16 Mar. 1944	Kalfaktor
Pie[c]k, Henry	10 Apr. 1895	Dutch	Ryswyk	6 Oct. 1943	Zeichner [architect]
Pintschuk, Wasilij	24 Oct. 1919	Russian	—	1 Sept. 1943	Kalfaktor
Pasfisil, Jan	19 Feb. 1895	Czech	—	1 Sept. 1943	Tierarzt
Reidel, Karl	16 Oct. 1902	German	—	1 Sept. 1943	Kapo
Robert, Johannes [Jan]	1 Mar. 1909	Dutch	Amsterdam	1 Sept. 1943	Bibliothekar [lawyer]
Sminnow, Iwan	15 Sept. 1918	Russian	—	3 Dec. 1943	Tierpfleger
Suard, Maurice	4 Jan. 1897	French	Angers	5 Dec. 1943	Chemiker
Schedenko, Pawel	17 Dec. 1925	Russian	—	15 Sept. 1943	Kalfaktor
Tkatichenko, Alex	9 July 1914	Russian	—	1 Sept. 1943	Tierpfleger
Tresoer, Bernard	17 Feb. 1917	Dutch	—	1 Sept. 1943	Laborant
Valter, Karl	17 Feb. 1909	Czech	—	13 Oct. 1943	Schreiber
Wagner, Christoph	19 June 1901	German	—	1 Sept. 1943	Desinfektor
[Waitz, Robert]	—	French	Strasbourg	30 Jan. 1945	—
de Wit, Martinus	4 Mar. 1921	Dutch	—	1 Sept. 1943	Laborant
Wolotowski, Wasilij	8 Aug. 1921	Russian	—	19 Apr. 1944	Kalfaktor

Source: AIP Fonds Balachowsky, Carnet de Buchenwald. The terminology and spellings follow those of Balachowsky.

12

From Medical Research to Biological Warfare

i. DDT and Medical Entomology

Campaigns against insects in the east became entwined with preparations for biological warfare. The idea of unleashing disease pathogens to destroy Germany's enemies fascinated disinfection experts, for it seemed to them that if a disease could be prevented, it should also be possible for epidemics to be deliberately spread. After all, the Germans had come close to such a strategy in creating the conditions to decimate the inmates of ghettos. The borderland between defensive and offensive germ warfare programmes was ill-defined: the fear that Germany's opponents were stockpiling arsenals of biological and chemical weapons spurred on offensive preparations. Consequently, disease-control programmes became radicalized, shifting from containment and prevention to strategies for total eradication of pathogens and their carriers.

Despite the intensity of German war-related research programmes, these lacked overall coordination: this was the case in medicine with the sporadic but failed attempts to produce penicillin. Axis vaccine production remained fragmented. The differences can be compared to the carefully orchestrated Allied project to develop an atom bomb and the nebulous German atomic strategy, so unclear as to render it controversial whether Nazi Germany was seriously interested in developing such weapons.[1] The contrast between the tightly organized Allied and multi-centred German research establishments led to divergent responses to DDT for pest control. Whereas the Germans clung to delousing by poison gas, the Allies adopted innovative DDT-based methods, and accelerated louse- and mosquito-control studies. It was said that for every 800 German prisoners of war infested with lice, there was one British case. In terms of medical organization the Allies showed greater ability to coordinate and instrumentalize scientific and technical discoveries. The innovative capacity of the Allied research contrasted with the organizational factionalism, rigidity, and historic fixations of the Germans, who increased their vulnerability to infection by embarking on their eastern offensives.

British researchers sought safer alternatives to hydrogen cyanide for delousing infested clothing, and from September 1941 a combined MRC and military entomological committee developed insect repellents.[2] The US relied on its Bureau of Entomology, with back-up from an Insect Control Committee of the Office of

---

[1] M. Walker, *German National Socialism and the Quest for Nuclear Power (1939–1949)* (Cambridge, 1989).

[2] PRO FD1/6448 Military Personnel Research Committee. The Entomological Sub-committee met from 6 Jan. 1942 until 9 Mar. 1945.

Scientific Research and Development. In the Soviet Union the Central Disinfection Institute of the Peoples' Commissariat for Health and the Institute for Sanitary Research of the Red Army developed an anti-louse soap for clothes and to impregnate bedding, cleaning fluids, and a powder for use at the front. The Allies were sceptical of delousing showers and fumigation chambers, for no sooner was a soldier deloused than reinfestation could occur. Because the British and Americans encountered typhus primarily in North Africa where the front was constantly moving, fixed delousing installations had little attraction.[3]

After experimenting with individual gas-bags for louse fumigation, the Allied scientists concentrated their efforts on impregnating uniforms with chemical powders to deter lice.[4] In March 1943 an outbreak of typhus in an Egyptian village was used to test a novel powder, called MYL; later that year MYL was compared to DDT in its effects on the inmates of an Algiers prison as a 'closed population' and on a civilian settlement with the cooperation of Sergent of the Algiers Pasteur Institute. The Rockefeller medical expert Fred Soper achieved a breakthrough when he invented a DDT dusting gun suitable for spraying clothed persons, overcoming the difficulty of persuading Muslim women to remove their clothing. This device to improve civilian compliance was hailed as a quick and easy method of tackling reservoirs of infection, when the Allies organized trial DDT-dusting programmes in Morocco, Tunis, and Sicily.[5]

Compared with the regimentation involved in delousing by means of showers, DDT was adaptable and flexible for field applications: it could be used as a powder for dealing with body lice, as a solution for the elimination of bedbugs and flies, or as a spray. Chemists seeking a moth-proofing agent for the Basle firm of J. R. Geigy in 1939 discovered its properties as an insecticide, and the product was patented in March 1940. Geigy offered the product to the Allies and the Axis powers, and from the summer of 1942 exported substantial quantities of DDT to the United States. American and British military researchers conducted extensive experiments, and in 1943 a report was received from Basle that the product was effective against the body louse. A British Insecticides Development Panel tested powders, solutions,

[3] NAW RG 112 USATC Box 37 C. H. Stuart-Harris, Army Pathology Advisory Committee, 19 July 1943; Report from Emergency Vaccine Laboratory, May 1943, on Typhus Research; T. E. Boldyrev, 'Problems of Epidemiology in War-time', in E. B. Babsky, I. G. Kochergin, and V. V. Parin (eds.), *Microbiology and Epidemiology* (London, 1945), 11–12; F. S. Hanenya and S. V. Zhuravlev, 'Insect Preparations for the Control of Pediculosis', *Microbiology and Epidemiology*, 39–47; PRO AVIA 42/63 British Central Scientific Office, Antilouse preparations, 1942–5, Office of Scientific Advisers Ministry of Production 13 July 1943 comparing the German and Russian antilouse powders.

[4] NAW RG7 Bureau of Entomology and Plant Quarantine; History of Development; R. Latta, review of the Louse Fumigation Work, 27 Dec. 1944; H. L. Haller and S. J. Cristol, 'The Development of New Insecticides', in E. C. Andrus, *et al.*, *Advances in Military Medicine* (Boston, 1948), 621–3; John H. Perkins, 'Reshaping Technology in Wartime: The Effect of Military Goals on Entomological Research and Insect Control Practices', *Technology and Culture*, 19 (1978), 169–86.

[5] PRO AVIA 42/63 British Central Scientific Office, Antilouse preparations, 1942–5; P. A. Buxton to E. Mellanby, 22 Sept. 1942 on MYL, report on visit of British delegation, 14 Oct. 1942; F. L. Soper, *et al.*, 'Louse-Powder Studies in North Africa (1943)', *Archives de l'Institut Pasteur d'Algérie*, 23 (1945), 183–223 repr. in J. A. Kerr (ed.), *Building the Health Bridge. Selections from the Works of Fred L. Soper, M.D.* (Bloomington, Ind., 1970), 357–83; *Notice sur l'Institut Pasteur d'Algérie* (Algiers, 1949), ii. 244–5; Cowdrey, *Bayne-Jones*, 154.

emulsions, and suspensions, and the effects of impregnating uniforms with DDT. At the Porton Down Chemical Defence Establishment research into DDT was a high priority from 1943, taking its place alongside chemical and biological warfare preparations. Scientists found this new wonder substance to be non-toxic for humans (a view that was later reversed). A research network in the US used analytical chemical methods to prepare pure, stable DDT of differing grades and in forms convenient for storage and use. Once Allied scientists showed DDT to be effective on a wide range of insects, the superior Allied war economy produced the miracle substance on a large scale.[6] That people could be 'dusted' without being undressed, allowed whole populations to be rapidly deloused: from January to 20 February 1944 there were 1,750,000 DDT dustings.[7]

German scientists resented how economic retrenchment and the lack of overseas territories impeded the development of medical entomology.[8] From 1933 applications for medical entomological funding to the DFG were supported by the expected acquisition of new colonies.[9] The two main research centres were the Hamburg Tropical Institute and the zoological department of the Reichsanstalt für Wasser- und Luftgüte in Berlin. These institutions continued approaches, dating from the First World War rather than developing fundamentally new strategies.[10]

The expert on the life-cycle and behaviour of lice, Hase, exemplifies how the echoes of First World War anti-louse campaigns continued to shape measures. In September 1939 Hase established a military station for research into pest eradication. He deployed physiological and ecological approaches, combined with analysis of instinct and behaviour. In conjunction with the Reich Ministry of the Interior and the army he trained 2,000 health inspectors, disinfectors, and pest exterminators in delousing procedures, and his course became a standard publication.[11] Although his First World War experience made him sceptical of anti-louse powders, he studied the sense of smell in lice and other insects, in order to establish whether any chemicals would repel lice. By 1943 the project was DDT-related.[12]

Medical entomology became a hornets' nest of warring military and SS factions.

---

[6] For a bibliography of US DDT research see Andrus, *Advances*, 815–19.

[7] F. H. Green and G. Covell (eds.), *History of the Second World War. United Kingdom Medical Series. Medical Research* (London, 1953), 160–1, 236–7; *The Story of DDT* (War Office Film, 1944, Imperial War Museum reference number CVN 238 0 PSA reels 1–3); J. L. Burn, *DDT in Disinfection* (Salford, 1945); G. B. Carter, *Porton Down. 75 Years of Chemical and Biological Research* (London, 1992), 48.

[8] BAK R 73/ 12900 Martini file, Bemerkungen über die heutige Lage der medizinischen Entomologie in Deutschland, n.d.; Martini to DFG 19 Feb. 1938.

[9] Militärgeschichtliches Forschungsamt, *Germany and the Second World War* (Oxford, 1995), iii. 278–301, 'Ideas of German Ruling Circles Concerning a Colonial Empire'; BAK R 73/ 12900 Martini file, Zeiss to Sauerbruch 25 Nov. 1937 concerning the ending of Martini's Rockefeller funding.

[10] W. Reichmuth, 'Neuere Ergebnisse und Probleme der Schädlingsbekämpfung', Rodenwaldt, *et al.*, *FIAT Review of German Science 1939–1946. Hygiene*, pt. II, *Preventive and Industrial Medicine* (Wiesbaden, 1948), 22.

[11] A. Hase and W. Reichmuth, *Grundlagen der behelfsmässigen Entlausungsmassnahmen* (Berlin 1940).

[12] BAK R 73/ 11515 Hase to Reichsforschungsrat 4 Apr., 14 Dec. 1942; 11 June 1941; Mentzel to Hase 22 Apr. 1942 granting 2,500 marks, 14 Dec. 1942 granting 2,500 marks, 21 Apr. 1943 granting 4,000 marks; A. Hase, 'Bekämpfung der Körperverlausung mit Hülfe pulverförmiger Mittel, sowie Prüfverfahren von sog. Läusepudern', *Zeitschrift für hygienische Zoologie*, 35 (1943), 1–17.

Erich Martini of the Hamburg Institute for Maritime and Tropical Diseases generated much controversy despite his special expertise in malaria prevention; he had
assisted Koch, joined the Hamburg Tropical Institute in 1914, and embarked on
louse and malaria control work during the First World War. He joined the Nazi
Party in May 1933, and by the outbreak of war he formulated an ambitious research
strategy on insect-borne diseases. He envisaged a central Berlin institute, reinforced by peripheral stations at Posen and Kiev, all with military support.[13] His reissued textbook of medical entomology in 1941 (the first edition was in 1923) applied
ecological perspectives to epidemiology. Martini linked historical and environmental factors in ways similar to the geo-medical ideas of Zeiss and Mrugowsky.[14]
Epidemics resulted from the ecologically determined distribution of parasites, as
well as from the racial health of the infected population.[15] Martini transposed the
values of *Blut und Boden* ideology into preventive medicine; in practical terms, his
work was in line with Nazi thinking, with its praise of hydrocyanic acid for delousing. Martin Mayer, the teacher of Zeiss who was forced to emigrate, was to accuse
Martini of support for Nazi genocide.[16]

Martini turned medical entomology into an academic battlefield. He opposed
the appointment of Mühlens as Director of the Hamburg Tropical Institute, and
a bitter dispute erupted. In April 1939 Martini submitted to the Führer a violent
character-assassination of Mühlens. The upshot was that in 1940 Martini joined
an entomological laboratory of the Military Medical Academy in Berlin; the
Hamburg Institute panicked, as they believed that Martini was attempting to build
up a much larger research team and that the professorial magnates Zeiss and
Rodenwaldt lay behind these machinations. Zeiss had already crossed swords with
Mühlens in 1938 whom he accused of being unpatriotic in commending French
research, and Rodenwaldt was aggrieved at not being offered command of the
Hamburg Institute. The Hamburg Tropical Institute attempted to persuade the
naval high command to transfer its Marine Medical Academy to Hamburg. The SS
cultural organization, the Ahnenerbe, combined forces with the military hygiene
lobby of Rodenwaldt, Mrugowsky, and Zeiss to support Martini's research as
crucial for defending the Waffen-SS against typhus and lice. However, the bombing
of the Military Hygiene Institute in 1943 and of the Hamburg Tropical Institute in
1944 disrupted such strategically oriented entomology.[17]

With the crawling of entomologists to the military, by 1942 the SS was dissatisfied
with the research carried out on preventing human insect parasites. The president
of the Reich Biological Institute declined to cooperate with the SS, while allowing

[13] BAK R 73/ 12900 Martini file, DFG to Martini 28 Mar. 1939, 18 Mar. 1940 concerning research funds
for insect pests; BDC Martini file, interview with Wüst 9 Jan. 1942.

[14] E. Martini, *Lehrbuch der medizinischen Entomologie* (Jena, 1941).

[15] Id., *Wege der Seuchen. Lebensgemeinschaft, Kultur, Boden und Klima als Grundlage von Epidemien*
(Stuttgart, 1943).

[16] BNI 10/2, Martin Mayer to Martini 7 Dec. 1945.

[17] BAK R 73/ 12900, Erna Martini to DFG 5 Sept. 1944; Wess, 'Tropenmedizin und Kolonialpolitik',
49–51; Wulf, *Tropenmedizin*, 129–40; AHUB Hygienisches Institut Nr 192 Zeiss to Mühlens 2 Dec. 1937, 13
Jan. 1938; Mühlens to Reiter 7 Feb. 1938.

Hase to work for the Wehrmacht at the Military Medical Academy's department for pest control. Several other entomological institutes evaded the SS's requests for research on human hosts of insect pests.[18] This prompted the search for an alternative focus of cooperation between the SS and the biological sciences: the Institute for Hygiene and Medical Entomology of the Ahnenerbe was established at the Dachau concentration camp as part of the Waffen-SS strategic research institute. The Dachau Institute had an advisory board consisting of senior SS academics as well as the entomologist Martini (who stressed the priorities of the Waffen-SS) and Walther Trappmann, an expert on pesticides and plant diseases from the Reich Biological Institute. The board supervised an entomologist, Eduard May, who had philosophical pretensions, as he combated the pernicious 'Jewish' philosophies of relativism and rationalism on the basis of the ideas of the German nature philosophers Leibniz and Goethe. May was influenced by Hugo Dingler, who proselytized for a Nazi philosophy of nature encompassing a 'German physics'. Himmler demanded that the institute study insect life and pathology, and that its environmental and chemical programmes of extermination should target insect breeding-grounds. May studied whether there could be a mass-induced spread of malaria parasites to humans. The eradication of insects was a military priority of immediate benefit for troops in the field while promoting biological warfare.[19]

Despite the crudeness of Himmler's rhetoric of extermination, the resulting research was scientifically ambitious: in 1942 the SS established a research council to advance delousing, viral research, the cyclotron (for electromagnetic acceleration of charged atoms), and antisepsis research. Martini welcomed the intervention of the SS, and argued that Germany lagged behind the United States, Britain, France, and the Soviet Union in medical entomology, and so required a grand interdisciplinary scheme.[20] Mrugowsky was alarmed at a rival research organization within the SS, and only acquiesced when Sievers explained that the new entomological organization was one of a number of fields in which Himmler (an agriculturalist by training) was taking a close interest. In September 1942 Martini pressed May to join him on a research trip to observe delousing procedures for the Waffen-SS in Russia. Late in 1942 Mrugowsky brought May into contact with Fritz Steiniger of the newly founded German Institute for Medical Zoology at Riga.[21] With the backing of the SS's Ahnenerbe organization, May travelled widely to study

---

[18] BDC May file, Präsident der Biologischen Reichsanstalt to Ahnenerbe 7 Jan. 1942; Institut für Landwirtschaftliche Zoologie der Universität Berlin 7 Jan. 1942, Deutsches Entomologisches Institut der KWG 7 Jan. 1942 also declined. The Deutsches Hygiene Museum was keen on cooperation, letter from Michael to Ahenenerbe 13 Jan. 1942; 'Zum 60. Geburtstag von Prof. Dr. A. Hase', *Zeitschrift für hygienische Zoologie*, 34 (1942), 61.

[19] BDC May file, agreement of May and the Ahnenerbe 24 July 1942; Ahnenerbe to May 10 Sept. 1942 concerning the Beirat; Forschungsauftrag 'Menschenschädigende Insekten', 4 Oct. 1943; Demands of Himmler on May's plan to eradicate flies by other insects; Deichmann, *Biologists*, 264–9; on Dingler see K. Hentschel (ed.), *Physics and National Socialism* (Basel, 1996), pp. lxxvii, 251–2.

[20] BDC Martini file 15 Jan. 1942, Martini to Wüst; Protocol of discussion between Martini and Wüst 7 Jan. 1942; NAW T 580, roll 124 Entomologische Forschung.

[21] BDC Steiniger file, Mrugowsky to Steiniger 18 Dec. 1942.

pest control—to Spain in April 1943 and to Bulgaria in September 1943—to tackle the malaria problem. He then embarked on malaria experiments in Dachau, as well as on delousing campaigns in the east.[22]

May cooperated with the Hygiene Institute of the Waffen-SS and with Guntram Pflaum, who in 1943 became SS supremo for pest control. Coming to pest control through Nazi agitation and lacking any specialist expertise other than in cleaning high-class ladies hats, Pflaum was a *völkisch* ideologue and party political creature who did not defer to technical specialists. His Nazi roots went back to the freekorps Bund Oberland and to Hitler's Putsch of 1923. He then agitated for non-fermented fruit juice on behalf of the anti-alcohol movement, and opened a 'German-Christian' ladies hat shop and cleaners in Munich in 1933. When the Bund Oberland was incorporated into the SS, Pflaum became a willing conscript. From June 1937 until December 1940 he worked for the *Lebensborn* homes for single mothers. He then joined Himmler's personal staff, and in July 1941 Himmler gave Pflaum the task of locating pure German children 'of uncorrupted blood' among the the Volga Germans, and this assignment was extended to the whole of European Russia. He joined the Waffen-SS in November 1941 to fulfil this 'special mission'. By May 1943 Himmler entrusted Pflaum with the task of combating flies and mosquitoes; his inflated title was the 'Sonderbeauftragte des Reichsführers-SS für Schädlingsbekämpfung', but he was more familiarly known as the 'Reichsfliegendiktator'. Himmler was obsessed by pest control matters, firing off suggestions and requiring Pflaum's outfit to inspect all SS barracks, training camps, and *Lebensborn* homes in the Reich and the occupied territories. Pflaum's team arranged supplies of pest control materials to the SS and police, with the notable exception of Zyklon, while generally educating the SS on the dangers of insect pests. Pflaum operated in Russia in 1943, but as the German troops retreated he moved to Auschwitz in January 1944.[23] Here camp inmates were formed into a pest control squad, who were given the congenial task of producing slogans and brochures.[24]

Pflaum's staff of about seventy-five Jews and forty SS men in Auschwitz devised a method of exterminating house-flies on a biological basis by deploying a predatory species of wasp, and concocted soaps and insect repellents. The strategy generated such momentum that the energetic Pflaum hoped to organize a conference on pest

[22] BDC 468–625 Ahnenerbe to Mrugowsky, 23 Nov. 1942; Martini file, letters from Martini to May 14 Sept. 1942; from Martini to Sievers, 14 Sept. 1942; from May to Ahnenerbe 17 Sept. 1942; May file, Ahnenerbe to Winzer, Madrid 5 Apr. 1943; AHUB Hygienisches Institut Nr 192, Report of the Hygiene Institut der Waffen-SS 1941, Bl. 252. BAP .03 Reichsministerium für die besetzten Ostgebieten II.2 K45, 19 Nov. 1942, concerning delousing ovens in Tauroggen and Wirballen. BAK NS 21/ 33 on May and the SS Ahnenerbe. NS 21/ 910 and 911. NMT roll 30, frames 412–3, concerning interviews between Mrugowsky and Sievers; roll 16, frames 1008–11, correspondence of Sievers to Hirt, 17 Jan. 1942 and Hirt to Sievers 20 Jan. 1942.

[23] NAW microfilm A 0377 SS officers, Guntram Pflaum file, Himmler to Lorenz and Heydrich 11 July 1941, note on order of 16 Aug. 1941; B. Klieger, *Der Weg, dem wir gingen. Reportage einer höllischen Reise* (Brussels, 1960), 28–9.

[24] T. Seela, *Bücher und Bibliotheken in Nationalsozialistischen Konzentrationslagern. Das gedruckte Wort im antifaschistischen Widerstand der Häftlinge* (Munich, 1992), 147; B. Klieger, *Der Weg, den wir gingen*, 33.

control on 10 January 1945 when Auschwitz was in its final gasps.[25] Pflaum had power over all pest control products with the exception of Zyklon, which required the permission of the Reichsarzt SS with powers delegated to Mrugowsky's Hygiene Institute.[26] Detested by Peters, the unqualified but energetic Pflaum represented the threat of an SS takeover of pest control: the expert engineer and manager loathed the clothes cleaner who played his SS links for all that he was worth.

The irony about Pflaum's pest control office in Auschwitz is that Jewish prisoners shaped the concept of the parasite which was disseminated to the SS. The prisoners used German medical texts. Bernhard Klieger found the *Schädlingskommando* a not too unpleasant niche, when placed in charge of producing pest control propaganda for the SS. He produced jingles warning about the rapid spread of insects. The Jews working for Pflaum became known in the camp as the *Schädlinge*—a mark of distinction among the prisoners.[27]

Delousing aroused conflicts among researchers, Nazi high-ups, ideological fanatics, and maverick entrepreneurs. The medical research establishment was outraged at the prevalence of 'quack' typhus remedies. Hitler favoured an anti-louse powder, and alerted his physician, Theo Morell, about the typhus hazard during the winter of 1941–2. By February 1942 Morell developed a foul-smelling powder, Russla, derived from potassium xanthogenate. The business boomed with Wehrmacht contracts gained with the Führer's intervention, until tests in March 1944 showed the powder to be ineffective. The British tested samples of Russla powder captured in North Africa in July 1943, and reached an unfavourable verdict. Morell was indignant at the links between German companies and the Swiss in manufacturing the rival anti-louse powder, DDT. Morell counter-attacked by attempting to culture penicillin in his laboratory.[28]

In January 1943 the Committee for *Raumentwesung und Seuchengefahr* praised the virtues of a new German product for impregnating underwear known as Delicia.[29] Rose took a lead in disseminating knowledge about its efficacy at the opening of the Behring Institute Lemberg.[30] But by 1944 military medical officers

[25] BDC May file, Pflaum to Brandt from Auschwitz 2, 29 Dec. 1944; Brandt to Pflaum 26 Jan. 1945; Wulf, *Tropeninstitut*, 147 concerning the invitation to Zumpt of the Abteilung für Schädlingsbekämpfung of the Hamburg Institute for Tropical Medicine.

[26] BA-MA H 20/929 Instructions of 14 June 1944 concerning the Referat für Schädlingsbekämpfung der Waffen-SS und Polizei in (9a) Auschwitz 2/O.S.

[27] Pflaum, *Schädlinge*, 28–30.

[28] BA-MA H20/518 Bormann report 31 Dec. 1943–15 May 1944; D. Irving (ed.), *Adolf Hitler: The Medical Diaries. The Private Diaries of Dr Theo Morell* (London, 1983), 76–8; PRO AVIA 42/63 British Central Scientific Office, Antilouse preparations, 1942–5, Busvine 12 July 1943. On penicillin see BA-MA H20/857 note of 27 June 1944 by Heeres-Sanitäts-Inspektion wanting a report. For Morell's interest in culturing penicillin see letters of 18 Jan., 19 and 25 Apr. 1944; H 20/ 837 for penicillin as a military research priority 24 Aug. 1944; Deichmann, *Biologen*, 102–4.

[29] W. Christiansen, H. Kemper, G. Peters, *et al.*, *Richtlinien für die zweckentsprechende Auswahl von Mitteln, Apparaten und Verfahren zur Entwesung* (Frankfurt, 1943), 17.

[30] G. Rose, 'Fortschritte in der Bekämpfung der Kleiderlaus', *Reichsgesundheitsblatt*, 18 (1943), 53–7; W. Freyberg, 'Über ein neues Verfahren zur unmittelbaren und prophalyktischen Läusebekämpfung mit dem Stoffimprägniermittel "Delicia-Läusepräparat"', *Zeitschrift für hygienische Zoologie*, 36 (1944), 17–23.

conceded that soldiers disliked Delicia as causing skin irritations, and so the Military Medical Academy supported the introduction of another patent insecticide, the DDT-based Lauseto. Delicia was left to the civilians.[31]

Although Geigy struck deals with the pharmaceutical conglomerates Schering and IG-Farben, DDT production was limited in Germany. Rose and Mrugowsky supported the German contacts with Geigy during 1942, leading to acquisition of two DDT-derived products, Gesarol (patented in Germany in November 1943 and used for spraying) and Neocid powder. These were tested on insects in Termjuk in the Caucasus, by Mühlens in Greece, and by the special aerial forestry corps, which loomed large in plans for biological warfare. DDT-derived products included 'Gix' (an anti-louse fluid), 'Lauseto' (produced by Schering under licence from Geigy), 'Duolit', and 'Multocid', some of these being markedly different in chemical composition from the Geigy products. Intensive research was conducted on their composition, concentration, and effects, and the Allies avidly tested captured samples. The Germans failed to develop a cost-effective product for impregnating clothing, whereas the Allies successfully applied DDT to the underwear and uniforms of the liberating armies. The Germans became bogged down in resolving complex scientific issues, which the Allies ignored, including whether insects developed resistance to the use of DDT, and how to treat skin irritation resulting from handling DDT or wearing chemically impregnated clothing.[32]

The German medical lobby favouring DDT failed to achieve a breakthrough in its deployment. In February 1944 at a lecture in Basle, Rose considered that tests on impregnation of clothing were so successful that mass use of DDT should be a priority. Rose welcomed the DDT products as they showed up delousing installations as too costly, laborious, requiring too much in the way of technical equipment, and too static to control infected populations. He envisaged massive laundries for impregnation of clothing or that DDT could be distributed so that everyone could be responsible for their own protection. Medical researchers dreamt of DDT as finally eradicating typhus in 'under-civilized' areas on a cheap and simple basis; instead of an endless campaign against chronic infestation, any epidemic could be rapidly halted.[33]

German publicity for DDT began in earnest only in 1944.[34] In May 1944 at the fourth conference of military medical experts, held at the SS sanatorium of Hohen-

[31] BA-MA H 20/754 Generalarzt Prof. Dr Schreiber, Kommandeur der Lehrgruppe C der Militärärztliche Akademie; Bericht über meine Dienstreise zur Besichtigung von Lauseto-Entlausungseinrichtungen in der Wehrkreisen XX u XXI. Reisedauer 4. bis 7.10.1944.

[32] BAK R 86/ 3961 on reports of Gesarol tests. W. Reichmuth, 'Neuere Ergebnisse und Probleme der Schädlingsbekämpfung', Rodenwaldt, *et al.*, *FIAT Review of German Science 1939–1946. Hygiene*, pt. II, *Preventive and Industrial Medicine* (Wiesbaden, 1948), 35–57; PRO AVIA 42/64 Impregnated Clothing, Woodward to King 19 May 1944 for report on Lauseto, details were passed to the US on 27 May 1944; BNI Rose I file, Mrugowsky to Rose 16 May 1942.

[33] G. Rose, 'Fortschritte in der Bekämpfung des Läuse-Fleckfiebers', *Acta Tropica*, 1 (1944), 193–218.

[34] For a German reference to the Swiss patent see 'Patentschau', *Zeitschrift für hygienische Zoologie*, 36 (1944), 79.

lychen, DDT was high on the agenda. Handloser, the chief military medical officer, observed that after successful pilot schemes deploying new chemical products at the front, it was necessary to draw up guidelines concerning routine practices. However, the experts were divided. Rose compared the Swiss DDT product, Gesarol, and the German product, Gix, declaring with apocalyptic zeal that a new age was about to dawn with the 'systematic extermination of typhus'. The tropical medicine expert Rodenwaldt and the eugenicist Lenz were sceptics: they considered that evidence of mounting insect resistance meant that 'these new weapons' needed to be supplemented by traditional delousing procedures.[35] May aimed to develop an insecticide to exterminate mosquitoes, which needed not to be poisonous for humans and as specific as possible for mosquitoes so that the other flora and fauna would be protected.[36] These aims suggest dissatisfaction with DDT. Eyer, in charge of military typhus control and vaccines, also campaigned against the use of DDT.[37]

Rose's schemes were to be frustrated. By October 1944 the Germans managed to achieve only limited impregnation of clothing with DDT. Delousing became ever more chaotic. When the delousing stations in the east were inspected—for example, at Graudenz, Thorn, and Marienburg, which had been in service since the turn of the century—the military medical officer Schreiber noted that the lack of drying rooms meant that soldiers were handed back clothing which was impregnated but soaking wet.[38] Although the Germans were in principle keen on airborn spraying to eradicate mosquitoes, regular spraying was deemed to be impractical with the erosion of German airpower. By 1944 the problems in organizing large-scale production and distribution of DDT were insurmountable.[39]

The Germans clung to the regimented systems of disinfection and isolation, and had much faith in the use of highly toxic chemicals and the police round-ups of infected civilians. By comparison, the Allies were way ahead of the Germans in production of DDT, and had a record of disliking hydrocyanide. Ironically, the Germans showed greater awareness of the toxicity of DDT, problems of acquired resistance, and the ecological hazards of its deployment. Although the Allies could be criticized as naïve and over-hasty in their adoption of DDT, its use made sense for the immediate circumstances of the war. The Germans continued to deploy Zyklon for disinfection, and the labour-intensive louse-gut based vaccine. Tragically, at a time when Zyklon became outdated in scientific and field use, it became the prime means for perpetrating genocide.

[35] *Bericht über die 4. Arbeitstagung der Beratenden Ärzte vom 16. bis 18. Mai 1944 im SS-Lazarett Hohenlychen* (n.p., n.d.), 159–69, 185–9.

[36] BDC May file, May to Reichsforschungsrat, 31 Mar. 1944.

[37] NAW USATC Interrogation of Rose 25–26 June 1943.

[38] BA-MA H20/754 Generalarzt Prof Dr Schreiber. Bericht über meine Dienstreise zur Besichtigung von Lauseto-Entlausungseinrichtigungen in der Wehrkreisen XX u. XXI. Reisedauer 4. bis 7 Oct. 1944.

[39] H. Vondra, 'Die Malaria—ihre Problematik und Erforschung in Heer und Luftwaffe', Guth, *Sanitätswesen*, 109–26; NAW USATC, Interrogation of Rose by Bayne-Jones, 22 Mar. 1946.

ii. Biological Warfare

Nazi notions of medicine can be conceptualized as a massive process of biological warfare: vaccination and disease control, the bid to eradicate Bolshevism and world Jewry, and attempts to promote Germanic racial welfare were all integral to the cosmic racial struggle. Ironically, the development of biological warfare remained stunted. For in practice biological warfare showed neither coherence nor consistency, because what Hitler meant by defensive biological warfare measures remained unclear. As in other areas of epidemic control, experts clashed over biological weapons, and the vaccination and germ warfare programmes became linked.

German advocates of germ warfare hoped to paralyse the enemy by artificially inducing an epidemic. Humans, cattle, crops, and water reservoirs were potential targets for such a knock-out blow. Yet immense practical difficulties surrounded the storage and dissemination of pathogenic micro-organisms. Heinrich Kliewe, a former student of Gotschlich transferred his interests from disinfection to biological warfare. He believed that the Germans could control naturally occurring epidemics, enabling them to induce diseases among the enemy: 'The fear that Europe, especially Germany will be more and more menaced by the plague, is exaggerated. If orderly conditions prevail, every focus of plague can be shut off and rendered ineffective.'[40]

Leading figures in biological warfare profoundly disagreed over theoretical approaches to epidemiology. Mrugowsky opposed the biological weapons programme, because his holistic epidemiology pointed to the sheer difficulty of inducing an epidemic, which would not backfire on the Germans. Kliewe had no such academic qualms—he saw the spread of an infection as unproblematic. Kurt Blome, the Deputy Reich Physicians' Führer, engaged in experimental cancer research (his ostensible field of research), while taking charge of germ warfare. Yet far from the naïve enthusiasm of Kliewe, his scepticism was shaped by the geographical epidemiology derived from Pettenkofer.[41] Paradoxically, the epidemiological complexities of geo-medicine curbed the will to launch a biological warfare offensive.

Germ warfare specialists constructed a self-contained history to legitimate their shadowy sphere of operations. Kliewe reported that during the First World War retreating troops were accused of poisoning wells and that there were sporadic schemes (as in Bucharest during 1916) to infect horses and cattle with glanders or foot and mouth cultures. It was all too easy for malicious accusations of conspiratorial sabotage to be spread as the cause of an epidemic. The Russians attributed the outbreak of cholera on the Eastern Front in 1915 to the Germans

[40] NAW Records of the Surgeon General (Army), Biological Warfare, Specialised Files (= RG 112/ 295A/ Box 10 Current Intelligence, Kliewe report, 14 Aug. 1943, p. 64).
[41] F. Blome, *Arzt im Kampf—Erlebnisse und Gedanken* (Leipzig, 1942); F. Hansen, *Biologische Kriegsführing im Dritten Reich* (Frankfurt/M., 1993), 148–9.

poisoning wells, and the Germans accused the retreating Russians of similar acts. Indeed, the influenza epidemic of 1918–19 was blamed on the deliberate German spread of the 'influenza bacillus'—ironic, since most German bacteriologists mistakenly believed that influenza was spread by a bacterium discovered by Richard Pfeiffer in 1891.[42] In 1916 a German military medical officer, Dr Winter, proposed dropping glass balloons of plague bacilli from airships in order to infect rat populations in the port of London. The plan was rejected by the medical staff of the German high command: Winter blamed Jews, Roman Catholics, freemasons, and socialists for thwarting his 'heroic deed'.[43] By the 1930s germ warfare came to enjoy a semi-mythical status, as the horror lingered of some deadly disease being scattered from the skies over the cities of Europe.

Medical experts of the League of Nations had reassuringly agreed that bacteriological warfare was an impossibility, and Germany had signed the Geneva convention in 1925, which banned offensive biological warfare. But the Germans adopted a double standard: during the same year in a report for the Reich Army Ministry, the bacteriologist and pioneer of typhus vaccination, Otto, considered that it might be possible to induce localized epidemics, whereas the military medical officer Reimer hoped to unleash a catastrophe on the scale of the Hamburg cholera epidemic of 1892.[44] British journalists pointed an accusatory finger at Germany, suggesting that since at least the late 1920s—and certainly since 1931—there were biological warfare programmes with Soviet involvement. The Japanese also began secret biological warfare projects during the 1930s, but on lines independent from the Germans.[45] The British founded in 1936 a Biological Warfare Sub-committee of the Committee of Imperial Defence, involving leading bacteriologists. British intelligence in 1936 recorded how the Soviet stockpiles of plague bacilli spurred the Germans to form a group for experimental studies of biological defence at the Reich Health Office. The British Sub-committee for Bacteriological Warfare secured detailed information on a German course laid on for bacteriologists to prepare for defensive measures.[46] German secret agents were accused of preparing to poison the airducts of the Paris metro in 1933, counting colonies of airborne bacteria at the metro station of Pasteur, and Rose claimed to have caused infections in Poland in 1932. The evidence was reviewed by Kliewe in July 1941, accepting the efficacy of sabotage using

[42] NAW Records of the Surgeon General (Army), Biological Warfare, Specialised Files (= RG 112/ 295A/ Box 10 Current Intelligence, Kliewe report, 23 July 1941, pp. 7–14); R. de Flers, *Sur les chemins de la guerre* (Paris, 1919). On Pfeiffer's bacillus see Crosby, *Pandemic*, 269–81.

[43] NAW Records of the Surgeon General (Army), Biological Warfare, Specialised Files (= RG 112/ 295A/ Box 10 Current Intelligence, Winter, 'Reflections on the Pros and Cons of Bacterial Warfare', 56–63) Comment by Kliewe 14 Aug. 1943, pp. 63–4; L. Georges, *L'Arme bactériologique. Future concurrente des armes chimique et balistique. Tentatives allemandes répétées de son emploi de 1914 à 1918* (Paris, 1922).

[44] F. Hansen, *Biologische Kriegsführung im Dritten Reich* (Frankfurt/M., 1993), 38–42.

[45] S. H. Harris, *Factories of Death. Japan's Secret Biological Warfare Projects in Manchuria and China 1932–1945* (London, 1993); Hansen, *Biologische Kriegsführung*, 43–6.

[46] PRO WO 188/650.

glanders bacillus and of other activities of German secret agents between the First and Second World Wars.[47]

Throughout the Second World War the spectre lurked of a deadly type of biological warfare: all sorts of scenarios were foreseen involving release of disease-infested animal vectors like rats or of bombs containing breakable glass capsules filled with a cocktail of lethal germs. The ideal was that the attackers should unleash a disease for which they possessed an effective vaccine but which the other side did not have. Various offensive and defensive strategies were developed: in marked contrast to the exterminatory policies against civilian populations, the German armed forces only teetered on the brink of germ warfare. Yet the mentality surrounding germ warfare linked disease control with genocide.[48]

From the 1920s onwards the Soviets were rumoured to be building up immense stockpiles of chemical and biological weapons. The tensions surrounding the departure of Zeiss from the Soviet Union are revealing of a psychosis of terror concerning epidemic subversion. While the Germans feared 'Asiatic' epidemics, the Soviet authorities were concerned about epidemics from the west—in that German medical experts might unleash germ warfare. Zeiss complained of 'Asiatic insults' when the new health commissar accused him of developing a strain of the plague-like tularemia for germ warfare.[49]

In June 1943 Zeiss commented on documents captured by German intelligence, concerning a Soviet accusation made in May 1941 that he had used his time in the Soviet Union to plan bacteriological warfare. The Soviet secret service accused the German Red Cross expedition of 1921–4 of providing a cover for organizing a counter-revolutionary network of bacterial saboteurs based in hygiene institutes. Soviet intelligence denounced a network of forty-eight microbiologists for sabotage, and disseminating typhus, cholera, and paratyphoid germs. The outbreaks of gut and stomach diseases in the USSR between 1931 and 1939 gave substance to these accusations, as well as tularemia outbreaks between 1939 and 1941. The Soviet security watchdogs denounced Japanese attempts to deploy typhus germs in 1936 and Polish microbiologists at Lemberg for preparing to spread paratyphoid.[50] Zeiss replied that some of the researchers accused of being part of his subversive network were communists and Jews and one was a Pole, and these were his greatest opponents. However, a couple of those accused were indeed his good friends and the pharmacologist, Oskar Awgustowitsch Steppun, was an ethnic German who had studied in Heidelberg.[51]

The fear of alien scientists unleashing subversive germ warfare likewise gripped the Nazi authorities. At the Berlin Hygiene Institute, Jewish medical researchers

---

[47] W. Steed, 'Aerial Warfare: Secret German Plans', *The Nineteenth Century and After*, 106 (1934), 1–15; id, 'The Future of Warfare', ibid., 129–40; NAW Records of the Surgeon General (Army), Biological Warfare, Specialised Files (= RG 112/ 295A/ Box 10 Current Intelligence, Kliewe report, pp. 7–14, 48. This report formed the basis of Bayle, *Croix gammée*, 930–78.

[48] PRO WO 188/681, report by Roger Briault, Paris.

[49] AHUB Medical faculty 12a Zeiss file, Bl. 87–94, 17 June 1943.

[50] Ibid. Original dated 23 May 1941 signed V. Merkulov, Peoples Commissar of State Security, 3rd degree.

[51] AHUB Medical Faculty 12a Zeiss file, Bl. 46 response of Zeiss dated 17 June 1943.

were denounced in March 1933 for plotting germ warfare. A Nazi activist in the Institute, Dr Heide raised the alarm that Jewish researchers had unrestricted access to cultures of plague, cholera, and typhus. The Education Ministry undertook to secure all biological material in universities, restricting access to 'reliable persons'.[52] Zeiss could claim to be such a person, and he was appointed institute director. Anti-Semitism was reinforced by notions of Jews as sources of germs. In Hamburg, the Nazi harbour doctor condemned the Jewish transit hostels as epidemic hazards, and imposed daily inspections.[53] The Nazi authorities gave a new lease of life to the medieval prejudice against Jews as poisoners of wells.

German fears of bacterial sabotage increased during the war. The Germans blamed epidemics of typhoid in Poland on Polish agents—believing that there was a central laboratory distributing bacteria throughout Poland. SS doctors accused Poles of poisoning high-ranking Germans by recruiting waiters to add lethal bacteria to their meals or adulterating furniture polish.[54] Similarly, typhoid in Paris was attributed to French saboteurs. The epidemics arising from brutal occupation could be conveniently ascribed to the already victimized population.[55]

The Germans were convinced that the Soviets might use their stockpiles of chemical weapons against them, prompting Hitler to warn the Reichstag, 'Whoever fights with poison gas will be fought with poison gas'.[56] The Germans initially made defence against chemical weapons a priority. Given the ruthless perversion of disinfection technology in the Holocaust, and the readiness to undertake human experiments, the reluctance to develop offensive germ warfare appears inconsistent. For typhus served an exterminatory purpose, as it decimated the inhabitants of ghettos and camps. Moreover, the Germans feared bacteriological attacks, and were convinced that the Americans, British, and Russians were working together on a chemical offensive. In December 1942 the Epidemic Combat Commission accused the Russians of having a substantial germ warfare programme with three large-scale centres for research and testing. The Germans had a report from an agent, Dr Skrymnik, who had supposedly worked at a 'Biochemical Institute' at Vlatshisha near Moscow between 1936 and 1938, and who maintained that this was really a chemical warfare station. During the war, deserters and captured personnel provided further information: one told of Soviet experiments in Mongolia using pneumonic and bubonic plague bacteria, suggesting—in a macabre parallel to the Holocaust—that people in the locality were subsequently shot or killed with hydrocyanic acid.[57]

[52] BAP 49.01 Reichserziehungsministerium Nr 1368 Hygienisches Institut 1929–1938, Bl. 94, 97 Landeskriminalamt to Preussische Ministerium für Wissenschaft 20 Mar. 1933, and reply of 2 May 1933.

[53] STAH II F6 Bd III Wolter-Peeksen (Auswandererarzt), *Bericht über das Jahr 1935* Bl. 218.

[54] NMT roll 30, frame 418 evidence of Werner Kirchert.

[55] NAW RG 112/ 295A/ Box 10 Current Intelligence, Blome interview, p. 2; Kliewe memo 16 Dec. 1942, pp. 26, 35.

[56] Cited by Spiers, *Chemical Warfare*, 62.

[57] NAW RG 112/ 295A/ Box 10 Current Intelligence, 19, 31–3. The Germans believed that there were three chief centres: under Maslokovich in Leningrad, Nikanorov at Lakes Seliger and Aral, and Klimoshinsky in Moscow and Mongolia.

Alarmed at discovering French installations for germ warfare, in January 1941 the German High Command allocated laboratories for biological research to Kliewe at the Military Medical Academy in Berlin. This marked the beginning of the German biological warfare programme. Kliewe was a bacteriologist and expert on disinfection, who had from 1928 directed the bacteriological laboratory of the state of Hessen, as well as the state disinfectors school, publishing a standard manual on disinfection procedures. In 1933 he joined the NSDAP.[58] From 1939 he served at the Military Medical Academy Berlin in the department of hygiene, and was dispatched to the bacteriological laboratories of Cracow, Danzig, and Warsaw, and finally to inspect French laboratories in 1940. His ardour for germ warfare contrasted with the scepticism of many more eminent bacteriologists, and so the programme devolved to a disinfection specialist of low-grade academic status. A panel of bacteriologists and virologists evaluated evidence of French germ warfare research: they consulted the Institutes for Experimental Therapy at Frankfurt and Marburg, the bacteriologists Otto and Zeiss, as well as the Behringwerke manager Demnitz, who were all involved in anti-typhus measures. Zeiss provided information on the preparations of the Russians for biological warfare. In 1941 the Behringwerke offered to supply Kliewe with plague and tularemia bacilli. Yet, overall the opinion of leading bacteriologists was that this form of warfare was impracticable.[59]

The biological warriors were confronted with the Herculean task of how to induce a large-scale epidemic. Assuming that once released, bacteria would inexorably spread, germ warfare enthusiasts ignored fundamental issues of the transmission and process of infection, and variations in virulence. They considered using plague strains, and searched for suitable vaccines for their own side. Kliewe carried out field experiments when he failed to spread bacteria using aerosol sprays; atomizers were supplied by the Vichy state concerned about a possible biological offensive from England. He considered spreading epidemics by dropping glass or metal canisters filled with bacteria; anthrax spores or the foot-and-mouth virus might be dried on hay or mixed into animal feed. The possibility of a deadly combination of poison gas and bacteria was contemplated. It was also necessary to defend crops against an expected British air drop of Colorado beetles, or of infected potato tubers. Agriculturalists experimented on fast-growing weeds that could choke crops. In response to the Colorado beetle scare, the Ahnenerbe research division of the SS ordered its entomological laboratory to prepare defensive measures.[60]

Frenetic research activity was generated by anticipated Allied use of poison gas. Gas warfare manuals dealt extensively with detoxifying measures. This might be

    [58] H. Kliewe, *Leitfaden der Entseuchung und Entwesung* (Stuttgart, 1937); Hansen, *Biologische Kriegsführung*, 83–7.
    [59] NAW RG 112/ 295A/ Box 10 Current Intelligence, ALSOS Report, pp. 6, 129, concerning Zeiss; Bayle, *Croix gammée*, 935.
    [60] NAW RG 112/ 295A/ Box 10 Current Intelligence, pp. 14–15, 20–23; Kliewe report, Berlin 28 Jan. 1943, pp. 29, 41. Stubbe of the KWG conducted the weed experiments; see BW report, p. 105; concerning Blome and the SS, pp. 108–10; concerning atomizers, p. 121; Blome interrogation, pp. 17–18.

interpreted in defensive terms, but given that the Germans were deploying poison gas against civilians, the safety of the perpetrators was a priority.[61] While Hitler only reversed his opposition to gas warfare late in 1944, the question arises whether his strategic caution was deliberate: he might have wished to maintain the secrecy of the stockpiles of nerve gas, bombs, and shells in order not to arouse Allied concern or indeed provoke reprisals. Or he might have intended that the deployment of hydrocyanic acid in the Holocaust should not be disrupted by the gas manufacturing plants and installations being classed as significant strategic targets. Military historians have tended to treat the history of German gas and biological warfare preparations in purely strategic terms without drawing any links to the uses of the same poisons in the Holocaust. While such approaches reflect the lack of concern with the Holocaust among Allied military strategists during the war, the German linkages should not be overlooked.[62]

The reasons for Hitler's reticence about biological weapons are obscure. Certain German medical officials did not take biological warfare seriously, as Reich Medical Führer Conti or Bieber, the RMdI administrator concerned with anti-typhus measures. The reluctance to unleash gas warfare hampered preparations for biological warfare. Hitler's prioritizing of pest control could be interpreted as having human extermination in mind, particularly because of the transfer of eradication methods from animal to human pests. Maintaining the secrecy of the Final Solution may have meant tactical caution in mounting any biological or poison gas military offensives. It was possible for the British intelligence to note the increased activity at the Ludwigshafen chemical plant producing the lethal carbon monoxide canisters, but no links were made to euthanasia or the mass killings of Jews.[63]

There were, however, sinister German projects. In 1936 an IG-Farben insecticide researcher, Gerhard Schrader, discovered a deadly nerve gas, tabun. In 1938 Schrader discovered an even more poisonous compound, which he named sarin. Between 1940 and 1943 an immense factory was built at Dyhernfurth near Breslau in Silesia to produce nerve gas shells, resulting in horrific accidents and poisoning of the workforce, but nurturing the hope that the stockpiles of shells might be Hitler's victory weapon. Yet operationalizing sarin was mercifully paralyzed by the dictatorial command structure, and hesitations in deploying a weapon with unforeseen consequences.[64]

In May 1942 Hitler ordered that biological warfare was to be defensive, and that German research should concentrate on combating biological pests. In any case Field Marshall Wilhelm Keitel and fellow generals in the High Command found biological warfare distasteful. The cooperation between the various medical, veterinary, agricultural, and military agencies—linked under the codename 'Blitzarbeiter' in early 1943—was only sporadic. The chief military medical officer,

[61] Oberkommando der Wehrmacht, *Kampfstoffverletzungen* (Berlin, 1943), pp. 29–31.
[62] Spiers, *Chemical Warfare.*   [63] Ibid., 67–8.
[64] Harris and Paxman, *A Higher Form of Killing*, 53–6; Spiers, *Chemical Warfare*, 5–6. For British tests on 'saran' see PRO AVIA 42/64 British Central Scientific Office, Impregnated Clothing, 13 Sept. 1943, Buxton to Taylor.

Handloser, objected that the chemical warfare division of the Army Ordnance Office had gained the upper hand in the new organization.[65] In March 1943 Hitler's tone became more aggressive: he ordered scientists to 'complete defensive measures against the enemy use of bacteria with all possible zeal and to hold the means of defense in easy readiness'. The germ warfare personnel argued: 'In order to give suitable protective regulations, the enemy's technique of introduction must be tested. Therefore the experiments planned are not at variance with the Führer's order.'[66] This crypto-offensive strategy involved elaborate measures, although deployment was curbed. The German advocates of biological warfare felt that the Führer was badly advised. They considered defensive measures could only be successful if there was offensive research.[67] Given that the Führer had only restricted attacks with germs targeting humans, the biological warriors supported animal disease offensives from June 1942. Yet here what could be undertaken was limited. For the danger was that experimental trials of a virulent micro-organism (such as rinderpest) might contaminate German livestock.[68]

In 1942 Zeiss became Kliewe's superior at the department of hygiene of the Military Medical Academy, and he attained at least nominal control of biological warfare research facilities, although in practice Kliewe worked under the army with some links to Mrugowsky's institute and the security services. In December 1942 Kliewe attempted to reverse the hostility of the German Chief of General Staff to biological warfare by arguing that the Russians were preparing to unleash plague bacteria—the only evidence being that they held stocks of anti-plague serum and vaccine.[69] Kliewe conjured up all sorts of dastardly scenarios by saboteurs in order to magnify the threat of a biological offensive against the Germans. He reported on the placing of louse excrement in wardrobes, and in gifts of sweets or cigarettes to soldiers so as to induce typhus, and that poisons, strong medicines, and typhoid bacilli were slipped into drinks or injected into eggs. Lengthy catalogues were compiled of incidents of sabotage resulting in mysterious illnesses and of acts of resistance by barbers, kitchen maids and medical personnel in Russia, Poland, and France. For example, in July 1943 the Germans claimed to have found evidence that Ukrainian saboteurs caused typhoid outbreaks in a Kiev military hospital.[70] The Germans considered exchanging prisoners of war who had been given an infected meal, and so producing an epidemic of cholera, but rejected the plan on grounds of practicality.[71]

---

[65] NAW RG 112/ 295A/ Box 10 Current Intelligence, Alsos Report, pp. 12, 20–1, 115–16. See also RG 330 German BW Organisation. Deichmann, *Biologen*, 213; Hansen, *Biologische Kriegsführung*, 158–61.

[66] NAW RG 112/ 295A/ Box 10 Current Intelligence, 39–40.

[67] Ibid., 20 Aug. 1945, H. I. Cole to G. Merck, Final Résumé of German BW Activities, pp. 121–2 concerning Bieber and Conti.

[68] NAW RG 112/ 295A/ Box 10 Current Intelligence, p. 50.

[69] Ibid., Kliewe memo, 16 Dec. 1942, p. 26; Hansen, *Biologische Kriegsführung*, 87.

[70] NAW RG 112/ 295A/ Box 10 Current Intelligence, Würfler memo, 23 Sept. 1943, pp. 73–4.

[71] Ibid., Kliewe memo, 3 May 1943, pp. 44, 62–3; 'Protective and defensive measures against sabotage activity with bacteria', 5 Sept. 1943, pp. 69–70, 82–3.

Scientific problems compounded the organizational difficulties: despite all the rhetoric concerning the 'Jewish virus' and the take-off of virus research, bacteriologists debated what a virus actually was. These medical uncertainties meant that deliberate contamination was problematic as it was not always known exactly what the infective agent was and how, as in the case of foot-and-mouth disease, it might be spread. Kliewe held a meeting in March 1943 with the chemical warfare section of the Army Ordnance Office; scientific difficulties over whether viruses were organisms or chemical bodies impeded offensive schemes. Scientists debated how the foot-and-mouth virus could be bound to chopped straw, and whether isolated cases of a disease could develop into an epidemic remained problematic. Knowledge of how in practice a large-scale epidemic could be induced was simply lacking. To remedy such deficiencies Blome demanded human experiments on disease causation.[72]

Blome's suggestion triggered the formation of a research group rivalling that of Kliewe and the military. Backed by Goering, the Supreme Command and Himmler, Blome was commissioned to take new initiatives on biological warfare. Blome had a classic Nazi pedigree as a veteran frontline soldier of the First World War, Freikorps fighter, and ultra-right activist. He had trained under Reiter, the Nazi Director of the Reich Health Office, and although only a Nazi Party member since 1931, his tireless right-wing activities led to his appointment as head of the German Red Cross (a position he had to cede to Grawitz because of his SA connections) and as the deputy Reich Physicians' Führer in 1939. With much reluctance General Keitel passed on details of military sponsored work on biological warfare, and allowed Blome access to Blitzarbeiter papers. Blome gained increased responsibilities in medical research; his brief of 'cancer research' provided a cover for his biological warfare activities and enabled the resources of the Reichsforschungsrat to be tapped. Work began on construction of a laboratory complex at Nesselstedt near Posen where it was integrated with the 'Reich University' in May 1944. The planned installations for biological warfare experiments incorporated a cremation furnace, indicating the intention to experiment on lethal biological materials.[73] Mrugowsky prevented Ding's transfer to Nesselstedt so as not to disrupt the Buchenwald vaccine research, and instead an SS bacteriologist, Karl Gross, was seconded in November 1943 from Mrugowsky's Hygiene Institute. Human experiments with plague bacilli were planned for defensive and offensive measures, and Gross experimented on prisoners at Mauthausen. When the SS official Sievers in December 1944 visited Gross at Nesselstedt in December 1944, he raised possibilities for collaboration with the entomologist May at Dachau, and shortly afterwards contacted Mrugowsky. However, the building of Nesselstedt was never completed, and Blome suspected Gross of deliberately putting off the start of the dangerous

---

[72] NAW RG 112/ 295A/ Box 10 Current Intelligence, Kliewe memo 16 Dec. 1942, pp. 37–8, 49, memo 24 Nov. 1943, p. 72.
[73] Hansen, *Biologische Kriegsführung*, 178–9.

plague work.[74] After the war Blome vehemently denied that any of the planned human experiments had ever taken place.[75]

The SS favoured an offensive approach to biological and chemical warfare. Blome consulted with Himmler on at least five occasions. Himmler's interest in biological weapons was aroused by the killing of Heydrich with a hand grenade infected with botulism bacterium.[76] Himmler offered concentration camp facilities for plague research, and obtained a strain of rinderpest virus (which turned out to be non-virulent). While Himmler hoped in 1944 that a major epidemic could delay the Allied invasion forces, in practice the SS had committed hardly any resources to such a programme.[77] Himmler, as an erstwhile agriculturalist and fertilizer salesman, appreciated the dangers of crop parasites like grain rust and Colorado beetles, which could exterminate food plants. SS experts—Blome, Sievers, and May—established that Germany lacked insecticides for routine use, so that in the event of major enemy sabotage reserves were unavailable. Blome backed May's scheme of inducing a malaria epidemic by unleashing hordes of malarial mosquitoes in an enemy held region.[78]

Attempts by the SS to establish links with the massive Japanese biological warfare programmes failed. In 1944 Himmler encouraged preparation of arsenic-free and organic insecticides that would not be toxic for humans or animals (DDT seems to have been placed in the non-toxic category). A young SS officer from the Munich Hygiene Institute, Horst Strassburger, urged Himmler to sponsor a plan which involved plague-infested rats swimming ashore from submarines. This was the reverse scenario of a German scare that the Allies were to unleash plague-infested rats by dropping them in containers attached to parachutes. Blome's experiments showed that rats had no idea where the shore might be, and that many drowned, and the bacteriologist Rose was also sceptical. Infighting and the low calibre of the involved personnel meant that the Germans were never in a position to undertake a major offensive using biological weapons.[79]

Mrugowsky drew up defence measures against epidemics. He had advised Grawitz and Himmler in 1939 that a biological offensive was not practicable;

[74] NAW RG 112/ 295A/ Box 10 Current Intelligence, US Alsos Report on German Biological Warfare (by Barnes, Cromartie, Henze, and Hofer), introduction, pp. 12–16; Blome interrogation, 30 July 1945, pp. 3–8; NAW microfilm 1019/roll 47 Mrugowsky interrogation 17 Oct. 1946, p. 8; on Blome see Hansen, *Biologische Kriegsführung*, 52–69; on Poznań see B. Piotrowski, *W Służbie Rasizmu i Bezprawia. 'Uniwersytet Rzeszy' w Poznaniu 1941–1945* (Poznań, 1984); Boston University, Alexander Papers, Box 58 Sievers diary, entries for 17, 19 Dec. 1944.

[75] Klee, *Auschwitz*, 90–1.

[76] Harris and Paxman, *A Higher Form of Killing*, 116; Hansen, *Biologische Kriegsführung*, 144.

[77] NAW RG 112/ 295A/ Box 10 Current Intelligence, US Alsos Report on German Biological Warfare (by Barnes, Cromartie, Henze, and Hofer), introduction, pp. 12–16; Blome interrogation, 30 July 1945, pp. 3–8, 13.

[78] BDC Eduard May files. Deichmann, *Biologen*, 219–22.

[79] NAW RG 112/ 295A/ Box 10 Current Intelligence, US Alsos Report on German Biological Warfare (by Barnes, Cromartie, Henze, and Hofer), 108–10, concerning Blome pp. 121, 131–2; Hansen, *Biologische Kriegsführung*, 155–7.

because the laws of how an epidemic spread were unknown, a germ warfare offensive might backfire. This report was said to have shaped Hitler's scruples concerning biological weapons. Mrugowsky's concerns were evident in that some of the Waffen-SS Hygiene Institute's activities were to counter enemy offensive action in poisoning water supplies. In August 1944 Grawitz sent Himmler another report by Mrugowsky on measures to counter a germ warfare attack.[80]

Kliewe resented the division of authority between biological warfare groups.[81] In September 1943 he pressed for a new initiative to alert the Führer to the urgency of a large-scale German bacteriological offensive that would include an attack on the United States.[82] The gravity of the situation dragged epidemiologists into the murky sphere of biological warfare: Kliewe consulted top medical officials, notably Conti, as well as the aged Heidelberg emeritus in bacteriology, Gotschlich, and the ubiquitous Hase with the aim of establishing a new scientific grouping for biological warfare.[83]

On the Eastern Front German bacteriologists tested germ-bearing powders in explosive canisters: initially typhus rickettsiae were deployed, and it was planned to spray rickettsiae of Rocky Mountain Spotted Fever, or to disseminate them by canisters in bombs and rockets.[84] Blome considered that the aerial corps used to spray forests in Southern Russia with DDT could disseminate pathogens and poisons.[85] But there was pessimism as to the feasibility of inducing an epidemic in Europe, because of higher levels of sanitation. Gotschlich pointed out that if water reservoirs were to be poisoned with cholera or typhoid bacteria, a disinfectant like chlorine would be an adequate safeguard.[86]

The Allies screened German prisoners of war, and collected fragmentary information about German biological warfare research. The reports were largely exaggerated, predicting that the Germans were preparing to drop over 250,000 rats infected with a cocktail of plague and typhus. By 1944 the Allies were worried that the Germans might unleash a deadly biological weapon as a final act of desperation.[87] The American verdict on German biological warfare was that the personnel was inadequate and mediocre, and that bickering, inaccurate intelligence, and

[80] NMT roll 38, frames 1112–13; roll 16, frame 983, concerning Kliewe's report 22 May 1944; frame 987, Blome's report, 18 Aug. 1944; NAW RG 112/ 295A/ Box 10 Current Intelligence, ALSOS Report, 30 Mar. 1943, p. 106, concerning Mrugowsky, pp. 123–5; Bayle, *Croix gammée*, 974–5; NAW M 1019/ roll 47 Mrugowsky interrogation, 17 Oct. 1946, pp. 11–12; Hansen, *Biologische Kriegsführung*, 82, 145–6 (re Gross). For human experiments by Gross see BAK NS 4/ Ma1–35.

[81] NAW RG 112/ 295A/ Box 10 Current Intelligence, Kliewe memo, 8 July 1943, pp. 49–50; Bayle, *Croix gammée*, 955; Hansen, *Biologische Kriegsführung*, 137–40.

[82] NAW RG 112/ 295A/ Box 10 Current Intelligence, Kliewe memo, 23 Sept. 1943, pp. 70–1.

[83] NAW RG 112/ 295A/ Box 10 Current Intelligence, Kliewe memo, 7 Oct. 1943 (re Gotschlich), 24 Oct. 1943 (re Conti) pp. 77–9; Hansen, *Biologische Kriegsführung*, 154 Groehler, *Der Lautlose Tod*, 240–2 confuses Hase with Ludwig Werner Haase, a chemist who forced prisoners at Neuengamme to drink contaminated water; Klee, *Auschwitz*, 177.

[84] NAW RG 112/ 295A/ Box 10 Current Intelligence, Information on Preparations for Biological Warfare, 18 and 27 May 1944.

[85] Ibid., 105.

[86] Hansen, *Biologische Kriegsführung*, 154.

[87] PRO WO 188/688 BW Reports, Interrogation of prisoners, 31 Oct. 1944.

petty jealousy handicapped the programme.[88] This critique can be applied to other aspects of the German medical war effort. To such structural flaws should be added a scientifically based reticence: holistic epidemiologists, who considered that the spread of disease depended on a range of geographical, social, and biological factors, were pessimistic about inducing a mass epidemic. The Germans clung to regimented delousing procedures, and to the labour-intensive louse-gut vaccine of Weigl, which was difficult to produce in adequate quantities. They lacked the ability to develop and deploy DDT; although this wonder dust was exposed as ecologically flawed in the longer term, it provided an effective means to control louse-infested populations. As the German sanitary measures became more draconian, they accelerated genocide.

[88] NAW RG 112/ 295A/ Box 10 Current Intelligence, 20 Aug. 1945, H. I. Cole to G. Merck, Final Résumé of German BW Activities.

13

Clinical Trials on Trial

i. Final Solutions

Before the War ended, allied medical experts devised stringent measures to prevent a massive 'blow up' of epidemic typhus in Germany. The French typhus expert Lemierre convinced the Americans that in the inevitable post-war chaos there was a grave risk of typhus epidemics in prisoner of war and concentration camps. These fears were offset by the Naples typhus epidemic of 1943–4, where it was claimed that mass DDT dusting had halted a major epidemic. This apparent success inspired schemes for delousing of civilians and detainees on a vast scale. The preventive measures raise issues of the values held by the victorious medical élite. The pressures of epidemics, the need for pharmaceutical products, and the onset of the Cold War all militated for indulgence toward the wartime scientific atrocities.

In November 1944 the United States of America Typhus Commission (USATC) suggested that typhus specialists should be drafted into Germany: the Commission hoped that the Germans would allow a pilot team to immunize all of the 40,000 US prisoners, and ideally British, French, and Russian prisoners as well as concentration camp internees. Part of the reciprocal deal was to immunize all German medical personnel, as there were sporadic typhus outbreaks throughout Germany. General Leon Fox, the Field Director of the USATC, was characteristically outspoken: he pleaded with the typhus supremo Bayne-Jones: 'We do not need, and I for one do not want to see a typhus epidemic in Germany. We have them whipped without it, and if it comes the ones that will suffer most are not the German criminals, but the poor devils that have been herded around in their concentration camps.'[1]

In the event, the words were prophetic. Despite such bad omens as the floods of refugees from the east, and marauding rats on bomb-sites, epidemics were localized. Typhus epidemics were mainly confined to the concentration camps, which in the final months of the war became sanitary nightmares.[2] The questions arise whether the final lethal ploy by the Germans in abandoning concentration camps without water or sanitation and thereby causing typhus to erupt could have been prevented either if the Allies or the International Committee of the Red Cross had

[1] NAW RG 112 USATC Box 33 Prisoners of War, LAF to SBJ 2 Nov. 1944, 17 Nov. 1944, Vaccination of American Typhus Prisoners in Germany. Memorandum 18 Nov. 1944; NLM Bayne Jones Papers, 'Health in Axis Europe', 30. For Fox see United Nations Archives, New York, UNRRA papers, 4/1.00.0.0.:26:13, Health Division.

[2] E. Rodenwaldt, *Ein Tropenarzt erzählt sein Leben* (Stuttgart, 1957), 464 on the role of German military units in disinfecting refugees from the east.

negotiated with the Germans. Typhus had a devastating effect on victims who were already at the margins of existence. During the final months of the war survivors of the death marches from disbanded concentration camps were accused of spreading typhus, and the arrival of wave upon wave of exhausted and famished prisoners exacerbated overcrowding in Belsen and Buchenwald. The marches were calculated killing exercises, with cold, exhaustion, hunger, diseases, and the brutal guards taking their toll.[3] Typhus even provided a pretext for continuing euthanasia after the war: at the Kaufbeuren asylum patients were found to be riddled with scabies, lice, and other vermin, and the staff attributed their final execution of a child on 29 May 1945 (33 days after US occupation) to typhus.[4]

In the winter of 1944–5 typhus epidemics erupted in the 'detention' and 'convalescent camp' of Bergen-Belsen; overcrowding, starvation, neglect of basic sanitation, and sporadic violence by the guards had transformed this into a death camp. On 12 April 1945 the commanding officer of the First German Parachute Army informed the advancing British that there were 1,500 cases of typhus in the camp consisting of 'criminals and anti-Nazis'. *The Times* reported that the Germans declared that 'the responsibility was international, in the interests of health'. The British commander agreed a truce, Himmler apparently being involved in the negotiations. The German military authorities were to place notices and white flags around the surrounding area warning of the danger of typhus. The SS were permitted to leave the camp, while Hungarian and German armed guards were to remain in place for a week before being allowed to return to their lines. The British did not enter the camp until the afternoon of 15 April, and came with only a small medical team as tending the British and German war casualties had priority.[5]

This curious episode demonstrates that even if a general agreement to assist concentration camp prisoners was not possible, localized agreements were. The Germans grossly understated the extent of typhus at Belsen, and used its presence as a shield to mask severe starvation and epidemics: the ploy kept the Allies at bay while allowing tactical troop movements, and did nothing to prevent the ravages of starvation, water shortage, and rampaging diseases. Belsen was a medical calamity, with estimates of typhus cases varying from 3,500 to 20,000—the internees were so covered with dirt, sores, scabies, and vermin that it was difficult to distinguish a typhus rash; after liberation 13,000 deaths occurred, leaving approximately 30,000 survivors. The medical horrors at this camp show how the exterminatory regime continued once the gas chambers ceased to function. Typhus was just one of a

[3] State of Israel, *The Trial of Adolf Eichmann* (Jerusalem, 1992–5), 109.

[4] H. Friedlander, *The Origins of Nazi Genocide* (Chapet Hill, NC, 1995), 162–3.

[5] CMAC RAMC 792/3/1–11. 1213/2/12 agreement between the British and German military authorities; NAW RG 112/710/box 1109, a US medical intelligence report of 13 Apr. 1944 states that three typhus hospitals were in operation, that several thousand political prisoners were held in the area, and that 'the Germans have asked that this area be declared an open zone'; 'Typhus Causes a Truce. British to Guard Prison Camp', *The Times* (14 Apr. 1945), reprinted 'On This Day', *The Times* (14 Apr. 1997); 'Belsen Concentration Camp. The Medical Services Take Over', *Lancet* (12 May 1945), 604–5; P. Kemp, 'The British Army and the Liberation of Belsen April 1945'. *Journal of Holocaust Education*, 5 (1996), 134–48.

lethal cocktail of diseases at Belsen that included 10,000 suffering from famine oedema, 20,000 cases of dysentery, and 10,000 cases of tuberculosis.[6]

The British drew up a 'plan of attack' to eradicate typhus in the camp, so that the epidemic should not spread. Troops (but not detainees) were vaccinated—and even so there were fourteen cases of typhus among the British military personnel; louse-infested barracks were burnt; mass burials were undertaken—the piles of bodies were bulldozed into pits, and the crematorium was dismantled.[7] Liberation of a camp meant imposing quarantine restrictions, so that the prisoners remained detainees. Squads equipped with dusting 'guns' organized a 'human laundry', although the frail condition of internees meant that dusting was painfully slow.[8]

Emergency relief included medical research. The haematologist Janet Vaughan led the Medical Research Council team to experiment with an intravenous hydrolosyte and with 'Amigen' (an American enzyme product). An UNRRA team also administered an experimental 'Bengal famine mixture'. Vaughan observed how the research terrified patients, who believed they were to receive a lethal injection: 'the majority of the patients were Russians, Poles, Yugoslavs, and Czechs—people with whom we had no common language, and to whom we could not explain what we were trying to do. Many of them were people who had come to regard the medical profession as men and women who came to torture rather than to heal. When we went up to our patients with a stomach tube they would curl themselves up and say 'Nicht crematorium'. We gradually realized that it had been the custom in the case of moribund patients to inject them with benzene in order to paralyze them before taking them to the crematorium. That attitude made treatment rather more difficult than it might otherwise have been.' She concluded that milk flavoured with tea or coffee would have been more appropriate than the products being tested. 'What these people require is simple nursing and frequent small feeds. They want to be washed and made comfortable.'[9] The camp inmates became in effect experimental material for nutritionists who visited the camp to evaluate feeding methods and take blood profiles before entering the starvation areas of the

---

[6] H. Lavsky, 'The Day After: Bergen-Belsen from Concentration Camp to the Centre of the Jewish Survivors in Germany', *German History*, 11 (1993), 36–59; W. F. R. Collis, 'Belsen Camp: A Preliminary Report', *British Medical Journal* (9 June 1945), 814–16; Lepscombe in *Lancet* (8 Sept. 1945); CMAC RAMC 1218/2/15 H. L. Glyn Hughes, 'German Concentration Camps—Early Measures at Belsen'; 1218/2/18 Anny Pfister, 'Memories of a Red Cross Nurse', typescript, n.d. Papers of Glyn Hughes, critical annotations on R. Barton, 'Belsen', *History of the Second World War*, 7/15 (1968), 3081–5.

[7] W. A. Davis, 'Typhus at Belsen. I. Control of the Typhus Epidemic', *American Journal of Hygiene*, 46 (1947), 66–83, also *Annals of Internal Medicine* (1951), 448–65.

[8] NAW RG 112 Box 1110, W. A. Davis, 'Typhus at Belsen', MS approved 31 Jan. 1947; Memoir of Eryl Hall Williams, 'Belsen in History and Memory', *Journal of Holocaust Education*, 5 (1996), 223.

[9] CMAC RAMC 792/3/4 Janet Vaughan, report concerning the treatment of starvation, report to the War Office and MRC, 24 May 1945; Janet Vaughan papers, Wellcome Unit for the History of Medicine, Oxford; 'Experiences of Belsen Camp', paper to the Inter-Allied Conference on Military Medicine, 4 June 1945; C. E. Dent, Rosalind Pitt Rivers, and Janet Vaughan, 'Report on the Comparative Value of Hydrolysates, Milk and Serum in the Treatment of Starvation, Based on Observations Made at Belsen Camp', Medical Research Council, Protein Requirements Committee; W. R. F. Collis, 'Belsen Camp: A Preliminary Report', *British Medical Journal* (9 June 1945), 814–16; Kemp, 'Belsen', 141.

Netherlands.[10] Vaughan realized the difficulties of her position, and some British doctors criticized such opportunistic experimentation.

The USATC conducted chemotherapeutic and clinical studies in US-liberated camps. The US army occupied Dachau on 1 May 1945, where a typhus epidemic had been raging since October 1944; faced by over 4,000 typhus cases and piles of corpses, the camp was promptly quarantined. US medical researchers tested a new drug, PABA, on the inmates, developed at the Rockefeller Foundation laboratory in 1942, and then tried in Egypt; there followed disagreement among researchers as to the therapeutic value of their chemotherapeutic arsenal.[11] The camps provided opportunities too good to miss for clinical research on confined populations. In defence, it could be pointed out (for there were virtually no criticisms at the time) that given that there was medical doubt as to how best to save the lives of starving and diseased populations, some trial and error was permissible. Yet military medical authorities sought to use the camp inmates to gain knowledge of conditions that might be encountered in future military operations.[12]

Buchenwald contained a 'small camp' crowded with 'living dead' where Jews who had survived the ordeal of transfer from other concentration camps were held in atrocious conditions, and even after liberation remained sealed off from the rest of the camp. All prisoners had to undergo DDT dusting, as well as delousing with a mass shower and a cuprex dip. However, many evaded the delousing procedures, and incoming displaced persons were not deloused immediately and retained freedom of movement.[13] Sixty-two cases of typhus were isolated in a hospital ward (although if properly deloused, isolation would have been superfluous). Many others died from inappropriate feeding of too rich food.[14]

While the typhus problem was most acute in the liberated camps, it also shaped responses to 'displaced persons' (DPs) and German civilians. Escapees from concentration camps were considered to be spreading typhus, and the medical personnel in UNRRA and SHAEF militated against swift repatriation as liable to spread typhus.[15] Allied policy was to collect and incarcerate such persons on medical grounds in DP camps. The label DP covered a range of civilians in Germany and elsewhere, ranging from the victims in concentration camps to ethnic Ukrainians (including an SS regiment) fleeing the liberating armies. DP was officially regarded

[10] CMAC RAMC 1103, *An Account of the Operation of the Second Army in Europe 1944–45*, ii. 415–27. The nutritionists were Jack Drummond and V. P. Sydenstricker.

[11] Bayne-Jones, 'Typhus Fevers', 240, 245, 248; NAW RG 112, 710/1109 'Typhus in Germany', 42–3; A. Youmans, *et al.*, 'A Report on the Activities of the USA Typhus Commission at the Dachau Concentration Camp, 10 May 1945–10 June 1945; A. Youmans, 'Progress in Rickettsial Disease Therapy. With Special Reference to Paraminobenzoic Acid', *Lancet*, 67 (1947), 60–3; J. C. Snyder, 'Typhus Fever in the Second World War', cited as offprint. For quarantine restrictions see Kafka, *Weg*, 69. 12 Collis, 'Belsen Camp', passim.

[13] NLM, Bayne-Jones Papers, Investigation of Typhus Fever at Camp Buchenwald, 23 May 1945; NAW RG 331 SHAEF G-5, 17.11, Jacket 10 Box 151/Buchenwald archives Sign 76 7–17, Buchenwald. A Preliminary Report by Egon W. Fleck, Civ. and 1st Lt Edward A. Tenenbaum, 24.IV.45; Abzug, *Vicious Heart*, 55.

[14] D. A. Hackett, *The Buchenwald Report* (Boulder, Colo., 1995), 6.

[15] United Nations Archives, New York, UNRRA papers, PAG 4/1.3.1.5.0.0:10, Goodman to Sawyer 12 June 1945.

as a desirable status, placing the person above the disorder of local economies. Yet the term was depersonalizing—a lowest common denominator, reflecting a sense that here were groups that simply needed to be 'collected', 'sorted', 'classified', and 'replaced', even though 'repatriation' might be precisely what the refugees were seeking to avoid. Registration, delousing, medical inspection, soap, blankets, and food were priorities. DPs were suspect as potentially criminal, disorderly, and diseased, and so required detention, and sanitary processing by delousing and DDT dusting. Added to basic concerns with food, water, and sanitation came the fear that 'DPs' carried disease, and would cause epidemics on the same vast scale as after the First World War. In addition to typhus, there were outbreaks of plague, diphtheria, smallpox, and tuberculosis, and syphilis was rampant. Segregation of the sick brought further emotional traumas.[16] In terms of rehabilitating populations previously classed as vermin, the status and conditions of DPs remained degraded. Their treatment reflected not so much concern for individual welfare but that reduction of epidemic risks should protect the occupying authorities and maintain order.

Problems of sanitation and social control intertwined. At a camp at Neustadt in the Rhineland, a riot erupted among the internees, due to a combination of ethnic tensions and not being habituated to the use of western lavatories.[17] DDT dusting was resented as undignified and violating privacy. At Nammen it was reported that ninety out of every 100 DPs endured dusting 'very unwillingly . . . or try to escape'.[18] Vaccination was less unpopular, but sometimes also resisted.

The invading armies first encountered several hundred typhus cases in the Rhineland. From March to June 1945 the US Army Typhus Case Finding team found more than 15,000 cases in over 500 localities of the inner Reich. Diseased civilians were hospitalized in camps, and deloused.[19] As long as Germany was still overflowing with camps for prisoners of war, Nazi suspects, or displaced persons, the threat of typhus remained. From April 1945 the occupying authorities imposed a strict cordon sanitaire along the Rhine, stretching from the Swiss border to the Rhine and Waal rivers to the North Sea—to include areas of the Netherlands which had suffered acute starvation in the final throes of German occupation. Travel required disinfestation and delousing: for a brief period the epidemic prevention procedures imposed control and surveillance at a time of post-war turbulence.[20] Momentarily, the cordon sanitaire represented a new divide—temporarily moved westwards—between civilized Western Europe and the devastated European heartland. A US officer, Colonel John E. Gordon, the Chief of Preventive Medicine, commented on the atavistic chaos confronting the Allies:

The Rhineland in those days of March 1945 could scarcely be believed by those who saw it—it is beyond the appreciation of those who did not. It was Wild West, the hordes of Genghis

---

[16] Wyman, *DP*, 49–51; UNRRA Medical Manual, Health and Medical Care of Displaced Persons, typescript in Wiener Library 473/271.

[17] Wyman, *DP*, 39.   [18] Ibid., 50.

[19] NAW 112/710/1110, pp. 22–39; Leiby, *Public Health*, 141.

[20] NLM Bayne-Jones Papers, Final Report of Typhus Fever Control, 11 May 1945; Bayne-Jones, 'Typhus Fevers', 244–5.

Khan, the Klondike gold rush, and Napoleon's retreat from Moscow all rolled up into one. Such was typhus in the Rhineland.[21]

Once the war ended, DDT dusting was stringently applied at crossing points between the allied zones of occupation, and a priority was a sanitary barrier along the entire eastern border of the American zone to handle refugees. Posters pointed to the risks of louse-infested *Ostflüchtlinge*. Delousing was required before a ration card could be issued. DDT hand and power dusters were delivered to every district, and typhus case-finding became a responsibility of German health authorities and physicians. Newsreels show how the face, and upper and lower body were 'dusted', evincing reactions of disgust of those undergoing the procedure.[22]

Officially, there were 4,000 reported cases of typhus in Germany during April–May 1945; these statistics must be assumed to be a severe underestimate—a peak of 6,590 cases between 19 May and 15 June is perhaps more realistic. But rates climbed to over 15,000 cases by August 1945. There was continued need for vigilance against epidemics that might resurge due to overcrowding, malnutrition, and destruction of sanitary facilities, and threaten the occupying armies. Public health posters proclaimed that it was no shame to harbour lice, but that combing and washing were necessary. The British public health authorities in Carinthia ordered that all refugees from Yugoslavia were to be held for fourteen days as potential typhus contacts. Detention and dusting went with education and propaganda. Once the threat of epidemics diminished, public health became a low priority to the British, French, and US military governments.[23] By 1946 the Bavarian authorities took over security functions in medical inspection centres for new waves of refugees from the east, including the Sudeten Germans. The Western allies favoured decentralization and allowing the German states a free hand in questions of public health.[24]

The Soviet Medical Administration (SMAD), established in July 1945, gave priority to mobilizing medical resources against epidemics, not least because a massive typhus epidemic in 1945 erupted in East Prussia (soon to be divided between the USSR and Poland). Mecklenburg and Brandenburg were devasted by the final months' combat, economic shortages, overcrowding, and the influx of Germans from the East. A sanitary report in June 1946 said that the starving and deprived population of Frankfurt am Oder was so enfeebled that people could not be made to undress for delousing. Disinfectants and soap were often lacking, and

[21] Bayne-Jones, 'Typhus Fever', 243.
[22] NAW OMGUS RG 260/box 554, 'Typhus and Typhoid'; A. W. Kenner, 'Control of Typhus Fever', 26 Sept. 1945; Kubin, Public Health and Welfare Branch, Military Government Typhus Control Program 10 Oct. 1946; J. C. Snyder, 'Recommended Policy for Control of Typhus Fever in Germany and Austria'. For a poster dating from 1946 see K. Sträter, 'Fleckfieber', in H. Schadewaldt (ed.), *Die Rückkehr der Seuchen* (Cologne, 1994), 135.
[23] BAK R 86/3888 *Merkblatt über Läusebekämpfung*, herausgegeben vom Institut für allgemeine Hygiene und vormals Reichsgesundheitsamt, 1946; H.-U. Sons, *Gesundheitspolitik während der Besatzungszeit: das öffentliche Gesundheitswesen in Nordrhein-Westfalen 1945–1949* (Wuppertal, 1983); PRO FO 1020/2649 f. 53 on illegal entrants from Yugoslavia; FO 1020/2662 measures of 29 Nov. 45.
[24] Leiby, *Public Health*, 102–3, 149–50.

the medical personnel was at risk from infection.[25] SMAD launched energetic measures to control epidemic diseases by means of registration and compulsory
hospitalization, while pressing for socialized medicine in polyclinics.[26] Infectious
diseases and health problems forced an easing of de-Nazification, as shortages of
doctors meant keeping on some from the old guard of ex-Nazi medical experts.
Compulsory service on the *Seuchenfront* was a way for 'tainted' doctors to be reha-
bilitated, as an alternative to the penalties of a de-Nazification tribunal.[27]

The USATC and the United Nations Relief Administration Agency (UNRAA)
would have liked to intervene extensively in Eastern Europe against typhus. At
the end of hostilities an estimated fourteen million civilians were on the move
throughout Europe. There were small armies of children, perhaps amounting to a
quarter of the refugees. In addition there were the homeless as a result of bombing,
and about ten million Wehrmacht veterans, and non-German SS detachments like
the ill-fated Cossacks and more fortunate Ukrainians. Later in 1945 came a further
twelve million expelled ethnic Germans from the east—from the newly acquired
Polish territories, East Prussia, and the Sudetenland.[28] Such a situation meant that
in 1945–6 fluid population movements in Europe appeared as a threat to international health. Yet despite localized outbreaks of typhus in France among prisoners,
deportees, and those being repatriated, and in Denmark, the Netherlands, and
England and Wales, the disease was in terminal decline.[29]

The medical situation in the east held a more menacing potential. In May 1945
the Czech government in exile sent a relief expedition to combat the outbreak of
typhus in the concentration camp of Terezin (Theresienstadt), where other infectious and chronic diseases included dysentery, starvation from hunger oedema,
and tuberculosis.[30] The USATC was concerned about the threat of a Polish typhus
epidemic, because it was believed that, as in the wake of the First World War, repatriated prisoners of war and refugees returning from the east might be typhus carriers. Equipped with supplies from the USATC, and in constant touch with US
Army agencies, an UNRRA mission entered Poland in May 1945. Weigl abandoned
Lvov which reverted to the Soviets, and achieved an honoured position in the new
Poland. Although the fear of epidemics from the east was not as intensive as after
the First World War, it was still prone to exaggeration.[31]

[25] G. Moser, 'Das Gesundheitswesen in Mecklenburg und Vorpommern nach 1945: Nationalsozialis-
tisches Erbe, politischer Anspruch, medizinischer Versorgungsnotstand', *Rostocker medizinische
Beiträge*, 5 (1996), 135–58. A.-S. Ernst, '*Die beste Prophylaxe ist der Sozialismus'. Ärzte und medizinische
Hochschullehrer in der SBZ/DDR 1945–1961* (Munster, 1997), 171–2.

[26] S. Kirchberger, 'Public-Health Policy in Germany, 1945–1949: Continuity and a New Beginning', in
D. W. Light and A. Schuller (eds.), *Political Values and Health Care: The German Experience* (Cambridge,
Mass., 1986), 186–238.

[27] H. Domeinski, 'Zur Entnazifizierung der Ärzteschaft im Lande Thüringen', in A. Thom and H.
Spaar (eds.), *Medizin im Faschismus* (Berlin, 1983), 320–7. Ernst, 'Prophylaxe', 182–6.

[28] Wyman, *DP*, 17–25.

[29] N. M. Goodman, *International Health Organizations and their Work*, 12; 'Note on Localised Epidemics of Exanthematic Typhus amongst Prisoners of War in France', *Bulletin OIHP* (1946), 259–64.

[30] E. H Strach, personal communication, 22 Sept. 1995. Dr Strach was a physician on the expedition.

[31] Bayne-Jones, 'Typhus Fevers', 251.

UNRRA was headed by former Rockefeller Foundation personnel, who used the agency for massive injections of medical supplies to 'non-enemy' countries, while promoting a scheme for a European Health Planning Commission. The Health Division was under Wilbur Sawyer, the European Regional Office was under Andrew Topping—both militated for energetic prevention against typhus 'as a serious threat still exists'.[32] Eighty per cent of all UNRRA's supplies went to Europe, and 86 per cent of these (with substantial consignments of DDT, vaccines, sulfa drugs, and penicillin) went to Austria, Italy, Czechoslovakia, Greece, Poland, and Yugoslavia—in part to preserve what were considered the most backward parts of Europe from a severe epidemic, but in part to avoid what were deemed the errors of the ARA in 1919 in providing assistance rather than promoting social reform.[33] The USATC monitored conditions in Yugoslavia and Greece, despite frustrations that these were areas of British influence. The Rockefeller Foundation was able to overcome resistance to US medical involvement in Greece. In August 1944 the USATC entered Yugoslavia. Despite surprise concerning the absence of a Yugoslav epidemic after the war, by 1945 DDT, dust guns, and vaccines were flown in on a large scale with the support of Tito. Although the US Congress could not countenance aid to Russia, UNRRA supplies went to Belarus and Ukraine.[34] By June 1945 the US authorities established that the epidemiological trend was one of 'progressive improvement', and the risk of an epidemic was deemed to have passed.[35] The decline of typhus was attributed to 'the rain of DDT louse powder that had been sprinkled over millions of persons' and to now ample supplies of vaccines, including captured batches of vaccines from Cracow and Lwów. The US zone of occupation in Germany was allocated supplies in 1946 for 12 million dustings.[36]

As epidemic hazards declined, migration again became possible. When Ellis Island closed in 1943, the Holocaust was at its height: terminating migration had fatal consequences for Europe's 'surplus' populations. Closing the door to refugees in the hope that they might secure improved conditions under Nazi rule (and not exacerbate the political tensions in Palestine) had tragic consequences. The medical techniques of disinfestation, fumigation, and disinfection which were devised to facilitate safe migration were unleashed by the Nazis for genocide. With the end of the war a new climate of compassion slowly dawned: in May 1946 the first shipload of refugees, consisting of former concentration camp prisoners, left Bremen for the United States—a sign that the era of hostility to Jewish migrants was passing.[37]

The defeat of Nazism thus meant the demise of typhus. The presence of the disease in concentration camps provided crucial evidence for epidemic typhus as a product of Nazi barbarism. By August 1945 epidemic typhus was believed to be

---

[32] UN archives, New York, UNRRA papers, PAG 4/4.2:16 W. A. Sawyer 'Health Problems Facing UNRRA', 1945.

[33] R. Ford, *UNRRA in Europe 1945–1947* (London, 1947).

[34] Bayne-Jones, 'Typhus Fevers', 255–6.   [35] Ibid., 245.   [36] Ibid., 249–50.

[37] 'Erstes Auswanderungsschiff nach USA', *Weser Kurier* (15 May 1946).

'extinct' in the US zone.[38] Post-war economic reconstruction, the Cold War, and mounting enthusiasm for basic research on genetics and molecular biology cleared away the intellectual constructs of epidemic threats and parasites, as if these were so much wartime rubble. The new political divide between Western capitalism and Eastern communism emerged as axiomatic for the post-war world. The 'iron curtain' as a military, political, and economic frontier meant that epidemiological divisions between European civilization and Asiatic barbarism were redundant.

ii. The Survival of the Behringwerke

The fear of an epidemic recrudesence in 1945 meant that the Americans wished to maintain the Behringwerke as a functioning entity. Given the integration of this plant into the Nazi economic and medical structures, the US overseers of the factory were confronted by the problem of maintaining production while seeking to excise Nazi elements. Extricating the works from the IG-Farben complex, and reorienting production to post-war requirements became less of a problem than dealing with those technical experts who were NSDAP and SS members. The Managing Director, Albert Demnitz, maintained his position as in formal terms he was not an NSDAP member: the US overseers did not appreciate the extent to which he was involved in the Nazi medical war effort. Demnitz presented himself as having fought the NSDAP and Deutsche Arbeitsfront to preserve the factory's autonomy. But this expressed more his strategy of sustaining the factory's survival, and supporting as far as possible those tainted by Nazism.[39] The history of the Behringwerke exemplifies the problem of de-Nazifying German industry. Were the continuities as seamless, or was there a fundamental restructuring of West German medical organizations and élites?

Tracing the history of typhus vaccine production at the Behringwerke suggests that the plant's managers tried at all costs to preserve the autonomy of the concern; Nazi personnel would be sacrificed, but only if absolutely necessary. Shortly before the Soviet occupation of Lemberg, its Behring Institute was evacuated; Richard Haas resumed typhus vaccine production at Marburg in August 1944, exploiting Polish and Soviet prisoners and labour conscripts to serve as louse-feeders. As the supply of rabbits ceased in the last months of the war, the Weigl technique was deemed the most suitable, but reliance on *Ostarbeiter* as louse-feeders became impossible after the war.[40] The Behringwerke were inspected by US Combined Intelligence Objectives Sub-committee (CIOS) teams in April 1945 with a view to restarting production. The US verdict was that although the plant was less efficiently organized than an American firm, it ought to be kept going. The Behringwerke continued to produce vaccines deemed necessary for public health, and

---

[38] Bayne-Jones, 'Typhus Fevers', 249.
[39] Behring-Archive, Spruchkammerangelegenheiten 1945–8, Demnitz to Review Board of the County of Marburg, 5 Nov. 1945.
[40] Bayer-Archiv, Leverkusen, 169/17 Besprechung in Marburg am 18. und 19.8.44.

Bieling convinced the Americans that the Behring vaccine was as potent as the US vaccine.[41]

Haas was investigated from April 1945 by Allied intelligence teams because of his Waffen-SS links while director of the Lemberg outpost. The Behringwerke felt that it could not retain his services, but in 1955 he became professor of microbiology in Freiburg. His wartime research at Lemberg laid the foundations for his becoming one of post-war Germany's leading virologists; his assistant, Gönnert, remained at the successor company of Bayer, while gaining the position of *Dozent* in tropical medicine at the University of Cologne. Bieling continued at the Behringwerke at a time when vaccine production was a priority, and he carried out vaccine tests for the Americans; although not an NSDAP member, by 1947 he was regarded as compromised by Nazi connections; his salvation was to activate a contact with Austrian bacteriology dating back to IG-Farben's acquisition of the Austrian serum works after the Anschluss. Bieling was appointed professor of hygiene in Vienna in 1951—maintaining a traditional concern with infections from the east as he took a prominent role in developing WHO programmes in virology.[42] While the links between academics, the Nazi state, and vaccine production were severed, researchers active in the east had brilliant academic careers.[43]

The clinging on of the old guard was indicated when in September 1947 the Behringwerke published a booklet on typhus, which used a text prepared in 1944: not only were sanitary regulations of 1942 extensively cited, so was literature by Mrugowsky, Haagen, Wohlrab, and Zeiss and Rodenwaldt that stigmatized Jews as typhus carriers.[44] The Behringwerke endured accusations made as part of the IG-Farben trial, and by Kogon as part of his critique of the SS state. Under Demnitz the plant remained a major force in production of vaccines.

The Behring cult was sustained: as an ideological concession, Paul Ehrlich was reinstated in the German medical pantheon and jointly honoured with Emil von Behring in 1954.[45] Medical historians continued to proclaim great heroes, so legitimating German medical science at a time when the Nazi abuses rendered it suspect. The professors of hygiene Rodenwaldt and Pfannenstiel produced a stream of

[41] Office of the Military Government of Hessian State (OMGHS). Production Control Agency (SHAEF), Industrial Investigation Report on Behringwerke, pp. 5–9, 12–13; Hessisches Staatsarchiv, Marburg, OMGHS 17/165–2/1, copy kindly made available by the Behringwerke; NAW OMGUS RG 260 Box 554 'Typhus and Typhoid', J. G. Feinberg, US Forces European Theater, 23 Aug. 1945.

[42] For Bieling see Homberger, *Behringwerke*, 92; NAW OMGUS RG 260/Box 554, 'Typhus and Typhoid', Bieling, Typhus Vaccine from Rabbit Lungs No. 21 18.II.46; J. Feinberg, 23 Aug. 1946, Typhus Vaccine; Behring-Archiv, Spruchkammerangelegenheiten 1945–8, Aktennotiz 29 Jan. 1947. For Haas see the legitimatory K. Munk, *Virologie in Deutschland* (Basel, 1995), 70–2, 142–3, also p. 138; E. Seidler, *Die Medizinische Fakultät der Albert-Ludwigs-Universität Freiburg im Breisgau* (Berlin, 1991), 461; Behring-Archiv, Spruchkammerangelegenheiten 1945–8.

[43] Bayer-Archiv, Leverkusen, 169/17 Besprechung in Marburg am 18. und 19.8.44.

[44] *Das Fleckfieber und seine Verhütung durch die Schutzimpfung* (Marburg, 1947).

[45] 'Hundertjahrfeier der Geburtstage von Paul Ehrlich und Emil von Behring in Frankfurt-Main, Marburg-Lahn und Hoechst', *Behringwerk-Mitteilungen*, 29 (1954). The Zeiss-Bieling biography was reissued as R. Bieling, *Der Tod hatte das Nachsehen. Emil von Behring Gestalt und Werk*, 3rd edn. (Bielefeld, 1954).

historical works, looking back to the origins of epidemic controls.[46] Bieling fostered the history of medicine on conservative lines in Vienna, including the republication of the Behring biography, although removing the passages on anti-Semitism and, true to his convictions, according due homage to the noble qualities of Behring's wife.[47] German medical history as an academic discipline was a seamless web of continuity with hardly a break in 1945. The former SS officer active in the east, Josef Gottlieb, held an academic position at the University of Saarbrücken; he had compiled a Nazi classic on German medical heroes. Medical history meant providing the old guard with a pedigree of respectability, while allowing them to project an image of a profession based on the forward march of clinical research.

iii. Perpetrators as Survivors

All sides concurred that advances in scientific and preventive medicine had 'conquered' typhus. Medical scientists were in a dilemma when confronted by Nazi human experiments: if the Nazi abuse of medicine was to be too severely condemned, this could retard clinical research at a time when it was strategically important to harness medicine to Cold War demands for expertise on the effects of radioactivity. Allied scientists expected to find rich pickings in German wartime medical records which might be relevant for some future conflict. Moreover, Allied medical researchers were prepared to cut some ethical corners on matters like informed consent, although most were mortified by the callous brutality of German medical atrocities. The combination of the strategic demands of the Cold War and the sense that clinical progress should not be impeded meant that investigations of medical crimes and prosecutions were progressively played down, as the perpetrators became increasingly immune from prosecution.

The Allied liberators of the concentration camps were so unprepared for the horrific conditions which they found that at first they were uncertain at how to investigate lethal medical experiments. Despite the international notoriety of Ding's wartime paper comparing typhus vaccines, the Americans were surprised to find at Buchenwald an intact concentration camp with its battery of cremation furnaces and medical research blocks.[48] On 16 April 1945 an intelligence team of the psychological warfare division set out to study the conditions in Buchenwald.[49] Fortuitously realizing the complexity of the situation, advice was sought from Eugen Kogon, Ding's prisoner-secretary, who contributed an analysis of the camp,

[46] e.g. E. Rodenwaldt (ed.), 'Die Gesundheitsgesetzgebung des Magistrato della sanità Venedigs, 1486–1550', *Sitzungsberichte der Heidelberger Akademie der Wissenschaften*, mathematisch-naturwissenschaftliche Klasse (1956), 1.

[47] R. Bieling, *Der Tod hatte das Nachsehen*, 6, 179–80.

[48] NLM, Bayne-Jones papers, Final Report of Typhus Fever Control, 11 May 1945.

[49] NAW RG 331 SHAEF G–5, 17.11, Jacket 10 Box 151/Buchenwald archives Sign 76 7–17, Buchenwald. A Preliminary Report by Egon W. Fleck, Civ. and 1st Lt Edward A. Tenenbaum, 24 Apr. 1945. A copy is also in PRO FO 371/46796.

20. Epidemic warning-signs at Terezín (Theresienstadt)

as well as of the typhus experiments.[50] The resulting report caught the attention
of Richard Crossman, who was attached to the Psychological Warfare Division in
Paris. Crossman, concerned to document fully Nazi concentration camps, recommended the expansion and publication of Kogon's report.[51]

The 'discovery' of the Nazi atrocities triggered a barrage of publicity. A British
Parliamentary delegation (including Lord Addison, who had been instrumental in
establishing the LNHO after the First World War) visited Buchenwald at General
Eisenhower's invitation, on 21 April 1945, to 'find out the truth' concerning the Nazi

---

[50] These have been republished as Hackett, *The Buchenwald Report.*
[51] Ibid., 18; E. Kogon, *Der SS-Staat. Das System der deutschen Konzentrationslager* (Munich: Karl Alber
Verlag, 1946), 23rd edn. (Munich, 1993), preface to 1970 edn., pp. 5–12.

21. 'Human laundry', Belsen

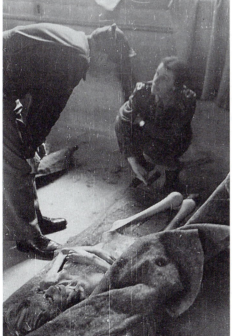

22. 'Janet Vaughan with one of her patients'

horrors. They encountered 'the odour of dissolution and disease', the still verminous huts, and evidence of the overcrowding, forced labour, and of gruesome
sterilization experiments.[52] Once Kogon supplied copious details of the Buchenwald typhus experiments, these became a legal battlefield at the Nuremberg
Medical Trial, which ran from December 1946 until July 1947.

Part of Kogon's evidence was the 'diary' of Ding, which became a crucial prosecution document in the strategy of linking atrocities committed in outlying
concentration camps with senior figures, notably Mrugowsky. Mrugowsky pointed
out that it contained numerous inaccuracies. Some were minor: the 'diary' gave the
date of the opening ceremony of the Behring Institute, Lemberg as 15–18 December
1942, instead of 10 December. Others were more significant in attributing Mrugowsky's attendance at the crucial meeting of December 1941 when human experiments were decided on, when he could demonstrate that he was in Russia. The
'diary' was attacked as retrospectively compiled close to the end of the war, when
Kogon had persuaded Ding that it would be to his advantage to provide documentation on the human experiments.[53] Oblivious to such niceties, the US prosecutors
focused on the human experiments as proving the involvement of Himmler and
the SS at the highest level. This strategy shifted the burden of guilt away from ambitious and reckless scientists by demonstrating that the prime guilt lay with leading
Nazis rather than with medical researchers who exploited the camps to demonstrate their scientific prowess.[54]

The Allied difficulty was whom to prosecute. Some Nazi medical experimenters
defiantly took their own lives: the SS medical supremo, Grawitz, and Lolling killed
themselves prior to arrest, and Ding committed suicide as did Conti in October
1945, while in prison at Nuremberg. The pioneer of geopolitics, Haushofer, against
whom the Allies considered mounting a prosecution, committed suicide in March
1946.[55] Fortuitously, Gildemeister, the president of the Robert Koch Institute, died
in 1945, apparently from natural causes.

The disinfection expert, Gerstein, approached two Allied CIOS officers, Major
D. C. Evans and J. W. Haught in late April 1945 at Rottweil in the Black Forest.
He declared that he was ready to testify against the perpetrators, as he wished that
those responsible for poison gassing should be tried. He was handed over to French
custody but his interrogators treated his evidence with considerable suspicion. He
was found hanged in his cell on 17 July 1945, one interpretation being that he committed suicide tortured by his own sense of guilt at having been involved in human
gassings. His aim that those responsible for the poison gassings should be convicted was to be only partially realized.[56]

---

[52] *Buchenwald Camp, The Report of a Parliamentary Delegation* (London, 1945). Hackett, *Buchenwald Report*, 9–15. PRO FO 371/46796 on the delegation.

[53] NMT roll 16, frame 889. The diary was filmed by Ernst Klee.   [54] Klee, *Auschwitz*, 47–59.

[55] R. W. Cooper, *The Nuremberg Trial* (Harmondsworth, 1947), 109–13.

[56] YVA, Gerstein file biographical notes Rottweil 26 Apr. 1945; 'Le Rapport du Major D. C. Evans et de Mr I. Id. Haupt. CIOS Consolidated Advance Field Team (VII)' (Original in Archives du Centre de Documentation Juive Contemporaine, Doc CDLVIII-83a).

The deceit of disguising the gas chambers as delousing installations and the genocidal abuse of Zyklon went largely unpunished. Only in the British zone was Zyklon supply treated with any severity. In March 1946 a military court condemned Bruno Tesch to death for suggesting Zyklon B as a 'more efficient and hygienic means of mass execution' and for having supplied poison gas to Auschwitz for mass murder.[57] The techniques of the killing process were scrutinized by British chemical warfare experts from Porton Down, who puzzled over a Dachau gas chamber in March 1946. This suggests that Zyklon did not arouse concern among the British during the war, but that after the war there was interest in its neurological effects. The British officer who had located Gerstein reported in January 1948: 'Considerable time was spent in trying to discover reliable data on which to calculate what concentrations of HCN were used for the extermination of victims. It would appear, however, that no controlled experiments were carried out on a scientific basis. The chief object was to kill the victims as quickly as possible so as to make room for the next batch.' The hunt was on for evidence of experiments with nerve gases so that such chemical weapons could be developed.[58]

The IG-Farben Trial in Nuremberg in 1948 was unable to resolve whether the producing firms' employees knew of the murderous use of Zyklon when fulfilling the steadily mounting orders placed by concentration camps. But Peters, the managing director of DEGESCH, after an initial sentence of five years in 1949 for complicity in murder, was acquitted in 1955. He claimed that he attributed no special significance to the Auschwitz camp, and remarkably the killing of the incurable and mentally deficient was accepted by his interrogators as legitimate. Hermann Schlosser, the chairman of DEGUSSA and long-term board member of DEGESCH, was released in April 1948, and set about developing new production facilities and products for hydrocyanic acid derivatives.[59] Other prosecutions of the abuse of poison gas collapsed. DEGESCH resumed production of Zyklon B, and supplies were required for disinfestation in camps and military installations by the Allies and UNRRA.[60] Bayer, one of the successor firms of IG-Farben, after some hesitation took over IG's role as a major shareholder in 1954.[61] Zyklon reverted to use as an insecticide.

---

[57] Trial transcripts in IfZ and PRO WO 235/83. Also convicted was Tesch's Prokurist, Karl Weinbacher, but Joachim Drosihn was acquitted.

[58] PRO WO 195/9678 D. C. Evans, 'German CW Experiments on Human Beings', report dated 12 Jan. 1948 for Ministry of Supply, Advisory Council on Scientific Research and Technical Development, Chemical Defence Advisory Board, p. 4, copy in Wiener Library Kh (1). Report cited by Observer Films (1995): 'The Secrets of Porton Down', Granada Presentation for ITV.

[59] *Sonne und Mond*, 148–9, 243–51; Degussa Firmenarchiv, Rechtsabteilung, 'Tatsachen zum Thema Zyklon B'. I. Sagel-Grande, H. H. Fuchs, C. F. Rüter (eds.), *Justiz und NS-Verbrechen* (Amsterdam, 1975), vol. 13, 105–204.

[60] *Sonne und Mond*, 149.

[61] Bayer-Archiv IG Fremdfirmen Degussa 6.14 Bd 1/2, Aktennotiz über Besprechung mit dem Geschäftsführer Herrn Stiege, 11 Nov. 1949; Degesch to Bayer 14 Oct. 1954; agreement of Bayer, Degussa and Theo Goldschmidt AG 11 Oct. 1954; K. Tscharnke, 'Nach 45 weiterproduziert, 'als wäre nichts passiert'; Giftgas Zyklon B und die Expansionspläne der Firma Degesch', *Aachener Nachrichten* (29 Sept. 1987).

There was a widespread sense that there had been in fact no element of criminality or abuse of medical power—merely a small number of fanatical Nazi leaders. At the Hamburg Institute of Tropical Diseases an era ended in June 1945 with the death from natural causes of Bernhard Nocht, the Institute's icon and aged Nazi founder. Nauck, the advocate of German colonies, ghettoization, and clinical tests in the Warsaw ghetto hospital became acting director in December 1943, and was confirmed in office in December 1947; this former Nazi Party member attained an influential position as rector of Hamburg University. He energetically supplied Rose with scientific ammunition to secure his release from Allied custody. That Erich Martini was penalized by an Allied tribunal resulted from his long-standing feud with the Nocht Institute leadership.[62]

The case of the virologist Haagen well illustrates the sense of indignation among German scientists that disinterested benefactors of humanity were being victimized. In 1945 Haagen was arrested but released by the Americans, and then conducted virus research at the invitation of the Soviet Medical Administration which was interested in the potential of virology for germ warfare. His work for the Soviet authorities enhanced his interest to the British and US investigators: he was arrested by the British Military Police in December 1946 (the month that the Nuremberg Medical Trial began) having been lured into the western sector of Berlin. After testifying at Nuremberg, Haagen was tried in France in 1952, but was released in 1955 when the DFG resumed support of his virological research. When on trial he declared that he should instead have received a Nobel Prize (he had prior to the war developed a successful yellow fever vaccine). His belief that his 'guinea-pigs'—including the hundreds transported from Auschwitz to Natzweiler—served legitimate scientific ends illuminated the reckless dedication to science.[63] Haagen's defence of his scientific record echoed the unrepentant stance of his RKI colleagues, notably Schilling who insisted that his experiments were justified as in the long-term interests of scientific progress, and Gerhard Rose who led a counter-attack by German medical researchers at the Nuremberg Medical Trial.

Zeiss, wheelchair-bound with Parkinson's disease but still at work at the Berlin Hygiene Institute, expected to resume cooperation with the Soviet liberators of Berlin. He even contacted Henry Sigerist in Baltimore to renew their cooperation. He was arrested in the autumn of 1945 along with his friend Sütterlin (also a veteran of the German Red Cross expedition), tried on the old charge of having been a spy until his departure from the Soviet Union in 1932, and died in custody in a prison hospital in Vladimir in 1949. A colleague reported that the prison medical staff honoured him for his earlier typhus and plague studies in the Soviet

---

[62] Wulf, *Hamburger Tropeninstitut*, 140–2. STAH BNI papers, Schriftwechsel in der Angelegenheit Dr med Gerhart Rose, Nauck to Rose 30 May 1946.

[63] I. Simon, 'Les Médecins criminels nazis Bickenbach, Haagen et Hirt du camp de Struthof et le procès de Metz', *Revue d'histoire de la médecine hébraïque*, 6/3 (1952/3), 133–42; P. Hoedeman, *Hitler or Hippocrates: Medical Experiments and Euthanasia in the Third Reich* (Lewes, 1991), 136–8; Hubenstorf, ' "Aber es Kommt mir doch so vor" ', 452–3.

Union.[64] Despite such casualties among the standard-bearers of German medical science, the majority of researchers found themselves immune from scrutiny by the occupying authorities.

As the interdisciplinary web of typhus prevention was dismembered, a small academic army landed up in senior academic posts. Kurt Scharlau, the geographer of the Hygiene Institute of the Waffen-SS, became associate professor of geography in Marburg. Buurmann moved from the medical department of the Generalgouvernement to the medical administration in the British zone, where he was joined by other colleagues from the east. Fritz Steiniger was associate professor of hygiene in Hannover, where he took charge of the state department for pest control. Wohlrab returned from Poland to become typhus commissioner in Thuringia, and then moved west to the state institute for infectious diseases at Hannover. Steiniger and Wohlrab co-edited the journal *Gesundheitswesen und Desinfektion* where Hagen defended his sanitary policies in Warsaw.[65] Kudicke was in 1946 honorary professor of hygiene in Frankfurt. Habs, dismissed as an SS officer from the chair of hygiene at Hamburg in 1945, was held in detention for twenty months, but in 1950 succeeded Rodenwaldt in Heidelberg, and went on to become medical advisor to the Federal German government. In 1951 the former Dachau entomologist Eduard May was appointed professor of philosophy at the Free University Berlin, where he developed the naturalistic *Weltanschauung* which had been prevalent in the Third Reich. Weyer retained his position as head of the entomological department of the Hamburg Tropical Institute from 1942 until 1969, unaffected by his period at the Warsaw Hygiene Institute. Eyer was promptly appointed to a chair of hygiene in Bonn in 1946, and he ended his career as director of the Pettenkofer Institute in Munich. Wilhelm Hagen, the former Warsaw medical officer, had been dismissed in February 1943 because the SS denounced his anti-tuberculosis measures as too favourable to the Poles; Hagen was by 1956 president of the Bundesgesundheitsamt, boosted by the clash with the Nazi leadership over his concern for the health of the Polish population (ignoring the Jews in the ghetto). Hagen's opponent Walbaum was dismissed late in 1942 as he too had fallen foul of the SS: he successfully avoided extradition to Poland in 1949 and indictment in the Federal Republic in 1968.[66] The appointments of Bieling and Haas show how combating epidemics in the east was a passport to a senior position in public health in the Federal Republic or Austria—indeed, typhus research provided credentials in virology which could then be applied to new problems like polio.

Few from the German bacteriological élite were brought to trial. In December

[64] P. Diepgen, 'Verstorbene innerhalb des deutschen Sprachgebietes seit Herbst 1939', *Centaurus* (1950–1), 81–6, 167–73; H. Harmsen, 'In memoriam Prof. Dr med. Heinz Zeiss', *Zentralblatt für Bakteriologie, Parasitenkunde, Infektionskrankheiten*, 157 (1957), 161–4; R. Bieling, *Der Tod hatte das Nachsehen*, 6.

[65] W. Hagen, 'Krieg, Hunger und Pestilenz in Warschau 1939–1943', *Gesundheitswesen und Desinfektion*, 8/9 (1973), 115–43.

[66] For careers see *Kürschners Deutscher Gelehrten-Kalender* (Berlin, 1954); *Kürschners Deutscher Gelehrten-Kalender 1970* (Berlin, 1971). Note that Kudicke who retired to Frankfurt was 69 in 1945. Browning, 'Genocide and Public Health', 165–8.

1945 the US authorities found the former director of the department for tropical medicine of the RKI, Claus Schilling, guilty of murder for malaria experiments; he had deliberately infected prisoners to examine variations in the course of the disease among different blood groups at the Dachau concentration camp. Schilling received a death sentence, carried out in May 1946.[67] But other experimentalists were more fortunate: the Waffen-SS bacteriologist Karl Josef Gross, who experimented on typhus in Mauthausen and pressed for plague experiments at the biological warfare establishment of Nesselstedt, practised after the war in nearby Linz.[68]

Hans Münch, the bacteriologist at Raisko and Auschwitz, was prosecuted at the major Auschwitz trial in Poland, and acquitted with the support of prisoner-physicians and former experimental subjects: he argued that his experiments were benign, intended to save the lives of persons otherwise earmarked for death.[69] He did not mention giving lethal injections and undertaking selections for the gas chambers. Only a minority in exposed positions (as Mrugowsky and Rose) were convicted. Robert J. Lifton observed that the *Weltanschauung* of an anonymized physician who had refused to take part in SS selections remained that of a Nazi.[70] Doctors who continued in practice, privately sustained authoritarian and Nazi convictions.

For strategic and economic reasons the Allies were interested in identifying the positive achievements of Nazi medical science. German scientists were interrogated, and CIOS documented what could be extracted from Eyer, Otto Fischer, and Schilling while in custody.[71] Some scientists were asked to review their specialisms under the auspices of FIAT, 'the Field Information Agency, Technical, a joint US and British venture. In mid-1947, just coinciding with the ending of the Nuremberg Medical Trial, FIAT reports were issued. Military authorities demanded knowledge of what had gone on in biological warfare and aviation medicine. These German-authored peer reviews dealing with 'progress' in such areas as general medicine and hygiene ignored all issues concerned with human experiments or the role of the SS. Thus the Buchenwald atrocities of Ding were simply mentioned by the virologist Bieling as an objective contribution to vaccine testing and serological diagnosis, or that of Haagen to the development of a dried serum, overlooking the hundreds of deaths resulting from the scientific butchery. Kogon's analysis of the SS-State became a source of information on clinical trials rather than human slaughter. The FIAT authors sanguinely hoped that the reports would allow German science to be internationally reintegrated as serving 'all humanity'.[72]

German bacteriologists used the reports to legitimate their expert credentials

[67] Ost, 'Malaria-Versuchsstation', 187–9; Hackett, *Buchenwald Report*, 370–1; CIOS, *Tropical Medicines*, 10–11.   [68] Klee, *Auschwitz*, 162.

[69] Personal communication, B. Schirra, May 1997. B. Schirra, 'Die Erinnerung der Täter', *Der Spiegel*, 40 (1998), 90–100. A. Smoltczyk, 'Der Doktor und sein Opfer', *Der Spiegel*, 14 (1999), 116–23.

[70] Lifton, *Nazi Doctors*, 325–34.

[71] CIOS, *Tropical Medicines and Other Medical Subjects in Germany* (London, n.d.).

[72] R. Bieling and H. Heinlein, 'Fleckfieber', in Bieling and Heinlein, *FIAT Review of German Science 1939–1946. Virus Diseases of Man* (Wiesbaden, 1947), 113, 129, 122, 127. Also 'Einleitung'.

and to trumpet their achievements. Rodenwaldt and Martini assessed epidemiology and the ravages of disease-carrying insects. The section on lice was a bald summary of their reproduction, variation, and control, noting work on louse eradication and the incidence of lice among different ethnic groups. Such objective terms conveyed a sense of medical triumphalism.[73] Reichmuth of the former Military Medical Academy was more forthcoming in describing how military priorities determined the selection of parasites as targets of intensive disinfestation research; he highlighted the central role of Hase in applications of hydrocyanic acid.[74] The virologist Bieling was assisted by the chemical warfare enthusiast Kliewe, who remained a strategic adviser in the Federal Republic.[75] Nauck reviewed the achievements of wartime tropical medicine.[76] The reports stressed how scientific innovation provided the basis for the containment of typhus and lice. Strategic and ideological motives had evaporated.

The new edition of the Zeiss–Rodenwaldt 'World Epidemics Atlas' in 1952 showed how geo-medical mapping which Zeiss limited to areas of military significance survived into the Cold War era. Initial support for the project came from the Bureau of Medicine and Surgery of the US Navy Department, which translated a text provided by German military medical experts. The details of epidemics in the east could be relevant in the event of a future war. The sections on louse-borne typhus were compiled by Felix von Bormann, who was imprisoned by the Allies until 1947 and lost his status at the Hamburg Institute for having experimented on Soviet prisoners of war. Yet Bormann continued as part of the resuscitated group of geo-medical observers of the east. In looking forward to a 'final cleansing' when typhus would be wiped out, he provided a racial interpretation, arguing that only where the civilized European races penetrated had typhus declined.[77] He used a European map dating from 1937 as he plotted the outbreaks of the disease in the course of the ebb and flow of the German advance and retreat. With the lack of an official history of German military medicine in the Second World War, the atlas provided the next best thing. Rodenwaldt and the medical geographer Jusatz established a Geomedical Research Unit in Heidelberg, and the atlas represented a network of conservative epidemiologists including the demographer, Burgdörfer,

[73] E. Martini, 'Krankheiten übertragende Insekten', in E. Rodenwaldt, *et al.*, *FIAT Review of German Science 1939–1946. Hygiene*, pt. III, *Epidemiology*, 333–52.

[74] W. Reichmuth, 'Neuere Ergebnisse und Probleme der Schädlingsbekämpfung', in Rodenwaldt, *et al.*, *FIAT Review of German Science 1939–1946. Hygiene*, pt. II, *Preventive and Industrial Medicine* (Wiesbaden, 1948), 21–62.

[75] Further relevant reports include K. Brass, 'Das Fleckfieber', in F. Büchner, *et al.*, *FIAT Review of German Science 1939–1946. Special Pathology*, pt. I (Wiesbaden, 1948), 27–42; K. Beckmann, 'Rickettsiosen', in R. Schoen, *FIAT Review of German Science 1939–1946. Internal Medicine*, pt. I (Wiesbaden, 1948), 57–95; F. Eichholtz and R. Muschaweck, 'Desinfektionsmittel', in Eichholtz, *et al.*, *FIAT Review of German Science 1939–1946. Pharmacology and Toxicology*, pt. III (Wiesbaden, 1948), 1–22.

[76] E. G. Nauck, *et al.*, *FIAT Review of German Science 1939–1946. Tropical Medicine and Parasitology* (Wiesbaden, 1948).

[77] F. von Bormann, 'The Occurrence of Louse-Borne Typhus in the World 1920–1955', *World Epidemics Atlas*, iii. 86–92, map (p. 97).

and Scharlau from the SS Hygiene Institute: having established its strategic utility in the Cold War, the cult of geo-medicine lived on.[78]

iv. Clinical Trials on Trial

Concern over health conditions, the expectation that the Germans had conducted strategically important research, and the onset of the Cold War meant turning a blind eye to genocidal atrocities and to Nazi Party and SS activities. Yet Allied medical experts could not totally overlook moral issues, and a delicate operation was conducted to condemn the human experiments as 'medical war crimes': by making sure that the prime guilt lay with the SS, medical science and its experimental procedures could be exonerated. It was in the interests both of the Germans and the Allied medical élites that clinical research should not be impeded, and the Cold War made such exoneration easier. While the German typhus experts doggedly defended their position at the Nuremberg Medical Trial, the Allies were concerned that the Trial should not undermine public confidence in the medical sciences.

At the first great Nuremberg trial—that of the major German war criminals— witnesses like the former Buchenwald prisoner Balachowsky provided eloquent testimony concerning the horrors of the Nazi human experiments. The trial, which ran from November 1945 until October 1946, publicized German medical and racial atrocities, and confirmed legal accountability for 'crimes against humanity', the legal construct used to prosecute the medical war crimes. The Allies opted neither for an international tribunal under the authority of the UN, nor to prosecute in the name of the millions of, in effect, stateless Jews, gypsies, and other victims. In its defence the military authority of four-power rule conferred powers to detain, investigate, and prosecute. But joint action as a military tribunal of the four Allied powers had its drawbacks, as the Germans began a campaign of resistance against 'victor's justice'. The trial had some lapses, as when the Soviet Union attempted to shift the guilt for the Katýn massacre onto the Germans.[79] But on the whole the Nuremberg trial successfully made the public aware of the genocidal activities of the Nazi élite.

The origins of the successor Nuremberg medical trial lie with the FIAT and CIOS investigations of biological warfare and vaccine production, which came across cases of fatal or disabling human experiments. The investigators noted that Schilling lacked the consent of his experimental subjects, and that many died. In December 1945 the chief medical investigator for the British FIAT, John West Thompson, urged prosecution, of 'medical war crimes'. On 15 May 1946 these problems were discussed at the US FIAT at the former IG-Farben offices of the Hoechst chemical manufacturers by American, French, and British medical and legal repre-

---

[78] W. Fricke and J. Schweikart, *Krankheit und Raum. Dem Pionier der Geomedizin Helmut Jusatz zum Gedenken* (Stuttgart, 1995).

[79] T. Taylor, *Anatomy of the Nuremberg Trials* (Boston, 1992).

sentatives.[80] British war crimes investigators had collected a large quantity of evidence on criminal medical experiments, and had segregated captured perpetrators of experimental wound infections from Hohenlychen and Ravensbrück for a special trial. The bacteriologist Pierre Lépine of the Pasteur Institute stated that the French had gathered sufficient evidence for a prosecution, thanks to Balachowsky and other interned French doctors who could provide first-hand evidence. Lépine wanted a moral condemnation, again in the name of the four powers. It was hoped that the British, French, and US FIAT organizations would co-operate.[81]

On 19 June 1946 a French government decree appointed four doctors, a biologist, and the director of the war crimes investigations to form a Commission on Medical Crimes. Meeting at the Pasteur Institute had a symbolic significance: now the heirs of Pasteur would sit in justice over the misdeeds perpetrated in the tradition of Robert Koch as an icon of German medicine. At the Pasteur Institute in July 1946 René Legroux headed this scientific commission, passing information to the UN War Crimes Commission—established as a British initiative in 1943, the UN Comission merely monitoring prosecutions and collating evidence.[82] The scientific commission formed the basis of an International Scientific Commission for the Investigation of Medical War Crimes, supported by the British and French. The process of peer review would judge the Nazi research according to the procedures of science. The British sent a highly energetic team of investigators, who had begun by investigating the fate of tortured female Special Operations Executive soldiers; the pathologist Keith Mant broadened out the scope of the investigation to the complete range of criminal medical activities in Ravensbrück. This involved gathering testimonies from the mainly Polish survivors of the human experiments, at least those who could be interviewed either in western Europe or Scandinavia. The Americans, who had far less evidence on experimental infections, promised to join the commission but did not do so. They were represented at the Pasteur Institute by Andrew Ivy, a professor of physiology at the University of Illinois College of Medicine, and a founder of the Naval Medical Research Institute; as a diehard experimentalist, he covered up the record of US medical experiments on prisoners and others unable to give informed consent. Ivy undertook to persuade the US government to ask for an advisory commission similar to the French Tribunal.[83]

The Tribunal's investigations remained confidential as potentially disrupting clinical research: faced by French demands for ethical evaluation at the Pasteur Institute in July 1946, Ivy cautioned that 'unless appropriate care is taken the

---

[80] PRO WO 309/471 International Scientific Commission for the Investigation of Medical War Crimes; CIOS, *Tropical Medicines*, 10–11.

[81] PRO WO 309/471 International Scientific Commission for the Investigation of Medical War Crimes. For background to Allied war crimes policies see T. Bower, *The Pledge Betrayed. America and Britain and the Denazification of Post-War Germany* (New York, 1982).

[82] UN War Crimes Commission, *German Medical War Crimes, A Summary of Information* (London, n.d. [1947]).

[83] P. J. Weindling, 'Ärzte als Richter: Internationale Reaktionen auf die Medizinverbrechen des Nürnberger Ärzteprozesses in den Jahren 1946–1947', in C. Wiesemann and A. Frewer (eds), *Medizin und Ethik im Zeichen von Auschwitz. 50 Jahre Nürnberger Ärzteprozess* (Erlangen and Jena, 1996), 31–44.

publicity associated with the trial of the experimenters ... may so stir public opinion against the use of humans in any experiment whatsoever that a hindrance will thereby result to the progress of science'. Concern arose that if the condemnation of German medical research was excessively severe, this would jeopardize not only the continuing development of medicine in Germany, faced by severe problems of epidemic infections in the post-war aftermath, but also clinical trials more generally. To remedy this situation Ivy proposed a new 'outline of principles and rules of experimentation':

1. The consent of the subject is required. Volunteers should be told of hazards and insurance should be provided.
2. Experiments should be based on animal experiments, and the results should be beneficial for the good of society.
3. Experiments should avoid unnecessary physical and mental suffering and injury, should be carried out by qualified persons and should not be conducted if the outcome will be death or disability.[84]

The first formulation of what became known as the 'Nuremberg code', to prevent reckless human experiments, thus occurred at the Pasteur Institute, and was in response to the French demand for ethical guidelines. It coincided with US interest in mounting a medical trial, which emerged only in the summer of 1946. At this point the story diverges between Anglo-French attempts to launch an authoritative international commission on medical war crimes and the American prosecution at Nuremberg. The French invited the Russians in July 1946 to the international commission but received no reply. In October 1946 the British prime minister, Clement Attlee, appointed Lord Moran, Churchill's physician, to lead a delegation of British medical scientists to evaluate the German human medical experiments.[85] Moran steered the proceedings so that the state (by which was meant the totalitarian state in all its forms) rather than unethical medical research was the prime culprit. His diagnosis broadened out the initial targeting of SS leaders as the main culprits to attributing the medical misdemeanours to the corrupting force of the state.

The Nuremberg medical trial ran from 9 December 1946 until 19 August 1947.[86] Deteriorating relations with the Soviets made any four-power prosecutions problematic. The US prosecutors had initially wanted to mount a trial of German financiers and manufacturers like Krupp von Bohlen und Halbach (the patron of Vogt) and Friedrich Flick, particularly for their exploitation of slave labour. But domestic right-wing pressure made it politic to look for an easier target—the Nazi medical establishment appeared to provide horrendous examples of clear-cut guilt. Administratively, the medical case, with its twenty-three defendants (including three SS administrators: Viktor Brack, Rudolf Brandt, and Wolfram Sievers),

[84] AIP Fonds Lépine, International Commission on Medical War Crimes.
[85] The delegation consisted of Henry Dale, Sydney Smith (Edinburgh), Sweeney (St. Thomas'), and W. G. Barnard (RCP). For background see *Scientific Results of German Medical Warcrimes. Report of an Enquiry under the Chairmanship of Lord Moran, MC, MD* (London, 1949).
[86] *Records of the United States Nuernberg War Crimes Trials 'United States of America v. Karl Brandt et al.' (Case I) November 21, 1946–August 20, 1947,* Microfilm Publications (Washington, DC, 1974) M 887.

was the first of twelve prosecutions of major sectors of the Nazi regime, conducted by the US.[87]

The typhus experiments were a major feature of the medical trial, which focused on the criminality of Nazi medical research rather than genocide as perpetrated by those responsible for ghettoization, murderous routines in concentration camps, and the processes of human extermination. The US prosecutors brushed aside Raphael Lemkin's concerns with the medical pursuit of genocide, a concept which involved total eradication of an ethnic, political, religious, or cultural group. Lemkin while in pre-war Poland had attempted to develop legal safeguards for minorities, sensing their vulnerability in the post-Versailles successor states. The US prosecution worked with a less comprehensive concept of 'crimes against humanity' which did not require establishing whether there were plans to eradicate any ethnic group. The prosecutors hoped that demonstrating that the human experiments were authorized by the SS would show that these were a clear-cut case of Nazi crimes.[88]

Telford Taylor, the chief prosecution lawyer, was briefed by the émigré neurologist Leo Alexander in mounting the argument that 'the poison of Nazi doctrine' corrupted men 'exceptionally qualified to form a moral and professional judgement'. Human experiments were defined as 'thanatology', by which was meant the science of producing death: 'not how to rescue or cure, but how to destroy or kill.'[89] As the typhus experiments involved comparison of a vaccinated group to an unvaccinated 'control' group, the verdict of 'thanatology' seems to be misapplied. The legitimation of the experiments was that a small human sacrifice of lives of a lower order (i.e. Russians, Jews, etc.) would assist the saving of lives of officers and soldiers on a vast scale. The American prosecution denied the scientific validity of the German experiments, and pointed to the gratuitous cruelty, so that once victims had entered 'the experimental mill', death was to be expected.

The defence counsel counter-attacked that unethical experiments were committed among the Allies: Rose, who obtained information from the Hamburg Tropical Institute on human experiments by French and US researchers, made much of US human experiments and the sterilizing of prisoners.[90] The case of R. P. Strong (the leader of American typhus expeditions to Serbia in 1914 and Poland in 1919) who had vaccinated 900 persons with a live plague bacillus and twenty-nine persons with a beriberi vaccine was compared by Rose to Haagen's experiments with live typhus vaccine. Ivy conceded that the extent of typhus from 1943 justified vaccine experiments, and that in a US penitentiary, a medical researcher would not

---

[87] NAW RG 153 Records of the Judge Advocate General (Army). War Crimes Branch. Nuremberg Administrative Files 84-1 Box 1 folder II.

[88] R. Lemkin, *Axis Rule in Occupied Europe* (New York, 1944).

[89] G. J. Annas and M. A. Grodin, *The Nazi Doctors and the Nuremberg Code* (Oxford, 1992), 70.

[90] For a cautionary attitiude to sterilization see The Committee of the American Neurological Association for the Investigation of Eugenical Sterilization: A. Myerson, J. B. Ayer, T. J. Putnam, et al., *Eugenical Sterilization. A Reorientation of the Problem* (New York, 1936). STAH Bernard-Nocht-Institut, Schriftwechsel in der Angelegenheit Dr med. Gerhard Rose, Prof. Nauck 'Material über Menschenversuche'.

normally query the circumstances in which prisoners volunteered. Yet overall, the US position was that the German medical experiments amounted to little more than sadistic butchery. The German position was that the experiments did not differ substantially from coercive human experiments conducted in the United States. The US defence insisted that any American experimentation in penitentiaries or on psychiatric patients was humane and fundamentally scientific.[91]

Criminal justice grappled with research ethics: hands-on murder, involving injections or shooting poisoned bullets, could receive the death penalty. The 'experimental' executions by Mrugowsky were decisive in securing his conviction, although this left unresolved his complicity in genocide for distributing Zyklon and his endorsement of a genocidal regime of typhus prevention. Kogon, the internee who provided evidence on the Buchenwald experiments, considered Mrugowsky 'not a simple criminal, but a complex fellow with multiple motives'.[92] The defence argument that the doctors were in effect soldiers acting under orders was not accepted. Pleas for clemency, directed initially to President Truman and then General Clay as commander of the US occupation forces, raised awkward questions about the legal basis of the prosecutions but were summarily rejected. Photographs show that Mrugowsky continued to wear the military tunic of a prisoner of war for the trial–indeed, he was one of ten defendants so attired. His last words before his execution subordinated his medical identity to that of a soldier. He protested: 'I die as a German officer sentenced by a brutal enemy and conscious that I never committed the crimes charged against me.'[93] Although during the war Mrugowsky had sustained a greater intellectual breadth in his epidemiological and medical research than many diehard Nazis, in the context of the trial his military and SS identities became the overwhelming explanation for abuses of medical power. What now was clearly Mrugowsky's presence at acts of hands-on murder— notably experimental shootings at Sachsenhausen of Russian prisoners with bullets poisoned with acontine, when Mrugowsky compiled a medical report on how the victims died—eclipsed his argument that Ding committed atrocities at Buchenwald without his knowledge.[94] The perpetrators of the typhus experiments were severely punished: death sentences were passed on Waldemar Hoven (camp doctor in Buchenwald) and Mrugowsky. Handloser, as chief military medical officer, and Rose received sentences of life imprisonment. The Ravensbrück sulphonamide experiments earned a death sentence for Gebhardt, and prison terms for the camp doctors Fritz Fischer (for life) and Herta Oberheuser.

The prosecution's chief medical experts Alexander and Ivy developed an ethical stance on the basis of the deliberations at the Pasteur Institute. Alexander argued in December 1946 that the Nazi medical experiments were fundamentally unscientific, sadistic, and primitive. Denigrating Nazi research cleared the way for permis-

---

[91] Bayle, *Croix gammée*, 1240, 1258, 1260. J. M. Harkness, 'Nuremberg and the Issue of Wartime Experiments on US Prisoners: The Green Committee', *Journal of the American Medical Association*, 276 (1996), 1672–5. STAN, KV Prozesse, Fall 1, Te 10 Rose—Closing Brief of the Defence, 87–93.
[92] NAW M 1019/roll 36 Kogon interrogation, 13.   [93] Annas and Grodin, *Nuremberg*, 106.
[94] Mrugowsky report to Widman 12 Sept. 1944, BDC Ding file.

sable human experiments. Ivy had argued at the Pasteur Institute for the legitimacy of scientifically valid experiments, for which animal experiments were an essential preliminary; these principles were presented to the Nuremberg judges in December 1946 when they were also endorsed by the American Medical Association.[95] Alexander added that consent of the subject must be free from duress and be on the basis of sufficient information to understand the aims of the experiment; the overall purpose must be to cure, treat, or prevent illness. Alexander conceded that risky experiments were justified if there was no alternative, and if the problem to be solved merited greater risks; but a safeguard was that the experimenter should undergo the same risks as the subjects. A set of ten principles were pronounced by the US judges in order to erect moral, ethical, and legal criteria to ascertain the level of criminality, a key innovation being what Alexander termed 'legally valid consent'.[96] Called the Nuremberg Code, this has established informed consent as an axiom of clinical research. Yet for medical researchers who were themselves vulnerable to criticism for their practices, the Code was a permissive document, seeking to allay any public outrage at the German atrocities, while leaving unregulated what constituted valid consent. For the Allied medical experts feared that any more radical probing of medical procedures would undermine public confidence in medical research. The Code had an international impact, but was slower to determine actual practice. In 1947 the UN Commission on Human Rights accepted the principle that 'no one shall be subjected without his free consent to medical or scientific experimentation'.[97]

The West German Chamber of Physicians sent a group of observers, led by Alexander Mitscherlich, a psychiatrist. His assistants on the commission, the medical student, Fred Mielke, and a psychiatrist, Alice Platen-Hallermund, were conscientious observers of the trial: they were a lonely pair at Nuremberg, on the one hand ostracized by the Allies, and on the other disliking attempts by Karl Brandt and the German defence to inveigle them into condemning wholesale the proceedings. Indeed, leading German physicians attacked not their colleagues on trial but the observers for their 'betrayal'. Mitscherlich diagnosed that the crimes were in large part the result of an 'aggressive search for truth', thereby implicating science rather than Nazi ideology. His courageous analysis earned him the lifelong hostility of his medical colleagues as a *Nestbeschmützer*.[98] Platen-Hallermund preferred to side with the Catholic democrat Kogon in blaming Nazi totalitarianism and Hitler's attempt to scientize anti-Semitism. She wrote a nuanced and

---

[95] A. C. Ivy, 'Nazi War Crimes of a Medical Nature', *Journal of the American Medical Association*, 139 (1949), 131–40; 'Supplementary Report of the Judicial Council', ibid., 132 (1946), 1090.

[96] L. Alexander, 'Ethical and Non-ethical Experimentation on Human Beings', in NAW RG 153/86-3-1/Box 10/Book 3 (written ca. Dec. 1946). Alexander, 'Ethics of Human Experimentation', *Psychiatric Journal of the University of Ottawa*, 1 (1976), 40–6.

[97] S. Perley, S. S. Fluss, Z. Bankowski, and F. Simon, 'The Nuremberg Code: An International Overview', in Annas and Grodin, *Nuremberg Code*, 149–73; French and Israeli proposals introduced the term 'informed consent' in 1948–9.

[98] Cited by C. Pross, 'Nazi Doctors, German Medicine and Historical Truth', in Annas and Grodin, *Nazi Doctors*, 38.

wide-ranging account of Nazi euthanasia, documenting terror and resistance.[99] Yet the German medical profession was by and large disinterested in these explanations. When Mitscherlich produced an eloquent digest of the proceedings for circulation to every physician, a few of the 10,000 copies were sent to such bodies as the World Medical Association—so rehabilitating German medicine—but professional disinterest meant that there was virtually no circulation within Germany.[100] While an American edition appeared under the title of *Doctors of Infamy*, it was not until 1960 that a German paperback was published, in which the Buchenwald and other typhus experiments received prominent attention.[101]

Rather than any wholesale condemnation of experimental medicine, the Allied strategy was to argue for safeguards against the abuse of clinical trials. Having condemned the German experiments for political, psychological, and scientific reasons, it was possible to legitimate further clinical trials and to argue for a relatively permissive code. There was a lively medical discussion during 1945–6 on whether it was legitimate to utilize the scientific data obtained from Nazi human experiments. An editorial in the *British Medical Journal* diagnosed the problem as political: 'the surrender, in fact, of the individual conscience to the mass mind of the totalitarian state.' Letters to the *Lancet* argued that scientific results of Nazi medical experiments should be published and used, although the *British Medical Journal* observed that however useful any such experiment might be, this did not condone the methods by which the information had been gained.[102] Paradoxically, the more the German experiments were condoned as scientifically valid, the weaker the US prosecution strategy became.

The utilitarian climate of opinion among many Allied medical researchers was eloquently expressed by Kenneth Mellanby, a medical entomologist, who persuaded the *British Medical Journal* to designate him its official correspondent at Nuremberg. Mellanby had been involved in extensive clinical trials for the Medical Research Council, concerning scabies (caused by an itch mite burrowing under the skin) during the war. In 1945 he published on experiments on conscientious objectors as *Human Guinea Pigs*. While he was scathing about their political opinions, he respected their cooperation. But his attitude to the victims of Nazi medical crimes was less indulgent. He believed: 'The victims were dead; if their sufferings could in any way add to medical knowledge and help others, surely this would be something that they themselves would have preferred.' His aim was to 'rescue the records' of human experiments or at least to create a climate of opinion to enable the Medical Research Council to evaluate these; he decided to begin his search for 'the records'

    [99] A. Platen-Hallermund, *Die Tötung Geisteskranker in Deutschland* (Frankfurt/M., 1948); Alice Ricciardi-von Platen, personal information, Oxford 13 Mar. 1998; E. Kogon, *Ideologie und Praxis der Unmenschlichkeit. Erfahrungen mit dem Nationalsozialismus* (Weinheim, 1995), 137.
    [100] E. BenGershom, 'From Haeckel to Hackethal: Lessons from Nazi Medicine for Students and Practitioners of Medicine', *Holocaust and Genocide Studies*, 5 (1990), 73–86.
    [101] A. Mitscherlich and F. Mielke, *Doctors of Infamy* (New York, 1949).
    [102] 'Doctors on Trial', *British Medical Journal* (25 Jan. 1947), 143.

at the Nuremberg medical trial.[103] Mellanby reviewed the proceedings in the *British Medical Journal* of January 1947. He questioned the prosecution's verdict that 'practically no results of any value were obtained in any of the work':

From what we already know of the typhus work it is clear that a useful evaluation of the various vaccines was obtained; some of these results have already been published.

Mellanby praised the notorious paper that Ding published in 1943 in the *Zeitschrift für Hygiene*. In 1943 this paper had caused concern to the *Lancet* that the Germans were experimenting on Allied prisoners of war. Mellanby claimed that Ding's vaccine test was an 'important and unique piece of medical research', that 'formed the basis not only of German, but also of British and Allied anti-typhus policy . . . for every victim of his experiments 20,000 others might have been saved'. This reflected the arguments of the defence lawyers as regards the German army, but Mellanby's views had no historical foundation as the Allies were firmly committed to the Cox vaccine. He justified the malaria experiments of Claus Schilling at the 'reasonably humane' Dachau camp, dismissing the reported numbers of deaths— several hundred out of a thousand experimental subjects—as exaggerated.[104] While conceding the German failure to obtain informed consent, Mellanby was convinced that there might be data worth salvaging, although the testimony of the victims of the experiments established that 'little of the work had been properly planned, few of the investigators were competent, there was a lot of very inaccurate recording and even some deliberate falsification of results'. It was tragic that 'little of value was discovered as the result of this appalling sacrifice of human lives'.[105] Yet overall, Mellanby endorsed a utilitarian legitimation to Nazi clinical experiments as of long-term benefit. The German defence at Nuremberg seized on Mellanby's views as useful ammunition in support of their stance that the German and Allied research ethics hardly differed.

Mellanby's defence of scientific freedom occurred at a time when many scientists were turning against ideas of social planning as synonymous with socialism, while at the same time demanding massive research resources for ever larger batteries of equipment and laboratory facilities. He opposed organized team research and the 'red tape' of large-scale organizations.[106] Confronting central state direction of science as part of social planning and strategic research, critics attacked large-scale state-controlled research as ushering in a Soviet-style totalitarianism. Nazi medical atrocities were ascribed to the ills of excessive state regimentation. Protecting the scientist's autonomy meant shifting responsibility for Nazi human experiments on to the totalitarian state—a convenient target at a time of rising East–West

[103] K. Mellanby, *Human Guinea Pigs* (London, 1945). The first edition makes no reference to Nazi human experiments, in contrast to the second edition (London, 1973), pp. 181–6. P. J. Weindling, 'Human Guinea Pigs and the Ethics of Experimentation: The *BMJ*'s Correspondent at the Nuremberg Medical Trial', *British Medical Journal*, 313 (1996), 1467–70.

[104] Mellanby, *Human Guinea Pigs* (1973), 187. Rose supported the medical value of the Buchenwald human experiments; see Bayle, *Croix gammée*, 1250–1.

[105] Mellanby, *Human Guinea Pigs* (1973), 196.   [106] Ibid. (1945), preface.

tensions. Scientists wanted power and resources without having their hands tied by public accountability.

Similar ideas of freedom from the corruptions of state power pervaded medicine. In September 1946 an international medical conference was held at the British Medical Association (BMA) in London to launch the World Medical Association as a physicians' association to counterbalance the public health orientation of the nascent World Health Organization. Charles Hill, the avuncular radio doctor, aimed to generate a current of opinion against state medicine. The BMA followed Moran in attributing the Nazi medical crimes to state interference in medicine. In November 1946 a BMA official diagnosed the ills of scientific medical research: 'It is clear from the events of the past fifteen years that material achievement and scientific progress unless harnessed to a humanitarian motive and moral dynamic become the tools of totalitarian ideologies.' A BMA pamphlet issued in June 1947 condemned Nazi doctors as

their amoral methods were the result of training and conditioning to regard science as an instrument in the hands of the state to be applied in any way desired by its rulers. It is to be assumed that initially they did not realise that ideas of those who held political power would lead to the denial of the fundamental values on which medicine is based.

The resulting code stressed the prime duty of the physician to the individual patient: it was the counterpart of the defence of professional powers against state encroachments.[107] Medical ethics was shaped by national political contingencies and professional issues.

The debate on medical research as an arm of state power raised the questions whether the results of Nazi human experiments were indeed medically useful, or whether the poison of Nazism crippled scientific endeavours. Moran convened a commission of six experts to evaluate the medical experiments dealt with at the Nuremberg medical trial. While the tribunal condemned Nazi human experiments as incompetent and racist, this implied that medical research was in general properly conducted and deserved a clean bill of health. C. P. Blacker, the president of the Eugenics Society, demarcated between the unscientific barbarism of the X-ray sterilizations at Auschwitz, and eugenics itself as humane, enlightened, and thoroughly scientific.[108] The bacteriologist Ronald Hare concluded that although the German bacteriological experiments were extensive, they 'added very little to the knowledge of the problems investigated'. Ding was singled out for having worked for three months at the Pasteur Institute, but Hare supported the view that the bulk of the work was left to untrained subordinates. That Nazi human experiments were condemned as incompetent saved the reputation of western science.

Moran produced a terse five-page report that stood in marked contrast to the

[107] BMA archives, W001 World Medical Association. International Relations Committee, memo by D. E. Claxton, Assistant Secretary to the BMA. International Relations. General File 19/3/19, Medical War Crimes, BMA pamphlet on 'War Crimes and Medicine'. 108 C. P. Blacker, 'Eugenic Experiments Conducted by the Nazis on Human Subjects', *Eugenics Review*, 44 (1952), 9–19.

[108] C. P. Blacker, 'Eugenic Experiments Conducted by the Nazis on Human Subjects', *Eugenics Review*, 44 (1952), 9–19.

verbose legal wrangles of the Nuremberg prosecution, contained in the bulky volumes of trial proceedings and documents. He angrily stated that a moral analysis would have required American cooperation.[109] The brevity of the British response can be attributed to the concern with the iniquities of state medicine for health care and medical research.[110] Moran was embroiled in the mounting outrage at the implementation of the National Health Service and at Aneurin Bevan as 'Medical Service Dictator'. Whereas Hill of the BMA spoke of doctors confronting 'Bevan or Belsen', Moran was more conciliatory.[111] The perfunctory Foreign Office report on German medical war crimes produced by Moran in 1949 reflected his outrage at British officialdom rather than at Nazi brutality. While Moran dealt with Nazi war crimes, he was in fact preoccupied with the BMA's war against government medical reforms.[112]

Having fought a successful scientific war culminating in the atom bomb, Allied scientists were divided between those seeking to research the effects of nuclear radiation, and a minority questioning the ethics of science for strategic ends. The British led the way in restarting the motor of German scientific advance. The physiologist Sir Henry Dale, who had a profound respect for German medical research, devised the new name Max Planck-Gesellschaft for the successor organization to the Kaiser Wilhelm Gesellschaft, which was formally established in September 1946.[113] The integration of German science into western structures resulted in turning an official blind eye towards former Nazi medical researchers.

The medical trial with its wholesale denunciation of the typhus experiments served to further an ethical double standard. Science under totalitarianism was inherently degrading and coercive, whereas liberal science provided inherent safeguards for experimental subjects. Allied radiation experiments from 1945 on civilian populations show that military demands continued to prompt violations of the new ethical codes. German chemical weapons, especially the nerve gas Sarin, were potentially of use. The Chemical Defense Advisory Board scrutinized the evidence of German chemistry for weapons research, urged the arrest of involved personnel in order to pump them for information, scoured the testimonies and other evidence presented at the war crimes trials, and captured documents for information. The United States recruited medical researchers whose expertise could be applied to strategic problems.[114] The biological warfare expert Blome, arrested in May 1945 and interrogated by his Allied counterparts, was acquitted in the Nuremberg medical trial. He was recruited in 1951 by the US Army Chemical Corps, yet his Nazi

[109] Foreign Office, *Scientific Results of German Medical War Crimes* (London, 1949), 4–5.

[110] C. Webster, 'The Metamorphosis of Dawson of Penn', in D. Porter and R. Porter, *Doctors, Politics and Society*, 212–28.

[111] C. Webster, *Problems of Health Care*, i (London, 1988), 99–101, 110, 116.

[112] R. Lovell, *Churchill's Doctor. A Biography of Lord Moran* (London, 1992), 289–90.

[113] M. Heinemann, 'Der Wiederaufbau der Kaiser-Wilhelm-Gesellschaft und die Neugrundungen der Max-Planck Gesellschaft (1945–1949)', in R. Vierhaus and B. vom Brocke (eds.), *Forschung im Spannungsfeld von Politik und Gesellschaft. Geschichte und Struktur der Kaiser-Wilhelm-/Max-Planck-Gesellschaft* (Stuttgart, 1990), 407–70.

[114] Heinemann, 'Wiederaufbau', 439–40; T. Bower, *The Paper Clip Conspiracy* (London, 1987).

pedigree and lack of expertise in microbiology meant that his planned move to the US was scrapped.[115] Operation Paperclip fed German medical researchers to satiate the appetite of US strategic requirements. Kliewe provided US interrogators with a full reconstruction of the germ warfare programme. That the Germans had carried out human experiments was seen as of strategic value. Allied sympathizers with the accused German scientists were prepared to override the niceties of such principles as informed consent, and to take risks concerning minor disabilities to their experimental subjects.

The post-war thirst for strategically relevant medical know-how meant that programmes for human experiments continued, but the line was firmly drawn against deliberate infection and lethal experiments. Medical science was to be disengaged from the corruptions of the totalitarian state, leaving it open for former combatants in the war on disease from the east to be recruited by those concerned with the defence of western freedoms. Medical progress and strategic priorities might still involve the occasional accidental fatality, and exploit prisoners and mental defectives, but systematic human butchery of the reckless and unrestrained Nazi experimenters was beyond the pale. What was left intact was the conviction that medical research should exercise widespread powers and command extensive resources, while being immune from public scrutiny except in the most dire of cases.

v. Eradicating Diseases, Eradicating Peoples

While Nazi medicine embarked on genocidal anti-epidemic measures, the question arises whether medicine emerged from the war with a hardened scientistic militancy—poised to embark on a global scientific drive to eradicate diseases? US public health experts pointed to the 'importance of stamping out disease at its source, in place of the older methods'.[116] By this was meant not just prevention and control, but intensive local vaccination campaigns and saturation with DDT and new drugs. Anti-typhus measures were a starting-point, as the US adopted a policy of free distribution of vaccines, and once the threat of typhus evaporated, other epidemic perils were targeted.

New approaches to the prevention of diseases required a root and branch extermination of vectors and of disease-inducing organisms. Preventive medicine had relied on containment and control of diseases, or the building up of powers of resistance by means of artificial immunization. Between the wars it was hoped that typhus would die out of its own volition. Signs of the new thinking were evident in the campaign by Fred Soper and the Rockefeller Foundation to eradicate mosquitoes; they joined forces with the Egyptian government and Allied military forces between 1943 and 1945. While Soper formulated an eradication concept in 1936,

[115] Hansen, *Biologische Kriegsführung*, 162–74.
[116] J. L. Brand, 'The United States Public Health Service and International Health, 1945–1950', *Bulletin of the History of Medicine*, 63 (1989), 590.

medical backing for total eradication did not gain ground until the Second World War.[117] Although previously considered and sporadically pursued, total eradication of a disease by rendering either the pathogen or the vector extinct as a species no longer appeared to be Utopian amidst the wartime acceleration of medical research and general devastation. The post-war ideology was very much that of basic medical research to target and conquer diseases.

There was a brief period of optimism that the imposition of scientifically proven and rational policies would cure the world of its political, medical, and environmental ills. Visionary scientists took command of international organizations: Stampar, the protégé of the Rockefeller Foundation and of Rajchman, having been imprisoned by the Nazis during the War, became Chairman of the Interim Commission and first president of the World Health Organization. At the end of 1946 Rajchman, the former director of the LNHO, gained acceptance for his suggestion that UNRRA's residual funds should be transferred to the International Children's Emergency Fund (UNICEF).[118] UNRRA was failing in its mission to reshape medical services in liberated countries; but its substantial aid contrasted with the punitive hunger blockade after the First World War.[119]

After a series of preparatory conferences the World Health Organization was finally established in April 1948. Crucial differences to the LNHO were that experts were sovereign, and that it was no longer so eurocentric. Experts found new fields of activities, reinforced by enthusiasm for world health. Typhus joined the ranks of diseases wiped out—it was claimed—by modern medical technologies. Soper observed that Zinsser's prophecy that typhus would live for centuries even though confined to 'the zoological garden of controlled diseases' was rendered redundant by the wartime chemical attack with DDT.

Typhus vanished from Europe after the summer of 1945, then from Africa (apart from Ethiopia between 1951 and 1956), from central and South America during the 1950s, and finally from Asia after a brief flare up in the wake of the Korean War. Experts claimed that DDT, new vaccines, and delousing routines effectively controlled and wiped out the disease.[120] In 1951 Soper as president of the Pan American Sanitary Bureau predicted the eventual eradication of typhus providing that international organizations could expand eradication programmes.[121] As the new antibiotics became available for bacterial infections, typhus rickettsiae were shifted back into the class of bacteria.

---

[117] F. L. Soper, *Building the Health Bridge* (Bloomington, Ind., 1970); M. Cueto, 'The Cycles of Eradication: The Rockefeller Foundation and Latin American Public Health, 1918–1949', in Weindling, *International Health*, 222–43.

[118] E. H. Hinman, *World Eradication of Infectious Diseases* (New York, 1967), 39–42; G. Woodbridge, *UNRRA. The History of the United Nations Relief and Rehabilitation Administration* (New York, 1950), i. 306; M. Black, *The Children and the Nations: The Story of UNICEF* (New York, 1986).

[119] 'The Tasks of UNRRA. Medical Services in Liberated Countries', *British Medical Journal* (9 June 1945), 816–17.

[120] *Les Dix Premières Années de l'Organisation Mondiale de la Santé* (Geneva, 1958), 270–1.

[121] F. Soper, 'The Elephant Never Forgets', *American Journal of Tropical Medicine and Hygiene*, 1 (1952), 361–8, repr. in Kerr, *Health Bridge*, 322–9.

As the threat of typhus receded, medical entomologists shifted their efforts to the intractable problem of malaria. Post-war efforts were concentrated against malaria as DDT eradication programmes were unleashed on a global scale. Chemical spraying promised a final solution to the problem of insect pests. In 1948 this tide of optimism was expressed in the award of a Nobel Prize to the Swiss chemist, Paul Hermann Müller, who had discovered the efficacy of DDT.[122] Nauck, who retained his position as director of the Hamburg Tropical Institute, joined the international medical campaign for the global eradication of malaria.[123]

Just as the dropping of the atomic bomb and ensuing nuclear tests provoked a critical public reaction when it was observed how radiation could cause cancers and mutations, the tide began to turn against insecticides during the 1950s. Eradication programmes were thwarted by resistance to insecticides, and unexpected side-effects. Strains of insects resistant to hydrogen cyanide were detected.[124] On 16 April 1945 *Time* warned that DDT damaged trees and wildlife. By 1949 it was observed how insects were becoming resistant to DDT in Italy, and a stronger cocktail of poisons also began to fail by the early 1950s. The cycle of indiscriminate use of DDT sprays, and resistance, was repeated between 1944 and 1947 in Denmark, and louse control programmes came to grief in Spain and Egypt by 1948, and in war-ravaged Korea and Japan between 1945 and 1951. Tests on lice collected from vagrants and refugees showed how DDT was becoming ineffective for the control of lice.[125] There followed concern about the accumulation of DDT in body tissues, and pollution. Rachel Carson's best-seller, *Silent Spring*, condemned how DDT spraying poisoned not just the targeted disease-vectors but whole swathes of wildlife in the countryside. A nightmare scenario was that mass chemical treatment was turning fields, forests, and waters into poisonous death-traps, withering vegetation, and silencing terrestrial inhabitants.[126]

The exterminatory approach to world health was based on the opinion that typhus had been eradicated by DDT and the Cox vaccine. The malaria eradication programme, first proposed in 1948, was launched by the WHO in 1955, and the smallpox and polio eradication programmes followed despite the criticisms that the eradication concept was unrealistic given the intricate adaptive relationships between humans and microorganisms.[127] Ignoring problems of endemicity and resistance, infectious diseases seemed to be a problem solved by modern medical

[122] P. H. Müller, 'Dichlorodiphyltrichoroathan und neuere Inzekticide', *Les Prix Nobel en 1948* (Stockholm, 1948), 122–32.

[123] E. G. Nauck, *Die Ausrottung der Malaria als Aufgabe der internationalen Forschung* (Hamburg, 1958).

[124] WHO, *Vector Control* (Geneva, 1963); J. R. Busvine, *Disease Transmission by Insects* (Berlin, 1993), 224–7.

[125] WHO, *Insect Resistance and Vector Control* (Geneva, 1958); A. W. A. Brown, *Insecticide Resistance in Arthropods* (Geneva, 1958); WHO, *Vector Control* (Geneva, 1963); R. Carson, *Silent Spring* (London, 1963), 217–20.

[126] Carson, *Silent Spring*. For criticism of Carson as exaggerated see Busvine, *Disease Transmission*, 231–3.

[127] D. Baxby, 'The Communicability of Smallpox, and the Role of Vaccination in its Eradication', unpub. paper.

research; in time public health strategies of isolation were meant to eradicate micro-organisms or their carriers.[128] There were wildly optimistic hopes concerning the powers of antibiotics, notably of penicillin as a new wonder drug. Saturation of populations with antibiotics was intended to eradicate syphilis and related diseases like yaws.[129] Medical strategies of disease control involved destroying a complete species of disease-carriers.

The post-war climate of medical triumphalism and eradication continued wartime efforts to deploy medical resources against disease outbreaks, often magnified into potential epidemics. When confronted by epidemics in the liberated concentration camps, medical researchers achieved remarkably little in terms of cure and control. Here a comparison may be drawn with the Allied interventions to delouse in Eastern Europe after the First World War. Although there were intense flare-ups of typhus during the Second World War, an epidemic on the scale of the Russian typhus epidemic of 1921–3 did not occur. One might argue that there were more victims of anti-typhus measures than of the disease itself, once the genocidal fiction of delousing is taken into account.

vi. Final Reflections

Holocaust history has rightly recognized the importance of the eugenic schemes for racial engineering, the *Generalplan Ost* as the context for extermination policies. I have suggested that underpinning this was what amounted to a *Seuchenplan Ost*—this involved a range of ruthless anti-epidemic strategies leading to genocide of peoples on the pretext of being potential disease carriers. Moreover, longer-term factors need to be taken into account, as illustrated by the remarkable medical career of Zeiss, from being seconded to the Ottoman army, to leading the campaign for a genocidal geo-medicine in the east. The involved medical personae reveal a combination of professional, ideological, scientific, and personal motives. Their conviction became crucial that German medicine should take a central role in the east to promote settlement and sustain ethnic German communities. I have alluded to the importance of the Russian origins of such doctors as von Bormann, Nauck, and Waegner. Others were born in the 'lost' territories of the east—in Bromberg, Posen, etc. Some rallied to the cause like Hase, seeing the east as a vast experimental terrain. Zeiss exemplifies a career dedicated to preservation of the lives of ethnic German 'colonists'.

Was bacteriology inherently exterminatory, culminating in programmes of eradicating diseases by eradicating peoples? I have shown that a number of bacteriologists associated with Koch espoused anti-Semitism and increasingly reckless human experiments. Koch's assistant in East Africa, Kudicke, took a prominent role in Warsaw public health, although he sided with Hagen in stabilizing the epidemic

---

[128] F. Fenner, *et al.*, *Smallpox and its Eradication* (Geneva, 1988), 367–92.
[129] A. J. Silman and S. P. A. Allwright, *Elimination or Reduction of Diseases? Opportunities for Health Service Action in Europe* (Oxford, 1988).

situation, rather than with the exterminatory Walbaum. The researchers at the Hamburg Tropical Institute, presided over by Koch's former assistant, Nocht, also took a prominent role in the east. Yet, medically, most adulterated Koch's strict bacteriological causality with geo-medicine. Social contingencies mixed with epidemiological perceptions.

Despite the impulses of medical leaders in Nazi Germany to implement strongly authoritarian measures against typhus, these did as much to spread as to contain the disease. Under Nazism authoritarian traits within the structure of medical thinking were taken to an extreme. As anti-Semitism and anti-epidemic measures became intertwined, so the problem of typhus came to facilitate the destruction of millions, treated as human vermin and subjected to the deception of delousing.

Public health experts strengthened the formation of a European order based on ethnically homogenous nations. Typhus epidemics accelerated international efforts to secure new frontiers in the wake of the First World War; by the time of the Second World War disease control camouflaged exterminatory medical policies. Ethnic diversity and mass migration were casualties of the closure of national frontiers so as to exclude migrant disease-carriers. Medicine emerges as an arm of state politics and biologically based welfare measures, primarily in defending borders and reinforcing schemes of conquest and racial cleansing. Sanitary controls were to keep the national stock free from racial pollution, while border controls were to exclude the nuisance of disease carriers.

The German eradication project relying on Zyklon required massive and brutal coercion. Fixed delousing facilities met with evasion, and were criticized as promoting infection; there were innumerable operating problems. It is arguable whether preventive measures based on delousing were effective other than in circumscribed areas, and experience showed that delousing was a haphazard and brutal process which could actually spread lice. Where typhus was endemic, it was difficult to eradicate. Where typhus had already died out, it is doubtful whether it could have achieved general epidemic proportions as long as there were sanitary facilities and people habitually washed their bodies and clothing.

Typhus control represented a scientized strategy to exclude ethnic undesirables. The association of Eastern European 'Asiatics' with lice, filth, and disease prompted draconian control measures. These gave a scientific cutting-edge to Nazi racial anti-Semitism on an organized basis. Typhus prevention involved rationales, procedures, and personnel for subjecting whole populations to shaving and showering as hygienic routines. Hygienic procedures meant that large groups could be controlled, confined, and, in the hands of racial fanatics, ultimately eliminated. Hygienic practices do not provide an explanation for the Holocaust—'inefficient' practices of the police battalions and death marches were highly effective in causing innumerable deaths and mass suffering. Nor does typhus prevention provide a simple story of enforcing compliance with the lethal fiction of delousing. But epidemic prevention provided genocidal perpetrators with persuasive medical rationales and powerful killing methods.

The threat of typhus, magnified as a New Black Death or Jewish plague, was grossly exaggerated, for as long as there was a basic sanitary structure and a population willing to change and launder clothes, then the disease might be localized but was hardly likely to ravage Europe. The danger arose where the sanitary structures were destroyed as in the Nazi concentration camps and ghettos. There has remained an uneasy sense that a recrudescence of infectious diseases on the eastern margins of Europe can recur, especially at times of increased ethnic tensions. The closing of the open door to migrants seeking to escape poverty and persecution in Europe had fatal repercussions. Interventive policies of assistance to eradicate an epidemic at its source were primarily in the strategic interests of the donor countries and of privileged medical élites, and generally failed to alleviate the suffering of afflicted minorities—imposing containment rendered the deprived and persecuted vulnerable to disease, starvation, and genocide. Typhus, caught between professional and international conflict, dissolved into a series of metaphors, legitimating a range of coercive hygienic measures. A disease was thus not so much a pathogenic invasion of the body but an artefact constructed by researchers and racists to secure racially purified states.

The diseased visions of typhus patients may be construed as representing emancipation from the tortures of medical and racial oppression. Compliance with the genocidal fiction of typhus was only sporadic. The oppressed learned to manipulate the German fear of the disease in their struggle to keep their persecutors at bay. Survivors' testimonies and the radical critique of German typhus epidemiology, vaccine research, and control measures—notably by Fleck and Hirszfeld—demonstrate the genocidal nature of Nazi notions of typhus. Many Jews under German occupation well understood the artificiality—and the deadly dangers—of disease categories relying on racist stereotypes, and the need to avoid as far as possible being lured into any medical trap as potentially lethal.

The post-war debris left by typhus consisted of a range of hazards: megalomaniac notions of disease eradication, toxic chemicals, research on persons unable to give their consent, Nazi physicians continuing in positions of authority, half-hearted Allied interest in prosecuting the perpetrators of war crimes, and German animosity against such prosecutions. But popular responses of survival and resistance to medical excesses left a challenging legacy as the morbid delusions of typhus victims became part of the fabric of post-war norms. Resistance to the genocidal thrust of Nazi anti-typhus measures provides an ethical warning that all programmes of disease eradication must be free from coercive experimentation and differential evaluations of human lives. Preventing disease should be accompanied by preventing the definition of any new species of infectious human parasite.

Appendix I

Typhus Statistics in Germany, Poland, Russia, and the Ukraine

Germany

Year	Cases	Deaths
1876		207
1877		240/114[1]
1878		647/223
1879		313/202
1880		323/209
1881		611/253
1882		422/118
1883		131/60
1884	Case statistics date	128/39
1885	from the Reich Law on	63/34
1886	Infectious Diseases	69/22
1887		97/49
1888		65/33
1889		13/16
1890		33/6
1891		22/12
1892		31/16
1893		26/15
1894		58/32
1895		16/19
1896		13/24
1897		11/7
1898		6/2
1899		11/18

[1] Sources: League of Nations, 'Typhus', *Monthly Epidemiological Report of the Health Section of the Secretariat*, 8 (1929); second column: *Statistisches Jahrbuch für das deutsche Reich*, 1– (1880–). The figure for overall deaths refers only to towns with over 15,000 inhabitants until 1912. The figures of cases and the third set of deaths between 1901 and 1914 derive form BAK R86/1039 Bd 1. Typhus deaths were concentrated in certain regions:

Year	Baltic coastal region	Oder-Warthe region	Saxon-Brandenburg Basin
1877	24	65	1
1878	112	77	28
1879	5	70	122
1880	73	32	27
1881	182	24	27
1882	67	34	2
1883	16	11	9

Year	Cases	Deaths
1900		17/14
1901	2	13/18
1902	1	0/12
1903	6	0/13/1
1904	2	1/7/1
1905	16	4/0/0
1906	3	5/0/0
1907	17	5/0/2
[1908	8/9	2]3/1/[2]
[1909	7/7	0]2/0
[1910	18/4	4]4/0
[1911	6/12	1]1/1
1912	[8]/6	0/0/0
1913	6/6	3/0
1914	14/4	6/7/0
1915	573	669
Prussia[3]	[6542]	[1311]
1916	120	358
	[110]	[157]
1917	273	502
	[271]	[356]
1918	379	535
	[299]	[401]
	659	71
1 Dec. 1918–3	1,980	
May 1919		
1919	3,549	527
	[2289]	[643]
	3758	327
1920	483	67
	[470]	[86]
1921	533/427	54
	[299]	[100]
1922	386/382[4]	51
	[429]	[94]
1923	27	11
	[16]	[12]
1924	8[5]	1

[2] Figures in square brackets are for Prussia, taken from *25 Jahre der preussischen Medizinalverwaltung*, 158–9. The high wartime rates includes prisoners of war. Discrepancies in the period 1918–20 arise from whether military, migrants, seasonal workers, and prisoners of war were included.

[3] Peiper, 'Fleckfieber in Preussen', 6.

[4] The second figures for cases in 1921–2, and for 1913 are from B. Möllers, *Gesundheitswesen und Wohlfahrtspflege im Deutschen Reiche* (Berlin, 1923), 236.

[5] Reported cases taken from Ries, 61. The 1919 rates includes prisoners of war, otherwise the figures 1914–24 are for the civilian population. See also *Medizinalstatische Mitteilungen aus dem Reichsgesundheitsamte*, 1–23 (1893–1925).

Year	Cases	Deaths	
	[10]	[3]	
1925	8	5[6]	
	[3]	[4]	
1926	3	1	
1927	7	0	
1928	2	0	
1929	1[7]	1	
1930		0	
1931		1	
1932		2	
1933		1	
1934		0	
1935		0	
1936		0	
1938		1	
1939	8[8]	0	
1940	556	95[9]	
1941	2,340	385	(includes 118 deaths in Prussia and 255 in Wartheland)[10]
1942	2,375	187	(includes 1246 cases in Prussia)[11]
1943	5,000[12]		
	973	88	(677 cases in Prussia, until 3 Apr.)[13]
May	296		
June	274[14]		
1944			
May	2,492		
June	2,225		
July	451[15]		

[6] K. Glaser, *Vom Reichsgesundheitsamt zum Bundesgesundheitsamt* (Stuttgart, 1960), 56 gives deaths from typhus as follows: 1921: 41, 1922: 41, 1923: 5, 1924: 8, 1925: 2 (out of 3 cases).

[7] League of Nations, 'Typhus', *Monthly Epidemiological Report of the Health Section of the Secretariat*, 8 (1929), 474 for 1919–29.

[8] NAW 112/710/1110 'Epidemiology. Typhus Fever'.

[9] Ries, 77.

[10] *Bulletin OIHP*, 34 (1942), 185. Ries, 77 gives 1969 cases and 326 deaths for 1941.

[11] *Bulletin OIHP*, 35 (1943), 186–7.

[12] NAW RG 112, 710 box 1110, 'Typhus Fever in Germany', Fig. 1. The statistics 1939–43 correspond to those of the LNHO, and thereafter an upward trend is recorded. There is no official record for 1944.

[13] *Bulletin OIHP*, 35 (1943), 555–6, repeated 36 (1944), 84–5. This period (3 Jan.–3 Apr.) is the last set of statistics for Germany.

[14] BAK R 86/4148 it was claimed that only 19 of the 296 cases were Germans and that only 14 of the 274 cases were Germans.

[15] BAK R 86/4148 Seuchenstand, Juni 1944.

Year	Cases	Deaths
1945	16,506 in US zone till June	
1945		

Weekly figures in US zone:

1–6 Apr. 1945	449	
11–17 Aug. 1945	14,598[16]	

Federal Republic of Germany

Year		Deaths
1951		12
1953		3
1954		2
1955		2
1956		0
1957		1
1958		2
1959		2
1960		4
1961		4
1962		0
1963		1
1964		1
1965		0

Poland

Year	Cases	Deaths	Cases	Deaths

Congress Poland

1912		145[17]		

annual average, US est. 6,500[18]

Government General

GERMAN OCCUPATION			AUSTRIAN OCCUPATION	
1915	1,244	1,357	11,294	1,328
1916	16,285/34,538	1,269	10,446	1,175
1917	29,616/43,840	2,328	15,645	—
1918				
–1 Dec	30,567/97,082/[19]	73,380	5,670[20]	

[16] Leiby, *Public Health*, 145.

[17] *Rocznik Satstyczny Krolestwa Polskiego* (1914), 233 cited in Frey, *Bilder*, 45.

[18] RAC RF 1.1/789/2/11, H. A. Shaw, 4 May 1920.

[19] Frey, 'Gesundheitswesen', 644; id., *Bilder*, 91. The second column refers to statistics given by Rajchman in *International Health Conference April 13–17 1920*, 32, 82.

[20] J. Kostrzewski, 'Dur wysypkowy (*Typhus exanthematicus*)', in id. (ed.), *Choroby Zakaźne w Polsce i ich Zwalczanie w Latach 1919–1962* (Warsaw, 1964), 445. Also 'Typhus', *Monthly Epidemiological Reports* (1929), 482.

Year	Cases	Deaths
Poland		
1919	219,066/231,206	18,640/19,891
1920	168,097	22,575[21]
1921	49,547	4,199
1922	42,724	3,199
1923	11,185	898
1924	7,706	666
1925	3,950	320
1926	3,574	266
1927	2,948	265
1928	2,401	161
1929	1,988	146
1930	1,639	112
1931	2,154	144
1932	2,424	185
1933	3,453	200
1934	5,127	303
1935	4,149	249
1936	3,757	234[22]
1937	3,477	196
1938	3,557	184[23]
1939	3,291	121
Government General		
1940	7,900	404[24]
1941	72,439	3,925
1942	88,609	5,843
1943	25,814	
1944	8,271	
Poland		
1945	15,803	1,285
1946	3,518	296
1947	535	39
1948	391	21
1949	389	10
1950	214	12
1951	211	20

[21] Walbaum, in du Prel, *Das Generalgouvernement*, 192; Strong, 'Anti-typhus Campaign', 198–9.

[22] M. Hanecki, B. Neuman, and J. Czajka, *Służba Zdrowia w Polsce* (Warsaw, 1956), 38 for statistics 1919–35.

[23] League of Nations, *Annual Epidemiological Report. Corrected Statistics of Notifiable Diseases for the Year 1938* (Geneva, 1941), 14.

[24] Ries, 77.

Year	Cases	Deaths
1952	219	17
1953	350	9
1954	369	12
1955	392	12
1956	433	7
1957	369	4
1958	287	1
1959	273	
1960	265	4
1961	209	8
1962	151	2[25]

Russia/Soviet Union

Year	Cases	Deaths
1905	76,831	6,241
1906	52,412	4,035
1907	51,984	3,639
1908	103,259	7,455
1909	180,724	10,501
1910	138,577	9,696
1911	120,671	7,647
1912	100,928	4,846
1913	118,419	7,251
1914	89,643[26]	
1918	141,638/700,000	
1919	2,340,691/6,600,000	
1920	3,945,574/6,500,000	
1921	698,449/1,200,000[27]	
1922	1,467,955/1,441,433	
1923	242,890/244,124	
1924	126,865/125,474	
1925	70,415/71,010	
1926	55,817/55,841	
1927	41,449/40,818[28]	
1928	31,090[29]	
1931	17,828	
1932	78,132	

[25] J. Kostrzewski, 'Dur wysypkowy (*Typhus exanthematicus*)', 441, 447 (includes statistics from 1919–62).

[26] 'Typhus', *Monthly Epidemiological Reports* (1929), 479.

[27] The second column contains estimates by Tarasevich.

[28] 'Typhus', *Monthly Epidemiological Reports*, 474.

[29] Ries, 62 for statistics 1918–28.

Year	Cases	Deaths
1933	35,218	
1934	56,194	

Year	Cases	Deaths
1936	45,409/55,954[30]	
1937	58,042	
1938	45,703[31]	
1980	1,100	
1985	500	
1989	300[32]	

Ukraine

Year	Cases	Deaths
1920	591,842	
1921	110,891	
1922	344,843	
1923	31,307	

[30] League of Nations, *Annual Epidemiological Report. Corrected Statistics of Notifiable Diseases for the Year 1938* (Geneva, 1941), 60. The USSR ceased to issue epidemiological data in April 1937.

[31] Ries, 76 for 1936–8 rates for European Russia.

[32] Patterson, 'Typhus and its Control', 381.

1924	14,219
1925	9,123

Appendix II

Typhus Vaccines and Sera, 1876–1944

The bacteriological phase

Mochutkovskii	1876	Odessa	convalascent serum
Otto	1917	Berlin	convalescent serum
Ashesov	1918–20	South Russia	inactivated human serum
Ashesov	1918–20	South Russia	horse serum therapy
Nicolle, Conseil	1920	Pasteur Institute, Tunis	convalescent serum
Bacot, Arkwright	1922	Egypt	convalescent serum

The biological phase

Rocha Lima	1917/18	Hamburg	louse faeces
Weigl	1930	Lwów	louse intestines
Blanc	1937	Casablanca	louse faeces
Eyer, Weigl	1939	Cracow	louse intestines

The viral phase

Yolk sac vaccines

Cox	1938–40	USA	yolk sac
Zinsser, Plotz, Enders	1939	Boston	agar & yolk sac
Otto, Wohlrab,	1939	Frankfurt	yolk sac
Gildemeister, Haagen	1940	Berlin	mouse brain/yolk sac
Behringwerk	1942	Marburg	yolk sac
Behringwerk	1942	Lemberg	yolk sac
Propper-Gaschenkov	1941/2	Moscow	yolk sac (Cox)
Smorodintsev	1942	Moscow/	yolk sac (Otto strain)
		Tomsk	yolk sac (Cox)
	c.1943	Rome	chick embryo
Darsin	1943	Riga	
Haagen	1944	Strassburg	dry vaccine

Mammalian tissues

Nigg, Landsteiner	1930	New York	cell cultures
Castaneda	1939	Mexico	mouse lungs
Laigret, Durand	1939	Tunis	mouse brains
Durand, Sparrow	1939	Tunis	mouse lungs
Castaneda	1940	Mexico	rat lung
Durand, Giroud	1940	Tunis Paris	mouse lung
Panthier	1941/2	Algiers	rabbit lung

Madsen, *et al.*	1941	Copenhagen	mouse lungs
Ciuca	1942	Bucharest	dog lung
Ding	1943	Buchenwald	rabbit lung
ASID	1943	Kiev	

Other types

| Fleck | 1942 | Lemberg | human urine |

SELECT BIBLIOGRAPHY

1. Archives

Austria

VIENNA
Österreichisches Staatsarchiv (ÖSA)
 Allgemeine Verwaltungsarchiv, Ministerium des Inneren, 'S'–Akten (Sanitätsakten) 1911–18
 Archiv der Republik (AdR), Staatsamt für soziale Verwaltung, Volksgesundheit
 Kriegsarchiv

France

PARIS
Archives de l'Institut Pasteur (AIP)
 Direction
 Fonds Lépine
 Fonds Sparrow

Germany

BERLIN
Archiv der Humboldt Universität, Berlin (AHUB)
 Medizinische Fakultät
 Hygienisches Institut
 Nachlass Grotjahn
 Nachlass Zeiss
 Universitätskurator Berlin Personalakten, Joachim Mrugowsky, Olsen, Zeiss
Bundesarchiv Berlin (BAB)/Berlin Document Center (BDC)
 R6/33, 605 Zentrale für Ostforschung
 Filmarchiv der Persönlichkeiten
 NSDAP, SS, SS-Ahnenerbe, Reichsärztekammer, Reichsforschungsrat
Archiv zur Geschichte der Max-Planck-Gesellschaft, Berlin
 1 Abt. Rep 0001A Gesetz zur Wiederherstellung des Berufsbeamtentums—KWI Hirn-forschung 1933–4
 Abteilung V Repositur 13 Haber
Geheimes Staatsarchiv Berlin-Dahlem (GSTA PK I. HA)
 Rep 76 VIII B Medizinalverwaltung
 Rep 84a Justizministerium
 Rep 92 Nachlass Althoff
Staatsbibliothek Preussischer Kulturbesitz, Berlin
 Nachlass Gerhart Hauptmann
 Nachlass 156 Erich Wernicke

BIELEFELD
Evangelisches Landeskirchenarchiv Westfalen (LkA EKvW)
  Nachlass Gerstein

BONN
  Archiv des Auswärtigen Amtes (AA)

BREMEN
  Staatsarchiv (STAB)

DÜSSELDORF
  Oskar-Vogt-Institut
  Nachlass Vogt

ESSEN
Historisches Archiv Friedrich Krupp
  FAH 4E 266

FRANKFURT AM MAIN
  DEGUSSA Firmenarchiv
Stadtarchiv
  Akten des Magistrats, Hygienisches Institut V 320

FREIBURG IM BREISGAU
Bundesarchiv–Militärarchiv (BA–MA)
  H 20
Aschoff-Archiv, Institut für Geschichte der Medizin, Universität Freiburg

HAMBURG
Bernhard-Nocht Institut (BNI)
Staatsarchiv (STAH)
  Bernhard Nocht-Institut
  Hafenarzt
  Senat

KOBLENZ
Bundesarchiv (BAK)
  R3/361 Reichsministerium für Rüstung und Kriegsproduktion: Arbeitsausschuss für
Raumentwesungs- und Seuchenabwehrmittel
  R 6 Reichsministerium für die besetzten Ostgebiete
  R 21 Reichsministerium für Erziehung, Wissenschaft und Volksbildung/101 KWI Hirn-
forschung; /11061 Institut für Experimentelle Therapie 'Emil von Behring'
  R 73 Notgemeinschaft der Deutschen Wissenschaft
  R 86 Reichsgesundheitsamt
  R 90 Reichskommissar für das Ostland
  R 94 Reichskommissar für die Ukraine
  R 168 Biologische Reichsanstalt
  NS 4 Konzentrationslager
  NS 21 SS-Ahnenerbe
  NS 31 SS-Hauptamt: Sanitätsamt
  NS 33 SS-Führungshauptamt: Sanitätswesen

LEVERKUSEN
Bayer Archiv
　IG Fremdfirmen 6.14 Bd 1
　Pharma Verkauf Länderberichte

MARBURG
Behring-Archiv
　Behring-Feier
　Lemberg

MUNICH
Hauptstaatsarchiv
　BHSTA MWi
　ML Ministerium für Landwirtschaft
Hauptstaatsarchiv Abteilung IV = Kriegsarchiv (BHK)
Institut für Zeitgeschichte (IfZ)
Universitätsarchiv
　Escherich files

NÜRNBERG (STAN)
Staatsarchiv
　502 Kriegsverbrecherprozess KV-Anklage, Interrogations, KV-Verteidigung

POTSDAM
Bundesarchiv (BAP)[1]
　09.02 Deutsche Botschaft Moskau
　11.03 Reichsministerium für die Besetzten Ostgebiete
　15.01 Reichsministerium des Inneren
　49.01 Reichserziehungsministerium

WEIMAR
Gedenkstätte Buchenwald

Israel

Yad Vashem Archives (YVA)

Poland

WARSAW
Archives of National Institute of Hygiene, Warsaw
National Archives
　Halbjahresbericht des Verwaltungschefs bei dem Generalgouvernement Warschau

Russia

MOSCOW
General Archive of the Russian Federation (GARF)
　5446/37/40/

Switzerland

GENEVA
League of Nations Archives (LNA)
　R 811, 812, 816, 823

---
[1] Now Bundesarchiv, Berlin.

United Kingdom

HEREFORD
Herefordshire Records Office
   Records of the Newman Family of Leominster M4

LONDON
BMA Archives, W001 World Medical Association
Public Record Office
   FD 1 Medical Research Council
   MH 55 Ministry of Health
   WO 188, 195 War Office
Wellcome Institute for the History of Medicine
   Royal Army Medical Corps Collection
Wiener Library
   D. C. Evans, 'German CW Experiments on Human Beings', report dated 12 Jan. 1948 for Ministry of Supply, Advisory Council on Scientific Research and Technical Development, Chemical Defence Advisory Board Kh (1)
   473/271 UNRRA Medical Manual. Health and Medical Care of Displaced Persons

MAIDSTONE
Cremation Society of Great Britain
   International Cremation Congresses

OXFORD
Bodleian Library
   Addison Papers
   Bod MSS Eng misc. d. 673 Evelyn Sharp Nevinson Papers
Wellcome Unit for the History of Medicine (now dispersed)
   Chalke Papers
   Hahn Papers
   Vaughan Papers

United States of America

BETHESDA, MD.
National Library of Medicine
   Bayne Jones Papers

BOSTON, MASS.
Boston University
   Leo Alexander Papers
Countway Library, Boston (CLB), Archives
   GA 82, Strong Papers
   Zinsser Papers
   Zinsser Reprints

NEW YORK, NY
YIVO Institute
   Papers on typhus and delousing in the Warsaw ghetto
United Nations Archives
   UNRRA papers

POCANTICO HILLS, TARRYTOWN, NY
Rockefeller Archive Center (RAC)
  Rockefeller Foundation (RF)
  International Health Board (IHB)

WASHINGTON, DC
National Archives, Washington, DC (NAW)
  RG 90 Records of the Public Health Service
  RG 112 USA Typhus Commission (USATC)
  RG 112/295A/ Box 10 Current Intelligence, US Alsos Report on German Biological Warfare
  RG 153 War Crimes Case Number 12-390, The Buchenwald Case
  RG 260 Records of the Office of Military Government for Germany OMGUS
  RG 331 SHAEF G-5
  Berlin Document Center microfilms
Microfilm Publications
  M887 Records of the United States Nuernberg War Crimes Trials, United States of America, Karl Brandt, et al. (Case 1) 21 November 1946–20 August 1947
  T 580, T175
  M 1019, Records of the United States Nuernberg War Crimes Trials Interrogations
US Holocaust Museum, Washington DC
  survivors' testimonies

2. Interviews

Isaac Arbus, New York Nov. 1996
Keith Mant, Walton-on-Thames, 1995–99.
Claudette Bloch Kennedy, Oxford 28
Ephraim Oshry, New York 6 Dec. 1998
Edith Geyl-Wernicke, daughter of Erich Wernicke, Mar. 1997
Alice Ricciardi-von Platen, March 1998
Gertraud Rudart and Hartmut Mrugowsky, Rostock, March 1999

3. Periodicals and Official Publications

Annual Report of the Epidemic Commission of the League of Nations (1921–   )
Arbeiten aus dem kaiserlichen Gesundheitsamte, 1 (1886–   )
Behring zum Gedächtnis (Berlin, 1942)
Bericht über die 4. Arbeistagung der Beratenden Ärzte vom 16. bis 18. Mai 1944 im SS-Lazarett Hohenlychen, 159–69, 185–9
Bildbericht für die Teilnehmer der Behring-Erinnerungsfeier vom 4. bis 6. Dezember 1940 in Marburg-Lahn (Marburg, n.d.)
Blätter des Deutschen Roten Kreuzes, 1–   (1922–   )
Bulletin of the League of Red Cross Societies, 1–   (1919–   )
Bulletin of War Medicine, 1–   (1942–   )
CIOS Reports Item No. 24 Medical
Desinfektion und Schädlingsbekämpfung, 35 (1943)
Deutsch-Russische Medizinische Zeitschrift, 1 (Oct. 1925)–4 (1928)
Deutsche Medizinische Wochenschrift

Die Flamme, (1918); NS, 12 (1936/7)
Der praktische Desinfektor, 13 (1921)–31 (1939)
European Health Conference (1922)
FIAT Review of German Science 1939–1946. Hygiene Part II Preventive and Industrial Medicine, (Wiesbaden, 1948)
International Health Conference April 13–17 1920 (London, 1920)
International Journal of Public Health, 1–2 (1920–1)
League of Nations, *Minutes of the Health Committee* (1922–   )
League of Nations. Monthly Epidemiological Report of the Health Section of the Secretariat
Mitteilungen aus dem kaiserlichen Gesundheitsamte, 1–   (1881–   )
Münchener medizinische Wochenschrift
Pharos, 4 (1937)
Quarterly Bulletin of the Health Organzation, 1 (1932)
State of Israel, *The Trial of Adolf Eichmann: Record of the Proceedings in the District Court of Jerusalem* (Jerusalem, 1992–5)
State Museum of Auschwitz-Birkenau, *Death Books from Auschwitz. Remnants* (Munich, 1995), 1–3
Trial of German Major War Criminals (London, 1946)
Zeitschrift für angewandte Entomologie
Zeitschrift für Desinfektion, 21 (1929)
Zeitschift für Desinfektions- und Gesundheitswesen (1930)
Zeitschrift für Geopolitik
Zeitschrift für Hygiene und Infektionskrankheiten
Zeitschrift für hygienische Zoologie und Schädlingsbekämpfung, 28 (1936)–36 (1944)
Zeitschrift für Schädlingsbekämpfung, 28 (1936)–33 (1941); also as part of previous title
Zentralblatt für Feuerbestattung, 1 (1929)–6 (1933–4)

4. Books and Articles

25 Jahre Preussische Medizinalverwaltung seit Erlass des Kreisarztgesetzes 1901–1926 (Berlin, 1927)
Adelsberger, L., *Auschwitz. A Doctor's Story* (Boston, 1995)
Adler, H. G., *Theresienstadt. Das Antlitz einer Zwangsgemeinschaft* (Tübingen, 1995)
Aly, G., *Endlösung. Völkerverschiebung und der Mord an den europäischen Juden* (Frankfurt/M., 1995)
Aschheim, S. E., *Brothers and Strangers. The Eastern European Jew in German and German Jewish Consciousness, 1800–1923* (Madison, Wis., 1982)
—— *The Nietzsche Legacy in Germany 1890–1990* (Berkeley, Calif., 1992)
Aschoff, Ludwig, *Ein Gelehrtenleben in Briefen an die Familie* (Freiburg, 1966)
Babsky, E. B., I. G. Kochergin, and V. V. Parin (eds.), *Microbiology and Epidemiology* (London, 1945)
Balinska, M. A., *Une vie pour l'humanitaire. Ludwik Rajchman 1881–1965* (Paris, 1995)
Baumgart, W., *Deutsche Ostpolitik 1918. Vom Brest-Litowsk bis zum Ende des Ersten Weltkrieges* (Vienna and Munich, 1966)
Bayne-Jones, S., 'Typhus Fevers', in E. C. Hoff (ed.), *Communicable Diseases* (Washington, DC, 1964) (also publ. as E. C. Hoff (ed.), *Preventive Medicine in World War II,* vol. vii)
Behring, E. von, 'Einleitende Bemerkungen über die ätiologischen Therapie von ansteckenden Krankheiten', *Gesammelte Abhandlungen zur ätiologischen Therapie von ansteckenden Krankheiten* (Leipzig, 1893)

Bein, A., 'The Jewish Parasite. Notes on the Semantics of the Jewish Problem with Special Reference to Germany', *Leo Baeck Institute Yearbook*, 9 (1964), 3–40

Beneden, P. J. van, *Die Schmarotzer* (Leipzig, 1876)

Bieling, R., *Viruskrankheiten*, 2nd edn. (Leipzig, 1944)

—— *Der Tod hatte das Nachsehen. Emil von Behring Gestalt und Werk*, 3rd edn. (Bielefeld, 1954)

Blättler, F., *Warschau 1942. Tatsachenbericht eines Motorfahrers der zweiten schweizerischen Aerztemission 1942 in Polen* (Zurich, 1945)

Brillot, J., 'L'Argent sans mémoire: Degussa-Degesch', *Le Monde Juif*, 151 (1994), 7–81

Browning, C. R., 'Genocide and Public Health: German Doctors and Polish Jews, 1939–1941', in id. (ed.), *The Path to Genocide. Essays on Launching the Final Solution* (Cambridge, 1992), 145–68

Burleigh, M., *Germany Turns Eastwards. A Study of Ostforschung in the Third Reich* (Cambridge, 1988)

—— *Death and Deliverance. 'Euthanasia' in Germany 1900–1945* (Cambridge, 1995)

Burrin, P., *Hitler and the Jews: The Genesis of the Holocaust*, 1st edn. (London, 1993); 2nd edn. (London, 1994)

Busvine, J. R., *Insects, Hygiene and History* (London, 1976)

—— *Disease Transmission by Insects. Its Discovery and Ninety Years of Effort to Prevent It* (Berlin, 1993)

Byam, W., *Trench Fever: A Louse Borne Disease* (Oxford, 1919)

Cornebise, A., *Typhus and Doughboys: The American Polish Typhus Relief Expedition, 1919–1921* (Neward, NY, 1982)

Dallin, A., *German Rule in Russia 1941–1945. A Study of Occupation Policies* (London, 1957)

DEGUSSA, *It All Began in Frankfurt. Landmarks in the History of Degussa AG* (Frankfurt/M., 1989)

Deichmann, U., *Biologen unter Hitler. Vertreibung, Karrieren, Forschung* (Frankfurt/M., 1992)

—— *Im Zeichen von Sonne und Mond. Von der Frankfurter Münzscheiderei zum Weltunternehmen Degussa AG* (Frankfurt/M., 1993)

Ding, E., 'Über die Schutzwirkung verschiedener Fleckfieberimpfstoffe beim Menschen und den Fleckfieberverlauf nach Schutzimpfung', *Zeitschrift für Hygiene*, 124 (1943), 670–82

Dvorjetski, M., *Le Ghetto de Vilna (rapport sanitaire)* (Geneva, 1946)

—— (also Dworzecki), *Histoire de la résistance anti-nazie juive (1933–1945)* (Tel Aviv, 1965)

Eckart, W. U., 'Medizin und auswärtige Kulturpolitik der Republik von Weimar-Deutschland und die Sowjetunion 1920–1932', *Medizin, Gesellschaft und Geschichte*, 10 (1993), 105–42

—— *Medizin und Kolonialimperialismus. Deutschland 1884–1945* (Paderborn, 1997)

Elkeles, B., 'Medizinische Menschenversuche gegen Ende des 19. Jahrhunderts und der Fall Neisser', *Medizinhistorisches Journal*, 20 (1985), 135–48

Escherich, K., *Die angewandte Entomologie in den Vereinigten Staaten* (Berlin, 1913)

—— *Leben und Forschen. Kampf um eine Wissenschaft*, 2nd edn. (Stuttgart, 1949)

Evans, R. J., *Death in Hamburg. Society and Politics in the Cholera Years 1830–1910* (Oxford, 1987)

Eyer, H., 'Fleckfieber', in S. Handloser and W. Hoffmann (eds.), *Wehrhygiene* (Berlin, 1944)

Farley, J., 'Parasites and the Germ Theory of Disease', *Milbank Quarterly*, 67, suppl. 1 (1989), 50–68

Fischer, H., *Der deutsche Sanitätsdienst 1921–1945. Organisation, Dokumente und persönliche Erfahrungen*, 6 vols. (Osnabrück, 1982–91)

Fisher, H. H., *The Famine in Soviet Russia, 1919–1923: The Operations of the American Relief Administration* (New York, 1927)

Frey, G., 'Das Gesundheitswesen im Deutschen Verwaltungsgebiet von Polen in den Jahren 1914–1918', *Arbeiten aus dem Reichsgesundheitsamt*, 51 (1919), 583–733

—— *Bilder aus dem Gesundheitswesen in Polen (Kongress-Polen) aus der Zeit der deutschen Verwaltung* (1919) (also publ. as *Beiträge zur Polnischen Landeskunde*, ser. B, vol. 7)

Friedberger, E., *Zur Entwicklung der Hygiene im Weltkrieg* (Jena, 1919)

Friedlander, H., *The Origins of Nazi Genocide. From Euthanasia to the Final Solution* (Chapel Hill, NC, 1995)

Gerhardt, O., *Stationen einer Idee. Behrings schicksalsvoller Weg* (Berlin, 1941)

Gilbert, M., *Winston S. Churchill*, iv, *1916–1922* (London, 1975)

—— *Auschwitz and the Allies*, 1st edn. (London, 1981)

Groehler, O., *Der lautlose Tod. Einsatz und Entwicklung deutscher Giftgase von 1914 bis 1945* (Hamburg, 1989)

Grove, D. I., *A History of Human Helminthology* (Wallingford, 1990)

Güthoff, W., 'Zur Epidemiologie und Bekämpfung der Seuchengeschehens in Sowjetrussland von 1918–1924', med. diss., Humboldt-Universität, Berlin, 1986

Gutman, I. (ed.), *Im Warschauer Getto. Das Tagebuch des Adam Czerniakow 1939–1942* (Munich, 1986)

Haber, L. F., *The Poisonous Cloud. Chemical Warfare in the First World War* (Oxford, 1986)

Hackett, D. A., *The Buchenwald Report* (Boulder, Col., 1995)

Hallier, E., *Die Pflanzlichen Parasiten des menschlichen Körpers für Ärzte, Botaniker und Studierende zugleich Anleitung in das Studium der niederen Organismen* (Leipzig, 1866)

Hamann, B., *Hitlers Wien. Lehrjahre eines Diktators* (Munich, 1996)

Hamperl, H., *Werdegang und Lebensweg eines Pathologen* (Stuttgart and New York, 1972)

Handloser, S. and W. Hoffmann (eds.), *Wehrhygiene* (Berlin, 1944)

Hansen, F., *Biologische Kriegsführing im Dritten Reich* (Frankfurt/M., 1993)

Harden, V. A., 'Rocky Mountain Spotted Fever Research and the Development of the Insect Vector Theory, 1900–1930', *Bulletin of the History of Medicine*, 59 (1985), 449–66

—— *Rocky Mountain Spotted Fever. History of a Twentieth-century Disease* (Baltimore, Md., 1990)

Hase, A., *Beiträge zur Biologie des Kleiderlaus* (Flugschriften der Deutschen Gesellschaft für angewandte Entomologie, 1) (Berlin, 1915)

—— 'Bekämpfung der Körperverlausung mit Hülfe pulverförmiger Mittel, sowie Prüfverfahren von sog. Läusepudern', *Zeitschrift für hygienische Zoologie*, 35 (1943), 1–17

—— 'Die Zoologie und ihre Leistungen im Kriege 1914/18. Zugleich ein Beitrag zur Frage der angewandten Zoologie in Deutschland', *Die Naturwissenschaften*, 9 (1919), 105–12

—— and W. Reichmuth, *Grundlagen der behelfsmässigen Entlausungsmassnahmen* (Berlin, 1940)

Hayes, P., *Industry and Ideology. IG-Farben in the Nazi Era* (Cambridge, 1987)

Heiss, G. and O. Rathkolb, *Asylland wider Willen. Flüchtlinge in Österreich im europäischen Kontext seit 1914* (Vienna, 1995)

Henneberg, G., K. Janitschke, M. Stürzbecher, *et al.* (eds.), *Robert Koch*, ii, *Teil 1882–1908. Nach Fragmenten von Bruno Heymann* (Berlin, 1997)

Herbert, C., 'Rat Worship and Taboo in Mayhew's London', *Representations*, 23 (1988), 1–24

Hetsch, H., 'Flecktyphus in Deutschland im 19. Jahrhundert', *Zeitschrift für Hygiene*, 124 (1942–3), 241–9

Heymann, B., *Robert Koch*, i, *Teil 1843–1882* (Leipzig, 1932)

Hilberg, R., *The Destruction of the European Jews*, 3 vols., rev. edn. (New York, 1985)

Hilger, G. and A. G. Meyer, *The Incompatible Allies. A Memoir History of German-Soviet Relations* (London, 1953)

Hirsch, A., *Handbook of Geographical and Historical Pathology* (London, 1883)

Hirszfeld owna, H, (ed.), *The Story of One Life* (Fort Knox, Ky., n.d.), tr. of L. Hirszfeld, *Historia jednego życia* (Warsaw, 1946)

His, W., *Die Front der Ärzte* (Bielefeld and Leipzig, 1931)

Hoeppli, R., *Parasites and Parasitic Infections in Early Medicine and Science* (Singapore City, 1959)

Hoffmann, W. (ed.) *Die deutschen Ärzte im Weltkriege* (Berlin, 1920)

Horn, H. and W. Thom, *Carl Flügge (1847–1923). Integrator der Hygiene* (Wiesbaden, 1992)

Howard, L. O., *A History of Applied Entomology* (Washington, DC, 1930)

—— *Fighting the Insects. The Study of an Entomologist* (New York, 1933)

Hubenstorf, M., 'Aber es kommt mir doch so vor, als ob Sie dabei nichts verloren hätten. Zum Exodus von Wissenschaftlern aus den staatlichen Forschungsinstituten Berlins im Bereich des öffentlichen Gesundheitswesens', W. Fischer *et al.*, *Exodus von Wissenschaften aus Berlin* (Berlin, 1994), 355–460.

Huet, M., *Le Pommier et l'olivier. Charles Nicolle, une biographie (1866–1936)* (n.p., 1995)

Jansen, S., 'Männer, Insekten und Krieg: Zur Geschichte der angewandten Entomologie in Deutschland, 1900–1925', *Geschlechterverhältnisse in Medizin, Naturwissenschaft und Technik* (Bassum, 1996)

Kielar, W., *Anus Mundi. Five Years in Auschwitz* (London, 1981)

Klukowski, Z., *Diary from the Years of Occupation 1939–44* (Urbana, Ohio, 1993)

Koch, R., *Gesammelte Werke von Robert Koch*, ed. J. Schwalbe, 3 vols. (Leipzig, 1912)

—— M. Beck, and F. Kleine, 'Bericht über die Tätigkeit die zur Erforschung der Schlafkrankheit im Jahre 1906/07 nach Ostafrika entsandten Kommission', *Arbeiten aus dem Kaiserlichen Gesundheitsamte*, 31 (1911)

Kogon, E., *Der SS-Staat. Das System der deutschen Konzentrationslager*, 23rd edn. (Munich, 1993)

—— H. Langbein, A. Rückerl, *et al.*, *Nationalsozialistische Massentötungen durch Giftgas. Eine Dokumentation* (Frankfurt/M., 1983), tr. as *Nazi Mass Murder: A Documentary History of the Use of Poison Gas* (New Haven, Conn., 1993)

Kraut, A. M., *Silent Travellers. Germs, Genes and the 'Immigrant Menace'* (New York, 1994)

Küchenmeister, F. (tr. E. Lankester), *On Animal and Vegetable Parasites of the Human Body. A Manual of their Natural History, Diagnosis and Treatment*, 2 vols. (London, 1857)

Kudicke, R., 'Ausbreitung und Bekämpfung des Fleckfiebers', *Schriftenreihe für Seuchenbekämpfung*, 1 (1944), 5–21

Labisch, A., *Homo Hygienicus. Gesundheit und Medizin in der Neuzeit* (Frankfurt/M., 1992)

Ladd, B., 'Public Baths and Civic Improvement in Nineteenth-century Germany', *Journal of Urban History*, 14 (1987–8), 342–93

—— *Urban Planning and Civic Order in Germany, 1860–1914* (Cambridge, Mass., 1990)

Langbein, H., *Der Auschwitz Prozess. Eine Dokumentation* (Vienna, 1965)

—— *Menschen in Auschwitz* (Vienna, 1972)

—— *Against All Hope. Resistance in the Nazi Concentration Camps* (London, 1994)

Leuckart, R., *Die menschlichen Parasiten und die von Ihnen herrührenden Krankheiten. Ein*

Hand- und Lehrbuch für Naturforscher und Aerzte, 2 vols. (Leipzig and Heidelberg, 1863, 1876; 2 edn., 1879)

Leven, K.-H., 'Fleckfieber beim deutschen Heer während des Krieges gegen die Sowjet-Union (1941–1945)', in E. Guth (ed.), *Sanitätswesen im Zweiten Weltkrieg* (Herford, 1990), 127–65

Liepmann, H., *Death from the Skies. A Study of Gas and Microbial Warfare* (London, 1937)

Lifton R. J., *The Nazi Doctors. Medical Killing and the Psychology of Genocide* (London, 1986)

Litthauer, K., *Ueber Einrichtung von Desinfectionsanstalten* (Leipzig and Berlin, 1889)

Long, J. C., 'The Volga Germans and the Famine of 1921', *Russian Review*, 51 (1992)

Lubarsch, O., *Ein bewegtes Gelehrtenleben* (Berlin, 1931)

MacKenzie, M. D., *Medical Relief in Europe* (London, 1942)

—— 'Louse-borne Typhus Fever', in A. Hurst, *Medical Diseases of War* (London, 1944)

Markel, H., *Quarantine. East European Jewish Immigrants and the New York City Epidemics of 1892* (Baltimore, Md., 1996)

Martini, E., 'Praktisch-entomologische Erinnerungen aus dem Weltkriege', *Zeitschrift für hygienische Zoologie*, 32 (1938), 51–8, 65–78

—— *Wege der Seuchen. Lebensgemeinschaft, Kultur, Boden und Klima als Grundlage von Epidemien*, 2nd edn. (Stuttgart, 1943)

Mendelsohn, J. A., 'Cultures of Bacteriology: Formation and Transformation of a Science in France and Germany, 1870–1914', Ph.D. thesis, Princeton, 1996

Micheels, L., *Doctor #117641. A Holocaust Memoir* (New Haven, Conn., 1989)

Mitchell, J. M., I. N. Ashesov, and G. P. N. Richardson, *Typhus Fever with Special Reference to Russian Epidemics* (London, 1922)

Möllers, B., *Robert Koch: Persönlichkeit und Lebenswerk, 1843–1910* (Hanover, 1951)

Mrugowsky, J., *Über den Bakteriengehalt von Anatomie-Leichen* (Halle, 1933)

—— 'Jüdisches und deutsches Soldatentum. Ein Beitrag zur Rassenseelenforschung', *NS Monatshefte*, 7/76 (1936), 635–8

—— 'Über die Desinfektion bei Infektionskrankheiten in der täglichen Praxis', *Der Öffentliche Gesundheitsdienst*, 1 (1936), 817–23

—— 'Die Bekämpfung der ansteckenden Krankheiten durch Desinfektion', *Der praktische Desinfektor*, 29 (1937), 235–44, 322–8, 352–8

—— *Biologie eines Mansfeldschen Bergmannsdorfes* (Berlin, n.d. [1938])

—— 'Zur Hygiene ländlicher Arbeiterwohnungen', *Zeitschrift für Hygiene*, 120 (1938), 402–504

—— 'Behring und die Serumtherapie', *Der Öffentliche Gesundheitsdienst*, 6 (1940), 523–6

—— *Untersuchung und Beurteilung von Wasser und Brunnen an Ort und Stelle* (Berlin, 1941)

—— 'Die Seuchenlage im europäischen Teil der UdSSR', *Der praktische Desinfektor*, 34 (1942), 115–21

—— 'Die Seuchenlage in europäischen Russland', *Medizinische Klinik*, 38 (1942), 625–9

—— 'Typischer und atypischer Krankheitsverlauf beim Fleckfieber', *Medizinische Klinik*, 38 (1942), 192–6, 221–3

Mühlens, P., 'Die Hunger- und Seuchenkatastrophe in Russland', *Münchener Medizinische Wochenschrift* (1922), 1444

Nicolle, C., C. Comte, and E. Conseil, 'Experimental Transmission of Exanthematic Typhus through Body Lice', in N. Hahon, *Selected Papers on the Pathogenic Rickettsiae* (Cambridge, Mass., 1968), 37–40

Nuttall, G. H., 'The Part Played by *Pediculus Humanus* in the Causation of Disease', *Parasitology*, 10 (1918), 68–71

Nyhart, L., *Biology Takes Form. Animal Morphology and the German Universities. 1800–1900* (Chicago, 1995)

Ost, E., 'Die Malaria-Versuchsstation im Konzentrationslager Dachau', *Dachauer Hefte*, 4 (1993), 174–89

Otto, R., Fleckfieber (Typhus exanthematicus)', in W. Hoffmann (ed.), *Handbuch der ärztlichen Erfahrungen im ersten Weltkriege* (Leipzig, 1922), 403–60

Pawlowicz, S., *I Will Survive* (London, 1966)

Peiper, O., 'Das Fleckfieber in Preussen 1918–1920', *Veröffentlichungen aus dem Gebiete der Medizinalverwaltung*, 19 (1921), 3–23

Pelt, R. J. van and D. Dwork, *Auschwitz 1270 to the Present* (New Haven, Conn., 1996)

Peters, G., *Blausäure zur Schädlingsbekämpfung* (Stuttgart, 1933)

Pinkus, B. and I. Fleischhauer, *Die Deutsche in der Sowjetunion* (Baden-Baden, 1987)

Pistor, M., *Geschichte der preussischen Medizinalverwaltung* (Berlin, 1909)

Pressac, J.-C., *Auschwitz: Technique and Operation of the Gas Chambers* (New York, 1989)

—— *Les Crématoires d'Auschwitz. La machinerie de meutre de masse* (Paris, 1993)

Rachmanowa, A., *Studenten, Liebe, Tscheka und Tod* (Salzburg, 1931)

Rather, L. J. (ed.), *Rudolf Virchow. Collected Reports on Public Health and Epidemiology* (Canton, Mass., 1985)

Ricketts, H. T., *Contributions to Medical Science by Howard Taylor Ricketts (1870–1910)* (Chicago, 1911)

Ries, H. H., 'Über die geschichtliche, insbesondere die kriegsgeschichtliche Bedeuting des Fleckfiebers', med. diss., Hamburg, 1944

Riley, J. C., 'Insects and the European Mortality Decline', *American Historical Review*, 91 (1986), 833–58

Rocha Lima, H. da, 'Zur Aetiologie des Fleckfiebers', *Berliner klinische Wochenschrift*, 53 (1916), 567–72, tr. in N. Hahon (ed.), *Selected Papers on the Pathogenic Rickettsiae* (Cambridge, Mass., 1968), 74–8

Rodenwaldt, E., *Ein Tropenarzt erzählt sein Leben* (Stuttgart, 1957)

Rogers, N., 'Germs with Legs: Flies, Disease and the New Public Health', *Bulletin of the History of Medicine*, 63 (1989), 599–617

Roland, C. G., *Courage under Siege. Starvation, Disease and Death in the Warsaw Ghetto* (New York and Oxford, 1992)

Rose, G., *Krieg nach dem Kriege* (Dortmund, 1920)

—— 'Fleckfieberfragen bei der Umsiedlung der Volksdeutschen aus dem Ostraum 1939', *Deutsche Medizinische Wochenschrift* (1941), 1262–5

—— 'Fleckfieberfragen der Heimat', *Die Gesundheitsführung. Ziel und Weg* (1942), 95–106

—— 'Fortschritte in der Bekämpfung der Kleiderlaus', *Reichsgesundheitsblatt*, 18 (1943), 53–7

—— 'Fortschritte in der Bekämpfung des Läuse-Fleckfiebers', *Acta Tropica*, 1 (1944), 193–218

Roth, K.-H., 'Von der Tropenheilkunde zur "Kolonialmedizin"', in A. Ebbinghaus, H. Kaupen-Haas, and K.-H. Roth (eds.), *Heilen und Vernichten im Mustergau Hamburg. Bevölkerungs- und Gesundheitspolitik im Dritten Reich* (Hamburg, 1984), 123–30

—— 'Ein Spezialunternehmen für Verbrennungskreisläufe: Konzernskizze DEGUSSA', 3/2 (1988), 8–44

Rousset, D., *The Other Kingdom* (New York, 1947)

Sackmann, W., 'Fleckfieber und Fleckfieberforschung zur Zeit des Ersten Weltkrieges. Zum Gedenken an Henrique da Rocha Lima (1879–1956)', *Gesnerus*, 37 (1980), 113–32

Schlich, T., 'Medicalisation and Secularisation: The Jewish Ritual Bath as a Problem of Hygiene (Germany 1820s–1840s)', *Social History of Medicine*, 8 (1995), 423–42

Schmidt-Ott, F., *Erlebtes und Erstrebtes 1860–1950* (Wiesbaden, 1952)

Schneider, U. and H. Stein, *IG-Farben—Buchenwald—Menschenversuche. Ein dokumentarischer Bericht* (Weimar-Buchenwald, 1986)

Schneider-Janessen, K., *Arzt im Krieg. Wie deutsche und russische Ärzte den zweiten Weltkrieg erlebten* (Frankfurt/M., 1993)

Schröder-Gudehus, B., *Deutsche Wissenschaft und internationale Zusammenarbeit 1914–1928* (Geneva, 1966)

Shelley, L., *Criminal Experiments on Human Beings in Auschwitz and War Research Laboratories. Twenty Women Prisoners' Accounts* (San Francisco, Calif., 1991)

Solomon, S. G., 'Social Hygiene in Soviet Medical Education, 1922–30', *Journal of the History of Medicine and Allied Sciences*, 45 (1990), 607–43

—— 'The Soviet-German Syphilis Expedition to Buriat Mongolia, 1928: Scientific Research on National Minorities', *Slavic Review*, 52 (1993)

—— and J. F. Hutchinson (eds.), *Health and Society in Revolutionary Russia* (Bloomington and Indianapolis, Ind., 1990)

Steiniger, F., 'Dorfbäder als behelfsmässige Entlausungsanlagen', *Zeitschrift für hygienische Zoologie*, 35 (1943), 57–62

—— 'Einiges über die häufigsten Entlausungsfehler', *Veröffentlichungen aus dem Gebiets des Volksgesundheitsdienstes*, 57/2 (1943), 99–140

—— 'Soll man bestehende Badeanstalten in Entlausungsanlagen umbauen?', *Zeitschrift für hygienische Zoologie*, 35 (1943), 93–6

Stoltzenberg, D., *Fritz Haber* (Weinheim, 1994)

Strong, R. P., *Trench Fever. Report of the Commission of the Medical Research Committee of the American Red Cross* (Oxford, 1918)

—— G. C. Shattuck, A. W. Sellards, *et al.*, *Typhus Fever with Particular Reference to the Serbian Epidemic* (Cambridge, Mass., 1920)

Szajkowski, Z., 'Sufferings of Jewish Emigrants to America in Transit through Germany', *Jewish Social Studies*, 39 (1977), 105–16

Szöllösi-Janze, M., 'Von der Mehlmotte zum Holocaust. Fritz Haber und die chemische Schädlingsbekämpfung während und nach dem ersten Weltkrieg', in J. Kocka, H.-J. Puhle, and K. Tenfelde (eds.), *Von der Arbeiterbewegung zum modernen Sozialstaat* (Munich, 1994), 658–75

Tory, A., *Surviving the Holocaust. The Kovno Ghetto Diary* (London, 1991)

Trunk, I., 'Epidemics and Mortality in the Warsaw Ghetto, 1939–1942', *Yivo Annual of Social Science*, 8 (1953), 82–121

Unger, H., *Robert Koch. Roman eines grossen Lebens* (Berlin, 1936)

—— *Unvergängliches Erbe. Das Lebensweg Emil von Behrings* (Oldenburg I. O., 1941)

—— 'Prowazek, der Erforscher des Fleckfiebers', *Die Gesundheitsführung. Ziel und Weg* (1942), 256–60

Vondra, H., 'Malariaexperimente in Konzentrationslager und Heilanstalten während der Zeit des Nationalsozialismus', diss., Hannover, 1989

Wajnryb, A., 'Medizin im Ghetto Wilna', *Dachauer Hefte*, 4 (1993), 78–115

Walbaum, J., 'Fleckfieber und Volkszugehörigkeit in Polen', *MMW* 87 (1940), 567–8

—— *Kampf den Seuchen! Deutscher Ärzte-Einsatz im Osten. Die Aufarbeit im Gesundheitswesen des Generalgouvernements* (Cracow, 1941)

Weindling, P. J., 'German-Soviet Co-operation in Science: The Case of the Laboratory for Racial Research, 1931–1938', *Nuncius. Annali di Storia Scienze*, 1 (1986), 103–9

—— *Health, Race and German Politics between National Unification and Nazism, 1870–1945* (Cambridge, 1989)

—— 'Hygienepolitik als sozialintegrative Strategie im späten Deutschen Kaiserreich', in A. Labisch and R. Spree (eds.), *Medizinische Deutungsmacht im sozialen Wandel des 19. und frühen 20. Jahrhunderts* (Bonn, 1989)

—— 'German-Soviet Medical Co-operation and the Institute for Racial Research, 1927–ca. 1935', *German History*, 10 (1992), 177–206

—— 'Scientific Elites in *fin de siècle* Paris and Berlin: The Pasteur Institute and Robert Koch's Institute for Infectious Diseases Compared', in A. Cunningham and P. Williams (eds.), *Laboratory Medicine in the Nineteenth Century* (Cambridge, 1992), 170–88

—— 'Medicine and the Holocaust: The Case of Typhus', in I. Löwy (ed.), *Medicine and Change: Historical and Sociological Studies of Medical Innovation* (Montrouge and London, 1993), 447–64

—— 'Public Health and Political Stabilisation: Rockefeller Funding in Interwar Central/Eastern Europe', *Minerva*, 31 (1993), 253–67

—— 'Die weltanschaulichen Hintergründe der Fleckfieberbekämpfung im Zweiten Weltkrieg', in C. Meinel and P. Voswinckel (eds.), *Medizin, Naturwissenschaft, Technik und Nationalsozialismus—Kontinuitäten und Diskontinuitäten* (Stuttgart, 1994), 129–35

—— (ed.), *International Health Organisations and Movements 1918–1939* (Cambridge, 1995)

—— 'The First World War and the Campaigns against Lice: Comparing British and German Sanitary Measures', in W. Eckart and C. Gradmann (eds.), *Die Medizin und der Erste Weltkrieg* (Pfaffenweiler, 1996), 227–40

—— 'Purity and Epidemic Danger in German-occupied Poland during the First World War', *Paedagogica Historica*, 33 (1997), 825–32

Weiss, A., *Le Typhus exanthématique pendant la deuxième guerre mondiale en particulier dans les camps de concentration* (Paris, 1954)

Weissman, B. M., 'The American Relief Administration in Famine, 1921–1923: A Case Study in the Interaction between Opposing Political Systems', Ph.D. diss., Columbia University, 1968, pp. 123–7. Pub. (rev.) as id., *Herbert Hoover and Famine Relief to Soviet Russia, 1921–1923* (Stanford, Calif., 1974)

Wess, L., 'Tropenmedizin und Kolonialpolitik: Das Hamburger Institut für Schiffs- und Tropenkrankheiten 1918–1945', *1999*, 8/2 (1992), 38–61

—— 'Menschenversuche und Seuchenpolitik—Zwei unbekannte Kapitel aus der Geschichte der deutschen Tropenmedizin', *1999* 9/2 (1993), 10–50

Wilmanns, K., S. Gross Solomon, and J. Richter (eds.), *Lues, Lamas, Leninisten. Tagebuch einer Reise durch Russland in die Burjiatische Republik im Sommer 1926* (Pfaffenweiler, 1995)

Wohlrab, R., 'Flecktyphusbekämpfung im Generalgouvernement. Vortrag gehalten vor der Academia Real, Madrid und der Universität Valladolid', *Münchener Medizinische Wochenschrift*, 89 (1942), 483–8

Wulf, S., *Das Hamburger Tropeninstitut 1919 bis 1945* (Berlin, 1994)

Zeidler, M., *Reichswehr und Rote Armee 1920–1933* (Munich, 1993)

Zeiss, H., 'Der Kampf der feindlichen Wissenschaft gegen Deutschland', *Süddeutsche Monatshefte* (Nov. 1919), 157–62

—— 'Das Reichsinstitut für Epidemiologie und Mikrobiologie für den Südosten Russlands in Saratow an der Wolga', *Münchener Medizinische Wochenschrift* (1924), 1468–9

Zeiss, H., 'Die Bedeutung Russlands für die medizinischen geographischen Forschung', *Münchener Medizinische Wochenschrift* (1925), 1834–8

—— (ed.), *Otto Obermeier. Die Entdeckung von fadenförmigen Gebilden im Blut von Rückfallfieberkranken* (Leipzig, 1926)

—— 'Das neugegründete Forschungsinstitut für Geschichte der Naturwissenschaften in Moskau', *Archiv für Geschichte der Mathematik, der Naturwissenschaft und der Technik*, 11 (1929), 209–316

—— 'Der augenblickliche Stand medizinisch-geographischer Forschungen in der Sowjet-Union', *MMW* 73 (1931), 1447–9

—— 'Die Notwendigkeit einer deutschen Geomedizin', *Zeitschrift für Geopolitik*, 9 (1932), 474–84

—— 'Johann Peter Franks Tätigkeit in St Petersburg', *Klinische Wochenschrift*, 12 (1933), 353–6

—— 'Die nationalen Aufgaben der deutschen Hygiene', *Reichs-Gesundheitsblatt*, 52 (1936), 962–71

—— 'Die Geomedizin', *Grenzmärkische Forschungen*, 1 (1939), 42–57

—— 'Leben und Wirken Behrings', *Deutsche Medizinische Wochenschrift*, 67 (3 Jan. 1941), 16–19

—— 'Medizinische Kartographie und Seuchenbekämpfung', in id. (ed.), *Seuchen-Atlas* (Gotha, 1942–5)

—— 'Geomedizin und Seuchenbekämpfung', in S. Handloser and W. Hoffmann (eds.), *Wehrhygiene* (Berlin, 1944)

—— 'Medizinische Kartographie und Seuchenbekämpfung', *Petermanns Geographische Mitteilungen*, 90 (1944), 41–3

—— and R. Bieling, *Behring. Gestalt und Werk* (Berlin, 1941)

—— and E. Rodenwaldt, *Hygiene und Seuchenlehre* 4th edn. (Stuttgart, 1942)

Zinsser, H., *Rats, Lice and History* (Boston, 1935)

—— *As I Remember Him. The Biography of R.S.* (Boston, 1940)

INDEX

Abel, Rudolf 173 f.
Abramowicz, Owseij 364
Abrikosov, Alexei 191
Acridin 359
Adelsberger, Lucie vii, 5
Adorno, Theodor 9
aethyl oxide/T-gas 132, 298
Africa 106, 216, 242 f., 323 f., 423
  German colonies 207, 232
agriculture 34, 41, 46, 92, 193
  grain research 93
Ahnenenerbe, see SS
Aktion Reinhard 297 f., 304, 314
Aleppo 106, 108, 232
Alexander, Leo 415–17
Alexandria 75
Algeria, Algiers 14, 324, 331
Althoff, Friedrich 23, 40
Ambros, Otto 307
American Relief Administration 154–72
Andres, Adolf 92
Anhalt, Dr 364
Anigstein, Ludwik 216
anthrax 22, 29, 51, 89
anthropology 28, 37
Antin, Mary 68–9
anti-Semitism 70–1, 118, 145, 157, 203, 258, 296, 346
Arbeitsausschuss für Raumentwesung und
  Seuchenabwehrmittel 307 f., 379
Arbus, Isaak 4
Argflovine 178
Armenians 106, 108
Arndt, Hans-Joachim 192
Aronson, Hans 23, 241
Aschoff, Ludwig 28, 186, 189–91, 194
Asia/Asiatic diseases 17, 37, 73, 225, 250
ASID 357
Atebrin 286, 363
Atoxyl 34, 178, 244
Auhagen, Otto 204
Aurich (nurse) 175
Auschwitz/Oświęcim 3 f., 54, 66, 69, 130, 251, 253,
  259, 279, 298–315, 317, 319, 338, 339, 358 f.,
  363–7, 378 f.
  Hygiene Institute, see Raisko
Austria-Hungary 25, 34, 93, 95, 98
  Navy 94
Azov, sea of 105

Bacot, Arthur 89, 143, 209
bacteriology 9 f., 19, 24, 26, 49, 52, 67, 89, 98, 100,
  179, 182, 193, 209, 212–17, 251, 334, 365, 383

SS 236
Bahr, Willi 314
Bajohren 64, 67
Baku 194, 207, 213, 229
Balachowsky, Serge 324, 355, 359, 367–9, 412
Balkans 69, 73, 86, 105 f., 227, 236
Baltic 98, 105, 115, 135
Baltic Germans 111, 140, 225, 229
Banach, Stefan 351
Bartel, Guido 263
BASF 124, 294
baths vii, 15, 34, 38, 69, 97, 145, 193, 281, 287,
  289–92
  National Society for Construction of Public
    Baths 40, 82
  sauna 231, 289
  Turkish 36, 88
Baumkötter, Heinz 314
Baur, Erwin 47, 104, 189
Bavaria 93, 95, 117, 123, 126
Bayer 123, 178, 193, 359, 402
Bayne-Jones, Stanhope 332 f., 393
beetles 90
Behring, Else 233 f., 241
Behring, Emil von 10, 23, 49, 75, 78, 166, 193,
  233–44, 325, 402
Behring Institutes 241
  see also Lemberg
Behringwerke 192, 234, 242, 294, 325, 327, 333–5,
  341–51, 356, 360, 362, 386, 401–3
Bein, Alex vii, 30
Belarus, see White Russia
Belgrade 88
Belsen 394 f.
Bełżec 297 f., 304
Beneden, Pierre van 35, 44 n.
Berkowitz, Renzi Rosa 4
Berlin 13, 20, 27, 43, 51, 58, 66, 92, 119
  municipal disinfection 51, 121
  University Hygiene Institute 207, 225, 233, 235,
    384 f.
Bernsdorff 357
Beuthen/Bytom 54, 97
Białystok 97, 280
Bickhardt, R. 334
Bieber, Walter 344, 387
Bieling, Richard 233 f., 333, 341, 347, 349, 354, 359,
  362, 402, 409–11
Big, Arthur 351
Bilharz, Theodor 33
Billroth Foundation 157, 178, 182
Biologisches Reichsanstalt 46, 125, 133, 376

biological warfare 358, 383, 386–92
  and Hitler 387 f.
biology 34, 199
  applied 7, 95, 122
  see also entomology
Birger, Trudi 320
Blättler, Franz 273, 288
Blacker, C. P. 420
Blanc, Georges 15, 215 f., 358
Blaschko, Alfred 28
Bloch, Claudette 4, 367
Blome, Kurt 221, 347, 382, 389–91, 421 f.
blood 23, 43, 79, 90
'blood and soil'/Blut und Boden 250, 267, 376
Bludau, Heinrich 303 n., 342
Blue, Rupert 130
Blumenreuther, Carl 237
Bohemia 73
Bolsheviks 140, 142, 148, 150, 154, 164, 208
Borchardt, Moritz 186
border sanitary controls 66–72, 103–5
Bormann, Felix von 197 n., 255, 341, 362, 411, 425
Bormann, Martin 286, 288
Boston 69
botany vii, 123, 132, 229
Bothmann, von 314
Brack, Viktor 318, 413
Brandenburg 293 f.
Brandt, Karl 256, 293, 417
Brandt, Rudolf 414
Brauer, Ludolf 156 f., 237
Bremen 56, 59, 62, 64, 68, 132
Bremerhaven 59, 64
Bremer/Norddeutscher Lloyd 62, 64, 117, 132
Breslau/Wrocław 22 f., 51–4, 64, 97, 271
Bresslau, Ernst 120
Brest-Litovsk 97, 105
Brill, Nathan 214
British Medical Association (BMA) 420
Brockdorff-Rantzau, Ulrich 186–8, 190
Bromberg/Bydgoszcz 23, 54, 348, 425
Brücher, Ernst 229
Brunstein, Esther 4
Buchanan, George 144 n., 170
Bucharest 357, 382
Buchenwald 248, 251 f., 259, 315, 317, 339, 349–61, 394, 403
bugs/bedbugs 13, 84, 90, 247
Bukharin, Nikolai 199
Bukovina 74, 142, 212, 273
Bulgaria 73, 111, 159, 216, 230, 245, 378
Bumke, Oswald 186
Buurmann, Otto 344, 346, 409

camel diseases 178, 193, 203
cancer 245, 389
Cannes sanitary conference 142–3
carbon monoxide 66, 119, 132, 255, 262, 293–8, 301, 304, 305, 311, 387

Carlebach, Emanuel 100
Carrel, Alexis 325
Carson, Rachel 424
Caucasus 96, 106, 191–4, 232, 342, 380
Céline/Louis Destouches 246
Chamberlain, Houston Stewart 24
Chapin, Charles 60
Chargraff, Erwin 217
Cherson 341
Chicherin, Grigori 159, 186
Chile 214
China 214 f., 242 f.
chlorine 13
Chodzko, Witold 103, 146
choleliathis 192
cholera 14, 29, 39, 44, 51 f., 58, 65, 70, 75, 105, 112, 148, 153, 160, 168, 170, 213, 228, 250, 382 f.
  Hamburg (1892) 62, 383
Churchill, Winston 92, 140, 142, 148 f.
Ciepielowsty, Marian 354 n., 368 f.
CIOS/Combined Intelligence Operations Sub-Committee 401, 410, 412
Ciuca, Michel 215
Clauberg, Carl 253, 366
Clay, Lucius Henry 416
Clemenceau, Georges 143
clothes 34, 37, 81 f., 89 f., 102
Cohn, Ferdinand vii, 22, 24, 30, 52 f.
Coler, Alwin von 49
Cologne 58
'colonists' German in Russia, *see* Ethnic Germans
Commonwealth Foundation 214
Conceil 75
concentration camps, WW1 98, 117
  sleeping sickness 26
Congo 27
Constantinopel 106
Conti, Leonardo 227, 237 f., 244, 253, 256, 267, 271, 293, 308, 327, 328 n., 334, 346 f., 360, 387, 391, 406
Coquillet, D. W. 46
Cossacks 193 f., 399
Cottbus 77, 79, 81
Cox, Herald 217, 331–3
  vaccine 343–6, 355, 369 f., 419, 424
Cracow/Krakau/Kraków 209, 334–7, 355, 365
  Vaccine Institute 350
  see also Eyer
Craigie Laboratories 331
cremation xi, 42–3, 102, 136–8, 235, 263–70, 294, 316–21, 339, 389
Crimea 14, 96, 105, 163
Crossman, Richard 404
Cumming, Hugh 130
Czechoslovakia 170, 216
  underground 315
Czerniakow, Adam 280
Czernowitz 74

Dachau 27, 252, 279, 315, 317, 359 f., 367, 389, 396, 407, 409, 419
   Institute for Hygiene and Medical Entomology 377 f.
Danzig/Gdańsk 58, 130, 242
Darré, Richard Walther 247 f.
Darsin 357
Darwinism 24, 31
DDT 247, 373–5, 379–81, 390, 392, 393, 395–8, 400, 422, 424
DEGESCH 91, 123 f., 126, 135, 261, 277, 299, 305–10, 357, 407
Degussa 47, 93, 95 f., 120 f., 123 f., 131, 133, 135, 306 f., 311, 407
Deinart, Adam 348
Delmotte, Hans 226, 366
delousing, origins of term 66
Demnitz Albert 341, 344, 349, 362, 386, 401
Denmark 327
   State Institute for Serum Therapy 350
dental gold 255, 307, 316 f.
Dessau sugar refiners/Dessauer Werke für Zucker und chemische Industrie 96, 134, 305, 309
Deutsch, Leon and Mina 280, 284
Deutsche Forschungsgemeinschaft (DFG) 206, 227, 338, 375, 408
Dietzsch, Arthur 355, 368
Ding(-Schuler), Erwin 231, 326, 350, 353–61, 389, 403, 406, 410, 419 f.
Dinges, Martin 198
Dingler, Hugo 377
diphtheria 23, 29, 51, 172
Dirksen, Herbert von 204 f., 206
disinfection 11, 38, 58, 61, 65, 67, 119, 166, 283, 310
disinfectors xi, 7, 41, 43, 51, 55, 64, 97, 99, 120, 227, 240, 248, 260–3, 294, 298, 302, 311
Dnieprpetrovsk/Dnjepropetrowsk 287, 339, 341
Dötzer , Walter 231, 326, 328 n.
Dora, camp 279
Doroschitz/Doroshicha 236
Dorpat/Tartu 186, 251, 287, 341, 357
Dostoyevsky, Fyodor 17, 154
Doty, Alvah 60 f.
DPs, Displaced Persons 396
Dresden 43, 137, 219
Drigalski, Wilhelm von 27
DRUSAG 191, 193
Düsseldorf 137
Duisberg, Carl 121
Durand, P. 324
   Durand–Giroud vaccine 367
DNVP (German National Peoples Party) 204, 226
DVP (German Peoples Party) 127, 226
Dvorjetsky, Marc/Dworzecki, Mark vii, 6, 281
dysentery 29, 51, 75, 83, 86, 105, 112, 256, 352, 395, 399

East Africa 26 f.
Eastern Marches 22, 53
   Society/Association 55 f., 96
Eberl, Irmfried 297
Edelman, Marek 3
Egypt 14, 33, 58, 90, 329, 396, 422
Ehrlich, Paul vii, 10, 22, 34, 86, 167, 200, 236, 239–41, 402
Eichmann, Adolf 298, 301, 303, 305, 315
   consults Tropeninstitut 337
Einstein, Albert 165
Ellis Island 59, 62, 400
Elsterowa, Olga 364
Engelhardt, Alexander von 237 f., 349
entomology/medical entomology xi, 34 f., 71, 82, 84, 89, 99, 357, 361, 373–81
Entress, Friedrich 312, 363
eradication of disease, *Ausrottung* 15, 22, 25, 28–30, 422–5
Erdmann, Rhoda 24
Erfurt 317
Escherich, Georg 123
Escherich, Karl 34, 46, 71, 92 f., 95, 119, 123, 126, 129, 207, 260
Estonia 170, 230, 256, 290, 341
   Koureme 281
   see also Dorpat/Tartu
ethnic Germans, in Russia vi, 158, 184, 193, 198, 203, 310, 317
eugenics/racial hygiene 27–9, 34, 119, 207, 227, 247, 420
   IFEO/International Federation of Eugenics Organisations 207
   Racial Hygiene Society 28
   Russian 183, 197
Europe 17, 62, 155, 228, 245, 250, 382
European health conference 168–71
European medicine 240, 245, 346
euthanasia 230, 255, 293–7, 303, 317 f., 320, 361, 394
Evans, D. C. 406, 407 n.
Ewald, Karl Joseph 10
exhibitions 51, 137, 263, 265
   Berlin Public Health 40
experiments, human, *see* human experiments
Eydtkuhnen 64, 69, 83, 117 f., 204, 275
Eyer, Hermann 231, 334 f., 347 f., 350–2, 354, 363, 409 f.
   and DDT 381

famine, Russian 153–9, 162–78
favus 62
Felix, Arthur 86, 332
FIAT, Field Information Agencies (Technical) 410, 412 f.
films, medical 4, 263, 273 f., 343
Finland 149, 170, 229, 246
Fischer, Alfons 233
Fischer, Eugen 176
Fischer, Otto 175, 181, 184, 231 f., 410

Fischer, Werner 218
fleas 13, 36, 38, 84, 213, 215
Fleck, Ernestina 365
Fleck, Ludwik 209, 306, 333 f., 357, 359, 363–5, 427
Flick, Friedrich 414
flies 34, 247, 303
Flügge, Carl 23, 51, 53 f., 70, 75, 82, 89, 92
Flury, Ferdinand 93, 125, 129
Foch, Ferdinand 142
Foerster, Otfried 186 f.
food 25
  meat inspection 29
forestry 48, 107, 122 f., 129, 207, 260, 267
Formaldehyde/formalin 9, 13, 31, 38, 53, 166
Fourneau, Ernest 327
Fox, Leon 393
Fraenkel/Fraenken, Carl 22
France 209, 240 f., 245, 307
  medical relief to Serbia 87
  Ministry of public health 325
  Occupied 325 f.
  Vichy 325 f., 386
Frank, Hans 340, 346 f., 351
Frank, Johann Peter 245, 335
Frankfurt am Main 27, 47, 92, 119, 167, 251
Frankfurt am Oder 115, 398
Freiburg im Breisgau 28
Frey, Gottfried 97, 168, 272
Fritzsch, Karl (Fritsch) 300, 313
Fry, Ruth 118

Gärtner, Wolfgang 161
Gaffky, Georg 40, 49
Galton, Francis 34
gas chambers 255, 260, 262, 298–315, 407
  mobile 132
  poison gas vans 295 f., 330
  warfare 91–3, 125, 196 f., 315, 338
gases 83, 89, 91–6, 106, 123, 196, 385
  see also carbon monoxide
Gassner, L. 309
Gebhardt, Karl 416
Geigy, J. R. 374, 380
Gelsenkirchen 25, 58
Generalgouvernement/Government General 97, 102
  (WW2) 228, 272, 275, 346
  pharmaceuticals 242
Generalplan Ost vi, 252
genetics 183, 189, 191–3, 195, 199, 206 f., 212, 229, 293
genocide, origins of concept 415
Genzken, Karl 237, 250 f., 357
geographical pathology 189, 195 f., 212, 256
geo-medicine 201–3, 215, 232, 250 f., 335, 348, 382, 411
Georgia 156, 182, 191
Gerhardt, Oswald 241
German East Africa 30, 178

German Order, see Teutonic Knights
Germanin (Bayer 205) 178, 193, 197, 210
Gerstein, Kurt 231, 251, 253, 259, 298, 301, 303, 305 f., 308 f., 313–15, 320, 406 f.
Gestalt 236, 257
ghettoes 271, 274 f., 280–4, 337 f., 373
  Białystock 280
  Grodno 280
  Lemberg 237, 335, 364 f.
  Neuhof 275
  Plöhnen 275
  see also Cracow; Kovno; Łódź/Litzmannstadt; Vilna; Warsaw
Gilchrist, Henry 143
Gildemeister, Eugen 55, 75, 218, 242, 326, 344, 350, 354, 358, 406
Giroud, Paul 217, 323, 326, 328, 331
Globocnik, Odilo 301, 304, 320
Godlewski, Emil 144
Goebbels, Joseph 152
Gönnert, Rudolf 348, 402
Göring, Hermann 344, 346, 347, 389
Goldscheider, Alfred 233–5
Goldschmidt, Richard 189
Goldschmidt, Theo 134
Golz, Bruno 348
Gorbunov, Nikolai Petrovitch 178 f., 193
Gorky, Maxim 154–6, 163 f.
Gossler, Gustav von 25
Gotschlich, Emil 58 f., 75, 226 n., 382, 391
Gottlieb, Josef 403
Graudenz/Grudziadz 381
Grawitz, Ernst Robert, Reichsarzt SS 221, 237, 247, 249–51, 296, 353, 360, 379, 389–91, 406
Graz 74, 247, 347
Great Britain 14, 146, 209, 315, 418–21
  Aliens Act 130
Greece 226, 230, 365, 380
Griesinger, Wilhelm 257
Grimm, Jacob 45
Gross, Karl Josef 389, 410
Gross, Walter 267
Gross-Rosen 253, 366
Grotjahn, Alfred 202, 211
Gruber, Max von 28, 104
Grünwaldt 339
Gumbinnen 53
Günther, Rolf 305
Gundel, Kay 291
Gusen 314, 359
gut infections 271
gypsies 8, 94, 256, 280, 312, 315, 345, 358, 361, 366, 412

Haagen, Eugen 218, 326, 335, 358, 361, 408, 410, 415
Haas, Ernest 327
Haas, Richard 327, 340, 346–52, 401 f.
Haber, Fritz 92–6, 120 f., 123 f., 125 f., 260, 266
Habs, Horst 409

Hach, Iwan 348
Hadamar 318
Haeckel, Ernst 201, 229, 266
Haecker, Valentin 248
Hafner, Desiré vii
Hagen, Wilhelm 275–8, 282 f., 409, 425
Hahn, Martin 53, 83, 104, 163
hair vii, 6, 99, 273, 291 f., 367
Haigh, W. E. 167, 169
Halberkann, Josef 79
Halle 58
Haller, Josef 144
Hallervorden, Karl 230
Hallier, Ernst 32, 42
Hamburg 40, 94, 129, 132, 135, 158, 197
    Eppendorf Hospital 68, 156
    Institute of Maritime and Tropical Diseases
        28, 58, 65 f., 74, 76, 106, 159 f., 176, 178, 194, 205,
        231, 323, 327, 337, 357 f., 376
    migration 59
    migration halls 64, 68, 131
Hamel, Carl 219
Hammerstein 84, 204
Hamperl, Herwig 191 f., 198
Handloser, Siegfried 230, 237 f., 256, 381, 388, 416
HAPAG 61, 114, 117
Harbauer, Max 269, 316
Hare, Ronald 420
Harmsen, Hans 207, 287
Hartheim 314
Hase, Albrecht 83, 89, 93 f., 96, 100 f., 119, 121,
    125 f., 128, 261 f., 298, 308, 375, 377, 391, 411, 425
Haskell, William 166
Haubold, Hellmut 245, 326 f., 356
Haught, J. W. 406
Hauptmann, Gerhart 154 f., 165
Haushofer, Karl 139, 201, 250, 406
Hautval, Adélaïde 363
headlice 67, 84
Heerdt, Walter 123, 125 f., 135, 299, 309
Heerdt-Lingler (Heli) 299, 309
Heess, Walther 295
Hegler, Carl Theodor 74
Heide 385
Heilsberg 118
Henke, Karl 229
Henkel 129
hepatitis 338, 360
heredity 34
Hess, Rudolf 227
Hetsch, Heinrich 90, 127
Heydrich, Reinhard 254, 297, 390
Heymann, Bruno 24, 27, 92, 235, 244
Heymonns, Richard 92, 95
Hilger, Gustav 159, 161, 171, 185, 188, 204
Hill, Charles 420 f.
Himmler, Heinrich 228, 254, 296, 301, 308, 317 f.,
    334, 338, 353, 358, 360, 366, 377 f., 389–91, 394,
    406

Hindenburg, Paul von 77, 204, 268
Hippocratic medicine 257
Hirsch, August 200
Hirszfeld, Ludwik viii, 276, 280, 282–4, 363 f., 427
Hirt, August 315, 358
His, Wilhelm 102, 105, 121, 157
history of medicine 9, 27, 200, 233–45, 402 f.
    of epidemics 250
Hitler, Adolf 19, 41, 48, 72, 122, 222, 240 f., 255,
    276, 287, 293, 296, 316, 379, 382, 385, 387 f.,
    391, 417
Hölderlin, Friedrich 257
Hoechst 233, 359 f., 412
Höfle 299
Höss, Rudolf 254, 292, 300, 305, 313, 317, 319
Hoetzsch, Otto 187, 204
Hoffmann, Wilhelm 119
Hohenlychen 380, 413
holism 249, 392
Holocaust, concept of vi
homosexuals 338
Hoover, Herbert 76, 154, 159, 163 f.
Horder, Lord 265
Hoske, Hans 230
hospitals 68, 87, 97, 172, 174
    Alexander Hospital, St Petersburg 178, 184
    Auschwitz 253
    Bremen 64
    concentration camp 292
    German Red Cross, Constantinople 86
    German, Kiev 388
    German, Simferpol 182
    German, Tiflis 105, 182, 184
    Jewish Hospital Berlin 244
    Jewish Hospital Lwów 364
    Jewish Hospital Warsaw/Czyste Hospital 280,
        338, 359
    Jewish Hospital Radom 362
    Kovno Ghetto 282
    Moscow 180
    Petrograd 175, 180
    SS 247, 366, 380
    trains 150
    Vilna ghetto 282
    Zamość 279
    see Hamburg, Eppendorf Hospital
Hoven, Waldemar 416
Hueppe, Ferdinand 24
Hufeland, Christoph Wilhelm 256
human experiments, clinical trials 15, 26 f., 178,
    248, 329, 338, 344 f., 355, 358–63, 365 f.
    German in Russia 178, 362
Humboldt, Alexander von 257
Hundertmark 339
Hungary 135, 230, 245, 334, 335
hunger oedema 172, 399
hydrocyanic acid 40–8, 91–6, 119, 121, 125–36, 289,
    295
    see also Zyklon

IG-Farben 134, 184, 198, 233, 241 f., 294, 306 f., 309,
327, 334, 337, 341 f., 346–9, 359, 380, 388, 401, 407
see also Bayer Behringwerte, Hoechst
Illowo/Iłowa 64
immunity, artificial, *see* vaccination
natural 85, 350
India 14
influenza 105, 111, 213, 274, 383
insects 34, 44, 46
see also entomology
Insterburg 64, 67
Institute for Experimental Therapy 29, 323, 386
International Office of Hygiene 59
international sanitary conferences 58
International Scientific Commission on Medical
War Crimes 413
Ireland 14
iron curtain, epidemic prevention wall 152, 177
Italy 61, 335
itchmites 84
Ivy, Andrew 413–6

Jadassohn, Josef 219
Japan 237, 241, 330, 383 f., 390
Jena 83, 96
Jerusalem 74, 159
Jews 3, 24, 41, 44, 97–100, 145, 164, 174, 258, 350–2
see also Judenfieber
Jochmann, Georg 78
Judenfieber, Jews as disease carriers vi, 70, 102,
104, 271, 274, 337, 389, 426 f.
Junkers 180, 184
Jusatz, Helmut 226, 411

Kafka, Franz 6 f., 42, 290
Kafka, Hanus 4
Kaftanov, Sergei 229
Kahr, General von 122
Kaiser Wilhelm Gesellschaft/Society 195, 421
Institutes: anthropology vii; biochemistry 94;
biology 229; brain research 188, 191, 195,
230; gas research 95; physical chemistry 94,
125, 129–30; psychiatry 234
Kalinin 193
Kallmeyer, Hellmut 295
Kamenev, Lev Borisovitsh 159
Kammerjäger 50, 127 f., 131, 261 f., 269
Katyn 246, 412
Kauen, *see* Kowno
Kaup, Ignaz 28, 114
Kazakhstan 202
Kazan/Kasan 160, 174 f.
Keitel, Wilhelm 387, 389
Kellogg, Vernon 166
Kharkov/Charkow 170, 189, 237, 243, 336 f., 342
Kielar, Wiesław 4, 279, 291
Kiev 19, 30, 148, 170, 228, 252, 287, 336, 341, 344,
376

Kinyoun, Joseph J. 61
Kirchner, Martin 49, 53, 104
Kisskalt Karl 28
Kitasato, Shibasaburo 10
Klemperer, Georg 186
Klieger, Bernhard 379,
Kliewe, Heinrich 261, 382 f., 386–9, 411, 422
Klukowski, Zygmunt 273, 279
Koch, Robert 9, 13, 19–30, 34 f., 44, 52, 62, 64 f., 70,
74, 78, 95, 166, 234, 241 f., 244, 249, 376, 413,
425
Koch's postulates 84, 426
König 308
Königsberg/Kaliningrad 117, 193, 299
University 53
Koerner, Moshe 6
Kogon, Eugen vii, xi, 248, 292, 354–6 n., 359,
402–6, 410, 416 f.
Kohn, Pinchas 10
Kok, Leo 290
Kolchak, Admiral 154
Kolin 48, 124, 134
Kollwitz, Käthe 158, 165
Koltsov, Nikolai 183, 191, 198
Kori, H. 317, 320
Korff-Petersen, Arthur 28
Korn, Milolasz 363
Kovno/Kauen/Kaunas 251, 273, 289, 341 f.
Ghetto 281 f.
Kraus, Friedrich 184, 195
Kress von Kressenstein, Friedrich 157
Krupp von Bohlen und Halbach, Gustav 187, 195,
414
Krupps 193
Kudicke, Robert 27, 48, 237, 243, 275, 344, 347, 365,
409, 425
Küchenmeister, Friedrich 31
Künsberg, Sonderkommando 246
Kuczynski, Max 202
Kuhn, Philalethes 140
Kulmhof/Chelmno 296, 301, 317, 319
Kunert, Herbert 243
Kyrgyzstan 193 f.

Laas, Ernst 192
Lagarde, Paul 71
Laigret, Jean 358
Landau, Léon 365 f.
Landsberg an der Warthe/Gorlsów Wielkopolski
116
Langbein, Hermann vii
Lange 305
Langerhans, Paul 44
Lassar, Oskar 39
Latvia 169 f., 230, 256
see also Riga
Lauenburg 117
laundering 12, 16

Lautenschläger, Carl 359
League of Nations 164, 170, 383
　Health Organization (LNHO)/Epidemic
　　Commission 135 f., 146 f., 166, 171 f., 175, 179,
　　210, 215, 218, 240, 242, 330
Lebensraum 207, 225, 229, 242, 250
Lechfeld 122
Leese, Arnold 203
Legroux, René 413
Lehmann, Karl Bernhard 126
Leipzig 64, 271
Lemberg/Lwów/Lvov 74, 209 f., 229, 236, 333 f.,
　　351, 363 f., 340, 384
　Behring Institute 237, 242, 327, 341, 345–52, 379,
　　401
Lemierre, André 323, 325, 328, 393
Lenin 148, 154, 164, 178–80, 185–8, 203, 230, 264
Lenin Institute for Brain Research 187 f., 205
Lenz, Fritz 14, 104, 176, 198, 229, 247, 258, 381
Lépine, Pierre 413
leprosy 11, 51, 53, 117, 282
Leuckart, Rudolf 31
Levi, Primo vii, 291
Lewin, Jacques 365
Lewis, Sinclair 135
Libau/Liepāja 65
lice viii, 10 f., 33, 36, 69, 84, 90, 132, 213, 247
　louse feeders 350–2 , 369
　see also headlice
Liebsch, Ernst 339
Liegnitz 112
Lifton, Robert J. 410
Lindner, Herbert 320
Lingler, Johann 135
Linnaeus, Carol 11
Lipschütz, Alexander 85
Lithuania 98, 14, 117, 169, 230, 255 f., 282, 290
Litvinov, Maxim 159, 164, 186 f., 198 f.
liver diseases 192
Liverpool School of Tropical Medicine 66
Łódź 97, 102, 228
　Ghetto 280, 292, 307
　Litzmannstadt 243
Loeffler, Friedrich 40, 49
Löwy, Yitshak 6
Lolling, Enno 252, 254, 311, 406
Loresch 175
Lubarsch, Otto 56, 186
Lublin 295, 304, 320
Luck 144
Ludendorff, Erich 105, 180
Lührs, Paul Erich 192, 206
Lunacharski, Anatoli 188, 193, 199
Lyck 115

McCoy, G. W. 212 f.
Mackenzie, Melville 172
Madagascar 337

Madsen, Thorvald 239
Majdanek 304, 314
malaria 29, 33, 74, 86, 105, 112, 153, 181, 243, 252,
　330, 339, 360 f., 378, 390, 424
　therapy 178
　vaccine 366
Maltzan, Georg Otto von 175
Manila 88 f.
Mansfeld miners 250
Mant, Keith 413
Mantegazza, Paolo 70
Marburg 233, 237–41, 244, 350
Marienburg 381
Marienwerder 53
Martini, Erich 6, 76 f., 79, 97, 121, 227, 304, 376,
　408, 411
Mauthausen 262, 292, 314, 317, 359, 389
May, Eduard 252 f., 377, 381, 390, 409
Mayer, Martin 176, 192, 194, 196, 376
measles 51
Mechnikov, Élie/Ilia Ilich 200, 233, 237
Mechnikov, Olga 233
　Metchnikov Bacteriological Institute 341
Mecklenburg 398
Medical Research Council (MRC) 89, 330, 332,
　373, 395, 418
Melitense 213
Melk gas chamber 315
Mellanby, Kenneth 418 f.
Memel/Klaipéda 53, 58, 117, 140
Mengele, Josef 253, 312, 317
Mennonites 166, 203
mental defectives 34
Mentzel, Rudolf 338
Merkel 267
Meseritz-Obrawalde 115
methylene blue 359
Mexico 213–15, 343
Meyer-Abich, Adolf 257
Mielke, Fred 417
migrants 42, 59 f., 115, 131, 169
　control stations 63
mikveh, Jewish ritual baths 41 f., 100, 144
Military Medicine 230
　Academy, Berlin 226, 335, 343, 354, 376 f., 380,
　　386, 388
　Senate 226
Minkowski, Oskar 186
Minsk 148, 153, 163, 167, 180, 287, 339
Mitscherlich, Alexander 417
Mogilev 295, 317
Moleschott, Jacob 42
Molotov, Viacheslav 199, 205
Montenegro 89
Mooser, Hermann 214, 328, 343 f.
Moran, Lord 414, 421
Morel, Theo 247, 379
Morocco 215

Moscow 170, 177, 195, 233
  Bacteriological station 179, 184
  Institute of racial pathology 189–99, 205–7
  School of Medicine 210
Moses, Julius 157
mosquitoes 84, 247, 250, 361, 373, 381, 390
Mrugowsky, Joachim 231, 237 f., 240, 250–9, 303,
    305, 308, 310, 326, 339, 341–3, 345, 349, 352–7,
    359, 362, 366–8, 376 f., 379 f., 382, 390, 406, 416
  biological wafare 389–91
Murchison, Charles 12, 257
Mühlens, Peter 74, 106, 108, 159–62, 166, 168 f.,
    173 f., 176–81, 184, 226, 231 f., 243, 337, 357,
    376, 380
Mühling, Paul 264
Muhsfeldt, Erich 320 f.
Müller, Friedrich von 23
Müller, Heinrich 305
Müller, Paul Hermann 424
Münch, Hans 248, 253, 259, 365–7, 410
Muller, Hermann 206
Munk, Fritz 85
Muntsch, Otto 197 f., 226
Murthum, Adolf 342
Musleims 99, 106, 374
Mussolini, Benito 219
Myslowitz 64, 67

Naganal 178, 193
Nałęcz-Sobieszczański, Mieczysław 272
Nansen, Fridtjof 142, 154, 159, 164 f.
Naples 61, 393
  Zoological Station 190
Napoleon 75
Natzweiler 315, 357 f.
Nauck, Ernst Georg 160, 174 f., 192, 194 f., 205,
    206, 232, 243, 323, 337 f., 408, 424 f.
Nazi Party 204
  cremation 267
  Hauptamt für Volksgesundheit 261
Nazim, Dr 108
Netherlands 166, 327, 365
Neuengamme 252, 275, 314, 357
Neufeld, Fred 25, 76
Neumann, Heinrich 341, 344, 347 f., 359
New York 48, 60
  Museum of Natural History 131
  see also Ellis Island
Newman, George 146
Nicolle, Charles 14 f., 69, 75, 87 f., 213–15, 221
Niedermeyer, Oskar von 180, 207
Nietzsche, Friedrich 235
Nikanorov, Sergei 171, 194, 212
Noack, Ernst 53
Nobel prizes 124, 408, 424
Nocht, Bernhard 49, 65–8, 74, 77–9, 106, 119, 168,
    179, 184, 210 f., 232, 408, 426
Nocht-Giemsa fumigation 132
Nonne, Max 186

Norddeutsche Lloyd, *see* Bremer Lloyd
North Africa 77
Norway 164
Notgemeinschaft der deutschen
    Wissenschaften/Emergency Fund for
    German Science 178, 185, 190 f., 206
notification of infections 51
Nuremberg 158, 271
  Code 414, 417
  IG–Farben Trial 407
  International military tribunal 303, 369, 412
  Medical Trial 89, 139, 254, 322, 333, 352–4, 361,
    369, 406, 410, 413–21
Nuttall, George 82, 89 f., 207

Oberheuser, Herta 416
Obermeier, Otto 233
Oderberg-Ratibor 64
Olsen, Otto 211, 219, 221, 245
Oppeln 53
Oranienburg 222, 249
  disinfectors school 303, 311
Oshry, Ephraim 273, 281
Ostforschung 238
Ostjuden 8, 41, 56, 71, 103, 112, 114 f., 117 f., 158
Ostmark, *see* Eastern Marches
Ostministerium, *see* Reichsministerium für die
    besetzten Ostgebieten
Ostroleka 97
Ostrowo 64
Otter, Göran van 304
Ottlotschen 64
Otto, Richard 14, 86, 99, 150, 160, 168, 217, 323, 333,
    345, 347, 355, 364, 383, 386
Oxford grease 75

Paget, Muriel 87, 149
Pan-German League 96, 104
Paracelsus 20, 235
parasitology 33
parasites 34, 260, 262, 308
  human 376
paratyphoid 213, 252, 384
Paris 59
Pascual, Marcellino 220
Pasteur, Louis 12, 15, 28, 34, 42, 85, 237, 413
  metro station 383
Pasteur Institute 74, 195, 201 214, 241, 324, 327 f.,
    331, 334, 347, 354, 356, 368, 413, 420
  Algiers 15, 324, 331, 374
  Casablanca 358
  Moscow 184
  Tunis 15, 213, 358
pathology 12, 16, 190, 192, 195
Pavlov, Ivan 155, 183
Pawlowicz, Sala 3, 292
pedlars 14, 102
pellegra 65, 192
penicillin 379, 400, 425

Pesch, Karl 230
Peters, Armin 304
Peters, Gerhard 134, 254 f., 261 f., 299, 301 f., 305–8,
    321, 379, 407
    Oberingenieur 267
Pettenkofer, Max von 20, 85, 228, 249, 382
Pfannenstiel, Wilhelm 237, 244, 247, 298, 304, 402
Pflaum, Guntram 308, 378 f.
Pfeiffer, Richard 383
Pilsudski, Jozef 116
Pittaluga, Gustavo 220
plague 16, 51, 58, 65, 382 f., 385, 391
Plate, Ludwig 83
Platen-Hallermund, Alice 417
Płock 97
Plotz, Harry 88
Plotzk 69
pneumonia 213 f., 292
Pohl, Oswald 317
Poland 75, 90, 96 f., 103, 140, 144–8, 168–70, 214,
    229, 334, 383
    as diseased 112, 115
Poles 56, 170, 348, 362, 366
polio 409, 424
Polotsk, Połock 153
Polskrow 144
pork 58
port health 14, 60, 64 f., 130
Porton Down 375, 407
Posen/Poznań 50, 67, 75, 97, 318, 339, 346, 376, 389,
    425
    control stations 64
    grand duchy of 52, 54
    Hygiene Institute 54 f., 75
    Reich University 318, 389
Prague 74, 209, 230, 264
    German University 94
Prausnitz, Carl 220
Preussisch-Holland/Pasłęk 118
Priessnitz, Vincenz 39
Prinzing, Friedrich 75
prisoners of war 77–81, 164, 275, 315, 357, 393
    Soviet, as victims of human experiments 362
prostitutes 25, 98
prontosil 363
Prostken 64, 115, 117
Prowazek, Stanislaus von 16, 28, 74, 76, 78 f., 85,
    241
Prüfer, Karl 266, 319, 321
Prussia 18
    army 14, 22, 40
    East Prussia 53 f., 111, 117, 289, 398
    Health council 137
    Institute for Infectious Diseases *see* RKI
    Ministry of Agriculture 94 f.; Education 95;
        Finance 95; Interior 94 f., 117; War 75, 92–5;
        Welfare 133
    West Prussia 53 f., 97, 111
prussic acid, *see* hydrocyanic acid

Przemysl 219
psychiatry 39
Pyjoff 171

Quakers 165, 172, 175
quarantine 51, 58–60, 62, 69, 87, 98, 105, 111, 117,
    148, 172, 273
Quisling, Vidkun 165

Rabinowitsch-Kempner, Lydia 24
Rabl, Rudolf 192
race 64, 70, 88, 98, 181, 189, 195, 249, 332
Race Political Office 271
racial pathology 189
Ragusa 73
railways 69, 88, 90, 160, 169, 175
    fumigation 310
Raisko Hygiene Institute/Botanical Station 251,
    253 f., 365–7, 410
Rajchman, Ludwik 130, 135, 146, 167–9, 171, 211,
    218, 423
Rapallo 185
Rascher, Sigmund 315
Rathenau, Walter 155
Ratibor/Raciborz 68
rats 12, 29, 34, 52, 90, 214, 303, 319, 358, 390 f.
    blood 214 f.
    catchers 66, 128
Raumentwesung und Seuchengefahr, committee
    for 307 f., 379
Ravensbrück 254, 359, 364, 413, 416
Reche, Otto 196, 272
Reclam, Carl 42
Red Army 150, 180, 185, 197, 205, 374
Red Cross:
    American 76, 87 f., 142, 181, 344
    British 87
    disguise 296, 313
    Dutch 181
    German 86, 117, 155–68, 178, 180–2, 184, 187,
        204, 221, 231, 311, 389
    ICRC/International Committee of the
        Red Cross 141, 164, 204, 328, 330, 368, 393
    LRCS/League of Red Cross Societies 142–5,
        170, 181, 245
    Russian 173, 181
    Swedish 181
    Swiss 343
Reichsarbeitsgemeinschaft für
    Schädlingsbekämpfung 262
Reich:
    Biological Institute 376
    Chamber of Physicians 245
    Colonial Office, Reich 66
    Finance ministry 123, 180
    Foreign office 148, 155–8, 166, 180, 190, 193, 195,
        199, 204
    Health Office 13, 22, 25, 34, 49, 115, 126, 131 f.,
        157, 166, 207, 220, 244 f., 308, 345, 383

Reich (*cont*):
 Institute for Air and Water/Wasser und
  Luftgüte Berlin 311, 375
 Interior Ministry (RMdI) 156, 158, 179 f., 198,
  275, 308, 311, 334, 344, 375
 Justice Ministry 132
 Medical Chamber 326
 navy 25, 40
 Security Office 304
 War Ministry 180
 Weapons and Munitions Ministry 307 f.
Reichsforschungsrat 389
Reichsministerium für die besetzten
  Ostgebieten/Ostministerium 289, 341 f., 345
Reichstag 121
Reichswehr 134, 180, 196 f., 205
Reichmuth 310 n., 411
Reinhardt, Rudolf 244
Reiter, Hans 220 f., 237 f., 245, 268, 344, 389
relapsing fever 34, 151, 181, 200
religion 64, 70, 99
Remak, Robert 51
Richet, Charles 367
Ricketts, Howard Taylor 16, 78
rickettsiae 78, 85, 202, 214, 216, 335, 345, 350, 357 f.
Riga 91, 94, 287, 289, 294–6, 341 f., 357
 Institute of Medical Zoology 250, 289, 349, 352,
  377
 Treaty of 164
Rimpau, Wilhelm 28, 177, 218
Robert, Jan 368
Robert Koch Institute (RLI) 5, 24 f., 49, 115, 217,
  242 f., 326, 330, 338, 343, 358
Rocha-Lima, Henrique 74, 76, 78 f., 86
Rockefeller Foundation 76, 145 f., 167, 195, 210,
  216, 218, 241, 343 f., 396, 400, 422 f.
 Laboratories 217
Rocky Mountain Spotted Fever 391
Rodenwaldt, Ernst 78, 83, 106, 176, 226 f., 232, 243,
  250, 311, 335, 376, 381, 402, 411
Roessler, Heinrich 47–8, 95, 120
Roman Catholicism 266, 268, 280
 cremation 44, 318
Romania 97, 149, 215, 245, 273
Rose, Gerhard 139, 242–4, 250, 308, 310, 330, 334,
  358, 360 f., 379, 380 f., 383, 390, 408, 415
Rosenau, Milton 60
Rosenberg, Alfred 229, 255, 287
Rosenheim 83
Rostock 205
Rott, Fritz 221
Rousset, David 290
Roux, Emil 235
Rowiński, Mirosław 271
Royal Army Medical Corps 87, 89
Rubner, Max 40, 82
Rüdin, Ernst 234
Ruhleben 63–5
Russia 14, 77, 84–6, 90, 168–70, 357

 as diseased 112, 153
 Jewish migrants 60
 Revolution 111
 see also Soviet Union
Rust, Bernhard 229, 236
Rutenol 359 f.

SA (Sturmabtailung) 205, 234
St Petersburg 76, 105, 178, 195
 Petrograd 153, 160, 178, 180
Sachsenhausen 218, 221, 249, 275, 284, 305, 311,
  314, 338, 357, 360, 416
Sakir, Benhaeddin 108
Salvarsan 179, 363
sanitary depot 246
Sarajevo 73, 94
Saratov 130, 162, 165, 177, 181, 185, 197, 207
 cremation 264
Sarkisov, Semion A. 191
Save the Children Fund 161 f., 165 f., 175
Sawyer, Wilbur 217, 400
scabies vii, 149, 394, 418
scarlet fever 51, 172
Scharlau, Kurt 251, 409, 411
Scheele, Carl Wilhelm 46
Schering 38, 380
Schilling, Claus 27, 106, 218, 242, 359 f., 410, 419
Schilling, Viktor 106, 160
Schlosser 407
Schmidt-Ott, Friedrich 185, 188, 191
Schneidemühl 79
Schopenhauer, Arthur 235
Schreiber 381
Schumann, Horst 366
Schweitzer, Albert 231
Schmidt-Ott, Friedrich 106, 189, 193, 206
Schmitz-Formes 362
Schrader, Gerhard 387
Schumann, Horst 253, 299
Schwanenberger, Dr 364
Scottish Women's Hospitals 87
scrub typhus 16
Seeckt, Hans von 179
Seeman, Jacob and Anna 364 f.
Seifert, Paul 178
Semashko, Nikolai 171, 178, 181, 183 f., 191, 193
Serbia 5, 73, 75–7, 87, 89, 99, 295
sera, cholera 106
 convalescent 86
 diphtheria 181, 336
 gas oedema 336
 plague 336
 research 99
 typhus 106, 181, 363
 serum therapy 23, 235
Sergent, Édmond 331, 374
serology 192, 198, 251
sexually transmitted diseases 51, 98, 149, 160, 179
shaving 99–100, 284, 290

Shaw, Bernard 165
shipping 46, 62, 66, 83, 119
showers 39 f., 41, 65, 67, 81, 97 f., 292, 294, 296, 317
Sievers, Wolfram 357, 360, 377, 389 f., 414
Sigerist, Henry 213, 408
Sikora, Hilda 76, 338
Silesia 13, 39, 53, 97, 115, 139, 157, 242
Skrymnik, Dr 385
sleeping sickness 29, 178
Slupetzky, Anton 262, 309, 314
smallpox 51 f., 58, 83, 111, 160, 169, 397, 424
Snyder 216
soap 38, 181, 274, 280, 282, 290, 302, 374, 378, 390
Sobibor 255, 297, 302
sodium cyanide 38
Sokal 86
Solovyev, Zinovii Petrovich 178
Sontochin 361
Soper, Fred 374, 422
South Tyrol 114
Soviet Union 176–8, 237, 273, 414
    Health Commissariat 205, 209, 334
Soviet Medical Administration (SMAD) 398
Sparrow, Helena 215, 324 f.
Spain 76, 323, 329, 334, 378
SS 251, 333, 353, 360, 336
    Ahnenerbe 252, 338, 358, 376, 386
    and poison gas 305
    see also Waffen-SS
Spann, Othmar 248
Speer, Albert 308, 310
Stabenow, Paul 131
Staemmler, Siegfried 23
Stalin, Joseph 165, 186 f., 196, 205, 229
Stalingrad 287
Stampar, Andrija 220, 423
Stangl, Fritz 297
Stargard 117
Steiniger, Fritz 250, 288, 377, 409
Stensch 118
Steppun, Oskar Augustovich 384
sterilization 366
    steam 318
    X-ray experiments 253, 363, 420
Sticker, Georg 12
Stoltzenberg, Hugo 128, 134, 196 f.
Strachey, Lytton 235
Stralkowo 150
Stralsund 58
Strasburger, Eduard 52
Strassburg/Strasbourg 140, 315, 339, 358
Strassburger, Horst 390
Strauss, Hermann 244, 282
Strong, Richard 87 f., 144, 415
Strümpell, Adolf 186
Stutthof 314, 320
Sudhoff, Karl 200 f.
sulphonamide drugs 338, 359, 364
Sütterlin, Theodor 175, 261, 408

Sweden 76, 164, 231, 304, 323
    cremation 138
Swiss Serum and Vaccine Institute 344
Switzerland 95, 166, 323, 329, 343, 381
syphilis 25, 62, 98, 111, 178, 202, 252, 368, 397, 425
    German–Soviet expedition 193
    and Lenin 186, 230

Taganrog 149
Tandler, Julius 114, 195
Taresevich, Lev 171 f., 212
    Institute 207
Tartars 181
TASCH 95 f., 120, 123 f., 128
Taskent 207
Tauroggen 289
Taute, Bruno 140, 211
Tesch, Bruno 129–31, 299, 305, 308, 311, 314
Tesch and Stabenow (Testa) 130–2, 299, 305, 314, 357
tetanus 23, 75, 253
Teutonic Knights 54 f., 238, 268
Thennard-Neumann, Ernst 243
Theresienstadt/Terezín 4, 244, 280, 315, 399
Thompson, John West 412 f.
Thorn/Torunn 64, 97, 381
Tiflis 105, 156, 188, 190 f., 193, 198 f., 205, 342
Tilsit 64, 67, 117, 348
Timoféef-Ressovsky, Nikolai 188, 191, 199, 206
Tirpitz , Alfred von 105
Tito, Marshall 400
Tjaden, Hermann 28, 67–8, 76
Topf 264, 266, 317–20
Topping, Andrew 400
Tovsukha, I. P. 188
trachoma 51 f., 62, 65, 170
trains, delousing 106, 114, 251 f.
Trappmann, Walther 377
Treblinka 255, 276, 296, 304, 314
Tréfouel, Jacques 327, 328 n., 369
trench fever 89, 112, 336
tropical medicine 65 f., 195, 207, 210, 303
Trotsky 159, 165, 186, 203
Trunk, Isaiah vii f., 276
Trusen, Peter 42
trypanosomiasis 178, 193
tuberculosis 10, 25, 51, 70, 86 f., 111, 146, 179, 271, 284, 395, 399
    as pretext for genocide 276, 288
    tularemia 193 f., 384, 386
Tunis 15, 88, 326
Turin 44
Turkey 73–4, 76, 86, 105 f., 215
typhoid 29, 74–5, 83, 86, 106, 112, 148, 162, 256, 385
typhus, 51, 65, 69, 75, 77, 83, 86, 103 f., 111 f., 146, 156, 255–6, 271, 290, 365, 393–9
    Commissar 97, 277
    definition 9, 34
    epidemics in Russia 255
    serum 363

Uganda 26
Uhlenbroock, Kurt 312
Uhlenhuth, Paul 140, 237
Ukraine 86, 96, 98, 105, 167 f., 170, 181, 189, 192,
    235 f., 242, 251, 252, 273, 334, 339, 342, 348, 400
Umschweif, Bernhard and Nusia 364 f.
Unger, Hellmuth 23, 241, 293
Ungeziefer 6 f., 15, 41, 75, 114
United Nations 412
    Commission on Human Rights 417
    United Nations Relief and Rehabilitation
        Administration (UNRRA) 395 f., 399 f., 407,
        423
    United Nations War Crimes Commission
        (UNWCC) 413
United States 58–9, 76, 206, 214, 329, 344
    Army Chemical Corps 421
    Bureau of Entomology 373
    Public Health Service 130, 212 f.
    United States of America Typhus Commission
        (USATC) 329, 331, 393, 397, 399 f.
Uralsk 193 f.

vaccination 84, 284
vaccines 10, 215, 322–72
    cholera 336, 360
    gas gangrene 336, 360
    rabies 366
    tetanus 366
    typhoid 169, 360
    typhus 242, 358; Castaneda 331; Cox/chick
        embryo 329, 331, 345, 347, 356; louse guts 86,
        333 f., 343, 345, 350; mouse and rat liver 361;
        mouse lung 334, 347; rabbit lung 347, 356;
        urine 364; yellow fever 336, 349; *see also*
        smallpox
vagabonds, vagrants 13, 25, 39, 89
Valery-Radot, Louis Pasteur 324
Vassal, J. 15
Vaughan, Janet 395 f.
Vavilov, Sergei 197, 229
venereal disease, *see* sexually transmitted
    diseases, syphilis
Ventox 125, 133
Versailles Treaty 139, 141, 146, 155, 167, 183, 186, 233,
    241 f.
Vertilgung 29
veterinary medicine 192 f.
Vetter, Hellmuth 359
Vienna 43, 58, 71, 103, 231, 241, 329, 347, 402 f.
Vilna 94, 96, 99, 104, 144 f., 160,
    ghetto vi, 6, 281 f., 363
Virchow, Rudolf 11, 23, 25, 40, 42, 161, 195, 241, 257,
    276
virology/virus 16, 19, 213, 216 f., 329, 360, 386, 389
Vladimirski, Mikhail 191
Vogt, Oskar 186–8, 190 f., 194 f., 199, 205 f.
Volga Germans 150, 160, 164, 175, 192, 198, 203 f.,
    252, 378

Volga region 196
Volhynia 89, 273
    fever 252
Volksdeutsche Mittelstelle 245
Voss, Hermann 318

Waegner, Harald 243, 256, 290, 425
Waffen-SS 253, 256, 313, 358, 372, 378
    Academy, Graz 347
    Hygiene Institute 226, 231, 246–59, 303, 305,
        339, 367, 379
    Institute for Military Science/Strategic
        Research Institute 358, 377
Wagner, Gerhard 293
Wajnryb, Abraham 6, 282
Walbaum, Jost 243, 272, 274, 337, 409, 426
Waldmann, Anton 226
Wales 14
Warburg, Otto 94
Wargon, Joseph 284
Warsaw 3, 86 f., 90, 97, 100, 102 f., 104, 136, 168,
    280, 326
    Ghetto vii, 3, 273, 275–7, 283 f., 289, 344, 363 f.
    Hygiene Institute 27, 215, 242 f., 275, 277, 284,
        334, 337 f., 344 f., 363
Wassermann, August von vii, 22, 236, 240
    tests 62, 184
water 77, 97, 252, 276, 303
Weber, Bruno 365 f.
Weigl, Rudolf 209, 214–18, 235 f., 333–5, 346,
    348–5, 354, 363, 365, 399
Weil, Edmund 86
Weil–Felix test 17, 86, 214
Weiss, A. 4
Wernicke, Erich 10, 49, 54, 116, 233
Wettstein, Fritz von 229
Weyer, Fritz 337, 409
Weyl, Theodor 45
Wheeler-Hill, Erik 357
White, Norman 148, 179, 211
White Russia 89, 170, 400
Widmann, Albert 293, 295
Wilmowski, Tilo 188 n.
Wilson, Thomas Woodrow 141, 143
Winter, Dr 383
Wirballen 289
Wirth, Christian 297, 301, 304
Wohlrab, Rudolf 243, 277, 323, 337, 345, 347, 355
Wollman, Eugène and Elizabeth 324
Wolter, Friedrich 200
World Health Organization (WHO) 420, 424
World Medical Association 418, 420
worms 31–3, 44
Württemberg 95
Wüstinger, Herbert 299, 301, 309
Wydowski, Bogdan 4

yellow fever 33, 51, 58, 336, 349, 360, 410
Yersin, Alexandre 15

Zahn, Gerhard 341, 344, 346, 348 f.
Zamość 273, 279
Zeiss, Heinz ix, 78, 86, 106, 108, 176–8, 182–5,
    189 f., 192–5, 198–204, 210, 225–8, 231–5,
    243–5, 247, 263–9, 311, 316, 335, 337 f., 348, 353,
    376, 384, 386, 388, 408 f., 411, 425
  and human experiments 362

  and Nazism 250
Zibulkowa 4
Zinsser, Hans 13, 88, 171, 179, 213–17, 218, 250, 423
Zumpt, Fritz 243, 339
Zurich 43, 343
Zyklon 125, 126–36, 178, 247, 254, 259 f., 262, 277,
    297, 299–315, 317, 319, 327, 378, 381, 407, 426

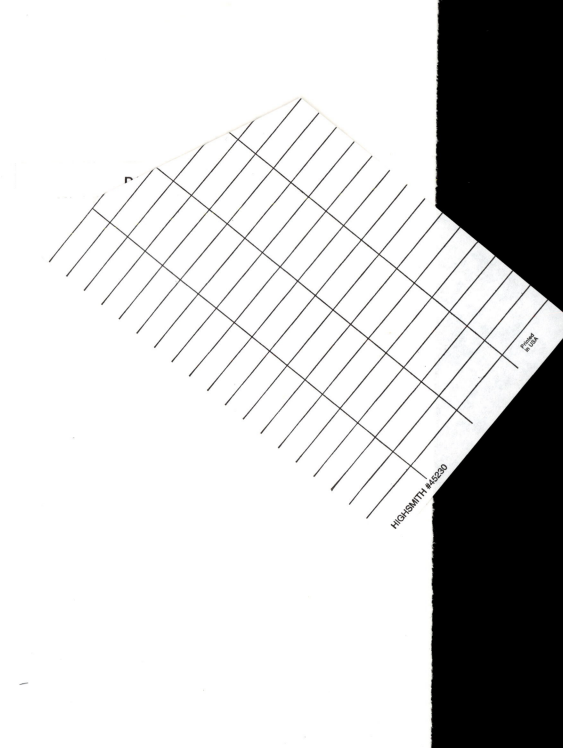

HIGHSMITH #45230

Printed in USA